MW01203881

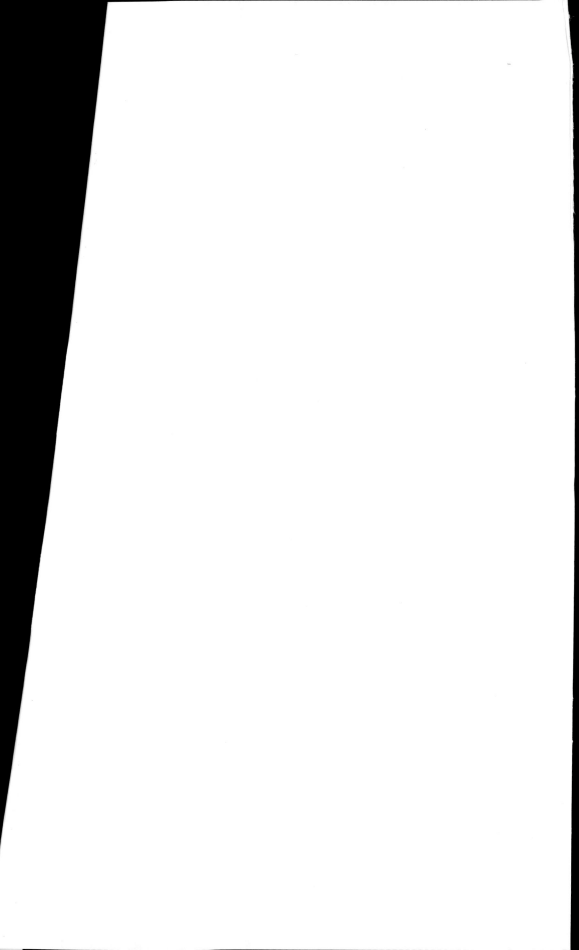

To Save Sin

To Save Sinners

A Critical Evaluation of the Multiple Intentions
View of the Atonement

Michael Riccardi

FOREWORD BY
John MacArthur

WIPF & STOCK · Eugene, Oregon

TO SAVE SINNERS
A Critical Evaluation of the Multiple Intentions View of the Atonement

Copyright © 2023 Michael Riccardi. All rights reserved. Except for brief quotations in critical publications or reviews, no part of this book may be reproduced in any manner without prior written permission from the publisher. Write: Permissions, Wipf and Stock Publishers, 199 W. 8th Ave., Suite 3, Eugene, OR 97401.

Wipf & Stock
An Imprint of Wipf and Stock Publishers
199 W. 8th Ave., Suite 3
Eugene, OR 97401

www.wipfandstock.com

PAPERBACK ISBN: 978-1-6667-4610-5
HARDCOVER ISBN: 978-1-6667-4611-2
EBOOK ISBN: 978-1-6667-4612-9

04/10/23

Contents

Foreword

BY JOHN MacARTHUR

In the middle of the Old Testament canon sits the drama of Job. His story actually took place in the days chronicled in Genesis. It is a saga from the days soon after God had drowned the whole of humanity in the judgment of the universal flood, and after the judgment at the tower of Babel, when God separated people by language. Job's adventure into and out of deep trouble occurred before Moses and the giving of the law; before the captivity, the plagues, and the exodus out of Egypt; before there was a nation of Israel; before God's covenant with Abraham—even before Abraham himself.

Job's story commences with the new humanity that came out of the ark. And it raises a critical question. Since only eight people, Noah and his family, escaped the judgment that killed everyone else, one profound lesson was etched in the minds of those who lived after it. With such a devastating judgment looming in recent memory, it was clear to everyone that God was holy and righteous, and that his wrath is justly stirred up against the sins of humanity. The question above all questions was left hanging over human life. It shows up three times in Job's story:

> Job 9:2—". . . how can a man be in the right before God?"
>
> Job 15:14—"What is man, that he shall be pure . . . righteous?"
>
> Job 25:4–6—"How then can mortal man be right with God?
>
> Or how can he be pure who is born of woman?
>
> Behold even the moon has no brightness,
>
> And the stars are not pure in His sight;
>
> How much less mortal man, that maggot,
>
> And the son of man, that worm!"

That is the ultimate question that all religion exists to answer. The human race needs to know how to be right with God, so as to escape his judgment and enjoy his favor in time and eternity. The universality and pervasiveness of religion reveals the extent of human urgency for an answer.

In Psalm 143:1–6, David exposes the heart cry of a sinner for God to rescue him from judgment and accept him as righteous. He prayed:

¹ O Yahweh, hear my prayer,

Give ear to my supplications!

Answer me in Your faithfulness, in Your righteousness!

² And do not enter into judgment with Your slave,

For no one living is righteous in Your sight.

³ For the enemy has pursued my soul;

He has crushed my life to the ground;

He has made me inhabit dark places, like those who have long been dead.

⁴ Therefore my spirit was faint within me;

My heart was appalled within me.

⁵ I remember the days of old;

I meditate on all You have done;

I muse on the work of Your hands.

⁶ I stretch out my hands to You;

My soul reaches for You like a weary land. Selah.

David knew he was incapable of being righteous, yet he knew God required perfect righteousness to allow him to enter his presence. He was pleading, as in Job, for the answer to the ultimate question: How can I be righteous before God?

This is the question only the Bible answers accurately, thus setting itself up as the authoritative truth rising over all the lies of religion.

The most critical riddle in the OT is focused on the same issue, looking at it from God's side. That riddle is expressed in Exodus 34:6–7:

⁶ Then Yahweh passed by in front of him and called out, "Yahweh, Yahweh God, compassionate and gracious, slow to anger, and abounding in loving-kindness and truth; ⁷ who keeps lovingkindness for thousands, who forgives iniquity, transgression, and sin; yet He will by no means leave the guilty unpunished, visiting the iniquity of fathers on the children and on the grandchildren to the third and fourth generations."

How can God who is holy and just, at the same time, be gracious and compassionate and forgiving; yet, not clear the guilty? The prophet Isaiah gives the answer to the riddle in Isaiah 53:4–6:

⁴ Surely our griefs He Himself bore,

And our sorrows He carried;

Yet we ourselves esteemed Him stricken,

Smitten of God, and afflicted.

> [5] But He was pierced through for our transgressions,
>
> He was crushed for our iniquities;
>
> The chastening for our peace fell upon Him,
>
> And by His wounds we are healed.
>
> [6] All of us like sheep have gone astray,
>
> Each of us has turned to his own way;
>
> But Yahweh has caused the iniquity of us all
>
> To fall on Him.

The servant of God, the Messiah, the Lord Jesus Christ, is the answer to the question in Job and the riddle in Exodus. Here is the incomparable good news—the gospel: Jesus Christ, Son of God, Son of Man, Lord and Savior, came to die under the judgment of God for the sins of his people. This most gracious and glorious of all truths is summed up by Paul in 2 Corinthians 5:21: "He made Him who knew no sin to be sin on our behalf, so that we might become the righteousness of God in Him." The gospel is the greatest gift heaven has given to sinners. And it is a gateway to joy and blessing forever.

We live in constant gratitude for the cross of Jesus Christ. We worship in exuberant praise to our substitute, our Savior, our Redeemer who has delivered us from the wrath of God by the sacrifice of himself in our place. We sing songs of our Lord, our brother, our friend who atoned for our sins. All our joy, all our praise, all our hope, all our love and obedience are offered in gratitude that rises up in our hearts for the glory of gospel truth that secured for us eternal blessing. So great a salvation leading to great praise rises from our deepest understanding of the riches of gospel theology.

After a lifetime of drawing daily from the well of salvation and drinking deeply of its grace, its sweetness is still increasing—so that my soul longs to drink even more. Isaiah captures this satisfaction:

> Then you will say in that day,
>
> "I will give thanks to You, O Yahweh;
>
> For although You were angry with me,
>
> Your anger is turned away,
>
> And You comfort me.
>
> Behold, God is my salvation,
>
> I will trust and not dread;
>
> For Yah—Yahweh Himself—is my strength and song,
>
> And He has become my salvation."
>
> Therefore you will joyously draw water
>
> From the springs of salvation.
>
> (Isa 12:1–3)

In this exceptional defense of the integrity of our Savior's work on the cross, Michael Riccardi lowers the bucket into the depths of salvation's well to draw up the water of life and give us all a taste of that water from its deepest, most undisturbed place. Drink deeply and be refreshed.

List of Abbreviations

ANF	*Ante-Nicene Fathers*
AOTC	Apollos Old Testament Commentary
BDAG	Danker, Frederick W., Walter Bauer, William F. Arndt, and F. Wilbur Gingrich, *A Greek-English Lexicon of the New Testament and Other Early Christian Literature*, 3rd ed.
BECNT	Baker Exegetical Commentary on the New Testament
BETS	*Bulletin of the Evangelical Theological Society*
BSac	*Biblotheca Sacra*
EBC	Expositor's Bible Commentary
EQ	*Evangelical Quarterly*
HALOT	*The Hebrew and Aramaic Lexicon of the Old Testament*
ICC	International Critical Commentary
JBL	*Journal of Biblical Literature*
JETS	*Journal of the Evangelical Theological Society*
JTS	*Journal of Theological Studies*
MNTC	MacArthur New Testament Commentary
MSJ	*The Master's Seminary Journal*
NAC	New American Commentary
NIBC	New International Bible Commentary
NICNT	New International Commentary on the New Testament
NICOT	New International Commentary on the Old Testament
NIDOTTE	*New International Dictionary of Old Testament Theology and Exegesis*
NIDNTTE	*New International Dictionary of New Testament Theology and Exegesis*
NIGTC	New International Greek Testament Commentary

NPNF1	*Nicene and Post-Nicene Fathers*, series 1
NPNF2	*Nicene and Post-Nicene Fathers*, series 2
PL	*Patrologia Latina*
PNTC	Pillar New Testament Commentary
SBJT	*Southern Baptist Journal of Theology*
SJT	*Scottish Journal of Theology*
TDNT	*Theological Dictionary of the New Testament*
TDOT	*Theological Dictionary of the Old Testament*
TNTC	Tyndale New Testament Commentaries
TWOT	*Theological Wordbook of the Old Testament*
WBC	Word Biblical Commentary
WTJ	*Westminster Theological Journal*
ZECNT	Zondervan Exegetical Commentary on the New Testament

Introduction

FOR WHOM DID CHRIST die? For someone familiar with the history of theology or acquainted with contemporary theological debates among even conservative evangelical Christians, the mere asking of that question can cause one to brace for heated conflict. For some, emotions run high if it is even implied that the work of the Savior does not extend to all alike, for such would be to call into question the genuineness of both God's love and his justice toward his creatures. For others, tempers flare at the suggestion that Christ's atoning work extends any further than God's own people, the elect who will finally be saved, for such would be to undermine the absolute sovereignty of God and the efficacy of Christ's sufficient cross work. Yet the question remains: On whose behalf did Christ offer himself a substitutionary sacrifice (cf. Isa 53:4–6; Heb 9:26)? Against whose sins did he satisfy the Father's wrath (cf. Rom 3:25; 1 John 2:2)? Whom did Christ reconcile to God (Rom 5:10; 2 Cor 5:18; Col 1:20) and redeem out of slavery to sin (Acts 20:28; 1 Pet 1:18–19; Rev 5:9)? On whose behalf has the victorious Savior conquered sin, death, and Satan (Heb 2:14–15)? In short, one may summarize the question with Louis Berkhof's famous query: "Did the Father in sending Christ, and did Christ in coming into the world, to make atonement for sin, do this with the design or for the purpose of saving only the elect or all men?"[1]

Answers to these questions have traditionally fallen into two broad categories. Advocates of what is variably called "universal atonement," "general atonement," or "unlimited atonement" contend that Christ has paid for the sins of every human person who has ever lived or will live, without exception.[2] They support this claim by

1. Berkhof, *Systematic Theology*, 394. Thus, he also aptly captures what the point of concern is *not*: "The question with which we are concerned at this point is not (a) whether the satisfaction rendered by Christ was in itself sufficient for the salvation of all men, since this is admitted by all; (b) whether the saving benefits are actually applied to every man, for the great majority of those who teach a universal atonement do not believe that all are actually saved; (c) whether the bona fide offer of salvation is made to all that hear the gospel, on the condition of repentance and faith, since the Reformed Churches do not call this into question; nor (d) whether any of the fruits of the death of Christ accrue to the benefit of the non-elect in virtue of their close association with the people of God, since this is explicitly taught by many Reformed scholars" (Berkhof, *Systematic Theology*, 393–94).

2. This school may be referred to under the broad heading of "universalism," whose proponents are "universalists." This is to be distinguished from that universalism which holds that all people without exception will finally be saved. Rather, they are so denominated in this context because they believe

appealing to the many passages of Scripture characterizing Christ's death as extending to "all" (1 Tim 2:6), to "everyone" (Heb 2:9), and to "the world" (John 3:16),[3] as well as texts that emphasize the universal saving will of God (1 Tim 2:4)[4] and the free offer of the gospel to all without exception (Matt 11:28).[5] On the other hand, advocates of what is variably called "particular redemption," "definite atonement," or "limited atonement" contend that Christ has paid for the sins of only those whom the Father has unconditionally elected in eternity past, those who will not fail to be regenerated by the Holy Spirit and finally be saved.[6] They support this claim by appealing to Scripture's emphasis on the actuality and efficacy of Christ's atonement (Gal 3:13; Eph 1:7; 1 Pet 2:24) such that those for whom Christ died could not fail to be finally saved:[7] texts speaking of Christ's death extending to particular individuals, distinguished from the world at large, such as his "sheep" (John 10:14–29), his "friends" (John 15:13), his "church" (Eph 5:25), the "elect" (Rom 8:33), and those the Father had given him (e.g., John 17:2);[8] texts testifying to the unity of Trinitarian work in salvation, arguing that the Father and Spirit cannot work to save some while the Son works to save all (John 6:37–39; Eph 1:3–14);[9] and texts grounding salvation in union with Christ both in his death and resurrection (Rom 6:5–8).[10]

Christ's atonement extends universally to all people without exception. Hence appear those labels such as "hypothetical universalism" and "Calvinistic universalists" to describe those who subscribe to unconditional election and irresistible grace, but not to a strict particular atonement.

3. E.g., Marshall, "For All, for All," 338; Lightner, *Death Christ Died*, 70.

4. E.g, Demarest, *Cross and Salvation*, 191.

5. E.g., Chafer, "For Whom Did Christ Die?," 315–16; Douty, *Death of Christ*, 45–49; Lightner, *Death Christ Died*, 114–18; Miethe, "Universal Power of the Atonement," 83–85; and Picirilli, *Grace, Faith, Free Will*, 115–18.

6. This school may be referred to under the broad heading of "particularism," whose proponents are "particularists." Many contemporary particularists acknowledge the traditional terminology for their view—"limited atonement"—to be unfortunate and potentially misleading. Particularists have no desire to cast the infinite worth, merit, and value of Christ's atonement as limited; the limitation is exclusively with respect to the extent of Christ's sacrifice. Further, particularists often urge that all positions hold to some form of limitation in the atonement, unless one is prepared to accept universal final salvation. They insist that "particular redemption" or "definite atonement" are better monikers for their position. See, e.g., Nicole, "Case for Definite Atonement," 200.

7. E.g., MacArthur and Mayhue, *Biblical Doctrine*, 548–53.

8. E.g., Boice and Ryken, *The Doctrines of Grace*, 125.

9. E.g., Reymond, *New Systematic Theology*, 678.

10. E.g., Murray, *Redemption Accomplished and Applied*, 70; Wellum, "New Covenant Work of Christ," 517–39.

Brief Historical Survey

The debate between universalism and particularism[11] has raged throughout the history of Christianity.[12] As happens with much of the history of doctrine, however, systematized formulations of the extent of the atonement awaited particular historical controversies, most notably the conflicts of the Protestant Reformation leading to the Synod of Dort in the sixteenth and early seventeenth centuries.[13] In that time, the two major schools of thought were represented in the second article of the Remonstrance[14] and Article VIII of the second head in the Canons of the Synod of Dort.[15] Though the Synod of Dort aimed to clarify the Reformed church's position on the extent of the atonement, and though particularism did become the majority view of Reformed orthodoxy, most notably standardized by John Owen's

---

11. Note this author's preference for "universalism" and "particularism" as labels for the two broad categories of views of the extent of the atonement outlined above.

12. For general historical treatments of the extent of the atonement before the Synod of Dort, see Blacketer, "Definite Atonement in Historical Perspective," 304–23; Godfrey, "Reformed Thought on the Extent of the Atonement to 1618," 133–34; and Rainbow, *Will of God and the Cross*.

For evidence of particularistic thought in the patristics, see Williams, *For Whom Did Christ Die?*, 2–30, and Haykin, "We Trust in the Saving Blood," 57–74.

For evidence of particularism in the Medieval church, see Hogg, "'Sufficient for All, Efficient for Some,'" 76–80.

For a survey of the relevant literature on Calvin's view of the extent of the atonement, see Muller, "Calvin on Christ's Satisfaction and Its Efficacy," 70–73, especially notes 2 and 7. In addition to those listed in Muller, for a rebuttal of the view that Beza was the originator of particular redemption, his views being discontinuous with Calvin's, see Letham, "Theodore Beza," 30; and Bray, "Theodore Beza's Doctrine of Predestination," 216, 238, 240; contra Armstrong, "Calvinism of Moise Amyraut," 41–42, 137–38; and Hall, "Calvin against the Calvinists," 27.

13. For analysis of the historical context of and doctrinal issues at play in the Synod of Dort, see Godfrey, "Tensions within International Calvinism"; Gatiss, "Synod of Dort and Definite Atonement," 143–63.

14. "Jesus Christ the Savior of the world died for all men and for every man, so that he obtained for them all, by his death on the cross, redemption and the forgiveness of sins; yet so that no one actually enjoys this forgiveness of sins except the believer, according to the word of the Gospel of John 3:16: 'God so loved the world that he gave his only-begotten Son, that whosoever believeth in him should not perish, but have everlasting life.' And in the First Epistle of John 2:2: 'And he is the propitiation for our sins; and not for ours only, but also for the sins of the whole world'" (Schaff, *Creeds of Christendom*, 3:546).

15. "For this was the sovereign counsel and most gracious will and purpose of God the Father, that the quickening and saving efficacy of the most precious death of his Son should extend to all the elect, for bestowing upon them alone the gift of justifying faith, thereby to bring them infallibly to salvation: that is, it was the will of God, that Christ by the blood of the cross, whereby he confirmed the new covenant, should effectually redeem out of every people, tribe, nation, and language, all those, and those only, who were from eternity chosen to salvation, and given to him by the Father; that he should confer upon them faith, which, together with all the other saving gifts of the Holy Spirit, he purchased for them by his death; should purge them from all sin, both original and actual, whether committed before or after believing; and having faithfully preserved them even to the end, should at last bring them free from every spot and blemish to the enjoyment of his glory in his own presence forever" (Schaff, *Creeds of Christendom*, 3:587).

famous tome, *The Death of Death in the Death of Christ*,[16] the controversy neverthe-less continued. There were several mediating views that both preceded and followed the Synod. These included the French hypothetical universalism of John Cameron and Moise Amyraut of the school at Saumur,[17] the British hypothetical universalism of James Ussher, John Davenant, and John Preston,[18] and the somewhat neonomian hypothetical universalism of Richard Baxter.[19]

The Multiple Intentions View

The debate has raged on through to the contemporary era of historical theology, with the heirs of both Remonstrant universalism[20] and Dortian particularism[21] contribut-ing to the discussion. Additionally, like the controversy of the seventeenth century, contemporary theology has seen no shortage of mediating views on the extent of the atonement, offering a better way than the two extremes. In addition to the so-called four-point Calvinism[22] of many theologians traveling the *via media*, there has emerged another mediating position. In the early 2000s, Professor Bruce Ware began circulat-ing a handout in his theology classes at Southern Seminary in which he began defend-ing what he called a "multiple intentions view" (MIV) of the atonement.[23] He laments that "much of the debate over the extent of the atonement is owing to the fact that a *single* intention (rather than multiple intentions) was sought by both sides." Instead, he avers that "God's intentions in the death of Christ are complex not simple, multiple not single."[24] What particularism and universalism see as an either-or decision—*either* Christ died to infallibly the secure the salvation of the elect alone, *or* he died to make

16. Owen, *Death of Death*, 139–428. Also representative of mainstream Reformed particularism were William Perkins, Francis Turretin, and later Herman Bavinck. For Perkins, see *Workes*; Muller, *Christ and the Decree*; and Moore, *English Hypothetical Universalism*, 27–68. For Turretin, see his *Institutes of Elenctic Theology*, 2:455–82. For Bavinck, see his *Reformed Dogmatics*, 3:455–75.

17. Amyraut, *Brief Traitté*. See also Armstrong, *Calvinism and the Amyraut Heresy*; Diaballah, "Controversy on Universal Grace," 165–99; and Nicole, "Moyse Amyraut."

18. Ussher, *Judgement*; Davenant, "Death of Christ." On John Preston, see the excellent presenta-tion of his thought and works in Moore, *English Hypothetical Universalism*, 71–169. On Ussher and Davenant, see Moore, *English Hypothetical Universalism*, 173–213.

19. Baxter, *Universal Redemption of Mankind*. For an attempt to prove that Baxter was a neono-mian, see Brown, "Not by Faith Alone," 133–52. For an attempt to exonerate Baxter, see Boersma, *Hot Peppercorn*.

20. E.g., Douty, *Death of Christ*; Miethe, "Universal Power of the Atonement"; and Picirilli, *Grace, Faith, Free Will*. See also Sailer, "Nature and Extent of the Atonement," 189–98.

21. E.g., Berkhof, *Systematic Theology*, 392–99; Boettner, *Reformed Doctrine of Predestination*, 150–61; Grudem, *Systematic Theology*, 594–603; White, *Potter's Freedom*, 251–80.

22. E.g., Chafer, *Systematic Theology*, 3:183–205; Lightner, *Death Christ Died*; Ryrie, *Basic The-ology*, 318–23; Thiessen, *Lectures in Systematic Theology*, 240–42; Walvoord, *Jesus Christ Our Lord*; Walvoord, "Reconciliation," 3–12.

23. Ware, "Outline." This was also presented at ETS 2010. Ware, "Select Support."

24. Ware, "Outline," 3.

possible, or available, the salvation of all without exception—the multiple intentions view holds that Christ died for both of these reasons. That is, there are both particular and universal intentions that God designed by the death of Christ.

In 2008, Dr. Ware supervised the PhD dissertation of Gary L. Shultz Jr., who wrote, "A Biblical and Theological Defense of a Multi-Intentioned View of the Extent of the Atonement,"[25] in which he aimed to develop Ware's thesis and to present "a full-length scholarly work explicitly explaining and defending a multi-intentioned view,"[26] which had not yet been done. Like Ware, Shultz laments that the traditional positions on the extent of the atonement "unnecessarily restrict God's intentions in sending his Son to die on the cross to a single intention," and therefore are unable to account "for all of the relevant biblical texts or the theological factors that impact the debate."[27] Instead, we ought to realize that "the atonement was neither merely provisional nor absolutely efficacious, but provisional for all and efficacious for some." Shultz states his thesis as follows:

> A multi-intentioned view holds that God the Father, in sending his Son to die on the cross, had both particular and general intentions for the atonement. In accordance with the Father's will, the Son then died to fulfill these multiple intentions. Based upon the Son's atoning death on the cross, the Spirit then works to apply the atonement in both particular and general ways.[28]

According to Shultz, God's particular intention in the atonement is to infallibly secure the salvation of the elect, just as particularists would claim. In addition, Shultz also claims that God intended that the Son pay the penalty for the sins of all people without exception to accomplish at least five other ends: "[1] to make the universal gospel call possible, [2] to make general grace (and not only salvific grace) possible, [3] to provide an additional basis of condemnation for those who reject the gospel, [4] to serve as the supreme example of God's character, and [5] to make the reconciliation of all things possible."[29]

After surveying the history of the debate over the extent of the atonement (chapter 2), Shultz argues, against particularism, that the universalistic passages of Scripture (e.g., John 3:16; 1 John 2:2) are best understood as teaching that Christ died for all without exception (chapter 3). He then attempts to make the biblical and theological case, also against particularism, that the atonement purchased these five benefits for all without exception (chapter 4). Finally, he argues, against

---

25. Shultz, "Defense." A version of this dissertation was later published as Shultz, *Multi-Intentioned View.*

26. Shultz, "Defense," 11n23.

27. Shultz, "Defense," 10–11.

28. Shultz, "Defense," 12.

29. Shultz, "Defense," 12.

universalism, that the Father designed for Christ to die to infallibly accomplish the salvation of his particular people (chapter 5).

The MIV has been gaining popularity in evangelical circles, as many regard it as the best of both worlds, a welcome alternative to the "extreme" positions of particularism and universalism that have generated such furious debate. Another key defense for the multiple intentions view has been offered by John Hammett in *Perspectives on the Extent of the Atonement: 3 Views*, edited by Andrew David Naselli and Mark A. Snoeberger.[30] Though Hammett acknowledges some differences from Ware and Shultz,[31] he nevertheless sees his view in the same broad category as theirs, arguing that there are universal, particular, and cosmic intentions in the atonement: that "Christ died in order to satisfy God's righteous wrath toward human sin by serving as the propitiation for all humans and thereby providing redemption and reconciliation for all humans;" that "another intention in Christ dying was actually to secure the salvation of some;" and "a third intention" in which Christ defeats "all the enemies believers face in this world."[32]

As the discussion continues, and as Ware's, Shultz's, and Hammett's contributions attest, Snoeberger's observation rings true: "New variations of hypothetical universalism, among which are located the multiple-intention view defended in this volume, are again making advances in the evangelical church."[33] Given that, it is appropriate for the advocates of the classic universalist and particularist positions to respond thoroughly to the merits of the more recent positions claiming to have found a better biblical and theological alternative. Shultz believes that the MIV is genuinely novel—that it "build[s] upon and go[es] beyond positions that have been proposed by Christian scholars in the past,"[34] and that it "is not an attempt to find a 'middle way' between Calvinism and Arminianism, or an attempt to incorporate Arminian elements into a Calvinistic soteriology," but approaches "the debate from a fresh perspective so that all of the Bible's teaching on the subject is properly emphasized,"[35] presumably in a way that he believes has not been done before.

Purpose and Thesis

In light of this, the purpose of this present work is to offer a critical evaluation of the MIV (as proposed by Ware, Hammett, and especially Shultz, among others) from the perspective of classic particularism. It will be demonstrated that, by failing to

30. Hammett, "Multiple-Intentions View," 143–94.

31. Hammett, "Multiple-Intentions View," 188–91.

32. Hammett, "Multiple-Intentions View," 149, 170, 184–85, respectively.

33. Snoeberger, "Introduction," 16.

34. Shultz, "Defense," 19.

35. Shultz, "Defense," 97. For how Shultz understands the MIV to differ from hypothetical universalism and contemporary four-point Calvinism, see Shultz, "Defense," 95–97.

adequately frame the issue in the context of Scripture's teaching concerning the nature and purpose of Christ's mediating work, the MIV bases its conviction that there are general intentions in the atonement on a mishandling of the universalistic texts. Therefore, it will further be demonstrated that, despite the criticisms levied by the MIV and other mediating views, classic particularism best accounts for all of the Bible's teaching concerning the nature, purpose, and extent of the atonement of Christ.

Limitations, Assumptions, and Contribution

Though the history of theology, and especially that of the doctrine of the extent of the atonement, is immensely important in the task of doctrinal synthesis, primary focus will be given to accurately ascertaining the meaning of individual biblical texts and synthesizing their meaning into a coherent theological whole. For the sake of space limitations, and also because there has been a wealth of historical research concerning the debate on the extent of the atonement, this project will not devote a separate section to historical survey, but instead will aim to bring relevant historical matters, arguments, and exegesis to bear on the discussion throughout.

As mentioned above, the scope of this present work aims to refute the multiple intentions view, whose advocates regard it as a genuinely novel position on the extent of the atonement. Therefore, while there will naturally be significant overlap, this project will not address the arguments of every opponent of particularism, whether Lutheranism, classic Arminianism, Wesleyan Arminianism, or the more traditional four-point Calvinism. Instead, its focus will be upon Ware, Shultz, and Hammett. In doing so, the present work will take for granted the various doctrines of the faith that these men and the present author share in common, but that are not always shared by each participant in this discussion. In addition to the evangelical commitments to the unity, inerrancy, and supreme authority of Scripture, these doctrinal assumptions include unconditional individual election, the distinction between the decretive, preceptive, and optative aspects of the will of God, and the representative headship of Adam and Christ.

Further, because Shultz's dissertation and subsequent monograph and journal articles[36] provide the most complete presentation of the multiple intentions view, the present volume gives special attention to his work. It aims to contribute to scholarship in this field by offering a full-length response to the most complete presentation of this novel view of the extent of Christ's atonement.

---

36. Shultz, "God's Purposes for the Nonelect," 145–63; Shultz, "Reconciliation of All Things," 442–59; and Shultz, "Why a Genuine Universal Gospel Call," 111–23.

Methodology

The present work offers a biblical and theological refutation of the multiple intentions view of the atonement, and therefore is by nature polemical. However, while this project will be necessarily polemical and therefore straightforward, it aims not to be contentious, avoiding the inflammatory rhetoric that can often mark this particular debate.[37] This author does not consider the disagreement between particularism and universalism to be a first-order disagreement. While not unimportant or merely trivial, it is an intramural debate between fellow Christians, and therefore is to be conducted with brotherly charity.[38]

The methodology employed will be exegetical-theological. It is first of all exegetical, reflecting the author's conviction that the sole infallible authority for the church's doctrine—the *norma normans non normata*—is Scripture alone. To exalt the authority and sufficiency of Scripture, the present work is grounded in a commitment to literal grammatical-historical exegesis. Thus, every truth claim defended in this project aims to be founded upon and in submission to the text of Scripture, interpreted in its context, according to the rules of grammar and the facts of history, in accordance with the intent of the original author.

Second, this project is also a work of theology, in which the exegetical conclusions of various texts of Scripture are held in conversation with one another and formed into a coherent whole—with no text amending, deemphasizing, or canceling out the import of any other text, but all held together consistently, recognizing that the single divine mind has authored them all. The Bible's doctrine of the extent of the atonement is not a product of a particular text or set of texts that explicitly states, "Jesus died for all people in history without exception," or, "Jesus died for the elect alone and so no one else." Rather, a biblical doctrine of the extent of the atonement is formulated similarly to the biblical doctrine of the Trinity—held together by the affirmation that the Father and Son are ὁμοούσιος, of the same substance, though such a term never appears in Scripture—or the biblical doctrine of the hypostatic union of divine and human natures in Christ, though no one text explicitly names Christ as one πρόσωπον subsisting in two φύσεων. As David and Jonathan Gibson put it,

> the diverse biblical parts demand the patient work of synthesis to portray the theological whole. . . . definite atonement is a *biblico-systematic* doctrine that arises from careful exegesis of atonement texts and synthesis with internally related doctrines. . . . When both exegetical and theological "domains of

37. Naselli, "John Owen's Argument for a Definite Atonement," 60–82.

38. My sentiments along these lines are echoed in an adapted comment from Garry Williams: "My argument for definite atonement should not be taken as an attempt to disenfranchise others who share central [evangelical] convictions, and for whom I am grateful to God for many reasons. Enough [evangelical] blood has been spilled by friendly fire. This chapter is simply intended to show brothers that at this point they are wrong, and that their positions, logically applied, will have consequences that they themselves would surely find alarming" (Williams, "Definite Intent," 462).

discourse" are respected as such *and* taken together, then reductionist objections to definite atonement lose their force and this reading of the meaning of the death of Christ emerges as profound and faithful.[39]

Thus, this project will aim to "respect" both exegetical and theological "domains of discourse," recognizing that exegesis is the foundation of theology and that theology is the necessary product of exegesis. The synthesis of (a) the exegesis of "atonement texts" with (b) the exegetical conclusions of other texts by which we arrive at doctrines intricately related to the atonement will yield a biblically faithful and theologically sound doctrine of the extent of the atonement.

This reflects the conviction that there is no conflict between faithful exegesis and sound theology. Sometimes, well-meaning opponents of particular redemption mistakenly divorce exegesis and theology by making the argument that particularism is theologically sound (because, for example, it provides for unity in the saving will of the Trinity, and because it is consistent with the other doctrines of grace, which these opponents affirm) but exegetically untenable (because of a set of passages that speak of Christ's death for "all" or for "the world"). However, such thinking misconceives theology as something other than the coherent holding together of the exegesis of individual texts of Scripture, and it misconceives exegesis as something other than that which must press to a conclusion and be coherently held together with the exegetical conclusions of the rest of Scripture. Genuine systematic theology must arise from sound exegesis, and genuine exegesis must issue in sound systematic theology; they can never be at odds with one another. Berkhof rightly observes, "There seems to be a lurking fear that the more we systematize the truth, the farther we wander from the presentation of it that is found in the Word of God." His reply is also accurate: there is no danger of sacrificing exegesis to "the system" so long as that system "is not based on the fundamental principles of some erring philosophy, but on the abiding principles of Scripture itself."[40] This is the standard at which this project aims.

Part 1 aims to present the multiple intentions view in the words of its own proponents, allowing them to explain it for themselves in the context of their own writings. The first part will survey the relevant work of Bruce Ware (chapter 1), whose brief classroom handout has served as a foundational articulation of the MIV; of Gary Shultz (chapter 2), whose PhD dissertation (subsequently published as a monograph) under the supervision of Dr. Ware remains the most thorough presentation of the MIV to date; and of John Hammett (chapter 3), whose 2015 essay is the most recent published defense of the MIV. Such a survey of the MIV in the words of its own adherents aims to ensure that the following critical evaluation will have properly represented its opponents.

39. Gibson and Gibson, "Sacred Theology," 38, emphases original.

40. Berkhof, *Systematic Theology*, 15.

Part 2 seeks to put forth a positive presentation of Scripture's teaching concerning the extent of the atonement in what will amount to a biblically faithful and theologically sound defense of particularism. Though it aims to be a positive presentation, it will nevertheless engage in conversation with the multiple intentions view at key points. Part 2 will begin by setting the redemptive work of Christ in the context of the Trinitarian plan of salvation, devised by the Father, Son, and Spirit in eternity past (chapter 4). The Son does not act independently, but accomplishes his saving mission in strict accordance with the Father's saving purpose (e.g., John 6:38). Second, it will survey Scripture's explicit commentary concerning the divine intention for the sending of the Son. It will be discovered that Scripture always explicitly names salvation—not merely the provision or possibility of salvation, and never, as the MIV suggests, the purchase of common grace or a well-meant gospel offer[41]—as the reason for which the Father has sent the Son into the world (chapter 5). Third, there will be a thorough examination of the nature of the atonement, which seeks to define what precisely Scripture says Christ accomplished in his atoning death. The various motifs of the atonement will be explored, including expiatory sacrifice, propitiation, reconciliation, and redemption, as well as the atonement's fundamental character as an efficacious penal substitution (chapters 6 and 7). Fourth, part 2 will set the atoning accomplishments of Christ in the light of his role as the great high priest of the New Covenant, exploring the unity of his priestly work of sacrifice and intercession, the particularity of the New Covenant promises, and how the high priest's salvific accomplishments necessarily follow unto application for those for whom they are accomplished (chapter 8). Finally, in the context of Scripture's teaching on the above subjects, we will examine three key texts that identify a particular people as the beneficiaries of the death of Christ (chapter 9).

Part 3 brings this vindication of particularism into confrontation with the multiple intentions view by responding to its exegesis of the universalistic passages of Scripture.[42] A substantial foundation of the MIV's case is that the many passages saying Christ died for "all" (chapter 10) and the "world" (chapter 11) are most naturally interpreted to mean that Christ died for all without exception. These texts, as well as those that seem to suggest Christ has died for those who will finally perish (chapter 12), it is argued, demand that there be a general aspect to the atonement. Part 3 examines each of those three categories of texts in their turn, and aims to demonstrate that, given the biblical and theological realities established in part 2, interpreting any of these texts to mean that Christ died for all without exception is untenable. It therefore also demonstrates how those texts are most faithfully interpreted in ways that cohere with particular redemption.

---

41. This is not to deny the existence of common grace or the well-meant offer of the gospel to all without exception. It is simply to say that the cross does not purchase these things.

42. This corresponds with Shultz's chapter 3, "A Biblical and Theological Explanation of Jesus Christ's Payment for the Sins of All People in the Atonement."

Part 4 turns to address what proponents of the MIV call the "general intentions" of the atonement.[43] Ware lists four general intentions, Shultz lists those four with an additional fifth, and Hammett lists two, both of which are discussed by Ware and Shultz. Part 4 isolates the three most compelling of these general intentions—the genuine universal gospel call (chapters 13 and 14), the provision of common grace (chapter 15), and the cosmic triumph over all sin (chapter 16)—and demonstrates that, while Scripture establishes the existence of each, none is ever said to be purchased by Christ's payment for the sins of all people.

A conclusion summarizes the arguments and findings of the entire project, synopsizes the inability of the multiple intentions view to account for the biblical data concerning the nature and extent of Christ's atonement, highlights the biblical and theological viability of particularism, and offers practical implications of particularism for the Christian's doctrine and life.

---

43. This corresponds with Shultz's chapter 4, "The General Intentions of the Atonement."

PART 1

An Introduction to the Multiple Intentions View

FEW THINGS ARE MORE lamented within contemporary evangelicalism than the extent to which charity has been absent in theological discourse. The phenomenon of social media has created an environment in which one does not have to go through the checkpoints of peer review in order to publish one's opinions, no matter how ill-founded and unsupported by sound argumentation. The result has been a low point in theological discourse, where question-begging, *ad hominem* fallacies, and straw-man argumentation have dominated. Nowhere has that been clearer than within the sphere of polemical theology. Though the present work is of necessity a work of polemical theology—a critical evaluation of the multiple intentions view of the extent of the atonement—it does not seek to imitate this degraded form of doctrinal discussion. Instead, it seeks to follow the hermeneutical golden rule: that one do unto *authors* as he would have them do unto himself.[1]

To this end, the purpose of the first part of this work is to present the multiple intentions view (hereafter MIV) in the words of its own proponents, allowing those who hold the position critiqued to explain it for themselves in the context of their own writings, before attempting any refutation.[2] These first three chapters, then, present the relevant work of three proponents of the MIV: Bruce Ware, whose brief classroom handout has served as a foundational articulation of the MIV; Gary Shultz, whose PhD dissertation under the supervision of Dr. Ware remains the most thorough presentation of the MIV to date; and John Hammett, whose 2015 essay is the most recent published defense of the MIV. A detailed, though not exhaustive, articulation of the MIV in its proponents' own words will ensure that the following critical evaluation will have accurately understood its target.

---

1. John Piper, *Think*, 45–46.

2. Occasionally, footnotes document concerns, questions, or perceived inconsistencies with the material presented. Such notes are only preliminary, foreshadowing the evaluation that will come in later chapters.

1

Bruce Ware

BRUCE A. WARE IS a former president of the Evangelical Theological Society, and currently serves as the T. Rupert and Lucille Coleman Professor of Christian Theology at The Southern Baptist Theological Seminary. Dr. Ware has made numerous contributions to several fields of evangelical theological scholarship over the past several decades.[1] In the early 2000s, he began distributing a handout in his theology classes entitled, "Extent of the Atonement: Outline of the Issue, Positions, Key Texts, and Key Theological Arguments."[2] In this handout, which eventually became widely disseminated online, Ware defended a mediating position concerning the extent of the atonement, a position that he variously labeled "un/limited atonement" (i.e., limited *and* unlimited atonement), "multiple intentions view," and "four point Calvinist position."[3] The presentation given in this handout has become the foundation for the MIV, providing a clear base upon which Ware's doctoral student, Gary Shultz, would develop a full-length scholarly defense of the MIV.[4] To present the MIV faithfully and on its own terms, one must begin with a thorough summary of this foundational document, while also considering some of Ware's other comments on the issue, which are sparse.

The Issue at Hand

Ware begins his outline by attempting to capture what is and is not the central issue in the debate over the extent of the atonement. He insists that the issue is not the sufficiency of the atonement, acknowledging that both the traditional "limited"

---

1. On the doctrine of God, see his *God's Lesser Glory*, *God's Greater Glory*, and "A Modified Calvinist Doctrine of God." On Trinitarianism, see his *Father, Son, and Holy Spirit*. On Christology, see *The Man Christ Jesus*. On soteriology, see Schreiner and Ware, *Still Sovereign*.

2. Ware, "Outline." This was also presented at ETS 2010. Ware, "Select Support."

3. Ware, "Outline," 3.

4. Shultz, "Defense." A version of this dissertation was later published as Shultz, *Multi-Intentioned View*.

and "unlimited"[5] positions agree that "[Christ's] death is sufficient for all."[6] Neither, Ware claims, is the issue the efficacy of the atonement, since both sides agree that "only those who truly and savingly believe in Christ . . . have Christ's payment for sin applied to their lives."[7] In other words, Ware believes that both traditional particularists and traditional universalists can rightly subscribe to the popular maxim that the atonement is sufficient for all but efficient only for the elect.[8] Neither sufficiency nor efficiency, he says, is a point of real disagreement between the two traditional positions.[9] Finally, Ware states that the debate concerning the extent of the atonement does not have to do with the free offer of the gospel, arguing that both traditional viewpoints believe the gospel must be preached to all people. While there is significant disagreement concerning whether a particular atonement is consistent with a bona fide offer of salvation to all (and in fact such is a significant argument in critiques of particularism), nevertheless, "all agree that all [without exception] are to be recipients of the gospel offer."[10]

Given that there is broad agreement between both camps on both the sufficiency and efficiency of the atonement, as well as on the necessity and propriety of the indiscriminate preaching of the gospel, Ware then defines what he believes is the central issue of the debate. He reveals this by asking several questions: "What is the *intention* of God in offering his Son as an atoning sacrifice? Is his intention *to save people* by his Son's death? . . . Or is his intention *to provide a payment* for any and all people, which payment is only effective at the point they savingly believe?"[11]

---

5. These are Ware's terms for the two major traditional views in the debate. See Ware, "Outline," 1–2. For clarity's sake, I once again note my preference for the terms "particularist" and "universalist." See footnote 2 of the Introduction (pages 1–2).

6. Ware, "Outline," 1.

7. Ware, "Outline," 1. Disagreement on the efficacy of the atonement centers upon whether the atonement is efficacious for all those for whom it was accomplished.

8. This phrase has its origins in the work of the Medieval theologian Peter Lombard, who wrote that Christ offers himself "for all, with respect to the sufficiency of the ransom, but for the elect alone with regard to its efficiency, because it effects salvation for the predestined alone" (pro omnibus, quantam ad pretii sufficientiam; sed pro electis tantum quantum ad efficaciam, quia praedestinatis tantum salutem effecit) (Lombard, *Sentences*, 2:128).

9. It seems Ware would agree, then, with Naselli, who comments, "It is not helpful when people define their position with the phrase 'sufficient for all, efficient for the elect.' . . . Arminians, hypothetical universalists, and Calvinists alike have used that elastic phrase to describe their positions; so using it to define one's position results in confusion rather than clarity and precision" (Naselli, "Conclusion," 219). Archibald explains, "The common solution in its medieval form is ambiguous. It does not distinguish between an efficiency based upon a limited intention and efficiency based upon a limited appropriation" (Archibald, "Comparative Study," 366). Only a minority of voices within the historical discussion have denied the sufficiency of Christ's atonement for all people. A contemporary example of that position would be Nettles, *By His Grace and for His Glory*, 305–22.

10. Ware, "Outline," 1.

11. Ware, "Outline," 1, emphasis added. This is reminiscent of Berkhof's classic statement in the framing of this debate: "The question does relate to the design of the atonement. Did the Father in sending Christ, and did Christ in coming into the world, to make atonement for sin, *do this with the*

The Traditional Positions

Having isolated the question at hand, Ware then goes on to summarize how the two traditional positions have answered this question. First, he presents the particularist view, which he calls the "limited atonement view" and the "five-point Calvinist position," as follows: "Christ died for the purpose of actually and certainly saving people from their sin, but since not all are in fact saved, it requires then that he died for and hence saved a certain people, viz., those whom the Father had given to him, viz., the elect."[12] He then cites several "key texts" of Scripture that seem to support this position, adding brief explanatory comments. John 6:37–40 teaches that those given to the Son by the Father will not fail to come to him in salvation; none of them will finally be lost. Several passages identify particular individuals as the beneficiaries of Christ's death: he died for his *sheep* (John 10:11, 15), purchased the *church* (Acts 20:28; Eph 5:25); was delivered for the *elect* (Rom 8:31–39); and gave himself for *us* (Titus 2:14).

He goes on to list a number of "key theological arguments" often used by particularists, including (a) the efficacy argument, which argues that Scripture teaches that Christ has come to effectually save his people, not merely provide a payment for them that may never actually save them; (b) the sovereignty argument, which Ware represents as follows: "If Christ died for all, and by this paid for the sins of all, then, because God is sovereign and his will cannot be thwarted, all would be saved. Since all are not saved, it must be the case that Christ died for those who are saved, viz., the elect"; (c) the ethical argument, which many recognize as the "double payment argument," namely, that it would be unjust for God to punish people in hell for the sins Christ has already paid for; and (d) the comprehensive payment argument, summarized in the following way: "If Christ paid for all the sin of all people, then he paid for their sin of unbelief (among other sins). If their sin of unbelief is paid for, then God cannot hold them accountable for their unbelief. But if he does so only the sin of the elect is paid for in Christ's death."[13]

Ware then turns to outline the universalist view, which he calls the "unlimited atonement view" and the "classic Arminian position," as follows:

> Christ died for the purpose of paying the penalty for the sin of all people making it possible for any and all to be saved. God loves all and wants all to be saved. In his love for all, he sent Christ to make the payment for the sin of all. Belief in Christ is necessary, however, to receive the benefits of Christ's death and be saved. The gospel must be preached to all, and, upon hearing the gospel, any can come because Christ died for the sins of all people in the world.[14]

---

design or for the purpose of saving only the elect or all men? That is the question, and that only is the question" (Berkhof, *Systematic Theology*, 394).

12. Ware, "Outline," 1.

13. Ware, "Outline," 2.

14. Ware, "Outline," 2.

Once again, Ware cites and briefly comments on "key texts." First Timothy 4:10 indicates that there is a sense in which Christ is Savior of unbelievers, but a special sense in which he is Savior of believers. Second Peter 2:1 names unregenerate false teachers as those whom the Master has bought (ἀγοράσαντα, redeemed). First John 2:2 and 4:14 speak of Christ being the propitiation not only of "our" sins, but of the sins of the "whole world," and, given the use of the term "world" in 1 John, it is doubtful that this refers to the world of the elect. Several passages designate the beneficiaries of Christ's death with universal terms like "all" (2 Cor 5:14–15, 19; 1 Tim 2:6), while several others identify a universal love (John 3:16; Rom 5:6–8) and a universal saving will (1 Tim 2:4; 2 Pet 3:9) of God.

Turning then to "key theological arguments" that universalists often use to support their view, Ware summarizes (a) the universal divine love argument, which reasons that if God loves all equally and desires all to be saved, he would never send Christ to die for only some; and (b) the universal gospel offer argument, which reasons that a universal offer of salvation requires a universal provision of atonement, for "if no payment has been made for the non-elect, then we cannot say to the non-elect that God offers salvation *to them*."[15] Ware also refers to two other arguments—(c) the part-to-whole argument and (d) the necessity-of-saving-faith argument—which he does not develop here but presents later as support for the MIV. It is worth noting, then, that Ware regards at least these two of the key arguments for MIV to be equally supportive of universal atonement.

The Multiple Intentions View

Having outlined the two traditional positions concerning the extent of the atonement, Ware then introduces his proposal for a mediating third way, which he dubs "un/limited atonement," the "multiple intentions view," and the "four point Calvinist position," the central tenet of which is that "God's intentions in the death of Christ are complex not simple, multiple not single."[16] In fact, he avers that "much of the debate over the issue of the extent of the atonement is owing to the fact that a *single* intention (rather than multiple intentions) was sought by both sides," and that "any single intention view will have difficulty reconciling its position with one or more strain of biblical teaching." However, "as soon as one admits *multiple intentions* for the atonement, one then can account for the variety of biblical teaching."[17] Ware's answer, therefore, to the earlier questions

15. Ware, "Outline," 2.

16. Ware, "Outline," 3.

17. Ware, "Outline," 3, 4, emphases original. One supposes that Ware here intends to speak of the variety of biblical *terminology*, for, unless one is prepared to admit contradictions in Scripture, there can be no genuine variety of biblical *teaching*. Note also that for Ware a special burden of the MIV is to explain the apparent contradictions between Scripture's particularist and universalist language. Ostensibly, Ware believes that neither particularists nor universalists have offered satisfactory accounts for the variety of biblical *terminology* with respect to the extent of the atonement.

asked in order to frame the issue at hand is not to choose one response over the other, but rather it is to say that God's intention in offering Christ was *both* to "secur[e] the sure and certain salvation of his own, his elect," *and* to "pa[y] the penalty for the sin of all people making it possible for all who believe to be saved."[18] By framing the issue as a both-and proposition, rather than an either-or proposition, Ware argues that one can have the "best of both sides," capitalizing on the strengths of both particularism and universalism while also eschewing their weaknesses.[19]

Besides these two intentions, called (1) the "limited scope purpose" and (2) the "limitless scope purpose," respectively, Ware lists three others: (3) the "bona fide offer purpose," that is, Christ's death for all without exception legitimizes the universal gospel offer; (4) the "just condemnation purpose," which provides the ground for God to justly hold accountable those who reject the gospel offer; and (5) the "cosmic triumph purpose," namely, the defeat of all sin and the reconciliation of all things to the Father. Note that only the first intention, the limited scope purpose, is particular to the elect, whereas the other four intentions are universal.

Ware then offers five categories of supporting biblical texts that correspond to the five purposes, or intentions, for the atonement outlined above, followed by several key theological arguments. For ease of presentation, I will discuss the supporting theological arguments alongside the supporting biblical texts. In the first place, Ware cites all of the texts previously cited in favor of the particularist view (i.e., John 6:37–40; 10:11, 15; Acts 20:28; Rom 8:31–39; 2 Cor 5:15; Eph 5:25; Titus 2:14) as support for the limited scope purpose. He comments, "Christ *did* die for the sin of the elect in a very specific and intentional manner, in order to secure their sure and certain salvation, which salvation would be theirs through, but not apart from, saving faith. . . . Scripture clearly presents Christ as dying for his own. . . . [I]n a particular and intentional sense he died to save those given him by the Father."[20] This is precisely the particularist position, a key tenet that the universalist cannot affirm.[21]

18. Ware, "Outline," 3.

19. Ware elsewhere calls the MIV "this both/and model" (Ware, "Foreword," in Shultz, *Multi-Intentioned View*, xi). It is worth noting that this seems to be something of a pattern in Ware's theological method: (1) his view of compatibilist middle knowledge seeks the *via media* between Calvinistic determinism and free will theism; (2) his doctrine of relational mutability is a compromise between the divine immutability of classical theism and the divine mutability of open theism; and (3) his functional kenotic Christology is something of a synthesis between classical Christology and ontological kenoticism. For the first two distinctions, see footnote 1 of this chapter. For the final distinction, see Wellum, *God the Son Incarnate*, 373–419.

20. Ware, "Outline," 3, 4, emphasis original.

21. Ware clarifies that the MIV does reject universalist argumentation on several fronts. "For example, four point Calvinism [i.e., MIV] will deny that the universal love of God or God's universal desire that all be saved demands unlimited atonement. Rather, as with five point Calvinism, this view will argue that there is a sense in which God does love all and want all saved, but Scripture also clearly affirms God's special love only for the elect (e.g., Isa 43:3–4; Eph 3–5 [*sic*]; Rom 9:10–13) manifest in his elective purpose to choose, call and save only some (e.g., Eph 1:3–5; Rom 8:29–30), to the glory of his name (Eph 1:6, 12, 14; Rom 9:22–24)" (Ware, "Outline," 3).

However, what distinguishes the MIV from particularism here is that "these texts are not seen as describing the *only* sense in which Christ died for sin."[22] That is to say, for example, that Jesus' comments about his laying his life down for his sheep do not rule out the possibility that he also died for the goats; it is simply not what he chose to emphasize in John 10. His emphasis on the elect, however, should not be taken to imply exclusion of the non-elect. Ware calls this the "part-to-whole argument," stating, "Yes, some passages say that Christ died for his own, his sheep, his church, but no passage says he died *only* for the elect. His death can be for all people while only those who believe are actually saved by his death. His death for his own, then, is part of the larger whole in which he died also for the world."[23]

Not only does Ware argue that no texts say Christ died only for his sheep; he also argues that other texts of Scripture say the opposite. These texts comprise the support for Ware's second category, the limitless scope purpose, and are the same texts and explanations presented in support of the universalist view above (1 Tim 4:10; 2 Pet 2:1; 1 John 2:2; 4:14; 1 Tim 2:6; 2 Cor 5:14–15, 19).[24] He comments, "Scripture just as surely speaks of a breadth of Christ's atoning work that extends to the whole world. The real issue here is what reading of these texts best accounts for what they say. The limited atonement position appears here to strain the natural and intended meaning of texts."[25]

A third category of texts is cited in support of Ware's bona fide offer purpose (Matt 28:18–20; Luke 24:46–47; John 6:35, 40; Rom 10:13), which he describes as "texts which stress the necessity of the proclamation of the gospel of Christ's death and resurrection on behalf of the world."[26] Ware argues, "Since we are commanded to preach the gospel to all people . . . , the unlimited atoning sacrifice of Christ renders this offer of salvation fully and uncompromisingly genuine."[27] Apparently, then, Ware does not believe that a particular redemption is compatible with a genuine universal offer of salvation, though he does not argue for why this is so, nor engage with particularist arguments to the contrary. Related to this, he cites both John 3:18 and

---

22. Ware, "Outline," 3, emphasis original.

23. Ware, "Outline," 5.

24. The order of references reflects Ware's own presentation. Note that he does not here repeat the citations of John 3:16; Rom 5:6–8; 1 Tim 2:4; and 2 Pet 3:9, which did appear in the section defending the unlimited atonement view.

25. Ware, "Outline," 4. Elsewhere he asks, "Might there be a way forward to incorporate more naturally all that Scripture teaches concerning Christ's death . . .?" (Ware, "Foreword," xi). As will become apparent, a crucial point of contention between universalism, particularism, and the MIV concerns what the natural reading of any particular text is. No one camp argues explicitly for what they believe to be an unnatural reading of Scripture. The matter in question, however, is whether what one supposes to be the natural reading is in fact the author's intended meaning, rather than a merely superficial reading. See chapter 2, footnote 21. These matters are more fully addressed in part 3, where the MIV's exegesis of universalistic texts is examined.

26. Ware, "Outline," 3.

27. Ware, "Outline," 4.

John 12:48 as texts "which indicate that rejecting Christ is a further basis for judgment," and asserts that those who reject Christ "can only be rightly held accountable for rejecting what was offered them if a *real* offer had been made to them." Therefore, "Christ died for the purpose of providing an additional basis for condemnation" for such persons as reject him.[28] Similar to the bona fide offer purpose, the just condemnation purpose rests upon an assumption concerning what makes an offer genuine or illegitimate (and therefore what makes condemnation for rejecting that offer just or unjust), which assumption is not here argued for.[29]

A fifth selection of texts is cited in support of the cosmic triumph purpose, texts that seem to indicate that the extent of Christ's atonement is not only broader than the elect alone, but broader even than all human beings whether elect or non-elect, namely, extending to the entire created order itself (i.e., Rom 8:20–23; 1 Cor 15:24–28; Eph 1:9–10; Phil 3:21; Col 1:19–20). Ware argues, "Were Christ to die for the sin of the elect only . . . this would leave sin that stands outside of his atoning work and hence outside of his victorious triumph over sin."[30] In other words, not only must the penalty for sins be paid by Christ's cross, but sin's "power must be defeated that *all might be conquered and laid at the feet of the Father*."[31] Apparently, for Ware, the judgment and punishment of his enemies are not means by which Christ conquers sin; sin can only be defeated and eradicated through some sort of atonement. Since the effects of sin have penetrated beyond individual human beings to infect and affect the entire cosmos, one universal intention for Christ's death is to atone for such sin on a cosmic level. Colossians 1:20 is especially significant for Ware in this regard, because it identifies both the universal scope of Christ's reconciliation ("and through Him to reconcile all things to Himself . . . through Him, I say, whether things on earth or things in heaven") and that the means of this universal reconciliation is Christ's cross work ("having made peace through the blood of His cross"). Colossians 1:23 demonstrates that though this reconciliation is universal, universal final salvation is not in view, since the benefits of this universal reconciliation are apprehended only upon the condition of faith ("if indeed you continue in the faith firmly established and steadfast").

Ware brings his arguments from Colossians 1 to a logically consistent though striking conclusion: "So, the reconciliation of Col 1:20 is one in which the rebellion is over, yet God's conquered foes do not share in his glory. In this sense, all those in hell stand reconciled to God, i.e., they are no longer rebels and their sinful disregard for God has been crushed and is ended."[32] Elsewhere he comments, "Those in hell, who never put their faith in Christ and so were never saved, are under the

28. Ware, "Outline," 3, 4, emphasis original.

29. What constitutes the genuineness of an offer is addressed in part 4.

30. Ware, "Outline," 4.

31. Ware, "Outline," 4, emphasis original.

32. Ware, "Outline," 4.

just judgment of God for their sin, even though *Christ has paid the penalty for their sin.*"[33] According to Ware, the MIV entails an understanding of the reconciliation accomplished by Christ's cross wherein one may be reconciled to God and yet not delivered from eternal punishment in hell.[34] Indeed, Ware says, "This reconciliation must be one which includes a sense in which those outside of Christ, consigned to eternal punishment in hell, are at peace with God."[35]

Ware then offers one final argument in support of the MIV and against particularism, which he calls the "necessity of saving faith argument." He contends,

> If, as limited atonement proponents [i.e., particularists] say, Christ died actually and certainly to *save* people (i.e., the elect), and not merely [to] make their salvation possible, then it follows that nothing else is needed for the elect to be saved. . . . But is it not true that the elect are born into this world under the condemnation of God, dead in their sin, and facing the impending wrath of God (e.g., Eph. 2:1–3)? Is not saving faith required *for the elect to be saved*? If so, how can it be said of the death of Christ *in itself* that by his death *alone* he saved those for whom he died? . . . [W]e cannot speak correctly of Christ's death as actually and certainly *saving* the elect. No, even here, the payment made by his death on behalf of the elect renders their salvation *possible* while that salvation becomes *actual* only upon their exercising saving faith.[36]

In other words, because the benefits of the redemption purchased on the cross are not immediately *applied* to the intended beneficiaries, therefore, the *accomplishment* of that redemption is best understood as potential, or possible, rather than actual. One wonders, however, how this harmonizes with Ware's earlier comments, namely, that "Christ died for the purpose of *securing* the sure and certain salvation of his own, his elect."[37] Securing the sure and certain salvation of some, on the one hand, and making their salvation possible, on the other, are two different propositions. Nevertheless, Ware's handout ends on this note without a summary or conclusion.[38]

---

33. Personal correspondence from Bruce Ware, cited in Piper, "My Glory," 648–49, emphasis original.

34. Mark Driscoll and Gerry Breshears, other proponents of the MIV, concur with this tenet, citing Ware: "In this sense all those in hell will stand reconciled to God, but not in a saving way as the universalists falsely teach. In hell unrepentant and unforgiven sinners are no longer rebels, and their sinful disregard for God has been crushed and ended" (Driscoll and Breshears, *Death by Love*, 174). Evaluative comments must await later chapters, but one wonders how sinners may be unrepentant but also no longer rebels, for to desist from rebellion is to repent of it.

35. Personal correspondence from Bruce Ware, as cited in Piper, "My Glory," 653.

36. Ware, "Outline," 5, emphasis original.

37. Ware, "Outline," 3, emphasis added.

38. This is not meant as a criticism, for one cannot expect a class handout to provide the detail of a journal article or book chapter. It is simply an explanation for the present author's abrupt ending of Ware's treatment.

2

Gary Shultz

GARY L. SHULTZ JR. currently serves as the senior pastor at First Baptist Church of Tallahassee, Florida, and has served as an adjunct professor for both Liberty University Online and Baptist Bible Theological Seminary. He holds a PhD from The Southern Baptist Theological Seminary, which he completed in 2008 under the supervision of Bruce Ware. His doctoral dissertation, "A Biblical and Theological Defense of a Multi-Intentioned View of the Extent of the Atonement,"[1] was the catalyst for several other publications, including several journal articles[2] and a monograph published by Wipf and Stock in 2013.[3] The presentation of Shultz's views will primarily be gleaned from his dissertation and monograph. His work is self-consciously designed to develop Ware's thesis and to present "a full-length scholarly work explicitly explaining and defending a multi-intentioned view," which had not yet been done.[4] To the present time, Shultz's work remains the most thorough presentation of the multiple intentions view of the extent of the atonement, and therefore it is worth significant attention in outlining this position.

The Traditional Framework

Shultz begins by offering his definition of Christ's atonement: "When we speak of Christ's atonement, or his atoning sacrifice, we are referring to what Christ accomplished to make salvation possible, or penal substitution, in which God gave himself in the person of Jesus Christ to suffer the punishment of death rightly due to fallen sinners as the consequence of sin."[5] He then briefly further explains his commitment to penal substitution. It is of note that from the outset Shultz casts atonement

---

1. Shultz, "Defense."

2. Shultz, "God's Purposes for the Nonelect," 145–63; Shultz, "Reconciliation of All Things," 442–59; and Shultz, "Why a Genuine Universal Gospel Call," 111–23.

3. Shultz, *Multi-Intentioned View.*

4. Shultz, "Defense," 11n23. He states that his work is designed "to fill that void" (Shultz, *Multi-Intentioned View*, 8).

5. Shultz, *Multi-Intentioned View*, 2n4.

as that which makes salvation "possible," a term he uses profusely to describe what Christ accomplished on the cross.

Shultz summarizes the issue at hand as follows: "Either Jesus died only for those who experience the saving benefits of his atonement [particularism], or he died for all people regardless of their salvific destiny [universalism]."[6] Just a bit later, he elaborates, "The debate over the extent of the atonement centers on the intent or purpose of the atonement." After then citing Berkhof's famous portrayal of the issue,[7] he continues, "Particular redemption holds that God's intention was effectually to bring about salvation for a specific group of people, and therefore Christ died only for those people. Unlimited atonement holds that God's intention of the atonement was to provide a payment for the sins of all people, a payment that becomes effective at the moment of saving faith, and therefore there is no one for whom Christ did not die."[8] Like Ware, Shultz sees little use in appealing to the oft-quoted sufficiency/efficiency formula, since "both positions generally agree that Christ's death is sufficient for all sin and is efficacious for all who truly believe."[9]

He then commences his introduction in earnest by surveying the two traditional evangelical positions on the extent of the atonement. He defines particular redemption as asserting "that God offered his Son, Jesus Christ, as an atoning sacrifice in order to save a particular group of people, his elect, and therefore Christ only paid for the sins of the elect. Christ's death did not make salvation possible for all people."[10] Shultz lists several texts which particularists cite in support of their position, substantially similar to Ware's list (i.e., Matt 1:21; John 6:37–40; 10:11, 15; Acts 20:28; Rom 8:31–39; 2 Cor 5:15; Eph 5:25; Titus 2:14; Rev 5:9). He goes on to enumerate six biblical and theological arguments employed by particularists. Three of these correspond to Ware's summary of particularism's arguments: the sovereignty argument, the ethical argument, and the efficacy argument.[11] In addition to these three, Shultz specifies the argument of priestly unity, i.e., that both of Christ's priestly actions of atonement and intercession must be coextensive (cf. John 17; especially verse 9); the argument of Trinitarian unity, i.e., that universalism creates conflict within the Trinity by having the Son atoning for a larger group than the Father chooses and the Spirit regenerates (cf. Eph 1:3–14); and the argument that universalism undermines union with Christ by suggesting that those united with Christ in his death are not also united with him in his resurrection (cf. Rom 6:5–8).

Turning to universalism, he defines unlimited atonement as asserting "that God offered his Son as an atoning sacrifice in order to pay for the sins of everyone in the

---

6. Shultz, *Multi-Intentioned View*, 2.

7. See chapter 1, footnote 11.

8. Shultz, *Multi-Intentioned View*, 5.

9. Shultz, "Defense," 6; cf. footnotes 10 and 11 of this chapter.

10. Shultz, "Defense," 2.

11. Shultz, "Defense," 2–3; cf. Ware, "Outline," 2.

entire world. This atonement then makes salvation possible for all people, without exception, and becomes effective when accepted by the individual through faith."[12] Shultz then lists a number of texts that universalists cite in support of their position, once again quite similar to Ware's list (i.e., Isa 53:6; John 3:16; Rom 5:6–8; 2 Cor 5:14–15; 1 Tim 2:4–6; 4:10; 2 Pet 2:1; 3:9; 1 John 2:2; 4:14), and presents six biblical and theological arguments employed by universalists, four of which correspond to Ware's summary: the universal divine love argument (which includes the divine desire of the salvation of all without exception, but which Shultz separates into a second argument), the universal gospel offer argument, the necessity-of-saving-faith argument, and the part-to-whole argument.[13] Shultz adds one other argument to Ware's presentation, though it is little more than an assertion rejecting the double payment argument.[14]

The Need for a Multi-Intentioned Approach

After outlining the traditional positions on both sides of this debate, Shultz argues for the need for an alternative, observing that "the way the issue is normally framed . . . leads one to assume that there is only one purpose . . . in the atonement. . . . Either Christ only died for the salvation of the elect, or he only died to pay for the sins of humanity."[15] He laments that the traditional positions thus "unnecessarily restrict God's intentions in sending his Son to die on the cross to a single intention," and therefore are unable to account "for all of the relevant biblical texts or the theological factors that impact the debate.[16] Indeed, "focusing on only one purpose leads one to contradict other aspects of biblical teaching."[17] Particularists, he claims, seem to contradict texts that speak of Christ's atonement extending to "all" and the "world," and they have difficulty explaining how a universal gospel call fits with a particular redemption. Universalists, on the other hand, struggle to account for the texts that cast the atonement in particularistic terms and thus present a unique relationship between Christ and his people in distinction from unbelievers.[18] Shultz also notes that unlimited atonement is not easily reconciled with the biblical doctrines of unconditional election, God's absolute sovereignty in salvation, and monergistic regeneration.

Instead of this either-or approach, he claims that "Scripture seems to teach that Christ's atonement was for all people, but that the atonement did not accomplish the same things for all people. Instead of presenting just one intention in the atonement,

---

12. Shultz, *Multi-Intentioned View*, 3.

13. Shultz, *Multi-Intentioned View*, 4; cf. Ware, "Outline," 2–3, 5.

14. "God is not unfair in sending those whom Christ died for to hell as long as they are not in Christ through faith" (Shultz, *Multi-Intentioned View*, 3).

15. Shultz, *Multi-Intentioned View*, 5.

16. Shultz, "Defense," 10–11.

17. Shultz, *Multi-Intentioned View*, 6.

18. Shultz, "Defense," 11.

the Bible seems to present the atonement as having multiple intentions." He states the thesis of his work as follows:

> A multi-intentioned view holds that God the Father, in sending his Son to die on the cross, had both particular and general intentions for the atonement. In accordance with the Father's will, the Son then died to fulfill these multiple intentions. Based upon the Son's atoning death on the cross, the Spirit then works to apply the atonement in both particular and general ways. God's particular intention in the atonement was to secure the salvation of the elect. The Son fulfills this intention by sending the Holy Spirit to apply salvation to the elect on the basis of his atoning work. The Father's general intention in the atonement was for the Son to pay the penalty for the sins of all people.[19]

This thesis statement prompts three brief observations. First, it is evident from the beginning that Shultz is concerned to answer the particularist criticism that universal atonement introduces disunity in the Trinitarian work of salvation. According to Shultz, the Son's work is not broader than the Father's or the Spirit's; the Father has multiple intentions—both universal and particular—for the Son's atonement, which the Spirit carries out accordingly. Second, since paying for one's sins is presented as God's general intention while securing one's salvation is presented as his particular intention, Shultz apparently regards securing one's salvation to be something different than paying for one's sins. According to this, paying sin's penalty is not a sufficient condition to secure salvation. This will be an important distinction to bear in mind. Third, what must not be missed is that the MIV is a both-and proposition, whereas the traditional views take an either-or approach. The MIV attempts to reconcile the seemingly disparate biblical data not by explaining the universalistic texts in light of the particularistic texts (or vice versa) but by embracing both sets at face value, arguing that Christ dies *both* for the elect alone ("sheep," "church," "friends," etc.) *and* for all people without exception ("all," "world," etc.) *in different senses*.[20] It is in this way, the MIV contends that "the most likely interpretations of [all of] the biblical texts" are preserved.[21]

19. Shultz, "Defense," 12.

20. "God's multiple intentions in the atonement indicate that the atonement is in some ways for all people, but that it is for the elect in certain ways in which it is not for all people. The assertion that God had multiple intentions in the atonement, that he died with different intentions for the elect and the non-elect, is the primary way in which the multi-intentioned view differs from both particular redemption and unlimited atonement, since both of those positions understand Christ as dying in the same way for all for whom he died" (Shultz, "Defense," 12–13).

21. Shultz, *Multi-Intentioned View*, 9. As noted above, a key concern for the MIV is that the natural sense of all biblical texts must be preserved. It must be remembered, however, that no position sides against allowing Scripture to speak for itself. Despite the oft-cited caricature, no one prefers what they self-consciously admit is an unlikely interpretation of a text simply to remain loyal to a preconceived theological system. The crucial question is: By what standard is any particular interpretation to be judged more or less likely than another? When representatives of opposing views disagree on which interpretation is "most likely," what is the biblical basis for their claim? See chapter 1, footnote 25, as

Distinguishing the Multiple Intentions View

Shultz devotes the second chapter of his dissertation and subsequent book to surveying the history of the theological discussion of the extent of the atonement. While one
might quibble with some of his conclusions concerning the views of various theologians, his account is a faithful survey of the broad strokes of the historical debate.
Shultz hopes, among other things, that this historical survey provides the necessary
background to demonstrate that the MIV "fits into neither of the two historical positions on the extent of the atonement . . . because it holds to what each view rejects."[22]
Namely, the MIV "argues that Christ on the cross intended to certainly secure salvation for the elect and the elect alone," something no universalist could accept, while at
the same time affirming that "Christ paid for the sins of every single person, elect and
nonelect," which no particularist could confess.[23] In this way the MIV is genuinely
distinct from both classic particularism and classic universalism.

However, what about its relationship to other mediating views in the history of
the debate? Especially significant is Shultz's treatment of those positions that have
sought to mediate between the two majority views, such as the various strains of hypothetical universalism held by men such as Davenant, Amyraut, and Baxter, as well
as the "moderate Calvinism" of Lewis Sperry Chafer and Millard Erickson,[24] because
it helps clarify whether the MIV is a new instantiation of one of these older mediating positions or is a genuinely novel proposal. It seems clear that Shultz believes the
MIV to be genuinely novel, as he states that his goal in "setting forth the different
explanations of the extent of the atonement, particularly the ones most similar to
the multi-intentioned view, [is] to show how a multi-intentioned view endeavors
to build upon their strengths and improve upon their weaknesses."[25] It purports to
"build upon and go beyond positions that have been proposed by Christian scholars in the past,"[26] and "hopes to approach the debate from a fresh perspective so
that all of the Bible's teaching on the subject is properly emphasized."[27] Other views
may "have come close to it," but "there has yet to be a detailed explanation" of the
view Shultz is proposing.[28] Significantly, this means that the MIV does not understand itself to be merely a repurposed Amyraldianism, a reiteration of hypothetical

---

well as part 3, for detailed exegesis of the universalistic texts.

22. Shultz, "Defense," 95.

23. Shultz, "Defense," 95.

24. Shultz, "Defense," 59–73, 89–94; cf. Shultz, *Multi-Intentioned View*, 53.

25. Shultz, "Defense," 18.

26. Shultz, "Defense," 19.

27. Shultz, "Defense," 97.

28. Shultz, *Multi-Intentioned View*, 12.

universalism, or an alternative version of four-point Calvinism, but rather a distinct doctrinal formulation all its own.[29]

How does Shultz, then, understand the difference between the MIV and other mediating positions? He presents four points of distinction. First, the MIV teaches that "Christ actually paid for the sins of all people in order to accomplish his general purposes." Unlike the claims of Amyraldianism or hypothetical universalism, Jesus "did not hypothetically or conditionally pay for the sins of the nonelect."[30] Second, unlike the earlier views, the MIV does not restrict the universal aspects of the death of Christ to the single intention of making salvation available to all. Christ's universal atonement does not simply relate to the salvation of all people, whether possible or actual, but it is what accomplishes God's plan for all creation. Therefore, for the MIV, "there is . . . nothing 'conditional' or 'hypothetical' about the atonement; it accomplishes exactly what God wants it to accomplish."[31] By this claim, Shultz aims to avoid one of the most significant particularist criticisms of all forms of universalism, namely, that it renders Christ's cross work inefficacious.[32] Third, the MIV's insistence that the atonement did indeed secure the salvation of the elect distinguishes it from other "moderate Calvinist views," which "typically understand the atonement in and of itself to be only universal, and only the application of the atonement to be particular. In the [MIV] the atonement is for all, but it is not for all people in the same way."[33]

29. Here I intend only to observe Shultz's self-perception. Whether the MIV is genuinely distinct from these prior mediating systems awaits further evaluation. I suggest that the MIV is a less sophisticated species of British hypothetical universalism; see footnote 33 below.

30. Shultz, *Multi-Intentioned View*, 53. Shultz summarizes Amyraldianism as follows: "The atonement is only hypothetically or conditionally universal, however, for the salvation that the atonement provides is only effectual when the condition of faith is fulfilled" (Shultz, "Defense," 62). He cites Armstrong for support: "It is to be noted, of course, that each mention of the universality of the design of Christ's atonement is qualified by a 'provided that.' Amyraut is very much concerned that it be understood that the will of God which desires universal salvation is made on the condition that the stipulation be fulfilled, and if that stipulation is not fulfilled he does not will it. This is perhaps the most adequate definition of [Amyraut's] 'hypothetical universalism' which can be given" (Armstrong, *Calvinism and the Amyraut Heresy*, 212).

31. Shultz, *Multi-Intentioned View*, 53.

32. Whether he actually avoids legitimate criticism in this area is addressed in part 2. It is interesting to note, however, that he often says, and cites others with approbation who say, that the atonement made salvation "possible" or merely "available" (e.g., Shultz, *Multi-Intentioned View*, 2n4, 156; Shultz, "Defense," 157–58, 195n103, 206–7, 280). Also, see footnotes 58, 61, and 62 of this chapter.

33. Shultz, *Multi-Intentioned View*, 53. While this certainly distinguishes the MIV from several species of unlimited atonement, there is some question as to whether it genuinely distinguishes it from the particularly British strain of hypothetical universalism as represented by men such as James Ussher and John Davenant. For example, Davenant could say, "There was in Christ himself a will according to which he willed that his death should regard all men individually; and there was also a will according to which he willed that it should pertain to the elect alone. He willed that it should regard all the posterity of Adam who should be saved, and that it should actually save them all, provided that [see footnote 30 above] they should embrace it with a true faith. He willed that it should so pertain to the elect alone, that by the merit of it all things which relate to the obtaining of salvation, should be infallibly given to them. And in this sense we confess that the oblation of Christ is of the same extent

Fourth, Shultz distinguishes the MIV from those strains of unlimited atonement that see the atonement absolving man for some sins, whether the guilt of original sin, as in semi-Pelagianism, or all sins aside from unbelief, as in some variations of Arminianism; in the MIV, Christ has actually paid for all sins. Having outlined these four distinctions, Shultz concludes by repudiating common charges against mediating views on the extent of the atonement that are likely to be leveled against the MIV: "The multi-intentioned view is not an attempt to find a 'middle way' between Calvinism and Arminianism. Nor is it an attempt to incorporate Arminian elements into a Calvinistic soteriology. Instead, it is an attempt to highlight the truths of both particular redemption and unlimited atonement while avoiding their weaknesses."[34]

The Exegetical Case

After surveying the history of the debate over the extent of the atonement in chapter 2, in chapter 3 Shultz turns to "la[y] the foundation for the multi-intentioned view by demonstrating the biblical and theological basis for understanding the atonement as a penal substitutionary payment for the sins of all people, elect and nonelect."[35] He begins by observing that while particularists agree, as Roger Nicole has said, "that there are certain blessings short of salvation, which are the fruits of the work of Christ, which may terminate upon any and all men, and which do in fact substantially benefit some who will never attain unto salvation,"[36] nevertheless, particularists do not ground these non-saving benefits to the non-elect in a universal payment for sin.[37] The MIV, on the contrary, holds to that very proposition. Since God is absolutely sovereign, whatever non-saving benefits accrue to the non-elect as a result of the atonement must have been sovereignly designed by him. These are not merely the indirect results of a particular redemption but are the specifically designed general intentions of a universal payment for sins. Thus, "the idea that Christ paid for the sins of the elect and the nonelect is necessary in order to account [for] the general intentions that God had in the atonement," and "is therefore central to the multi-intentioned view."[38] In

---

as the predestination of God" (Davenant, "Dissertation," 2:380). This seems to locate some form of particularism in the atonement itself, not merely in its later application.

34. Shultz, *Multi-Intentioned View*, 53. It is curious, however, that while Shultz aims to thus substantively distinguish the MIV from these "moderate Calvinist" and "four-point Calvinist" mediating views, when he makes his exegetical case for a universal payment for the sins of all without exception, he relies heavily on the argumentation of the proponents of these very positions (e.g., Demarest, Erickson, and Lightner), as well as Arminians (e.g., Marshall). See part 3 for further development.

35. Shultz, "Defense," 276–77.

36. Nicole, "Case for Definite Atonement," 199.

37. See, for example, Bavinck, *Reformed Dogmatics*, 3:470–75; Berkhof, *Systematic Theology*, 438; Boettner, *Reformed Doctrine of Grace*, 160–61; Kuiper, *For Whom Did Christ Die?*, 78–81; and Murray, *Redemption Accomplished and Applied*, 61–62.

38. Shultz, "Defense," 100.

order for the MIV to stand, then, Shultz must prove that these non-saving benefits are indeed general intentions designed by God for the atonement, and that these general intentions are grounded specifically in a universal payment for sin. He argues that this proposition is demonstrated to be true by the many passages of Scripture that cast the extent of the atonement in universalistic terms, passages that ought to be interpreted as teaching that Christ atoned for the sins of all without exception.[39] According to Shultz, these texts are Isa 53:4–6; John 1:29; 3:16–17; 4:42; 6:51; 12:46–47; 2 Cor 5:14–15, 18–21; 1 Tim 2:4–6, 4:10; Titus 2:11; Heb 2:9; 2 Pet 2:1; 1 John 2:2; and 4:14, which he discusses in four sections: (1) Isa 53:4–6, (2) Johannine texts, (3), Pauline texts, and (4) texts from the General Epistles.[40]

In discussing the extent of the atonement from Isaiah 53, Shultz argues that the first-person plural pronouns throughout the passage refer to the nation of Israel as a whole, as opposed to the nations of 52:13–15 or the collective voice of the prophets.[41] This nation is comprised of both the elect remnant who were believers in Yahweh as well as the nonbelieving Jews who rejected him. Therefore, since the Servant bears the iniquities of the nation as a whole (53:4–5), and since the nation as a whole is comprised of both the elect remnant and the nonbelievers in Yahweh, then the Servant must bear the iniquities of the unbelievers as well as the believers.[42] Further, he argues that in verse 6 "the 'all' who have sinned is equated with the 'all' whose sins God laid upon the servant,"[43] and therefore the atonement is as coextensive as sin itself. Since sin has extended to all without exception, the parallel force of Isa 53:6 demands that the atonement be extended to all without exception.

39. It should be observed that, strictly speaking, this is not a valid syllogism. In what follows, Shultz does not actually prove that what particularists recognize as non-saving benefits indirectly resulting from the atonement are instead general intentions grounded in a universal payment for the sins of even the reprobate. It seems he assumes this to be true as a presupposition, and then observes that such a proposition coheres nicely with the universalistic texts, which ought to be interpreted universalistically in order to cohere with the general intentions. The argumentation thus takes a bit of a circular form. On the one hand, Shultz argues we should understand the universal benefits to be grounded in a universal atonement because Scripture employs terms like "all" and "world" to refer to Christ's work. On the other hand, we should understand the terms "all" and "world" to refer to all without exception (as opposed to, e.g., all without distinction) because of the existence of the universal benefits, which just must be grounded in the atonement. It seems this presupposition drives the exegesis that follows in his third and fourth chapters.

40. Shultz, *Multi-Intentioned View*, 56; cf. Shultz, "Defense," 100.

41. Shultz, *Multi-Intentioned View*, 57.

42. It is not clear whether Shultz considers that the speakers in this chapter are necessarily repentant Jews, and that they are likely eschatological Israel whom both Zechariah and the Apostle John describe as looking back on the Son whom they have pierced and mourning for him as an only Son (Zech 12:10; cf. Rev 1:7). In that case, the first-person plural pronouns would refer only to believing Israel. The universalistic language is explained by the fact that at that time all Israel would be believing Israel (cf. Rom 11:26). For a recent articulation of this view, see MacArthur, *Gospel According to God*, 38–39.

43. Shultz, *Multi-Intentioned View*, 57.

Turning to the Johannine texts, Shultz begins with John's Gospel, which, he observes, contains numerous texts that extend both God's love and Christ's death to the world (i.e., John 1:29; 3:16–17; 4:42; 6:33, 51; 12:47). He argues that John uses the term κόσμος in three different ways: the totality of creation, the world of humanity in general, or the world of humanity specifically in opposition to God. "There is no place in the Gospel of John," however, "where the term *kosmos* is used to refer to a limited group of people, such as believers or the elect, or Gentiles as opposed to Jews."[44] Therefore, particularist exegesis that understands some uses of κόσμος to refer to the elect alone is categorically rejected as "not possible" and not in accord with "the plain sense of the sayings."[45] In the case of John 3:16–17, reading κόσμος as "the elect" would require us to read John 3:18 as saying, "he 'of the elect' that believeth may be saved and he 'of the elect' that believeth not is condemned," which "would contradict the most basic point of Calvinism, namely, that God has elected from eternity past individuals and they alone will be saved."[46] The universalist interpretation "is so plain" and "so clearly expresses" a universal atonement that many particularists simply equivocate on the meaning of κόσμος.[47] In the case of 1 John 4:14, which identifies Jesus as the Savior of the world, we are told that "John most likely uses this phrase here to emphasize that Jesus has come in the flesh as the atoning sacrifice for all sin. . . . The term 'world' is used here to denote humanity in opposition to God, ascribing the widest possible scope to the saving purposes and activity of God."[48] For 1 John 2:2, which describes Jesus as "the propitiation for our sins; and not for ours only, but also for those of the whole world," Shultz surveys the numerous ways in which particularists interpret this distinction that do not require the "whole world" to mean all without exception.[49] He

44. Shultz, "Defense," 107–8. Interestingly, however, in the next paragraph Shultz says that John's use of κόσμος in John 4:42 is a reference to Gentiles as opposed to only Jews: "The Samaritans' statement in John 4:42 that Christ is the 'Savior of the World' [sic] means that he is not the Savior of the Jews alone, but that he came to be the Savior of all people, Jews and Gentiles" (Shultz, "Defense," 109). These instances demonstrate that κόσμος does sometimes refer to all without distinction as opposed to all without exception, phraseology that Bruce, whom Shultz cites approvingly, explicitly employs: "The 'world' embraces all without distinction of race, religion, or culture" (Bruce, *Gospel of John*, 53).

45. Shultz is here quoting Marshall (Shultz, "Defense," 108n34; cf. Marshall, "For All, for All," 338). These assertions are not argued for, however. Shultz often makes such assertions, appends a footnote in which one expects argumentation, but which in many cases merely contains the same assertion being made by a commentator without exegetical or theological argumentation. Shultz proves that others agree with his assertions, but too often he does not prove those assertions by presenting any argumentation. Specific evaluation awaits part 3.

46. Shultz is here quoting Lightner (*Multi-Intentioned View*, 62; cf. Lightner, *Death Christ Died*, 70).

47. Shultz, *Multi-Intentioned View*, 62.

48. Shultz, "Defense," 113–14. Once again, these statements comprise Shultz's handling of 1 John 4:14, but they are nowhere argued for, despite citations of authors who agree with these conclusions (e.g., Shultz, "Defense," 114n55; cf. Bruce, *Epistles of John*, 111).

49. These include: (1) John is distinguishing between Jews and Gentiles; (2) he is distinguishing between believers of that generation and believers of future generations; (3) he is emphasizing the exclusivity of Christ; i.e., he has made the only propitiation in the whole world; (4) he is simply stating

dismisses all but one of these arguments (for the fifth he has no response) with brief rejoinders, which he summarizes as follows: "None of these proposals does justice to the meaning of the words 'whole' or 'world', or the context of 1 John 2:2. . . . There is no clearer statement in Scripture indicating that Christ died to pay the penalty for the sins of all people."[50] First John 2:2 simply teaches a universal atonement, and no particularist explanation of the text does justice to the plain sense.

Coming to the Pauline texts, Shultz treats 2 Cor 5:14–15 first, arguing that "they who live" refers to a subcategory distinct from the "all" for whom Christ died. If both expressions referred to the same group, why would Paul not simply continue to use the word "all"? Therefore, Paul here teaches that Christ "died for all" without exception with the design that "they who live," i.e., believers, would no longer live for themselves but for him.[51] Second Corinthians 5:18–21 also supports a universal atonement, because "God was in Christ reconciling *the world* to Himself." Shultz here argues that reconciliation has both objective and subjective components. God objectively reconciles all without exception ("the world") to himself by means of Christ's universal atonement (which makes forgiveness available), but the enjoyment of that reconciliation is only subjectively experienced after man responds in faith to the gospel offer.[52] Shultz then turns to 1 Tim 2:3–6, where he claims that the "all" of verses 4 and 6 cannot mean merely "all sorts of people," as particularists advocate,

---

that Christ is the propitiation who is available to the whole world; (5) he is distinguishing between believers in his own inner circle versus those throughout the whole world; and (6) he is saying that from an eschatological perspective Christ will have saved the whole world because all his enemies will have been conquered in judgment.

50. Shultz, "Defense," 120.

51. Shultz, "Defense," 124. The particularist will respond that this conclusion is untenable because Paul says that the all for whom Christ died therefore (i.e., because of his death for them) themselves died to sin in him (cf. Rom 6:3–10). Shultz responds by arguing, "The death that the all died was not a death to sin or self, as this would indicate that all of humanity is saved" (Shultz, "Defense," 124n85). (Of course, this only follows if one accepts that the "all" must be interpreted to mean all people without exception.) Instead, "The death that all die in Christ's death is most likely the death that all deserve because of their sin. All have died in the sense that Christ in his death suffered the penalty for all sin, and therefore for all death" (Shultz, "Defense," 124n85).

52. See Shultz, "Defense," 126–31, especially footnotes 92–95. Also: "It is only those 'who live' and those who are 'in Christ' who are subjectively reconciled to God through faith, but all people are objectively reconciled to him" (Shultz, "Defense," 130). To substantiate this claim, Shultz quotes Marshall: "'God reconciles the world to himself' thus means: God acts in Christ to overlook the sins of mankind, so that on his side there is no barrier to the restoration of friendly relations. . . . But at the same time the indicative forms the basis for an imperative. Now people are commanded: 'be reconciled to God.' In view of what God has already done, this cannot be understood to mean that they must render God amenable to them by appropriate action. Rather God and Christ appeal to them to accept the fact that reconciliation has been accomplished *and to complete the action* by taking down the barrier on their side—the barrier of pride and disobedience and hatred of God. Let them put away their feelings against God and enter into a new relationship with him" (Marshall, "Meaning of Reconciliation," 123, emphasis added). Note that according to this definition, though reconciliation has been begun by God, it must be completed by man. Such an understanding of reconciliation is examined in part 2.

but instead must mean "all people without exception."[53] First Timothy 4:10 describes God as the Savior of all men but especially of believers. While particularists often claim that Paul uses σωτήρ here in a non-soteriological sense (i.e., in his common grace he often preserves and rescues both believers and nonbelievers from natural dangers, etc.), Shultz argues that this does not fit Paul's usage of this phrase in the Pastoral Epistles, where every other time its meaning is clearly soteriological.[54] Furthermore, such an interpretation requires Paul to use σωτήρ in two different ways, which is unacceptably awkward.[55] Instead, this verse teaches that God "has provided . . . salvation for all people in the ransom of Christ, but that he acts as Savior toward believers in a much more profound, deeper sense because it is only they who enter a saving relationship with him."[56] Finally, if this interpretation of 1 Tim 2:3–6 and 4:10 is correct, it is not likely that Titus 2:11 refers to God bringing salvation to all *kinds* of men, which would not fit the context.[57] Instead, it teaches that Christ's universal saving work "has made salvation available to all people."[58]

Turning to the General Epistles, Shultz discusses Heb 2:9, which says that Jesus "taste[d] death for everyone." "Everyone" ought not to be equated with the "many sons" brought to glory in verse 10, "those who are sanctified" in verse 11, the children of God in verses 13 and 14, those delivered from the bondage of death in verse 15, and God's people in verse 17. Instead, it ought to refer to each and every human being, since Christ fulfills Ps 8:4–6, which the author quotes in Heb 2:5–8, on behalf of humanity. He is therefore "united with all people in his incarnation and his death."[59]

---

53. Shultz, "Defense," 135–36, Once again, the actual argumentation here is sparse. His first argument is that verse 1 is best understood to refer to praying for all people without exception rather than all sorts of people, which "is clearly not the intent of the passage" (134n116). Second, "God is the only God and Christ is the only Mediator, and therefore God is the God of all and Christ is the Mediator for all" (135). Third, he simply asserts that "the focus of Paul's reasoning in this passage is that Christ is the ransom *for all*" (135); this is not an argument for why all should be read as all without exception. His fourth argument, which he calls "perhaps the most decisive one" (136), is that this interpretation accords with 1 Tim 4:10, which effectively shifts the interpretive burden to that text.

54. He lists 1 Tim 1:1; 2:3; Titus 1:3; 2:10; and 3:4 (Shultz, *Multi-Intentioned View*, 76).

55. Shultz, "Defense," 139. He cites Marshall for support: "This view . . . requires that the term be understood very awkwardly in two different senses with the two nouns that are dependent upon it, in a this-worldly nonspiritual sense with the former and in an eschatological spiritual sense with the latter" (Marshall, "For All, for All," 327).

56. Shultz, *Multi-Intentioned View*, 76.

57. Shultz, "Defense," 140–41.

58. Shultz, "Defense," 141. Shultz quotes Hiebert for support: "Salvation is available for all, but its saving effect is dependent upon the personal response of faith" (Hiebert, *Titus*, 440). Such argumentation seems to contradict Shultz's claims that the atonement was perfectly efficacious. See footnote 32 of this chapter.

59. This claim is neither argued for nor developed further, but it sounds similar to the Barthian view that since Christ assumed a genuine human nature, no one with a genuine human nature is untouched by his atoning work. Macleod's response to this is apposite: "His humanity is that of Everyman. But he is not Everyman. He is the man, Christ Jesus; and the only humanity united to him hypostatically is his own" (Macleod, *Person of Christ*, 202).

Shultz then addresses 2 Pet 2:1, which states that false teachers deny the Master who bought them. Particularists variably teach that in this verse δεσπότης refers not to the Son but to the Father, and that ἀγοράζω here is used in a non-soteriological sense. Shultz argues that both of these claims fail. First, δεσπότης explicitly refers to Christ in Jude 1:4, and Jude's letter parallels 2 Peter as they both are concerned to address the problem of false teachers. Second, ἀγοράζω must be soteriological, for this agrees with both the lexicography and the immediate context.[60] This is an effectual redemption, yet with both objective and subjective senses similar to reconciliation. Christ has objectively redeemed all, including false teachers, but such redemption is only subjectively appropriated through faith.[61]

Shultz concludes this chapter of exegesis by attempting to answer the objection that "Christ's payment for the sins of all people, elect and nonelect, ... would demand universalism [i.e., universal final salvation]."[62] He offers two reasons it does not. First,

> the Bible consistently differentiates between Christ's objective work in the atonement and the subjective application of that work to the believer. Christ's atonement actually accomplished reconciliation, redemption, and propitiation for all people, but all people are not saved because all people do not subjectively appropriate what Christ has done for them. In order to experience the reconciliation and redemption that Christ has accomplished in the atonement, one must be in Christ through faith. . . . Advocates of particular redemption err by collapsing the application and the provision of the atonement into the same act when the Bible separates them.[63]

According to Shultz, when particularists insist that the atonement "actually saves," they open themselves up to the criticism that faith is not necessary for salvation. However, Scripture teaches that until the elect come to faith, they are subject to

60. Shultz, "Defense," 148–49, especially footnotes 172–77.

61. "Just as Christ objectively reconciled the world but not all people are subjectively reconciled to him, Christ objectively redeemed the world, though all are not subjectively redeemed by him" (Shultz, "Defense," 149–50n177). He appeals to Chafer for support: "There is, then, a redemption which pays the price, but does not of necessity release the slave . . ." (Chafer, "For Whom Did Christ Die?," 313). One wonders how positing such a redemption that does not actually redeem is distinct from rendering Christ's atonement inefficacious. Shultz is aware of this criticism and attempts to answer it by appealing to the distinction between objective accomplishment and subjective application (Shultz, "Defense," 151–58; see especially footnotes 185–190 for examples of this criticism from particularists). Also see footnotes 32 and 58 of this chapter.

62. Shultz, "Defense," 151. It would either demand universal final salvation or it would undermine the efficacy of the atonement, a charge that Shultz also denies. See footnotes 32, 58, and 61 of this chapter.

63. Shultz, "Defense," 154, 155–56. One must note, however, the reversion from an "accomplishment" of redemption to merely a "provision" of atonement. Shultz seems to use these terms interchangeably, but they denote distinct concepts. "Accomplishment" denotes certainty and definiteness of application. "Provision" implies tentativeness and potentiality.

God's wrath (e.g., Eph 2:1–3). This proves some sort of inefficacy in the atonement.[64] A second reason a universal atonement does not entail universal final salvation is that, according to the MIV, Christ's atonement is not *merely* universal; it is *also* particular. There are *multiple* intentions in the atonement—both the provision of universal non-saving benefits and the securing of the certain salvation of the elect alone—and both universal and particular intentions are accomplished by Christ's payment for the sins of all people.[65]

The Multiple General Intentions

The universal, or general, intentions in the atonement are discussed in chapter 4. Therein Shultz argues that God intended that the Son pay the penalty for the sins of all people without exception to accomplish at least five other ends: "[1] to make the universal gospel call possible, [2] to make common grace (and not only salvific grace) possible, [3] to provide an additional basis of condemnation for those who reject the gospel, [4] to serve as the supreme revelation of God's character, and [5] to make the Christ's cosmic triumph over all sin possible."[66]

Shultz begins by insisting that "Jesus' payment for the sins of all people, elect and nonelect, was necessary for the universal gospel call to take place."[67] He gives four reasons for this. First, the content of the gospel, as summarized by Paul in 1 Cor 15:1–5, is that "Christ died for *our* sins." Since the word "our" includes both the preacher and the hearers of the gospel, and since the gospel is preached to unbelievers (and not merely the elect) in order to bring them to faith, then Christ has died for unbelievers as well as believers.[68] Second, Shultz argues that in 2 Cor 5:11–18 Paul declares that his motivation for preaching the gospel universally was a universal atonement. He cites Barnett: "Paul's sense of ongoing compulsion to evangelize ('controls') arose from his considered judgment ('we are convinced') when he understood that '[Christ had] died for all."[69] Third, he appeals to John 16:7–11, where Jesus teaches that, as a result

64. Here Shultz cites Ware's "necessity of saving faith" argument.

65. Shultz, "Defense," 159.

66. Shultz, *Multi-Intentioned View*, 89; cf. 89–121; Shultz, "Defense," 161; cf. 161–224. This material is also presented in Shultz's 2008 *BSac* article (Shultz, "God's Purposes for the Nonelect," 145–63).

67. Shultz, *Multi-Intentioned View*, 92. This material is also presented in Shultz's 2010 *EQ* article (Shultz, "Why a Genuine Universal Gospel Call," 111–23). This argument corresponds to Ware's "bona fide offer purpose" of the atonement (cf. Ware, "Outline," 4).

68. Shultz, *Multi-Intentioned View*, 93; cf. Shultz, "Defense," 168. It must be observed, however, that the proper antithesis is not between "elect" and "unbelievers," but between "elect" and "non-elect." There is such a thing as elect unbelievers, since all those whom God has chosen for salvation do not enter the world believing the gospel but must come to faith as a result of the regenerating work of the Holy Spirit. Shultz seems to unnecessarily equate "unbelievers" and "non-elect."

69. Shultz, *Multi-Intentioned View*, 94; cf. Barnett, *2 Corinthians*, 288. Shultz acknowledges that this argumentation depends on his interpretation of "all" and "world" in 2 Cor 5:14–19 to mean "all without exception," as was presented in his third chapter.

of his ascension, he will send the Holy Spirit to convict the world concerning sin, righteousness, and judgment. The "world" here refers to unbelievers, those who are hostile toward God, oppose his purposes, and hate him (cf. John 15:18–16:6).[70] Further, because Jesus explains that the Spirit only accomplishes this work among unbelievers because he will go away from them, and because he only ascends to the Father by virtue of his death and resurrection, therefore this universal work of the Spirit only occurs because of the atonement. If this universal work of the Spirit is grounded in the atonement of Christ, there must be some sense in which the atonement is universal.[71] Finally, Shultz insists that for the universal gospel call to be genuine there must be a universal provision upon which it is grounded, for "if Christ did not pay for the sins of the non-elect, then it is impossible to genuinely offer salvation to the non-elect, since there is no salvation available to offer them."[72]

Deviating from the order of his introduction, Shultz then turns to address a second, and related, general intention of the atonement, namely, that Christ's death "provided an additional condemnation for those who explicitly reject his payment for their sins."[73] The Scriptures indicate that unbelief is a ground for condemnation (e.g., John 3:18; John 8:24; 2 Pet 2:1, 20–21), and such condemnation could only be just if unbelievers reject a provision of salvation that is genuinely available to them.[74]

A third general intention of the atonement is the provision of common grace. While Shultz acknowledges that particularists stipulate that common grace is an indirect benefit or result of the atonement but is not itself purchased by a universal payment for sins, the MIV presses further by insisting that "non-salvific grace goes out to the nonelect on the basis of the atonement,"[75] and that the Holy Spirit's role in bringing about common grace (similar to his convicting the world of sin, John

---

70. As in footnote 68 of this chapter, it once again must be noted that Shultz is conflating the category of "unbelievers" with the category of "non-elect." It would seem that for Shultz's point to stand, the "world" must refer to the latter, but he argues only for the former.

71. Shultz, *Multi-Intentioned View*, 96.

72. Shultz, *Multi-Intentioned View*, 98. Shultz nowhere argues for the legitimacy of this claim but only asserts it, citing others' assertions, but not arguments. Chafer serves as an example: "To say on the one hand that Christ died only for the elect and on the other hand that his death is the ground on which salvation is offered to all men is perilously near contradiction" (Chafer, "For Whom Did Christ Die?," 315). Once again, the characteristics of a genuine offer will be explored in part 4.

73. Shultz, "Defense," 178. Note that "his payment for their sins" is assumed here, which begs the question. Shultz ought to have said, ". . . who explicitly reject the offer of the gospel."

74. Shultz, "Defense," 183. This argument corresponds to Ware's "just condemnation purpose" of the atonement, whom Shultz cites here: "Christ's death for the sins of those who reject him and are condemned (e.g., 2 Pet 2:1) insures [*sic*] that their judgment for rejecting Christ . . . is just, because they reject a real gift that is really, freely and graciously offered to them" (cf. Ware, "Outline," 4). One must observe, though, that particularists do not deny that the gospel is "really, freely, and graciously offered" even to the reprobate; they simply do not believe a universal provisional payment is necessary for such an offer to be genuine. Further explanation awaits part 4.

75. Shultz, "Defense," 186.

16:8) is a ministry he has only by virtue of the atonement.[76] The giving of all natural gifts and the restraining of sin and evil could not happen if God did not forestall his judgment of those outside of Christ (cf. 2 Pet 3:9). But God's patience in judgment is explicitly grounded in the atonement of Christ (Rom 3:23–25). "It is because of the atonement that God can justly forbear from punishing sin for as long as he desires, because sin has been punished in Christ,"[77] that is, "his wrath against humanity has been satisfied in the atonement."[78]

Fourth, Shultz argues that one of the purposes of Christ's atoning death was to supremely reveal the character of God. At the cross, both God's love (Rom 5:8; 1 John 4:9–10) and God's justice (Rom 3:23–26)—into one or the other of which broad categories all of God's attributes can be placed—are displayed in their fullness. Since God loves all (albeit in different ways, i.e., general and particular, saving and non-saving),[79] and since his justice "can potentially be seen by all people, the elect and nonelect,"[80] and since *both* are supremely revealed in the atonement, therefore the atonement is for all without exception.[81]

A fifth and final universal intention that God purposed in the atonement was "Christ's cosmic triumph over all sin, or the reconciliation of all things in Jesus Christ."[82] Colossians 1:19–20 teaches that Christ reconciled all things to the Father through the peace made by the blood of his cross. These "all things" that have been reconciled are the same "all things" that have been made through and for Jesus (cf. Col 1:16), which is to say all creation. He argues for this on four grounds. First, Shultz appeals to the *Christus Victor* theory of the atonement (Col 2:13–15; Heb 2:14–18), viewing it as complementary to penal substitution. Of this conquest over sin, he argues, "If Christ only paid for the sins of the elect in the atonement, then it would seem that there would be sin that would be outside of his atoning work, and thus there would be sin outside

---

76. "It is because this restraining of sin and evil is a work of the Holy Spirit that it results from the atonement, as all that the Holy Spirit does to restrain sin is based upon the Son's atoning death" (Shultz, "Defense," 191). See the above treatment of John 16:7–11, along with relevant references to Shultz's presentation.

77. Shultz, "Defense," 192–93.

78. Shultz, "Defense," 189.

79. Shultz, "Defense," 198–201.

80. Shultz, "Defense," 202. Note the language of potentiality. Since the universality posited here is predicated on all potentially seeing God's justice, one wonders if the most Shultz can say is that the atonement is potentially for all without exception.

81. "That the atonement is the supreme expression of God's love seems to suggest that the atonement is for all people, because God's love is for all people" (Shultz, "Defense," 198). "All people who repent of their sin and trust in the truth of the gospel are justified by God, and this act of salvation demonstrates God's justice because their sin has been paid for by Christ" (202).

82. Shultz, *Multi-Intentioned View*, 110. This corresponds to Ware's "cosmic triumph purpose" (Ware, "Outline," 4). Like Ware, Shultz seems to believe that sin can only be defeated and eradicated by atonement, not by the judgment and punishment of God's enemies whose sins they themselves will pay for throughout eternity. See pages 21 and following.

of his cosmic triumph."[83] In that case, his conquest over sin would not be total. Instead, Christ destroys the work of the devil (1 John 3:8)—which has had a cosmic extent—by taking away sins (1 John 3:5) even unto a cosmic extent.

Second, Shultz appeals to a two-stage understanding of the nature of reconciliation to avoid universal final salvation. This is critical to his argument. Such reconciliation is indeed universal (Eph 1:10; Col 1:20), but because Scripture rules out universal final salvation we must understand that this reconciliation cannot be the same for the elect and the non-elect. The elect are eventually reconciled in a salvific way (or subjectively), but the non-elect are reconciled in a non-salvific way (merely objectively), an understanding that accords with several texts that speak of reconciliation in this dual manner (e.g., Rom 5:10a vs. 5:10b; Col 1:20 vs. 1:21–23).[84] Shultz explains, "While the elect are subjectively reconciled to God during this life at the moment of their salvation, the nonelect never experience this aspect of reconciliation. In the eschaton the nonelect will be reconciled as God restores cosmic peace to his creation."[85] Such a reconciliation does not involve the forgiveness of sins or the reward of eternal life; those in hell will suffer the just punishment for their sins for eternity. Instead, this reconciliation means that "they have been decisively subdued to the will of God and can do nothing but serve his purposes. . . . The nonelect in hell will be reconciled in that they are no longer able to rebel against God because they will acknowledge Jesus for who He is," as Phil 2:9–11 teaches.[86] Indeed, while they are suffering in the lake of fire with Satan, "there will be peace even between God and the nonelect as a result of the atonement."[87]

A third reason that Christ's cosmic triumph over all sin must be based upon a universal atonement is that both the elect and the reprobate will experience an eschatological resurrection (John 5:26–28; 1 Cor 15:21–22). Their resurrection is grounded upon Christ's resurrection, and Christ's resurrection is grounded in his atonement.[88] Shultz explains, "Because the nonelect will be raised from the dead by the power of Christ's resurrection just as the elect will, it seems that they must have been included in Christ's atonement just as the elect were."[89] Shultz then gives a fourth and final reason, very similar to the third one. Since Jesus will rule over all creation (not merely the elect), and since his kingly rule is only given to him as a result of his atonement and resurrection (e.g., Rev 5:11–14), his atonement must be in

---

83. Shultz, *Multi-Intentioned View*, 112.

84. Shultz, "Defense," 213–15.

85. Shultz, "Defense," 215.

86. Shultz, "Defense," 215–16.

87. Shultz, "Defense," 216. This closely parallels Ware's comments discussed above. See pages 21–22 above.

88. Shultz, "Defense," 217–19.

89. Shultz, "Defense," 219–20.

some sense for all creation. In other words, the atonement that grounds a universal reign must itself be universal.[90]

The Particular Intention

Having made his exegetical case for universal intentions in the atonement in chapter 3, and having identified and explained those universal intentions in chapter 4, Shultz then turns to discuss the particular intention in the atonement, namely, the securing of the salvation of the elect. He explains, "We purposely use the word 'securing' here, as it preserves the difference between the accomplishment of salvation at the cross and the application of salvation by the Holy Spirit, or the objective and subjective aspects of the atonement."[91] This is a significant feature of Shultz's version of the MIV, which distinguishes it from nearly all other forms of non-particularism. Indeed, he says, "Christ died to secure the salvation of the elect alone,"[92] a statement very few non-particularists would make. He goes on to argue that the Bible teaches both an unconditional particular election and a particular monergistic regeneration, both of which cohere with particular redemption but not with unlimited atonement. Without a particular intention in the atonement, non-particularists cannot account for the unity in the saving work of all three persons of the Trinity,[93] a doctrine that is taught clearly in several passages of Scripture (Matt 11:25–27; John 5:19–21; 6:37–40; 10:26–30; 17:1–24; Eph 1:3–14).[94] Shultz also argues that the particularistic language that permeates Scripture is evidence of a special love of God for the elect, especially those passages that speak of Christ dying for a particular people (e.g., his "people," Matt 1:21; his "sheep," John 10:11, 14–15; his "friends," 15:12–14; "the church," Acts 20:28; Eph 5:22–33; and the "elect," Rom 8:31–39). This accords naturally with particularism but is unexplained by a universalism that demands that Christ's death extend to all equally because God's love extends to all equally.[95]

There are several key ways, however, in which the particularism Shultz advocates is distinct from traditional particularism. In the first place, he is careful to note that particularistic terms such as "sheep" and "elect" need not exclude a universal intention

90. Shultz, "Defense," 220–22.

91. Shultz, *Multi-Intentioned View*, 122.

92. Shultz, "Defense, 237.

93. "If the Son provided salvation for all, but the Father only intended to save some, then this introduces disjunction into the Godhead, as this implies that the Father and Son have different salvific goals. Most Moderate Calvinists, who hold together unconditional election and unlimited atonement, are open to this charge" (Shultz, *Multi-Intentioned View*, 125). Shultz surveys the Holy Spirit's particularistic work in effectual calling (140–43); regeneration, conversion, and justification (143–45); indwelling and filling (145–47); baptism into the body of Christ (147–48); sanctification, preservation, and perseverance (148–50); and glorification (150–51).

94. Shultz, *Multi-Intentioned View*, 133–37.

95. Shultz, *Multi-Intentioned View*, 129–33.

in the atonement, "because verses that limit the extent of the atonement to a particular group can easily be reconciled with verses that speak of Christ's atonement for all people."[96] In other words, Christ may have died for the sheep, but that does not mean he did not also die for the goats. This is borne out by Gal 2:20, in which Paul particularizes the atonement to himself but does not mean to exclude others, as if he were the only object of Christ's atonement. In Rom 8:33, which explicitly names the elect as the beneficiaries of the atonement, we should not think that Paul is referring to the elect alone; there he is commenting on Christ's death for the elect, but this does not rule out other passages that speak of his death for "all" and "the world."[97]

Secondly, early on in this chapter he makes a key concession. After insisting that the atonement secures the salvation of the elect alone, he goes on to say, however, "The atonement secured and made certain the salvation of the elect, but it did not technically 'save' the elect because no one is saved until he or she puts his or her faith in the gospel of Jesus Christ."[98] It seems, then, that there is a disjunction between atonement for sin on the one hand and salvation on the other; the cross does not save, per se, but only lays the groundwork for the Holy Spirit to come and save through his particular application of Christ's atonement.[99] For example, he says, "Christ secured the salvation of the elect in the atonement by dying for their sin in order to send the Holy Spirit to apply salvation to them."[100] Thus, the particularity does not seem to be in the atonement per se, except insofar as the atonement secures the Holy Spirit's regenerating ministry to the elect. But Shultz has also argued, in his chapters 3 and 4, from John 16:7–11 that Christ has purchased the Holy Spirit's work among the non-elect as well. Elsewhere, he says that the Holy Spirit's application of redemption to the elect is what "accomplish[es God's] particular purpose in the atonement,"[101] and that this is what "makes the redemption that Christ secured on the cross for the elect effective."[102] These statements seem to strongly imply that Christ's atonement

96. Shultz, *Multi-Intentioned View*, 132

97. Shultz, *Multi-Intentioned View*, 130n26.

98. Shultz, *Multi-Intentioned View*, 122. Yet elsewhere Shultz speaks of Jesus saving by the cross (e.g., 134).

99. This is reinforced by multiple references to the "saving works of the Holy Spirit" (e.g., Shultz, *Multi-Intentioned View*, 144, 148) and statements that "the Spirit saves" (151). However, this seems to be a view that Shultz is concerned to avoid, indeed, a view that he believes distinguishes the MIV from universal atonement. Earlier, he writes, "That God intended for the atonement to secure the salvation of the elect alone differentiates the multi-intentioned view from traditional unlimited atonement, which is unable to account for any particularity in the atonement because it understands the atonement to be a general payment for all sin that only provides salvation for all, and asserts that the particular saving acts of God are then found in the Father's election and the Spirit's saving work, but not the atonement" (125–26). Therefore, it is difficult to understand how the MIV differs from traditional unlimited atonement in this respect.

100. Shultz, *Multi-Intentioned View*, 123.

101. Shultz, *Multi-Intentioned View*, 138.

102. Shultz, *Multi-Intentioned View*, 148; cf. 140, where he cites Demarest, who says the Holy Spirit "applies, *makes effective*, and preserves the redemption Christ bought to those who believe" (Demarest,

is not itself effective and does not itself accomplish God's particular purpose toward the elect. In fact, Shultz later says, "the Son secured the salvation of the elect *by* sending forth the Holy Spirit to apply the salvific benefits of the atonement only to the elect."[103] If the Spirit's application of redemption is the means by which the Son secures the salvation of the elect, then it seems the cross is not that means. This is a key difference between the MIV and classic particularism.

Cross and Salvation, 44, emphasis added). Significantly, as a result, substitutionary sacrifice, redemption, reconciliation, and propitiation are redefined as no longer efficacious accomplishments for the elect, but general provisions for all (Shultz, *Multi-Intentioned View*, 138).

103. Shultz, *Multi-Intentioned View*, 152, emphasis added. Elsewhere: "*The way* that Christ secured the salvation of the elect was by sending the Spirit to only apply salvation to the elect" (154, emphasis added).

3

John Hammett

JOHN S. HAMMETT IS the John L. Dagg Senior Professor of Systematic Theology at Southeastern Baptist Theological Seminary. Dr. Hammett has made several contributions to evangelical theological discourse, especially in the discipline of ecclesiology.[1] In 2015 he contributed to *Perspectives on the Extent of the Atonement: 3 Views*, published by B&H Academic, in which he defended the multiple intentions view of the atonement in conversation with Carl Trueman (a particularist) and Grant Osborne with Thomas McCall (universalists).[2] Hammett's essay in that volume self-consciously builds on the work of Ware and especially of Shultz in developing the MIV, and is the most recent widely disseminated defense of the MIV in print. Therefore, his contribution must be consulted in any presentation or evaluation of the MIV.

Defining the Issue

After some introductory remarks, Hammett begins in a way similar to Ware and Shultz, namely, by defining the specific question that is of concern in the debate over the extent of the atonement. Like Shultz, he cites Berkhof's framing of the issue, noting that many "identify the key issue as the design or intent of God in the death of Christ," and ask the question, "For whom did Christ die?"[3] However, Hammett notes that some (presumably him included) believe that "Berkhof unnecessarily limits the question to an either-or dichotomy. Is it possible," he asks, "to relate the atonement both to the elect and to all, but in different senses?"[4] This sets the stage for the presentation of the multiple intentions view. The key question as Hammett sees it is not merely "For whom did Christ die?" but must be broadened to "What did God intend to accomplish by Christ's death?"[5]

---

1. See Hammett, *Biblical Foundations for Baptist Churches*, and idem, *40 Questions about Baptism and the Lord's Supper.*

2. Hammett, "Multiple-Intentions View," 143–94.

3. Hammett, "Multiple-Intentions View," 146–47. See chapter 1, footnote 11.

4. Hammett, "Multiple-Intentions View," 147.

5. Hammett, "Multiple-Intentions View," 148.

Hammett then offers definitions and descriptions of both definite atonement and universal atonement, differentiating them by both extent and efficacy. Definite atonement makes salvation not merely possible but certain, and that for the elect alone, whereas universal atonement makes salvation available generally to all without exception. The mediating views, variously designated as "hypothetical universalism," "Amyraldism," and "unlimited/limited atonement," all teach that the atonement is in some sense universal and in some sense limited.[6] He then states the thesis of his essay:

> This essay argues that there are three intentions in the atonement: universal, particular, and cosmic. It affirms that the atonement is in some sense universal and in some sense particular, but *multiple-intentions* best comprehends all of the biblical teaching on the atonement, particularly biblical teaching on the extent of the atonement.[7]

The Universal Intention

According to Hammett, the universal intention of God in the atonement was "to provide forgiveness of sins for all." In order to do this, God sent Christ "to serve as the substitute for all humanity," wherein he satisfied God's wrath "toward human sin by serving as the propitiation for all humans and thereby providing redemption and reconciliation for all humans."[8] Penal substitution, propitiation, redemption, and reconciliation are thus all benefits of the atonement enjoyed by all universally. However, because these are *provided*—as opposed to, e.g., secured to be definitively applied to all for whom they were purchased—not all people will finally be saved. He aims to substantiate these claims in light of biblical, historical, theological, and practical issues.

Hammett begins by appealing to the "*prima facie* biblical case" for universal aspects to the atonement, demonstrating once again that the plain-sense reading of "world" and "all" is a key concern for proponents of the MIV.[9] Hammett cites the Johannine use of "world" (cf. John 1:29; 3:16; 6:51; 1 John 2:2) as evidence for a universal intention, and, while he understands that there are different legitimate interpretations of "world," he cites numerous commentators who find it untenable to interpret it to mean "the elect."[10] He also finds the many "all" statements in the Pauline corpus to

6. Hammett, "Multiple-Intentions View," 148–49. Interestingly, though Hammett defines definite and universal atonement by extent *and* efficacy, he defines the MIV by extent alone, offering no comment on the efficacy.

7. Hammett, "Multiple-Intentions View," 149, emphasis original.

8. Hammett, "Multiple-Intentions View," 149.

9. Hammett, "Multiple-Intentions View," 149. Later he writes, "By far the most important advantage [of the MIV] is that it allows for the most natural exegesis both to universal and to particular texts" (183). See chapter 1, footnote 25, and chapter 2, footnote 21.

10. Hammett, "Multiple-Intentions View," 150. Two things must be observed here. First, it seems Hammett believes that interpreting the "world" as the elect is essential to the particularist case,

substantiate universality in the atonement, especially 1 Tim 2:6 and 4:10. Of these he writes, "Taken at face value, the wording of 1 Tim 2:6 . . . seems to indicate clearly a universal or general intention in the atonement, and a number of interpreters take it that way."[11] And since 1 Tim 4:10 says that God is in some sense the Savior of all people, even though he is in a different sense the Savior of those who believe, it is difficult to square with particularism, which holds that God is the Savior only of the elect. The particularist response that God is the Savior of the non-elect in some non-soteriological sense is unconvincing because σωτήρ is never used non-soteriologically in the Pastoral Epistles.[12] This does not entail universal final salvation because the divine provision is separate from the human appropriation, both of which are necessary for salvation. First Timothy 4:10 indicates that God has provided salvation for all, but only believers experience that salvation "precisely because they are believers."[13] Third, Hammett cites several texts that he believes teach that Christ died for some who will finally perish, and thus for more people than the elect alone (Rom 14:15: 1 Cor 8:11; Heb 10:29; 2 Pet 2:1). Speaking particularly of 2 Pet 2:1, Hammett argues, similarly to the above, that these false teachers were soteriologically bought by Christ by virtue of the universal divine provision on the cross but were never saved because they never personally appropriated that provision through faith. Particularists who claim that Peter was simply describing the false teachers by the judgment of charity give evidence of the fact that they "approach the verse with a commitment to definite atonement" and must "deny what [the] verse straightforwardly appears to affirm."[14]

After these biblical considerations, Hammett briefly surveys the historical debate on extent of the atonement, observing that "the majority position in Christian history is decidedly on the side of universal atonement."[15] He concludes that the historical re-

---

though several particularists do not take that interpretation of such texts, a point of which he seems to be aware in his later citation of Dabney (Hammett, "Multiple-Intentions View," 154n36). Second, Hammett does not offer exegetical argumentation for his view, but simply appeals to several other commentators who share his interpretation. This proves that there are published authors who agree with him, but it does not prove his assertions. See chapter 2, footnote 45 for similar observations concerning Shultz.

11. Hammett, "Multiple-Intentions View," 151. Once again, however, the appeal to "a number of interpreters" is moot, for one finds numerous proponents of each position, and, even if it could be proven that one view enjoys a majority of support, such matters are determined by grammatical-historical exegesis, not majority rule. Besides this, it should also be noted that it is not an argument to merely insist that the "face value" of the text "clearly" supports one's view. Similarly, when Hammett quotes George as saying, "Unless the context clearly requires a different interpretation, it is better to say that 'all means all,'" (Hammett, "Multiple-Intentions View," 152), it must be noted that this is to beg the question and assume a default interpretation of "all" that has not been argued for.

12. Hammett, "Multiple-Intentions View," 152–53. On this last point, Hammett appeals to Shultz's exegesis (Shultz, "Defense," 138).

13. Hammett, "Multiple-Intentions View," 154. One wonders whether by this comment Hammett intends to make the sinner's response the decisive or determinative cause of salvation.

14. Hammett, "Multiple-Intentions View," 157.

15. Hammett, "Multiple-Intentions View," 158; cf. 157–62. Hammett's presentation seems to

cord strengthens the case for universal atonement, but "The persistence of both views suggests that a multiple-intentions view . . . may be able to preserve the strengths of both sides and provide a more comprehensive explanation."[16]

Then, Hammett turns to answer four main theological objections to what he has presented so far. First, Hammett anticipates the particularist argument that because (a) God will certainly accomplish all he intends, (b) because the atonement is inherently efficacious, and (c) because it would be unjust to punish people for sins Christ has paid for, a universal atonement necessitates universal salvation. Hammett rebuts this objection by leaning heavily on the distinction between the universal objective provision of salvation and the particular subjective appropriation of salvation.[17] That is to say, "The payment Christ made for sins is not effectual apart from a faith-union with Christ," but is "of no value, ineffectual, and useless, until subjectively appropriated."[18] In other words, Christ did not effectually pay for sins by his atonement but simply provided a payment that may be applied on the basis of the sinner's decision. Second, he addresses the objection that universal atonement drives a wedge between Christ's priestly offering (i.e., his death) and his priestly intercession. These two works must be coextensive, and since John 17:9 restricts Christ's intercession to his people, therefore his death ought to be restricted to his people. Hammett counters by questioning the biblical foundation for the claim that the two priestly functions must be coextensive, and also by noting that Christ's prayer from the cross seems to provide evidence of Christ interceding for elect and reprobate alike (Luke 23:34).[19] Third, Hammett responds to the contention that universal atonement divides the persons of the Trinity, since the Son would die for a different number than the Father had chosen and than the Spirit will regenerate. In response, he contends that this argument needlessly narrows the Father's intent in the cross to saving his elect. If, alongside his particular intention to save some, he also intended Christ's death to make a universal provision for all, then there is no disruption.[20] Fourth, Hammett notes that particularists often claim universal atonement fails to account for the passages of Scripture that particularize his death for his people (Matt 1:21) and his sheep (John 10:11), and so on. He responds by noting that these passages do not indicate that Christ died *only* for his people or his sheep, but also comments that the MIV can give a fuller voice to these texts than a single-intentioned universal atonement can.

---

parallel considerably, though not exactly, with Shultz's survey (Shultz, "Defense," 19–97).

16. Hammett, "Multiple-Intentions View," 161.

17. Hammett, "Multiple-Intentions View," 162–65.

18. Hammett, "Multiple-Intentions View," 164–65. This corresponds to Ware's "necessity of saving faith" argument (Ware, "Outline," 5). Hammett here seems to explicitly affirm the inefficacy of the cross, something Shultz seemed very eager to uphold. For example, see Shultz, *Multi-Intentioned View*, 53, where he says the cross "accomplishes exactly what God wants it to accomplish."

19. Hammett, "Multiple-Intentions View," 165–66.

20. Hammett, "Multiple-Intentions View," 166.

Finally, Hammett concludes his case for a universal intention in the atonement by noting universalists' contention that particularism "provides an insufficient ground for evangelism by undercutting the well-meant gospel offer."[21] After providing a number of particularists' responses, he rejects them on the basis of Shultz's handling of 1 Cor 15—i.e., that "Christ died for our sins" must include believers and nonbelievers, and thus, ostensibly, the elect and reprobate. Hammett is careful to confess that he does not accuse particularists of insincerity or indolence in proclaiming the gospel, but he believes that a universal gospel offer "fits much more easily and completely" with a universal provision in the atonement.[22] Thus, on biblical, historical, theological, and practical grounds, Hammett is persuaded that there is a universal intention in the atonement.

The Particular Intention

This does not, however, rule out a particular intention in the atonement. In addition to this universal intention, Hammett argues that "another intention of God in sending Christ and another intention of Christ in dying was actually to secure the salvation of some."[23] He defends this both biblically and theologically while also offering answers to several theological objections.

Hammett begins his case for a particular intention in the atonement by noting that advocates of the MIV can employ many of the traditional biblical arguments for particular redemption, though with some modifications. For example, texts emphasizing that Christ has died for a particular group of people (e.g., Matt 1:21; John 10:11; Eph 5:25–27) point significantly to a particular intention in the atonement. Though these passages do not prove that Christ died *only* for his sheep, etc., and thus do not prove particularism to the exclusion of universalism, they do nevertheless indicate a particular intention that is not adequately addressed by proponents of a single-intentioned universal atonement. Secondly, these particularistic expressions are complemented by a number of texts that teach God has a special love for his elect people (e.g., Rom 8:31–39), though this does not rule out God's love for all people, albeit in a different way. Third, Scripture also emphasizes "the certainty and

21. Hammett, "Multiple-Intentions View," 167. Here he is citing Allen, "Atonement," 107.

22. Hammett, "Multiple-Intentions View," 169. Hammett seems to conflate "unbelievers" and "non-elect," as Shultz does. See chapter 2, footnote 70.

23. Hammett, "Multiple-Intentions View," 169–70. This represents a shift in the way Hammett has spoken of the salvation of the elect so far in this essay. Earlier on, he cast the atonement as making the same ineffectual provision for all without exception, which is subjectively applied to the elect through faith by the ministry of the Holy Spirit (Hammett, "Multiple-Intentions View," 154, 162n60). Christ has not made two accomplishments, one for all and one for the elect, but rather has accomplished a universal provision that will be made effective by the Holy Spirit. Now Hammett does present Christ as making two accomplishments, one of which actually infallibly secures the salvation of the elect. This confusion is also present in Shultz (see chapter 2, pages 39–41 and footnotes 99–103, as well as "An Internal Inconsistency" in chapter 4).

definiteness of the salvation provided through the cross."[24] Matthew 1:21 says that Jesus *will* save his people; Rom 5:9–10 says that we *have been* justified and *were* reconciled by the cross; Eph 5:25–27 says that Christ gave himself up for the church "with a purpose that seems to go beyond merely providing forgiveness: 'to make her holy . . . to present her to himself as a radiant church' (NIV)."[25] Particularism thus seems to honor the truth that Jesus is "Savior, not just Possibility-Maker," that God intends "not just to provide universal forgiveness through the atonement but actually to save some."[26] This, however, is not contradictory to a universal provision of salvation, but rather complementary to it.

Hammett then goes on to enumerate several other biblical arguments for particularism whose merit he questions. While many particularists point to the coherence between particular redemption and a particular unconditional election, "the lack of clear and explicit biblical connection of election and sovereignty to the intention of the atonement limits the strength of this argument."[27] Similarly, Hammett rejects the argument that because Christ's death procured the gift of saving faith for those for whom he died, penal substitution demands particularism. He responds by claiming that precisely how the cross "procures" faith is unclear; he sees a connection but develops it differently than traditional particularists.[28] Further, he finds logical the argument that definite atonement preserves the unity of the divine will in salvation, "but it is inferential more than explicit, and it is qualified by the evidence elsewhere in the New Testament that there is also a universal intention in the atonement."[29] Thus it

24. Hammett, "Multiple-Intentions View," 170. This is a curious phrase, for "certainty and definiteness" do not cohere naturally with the concept of the mere *provision* of salvation. Particularists will often speak of the certainty and definiteness of the salvation *accomplished* by Christ on the cross. The preference of the language of provision over accomplishment may be one of the ways in which Hammett intends to "modify" (Hammett, "Multiple-Intentions View," 170) traditional particularist argumentation, and thus it becomes noteworthy in distinguishing particularism from the MIV. See "Efficacious Accomplishment" in chapter 7.

25. Hammett, "Multiple-Intentions View," 170–71.

26. Hammett, "Multiple-Intentions View," 171. However, only a few pages later, Hammett approvingly quotes Vanhoozer who says, "The saving significance of Christ's death consists in making possible God's gift of the Holy Spirit" (Hammett, "Multiple-Intentions View," 176; cf. Vanhoozer, "Atonement in Postmodernity," 398–99). This both reinforces Jesus as "Possibility-Maker" and locates the saving efficacy in the atonement not in Christ's objective accomplishment but the Spirit's subjective application. Once again, see chapter 2, pages 39–41 and footnotes 99–103.

27. While Hammett leans on Shultz (and others) here (Hammett, "Multiple-Intentions View," 171; cf. Shultz, "Defense," 235–36), he differs from Shultz on the connection between election and atonement. As Shultz says, "The doctrine of election is closely related to the doctrine of the extent of the atonement, as the former refers to God's plan to save sinners and the latter refers to the enactment of God's plan to save sinners through Jesus Christ" (Shultz, *Multi-Intentioned View*, 124).

28. Hammett, "Multiple-Intentions View," 172. Note that Shultz says on this topic, "Because the Holy Spirit only bestows faith on the elect, faith must have been secured for the believer by the atonement just as all the other saving works of the Holy Spirit were secured by the atonement" (Shultz, *Multi-Intentioned View*, 144).

29. Hammett, "Multiple-Intentions View," 172.

is plain that the MIV does not simply embrace both universalism and particularism without modifying key aspects of each system.

He commences his theological rationale for a particular intention in the atonement by asking how the single event of Christ's death can both provide salvation for all and secure salvation for the elect. He argues that the objective accomplishment of the cross "removes the obstacles to fellowship with God," while the subjective application of salvation is what actually effects that fellowship.[30] The particular intention of the atonement is only achieved by the Spirit's power to cause one to place faith in the gospel. This subjective application and the objective provision of the cross "are so tightly linked that they may be properly recognized as two aspects of the one work of atonement."[31] The scope of the atonement is thus broadened to include not only the cross but also the Spirit's work of regeneration. They may legitimately be so linked, he argues, because of texts like John 7:39, which inextricably links the giving of the Spirit to the death, resurrection, and ascension of Christ.[32] He goes on to make his most unique contribution to the discussion, leveraging the moral influence theory of the atonement to explain how the subjective aspect of salvation is directly connected to the cross. The cross has a subjective moral influence on the elect after salvation, teaching us to love (1 John 4:19) and live for Christ (2 Cor 5:14). But Hammett argues that it also has a subjective moral influence on the elect in conversion, because the Spirit uses the foolishness of the message preached to bring some to faith (1 Cor 1:22–24; 2:2–5). He says, "The moral influence of the cross enlightens them to see the cross in a different way, not as foolishness but as wisdom and power. Such a view of the cross leads them to embrace it in faith and repentance. But such a response is not universal but particular."[33] Thus, what has traditionally been recognized to belong to regeneration, Hammett, by means of the moral influence theory, imports into the atonement itself. It is only in this way that the atonement is particular.

30. Hammett, "Multiple-Intentions View," 174. Note that removing obstacles to fellowship with God is not securing salvation for anyone.

31. Hammett, "Multiple-Intentions View," 174. Hammett is concerned to distinguish his view from those who locate the particularity of salvation solely in the Spirit's work of regeneration (Hammett, "Multiple-Intentions View," 171n96; cf. Strong, *Systematic Theology*, 773). This is because he rightly desires to maintain a symmetry of particularity for all three persons of the Trinity in the work of salvation. However, the move seems merely formal, for the particularity of Christ's work seems to be nothing more than the provision for the eventual work of the Holy Spirit. Calling the particular work of the Holy Spirit a second aspect of the one work of the atonement does not change this. See footnote 26 of this chapter.

32. Hammett, "Multiple-Intentions View," 175. He self-consciously leans on Shultz here (Hammett, "Multiple-Intentions View," 176; cf. Shultz, *Multi-Intentioned View* 123). It would seem, then, according to Hammett's paradigm, it is the Holy Spirit who is most properly designated our Savior, not Christ. Once again, refer to chapter 2, pages 39–41 and footnotes 99–103.

33. Hammett, "Multiple-Intentions View," 180. This has had significant impact on the development of the MIV, as is evident by the fact that while there is no mention of the moral influence theory in Shultz's dissertation, it is an argument he makes in his book, citing Hammett (Shultz, *Multi-Intentioned View*, 142).

Hammett then briefly responds to some theological objections to a particular intention in the atonement. In the first place, the universal texts and the genuine universal offer of the gospel are no argument against the MIV, because the MIV incorporates the universal intention right alongside the particular intention. Though universalists "see any assertion of a particular intention to secure the salvation of some as contrary to [the] universal love and universal saving will" of God, they must admit that "the Bible speaks of God's love in different ways."[34] Besides, this objection conflates fairness with justice; though God does not treat all equally, he does treat all fairly (cf. Matt 20:1–16).

The Cosmic Intention

Hammett then turns to his third and final intention in the atonement, namely, the cosmic intention. While the objective theories of the atonement (e.g., penal substitution) correlate well with the universal provision of forgiveness, and while the subjective theories of the atonement (e.g., moral influence) correlate well with the particular intention of subjective application of salvation, it is the *Christus Victor* theory of the atonement that correlates with a cosmic intention, in which all the enemies of believers are conquered by the cross.[35]

He begins his case for this cosmic intention by noting how 2 Cor 5:19 supports an objective, universal provision of reconciliation on the basis of the cross.[36] He goes on, however, to address Col 1:20, which extends reconciliation by the cross to "all things," i.e., all created things, as made clear by the same phrase in Col 1:16. This does not entail universal final salvation, since reconciliation ought to be understood as primarily objective—that is, not the actual abolition of alienation and enmity, but only the provision of such. Citing Melick, Hammett insists that in this context reconciliation must be defined as "all things being put in right relation to Christ," which, for those who are finally lost, involves judgment and punishment.[37] As a result, it will then be "right for God to relate to creation in a restored way because of what Christ accomplished on the cross."[38] Hammett also references Col 2:15; Heb 2:14–15; and Phil 2:9–11, which relate Christ's cosmic conquest to his death and resurrection. Hammett says he "know[s] of no one who explicitly objects to this cosmic intention of the cross," but notes that some particularists see it as ancillary to the issue of the atonement, a notion Hammett rejects.

34. Hammett, "Multiple-Intentions View," 181.

35. Hammett, "Multiple-Intentions View," 184.

36. Hammett, "Multiple-Intentions View," This is not thoroughly argued for, but he seems to follow Shultz's presentation. See Shultz, "Defense," 126–31.

37. Hammett, "Multiple-Intentions View," 185–86; cf. Melick, *Colossians*, 225. This is a significant revision of the soteriological concept of reconciliation, which is addressed in chapter 6. Under this definition, one may be reconciled to God while undergoing judgment and punishment. This parallels Ware's and Shultz's presentation. See chapter 1, pages 21–22, and chapter 2, pages 37–38.

38. Hammett, "Multiple-Intentions View," 186.

But this is precisely what is in dispute, that is, whether everything that results from the atonement (e.g., the restoration of the cosmos) is a direct benefit purchased by the cross or is only an indirect benefit as a result of the cross.

Other Intentions?

Hammett then turns to discuss other intentions of the atonement that have been proposed by other proponents of the MIV, or of some formulation like the MIV. Here he addresses those proffered by Ware and Shultz. Hammett believes the "genuine universal gospel call" and the "additional basis for condemnation" "seem more like results or outcomes of the universal intention of the atonement rather than separate and additional purposes or intentions of the atonement," since there are no biblical texts explicitly indicating such.[39] Thus, Hammett is not averse to distinguishing between that which results from the atonement and that which the atonement itself accomplishes. This will prove to be a key point in the particularist case against what Hammett calls the "cosmic intention" of the atonement. Against "the provision of common grace,"[40] Hammett notes that "the texts usually cited in support of common grace (e.g., Matt 5:45; Acts 14:17) seem to associate common grace more with the character of God (his love and kindness) than with the atonement of Christ. It makes logical sense . . . , but in the absence of more explicit biblical support I hesitate to affirm it."[41] Hammett does agree that the cross is "the supreme revelation of God's character," but locates this in the particular intention of the atonement, according to the subjective moral influence theory, since it is only those who are saved who accurately perceive God's character as revealed by the cross.[42] He also briefly repudiates the notion that the cross procures prevenient grace in the Arminian sense, as well as the prosperity gospel teaching that the cross secures physical healing and wealth.[43]

Hammett summarizes and concludes his case by reemphasizing that the MIV allows for a more natural exegesis of the relevant texts than do the traditional views, is more theologically comprehensive since it embraces what the traditional positions deny, and conveniently builds on the strengths and avoids the weaknesses of a single-intentioned particularism or universalism.[44]

---

39. Hammett, "Multiple-Intentions View," 190. Hammett does not interact with Shultz's exegetical defense of these intentions.

40. Shultz, "Defense," v.

41. Hammett, "Multiple-Intentions View," 190–91.

42. Hammett, "Multiple-Intentions View," 191.

43. Hammett, "Multiple-Intentions View," 191–92.

44. Hammett, "Multiple-Intentions View," 193.

Part 1 Summary and Conclusion

THE FOREGOING STUDY LEADS us, by way of summary, to highlight several key distinctives of the multiple intentions view of the extent of the atonement. Proponents of the MIV are driven by the central burden that neither traditional position in the debate over the extent of the atonement has given adequate voice to all of the Bible's teaching on the matter. According to the MIV, universalism fails to satisfactorily explain passages of Scripture that speak of Christ dying for a particular people, passages that speak of God's special love for his chosen people, and how a universal atonement can cohere with the biblical teachings of unconditional election and monergistic regeneration. On the other hand, particularism fails to do justice to the natural reading of the many passages of Scripture that cast the extent of Christ's atonement in the widest of terms, such as "all" and the "whole world." Particularism also struggles to coherently ground the well-meant offer of the gospel to all without exception, since no provisional atonement has been accomplished for the reprobate. The chief failure of each view is that they limit God's intention in the atonement to a single intention. The MIV proposes that we eschew this either-or dichotomy and embrace a both-and approach: God sent Christ, and Christ came to earth, with the intention that Christ would die *both* to make salvation available to all without exception *and* to infallibly secure the salvation of the elect alone. Thus, Jesus paid for the sins of the elect and the reprobate, but in different senses and to accomplish different purposes. The triune God had multiple intentions in the Son's atonement, particular *and* universal. In this way, the most natural reading of all the relevant passages of Scripture is preserved in a way that has not been done before, even by other mediating positions, from which the MIV is eager to distinguish itself as a genuinely novel proposal.

	Ware	Shultz	Hammett
1	Limited Scope	Secure Salvation for the Elect	Particular
2	Limitless Scope	(Pay for All Sins)	Universal
3	*Bona fide* Offer	Legitimize Universal Gospel Call	
4	Just Condemnation	Additional Basis for Condemnation	
5		Provide Common Grace	
6		Supremely Reveal God's Character	
7	Cosmic Triumph	Cosmic Triumph	Cosmic

Table 1: The Multiple Intentions of the Atonement

In addition to these two intentions concerning salvation, various proponents of the MIV propose several other intentions that God purposed in the atonement. Ware and Shultz have very similar positions here, holding that Christ's payment for the sins of all without exception has secured a well-meant gospel offer to all, has provided an additional basis for condemnation to those who reject the gospel, and grounds the reconciliation of the whole cosmos to Christ. Shultz adds two other intentions: the purchase of common grace and the supreme revelation of God's character. Hammett limits his multiple intentions to three: the universal, in which Christ provides redemption and reconciliation for all; the particular, in which he actually secures the salvation of some; and the cosmic, in which he conquers all the forces of wickedness in the entire created order. These other general intentions of the atonement are not merely indirect benefits that result from the atonement, as many particularists have often conceded, but are specifically grounded in a universal payment for the sins of all people.

The MIV makes some key theological moves in order to explain and support its handling of the various relevant texts of Scripture. Specifically, the traditional understandings of the achievements of the atonement (e.g., propitiation, redemption, reconciliation, etc.) are modified significantly. These benefits of the cross are not the particular accomplishments that will certainly be applied to all those for whom they were purchased; rather, they are benefits that are provided but may be rejected through unbelief. That is, there are those for whom Christ propitiates the Father's wrath who bear that wrath for eternity; there are those whom Christ has redeemed who will remain in their slavery to sin and death; and there are those whom Christ has reconciled to the Father who will suffer divine alienation in the lake of fire. The efficacy of these benefits—i.e., the particularity of the atonement—is located not in the cross itself, but in the cross's provision of sending the Holy Spirit, who applies the purchased provisions of the cross to the elect alone through faith. Much is made, then, of the distinction between the objective accomplishments or provisions of the cross, on the one hand, and the subjective application of salvation by the Holy Spirit. Substitutionary sacrifice, propitiation, reconciliation, and redemption are all objective provisions that may or may not be subjectively applied.

Further, it is significant that the MIV makes more use of the various theories of the nature of the atonement than the traditional positions. Whereas universal atonement has historically leaned heavily upon the governmental theory of the atonement, and whereas particular redemption has regarded the cross chiefly as a work of penal substitution (though neither major view has totally excluded other theories), the *Christus Victor* and moral influence theories figure much more prominently in the MIV. The *Christus Victor* theory coheres nicely with the cosmic intention of Christ's universal conquest of sin. A modified moral influence theory is employed to bring particularity back to the atonement, after it had been largely exported to the Spirit's work of regeneration. Since the particular intention of the atonement is accomplished by means of the Spirit's application of salvation, the atonement is broadened to include the Spirit's work. Thus, the regenerating, illuminating work of the Spirit in regeneration is regarded as an aspect of the cross, whose moral influence efficaciously persuades the elect to repent and believe the gospel.

It is without question that Ware, Shultz, and Hammett have made a winsome case for the MIV. It is difficult to take issue with a view that desires to mediate between the putative extremes of a long-held debate, a view that has embraced the best and repudiated the worst of each position, a view that allows all of the relevant passages of Scripture to be read in their most natural sense, and a view that makes theological sense of its exegetical conclusions. The question is, however, whether the MIV can sustain the claims its proponents have made for it—whether the exegetical and theological argumentation bears the weight of its attractive assertions. It is the contention of this present work that the exegesis and theological synthesis provided by the MIV's most significant proponents do not sustain their claims, and that when examined closely the MIV fails the tests of biblical comprehensiveness and theological consistency. The ensuing chapters aim to make that case.

A Defense of Particularism in Light of the Claims of the Multiple Intentions View

AT THE RISK OF being reductionistic, it is not inaccurate to say that the central burden of the multiple intentions view of the extent of the atonement is to be exegetically faithful to the text of Scripture—specifically, to give full weight to those passages of Scripture that cast the work of Christ in universalistic terms (e.g., he "gave Himself as a ransom for *all*," 1 Tim 2:6; "He Himself is the propitiation for our sins; and not for ours only, but also for those of the *whole world*," 1 John 2:2). For proponents of the MIV, these universal referents cannot be understood properly unless they are interpreted to refer to all people without exception. That central conviction grounds the claim that God has intentions for the atonement that are not limited to securing the salvation of a particular people, but rather general intentions, short of salvation, that extend to the elect and reprobate alike.

Because the interpretation of those universalistic passages is so central to the universalist's case, many contributions to the debate between particular versus universal atonement begin immediately with the exegesis of those passages. The particularist aims to explain why ostensibly universalistic language ought not to be interpreted as absolutely universal—i.e., all of all sorts, all without exception—but rather as indicating some of all sorts, all of some sorts, or all without distinction. Universalists respond that such interpretive moves do not accord with the plain sense of Scripture, and both sides furnish a cadre of commentators supporting their mutually exclusive claims. It is at this point that the conversation typically reaches a stalemate, or, worse, gives way to frustration and uncharitable discourse.

While the present work aims to challenge the MIV's handling of these universalistic texts (and thus undermine the ground for believing that there are general intentions in the atonement), it does not aim to do so merely by offering a plausible alternative interpretation of those texts along particularistic lines, and so to continue volleying proof texts and citations of disparate commentators back and forth with one another. Rather, the thesis of the present work is that the MIV misinterprets those universalistic passages preeminently by failing to adequately frame them in the context of the whole of Scripture's teaching concerning (a) atonement in general and (b) the purpose and nature of Christ's atoning work in particular. The MIV's interpretive conclusions concerning passages that cast the *scope* of Christ's atonement in universalistic terms fail because they contradict key tenets of the rest of Scripture's teaching concerning the *substance* of the atonement (i.e., what the atonement is) and the *scheme* of the atonement (i.e., what it is designed to accomplish).[1]

The aim of part 2, therefore, is to set forth that biblical teaching—to provide Scripture's framework concerning the purpose and nature of the atonement, and then to bring those truths to bear on the question of the extent of the atonement. This will amount to a biblically faithful and theologically sound positive argument for the doctrine of particular redemption—namely, that the Father's intention and design in sending Christ, and Christ's intention and design in dying in the place of sinners, was to save the elect (and them alone) by dying in their place as an atonement for their sins (and theirs alone), thus securing everything necessary to put them into possession of saving faith by the work of the Holy Spirit.[2] Though primarily intended to be a positive presentation, part 2 will also seek to engage in conversation with the MIV, demonstrating

---

1. This reflects the author's conviction that the biblical doctrine of the extent of the atonement is not a product of any particular text or set of texts that explicitly states, "Jesus died for all people in history without exception," or "Jesus died for the elect alone and no one else." Rather, a biblical doctrine of the extent of the atonement is formulated similarly to the biblical doctrine of the Trinity—held together by the affirmation that the Father and Son are ὁμοούσιος, of the same substance, though such a term never appears in Scripture—or the biblical doctrine of the hypostatic union of divine and human natures in Christ, though no one text explicitly names Christ as one πρόσωπον subsisting in two φύσεων. As David and Jonathan Gibson put it, ". . . the diverse biblical parts demand the patient work of synthesis to portray the theological whole. . . . definite atonement is a *biblico-systematic* doctrine that arises from careful exegesis of atonement texts and synthesis with internally related doctrines. . . . When both exegetical and theological 'domains of discourse' are respected as such *and* taken together, then reductionist objections to definite atonement lose their force and this reading of the meaning of the death of Christ emerges as profound and faithful" (Gibson and Gibson, "Sacred Theology," 38, emphases original).

2. Packer defines particular redemption as "Christ's actual substitutionary endurance of the penalty of sin in the place of certain specified sinners, through which God was reconciled to them, their liability to punishment was for ever destroyed, and a title of eternal life was secured for them" (Packer, "Saved by His Precious Blood," 119–20). David and Jonathan Gibson provide another helpful definition of particular redemption: "The doctrine of definite atonement states that, in the death of Jesus Christ, the triune God intended to achieve the redemption of every person given to the Son by the Father in eternity past, and to apply the accomplishments of his sacrifice to each of them by the Spirit. The death of Christ was intended to win the salvation of God's people alone" (Gibson and Gibson, "Sacred Theology," 34). This definition is careful to emphasize key biblical and theological themes that figure prominently in the formulation of a biblical doctrine of the extent of the atonement: the unity of the Trinity ("triune God"), the importance of the divine intention ("intended to save," "intended to win"), that redemption is efficaciously accomplished and not merely made possible ("achieve the redemption," "accomplishments of his sacrifice"), that atonement is circumscribed by divine rather than human choice ("given to the Son by the Father in eternity past"), and that that which the cross accomplished must certainly be applied ("and to apply the accomplishments of his sacrifice").

key places where the MIV fails to remain consistent with the biblical doctrines of the purpose and nature—and therefore the extent—of the atonement.

First, in chapter 4, the redemptive work of Christ will be set in the context of the Trinitarian plan of salvation, devised by the Father, Son, and Spirit in eternity past. By virtue of their own unity of essence (who they are), the persons of the Trinity must be perfectly united in all of their intentions (what they will) and acts (what they do). This is no less the case with respect to their work in salvation. Thus, the saving work of the Son must never be divorced from the saving work of the Father and the Spirit. Maintaining the unity of the Trinity in the work of salvation is of paramount importance to biblical faithfulness and theological orthodoxy. Therefore, it will be demonstrated that the Son did not undertake his atoning work independently but instead accomplished his saving mission in strict accordance with the eternal plan purposed by the Father in election and executed by the Spirit in regeneration. It will be shown that a particular redemption coheres most consistently with a particular election and a particular regeneration.

Second, chapter 5 will survey the statements of Scripture concerning the triune God's intention for sending the Son to atone for sins. In challenging a position whose definitional claim is that there are multiple intentions for Christ's atonement, it will be essential to examine those texts that comment directly on the intention, purpose, or aim of Christ's death. It will be discovered that Scripture always explicitly names salvation—not merely the provision or possibility of salvation, and never the so-called general intentions posited by the MIV—as the single, all-encompassing intention for which the Father sent the Son into the world to make atonement.

Third, chapters 6 and 7 will examine the Bible's teaching concerning the nature of the atonement, namely, what precisely Scripture says Christ accomplished in his atoning death. Particular attention will be given to the various motifs by which Scripture casts the penal substitutionary atonement, including expiatory sacrifice, propitiation, reconciliation, and redemption.[3] As was noted at the close of part 1, while the MIV presents itself as holding to both particularism and universalism in some form, it nevertheless fundamentally diverges from classic particularist definitions (which I will argue are biblical definitions) of the accomplishments of the cross. The MIV speaks of a substitution in which both the substitute and those in whose stead he stands receive punishment, a propitiation in which the anger of the one propitiated is nevertheless rekindled for eternity, a redemption in which slaves are never released from bondage, a reconciliation that leaves man and God eternally separated. It will be demonstrated that such conceptualizations of the central motifs of the atonement are both absent from and fundamentally at odds with the biblical data. Intimately related to this, I will survey Scripture's consistent presentation of Christ's work of

---

3. Though "conquest" is also a motif of the atonement (cf. Col 2:14–15; Heb 2:14–15), it bears little on the present discussion and so, in the interest of space limitations, will not be expounded upon. Its relevance is discussed in part 4.

atonement as an efficacious sacrifice—an offering that perfectly accomplished what it was intended to accomplish. It will be shown that the atonement is not, at bottom, a provision, a potentiality, or a possibility, but an efficacious accomplishment; that is, Christ did not by his death make men salvable or redeemable, or God placable or reconcilable, but he saved and redeemed men, and he propitiated God and reconciled him to man. As noted in the part 1, the proponents of the MIV are sensitive to the accusation that an atonement whose scope is broader than those finally saved must ultimately be inefficacious. While they aim to evade this charge in several ways, it will be demonstrated that it ultimately cannot be avoided.

Fourth, in chapter 8, the atoning accomplishments of Christ will be set in the light of his role as the great high priest and mediator of the New Covenant. It will be demonstrated that Christ exercises his priestly office in substantial continuity with the Levitical priests whose ministry he fulfills (except where the New Testament shows obvious discontinuities, e.g., Heb 10:11–12), and therefore that the priestly works of sacrifice and intercession are inextricably linked and must thus be coextensive. Christ offers himself as sacrifice for the very same number as those for whom he intercedes before the Father, which Scripture identifies as particular and not universal. It will also be shown that it is impossible to divorce Christ's atoning work as Savior from his identity as the mediator of the New Covenant, the promises of which are explicitly limited to those whom God chooses and eventually brings to himself in saving faith. Further, the relationship between impetration and application will be explored—i.e., that the high priest's salvific accomplishments cannot fail to be applied to those for whom they are accomplished, such that none for whom Christ has satisfied God's wrath can fail to escape his judgment in hell.

Finally, in the context of Scripture's teaching on the above subjects, chapter 9 will examine key texts that identify a particular people as the beneficiaries of the death of Christ. It should be noted that such exegesis of classic particularist proof texts comes long after the Bible's framework of the nature and purpose of the atonement has been set forth, so that these texts may be properly interpreted in the context of the full breadth of Scripture's teaching. While it is often argued that particularizing designations of the objects of Christ's death (e.g., "sheep") do not necessarily exclude others (e.g., "goats"), it will be demonstrated from select texts that such designations are intended by the biblical authors to be exclusive.

4

The Son's Redemptive Work in the Context of the Trinitarian Plan of Salvation

ONE OF THE GREATEST causes for confusion and misunderstanding concerning the nature and extent of the atonement is the failure to properly root the Son's saving mission in the eternal Trinitarian plan of salvation.[1]

Neither Unison nor Discord, but Harmony

The acts of the triune God in creation, providence, and salvation are inextricably grounded in the Trinitarian life of God himself. In other words, God does what he does because he is who he is. And the most essential comment one can make about the identity and being of God is that he is triune—that the single, undivided divine essence subsists eternally in three coequal, consubstantial persons: the Father, the Son, and the Holy Spirit (Matt 3:16–17; 28:19–20; 1 Cor 12:4–6; 2 Cor 13:14; Gal 4:4–6; Eph 4:4–6; Titus 3:4–6). Therefore, precisely because the *persons* of the Father, Son, and Holy Spirit can never be divided, neither can their *works* be divided (John 14:10).[2] As Letham explains, "in all God does, all three persons are directly involved. God's various actions, while particularly attributable—or appropriated—to one of the three are yet indivisibly those of all three working together in harmony."[3] So, for example, while

1. Portions of this section are adapted from the author's contributions to MacArthur and Mayhue, eds., *Biblical Doctrine*, 513–16, 545–58.

2. This doctrine of the inseparable operations is a fundamental axiom of classic Trinitarian theology. That is, *opera Trinitatis ad extra indivisa sunt*: the external works of the Trinity are undivided. See Muller, *Dictionary*, 213; Vidu, *Same God Who Works All Things*. Gibson offers a helpful summary: ". . . who God is in the history of redemption arises from who God is in himself. His act reflects his being. And if God's being lives in harmony—three persons in one God and one God in three persons mutually cohering and complementing each other—then when the same God acts in history in the economy of salvation, we should expect nothing less than the same harmony of purpose and love" (Gibson, "Trinitarian Work," 366).

3. Letham, "God, Incarnation, and Definite Atonement," 440, emphasis original. This language is to be distinguished from how Ware employs it in Ware, *Father, Son, and Holy Spirit*, 42, which is given more to social Trinitarianism than the traditional doctrine of inseparable operations grounded in a genuine unity of action, which is what the present author aims at here. The persons of the Trinity are not three centers of consciousness collaborating unto a common end, but three persons subsisting in

Scripture identifies God the Father as the creator of the world (Gen 1:1; 1 Cor 8:6a), creation is also attributed to the Son (John 1:3; 1 Cor 8:6b; Col 1:16) and to the Spirit (Gen 1:2; Ps 33:6). Thus, the church confesses that there are not three separate acts of creation, but that the one act of creation is by the Father through the Son in the Holy Spirit.[4] God's indivisible being is represented in his indivisible acts.

Nevertheless, the doctrine of inseparable operations must always be complemented by the doctrine of appropriations. That is to say, while no person of the Trinity acts apart from the other two, each divine act is appropriated, or attributed, to one of the persons in particular. Thus, as in the previous example, though the Son and the Spirit are not absent from creation, the Father is most often named as the subject of that work. For another, while the Son alone is the subject of the incarnation (John 1:14; Phil 2:6–7), nevertheless he is sent into the world by the Father (1 John 4:9) and is begotten in Mary's womb by the Holy Spirit (Luke 1:35). As Letham memorably illustrates, the doctrine of appropriations ensures that the persons of the Trinity work in harmony rather than in unison, while the doctrine of inseparable operations ensures that they are never in discord.[5]

The Triune Plan of Salvation

This principle of Trinitarian unity holds true for God's work of salvation as well. This means that the atoning work of Christ can never be adequately understood if it is considered in isolation from the saving work of the Father and the Holy Spirit. When the eternal Son took on flesh to dwell among man and accomplish our salvation by his atoning death, he was not acting as a rogue agent, divorced from the intentions and the actions of the other persons of the Trinity. Indeed, he openly declares, "For I have come down from heaven, not to do My own will, but the will of Him who sent Me" (John 6:38). Jesus self-consciously conducted every aspect of his ministry in strict accordance with the will of the Father—a will that was known to him in the eternal council of the Trinity, in which the Father, Son, and Spirit devised a plan to rescue fallen humanity from the effects of sin and death.

Scripture testifies of this eternal plan of salvation in several ways. In the first place, a number of passages of Scripture characterize the saving work of the Son as being divinely predetermined. In Ephesians 3, Paul teaches that the gospel accomplished in Christ's life, death, and resurrection, which Paul preached (3:6)—the unfathomable riches of Christ (3:8) that revealed the long-hidden mystery of the administration in which Jew and Gentile would dwell together in one body through faith in Messiah (3:5–6, 9)—was all accomplished "in accordance with the eternal purpose which He

---

the identical (undivided and simple) divine essence acting inseparably.

4. Augustine, *Gospel of John*, Tractate 20, in *NPNF1* 7:131–37 (*PL* 35:1556–64). See also Bavinck, *Reformed Dogmatics*, 2:319.

5. Letham, "God, Incarnation, and Definite Atonement," 442.

carried out in Christ Jesus our Lord" (Eph 3:11; cf. 1:9–11). That is, Christ's redemptive work was carried out according to a predetermined plan, namely, the Father's purpose (πρόθεσις) designed in eternity past,[6] which Eph 1:11 calls "the counsel of His will" (τὴν βουλὴν τοῦ θελήματος αὐτοῦ). Thus, when Jesus told the disciples of his impending betrayal at the Last Supper, he said, "For indeed, the Son of Man is going as it has been determined [κατὰ τὸ ὡρισμένον]" (Luke 22:22), or, as a leading Greek dictionary renders it, "in accordance with the (divine) decree."[7] The design of this treachery predated Judas; it had been irrevocably determined in eternity past. According to 2 Tim 1:9, God has saved us "according to His own purpose [πρόθεσιν] and grace which was granted us in Christ Jesus from all eternity [πρὸ χρόνων αἰωνίων]." So determinative is this eternal saving purpose of the triune God that the elect are said to have received grace in Christ before they even existed—indeed, before time began.[8] Even the events of the crucifixion itself are described as the execution of this eternal plan of salvation, for Jesus was "delivered over by the predetermined plan [τῇ ὡρισμένῃ βουλῇ] and foreknowledge of God" (Acts 2:23); his crucifiers only did "whatever [the Father's] hand and [the Father's] purpose [ἡ βουλή] predestined [προώρισεν] to occur" (Acts 4:28).

Secondly, besides such statements that the Son's atoning work was carried out according to the eternal divine plan, Scripture also explicitly identifies Jesus' saving mission as his obedience to the Father's will, which clearly indicates that this will had been made known to the Son in a prior agreement. In addition to John 6:38, already mentioned above, Jesus explained that the authority he had to lay down his life as a sacrifice for sin and to take it up again in victorious resurrection derived from the "commandment [he] received from [his] Father" (John 10:18). Hebrews identifies Christ as the prophesied Servant to come who characterized his self-offering for sin as readiness to come and do the will of the Father (Heb 10:7–9; cf. Ps 40:6–8). Indeed, at the outset of his ministry, Jesus says, "My food is to do the will of Him who sent Me and to accomplish His work" (John 4:34); then at the close of his ministry, as he prepares to return to the glory of the fellowship of the Father, which he had enjoyed from all eternity (John 17:5), he says, "I glorified You on the earth, having accomplished the work which You have given Me to do" (John 17:4). The work assigned to him in the triune council had been obediently discharged, and thus the κένωσις and ταπείνωσις of his incarnation and atonement are cast as matters of becoming obedient to the point of death on a cross (Phil 2:6–8).

A third category of biblical evidence for this pretemporal Trinitarian compact consists in passages that outline the Father and Son's roles in accomplishing salvation, in which the Father promises to reward the Son for the obedient completion of his mission. In Ps 2:7–8, the Son himself speaks of the Father's eternal decree in which

---

6. BDAG, 869.

7. BDAG, 723.

8. BDAG, 33.

he is promised to inherit the nations and to possess the ends of the earth.[9] The Father will put the Spirit upon the Son, his Servant, who will work righteousness among the nations (Isa 42:1–3; 49:6). He will send the Son, appointed as a covenant to the people, to give sight to the blind and to free the captives (Isa 42:6–7; 49:8). The Father will accomplish this not only by sending the Son into the world, but by sending him to intercede for sinners by bearing their iniquity unto death (Isa 53:10–12). But as a reward for rendering himself a guilt offering, the Son is promised to see his offspring, to prolong his days, and to prosper in the Father's good pleasure (Isa 53:10). Because he would justify the many by bearing their sin in the anguish of his soul, he is promised to see his reward unto satisfaction (Isa 53:11–12). Thus, the roles of the three persons of the Trinity according to this council of salvation become clear: the Father will send the Son into the world to accomplish salvation; the Son will accomplish that salvation by working righteousness and dying a substitutionary death for sinners; and the Spirit, whose role is most clearly revealed only in retrospect, will empower the Son throughout his saving mission—from birth (Luke 1:35), throughout life (Luke 4:1, 14), in death (Heb 9:14), and finally unto resurrection (Rom 8:11; 1 Tim 3:16)—and will eventually apply the salvation the Son has accomplished to all those whom the Father has chosen (Gal 4:4–6; Titus 3:5). The Father will then reward the Son for his obedience to this divine plan (Phil 2:8) by highly exalting him and exhibiting him to all as the Lord of heaven and earth (Phil 2:9–11).[10]

These realities demand a perfect and complete unity of purpose between the Father, the Son, and the Spirit with respect to salvation. Though the three persons are attributed different roles—the Father planning and sending, the Son living and dying and rising to accomplish salvation, and the Spirit empowering the Son and applying the Son's accomplishments to sinners—the external works of the Trinity are undivided such that no person works or wills out of accord with the others. While they work not in unison but in harmony, they indeed work in harmony and not in discord. The slightest rift in the saving will of the Father versus the saving will of the Son versus the saving will of the Spirit would undermine the consubstantiality of the persons of the Trinity.[11]

---

9. Plumer, *Psalms*, 43–45; Turretin, *Institutes of Elenctic Theology*, 1:294–95. See also Augustine, *Augustine on the Psalms*, 1:27; and Owen, *Mystery of the Gospel Vindicated*, in *Works*, 12:240–43.

10. Trueman summarizes the roles of the three persons of the Trinity in the plan of redemption: "In brief compass, the [plan] of redemption is that which establishes Christ as Mediator, defines the nature of his mediation, and assigns specific roles to each member of the Godhead. The Father appoints the Son as Mediator for the elect and sets the terms of his mediation. The Son voluntarily accepts the role of Mediator and the execution of the task in history. The Spirit agrees to be the agent of conception in the incarnation and to support Christ in the successful execution of his mediatorial role" (Trueman, "Atonement and the Covenant of Redemption," 214).

11. As Trueman helpfully argues, "Significantly, the *homoousian* means the interaction between Father and Son cannot be construed in any terms that would imply even the most mildly adversarial relationship"; such would be to "clearly tend toward tritheism" (Trueman, "Definite Atonement View," 26).

Trinitarian Unity a Biblical Doctrine

We see this Trinitarian unity reflected in key passages of Scripture that inextricably link the persons and their work in salvation, consistently presenting the Father's work in the plan of redemption, the Son's work in the accomplishment of redemption, and the Spirit's work in the application of redemption:

> . . . the Lord Jesus Christ, who gave Himself for our sins so that He might rescue us from this present evil age, according to the will of our God and Father. (Gal 1:4)

The Lord Jesus gave himself for our sins to accomplish redemption (v. 4a), so that we might be rescued from this present evil age, an implicit reference to the Spirit's application of redemption (v. 4b), according to the will of the Father as expressed in the plan of redemption.

> But when the fullness of the time came, God sent forth His Son, born of a woman, born under the Law, so that He might redeem those who were under the Law, that we might receive the adoption as sons. Because you are sons, God has sent forth the Spirit of His Son into our hearts, crying, "Abba! Father!" (Gal 4:4–6)

Here we see that the Father sends the Son into the world according to the plan of redemption (v. 4); the Son accomplishes redemption by redeeming those under the Law that they might be received as adopted sons (v. 5); and the Spirit applies that redemption by being sent into the hearts of the redeemed in regeneration (v. 6).

> Blessed be the God and Father of our Lord Jesus Christ, who has blessed us with every spiritual blessing in the heavenly places in Christ, just as He chose us in Him before the foundation of the world, that we would be holy and blameless before Him. In love He predestined us to adoption as sons through Jesus Christ to Himself . . . . In [the Beloved] we have redemption through His blood, the forgiveness of our trespasses, according to the riches of His grace . . . In Him, you also, after listening to the message of truth, the gospel of your salvation—having also believed, you were sealed in Him with the Holy Spirit of promise, who is given as a pledge of our inheritance, with a view to the redemption of God's own possession, to the praise of His glory. (Eph 1:3–5, 7, 13–14)

Paul's great hymn to the triune Savior in Ephesians 1 shows us that the Father plans redemption for those he chooses in eternity past (1:4–5); the Son accomplishes their redemption through his blood (1:7); the Spirit (implicitly in this verse) applies that blood-bought redemption unto the forgiveness of God's people (1:7), sealing them (1:13) for the time when the Spirit will consummate redemption by bringing God's people to their promised inheritance (1:14).

> But when the kindness of God our Savior and His love for mankind appeared, He saved us, not on the basis of deeds which we have done in righteousness, but according to His mercy, by the washing of regeneration and renewing by the Holy Spirit, whom He poured out upon us richly through Jesus Christ our Savior, so that being justified by His grace we would be made heirs according to the hope of eternal life. (Titus 3:4–7)

Here in Titus 3, the Father's plan for redemption is represented by a reference to the love and kindness of his predestining plan (3:4; cf. Eph 1:4–5, "in love He predestined us . . . according to the kind intention of His will"); the Son accomplishes redemption by saving us in mercy (3:5–6); the Spirit applies redemption by regenerating and renewing us unto justification and eternal life (3:6–7).

> . . . God, who has saved us and called us with a holy calling, not according to our works, but according to His own purpose and grace which was granted us in Christ Jesus from all eternity, but now has been revealed by the appearing of our Savior Christ Jesus, who abolished death and brought life and immortality to light through the gospel . . . (2 Tim 1:8–10)

In this passage, God is represented as having "saved us and called us with a holy calling," a reference to our effectual calling unto salvation by the Spirit (cf. Rom 8:28, 30; 1 Cor 1:9; Eph 4:4), which thus speaks of redemption applied. Such salvation was not according to our works, but according to the gracious, electing purpose of the Father in eternity past, which thus speaks of redemption planned. That plan has now been revealed by the atoning work of the Son whereby he abolished death and brought life and immortality, which thus speaks of redemption accomplished.

In summary, the predestining, electing work of the Father, the accomplishing, redemptive work of the Son, and the applying, regenerating work of the Spirit are wrought in perfect harmony. There is a perfect unity of purpose and intention in the saving will of the persons of the Trinity, for it is the identical, selfsame will. Therefore, the objects of these saving acts of God—election, atonement, and regeneration—must be coextensive. If any one person acts to save more or fewer sinners than any other person of the Trinity, they could not be said to be united in their saving will. The Father elects unto salvation; the Son redeems those the Father has chosen; and the Spirit gives life to those redeemed.

Particular Election, Particular Redemption

The question must be asked, then: Has the Father chosen all without exception to be saved, or has he chosen a particular people to be brought to himself in salvation? Is the Father's election universal or particular? Scripture answers in favor of the latter. This eternal plan of salvation was not devised on behalf of sinners in general, but only on behalf of those whom the Father had chosen to receive salvation. Romans 8:28–30 serves to establish this definitively. Those on whom the Father has set his foreknowing, electing love he also predestined; and those he predestined he also effectually called to life in regeneration; and those whom he called he also declared righteous in Christ through faith; and those whom he justified he also glorified. Since (a) all who are predestined and chosen are eventually justified and glorified, and since (b) not all without exception are justified and glorified—a fact admitted by all who do not embrace universal final salvation—therefore, it follows that (c) not all without exception have been predestined by the Father unto salvation. The designation "elect" (which appears a few verses later, Rom 8:33), against whom none can bring a charge, necessarily implies a category of those not elected who may indeed be justly charged for their sins and perish for them. As the following chapter makes clear, the Potter has fashioned from the same lump of clay both "vessels of wrath prepared for destruction" as well as "vessels of mercy . . . prepared beforehand for glory" (Rom 9:22–23). In his inscrutable wisdom, the Father has not chosen to save every human being without exception, but only a subset of those on whom he has set his sovereign love.[12]

Therefore, since the Father's election is particular and not universal, and since the Father and the Son must be perfectly united in their saving intention—indeed, since the Son's mission is birthed out of and circumscribed by the Father's eternal choice[13]—it must be that the Son's atonement is particular and not universal. Robert Reymond illustrates the impossibility of the alternative: "It is unthinkable to believe that Christ would say: 'I recognize, Father, that your election and your salvific intentions terminate upon only a portion of mankind, but because my love is more inclusive and expansive than yours, I am not satisfied to die only for those you have elected. I am going to die for everyone.'"[14] While few opponents of particularism would state their position in such terms, it is difficult to see how their view does not logically necessitate such a conclusion. A particular election (and a particular regeneration) coupled with a universal atonement inevitably introduces a disjunction between the persons of the Trinity. It is to "separate the Father and the Holy Spirit from the Son, when the very essence of God is that there is one purpose in which

12. The same is true for the ministry of the Spirit. Since (a) it is by the ministry of the Holy Spirit that redemption is applied unto regeneration, justification, and glorification (cf. Rom 8:30), clearly implying that none who are justified will fail to be glorified; and since (b) there are some who do indeed perish in their sins (Matt 7:13–14; 25:46; 2 Thess 1:8–9; Rev 20:15; cf. 14:11); therefore, (c) neither is the regenerating work of the Spirit universal, but particular.

13. That election circumscribes the atonement is substantiated by the previous passages cited. It is the Father's will that gives rise to the Son's mission (Gal 1:4); the Son redeems because the Father has sent him to do so (Gal 4:4–5); the Father has chosen us *in Christ* (Eph 1:4), having granted us grace from all eternity *in Christ Jesus* (2 Tim 1:9). As Gibson argues, "the elective purpose of God the Father ([Eph] 1:4) and the redemptive purpose of God the incarnate Son (5:27) are one and the same: to present the elect as the Son's bride, holy and blameless on the last day. More specifically, Christ's death is the *means* to accomplish the electing purpose of the Father. In short, election circumscribes atonement" (Gibson, "Trinitarian Work," 346).

14. Reymond, *New Systematic Theology*, 678.

they are united."[15] Gibson rightly observes, "This detracts from the indivisible, Trinitarian work of God in Christ—the Father and the Son united in their distinct works within the economy of salvation, as is the Son and the Spirit. Despite protests to the contrary, these various positions on the atonement cannot evade the accusation of a dysfunctional Trinity, where dissonance rather than harmony is the sounding note."[16] Unity in the Trinity demands a particular redemption.

Notwithstanding all this, the argument for particularism grounded in Trinitarian unity is not based merely upon logical deductions from orthodox Trinitarianism. It is explicit in the text of Scripture itself. If it is plain that the Father sent the Son to earth for a specific purpose and to accomplish a specific mission, and if Jesus explicitly identified the will of the Father as the driving motivation in all his saving work (cf. John 4:34; 6:38; 10:17–18; 17:4; Heb 10:7), what then was the will of the Father as Jesus understood it? The following passages answer that Jesus knew he was to be the representative and substitute for all those and only those whom the Father had chosen for salvation—a group he identifies as those given to him by the Father:

> *All that the Father gives Me* will come to Me, and the one who comes to Me I will certainly not cast out. For I have come down from heaven, not to do My own will, but the will of Him who sent Me. *This is the will of Him who sent Me*, that *of all that He has given Me I lose nothing*, but raise it up on the last day. For this is the will of My Father, that everyone who beholds the Son and believes in Him will have eternal life, and I Myself will raise him up on the last day. (John 6:37–40)

> I am the good shepherd, and I know My own and My own know Me, even as the Father knows Me and I know the Father; and *I lay down My life for the sheep*. . . . My Father, *who has given them to Me*, is greater than all; and no one is able to snatch them out of the Father's hand. (John 10:14–15, 29)

> Father, the hour has come; glorify Your Son, that the Son may glorify You, even as You gave Him authority over all flesh, that to *all whom You have given Him*, He may give eternal life. This is eternal life, that they may know You, the only true God, and Jesus Christ whom You have sent. . . I have manifested Your name to the men *whom You gave Me* out of the world; *they were Yours and You gave them to Me*, and they have kept Your word. . . . I ask on their behalf; I do not ask on behalf of the world, but of *those whom You have given Me; for they are Yours*; . . . Father, I desire that they also, *whom You*

15. Nicole, *Our Sovereign Savior*, 65.

16. Gibson, "Trinitarian Work," 368. Barnes writes, "If God decided in eternity past whom he would call and save—i.e. to whom he would give grace in Christ Jesus [2 Tim 1:9], if God decided in eternity past who would be united to Christ and thus receive his grace, then in what way can we say that Jesus Christ died to pay the penalty for sins and to remove the condemnation from those who are not part of this eternal decision? Are we to conclude that God on the one hand decided to pass over some and allow them to go their own way and not be saved, but yet on the other hand to 'save' them potentially by purchasing them, by paying their sins?" (Barnes, *Atonement Matters*, 95–96).

have given Me, be with Me where I am, so that they may see My glory which You have given Me, for You loved Me before the foundation of the world. (John 17:1–3, 6, 9, 24)

For both He who sanctifies and those who are sanctified are all from one Father; for which reason He is not ashamed to call them brethren, saying, "I will proclaim Your name to My brethren, in the midst of the congregation I will sing Your praise." And again, "I will put My trust in Him." And again, "Behold, I and the children *whom God has given Me*." Therefore, since the children share in flesh and blood, He Himself likewise also partook of the same, that through death He might render powerless him who had the power of death, that is, the devil, and might free those who through fear of death were subject to slavery all their lives. For assuredly He does not give help to angels, but He gives help to the descendant of Abraham. (Heb 2:11–16)

It is in the context of these passages, in which Jesus declares the inextricable connection between his mission and the Father's will (e.g., John 6:38; 17:4), that he also states that the Father has given to him a particular group of individuals, and that it is particularly on their behalf that he accomplishes his redemptive work. These individuals belonged to the Father ("they were Yours") in a way that the rest of the world did not (John 17:6), which can only refer to his foreknowing and predestining them unto salvation (Rom 8:30; cf. Eph 1:4–5; 2 Tim 1:9). At various points, Jesus calls these individuals his "own" (John 10:14) and his "sheep" (John 10:15),[17] whom he will never lose (John 6:39; 10:29); "brethren" (Heb 2:11–12), the "children" of the Father (Heb 2:11, 13–14);[18] and the "seed of Abraham" (Heb 2:16).[19] They are distinct from "the world" (John 17:9; cf. 17:2) and so are not all without exception; rather, they have been chosen out from among the world (John 17:6). Because the Father sovereignly draws them (John

---

17. Note that these sheep are so called not as a consequence of their faith in him; rather, existence as a sheep belonging to Christ is the prerequisite for saving faith, such that Jesus says, "But you do not believe *because* you are not of My sheep" (John 10:26). Therefore, Jesus' people exist as his sheep even before they trust in him for salvation. That is to say, they are those whom the Father has chosen and given to the Son, the elect. Note, then, especially in light of Jesus identifying the Pharisees as those who are not his sheep in John 10:26, that "Jesus lays down his life for a particular group of people (his sheep) in distinction from others (those who are not his sheep)" (Harmon, "For the Glory of the Father," 277). Indeed, for Jesus to say that he lays his life down for his sheep, and then immediately to identify certain persons to be not of his sheep, is to teach that he did not lay down his life for them, and so not for all without exception. For more on this, see "John 10:11–30: The Good Shepherd and His Sheep," in chapter 9.

18. Owen comments, "Their participation in flesh and blood moved him to partake of the same— not because all the world, all the posterity of Adam, but because the *children* were in that condition; for their sakes he sanctified himself" (Owen, *Death of Death*, 175).

19. Note that the writer does not say that the Son gives help to the posterity of Adam, which would seem to be required if Christ died for all without exception, but rather to the seed of Abraham, a designation that particularizes the objects of Christ's help to those who eventually follow in the steps of the faith of Abraham (cf. Rom 4:12–13, 16; Gal 3:7, 9, 29).

6:44, 65), these sheep come to Christ in faith (John 6:37), are freed from the slavery of death (Heb 2:14–15), and receive eternal life (John 6:40; 10:28; 17:2). They are the exclusive beneficiaries of the Son's intercession, which is denied to the rest of mankind (John 17:9); they will eventually be raised to everlasting life (John 6:40); and they will dwell with Christ forever in glory (John 17:24).[20] *These* are they for whom Christ died, and none of the above descriptors can be rightly applied to those who finally perish in their sins. Christ dies for his people (Matt 1:21), his friends (John 15:13), his church (Acts 20:28; Eph 5:25), a people for his own possession (Titus 2:14), the elect (Rom 8:33).

The MIV and Trinitarian Unity

Proponents of the MIV are not insensitive to the need for the Father, Son, and Spirit to be perfectly united in their saving work. Shultz recognizes that traditional non-particularist positions are vulnerable to this critique, saying, "If the Son provided salvation for all, but the Father only intended to save some, then this introduces disjunction into the Godhead, as this implies that the Father and the Son have different salvific goals. Most Moderate Calvinists, who hold together unconditional election and unlimited atonement, are open to this charge."[21] He explains,

> The multi-intentioned view avoids this charge by asserting that God the Father had multiple intentions for the atonement. The atonement not only accomplishes his elective purposes, but his purposes for the creation and the nonelect as well. The Holy Spirit then works among the nonelect and the elect on the basis of the atonement, fulfilling the Father and the Son's intentions. Each person of the Trinity has general and particular intentions for creation. The unity of the Trinity is therefore upheld by the multi-intentioned view. Unconditional election has to do with God's particular purposes, which are

20. Owen provides helpful clarity: "His own aim and intention, may be seen in nothing more manifestly than in the request that our Savior makes upon the accomplishment of the work about which he was sent; which certainly was neither for more nor less than God had engaged himself to him for. 'I have,' saith he, 'glorified thee on earth, I have finished the work which thou gavest me to do,' John 17:4. And now, what doth he require after the manifestation of his eternal glory, of which for a season he had emptied himself, verse 5? Clearly a full confluence of the love of God and fruits of that love upon all his elect, in faith, sanctification, and glory. God gave them unto him, and he sanctified himself to be a sacrifice for their sake, praying for their sanctification, verses 17–19; their preservation in peace, or communion with one another, and union with God, vv. 20–21. . .; and lastly, their glory, verse 24. . . . And in this, not one word concerning all and every one, but expressly the contrary, verse 9" (*Death of Death*, 171).

21. Shultz, *Multi-Intentioned View*, 125. In his dissertation, he calls these moderate Calvinists "four-point Calvinists" (Shultz, "Defense," 229n12). Shultz is correct that the moderate or four-point Calvinist position is vulnerable to the charge of Trinitarian disunity, as are semi-Pelagianism, Arminianism, Amyraldianism, and even British hypothetical universalism (see Gibson, "Trinitarian Work," 367–71; Letham, "God, Incarnation, and Definite Atonement," 442–43).

accomplished in the atonement, but these particular purposes do not rule out his general purposes, which are also accomplished in the atonement.[22]

In other words, proponents of the MIV would aim to affirm much, if not all, of what is presented above: the Father chooses some and not all, the Spirit regenerates some and not all, and therefore it is consistent that the Son secures the salvation of some and not all.[23] However, they would say that this relates only to God's *particular* intentions for the cross. There are also general intentions for the cross shared by all three persons of the Trinity. The claim is that the Father intends the atonement not only to secure the salvation of the elect but also to purchase common grace, which the Father then dispenses upon all without exception as a result of the atonement.[24] Further, it is claimed that the Spirit exercises a ministry of universal conviction as part of the universal gospel call (cf. John 16:7–11); and since the Spirit's ministry is contingent upon Christ's ascension to the Father (John 16:7), and since his ascension is contingent upon his resurrection, and since his resurrection is contingent upon his death, therefore the universal convicting ministry of the Spirit is purchased by the atonement.[25] Thus, according to Shultz, the Son's atoning work is not broader than the Father's or the Spirit's work; it is simply that the Father and the Spirit also have universal non-saving intentions tied to the atonement, and therefore the Son may die for all without Trinitarian discord.[26]

While part 2 is intended to be a positive argument for particularism, and while thorough criticism of these claims awaits the more extended analysis in part 4—especially the chapters regarding the relationship of the extent of the atonement to common grace and the universal gospel call—a preliminary cross-examination is here necessary in order to demonstrate that the MIV does not in fact legitimately escape the censure of Trinitarian disunity.

An Internal Inconsistency

In the first place, while positing both particular and universal aspects to the Father's and Spirit's work would theoretically cohere with an atonement that accomplishes one

22. Shultz, "Defense," 230n12; cf. 12. A similar model is presented in Daniel, *History and Theology of Calvinism*, 371; Knox, "Aspects of the Atonement," 1:262, 265; Lightner, *Death Christ Died*, 130. Douty calls it "a single transaction with a double intention" (Douty, *Treatise on the Extent of Christ's Atonement*, 60).

23. One might have simply said, "the Son atones for some and not all," but the MIV sees a disjunction between the concepts of atonement and securing salvation. Unlike particularism, the MIV claims that these are not the same, and that the latter does not necessarily follow from the former. That is, the Son atones for some whose salvation is not secured. See Shultz, "Defense," 130n26, as well as chapter 2, pages 25–26, 39–41.

24. E.g., Shultz, "Defense," 183–95.

25. E.g., Shultz, "Defense," 172–74.

26. Hammett, "Multiple-Intentions View," 166.

set of benefits for all without exception and another set of benefits for the elect alone, the proponents of the MIV do not consistently present the atonement in this way. The strength of the MIV in distinction to the so-called "moderate Calvinist" view that Shultz rejects is that the MIV (at times) conceives of the atonement as Christ accomplishing something different for the elect than for the reprobate.[27] There are two accomplishments: "Christ procured the offer and provision of salvation for all people on the cross, *and* he also procured the definite application of salvation for the elect on the cross."[28] It is not, as the "four-point Calvinist" claims, that the atonement is a universal provision of salvation made on behalf of all men alike, which is only subjectively applied to the elect through faith. Such a view is "unable to account for any particularity in the atonement because it understands the atonement to be a general payment for all sin that only provides salvation for all, and asserts that the particular saving acts of God are then found in the Father's election and the Spirit's saving work."[29] Such a view is thus vulnerable to charges of Trinitarian disunity, because it exports particularity from the Son's work of atonement to the Spirit's work of regeneration.[30]

However, at other times, both Shultz and Hammett present the atonement in precisely this way—conceiving of it as a single provision for all alike, which only later is subjectively applied (or made efficacious) to the elect.[31] Indeed, commenting

27. This is a strength only in a relative sense, namely, in that it could be seen to evade the charge of Trinitarian disunity. However, a double accomplishment is not without its own problems. First, as chapter 5 demonstrates, Scripture simply never speaks of God's universal *intention* for the atonement that purchases for the reprobate blessings short of salvation, but only of a divine intention for the atonement to bring to salvation those for whom it is accomplished. There is a not a universal economy of salvation that runs parallel to a particular economy, but a single economy of salvation in Christ (Eph 1:10; 3:9). Second, some have aptly argued that the doctrine of a double accomplishment—present in British hypothetical universalism as well as the MIV—"presents a confused Christ" with a "split personality," resolving to die to make men savable, some of whom (in the case of those who never hear the gospel) he sovereignly determines never to reveal the means by which they might be saved (Gibson, "Trinitarian Work," 369). Turretin represents the confused Christ this way: "I desire that to come to pass which I not only know will not and cannot take place, but also what I am unwilling should take place because I refuse to communicate that without which it can never be brought to pass as it depends upon myself alone" (Turretin, *Institutes of Elenctic Theology*, 2:467). Turretin also disputes the coherence of how Christ can die for the elect in one sense and die for the reprobate in another in a single act of dying (Turretin, *Institutes of Elenctic Theology*, 2:460). Thus, the double accomplishment model does not pass biblical and theological muster.

28. Shultz, "Defense," 176. Hammett agrees: ". . . another intention of God in sending Christ [i.e., in addition to providing salvation for all] and another intention of Christ in dying was actually to secure the salvation of some" (Hammett, "Multiple-Intentions View," 169–70). There are two distinct accomplishments here: one for all without exception and one for the elect alone.

29. Shultz, *Multi-Intentioned View*, 125–26.

30. Shultz, *Multi-Intentioned View*, 125. See footnote 21 of this chapter.

31. Shultz says, "Jesus Christ, in fulfilling the Father's intentions for his atonement, accomplished several objective realities that only the elect subjectively experience. . . . While God intended for these objective realities [i.e., penal substitution, propitiation, etc.] to accomplish his general purposes in the atonement, he also intended for them to subjectively applied to the elect, and only for the elect, in order to accomplish his particular purpose in the atonement. In order to fulfill this purpose, Jesus, on the basis of his atonement, sent the Holy Spirit to apply salvation to the elect" (Shultz, "Defense,"

on 1 John 2:2, Shultz says, "It is also important to note that Christ is the propitiation for 'our sins' (believers) *in the same way* that he is the propitiation for 'the sins of the whole world' (unbelievers)."[32] According to the two-accomplishments model of the atonement unique to the MIV, Shultz should have said here that Christ is the propitiation for the sins of believers such that he secures their salvation but is the propitiation for the sins of unbelievers such that he makes their salvation possible. Yet at this portion of his work, he believes the exegesis of 1 John 2 does not allow for that interpretation, which he later accepts. Similarly, he says, "Just as he did in 4:14, John [in 1 John 2:2] stresses that Christ's saving work encompasses the sins of all people so that the heretics in the community would know that their sins were forgivable on the basis of the atonement."[33] Yet if propitiation makes the reprobates' sin forgivable, and Christ is the propitiation for the sins of the elect and reprobate "in the same way," then (a) the atonement is a singular provision that is later applied, not two accomplishments, and (b) the elect's salvation is not secured by the atonement; their sins are only made forgivable, which forgiveness is applied and particularized by the Spirit.[34] This is the very exportation of particularity from atonement to application that Shultz (rightly) claimed was open to the charge of Trinitarian disunity. Indeed, Shultz is elsewhere constrained by the inconsistency of his position to admit the very

---

250–51; Shultz, *Multi-Intentioned View*, 138). On this scheme, propitiation is accomplished provisionally for all, and that universal provision is applied and made particular only by the Spirit's ministry, not by anything particularizing in the atonement itself. Hammett says, ". . . in addition to making a universal objective provision for the salvation of all, God works subjectively in the hearts of some to apply that provision to them, making that provision efficacious for them." (Hammett, "Multiple-Intentions View," 162n50; cf. 154). This is not an efficacious accomplishment of non-saving benefits for the reprobate, but a universal provision for elect and reprobate alike, which is only made efficacious for the elect by the Holy Spirit.

32. Shultz, "Defense," 116n59, emphasis added.

33. Shultz, "Defense," 116–17.

34. As another illustration of this, Shultz ("Defense," 156n196) approvingly cites Demarest, who says, "In terms of the Atonement's provision Christ died not merely for the elect but for all sinners in all times and places. Christ drank the cup of suffering for the sins of the entire world. He died as a substitute, a propitiation, a ransom, etc. for the universe of sinners. The non-elect had their sins paid for on the cross, even though through unbelief they do not personally appropriate the benefits of his work. Christ, in other words, provided salvation for more people than those to whom he purposed to apply its saving benefits" (Demarest, *Cross and Salvation,* 191). He then cites Ware, who says, ". . . we cannot speak correctly of Christ's death as actually and certainly *saving* the elect. No, even here, the payment made by his death on behalf of the elect renders their salvation *possible*" (Ware, "Outline," 5). These are clear affirmations of the same universal payment provided (note, not accomplished) for all, later particularized in the Spirit's application. Just a few pages later, however, Shultz says, "God also accomplishes the certain salvation of the elect through Christ's payment for the sins of all people" ("Defense," 159). This seems to revert to the two-accomplishments model. If God accomplishes the certain salvation of the elect via Christ's payment, why does Ware say we cannot speak of Christ's death as certainly saving the elect? This internal inconsistency makes it difficult to critique the MIV, for when a criticism is legitimately brought against the former model of atonement, they insist on their adherence to the latter, and vice versa. This incoherence ultimately stems from attempting to hold two mutually exclusive positions (particularism and universalism) together.

thing he previously denied: "The Son secured the salvation of the elect *by* sending forth the Holy Spirit to apply the salvific benefits of the atonement only to the elect";[35] and, "*The way* that Christ secured the salvation of the elect was by sending the Spirit to only apply salvation to the elect."[36] If the Spirit's application of redemption is the *way* and *means* by which the Son secures the salvation of the elect, then the cross cannot be that way and means. Christ is reduced to the very "Possibility-Maker" Hammett explicitly denies him to be.[37]

Thus, the claim that the Father, Son, and Spirit each have universal and particular intentions in their saving work is undermined. When pressed for consistency, the MIV's view of the particularity of the cross is discovered to be merely formal rather than substantive, and thus universal and not particular. There is therefore no particularity that corresponds with the Father's particular intention in election and the Spirit's particular work in regeneration, and Trinitarian unity is thus fatally undermined.

Purchase vs. Result

However, if one were to overlook this inconsistency and assume for the sake of argument that the MIV uniformly conceives of the atonement as two accomplishments—one particular and one universal—even in this case the MIV's claim of Trinitarian unity fails. This is because it fundamentally depends on (a) the Father and the Spirit working in all people without exception, not merely the elect alone, and on (b) the notion that such work is purchased by Christ's universal payment for all sins. In other words, it is not the mere existence of common grace or the existence of the Spirit's work in the hearts of the reprobate that would prove the MIV's case; particularism grants that God is good to all without exception (e.g., Ps 145:9; Matt 5:44–45) and that the Spirit restrains evil even in those who will finally perish in their sins (cf. 2 Thess 2:6–7). Rather, for the MIV's claim of Trinitarian unity to obtain, the atonement must *purchase* both the Father's common grace to mankind and the Spirit's ministry to the non-elect.

Yet the MIV never successfully demonstrates this to be the teaching of Scripture. It is simply not the case that everything the Father and Spirit accomplish in the

35. Shultz, *Multi-Intentioned View*, 152, emphasis added; Shultz, "Defense," 274.

36. Shultz, *Multi-Intentioned View*, 154, emphasis added. This notion is reinforced by multiple references to the "saving works of the Holy Spirit" (e.g., Shultz, "Defense," 144, 148) and statements that "the Spirit saves" ("Defense," 151). Hammett says the "objective accomplishment" of the cross merely "removes obstacles to fellowship with God"—which does not secure salvation for anyone—while the "subjective application" is what actually effects that fellowship. The particular intention is achieved only by the Spirit's power to cause one to have faith in the gospel, such that the Spirit's application and Christ's accomplishment are "two aspects of the one work of atonement" (Hammett, "Multiple-Intentions View," 174). Thus, the particularity of Christ's work is nothing more than laying the groundwork for the eventual particular, saving work of the Spirit. Despite hoping to avoid evacuating particularity from the Son's work, the MIV does just that, and therefore cannot maintain Trinitarian unity.

37. Hammett, "Multiple-Intentions View," 171.

world, short of salvation, must be purchased by the atonement. Christ does not have to pay for the sins of all people without exception for the Father to be merciful to his enemies or for the Spirit to restrain wickedness in them.[38] There may be benefits that indirectly accrue to the reprobate as a result of the atonement made solely for the elect,[39] but the results of the atonement must not be conflated with the atonement itself. Shultz aims to defend the notion that whatever the Spirit does in the world is a direct, purchased benefit of the atonement by observing that the coming of the Spirit is a consequence of Christ's ascension, which is a consequence of his resurrection, which is a consequence of his death. On this basis, it is argued, his death must be universal.[40] Yet we might with the same consistency observe that Christ's death is a consequence of his obedient life, and his obedient life is a consequence of his incarnation; however, we ought not to say that the ministry of the Spirit was purchased by the incarnation or obedient life of Christ. The ministry of the Spirit is as much a result of the atonement as it is of the incarnation, and Scripture explicitly declares the incarnation to have been designed with exclusively *salvific* intentions (John 3:17; 12:46; 1 Tim 1:15; Heb 10:5–10; 1 John 3:5; 4:9). The Son partook of flesh and blood because the children (Heb 2:14) whom the Father had given him (Heb 2:13) were of flesh and blood; he gives help to the seed of Abraham, not the posterity of Adam (Heb 2:16), and *therefore* had to be made like his *brethren* in all things in order to make propitiation for the sins of his people (Heb 2:17). Thus, the MIV fails to provide conclusive biblical or theological evidence that the common grace of the Father or the Spirit's work among the reprobate are purchased by the cross.[41]

The Spirit's Conviction Not Universal

Further, Shultz's basis for arguing for universality in the Spirit's work is that John 16:7–11 teaches that the Spirit convicts "the world" of sin, righteousness, and judgment, which Shultz believes refers, at least in part, to those who finally perish in

38. Indeed, if the atonement is the highest display of God's mercy and goodness to sinners (which mercy is the cause of the atonement), and if God is not free to be merciful to sinners apart from purchasing these blessings by atonement, the atonement would be thus conceived as the cause of itself, a logical impossibility. But the love and kindness of God are a *cause* of the atonement (John 3:16; Titus 3:4), not its consequence.

39. MacArthur and Mayhue give an example of this: "If God had not intended to save sinners through Christ's atonement, it is likely that he would have immediately visited justice on sinful man as he did the fallen angels (2 Pet. 2:4). Yet because God intended to save his people through Christ in the fullness of time, even those whom he will not ultimately save will have enjoyed the benefits of common grace, divine forbearance, and a temporary reprieve from divine judgment" (MacArthur and Mayhue, *Biblical Doctrine*, 544). This is not to say that the cross *purchased* these benefits; rather, it is to say that a particular redemption may have universal effects or results without requiring that it be a universal redemption. A full refutation of Shultz's claim that a universal gospel call and common grace require a universal atonement will be given in part 4.

40. For examples of this, see Shultz, "Defense," 100, 172–74, 218–19.

41. As noted, this will be more thoroughly argued in chapter 15.

their sins.[42] Yet if this claim is shown to be false, Shultz has no basis for arguing for a universal scope to the Spirit's ministry, and the MIV's case for Trinitarian unity fails. A more thorough interaction with this claim awaits part 4, yet a brief survey of the text shows just that. In order to make the case that "the world" refers at least in part to the reprobate, Shultz argues that the conviction of this text does not necessarily lead to conversion. However, Jesus notes that this convicting ministry of the Holy Spirit is for the disciples' advantage (16:7), which is likely a reference to their encouragement through the conversion of unbelievers (cf. Acts 2:36–38) and the relief from persecution (cf. John 16:2, 32–33) that would come when their persecutors became their brothers (cf. Acts 9:21).[43] Yet neither of these advantages would obtain if this conviction did not result in eventual conversion. If the Spirit convinced unbelievers that they were in sin for refusing to believe in Jesus (16:9), that he was indeed righteous as evidenced by his resurrection (16:10), and therefore that their judgment of him was satanically unrighteous (16:11), but such conviction was not effectual unto repentance and faith but only temporary, why would they not return to their vomit and persist in their unjust maltreatment of Jesus' followers? To what *advantage* would that convicting ministry be to the disciples? Instead, the "world" whom the Spirit will convict is best understood as those elect persons not yet brought to faith, the sheep not yet brought into the fold (John 10:16; 17:20) but who will not fail to be saved by the good shepherd (John 10:27–29; cf. 6:39). John 16:7–11 does not teach that the Spirit ineffectually convicts the reprobate, but effectually brings the unbelieving elect to repentance and faith in Christ.

Besides this, the burden of proof the MIV must meet to prove a universal aspect to the Spirit's work is not merely that he may work an ineffectual conviction in some of the reprobate. Rather, in order to prove universality in the Spirit's work, the MIV must demonstrate that the Spirit exercises this ministry in all persons throughout history without exception, for this is the breadth of the Father's common grace and the Son's supposed universal atonement. But it is granted by all sides that, in God's providential control of history, the Holy Spirit has not brought the gospel to the vast majority of persons who have lived, much less to all without exception. Gibson is correct when he concludes, "The unevangelized remain a problem for proponents of a universal atonement. In this regard, the Spirit underperforms and in so doing brings disharmony into the Trinity."[44]

---

42. Shultz, "Defense," 171–74; Shultz, "Why a Genuine Universal Gospel Call," 118–20. Shultz often conflates the category of unbelievers with the reprobate (see Shultz, *Multi-Intentioned View*, 93; Shultz, "Defense," 168). But there is such a thing as elect unbelievers, those chosen by God to receive salvation who have not yet come to faith in the Lord Jesus Christ. Each one of the elect were at one point part of the unbelieving "world." Shultz does not need to prove the Spirit's work amongst *unbelievers*, but amongst the *reprobate*.

43. Carson, "Function of the Paraclete," 564.

44. Gibson, "Trinitarian Work," 369.

Thus, even on the supposition of a twofold accomplishment, a position not without its own problems,[45] the MIV is unable to account for a universal aspect of the Spirit's work on the basis of the atonement, and thus fails to coherently safeguard Trinitarian unity in the atonement. If there were no other reason to reject the MIV, one finds sufficient ground here, for it cannot cohere with the cardinal doctrine of the Christian faith.

45. See footnote 27 of this chapter.

5

The Divine Intention for the Son's Atonement

IN THE PREVIOUS CHAPTER, it was established that Scripture presents all three persons of the Trinity as perfectly united in conceiving and carrying out the plan of salvation. What the Father intends in sending the Son into the world, what the Son intends in undertaking his atoning mission, and what the Spirit intends in empowering the Son to accomplish his mission and later applying his work are identical. They are the very same intention of the selfsame single will of the triune God. In this chapter, we come to address what precisely that intention was. Given that the persons of the Trinity are united in their saving intention and works, what does Scripture teach about what they intended the cross to accomplish?

It has long been granted that the central question to be answered in the debate over the extent of the atonement concerns God's *intention* for Christ's work. The majority of those engaging in this discussion agree that Berkhof's classic framing of the issue is accurate: "Did the Father in sending Christ, and did Christ in coming into the world, to make atonement for sin, do this with the *design* or for the *purpose* of saving only the elect or all men?"[1] Proponents of the MIV are no exception to this. For example, Shultz states, "In seeking to ascertain whom Christ died for on the cross, both particular redemption and unlimited atonement are actually attempting to explain the purpose or intent that God had in the atonement. . . . The debate over the extent of the atonement centers on the design or purpose of the atonement."[2] Thus, the question is not in dispute. The point of contention is not the sufficiency or efficiency of the atonement, whether the gospel ought to be preached to all indiscriminately, or whether the reprobate enjoy certain benefits short of salvation as indirect consequences of the cross, but rather whether God *intended* the atonement to provide something for all without exception or to accomplish something for the elect alone.

---

1. Berkhof, *Systematic Theology*, 394, emphasis mine. Most agree that the question of the extent of the atonement boils down to the question of its divine intent, whether they affirm universal atonement (e.g., Demarest, *Cross and Salvation*, 193; Lightner, *Death Christ Died*, 33; Picirilli, *Grace, Faith, and Free Will*, 103–4) or particular redemption, as Berkhof (e.g., Letham, *Work of Christ*, 225–26; Nicole, "Case for Definite Atonement," 200).

2. Shultz, "Defense," 5–6. Hammett agrees, saying the question of the debate is, "What did God *intend* to accomplish by Christ's death?" (Hammett, "Multiple-Intentions View," 148, emphasis added).

Ware helpfully frames the classic disagreement between particularism and universalism in terms of divine intention: "What is the *intention* of God in offering his Son as an atoning sacrifice? Is his intention *to save people* by his Son's death? . . . Or is his intention *to provide a payment* for any and all people, which payment is only effective at the point that they savingly believe?"[3] The MIV argues, however, that reducing the question to an either/or is illegitimate, for it "unnecessarily restrict[s] God's intentions in sending his son to die on the cross to a single intention."[4] Instead, they argue, we ought to affirm both, for the triune God "had both particular and general intentions for the atonement."[5] In other words, the MIV does affirm, along with particularists, that the Father intended the atonement to secure the salvation of the elect alone, that the Son dies for this purpose, and that the Spirit applies this secured salvation to the elect alone. But in addition to this, the MIV also claims that the Father intended the atonement to accomplish other benefits short of salvation for all people without exception, including "to provide forgiveness of sins for all,"[6] "making it possible for all who believe to be saved,"[7] "to make the universal gospel call possible," and to purchase common grace, among other things.[8]

But what does the Scripture say? How do the biblical authors cast the Father's intention for sending the Son into the world? How do they capture the design and purpose for Christ's atoning work? The discrepancy between the MIV and the biblical presentation is especially exposed by first considering the substance of the divine intention for the atonement rather than the scope of those for whom it was intended. In other words, we are concerned to discover *what* God intended the cross to accomplish before we consider *for whom* he intended to accomplish it. The remainder of this chapter will demonstrate that Scripture consistently and uniformly identifies the unified divine intention for the atonement as exclusively salvific. Contrary to the claims of the MIV, Scripture never identifies the intent of the atonement as making mere provisions, possibilities, or procurements that may or may not be applied. Instead, the writers of Scripture teach that the divine intention for the atonement was that Christ would actually save all those for whom he died, purchasing their redemption in such a way that they whom he redeemed cannot fail to be set free from sin unto salvation.[9]

---

3. Ware, "Outline," 1, emphasis added.

4. Shultz, "Defense," 10.

5. Shultz, "Defense," 12. Thus they aim at evading the charge of introducing disunity into the Trinity. See the previous chapter for my case that they are in fact susceptible to that charge.

6. Hammett, "Multiple-Intentions View," 149.

7. Ware, "Outline," 3.

8. Shultz, "Defense," 12.

9. As Macleod states, "Christ came to save: not to make salvation possible, or to contribute to it, or to attend to some parts of it, but actually to save. This salvation has two aspects, the forensic and the ontological, and these two aspects are inseparable. The cross secures both reconciliation and transformation. Its final decreed outcome is not mere salvability but . . . Christ making absolutely certain that those he loved will become partakers of the divine nature (2 Pet. 1:4). He would not merely *procure*

This will be borne out in two stages: first, by examining Scripture's explicit statements concerning the cross's intention; second, by examining Scripture's statements concerning the actual effects of Christ's death.[10]

The Salvific Intention of the Atonement

In the first place, the New Testament uniformly presents the intent and purpose of Christ's saving mission as the sure and certain *salvation* of those for whom he has come.

The Synoptic Gospels

The first such text that expresses a clear intention for the coming of the Son of Man is disputed as a textual variant. Those translations that have Matt 18:11 state, "For the Son of Man has come to save that which was lost." Though it is likely that this reading is unoriginal here, it was most likely an interpolation from Jesus' comment in Luke 19:10, "For the Son of Man has come to seek and to save that which was lost."[11] Both texts make clear that the intention for the coming of the Son of Man was to *save* the lost.

As James and John contend with one another for their own greatness in the kingdom of Jesus, the Lord rebukes their selfish ambition by teaching that leadership in his kingdom is marked by service (Matt 20:20–28; Mark 10:35–45), an example that has been modeled for them in his own life. In this context, Matt 20:28 and Mark 10:45 record another explicit statement of the divine intention for the Son's mission. He says, "The Son of Man did not come to be served, but to serve, and to give His life as a ransom for many." As Lane says, "The formulation 'The Son of man came . . .' places the entire statement in the context of Jesus' messianic mission (cf. Ch. 2:17). . . . The ransom metaphor sums up the purpose for which Jesus gave his life and defines the complete expression of his service."[12] This is why Christ has come. France comments, "This vicarious servant role is stated to be the *purpose* of Jesus' coming. . . . The vicarious death

---

eternal life for them: he would *give* it to them (John 17:2), ensuring a complete, seamless salvation, culminating in that moment when he would present them faultless in the presence of his glory with great joy (Jude 24). That is his ultimate satisfaction, and it was the prospect of it that sustained him as he poured out his soul to death (Isa. 53:12)" (Macleod, "Definite Atonement and the Divine Decree," 434–35).

10. This presentation follows the broad outline of John Owen in book 2, chapters 1–3, of *The Death of Death* (pages 200–220).

11. "Some MSS read verse 11 (as D K W X and many later MSS). But this cannot outweigh its omission from ℵ B L* Θ etc. and the likelihood that it was borrowed from Luke 19:10 to make a good connection between verse 10 and verses 12-14" (Morris, *Matthew*, 465n32). See also Metzger, *Textual Commentary*, 36.

12. Lane, *Mark*, 383.

of Jesus is thus firmly placed before us not as a historical accident but as his deliberate goal."[13] And this deliberate goal and purpose of Jesus' coming is identified as giving his life as a ransom, λύτρον, which originated in "practices of warfare, where it was the price paid to bring a prisoner of war out of his captivity"[14] and which comes to denote atonement both in the LXX and New Testament, as does its Hebrew counterpart in the Old Testament.[15] The Son of Man has come into the world with the intention that many who are enslaved to sin may be released into the freedom of salvation through the giving of his life as the substitutionary ransom price to be paid for them (cf. Rom 6:17–22; Rev 5:9). There is no word here about making these slaves redeemable or about providing for the possibility of their deliverance; Christ's intention is that the ransom price of his blood will free the many held captive to sin.[16]

A final text from the Synoptic Gospels is also of disputed origin. As the indignant disciples pressed Jesus to rain fire from heaven upon the Samaritan village that refused to provide them hospitality, Jesus rebuked their eagerness to see others destroyed. In Luke 9:56, he states that such destruction is out of accord with the purpose for which he has come into the world: "For the Son of Man did not come to destroy men's lives, but to save them." While the manuscript evidence is lacking, this comment is likely derived from Luke 19:10, as is the statement in Matt 18:11.[17] Once again, Jesus identifies the purpose for his atoning mission as the actual salvation of people's lives, not merely the provision for such. In addition to this, if this verse is received as authentic, or at the very least received as expressing an authentic saying of Jesus even if not at this point in Luke's gospel, the express negative intention—i.e., that the Son of Man did not come to destroy men's lives—seems to be at odds with one of the MIV's putative general intentions for the atonement, namely, the notion that "Christ died for the purpose of providing an additional basis for condemnation" for those who reject him.[18] It is difficult to see how the Son could not intend the destruction of lives while at the same time intending to provide grounds for their eternal condemnation.

Johannine Literature

In John 3:16–17, one of the most beloved passages in all of Scripture—as well as one of the most disputed passages in the atonement debate—we read, "For God so loved

---

13. France, *Matthew*, 763, emphasis original.

14. Morris, *Matthew*, 512–13; cf. Büschel, "λύτρον," *TDNT*, 4:340–49.

15. Edwards, *Mark*, 327.

16. Though we are here concerned to examine the divine intention for the atonement itself and not presently its scope, one ought to note Jesus' use of the particular designation "many" rather than "all," undoubtedly a reference to Isa 52:15 and 53:11–12. See the exegesis of that text in chapter 10.

17. Bock notes that both this and the variant in 9:55 "are absent from the early manuscripts as well as from a variety of uncials. The UBS-NA text is supported by P45, P75, א, A, B, C, L, W, D, X, and Y" (Bock, *Luke*, 2:973).

18. Ware, "Outline," 3–4; cf. Shultz, "Defense," 12, 178–79.

the world, that He gave His only begotten Son, that whoever believes in Him shall not perish, but have eternal life. For God did not send the Son into the world to judge the world, but that the world might be saved through Him." God's love for the world has caused him to give (δίδωμι) his only begotten Son, a reference not only to the giving of the Son in the incarnation but also in giving him over to death on the cross for sinners (cf. Rom 8:32; Gal 2:20, παραδίδωμι).[19] The purpose (ἵνα) for God giving the Son up to die is that those believing in Jesus would have eternal life: "His ultimate purpose is the salvation of those in the world who believe in him."[20] The elaborative comment in verse 17 serves only to emphasize this salvific intention: the Father sent the Son in order to (ἵνα) save the world through him. The express negative intention—i.e., the Father did not send the Son into the world to judge (κρίνω) the world—also seems to undermine the MIV's "just condemnation" purpose for the atonement.[21]

John 6:51 contains the statement from Jesus, "I am the living bread that came down out of heaven; if anyone eats of this bread, he will live forever; and the bread also which I will give for the life of the world is My flesh." The giving of his flesh can refer to nothing but his sacrifice on Calvary, and the key substitutionary preposition ὑπέρ strengthens that case given how often John employs it to refer to Christ's death on behalf of sinners (10:11, 15; 11:50, 51, 52; 13:37, 38; 15:13; 17:19; 18:14).[22] And Christ's intention in giving his flesh in death is to bring life to the world—that is, "so that [ἵνα] one may eat of it and not die" (John 6:50; cf. 3:16). Contrary to this, when Shultz cites John 6:51 as evidence for a universal intention in the atonement, he modifies Jesus' statement in a slight but significant way: ". . . he [Jesus] means that he gives his life (i.e., he dies) so that all people might have life."[23] It may be that by inserting the word "might" Shultz simply intends to give force to the subjunctive following the ἵνα clause in the previous verse (ἵνα τις ἐξ αὐτοῦ φάγῃ καὶ μὴ ἀποθάνῃ).[24] However, taking it in

19. Morris, *John*, 203.

20. Carson, *John*, 206.

21. It may be objected that John 5:27 (καὶ ἐξουσίαν ἔδωκεν αὐτῷ κρίσιν ποιεῖν) and John 9:39 (εἰς κρίμα ἐγὼ εἰς τὸν κόσμον τοῦτον ἦλθον) contradict the notion that Jesus did not come to judge or condemn the world. But in 5:27 and 9:39, the meaning of "judgment" is neutral, as is evident in that the result of judgment may be either positive (resurrection of life, 5:29; that the blind may see, 9:39) or negative (resurrection of judgment, 5:29; that the seeing become blind, 9:39). In 3:17, judgment is not considered as neutral; the negative connotation of judgment is in view, being opposed to the positive aspect of salvation. As Laney says, "the purpose of Christ's coming was redemptive. Yet, when His saving work is rejected, judgment results. Even though judgment results from unbelief, condemnatory judgment was not the purpose of the incarnation" (Laney, *John*, 82). Thus, it is true that condemnation results from the incarnation and the cross, but it is misguided to conclude, as the MIV does, that such condemnation is the Father's intention in the atonement.

22. Carson, *John*, 295; Morris, *John*, 331n123.

23. Shultz, "Defense," 109–10.

24. It is common for the use of the subjunctive in a ἵνα clause to express the purpose of an action that efficaciously achieves its intended result. As Wallace says, "We must not suppose that this use of the subjunctive necessarily implies any doubt about the fulfillment of the verbal action on the part of the speaker. . . . Not only is ἵνα used for result in the NT, but also for purpose-result. That is, it

the context of his overall argument, it seems he intends "might" to introduce a sense of uncertainty as to whether the stated intention achieves its result. In other words, Jesus dies in such a way that all without exception *might* have life, but also that they might not. It must be noted, though, that this is not what Jesus says. Instead, he says he will give his life as a sacrificial offering in death on behalf of the life of the world. That is, his intention in dying is that the world—whomever that may be—will have life, not merely the possibility of life. The same is true of his comments in John 10:10, where he says, "I came that they may have life [ἵνα ζωὴν ἔχωσιν], and have it abundantly." His intention is not merely the *procuring* but the *imparting* of abundant life.

In John 12:46–47, Jesus once again reaffirms that his purpose in coming into the world and undertaking his mission was not to condemn but to save and rescue. He says, "I have come as Light into the world, so that [ἵνα] everyone who believes in Me will not remain in darkness. If anyone hears My sayings and does not keep them, I do not judge him; for I did not come to judge [ἵνα κρίνω] the world, but to save [ἵνα σώσω] the world." Once again, the divine intention for the atonement could not be clearer. Christ intends for his atonement to deliver the believing ones from darkness, that is, to save the world. Yet Shultz comments, "Jesus makes salvation available to all people when he states that he did not come to judge the world, but to save the world in John 12:47."[25] The particularist does not dispute that the one who comes to Christ he will certainly not cast out; no one has come to Christ in repentance and faith for salvation only to find that no such salvation was available to him. But Shultz unwarrantedly injects the concept of availability into Jesus' statement here. According to John 12:46–47, Jesus does not come to make salvation *available*; he comes to *save* the world.

In the High Priestly Prayer of John 17, Jesus comments once again on the purpose of his atonement in verse 19: "For their sakes I sanctify Myself, that [ἵνα] they themselves also may be sanctified in truth." The prayer is aptly named, for on the eve of his crucifixion Jesus is coming to the pinnacle of his work as high priest for his people, as he prepares to make propitiation for them by his substitutionary death (cf. Heb 2:17; 3:1; 4:14–15; 5:5, 10; 6:20; 7:26; 8:1; 9:11). When he speaks of sanctifying himself, he refers to himself as the fulfillment of Levitical priesthood, who would need to be consecrated for their service (Exod 28:41; 29:1). He presents himself as the fulfillment especially of the high priest, who was required to make atonement for himself before interceding on behalf of the people (Lev 16:2–6). Thus, Jesus declares that he sanctifies or consecrates himself as the high priest of his people as he prepares for the ultimate day of atonement. Further, Jesus is not only the high priest who offers sacrifice in the

---

indicates *both the intention and its sure accomplishment*. . . . In other words, the NT writers employ the language to reflect their theology: what God purposes is what happens and, consequently, ἵνα is used to express both the divine purpose and the result" (Wallace, *Greek Grammar beyond the Basics*, 472, 473). He goes on to give John 3:16 and Phil 2:9–11 as examples of this use of the ἵνα + subjunctive, and it would be unfounded to introduce uncertainty into whether the believing ones will have eternal life (John 3:16) or whether every knee will bow and tongue confess the lordship of Christ (Phil 2:10–11).

25. Shultz, "Defense," 110.

presence of God, but he himself is the sacrifice offered (cf. Heb 9:12, 26, 28; 13:12). The Old Testament prescriptions also required the sacrifices to be consecrated (Exod 28:38; Num 18:9; Deut 15:19, 21), and thus Jesus also sanctifies himself to be offered as the once-for-all sacrifice that sanctifies the people for all time (Heb 10:14).[26] And once again, note the express purpose (ἵνα) for this sanctification of himself unto his atoning death: it is that they—that is, those whom the Father has given him (John 17:2, 6, 9, 20), the elect—would be sanctified in truth. Jesus intends his atonement to accomplish the actual, effectual sanctification of those for whom he dies.

Turning from John's Gospel to his first epistle, we find several other clear, categorical statements of intention for the Son's saving incarnation and atonement. First John 3:5 declares, "You know that He appeared in order to take away sins." In the context in which the churches of Asia are beset with the false teaching of indifference to sin, John explains that those who are united to and follow Christ can have nothing to do with sin, because their Savior has come into the world for the express purpose of taking away (ἵνα . . . ἄρῃ) sins.[27] Jesus accomplished this expiation by his atonement, for it is in his capacity as the "the Lamb of God" whose blood atones for sin that he "takes away [ὁ αἴρων] the sin of the world" (John 1:29).[28] Thus, Christ appeared in his incarnation to offer himself as the sacrificial Lamb of God with the intention that his atoning work would actually and effectively take away sin.

This purpose is reiterated from a slightly different angle in the following verses, as John declares categorically in 3:8: "The Son of God appeared for this purpose [εἰς τοῦτο], to destroy the works of the devil." Once again, the Son "appears" by his incarnation for the express purpose of destroying the devil's works, which he accomplishes by his death and resurrection (Heb 2:14–15).[29] These works of the devil are identified by the context as being the practice of sin (1 John 3:4, 6, 8–9) as opposed to the practice of righteousness (1 John 3:7, 10), results of Satan's wiles in tempting and enslaving men to sin.[30] To destroy Satan's work of man's enslavement to sin, the Son of God appeared to take away sin (1 John 3:5) by bearing it in himself as the Lamb of God (John 1:29). Christ did not intend by his atonement to potentially destroy sin, or to make it possible for sin to be destroyed; his intention was to actually destroy the works of the devil.

---

26. "The verb ἁγιάζω is used in LXX of the setting apart of both people and things for the service of God (more often of people than things). . . . The verb does not signify in itself a setting apart for death, but in this context the meaning can scarcely be anything else" (Morris, *John*, 647n56; cf. Carson, *John*, 567).

27. Marshall, *Epistles of John*, 177. "What John wants to stress is his purpose in coming: to 'take away [αἴρω, airō] sins'" (Yarbrough, *1–3 John*, 185).

28. Marshall, *Epistles of John*, 177.

29. Yarbrough, *1–3 John*, 188.

30. "*The task* of Jesus was to undo whatever the devil had achieved . . . . No doubt it is his 'work' of temptation and enslaving men that is in view" (Marshall, *Epistles of John*, 185, emphasis added). See also Yarbrough, *1–3 John*, 188; Bruce, *Epistles of John*, 91.

Another categorical statement concerning the Father's purpose for the atoning work of Christ comes in 1 John 4:9: "By this the love of God was manifested in us, that God has sent His only begotten Son into the world so that [ἵνα] we might live through Him." Once again, we see that it is the spiritual *life* of sinners at which the cross aims. As Yarbrough puts it, "God's very purpose in sending his Son into the world was to bring about the God-given life of regeneration."[31] The atoning work of Christ intends not the *potential* for the Spirit's work of regeneration, nor the *availability* of the Spirit's work of regeneration, but the actual possession and experience of new spiritual life imparted by the Holy Spirit, who is as united to the Son in his atoning work as the Son is united to the Father in his electing work.[32] Just a few verses later, John states in 4:14 that "the Father has sent the Son to be the Savior of the world." The "saving intent and effect" of "God's act of sending Christ"[33] is that he would be Savior—not that he would be *offered* as Savior, or become a *potential* Savior, but that he would *actually* save his people (cf. Matt 1:21) and thus properly be called Savior.

Pauline Epistles

In 2 Cor 5:14–21, Paul discloses to the church what motivates his endurance in ministry (5:14) despite overwhelming trials (5:12–13; cf. 4:8–12, 16–18). In addition to the fear of the Lord (5:11), that motivation is the love of Christ (5:14a) displayed in the gospel of his substitutionary death and resurrection (5:14b–15), the gift of new life in regeneration (5:16–17), reconciliation to God (5:18–20), and justification by the imputation of righteousness (5:19, 21). In this discussion of the saving work of God in Christ, two purpose clauses (ἵνα) appear, which give insight into Paul's doctrine of the divine intention for the cross. Specifically, in verse 15 he states that Christ "died for all, so that [ἵνα] they who live might no longer live for themselves, but for Him who died and rose again on their behalf." This teaches that Christ died with the intention that the objects of his death would live a life of sanctification, devoted no longer to themselves but to Christ above all else (cf. Titus 2:14; 1 Pet 2:24). The intention of the atonement was not merely to purchase salvability, but to purchase a salvation that would of necessity be applied unto the practical transformation of those for whom Christ died.[34] In verse 15 the aspect of the application of redemption in view is sanctification, while in verse 21 it is justification: "He made Him who knew no sin to be sin on our behalf, so that [ἵνα] we might become the righteousness of God in Him." Harris comments, "The

---

31. Yarbrough, *1–3 John*, 237.

32. "The purpose of His thus sending His Son is our blessing—'that we should receive life through him', for thus the ingressive force of the aorist *zēsōmen* may be expressed" (Bruce, *Epistles of John*, 107).

33. Yarbrough, *1–3 John*, 248.

34. As Harris says, "The intended result of the death of Christ was the Christian's renunciation of self-seeking and self-pleasing and the pursuit of a Christ-centered life filled with action for the benefit of others, as was Christ's life" (Harris, *2 Corinthians*, 422).

conjunction ἵνα here denotes a purpose, and, by implication, a result. . . . This desired result and achieved outcome was future to Christ's being 'made sin,' being true . . . of believers' present state."[35] Once again it must be observed that the subjunctive (ἵνα . . . γενώμεθα, "might") ought not to be read as introducing doubt into the achievement of the Father's purpose.[36] He did not make the Son to be sin so that sinners might *possibly* be counted righteousness; his intention for the death of Christ was that sinners would actually be credited with the righteousness of God.

In 2 Cor 8:9, Paul calls upon the grace of Christ to motivate the Corinthians to radical generosity: "For you know the grace of our Lord Jesus Christ, that though He was rich, yet for your sake He became poor, so that you through His poverty might become rich." The Lord Jesus renounced the spiritual riches of heaven in exchange for the poverty of life as a human being and death under the wrath of God. He became poor for the sakes of those for whom he came, with the intention that (ἵνα) the objects of his death would be made spiritually rich, partakers of the benefits secured by his death, which Paul elsewhere defines as reconciliation with God (5:18), forgiveness of sins (5:19), justification (5:21), and the indwelling Holy Spirit (1:22; 5:5).[37]

In the opening words of his letter to the Galatians, Paul identifies Christ as the one "who gave Himself for our sins so that He might rescue us from this present evil age, according to the will of our God and Father" (Gal 1:4). The self-giving (τοῦ δόντος) of the Son for our sins refers to his delivering himself up over to death on the cross (cf. 2:20, παραδόντος). The explicit purpose for this self-giving is so that (ὅπως) those for whom he gave himself would be rescued (ἐξαιρέω) or delivered out from (ἐκ) the evil of the present age, similar to how the Lord delivered Israel out from the bondage of their slavery in Egypt (Exod 3:8; 18:4, 8–10 LXX, ἐξαιρέω), a paradigm for the future redemption of the New Covenant (Ezek 34:27).[38] In the case of the exodus, the Lord's intent was to conclusively transplant Israel from the yoke of their bondage to the freedom of their redemption. So also in the cross, the Lord Jesus' intent, according to the will of God the Father, was not merely to make provision for such a rescue but to conclusively transfer his people from the kingdom of darkness to the kingdom of Christ (cf. Col 1:13–14).

In Gal 4:4–5, Paul writes, "But when the fullness of the time came, God sent forth His Son, born of a woman, born under the Law, so that He might redeem those who were under the Law, that we might receive the adoption as sons." The purpose (ἵνα) for which the Father sent the Son to earth (ἐξαποστέλλω) is the redemption (ἐξαγοράζω)

---

35. Harris, *2 Corinthians*, 454.

36. Wallace, *Greek Grammar beyond the Basics*, 472–73. See footnote 24 of this chapter.

37. Harris, *2 Corinthians*, 578–79.

38. Schreiner, *Galatians*, 76–77. Schreiner also states, "The purpose of Jesus' self-giving is [in v. 4] explained. Jesus died to rescue believers from the evil of this present age, which the Galatians were succumbing to by considering circumcision. Jesus' death is located in the will and purpose of God the Father, and hence it represents the fulfillment of God's saving purposes and thus fulfills OT prophecy" (76–77).

of those in bondage under the law, doomed to face death as the curse of sin (cf. Gal 3:13). Redemption "connotes liberation from enslavement, involving the payment of a price: the price of Christ's death."[39] Once again, it is redemption that is aimed at, not mere redeemability, and that redemption consists not merely in the payment of a price but the effectual release of those for whom the price was paid. Further, a second ἵνα clause in verse 5 identifies the purpose for this redemption: that the redeemed would receive the adoption as sons (υἱοθεσία). That is, the intent of the redemption purchased by Christ's cross work is to bring the redeemed into a proper relationship with God as members of his family, those who enjoy all the rights and privileges of the household of God (cf. Rom 8:15; Eph 1:5).[40] In his atonement, Christ aims for nothing short of the full application of salvation to those for whom he has died.

In Eph 5:22–33, Paul draws on the mystery of the Christ-church relationship to ground his ethical instruction on marriage. Husbands are to love their wives as Christ loved the church and gave himself up (παραδίδωμι) for her (5:25), once again referring to his atoning death on the cross (Eph 5:2; cf. Rom 8:32; Gal 2:20). The purpose for Christ's sacrificial death for the church is then stated in verses 26–27 by means of three ἵνα clauses: "so that He might sanctify her," "that He might present to Himself the church in all her glory," and "that she would be holy and blameless." These phrases describe the sanctification and eventual glorification of those for whom Christ died. Thus, Macleod is correct when he states, "The NT . . . insists on a divinely ordained link between the sacrifice of Christ and the subjective transformation of the sinner. . . . Clearly, [in Eph 5:25–27,] the intended outcome of the cross was not merely forgiveness, but holiness."[41]

In 1 Tim 1:15, we find what is perhaps the most plainspoken statement concerning the divine intention for the incarnation and atonement of Christ. Paul writes, "It is a trustworthy statement, deserving full acceptance, that Christ Jesus came into the world to save sinners, among whom I am foremost of all." The "faithful saying" formula (cf. 1 Tim 3:1; 4:9; 2 Tim 2:11; Titus 3:8) heightens the solemnity of Paul's dictum. And, as Knight says, "The keynote of the saying is the verb σῶσαι, which expresses the reason for Jesus' coming, namely, deliverance for sinners from their sin and from all its consequences."[42] Owen's comment on the proper representation of the atonement's intent from this passage is as perceptive as it is decisive. Paul does not say that Christ came to "open a door for [sinners] to come in if they will or can; not to make a way passable, that they *may* be saved; not to purchase reconciliation and pardon of his Father, which perhaps they shall never enjoy; but *actually* to save them

39. Moo, *Galatians*, 267.

40. Moo, *Galatians*, 268; cf. Schreiner, *Galatians*, 271.

41. Macleod, "Definite Atonement and the Divine Decree," 432. Owen adds, ". . . which last words express also the very aim and end of Christ in giving himself for any, even that they may be made fit for God, and brought nigh unto him" (Owen, *Death of Death*, 158).

42. Knight, *Pastoral Epistles*, 101.

from all the guilt and power of sin, and from the wrath of God for sin: which, if he doth not accomplish, he fails of the end of his coming."[43]

In 1 Tim 2:6, we find one of the most disputed comments in the debate over the extent of the atonement, namely, Paul's comment that Christ "gave Himself as a ransom for all." Because the focus so quickly centers on the scope of Christ's self-giving ("for all"), the substance of his self-giving—i.e., that he gives himself as a ransom—is often neglected. The term ἀντίλυτρον occurs nowhere else in Scripture, but is a compound composed of the familiar term λύτρον (Matt 20:28; Mark 10:45; see above) with the preposition ἀντί prefixed to it, indicating a quality of substitution.[44] Thus, Leon Morris translates it "substitute-ransom,"[45] and, as in Matt 20:28 and Mark 10:45, it carries with it connotations of the manumission of slaves from captivity. Thus, Christ gives his life with the intention of bringing slaves of sin into freedom by the ransom price of his blood. It can scarcely be conceived that the Son intends merely to pay the ransom price but does not necessarily intend by that price to free the captive. By paying a ransom price, one intends to secure the release of those ransomed. Therefore, the intent of this life-giving ransom payment is the actual freedom of those for whom it is made.

In great similarity to Gal 4:4–5 and Eph 5:25–27, Paul states in Titus 2:14 that the purpose of the Son's self-giving is "to redeem us from every lawless deed, and to purify for Himself a people for His own possession, zealous for good deeds." Once again, the unbreakable link between the accomplishment of Christ and its application is made plain: those for whom he gives himself are redeemed, and the ones he has redeemed he intends to purify for himself in sanctification, so that they might be fit for the presence of God. He is not merely providing the possibility for redemption and sanctification; he intends his atonement to redeem and sanctify unto final glorification (cf. Heb 2:10).

General Epistles

Hebrews 2:14–15 states, "Therefore, since the children share in flesh and blood, He Himself likewise also partook of the same, that through death He might render powerless him who had the power of death, that is, the devil, and might free those who through fear of death were subject to slavery all their lives." Verse 17 adds, "Therefore, He had to be made like His brethren in all things, so that He might become a merciful and faithful high priest in things pertaining to God, to make propitiation for the sins of the people." The author of salvation (2:10) accomplishes that salvation, first, by partaking of flesh and blood (2:14) on behalf of the children the Father had given him (2:13–14), and, second, by dying in their place ("through death," 2:14). The intention (ἵνα) for his death is the freedom of those who were subject to slavery through the fear

43. Owen, *Death of Death*, 209, emphasis added.

44. BDAG, 87; Harris, *Prepositions and Theology*, 50–52.

45. Morris, *Apostolic Preaching of the Cross*, 51.

of death. A second intention (ἵνα . . . εἰς τὸ) is declared in verse 17, namely, that as their high priest Christ came to make propitiation for the sins of the people. Propitiation (ἱλάσκομαι) refers to the efficacious satisfaction of divine wrath (e.g., Num 16:46–47; 25:11–13, LXX: ἐξιλάσκομαι).[46] In each case, then, the intention for the atonement is made clear. There is no indication that Christ intends his saving mission merely to provide a possible deliverance from the slavery of the fear of death.[47] Nor is there mention of a potential propitiation whereby God's wrath may be satisfied by some later appropriation. By his atonement, the author of salvation purposes to bring the many sons—the children whom the Father had given him (2:13, 2:14), his brethren (2:11, 17), the seed of Abraham (2:16), his people (2:17)—to glory (2:10) by freeing them from slavery (2:14–15) and satisfying the Father's wrath against them (2:17).

Hebrews 9:15 says, "For this reason He is the mediator of a new covenant, so that, since a death has taken place for the redemption of the transgressions that were committed under the first covenant, those who have been called may receive the promise of the eternal inheritance." Jesus' atoning death is virtually synonymous with his being the mediator of the New Covenant, for his blood is the "blood of the covenant" (Matt 26:28; Mark 14:24; cf. Luke 22:20). This death (θανάτου) that has taken place is Christ's death for the redemption of men from sin (ἀπολύτρωσιν τῶν . . . παραβάσεων; cf. Rom 3:24–25). The purpose (ὅπως) for Christ's New Covenant mediation through his redemptive death is that the called (οἱ κεκλημένοι)—that is, those who were foreknown and predestined by the Father, eventually effectually called unto salvation, namely, the elect (Rom 8:29–30, 33)—would receive (λαμβάνω, "to lay hold of") the promise of the eternal inheritance. In other words, Christ's death for redemption is intended not only to *purchase* or *provide* eternal life but to ensure the *application* and *reception* of eternal life for those for whom it was purchased.

Hebrews 13:12 says, "Therefore Jesus also, that He might sanctify the people through His own blood, suffered outside the gate." The suffering in view here is clearly the sacrificial death of Christ, akin to the offering of Levitical sacrifices (Heb 13:11), accomplished "through" the shedding of "His own blood." The purpose (ἵνα) for his atoning death is here described as the sanctification (ἁγιάζω) of the people whom he represented. Therefore, "His purpose was to set them apart to God by removing their guilt, and thus to enable them to have continuing access to God on the basis of forgiveness by expiation."[48] This sanctification refers to "qualifying them for an approach to God in worship"[49]

46. Morris, *Apostolic Preaching of the Cross*, 144–213.

47. Owen observes, "Nothing at all of the purchasing of a possible deliverance for all and every one; nay, all are not those children which God gave him [Heb 2:13], all are not delivered from death and him that had the power of it: and therefore it was not all for whom he then took flesh and blood" (Owen, *Death of Death*, 209–10).

48. Kent, *Hebrews*, 285. Bruce styles Jesus' intention in the atonement from this text as "bring[ing] them to God as worshipers purified in conscience" (Bruce, *Hebrews*, 380–81).

49. "The notion behind the action of 'sanctifying' or 'consecrating' the people is that of qualifying

Peter makes two comments concerning the intention of the atonement in his first epistle. First, in 1 Pet 2:24, he writes, "He Himself bore our sins in His body on the cross, so that we might die to sin and live to righteousness." The intention named here is the practical sanctification of those whose sins Christ bore in his body on the cross (cf. Isa 53:5). This is substantially the same as Paul's statement in 2 Cor 5:15. For further comment, see the discussion on that passage above. Second, 1 Pet 3:18 contains another clear affirmation of the intended purpose of the atonement, saying, "For Christ also died for sins once for all, the just for the unjust, so that He might bring us to God." The purpose (ἵνα) for Christ's substitutionary atonement (δίκαιος ὑπὲρ ἀδίκων) was that he would bring his people into the presence of God for eternal fellowship with him. As Davids puts it, "Jesus died in order that, so to speak, he might reach across the gulf between God and humanity and, taking our hand, lead us across the territory of the enemy into the presence of the Father who called us."[50] The atonement was not designed merely to remove obstacles to God or to make a way to God accessible, but rather to actually bring men and women to God.

Summary

The preceding survey demonstrates that the New Testament's characterization of the divine intention for Christ's atonement is uniformly and exclusively salvific. While we agree that Scripture teaches universal common grace (Matt 5:44–45), the necessity of universal gospel proclamation (Acts 17:30), and the final redemption of the cosmos (Rom 8:21), there is no mention of the Father or the Son intending the cross to accomplish those realities, and therefore there is no evidence to support the MIV's claims for multiple intentions in the atonement. Instead, this survey has shown that the divine intention for the atonement was to save sinners (Luke 19:10; John 3:16–17; 12:46–47; 1 Tim 1:15; 1 John 4:14), to satisfy divine wrath (Heb 2:17), to take away sin (1 John 3:5; cf. John 1:29), to impart spiritual life (John 6:51; 10:10; 1 John 4:9) and richness (2 Cor 8:9), to free captives from slavery (Matt 20:28; Mark 10:45; Heb 2:14–15; 1 Tim 2:6), to rescue from evil (Gal 1:4), to impute righteousness (2 Cor 5:21), to impart adoption (Gal 4:5), to sanctify his people (John 17:19; 2 Cor 5:15; Eph 5:25–27; Titus 2:14; Heb 13:12; 1 Pet 2:24), and to glorify them and bring them into the presence of God (Heb 2:10; 1 Pet 3:18).

---

them for an approach to God in worship. . . . The text ascribes to Jesus a unique and unrepeatable action without which the people could not have enjoyed unhindered access to God and the attainment of the 'perfection' that will finally culminate in the experience of glory" (Lane, *Hebrews 9–13*, 541).

50. Davids, *First Epistle of Peter*, 136.

The Salvific Effect of the Atonement

Given the omnipotence of the Father, Son, and Spirit—as Almighty God, for whom nothing is too difficult (Gen 18:14; Jer 32:17, 27), who accounts the inhabitants of the earth as nothing and accomplishes his will (Dan 4:35), even all his good pleasure (Isa 46:9–10; Pss 115:3; 135:6)—no purpose of the triune God can be thwarted (Job 42:2) but will be established and will stand forever (Ps 33:10–11; Isa 46:10). Therefore, whatever the triune God intends to accomplish by the atonement must certainly be effected. Gibson is correct when he notes that these purpose clauses and statements of intention "are not expressing wishful thinking in the form of a purpose clause— an unrealized potential; rather, they demonstrate a primary, intended goal that *will* be realized." Indeed, he asks, memorably, "If the triune God—Father, Son, and Holy Spirit—are for these ends, who then can be against them?"[51]

Given this, we ought to expect biblical testimony that the cross actually effected the intentions that God purposed. A survey of Scripture's teaching concerning the accomplishments of Christ on the cross reveals that this is precisely the case, as seen in the following ten areas:

1. Redemption: Our high priest has not merely intended redemption by his sacrificial offering, but he "obtained eternal redemption" through his own blood (Heb 9:12). Christ did not merely ensure that redemption would eventually occur through the sinner's repentance and faith. Rather, Scripture locates the accomplishment of redemption in the offering of his blood in the atoning work of the cross (cf. 9:15).

2. Expiation: Jesus did not merely appear with the intention of expiating sins (cf. 1 John 3:5) but did "put away sin by the sacrifice of Himself" (Heb 9:26). "The [Father] has caused the iniquity of us all to fall on [the Son]" (Isa 53:6), and so "He Himself *bore* our sins in His body on the cross" and in this way accomplished the healing of his people (1 Pet 2:24; cf. Isa 53:10–12). The efficacious language must be noted. Christ did not *potentially* bear our sins; he bore them. Nor does the text say that in bearing our sins he made us *healable*; no, "by His scourging we are *healed*" (Isa 53:5). The cross did not make spiritual healing possible; it healed those for whom it was intended.[52]

3. Definitive sanctification: Christ did not only intend to purify us from sin (cf. Titus 2:14), but he "made purification for sins" (Heb 1:3) such that "we *have been sanctified* through the offering of the body of Jesus Christ once for all" (Heb 10:10). The bridegroom of the church did not merely intend her definitive

---

51. Gibson, "Trinitarian Work," 367.

52. Owen comments, "Christ, then, so bare our iniquities by his death, that, by virtue of the stripes and afflictions which he underwent in his offering himself for us, this is certainly procured and effected, that we should go free, and not suffer any of those things which he underwent for us" (Owen, *Death of Death*, 212).

sanctification; he accomplished it, "having cleansed her by the washing of water with the word" (Eph 5:26).[53]

4. Reconciliation: Scripture does not teach that Christ merely made the Father reconcilable to sinners through his death; rather, it states that "we *were* reconciled to God through the death of His Son" (Rom 5:10), and again, "He has now reconciled you in His fleshly body through death" (Col 1:22; cf. 2 Cor 5:18–19; Eph 2:15–16).[54] The death of Christ of itself has reconciled his people to God.

5. Salvation: Not only has the Father sent the Son into the world with the intention of saving the world (cf. John 3:17; 12:47), but "the grace of God has appeared, bringing salvation to all men" (Titus 2:11). Shultz paraphrases Paul's words here as saying that "God's purposes in Christ's saving work [have] made salvation available to all people."[55] However, the text does not speak of the availability of salvation; it says that God's grace in Christ has actually brought salvation itself.[56]

6. Regeneration: Christ intended his death to bring spiritual life to the world (John 6:51; 10:10), and this he accomplished, for the bread of life "comes down out of heaven, and [in fact] gives life to the world" (John 6:33). As the good shepherd, he laid his life down for the sheep (John 10:15) and in this way gave eternal life to them (John 10:28). Through the gospel of his death, Christ "abolished death and brought life and immortality to light" (2 Tim 1:10), which is applied through the Spirit's work (1 Pet 1:1–3).

53. The aorist participle of means, καθαρίσας, indicates antecedent action, which communicates that this cleansing was definitively accomplished on the cross, even if later applied through faith in the preached word. See Hoehner, *Ephesians*, 750–52. Thielman notes, "Viewed from one angle, it happened when Christ gave himself for the church, since the purpose of this giving was to sanctify it, and its sanctification involved its cleansing. . . . This cleansing, sanctifying action was applied to them when they were washed in the verbal proclamation of the gospel, that is, when they heard the gospel preached, believed it, and were sealed as God's special people by the Holy Spirit" (Thielman, *Ephesians*, 383, 385).

54. A more through discussion of the doctrine of reconciliation appears in chapters 6 and 16. Briefly, however, the reconciliation accomplished by the cross is the forensic removal of the ground of God's enmity against sinners, which is especially clear in the parallel with justification in Rom 5:9–10 (cf. Murray, *Romans*, 1:172–75; Moo, *Romans*, 311–12). This reconciliation is said to be accomplished "through death" (Col 1:22), that is, "through the death of [God's] Son" (Rom 5:10), and not through faith. Thus it refers to an objective act achieved on the cross, for, as Owen argues, "If God doth only purpose and promise to lay aside his anger upon the death of Christ, but doth it not until our actual believing,—then . . . our faith is the proper procuring cause of reconciliation, the death of Christ but a requisite antecedent; which is not the Scripture phrase" (Owen, *Of the Death of Christ*, 10:453).

55. Shultz, "Defense," 141.

56. The proper scope of πᾶσιν ἀνθρώποις must be interpreted in light of the substance of σωτήριος; the latter must not be modified based upon a predetermined interpretation of the former. That "all men" do not in actuality have salvation brought to them is evidence that all without exception are not in view, but rather all classes and kinds of men, as fits the context, which speaks of older men (2:2), older women (2:3), young women (2:4), young men (2:6), and slaves (2:9) (Knight, *Pastoral Epistles*, 319).

7. Justification: The Father made the Son to be sin with the purpose that sinners would become the righteousness of God in him (2 Cor 5:21). This justification is accomplished by the grace of God "through the redemption which is in Christ Jesus" (Rom 3:23–25), which redemption was accomplished by Christ's bearing our curse on the cross (Gal 3:13), and which issues in the forgiveness of sins (Col 1:14). The redemption that accomplishes the forgiveness of sins must consist in justification, for justification consists (in part) in not having sin imputed to one's account (cf. Rom 4:6–7; 5:9).

8. Adoption: The redemption that accomplishes our forgiveness and justification also accomplishes our adoption (Gal 4:5), as God's eternal purpose for us (Eph 1:5) is carried out in Christ's atoning work.

9. Progressive sanctification: Christ gave himself for the church with the intention of sanctifying her (Eph 5:25–27), and this he does, as his blood is said to cleanse us from all sin (1 John 1:7) and to cleanse the conscience from dead works to serve the living God (Heb 9:14).

10. Glorification: Christ's intention in his substitutionary suffering was to bring us to God (1 Pet 3:18); this also his death actually accomplishes. The writer of Hebrews describes Christ's saving death as actually "bringing many sons to glory" (Heb 2:10), for it is on the basis of his death ("since a death has taken place for the redemption of the transgressions") that his people will "receive the promise of the eternal inheritance" (Heb 9:15).

Therefore, Scripture not only testifies that the divine *intention* for the cross was uniformly salvific; it also testifies that the cross effectually *accomplished* all of its salvific intentions. It could not be otherwise, for, as was mentioned, it is unthinkable to suppose that the triune God could fail to bring about any of his purposes. Such may only be ascribed to a being who lacks either the wisdom or power to carry out his plans; but it would be blasphemy to ascribe want of wisdom or power to the all-wise, omnipotent Lord of hosts.[57] As Owen quips, "The work effecteth what the workman intendeth. . . . Whatsoever the blessed Trinity intended by them, that was effected."[58]

Thus, Scripture's stated intention for the atoning death of Christ is that it would save, ransom, satisfy wrath, take away sin, redeem, impart spiritual life, justify, sanctify, and glorify. And Scripture's testimony of the actual effect of the atoning death of Christ is that by it Christ saved, ransomed, propitiated, expiated, redeemed, regenerated, justified, adopted, sanctified, and glorified all those for whom he died. Given these truths

---

57. See Boettner, *Reformed Doctrine of Predestination*, 156. Owen reasons, "Now, unless we will blasphemously ascribe want of wisdom, power, perfection, and sufficiency in working unto the agent, or affirm that the death and intercession of Christ were not suitable and proportioned for the attaining the end proposed by it to be effected, we must grant that the end of these is one and the same" (Owen, *Death of Death*, 201).

58. Owen, *Death of Death*, 201.

concerning the *intent* and *effect* of the atonement, the *extent* must be limited to those who actually partake in the intended and accomplished blessings.[59]

Jesus died to purchase the blessings of salvation precisely so that they would be applied to those for whom he purchased them. And yet, it cannot be said that all individuals without exception experience these blessings. Not all are called, justified, and glorified (cf. Rom 8:30); many walk the broad road to destruction rather than the narrow way unto salvation (Matt 7:13–14; cf. Matt 25:41, 46; Rev 20:15). Therefore, lest we grant that the triune God failed in his intention, the *intent* of the atonement is determinative of its *extent*: Christ did not die for all without exception but for the elect alone.

Multiple Intentions?

Similar to the presentation on Trinitarian unity, the MIV desires to affirm the above presentation concerning the intent and effect of the atonement. However, it does so by relegating it to what they call the "particular intention" of the cross. "God's particular intention in the atonement," says Shultz, "was to secure the salvation of the elect."[60] The above presentation refers to this particular intention. However, as stated above, the MIV claims that, in addition to this particular intention, God *also* intended the cross to accomplish other benefits, short of salvation, that accrue to the reprobate as well: providing forgiveness for all, making it possible for believers to be saved, making the universal gospel call possible, purchasing universal common grace, and more.

This, however, simply will not do, for there is no text of Scripture that expressly sets forth any universal intentions for the cross in the manner of the above passages. One searches the biblical witness in vain for a statement such as, "The Son of Man has come to provide forgiveness" (cf. Luke 19:10); or, "You know that He appeared to provide common grace" (cf. 1 John 3:5); or, "It is a trustworthy statement, deserving of full acceptance, that Christ Jesus came into the world to make it possible for sinners to be saved" (cf. 1 Tim 1:15). After observing how frequently and uniformly the New Testament explicitly identifies *salvation* as the intent of the atonement, to propose that these speak only of a particular intention and do not necessarily rule out general intentions,

---

59. Owen's conclusion regarding the *extent* is inescapable: "If the death and oblation of Jesus Christ (as a sacrifice to his Father) doth sanctify all them for whom it was a sacrifice; doth purge away their sin; redeem them from wrath, curse, and guilt; work for them peace and reconciliation with God; procure for them life and immortality; bearing their iniquities and healing all their diseases; — then died he only for those that are in the event sanctified, purged, redeemed, justified, freed from wrath and death, quickened, saved, etc.; but that all are not thus sanctified, freed, etc., is most apparent: and, therefore, they cannot be said to be the proper object of the death of Christ" (Owen, *Death of Death*, 214).

60. Shultz, "Defense," 12.

while at the same time failing to provide a single text that does speak of these general intentions, is to fallaciously argue from silence.[61]

The texts that Shultz cites in support of a universal provisional intention for the atonement teach no such thing, and in fact many of them argue instead for a salvific intent and are the very passages examined above (e.g., John 3:16–17; 6:51; 12:46–47; 2 Cor 5:14–21; 1 Tim 2:4–6; Titus 2:11–14; 1 John 4:14). A full refutation of Shultz's exegesis of these passages awaits part 3, but, in brief, his handling of these texts fails because he focuses on their scope to the neglect of their substance. Presuming that the plain meaning of "all" and "world" is all people without exception in the history of the world, he, along with the other interpreters of the MIV, recognizes that saying Christ's death saves (John 3:16–17), ransoms (1 Tim 2:6), or gives life (John 6:51) to all without exception leads to the doctrine of universal final salvation. Thus, the substance of the atonement as that which efficaciously saves and gives life is reinterpreted as merely providing salvation or making life available.[62] If Christ comes to save all, and all without exception are not saved, it is concluded that Christ has *not* come to save all but to render their salvation possible.[63] Efficacious accomplishment is reduced to possibility in order to interpret universalistic language to mean all without exception. Instead, rather than interpreting the substance of the atonement in light of its scope, the scope of the atonement ought to be interpreted in light of its substance. If Christ came to save all, and all without exception are not saved, it ought to be concluded that "all" speaks of the all who are actually saved—all without distinction rather than all without exception.

Besides this, two categories of the reprobate present an insuperable problem for the notion that God intends the cross to provide for the possibility of the salvation of all without exception. The first category is the unevangelized. It could not have been the Father's intention for the cross to make possible the salvation of all without exception, for the Father could not have intended to save, on the condition of faith in the gospel, those to whom he in his sovereign providence never intended (a) to send the gospel nor (b) to grant faith. In other words, if the Father does not intend to provide the means by which the possibility of salvation may be converted into actual salvation—namely, the hearing of the gospel message (Rom 10:14–17) as well as the sovereign gift of faith (Eph 2:8; Phil 1:29)—he cannot in any proper sense

---

61. Aside from the following paragraph, the MIV argues for universal non-saving intentions in the atonement by inferring that apparently universalistic language combined with apparently universal results of the cross must indicate universal intentions. Part 3 addresses the universalistic language, while part 4 addresses the universal results.

62. E.g., Shultz, "Defense," 109–10. See the above interaction with proponents of the MIV in the presentation of each of the passages in "The Salvific Intent of the Atonement."

63. E.g., Ware, who says, ". . . we cannot speak correctly of Christ's death as actually and certainly *saving* the elect. No, even here, the payment made by his death on behalf of the elect renders their salvation *possible*" (Ware, "Outline," 5; cf. Shultz, "Defense," 156–58).

be said to intend their salvation.[64] The second category is those already damned before the coming of Christ. It could not have been the Father's intention for the cross to make possible the salvation of those whose destiny was already sealed in hell at the time of the cross, for "it is appointed for men to die *once* and then comes judgment" (Heb 9:27). There is no possibility for a second chance at salvation after one has already perished in one's sins. Indeed, between heaven and hell "there is a great chasm *fixed*, so that those who wish to come over from here to you will not be able, and that none may cross over from there to us" (Luke 16:26).[65] The permanence of judgment in hell speaks to the Father's intention not to save those who enter there; he could not have intended the cross to make possible the salvation of those who had already entered into their condemnation. Thus, the existence of both the unevangelized and the already-damned demonstrates that there could not have been a genuinely universal intention in the atonement.

---

64. This is also the ground of the fundamental confusion that hypothetical universalism introduces into the divine decree. Macleod comments, "On the one hand, God decreed to redeem all men on condition that they receive the gospel; on the other, knowing that every human being is by nature indisposed to receive the gospel, he decreed to overcome this indisposition only in the elect. He will give *them* faith; the rest he will pass by—redeemed but reprobate. In effect there are two saving decrees: one to save everyone from the guilt of sin by the cross of Christ; and another, quite distinct, to redeem only some from its power. This, surely, exposes a lack of coherence in the divine mind" (Macleod, "Definite Atonement and the Divine Decree," 431).

65. For the verb "fixed" (ἐστήρικται), Reymond provides the gloss, "has been firmly fixed and stands permanently so" (Reymond, *New Systematic Theology*, 675).

6

The Nature of the Atonement, Part 1

IN THE PREVIOUS CHAPTER, it was demonstrated from Scripture that the divine intention for the atonement of Christ was to accomplish salvation for those for whom it was rendered.[1] As a result, it was concluded that since salvation is not enjoyed by all without exception, the extent of the atonement is limited to those particular individuals who eventually enjoy its benefits. The extent of the atonement was thus demonstrated to be a function of its intent, or its purpose. It was also briefly observed that Scripture teaches that the atonement effected precisely the salvation that God intended for it to accomplish.

In this chapter and the next, it is necessary to examine this doctrine more thoroughly and systematically. What is the *nature* of the atonement? What does Scripture say that Christ actually accomplished by his death on the cross? Similar to the intention of the atonement, the question of the extent of the atonement will also be shown to be a function of its nature. When one gives a conclusive, biblical answer to this question of *what* Christ accomplished, the question concerning *for whom* he has accomplished it becomes much clearer.

Scripture teaches the nature of Christ's atonement by describing it according to several themes, or motifs. These motifs emerge as a consequence of the various ways man's sin has broken the relationship between God and humanity. In man's rebellion against the commandments of God, he has become a lawbreaker. The standard of righteousness expressed in the divine law now holds man guilty and he is thus required to pay the penalty appropriate for offending God's infinite holiness: spiritual death (Rom 3:19; 6:23). Precisely because God is holy, his wrath is aroused against human sin, and, in accordance with perfect justice, that wrath must be satisfied in the just punishment of sinners in hell (Rom 1:18). God's holy anger against sin is the ground for enmity between God and man; whereas man was created for intimate fellowship with and enjoyment of God, there is only alienation and hostility between them (Isa 59:2; Col 1:21). Further, man's sin is not merely incidental to him but so afflicts his entire being that he is said to be in bondage to sin and death (John 8:34; Rom 6:16–20).

---

1. Portions of this and the next chapter are adapted from the author's contributions to MacArthur and Mayhue, eds., *Biblical Doctrine*, 519–35, 542, 548–51.

The reality of man's sin before a holy God requires atonement—a means of paying for sin, satisfying justice, and restoring the broken relationship. And yet man's slavery to sin renders him unable to pay the required penalty short of perishing eternally in hell. But the good news of the gospel is that the Father has appointed the Lord Jesus Christ to stand in the place of sinners and accomplish their atonement as their substitute. Thus, the atonement is most fundamentally a penal substitution (which will be expounded in chapter 7), but the motifs explain what sort of penal substitution the atonement was. By standing in the place of sinners, Jesus paid for their sin and guilt by offering himself as an expiatory sacrifice to God (1 Pet 2:24), propitiated the Father's wrath by bearing its full exercise in himself (Rom 3:25; Gal 3:13), reconciled God to man (Rom 5:9–10; Col 1:20–22), redeemed man from his slavery (1 Pet 1:18–19), and conquered sin and death (Heb 2:14–15). These motifs—expiatory sacrifice, propitiation, reconciliation, and redemption—define the nature of the penal substitutionary atonement that Christ accomplished by his death on the cross. When the biblical definitions of these motifs are respected, it becomes plain that the nature of the atonement is one of efficacious accomplishment, not one of potentiality or provision. That is, by his death, Christ actually took away sin, effectively appeased God's wrath, decisively overcame alienation, and genuinely freed sinners from slavery, all by actually bearing their punishment in himself as their substitute. In short, the cross *saved* sinners; it did not merely *provide* salvation or make salvation *possible*.

It will be demonstrated that the biblical understanding of the nature of Calvary's achievements requires us to take a particularist view of their extent. An atonement of unlimited efficacy must necessarily be restricted to those who enjoy its benefits—namely, the elect of God, and not all without exception.[2] It will be shown that, in order to extend at least some of the benefits of the atonement to all without exception, the MIV fatally compromises its efficacy, failing to remain consistent with the biblical definitions of the atonement's accomplishments.

2. Yet it should be noted that this restriction or limitation in extent is not an end in itself. The particularist's chief concern is not to exclude people from the benefits of Christ's glorious work. Rather, it is to safeguard the achievements of the cross from being robbed of their efficacy as a result of a desire to universalize their extent. In order to be able to say that Christ died for all without exception, the *substance* of the atonement must be reimagined as that which makes men savable rather than that which actually and decisively saves them. "What they give on the one hand they take away with the other," Owen says, "by suspending the enjoyment of [the benefits of the cross] on a condition by us to be fulfilled, not by [Christ] procured" (Owen, *Death of Death*, 226). Thus, as Trueman explains, "The concern that formulations of limited atonement are intended to protect is not the limitation of the atonement but its indicative nature, its glorious, powerful efficacy in dealing once and for all with the sins of God's people and guaranteeing their salvation" (Trueman, "Definite Atonement View," 61). Above all, what particularists are most concerned to preserve is the fully consistent affirmation of an atonement that actually atones.

Expiatory Sacrifice

The New Testament repeatedly identifies the atoning death of Christ as a sacrifice offered to take away sins: "But now once at the consummation of the ages He has been manifested to put away sin by the sacrifice of Himself" (Heb 9:26; cf. John 1:29; Eph 5:2; Heb 10:12; 1 John 3:5). Yet this imagery of sacrificial offering is rooted not merely in the New Testament but in the Old Testament's prescriptions for Israel's sacrificial worship to God, of which Christ's atonement is the antitype and fulfillment (cf. Heb 9:23; cf. Heb 7–10). Thus, it is impossible to adequately understand the significance of Christ's death as sacrifice without considering it in light of the Levitical law's categories for substitutionary atonement by sacrifice.[3] Such a study consistently reveals that from its inception in the law of God, the concepts of both efficacy and particularity are inherent in the concept of atonement. Atonement (a) is always that which accomplishes its intentions of taking away sin, satisfying wrath, and reconciling God and sinners, not merely making such things possible; and it is (b) always that which is accomplished on behalf of a specific group of persons rather than all people without exception.[4]

The Hebrew term most often translated as "atonement" is כָּפַר, the significance of which includes "to atone," "to wipe off," and "to cover."[5] Other glosses include "to appease," "to make amends," "to ransom,"[6] and "to avert wrath,"[7] the last of which will figure prominently in the below discussion of propitiation. Harris says it means "to atone by offering a substitute."[8] The first occurrence of the term in the context of

---

3. Several authors observe that this is a weakness in non-particularist presentations of the extent of the atonement. Trueman is correct, who says of Hammett's essay in defense of the MIV, "Hammett's problem flows from a failure to allow the Old Testament to set the categories for understanding the New. The Old Testament develops notions of sacrifice and substitution and provides the basic foundation for understanding the same in the New. We need to take the whole Bible seriously when we approach the death of Christ, and central to that task is making sure we set Christ's death in the same context that Paul and the other New Testament writers did. That context is not simply that of sin and salvation but also of the history of redemption as it develops in ancient Israel and then culminates in Christ. The context of the New Testament texts is thus not simply the New Testament but the Old Testament too. We must allow the Old Testament to shape how we understand substitution" (Trueman, "Response to Multiple-Intentions View," 205). At the close of his dissertation, Shultz lists as a need for further research a biblical theology of atonement, "especially from the Old Testament" (Schultz, "Defense," 288).

4. In this observation and the following presentation, I am indebted to the work of Barnes, *Atonement Matters*, 47–62.

5. *HALOT*, 493.

6. Averbeck, "כָּפַר," *NIDOTTE*, 3:681–82.

7. Steve Jeffery, Michael Ovey, and Andrew Sach add this final gloss and argue for it persuasively (Jeffery, Ovey, and Sach, *Pierced for Our Transgressions*, 45; cf. 44–48). David G. Peterson also lists forgiveness, cleansing, ransom, and the averting of God's wrath as four possible meanings of כָּפַר (Peterson, "Atonement in the Old Testament," 1–25).

8. Harris, "כָּפַר," *TWOT*, 1:452–53. Williamson summarizes, "While the Qal conveys the idea of 'to cover' (cf. Gen. 6:14), the Piel seems to connote either 'to ransom' (cf. Ex. 30:11–16; Num. 35:29–34) or 'to wipe clean' (i.e., 'to purge'; cf. Jer. 18:23, where it is used in parallel with 'to blot out')" (Williamson,

atonement is in Gen 32:20, wherein Jacob aims to appease (כָּפַר) Esau's anger with an offering (מִנְחָה) of livestock and thereby restore their relationship. The concepts of propitiation and reconciliation are thus already in play, and both the particularity and efficacy of this atoning offering are evident in that (a) it is offered on behalf of Jacob specifically and (b) Jacob expects that the gift will indeed effectively assuage his brother's anger and reconcile them to one another.

Its occurrences in the book of Exodus are associated with the consecration (cleansing) of the priests (Exod 29:33, 36–37), the yearly cleansing of the altar of incense (Exod 30:10), the atonement to be made in relation to the census tax (Exod 30:15–16), and, most significantly, Moses' attempt to intercede for the people's idolatry with the golden calf: "You yourselves have committed a great sin; and now I am going up to the LORD, perhaps I can make atonement [כָּפַר] for your sin" (Exod 32:30). Several features of this atonement are noteworthy. First, it is clearly substitutionary, as Moses is offering to make atonement for (בְּעַד), or on behalf of, Israel's sin; he even offers himself in their place (Exod 32:32). Second, this atonement is particular; it is for the sins of the camp of Israel and no one else for which Moses intercedes. Third, this atonement would involve the efficacious expiation of their sin—i.e., their sin would be taken away, or forgiven (Exod 32:32); forgiveness would not be made possible or available but would be accomplished.

Atonement figures exceptionally prominently in the book of Leviticus, the central burden of which is to explain how a holy God can dwell (cf. Exod 40:34–38) in the midst of a sinful people. The answer is given almost immediately; sinners will offer sacrifices to God that will atone for their sin and make them acceptable to dwell in his presence: "he shall offer [his sacrifice] at the doorway of the tent of meeting, that he may be accepted [רְצֹנוֹ] before the LORD. He shall lay his hand on the head of the burnt offering, that it may be accepted [רָצָה] for him to make atonement [כָּפַר] on his behalf" (Lev 1:3–4). The particularity of this sacrifice is evident, first, in that the sacrificial animal was to be brought by the sinner who was seeking atonement. As Williams notes, "Unless he was bringing a small bird, the worshiper himself killed the animal, gutted it, cut it up, and washed its entrails and legs, while the priest sprinkled the blood and placed the carcass on the fire. Thus from the outset of the offering the sacrifice was connected to the specific worshiper."[9] Secondly, the particularity and personal nature of the sacrifice is evident by the worshiper's laying his hand on the head of the burnt offering, which signifies an identification of the sinner with the substitute to the degree that the worshiper's sins would be transferred to the animal (cf. Lev 16:21).[10] Third, the repetition of the dative suffixes "for him" (לוֹ) and "on his behalf" (עָלָיו) emphasize the particular nature of this atoning sacrifice: it was for *him* and on *his* behalf that this substitutionary transfer of sin

---

"Because He Loved Your Forefathers," 225n1).

9. Williams, "Definite Intent," 475.

10. Rooker, *Leviticus*, 87.

took place.[11] Further, in addition to the particularity of this sacrifice, its efficacy is also evident. Such an offering would indeed make atonement for him, not just make atonement possible upon the fulfillment of a later condition; it would satisfy the demands of God (cf. Lev 1:9) and thereby make the worshiper *accepted*, not merely acceptable, in Yahweh's presence.

As with the burnt offering, the prescriptions for the sin offering in chapter 4 and the guilt offering in chapter 5 emphasize both particularity and efficacy. Once again, the hand-laying intimately links the worshiper to the sacrifice (Lev 4:4, 15, 24, 29, 33), so that it is plain that it is *his* sins that are punished in the death of the substitute. In 5:5–6, the sacrifice is explicitly conjoined to the confession of sin, which means that it was particularly for the sins that an individual confessed that the atonement was accomplished. In 4:20–21, the offering is specifically identified as "the sin offering for the assembly," that is, for the assembly of Israel alone, and not for the nations (cf. 9:7; 16:17; Num 15:25–26).[12] Atonement is made on behalf of the worshiper with regard to his specific sins ("on *his* behalf," 5:6; "for the sin which *he* has committed," 5:10; "atonement for *him* concerning *his* sin," 5:13; cf. 5:18, 26).[13] With regard to efficacy, it is noteworthy that in every instance in which the narrator comments on the atonement he has just prescribed, it is a reference to its efficacious accomplishment of its intent: "and they shall be forgiven" (4:20); "and he shall be forgiven" (4:26, 31, 35; 5:10, 13, 16, 18; 6:7; 19:22); "and she shall be clean" (12:8); "and he shall be clean" (14:20); "and it shall be clean" (14:53). There was no question as to whether the forgiveness or cleansing intended by the atonement would be accomplished. It has been correctly said that "the repetition of the laws for sacrifice would have indelibly impressed on the mind of the faithful Israelite that when the priest made atonement, he actually atoned, and that atonement brought about its intended effect of the forgiveness of sins."[14]

The pinnacle of the Old Testament sacrificial system was the Day of Atonement, in which Israel's high priest was to enter the most holy place in order to "make atonement for himself and for his household and for all the assembly of Israel" (Lev 16:17; cf. 16:24; 32–34). At the center of the Day of Atonement ceremonies were two goats: (1) the goat of sacrifice, which was to be slain and whose blood was to be sprinkled on the mercy seat as a substitutionary, life-for-life atonement (16:15–19; cf. 17:11); and (2) the scapegoat, upon whose head Aaron confessed all the sins of the people of Israel, and who was then banished into the wilderness (16:21–22). Instead of each

---

11. Milgrom, *Leviticus 1–16*, 153.

12. "What we must note at this point in redemptive history and revelation is that the focus of the atoning sacrifices was 'the people,' a technical term for Israel . . ." (Barnes, *Atonement Matters*, 50).

13. See Williams's literary analysis of Leviticus 4–5, in which he demonstrates that "the references to specific offenses committed by particular people at the beginning and end of each of the descriptions of the purification offerings are far from accidental. They deliberately employ elegantly varied forms of expression to make the same point again and again: the sacrifices were offered for and were effective for the specific offenses of particular people" ("Williams, "Definite Intent," 476; cf. 476–79).

14. MacArthur and Mayhue, eds., *Biblical Doctrine*, 542.

Israelite bearing their own guilt (5:1; 17:16; 20:17, 19), punishment (5:17; 22:16), and iniquity (7:18; 19:8), and being cut off from the holy presence of God (cf., e.g., 7:20–27; 17:4–14; 18:29), the innocent scapegoat bore the sins of the people and was banished in their place. By virtue of substitutionary sacrifice and the imputation of sin and guilt, God's people were released from their deserved punishment. The efficacy of the sacrifice is nearly self-evident. The assembly's sins were not made forgivable on the Day of Atonement; just as surely as the goat of sacrifice died and just as surely as the scapegoat was banished, Israel's sins had been taken away in the act of substitutionary sacrifice (Lev 16:30).[15] Further, the particularity of the sacrifice is evident as well. The high priest makes atonement "because of the impurities of *the sons of Israel* and because of *their* transgressions in regard to all *their* sins" (16:16); he makes atonement "for himself and for his household and *for all the assembly of Israel*" (16:17). This was not a sacrifice offered on behalf of the Gentile world; there was no yearly atonement that accomplished forgiveness for the Moabites or the Philistines. Aaron laid his hands on the head of the scapegoat and confessed over it "all the iniquities of *the sons of Israel*, and all *their* transgressions in regard to all *their* sins" (16:21). The sins of the Midianites and the Egyptians were not imputed to the scapegoat. This was a definite, particular atonement for the assembly of Israel and them alone.[16]

15. This is not to suggest that salvation came by means of these sacrifices, "for it is impossible for the blood of bulls and goats to take away sins" (Heb 10:4; cf. 9:9; 10:1). The sacrifices of the Old Covenant "looked forward to and derived their efficacy from Christ's final sacrifice (Rom. 3:24–26; Heb. 9:11–10:18). Nevertheless, on the basis of the work of Christ, God graciously allowed himself to be temporarily propitiated by the sacrifices he prescribed to Israel" (MacArthur and Mayhue, eds., *Biblical Doctrine*, 542n55).

16. The objection is often raised that because the assembly of Israel was a mixed community consisting of both genuine believers in Yahweh as well as unbelievers who were not ultimately saved, the Day of Atonement gives an example of an atonement offered for the "all" of the assembly but which was only effective for the remnant of believing ones. In the same way, it is argued, Christ's atonement was offered for all without exception but is effective only for those who appropriate it by faith (e.g., Driscoll and Breshears, *Death by Love*, 179).

Yet this is an apples-to-oranges comparison. It pictures the New Covenant as being made with all without exception while its benefits are applied only to the remnant of the church. Such is not the case; the New Covenant is only made with those who know Yahweh (Jer 31:34). Israel is not analogous to the world while the remnant is analogous to Christians. Rather, the Gentile nations are analogous to the unbelieving world and the Old Covenant community of Israel is analogous to the New Covenant community of those regenerated by the Spirit (cf. Jer 31:31–34). In both cases, atonement is made only for the people of God.

One distinction between Israel and the church is that the former was a mixed community of believers and unbelievers, while the latter, by definition, consists only of those who know the Lord (Jer 31:34). This means that all Israelites—elect and reprobate, believing and unbelieving—enjoyed the benefits of the covenant made with the nation, even the temporary satisfaction of God's wrath for the nation on the Day of Atonement. For example, even though Ahab was a wicked king who did not know Yahweh, he nevertheless would have received the covenant sign of circumcision (Gen 17:10) and would therefore have been privileged to eat the Passover (Exod 12:43–45, 48–49), and he lived in the land promised to David as the reigning king of Israel (cf. 2 Sam 7:10). He experienced the blessings of the national covenant even though he did not know the Lord. The same would have been true for the Day of Atonement. However, because the New Covenant community consists of the elect alone

Another significant event that colors the Old Testament doctrine of sacrificial atonement—even though the term כָּפַר does not appear—is the rite of the Passover. In order to pour out his wrath in judgment upon Egypt, God purposed to kill every firstborn animal and child throughout the nation (Exod 12:12). Though Israel was spared from the first nine plagues, they would not be spared from the tenth unless each family killed an unblemished lamb and put its blood on the doorposts of their house (Exod 12:3–7). If they followed this prescription, however, the blood would serve as a sign to the angel of Yahweh and his wrath of destruction would be turned away (Exod 12:13). Therefore, the Passover lamb died as a substitutionary sacrifice in the place of the firstborn children of the Jews. In this scene we once again observe both the particularity and the efficacy of expiatory sacrifice. The particularity is made plain by the fact that instructions for the escape of God's judgment were not given to all of Egypt but to the children of Israel alone. All were subject to the Lord's wrath, but only his people were given an atonement. Besides this, as Williamson observes, "The amount of flock animal consumed was to be directly proportionate to the number in each household (Ex. 12:4), suggesting that each animal slain provided for only a limited number of individuals. . . . Each lamb served a specific body of people and redeemed a prescribed household."[17] Further, those celebrating the Passover meal in years to come are limited to members of the covenant community; if it was to be extended outside the family of Israel, such a man was to become a proselyte worshiper of Yahweh and be circumcised (Exod 12:43–45, 48–49). That this sacrifice was efficacious is evident by the fact that God's wrath was indeed poured out on the Egyptians (Exod 12:29–30) but not on the Israelites.

Both the Passover and the Levitical sacrifices epitomized by the Day of Atonement foreshadow the atoning work of Christ by substitutionary sacrifice. When Jesus instituted the New Covenant in his blood at the Last Supper, the celebratory meal he shared with them was the commemoration of the Passover (Matt 26:17–29; Mark 14:12–25; Luke 22:7–20). Thus his death was the fulfillment of the Passover, for he is "our Passover lamb" who "has been sacrificed" (1 Cor 5:7, ESV), "the Lamb of God who takes away the sin of the world" (John 1:29) and by whose "precious blood, as of a lamb unblemished and spotless" sinners are redeemed from sin (1 Pet 1:18–19). Indeed, "Just as the blood of the slain lamb protected Israel from the execution of God's judgment, so also the blood of the slain Lamb, Jesus, now protects His people from the Father's wrath against their sin."[18] Similarly, the author of Hebrews identifies Christ as the fulfillment of all of the Levitical sacrifices. While they were ultimately unable to make the worshiper perfect in conscience as evidenced by their needed repetition (Heb 9:9; 10:1–4), the Lord Jesus Christ came and, "having offered one sacrifice for

---

(Jer 31:34), there is no analogous scenario in the New Covenant era. For more on this, see "The Old Covenant Priest and the Mixed Community of Israel" in chapter 8.

17. Williamson, "Because He Loved Your Forefathers," 231–32.

18. MacArthur and Mayhue, eds., *Biblical Doctrine*, 526.

sins for all time, 'sat down at the right hand of God.' . . . For by one offering he has perfected for all time those who are sanctified" (Heb 10:12, 14). He is especially the fulfillment of all aspects of the Day of Atonement ceremonies: the great high priest (cf. Heb 3:1; 8:1), who entered beyond the veil of the heavenly tabernacle (Heb 10:20), sprinkling the blood of sacrifice, namely, his own blood (Heb 9:21–22), which is better than the blood of bulls and goats (Heb 12:24; cf. Heb 10:4). He is the ἱλαστήριον (Rom 3:25; cf. Lev 16:2 LXX), the mercy seat upon which propitiation is made and where God's wrath against sin is turned away. And he is the scapegoat, the one who knew no sin made to be sin (2 Cor 5:21; 1 Pet 2:24) as the Father, as it were, laid his hands on the head of the Son, caused the iniquity of us all to fall on him (Isa 53:6), and banished him from the presence of the Lord (Matt 27:46; Heb 13:12). He is the great high priest who offers the sacrificial offering, the mercy seat upon which the offering is sprinkled, and the scapegoat who bears his people's sins in their place.

Because the Old Testament's doctrine of substitutionary atonement as expiatory sacrifice is fulfilled in Christ, it is legitimate to draw comparisons between the type and the antitype (except for where there are explicit discontinuities revealed; e.g., Heb 10:11–12). From the moment the concept of atonement was revealed by God to his people, it has signified that which is inherently efficacious on behalf of particular persons. Therefore, when the New Testament employs the same terminology to describe the atonement Christ accomplished by his death, it is proper to regard his atonement with the same inherent particularity and efficacy. This is only confirmed by the many texts that identify the scope of Christ's work as relating to a particular people—his sheep (John 10:14–15), his friends (John 15:13), his church (Acts 20:28; Eph 5:25), his people (Matt 1:21), the many (Matt 20:28; Mark 10:45) whom his Father had given him (John 6:37–40; 10:29; 17:2, 6, 9, 24; Heb 2:13)—and by those texts that cast the atonement as actually taking away sin (John 1:29; 1 John 3:5), healing (1 Pet 2:24), redeeming (Rev 5:9; cf. Eph 1:7), and so on.

Propitiation

As mentioned above, the concept of atonement as denoted by the term כָּפַר is not limited merely to expiation—the forgiveness, cleansing, removal of, or ransom from sin. Inherent in the term כָּפַר, as well as the New Testament counterpart, ἱλάσκομαι (which often translates כָּפַר in the Septuagint and is used to describe the death of Christ, Rom 3:25; Heb 2:17; 1 John 2:2; 4:10), is the concept of the turning away of divine wrath.[19] This was observed briefly in two early occurrences of כָּפַר. The first was when Jacob aimed to appease (כָּפַר) Esau's anger by presenting him with an offering (מִנְחָה) of livestock. This offering is intended to satisfy, or turn away, his brother's wrath from him, which was aroused because of Jacob's deception (Gen 32:20). The

19. Once again, see Jeffery, Ovey, and Sach, *Pierced for Our Transgressions*, 44–48; and Peterson, "Atonement in the Old Testament," 1–25.

second instance briefly examined was Moses' intercession on behalf of Israel after their idolatrous act of fashioning the golden calf (Exod 32:1–8), a blatant violation of the covenant law (20:3–5) they had just sworn to uphold (24:3, 7). Yahweh's response to this brazen idolatry was to be righteously aroused in wrath: "Now then let Me alone, that My anger [אַף] may burn against them and that I may destroy them; and I will make of you a great nation" (32:10). While God relented from this intention as a result of Moses' intercession (32:11–14), nevertheless the wrath of God was exercised against his people in the slaughter of three thousand idolaters that same day (32:27–28). On the next day, in order that Yahweh's wrath might be turned away from the nation, Moses told the people he intended to intercede on their behalf: "You yourselves have committed a great sin; and now I am going up to the LORD, perhaps I can make atonement [כִּפֶּר; ἐξιλάσωμαι, LXX] for your sin" (32:30). Moses understood that the Lord's wrath had been roused by the sin of the people, and his instinct was to "make atonement," which he attempted by offering himself as a substitute for the people who would bear God's wrath against them by being cut off from him (32:32). This demonstrates that כִּפֶּר and ἐξιλάσωμαι indeed denote propitiation and not merely expiation; inherent to the biblical concept of atonement (from its inception in the law of God) is the concept of turning away the wrath of God.

While such examples could be multiplied, two others will suffice. In Numbers 16, in response to Israel's mutiny against Moses and Aaron, Yahweh's wrath was again kindled against the people (16:45) in the form of a plague that killed 14,700 people (16:48–49). Moses describes this as wrath (קֶצֶף) having gone forth from the Lord, and his instinctive response (כִּי) is to instruct Aaron to make atonement (כִּפֶּר) for them by an offering of incense (16:46). When Aaron had done this, the plague was checked (16:47–48); the Lord's wrath had indeed been turned away by atonement.

A final example illustrates the same concept. In Numbers 25, the camp of Israel is found in a similar tangle of idolatry, because the people had been fornicating with the Moabites and worshiping their gods as a result (Num 25:1–3). The response from God, once again, is wrath: "And Yahweh was angry [אַף] against Israel" (25:3). His wrath was expressed in the form of a plague that consumed twenty-four thousand lives in Israel (25:8–9), and he ordered the execution of the guilty that his wrath might be turned away (25:4). In the midst of that judgment, however, an Israelite brazenly intended to commit the same sin in the sight of the whole assembly (25:6). Then one of the priests, Phinehas, arose and slew both the man and the woman (25:7–8). The text notes that in that moment the plague, which had been the manifestation of God's anger, was checked (25:8). Yahweh then announced that Phinehas's zeal for the Lord's righteousness had "turned away My wrath [הֵשִׁיב אֶת־חֲמָתִי] from the sons of Israel . . . so that I did not destroy the sons of Israel in My jealousy" (25:11). God then identifies this turning away of his wrath as כִּפֶּר: "he was jealous for his God and made atonement [וַיְכַפֵּר] for the sons of Israel" (25:13).

These texts substantiate that the biblical concept of propitiation—the efficacious satisfaction of or turning away of divine wrath—is synonymous with making atonement. In each scenario, when atonement was made, the wrath that had been expressed in the form of a plague was stopped. This propitiation was not provisional; the Israelites were not required to subjectively appropriate Phinehas's execution or Aaron's incense offering by the addition of any work of their own. Rather, the act of atonement itself was sufficient to turn away wrath.

Coming to the New Testament, we observe that the ἱλάσκομαι word group, which was used to translate כָּפַר in the Septuagint, is applied to the atoning death of Christ. This means that Scripture characterizes the death of Christ not merely as an expiatory sacrifice—that which takes away sin—but also as a propitiatory sacrifice—that which efficaciously satisfies divine wrath.[20] As MacArthur and Mayhue put it, "by receiving the full exercise of the Father's wrath against the sins of his people, Christ satisfied God's righteous anger against sin and thus turned away his wrath from us who, had it not been for our substitute, were bound to suffer it for ourselves."[21]

In particular, four New Testament texts describe Christ's atoning work as propitiation.[22] The first significant occurrence is in Rom 3:25, and its context once again testifies to the meaning of the efficacious satisfaction of divine wrath. By this point in the Epistle to the Romans, Paul has written two chapters explaining how the wrath of God (ὀργὴ θεοῦ) has been kindled against all mankind for their sins against him (Rom 1:18). In the case of the Gentiles, who did not have the law but who did see the divine character revealed in creation (1:19–20) and conscience (2:14–15), God displayed his wrath by giving them over to lusts, impurity, idolatry, degrading passions, homosexuality, and a depraved mind (1:24–28). In the case of the Jews, who did have the law but broke it anyway (2:1–4), they had been "storing up wrath for yourself in the day of wrath and revelation of the righteous judgment of God" (2:5). Those who are selfishly ambitious and obey unrighteousness can only expect "wrath and indignation" (2:8) from "the God who inflicts wrath" (3:5). Before the divine standard of perfect righteousness (cf. 3:22–23), every mouth has been closed and all the world is accountable to God (3:19). The attentive reader of the Epistle to the Romans

20. At the heart of the ἱλάσκομαι word group is the concept of the efficacious satisfaction of wrath. Glosses include "to cause to be favorably inclined or disposed," "propitiate," and "conciliate" (BDAG, 473). "The underlying purpose to change God's attitude from one of wrath to one of good-will and favor. . . . In short, propitiation appeases the offended person" (Silva, ed., "ἱλάσκομαι," NIDNTTE, 2:532–42). See also Morris, *Apostolic Preaching of the Cross*, 144–213; and Nicole, "C. H. Dodd and the Doctrine of Propitiation," 117–57.

21. MacArthur and Mayhue, eds., *Biblical Doctrine*, 528.

22. The term also appears in Luke 18:13, in which the penitent tax collector entreats God to be merciful—literally, to be propitious (ἱλάσθητί μοι)—to him, for no other reason than his sovereign grace. Informed by this lexical analysis, his entreaty is that God's wrath would be satisfied in his case and that he would look upon him with undeserved favor. The other occurrence comes in Heb 9:5, which refers to the literal mercy seat (ἱλαστήριον) of the ark of the covenant of the Old Testament tabernacle. While very much related, neither instance speaks directly to Christ's atonement.

is immediately confronted with the problem of divine wrath against human sin. If there is one question generated by the content of the early chapters of this letter, it is: How will the God who is righteously roused to wrath against sin save sinners while remaining righteous? How will the wrath of God be satisfied? That answer is given in 3:21–26: sinners may be credited with the righteousness of God on the basis of the redemption accomplished by Christ's cross, which righteousness they receive by grace through faith alone. But how is that just? What about God's wrath? In the redemption that Christ accomplished, "God put [him] forward [ὃν προέθετο ὁ θεὸς] as a propitiation by His blood [ἱλαστήριον . . . ἐν τῷ αὐτοῦ αἵματι], to be received by faith" (3:25, ESV). The Father has satisfied his wrath against sin by the sprinkling of the blood of his Son, the spotless Lamb, on the mercy seat (ἱλαστήριον) of the heavenly altar (cf. Heb 9:11–15, 23–24). He has punished his people's sins in the substitute, and thus his wrath has righteously been turned away from them.

Several comments on this text are useful to underscore the nature of Christ's propitiation. First, the subject of the sentence, and thus the initiator of this act of propitiation, is God. As Schreiner observes, despite protestations that it is "grotesque," "God himself took the initiative to satisfy and appease his own wrath."[23] Second, Christ is set forth as the propitiation. He is not merely the means of our propitiation; he *is* himself our propitiation. Third, the term ἱλαστήριον is identical to the term used for the mercy seat in the tabernacle, upon which the priest was to sprinkle the blood of the sacrifices (cf. Lev 16:15). While it is disputed as to how directly Paul intends to identify Christ with the mercy seat, an allusion is likely.[24] Christ is metaphorically described as the place whereupon his own sacrificial blood is sprinkled, with the result that atonement is made and divine wrath is satisfied. Yet this imagery ought not to be overplayed, for the basic meaning of ἱλαστήριον in this context is "propitiation" or "propitiatory sacrifice."[25] Fourth, the propitiation consists in the blood of Christ shed on the cross. Though ἐν τῷ αὐτοῦ αἵματι could function as the object of πίστεως, Paul "never elsewhere makes Christ's blood an object of faith."[26] Instead, the ἐν ought to be read as instrumental, identifying "Christ's blood as the means by which God's wrath is propitiated."[27] In other words, propitiation is the divine act of the Son according to the purpose of the Father (cf. Heb 2:17; 1 John 4:10). Finally, the benefits of this propitiation are received only through the sinner's faith apart from any works. The phrase διὰ [τῆς] πίστεως thus does not modify προέθετο, for that would mean that propitiation is not accomplished by God in Christ (as was shown above) but by human faith, a notion utterly foreign to the biblical concept of propitiation. Propitiation is accomplished by the Son through

---

23. Schreiner, *Romans*, 191.

24. See the discussion in Schreiner, *Romans*, 192–94, with whom I agree.

25. Morris, *Romans*, 181–82.

26. Moo, *Romans*, 237.

27. Moo, *Romans*, 237; cf. Schreiner, *Romans*, 194; Cranfield, *Romans*, 1:210.

the sprinkling of his blood. Instead, διὰ [τῆς] πίστεως modifies ἱλαστήριον and "indicates the means by which individuals appropriate the benefits of the sacrifice."[28] In other words, Christ's death effects the action of propitiation, impetrating the satisfaction of wrath for those for whom it is offered and thus ensuring that no one for whom Christ died will ever experience divine wrath themselves; however, though his people have a *right* to the propitiation purchased, they do not actually *possess* that propitiation until they believe. That which Christ effectively accomplishes (not merely provides) on the cross is thus applied through faith.[29] Christ's blood, not human faith, is the means of propitiation;[30] but it is God-granted faith, not works, whereby the sinner lays hold of the benefits of that propitiation.[31]

The second occurrence of the ἱλάσκομαι word group with reference to the death of Christ comes in Heb 2:17, and it no less than the others identifies Christ's atonement as an efficacious satisfaction of divine wrath. The author of Hebrews has spoken of God's wrath as the "just retribution" for every transgression or disobedience under the old covenant (2:2, ESV), retribution that must be expected by those in the present age who neglect so great a salvation as accomplished by Christ (2:3). Christ accomplished this salvation by "suffering" (2:10) and "tasting death" (2:9), indicating that the suffering of death is the just retribution of divine wrath against sin. This is only further confirmed by the comment that the slave master, Satan, enslaves by the power of death, which was overcome by the incarnation and atoning death of Christ (2:14–15). For *this* reason (ὅθεν)—that is, because the just retribution of death as the expression of God's wrath against sin threatened the children God had given him (cf. 2:13)—"He had to be made like His brethren in all things, so that He might become a merciful and faithful high priest in things pertaining to God, to make propitiation [εἰς τὸ ἱλάσκεσθαι] for the sins of the people" (2:17). The high priest satisfies divine wrath by bearing it himself, thus turning it away from his people and ensuring their glorification (2:10).[32]

28. Moo, *Romans*, 236. Or, as Cranfield puts it, it indicates that "the benefit resulting from the fulfillment of God's purpose that Jesus Christ should be ἱλαστήριον is to be accepted, appropriated, by faith" (Cranfield, *Romans 1–8*, 210).

29. See "The Relationship between Impetration and Application," in chapter 8, noting the distinction between this and the way it is presented and employed by advocates of the MIV.

30. Contra Shedd, who claims, "Atonement, in and by itself, separate from faith, saves no soul. Christ might have died precisely as he did, but if no one believed in him he would have died in vain.... It is only when the death of Christ has been actually confided [believed] in as atonement, that it is completely 'set forth' as God's propitiation for sin" (Shedd, *Dogmatic Theology*, 747).

31. As Calvin observes, though propitiation is efficaciously accomplished on the cross, "God is propitious to us as soon as we have our trust resting on the blood of Christ; for by faith we come to possession of this benefit" (Calvin, *Romans*, 143). Christ infallibly secures the elect's *right* to propitiation (impetration) even though they do not come into *possession* of this benefit until they believe (application).

32. O'Brien explains, "Our author assumes that divine wrath threatened his listeners, just as it threatened Moses' generation (3:7—4:13; 10:26–31; 12:29). Christ's sacrifice not only sets aside sin (9:26) and purifies people (1:3; 9:13–14); it also delivers men and women from judgment (10:26–31;

In 1 John 2, John comforts the believers in the Asian churches by reminding them that though they may sin, they nevertheless have "an Advocate with the Father, Jesus Christ the righteous" (2:1), who pleads their cause in his heavenly intercession before the Father. Their need of a righteous advocate implies divine displeasure in their case. For this reason, John immediately grounds Christ's heavenly intercession for sinners in his propitiatory death, whereby he decisively turned away God's displeasure on behalf of all those who repent and trust in him: "and He Himself is the propitiation [ἱλασμός] for our sins" (2:2).[33] This same context applies for the final occurrence of ἱλασμός at 4:10, where John makes a categorical statement about the love of God expressed in the propitiatory death of Christ: "In this is love, not that we loved God, but that He loved us and sent His Son to be the propitiation [ἱλασμός] for our sins." The love of God consists in his sending the Son of God to turn away the wrath of God from the people of God.

In summary, for Scripture to identify the atonement of Christ as a propitiation means that his atoning death efficaciously satisfied the righteous wrath of God against the sins of those for whom he offered himself. He was not set forth as a potential propitiation, but as a propitiation (Rom 3:25); the high priest does not make provisional propitiation for the sins of his people, but he makes propitiation (Heb 2:17). Thus, in the case of those for whom Christ is a propitiation, God's wrath is extinguished. For it ever to be roused again would indicate that the propitiation Christ made was insufficient, a most blasphemous notion. Therefore, there is no wrath left for God to execute upon the sinner for whom Christ has died as a propitiation. And yet, because there will be some who will have the wrath of God against their sins poured out on upon them in hell—indeed, some who were undergoing that wrath even as Jesus offered himself as a propitiation—it cannot be concluded that Christ has propitiated for all without exception.[34]

12:29) because wrath is averted. Here at 2:17, however, Hebrews does not indicate how this forgiveness and removal of wrath take place. The answer is reserved for the later expository chapters" (O'Brien, *Hebrews*, 122). Also see Morris, *Apostolic Preaching of the Cross*, 202–5.

33. Morris explains, "If we sinners need an advocate with God, then obviously we are in no good case, our misdeeds prevail against us, we are about to feel the hostility of God to all that is sinful. Under these circumstances we may well speak of Christ turning away the wrath of God, and thus ἱλασμός is a natural word in the context" (Morris, *Apostolic Preaching of the Cross*, 206–7; cf. Reymond, *New Systematic Theology*, 638).

34. In other words, precisely because the atonement is the efficacious satisfaction of wrath, the scenario that Ware proposes can never obtain, namely, that there are "those in hell, who never put their faith in Christ and so were never saved, [who] are under the just judgment of God for their sin, even though *Christ has paid the penalty for their sin*" (personal correspondence from Bruce Ware, cited in Piper, "My Glory," 648–49, emphasis original). Owen captures the thought well: "For whose sins he made satisfaction to the justice of God, for their sins justice is satisfied, or else his satisfaction was rejected as insufficient, . . . which to aver is blasphemy in the highest degree. But now the justice of God is not satisfied for all the sins of all and every man . . . . But that innumerable souls shall to eternity undergo the punishment due to their own sins, I hope needs, with Christians, no proving. Now, how can the justice of God require satisfaction of them for their sins, if it were before satisfied for them in Christ? To be satisfied, and to require satisfaction that it may be satisfied are contradictory" (Owen,

Reconciliation

In addition to incurring guilt and stirring up God to holy wrath, man's sin has also caused a breakdown in the relationship between God and man. That alienation was illustrated almost immediately after the entrance of sin, both in man's instinct to hide from God in shame (Gen 3:8) and in God's judgment in banishing man from his presence in the garden (Gen 3:22–24). Sin separates from God (Isa 59:2). It leaves man as God's enemy (Rom 5:10; Jas 4:4), hostile to him (Rom 8:7; Col 1:21) and alienated from him (Col 1:21). And yet this enmity is not merely one-sided. Man's sin is in moral conflict with God's holy justice, and the result is God's own hostility against sinners in return; his wrath abides on them (John 3:36; Eph 2:3) and will break over them unless the ground of the enmity is done away with.

Scripture presents the atoning death of Christ as a work of reconciliation precisely in order to answer this need. By his propitiatory sacrifice, Christ removes the ground of the enmity between God and men—i.e., the guilt of sin and the wrath of God—accomplishing peace where there was alienation and hostility: "while we were enemies, we were reconciled [κατηλλάγημεν] to God through the death of His Son" (Rom 5:10–11); God "reconciled [καταλλάσσων] us to Himself through Christ . . . God was in Christ reconciling the world to Himself" (2 Cor 5:18–19); "He has now reconciled [ἀποκατήλλαξεν] you in His fleshly body through death" (Col 1:20–22). The biblical concept of reconciliation is represented as "the exchange of hostility for a friendly relationship."[35] It "expresses the transformation of the relationship (of enmity) between God and human beings that has been brought about by the new Adam, Jesus Christ (Rom 5:12–19)."[36]

At least three significant characteristics of the biblical doctrine of the atonement as reconciliation emerge from the above passages. First, reconciliation is the work of God in Christ through the efficacy of his atoning death. This is evident by how consistently God is the subject of the action of reconciliation: "Now all these things are from *God*, who reconciled us to Himself" (2 Cor 5:18); "*God* was in Christ reconciling the world to Himself" (2 Cor 5:19); it was the Father's good pleasure "to reconcile all things to Himself" (Col 1:20); "*He* has now reconciled you" (Col 1:22). It was "while we were enemies"—continuing in open rebellion against God—that "we *were reconciled* [passive voice] to God through the death of His Son" (Rom 5:10). Sinners do not effect or activate this reconciliation by some action on their part. It is accomplished outside and independent of man. Sinners only passively *receive* as a gift the reconciliation accomplished by Christ's work (Rom 5:11).

Death of Death, 247).

35. BDAG, 521.

36. Silva (ed.), "ἀλλάσσω," *NIDNTTE*, 1:246. As Barrett says, "To reconcile is to end a relation of enmity, and to substitute for it one of peace and goodwill" (Barrett, *2 Corinthians*, 175).

Second, this objective reconciliation must be understood to be a finished work of Christ on the cross, and not something that is accomplished or completed by man. Now, it is true that reconciliation denotes the putting away of mutual alienation, and that man's hostility to God is not overcome until God grants repentance and faith; it is when sinners believe in Christ that they have "now *received* the reconciliation" (Rom 5:11).[37] But before they received it—that is, even before their conversion; indeed, while they were yet *enemies* of God—Scripture says sinners were reconciled to God through the death of Christ (Rom 5:10). It is through Christ's death on the cross that sinners are reconciled to God (Col 1:22), and not through their faith at the time of their conversion. That is because reconciliation denotes the putting away of the ground of the enmity between God and man, namely, man's sin, and man's sin is not put away by his faith but by Christ's death. Thus, "reconciliation was wrought on the cross before there was anything in man's heart to correspond."[38]

Third, and explanatory of the previous point, reconciliation is a fundamentally forensic reality. That is to say, the reconciliation that Christ accomplished on the cross was a legal rather than a transformative change. This becomes apparent when one observes the parallelism between reconciliation and justification in Rom 5:9–10, where "we were reconciled to God through the death of His Son" stands parallel to "having now been justified by His blood." This relationship is underscored in 2 Cor 5:19, where Paul defines God's reconciling work in Christ as "not counting [μὴ λογιζόμενος] their trespasses against them." This non-imputation of sin by virtue of the imputation of sin to a substitute (cf. 2 Cor 5:21) is precisely Paul's doctrine of justification, for the justified one is "the man to whom God credits righteousness [λογίζεται δικαιοσύνην] apart from works," namely, "the man whose sin the Lord will not take into account [οὐ μὴ λογίσηται]" (Rom 4:6–8). The forensic nature of reconciliation thus cannot be denied. Like propitiation, then, which speaks of "things pertaining to God" (Heb 2:17), reconciliation ought primarily to be understood as an objective rather than subjective reality; i.e., it has its effect in God rather than man. Whereas propitiation removes God's wrath against sinners, reconciliation removes God's enmity against sinners. MacArthur and Mayhue offer a clarifying explanation with the help of John Murray:

37. In other words, "now" refers to the subjective application of the benefits of salvation, experienced at conversion, to which Christ's act of reconciliation (again, while we were enemies) is antecedent. Paul also uses the term "now" to refer to the believer's having been justified (Rom 5:9), another aspect of the application of redemption. Thus, Christ's work of reconciliation is *finished* and *accomplished* on the cross, but it is *received* by and *applied* to the believing sinner at conversion.

38. Morris, *Apostolic Preaching of the Cross*, 225. As Forsyth put it, "Reconciliation was finished in Christ's death. Paul did not preach a gradual reconciliation. He preached what the old divines used to call the finished work. . . . He preached something done once for all" (Forsyth, *Work of Christ*, 86). Denny says, "The work of reconciliation, in the sense of the New Testament, is a work which is *finished*, and which we must conceive to be finished, *before the gospel is preached*" (Denny, *Death of Christ*, 103, emphasis original).

When we consider (1) that the Bible pictures reconciliation as a forensic act decisively accomplished by God in Christ and (2) that elect sinners who have not yet come to faith remain hostile to God, it is apparent that reconciliation "does not refer to the putting away of the subjective enmity in the heart of the person said to be reconciled, but to the alienation on the part of the person to whom we are said to be reconciled." Therefore, the mutual peace accomplished by the act of reconciliation is experienced as the result of reconciliation, when the regenerating work of the Holy Spirit overcomes man's hostility to God as the Spirit applies Christ's objective work to sinners, granting them the justifying faith by which they have peace with God (Rom. 5:1).[39]

The objective reconciliation accomplished by Christ on the cross thus must be distinguished from the mutual peace subjectively experienced at conversion. However, they must never be separated. Though Scripture distinguishes between the objective accomplishment of reconciliation and its subjective application, it never suggests that reconciliation may be objectively accomplished for a greater number than those to whom it is subjectively applied. As demonstrated in the previous chapter, Christ intends his atonement to purchase benefits precisely so that they may be applied, so that they might find their home as it were with those for whom they were purchased, not so they might be left suspended in midair. Thus, though there is a time gap between them, all those "reconciled to God through the death of His Son" (Rom 5:10) will indeed "receive the reconciliation" (Rom 5:11), lest Christ's work be rendered ineffectual.

The consequences of this reality for the extent of the atonement are significant. First, it must be observed that not all without exception will receive the reconciliation that is sure to follow its accomplishment. There are those who perish in their sins and are thus forever at enmity with God. As Owen puts it, reconciliation "is the renewing of lost friendship, the slaying of enmity, the making up of peace, the appeasing of God, and turning away of his wrath, attended with a non-imputation of iniquities; and, on our part, conversion to God by faith and repentance."[40] Indeed, since reconciliation consists in God not counting trespasses against sinners (2 Cor 5:19), and since such a non-imputation of sin is the substance of justification (cf. Rom 4:6–8; see above), if all without exception are reconciled, why are not all without exception justified?[41] The definition of those reconciled simply does not describe all without exception, and thus we can be sure that Christ has not reconciled through his death all without exception.

Because of this, in order to make provision for a universal aspect of the atonement, proponents of the MIV significantly modify the biblical definition of reconciliation. In a desire to read "the world" in 2 Cor 5:19 as a reference to all without

---

39. MacArthur and Mayhue, eds., *Biblical Doctrine*, 532–33, citing Murray, *Redemption Accomplished and Applied*, 38.

40. Owen, *Death of Death*, 264.

41. Owen, *Death of Death*, 264.

exception, Shultz redefines reconciliation as ineffectual, suggesting that there are those for whom reconciliation is accomplished to whom it will never be applied.[42] To support this claim, he appeals to Marshall's handling of reconciliation, in which he states, "Rather God and Christ appeal to them to accept the fact that reconciliation has been accomplished *and to complete the action* by taking down the barrier on their side—the barrier of pride and disobedience and hatred of God."[43] In order to support their universalism, Shultz and Marshall must redefine reconciliation no longer as that which is an objective work finished on the cross, but rather that which has been *begun* by God but must be *completed* by man. Given that Scripture characterizes the atonement itself as a work of reconciliation, this is nothing short of suggesting that the atonement itself must be completed by man.[44]

Besides this, proponents of the MIV redefine reconciliation in such a way that it may be applied to those who perish eternally in hell. Insisting that the "all things" reconciled by Christ in Col 1:20 refers even to the damned, Ware states, "In this sense, all those in hell stand reconciled to God, i.e., they are no longer rebels and their sinful disregard has been crushed and ended."[45] Elsewhere he says, "This reconciliation must be one which includes a sense in which those outside of Christ, consigned to eternal punishment in hell, are at peace with God."[46] Similarly, Hammett says that reconciliation must be defined as all things being put in right relation to Christ, which, for those who have rejected Christ and rebelled against him, "involves judgment and punishment."[47] This stretches language to its breaking point, bearing no resemblance to the biblical concept of reconciliation just expounded. There is no sense in which those in hell are at peace with God—a peace that is the result of the justification (Rom 5:1) that the MIV, inconsistently, does not believe extends to all without exception. There is no sense in which those experiencing eternal punishment for their sins can be said to have removed the ground of their enmity with God. As Piper says, what the MIV describes as reconciliation "is not reconciliation. It is ultimate banishment and alienation. This is not the peace Jesus purchased with his blood. This is the removal of those who would not make peace with God."[48]

42. Shultz, "Defense," 130.

43. Marshall, "Meaning of Reconciliation," 123, emphasis added.

44. Also see Hammett, "Multiple-Intentions View," 185–86.

45. Ware, "Outline," 4.

46. Personal correspondence from Bruce Ware, as cited in Piper, "My Glory," 653.

47. Hammett, "Multiple-Intentions View," 186; cf. Shultz, "Defense," 215–16.

48. Piper, "My Glory," 655.

7

The Nature of the Atonement, Part 2

IN THE PREVIOUS CHAPTER, we began discussing the nature of the atonement—what Scripture says Christ actually accomplished by his death on the cross. Understanding what the atonement is brings great clarity to the question concerning for whom it was accomplished. In other words, the extent of the atonement is, in part, a function of its nature. The previous chapter began this study of the nature of the atonement by examining the motifs of expiatory sacrifice, propitiation, and reconciliation. This chapter continues this study by focusing on redemption, penal substitution, and the atonement as an efficacious accomplishment rather than a provision or potentiality.

Redemption

As an expiatory sacrifice, the atoning death of Christ takes away sin by removing its guilt and penalty. As a propitiatory sacrifice, Christ's death satisfies the righteous wrath of God aroused by sin's offense to his justice. As reconciliation, the atonement removes the hostility and enmity that sin has interposed between God and man, restoring them to peace. In addition to these motifs, Scripture also characterizes the atonement as redemption (e.g., Rom 3:24; 1 Cor 1:30; Eph 1:7; Col 1:14; Heb 9:12, 15)—i.e., the ransom payment of the blood of Christ (1 Tim 2:6; 1 Pet 1:18–19) as the price that effects sinners' release from the bondage of sin (John 8:34; Rom 6:6, 16–18) and the curse of the law (Gal 3:13; 4:4–5).

The rich imagery employed by the above-referenced passages originates not in the New Testament but in the Old. Therefore, to understand the significance of Christ's death as redemption, it is necessary to discern the Old Testament background that serves as the foundation for the usage of these terms in the context of Christ's atonement. Terms for redemption figure prominently in the Pentateuch, especially in the Exodus narrative and later reflection upon Yahweh's redemption of Israel out of slavery in Egypt—an event that becomes paradigmatic not only for Yahweh's relationship with the nation but also for his future redemption of sinners of all nations from the bondage of sin.[1] They are גָּאַל,[2] פָּדָה,[3] and, to a lesser extent, כֹּפֶר.[4] The preponderance of the biblical data leads one to conclude that the fundamental meaning of redemption is the liberation from enslavement by the payment of a ransom price.

This is illustrated in the term גָּאַל, whose "primary thought is the general one of family obligation, and arising out of this is the narrower concept of the payment of price, of redemption."[5] This is the term that figures prominently in Boaz's redemption of Ruth as her kinsman-redeemer, in which Boaz bought the right to acquire Ruth and her family (cf. Ruth 2:20; 3:9–13; 4:1–14). It is also the term used in Leviticus 25, which lays out directives for the redemption of property surrendered in a time of extreme need. In the case that an Israelite had become so poor that he needed to sell his property (25:25) or even to sell himself into slavery (25:47), the law of God provided for his family to redeem him (25:47–55). It is a fundamentally commercial context: there is talk of a "purchaser" (קֹנֵהוּ), a "price" (כֶּסֶף), a "purchase price" (מִכְסַף מִקְנָתוֹ, LXX: λύτρον), and a "refund" (שׁוּב) (cf. also Lev 27:13–20, 27–33). This is the language of the market, of buying and selling. The family of the one who had been sold into slavery could redeem him out of his slavery by the payment of a ransom price. And of necessity, when that price was paid, the family member would be released and go free. The related term, פָּדָה, carries the same commercial connotations without the role for the familial relationship denoted by גָּאַל,[6] as it speaks of the substitute payment for the redemption of the firstborn (Exod 13:12–15; Num 3:40–49; 18:15–17) or of a slave-concubine (Exod 21:8, 11; Lev 19:20). The price that is paid is the כֹּפֶר. Without the paying of this substitutionary ransom price, the penalty must remain (Exod 30:12), but if it is paid a life is redeemed (Exod 21:28–30).[7]

These terms are also used of Yahweh's deliverance of his people from Egypt, which becomes paradigmatic for God's spiritual redemption of his people from sin. In Exod 6:6, Yahweh says, "I am the Lord, and I will bring you out [יָצָא] from under the burdens of the Egyptians, and I will deliver [נָצַל] you from their bondage. I will also redeem [גָּאַל] you with an outstretched arm and with great judgments" (Exod 6:6; cf. 3:7–8). David celebrates the Exodus in 2 Sam 7:23 and speaks of God's "people whom You have redeemed [פָּדָה] for Yourself from Egypt, from nations and

---

1. As Hendel notes, "Virtually every kind of religious literature in the Hebrew Bible—prose, narrative, liturgical poetry, didactic prose, and prophecy—celebrates the exodus as a foundational event" (Hendel, "Exodus in Biblical Memory," 601). And Alexander says, "What happened in Egypt becomes a paradigm for what God will do in the future" (Alexander, *Exodus*, 5–8).

2. *HALOT*, 1:169; Hubbard Jr., "גאל," *NIDOTTE*, 1:789–94.

3. *HALOT*, 3:912; Hubbard Jr., "פדה," *NIDOTTE*, 3:578–82.

4. *HALOT*, 2:495.

5. Morris, *Apostolic Preaching of the Cross*, 20.

6. Morris, *Apostolic Preaching of the Cross*, 22.

7. "In its biblical usage it refers to the sum paid to redeem a forfeited life" (Morris, *Apostolic Preaching of the Cross*, 24).

their gods" (cf. Deut 7:8; 9:26; 13:5; 15:15; 21:8; 24:18).[8] As with expiatory sacrifice, redemption is seen to be both particular and effective. Yahweh's redemption is announced for his people Israel alone, with emphasis on the distinction between them and the Egyptians (cf. 8:22–23, where the word פְּדֻת, a cognate of פָּדָה, is translated "division," and demonstrates Yahweh's discrimination between those who are and are not his people[9]). And his redemption of his people is effective; this was not a promise to provide for Israel's redemption or make them redeemable, but to effectively deliver them out of their slavery, for "the LORD *saved* Israel that day from the hand of the Egyptians" (Exod 14:30). Such redemption is so effective that those redeemed and ransomed by Yahweh will shout joyfully in Zion with everlasting joy upon their heads (Isa 35:9–10), for their transgressions will have been wiped out (Isa 44:22). There is no hint of potentiality or bare provision; to redeem is to secure the deliverance of a captive by the payment of the price.

Coming to the New Testament, the biblical writers often employ the Greek terms that translate the Hebrew words surveyed above, and they fall into two broad word groups: (1) λυτρόω, (ἀπο)λύτρωσις, (ἀντί)λύτρον;[10] and (2) (ἐξ)αγοράζω.[11] In the former word group, the same emphases are apparent as in the Old Testament, as Morris notes: "When they chose to use λύτρον (or its cognates) it was because they wanted a term which expressed in itself, and not simply by inference from the context, the idea of release by payment."[12] Thus, Jesus gives his life as a λύτρον for many (Matt 20:28; Mark 10:45), signifying that his life surrendered in death was the price by which those in whose place he substituted (ἀντί) would be delivered from the death that sin requires (cf. 1 Tim 2:6). Jesus defines his saving mission as a work of ransom, of which his life was the ransom price given in the stead of the many sinners whose freedom he purchased. His life was the substitute-ransom given for their lives (cf. Exod 21:30; 30:12) and thus must issue in their release. Peter says that Christ's people were redeemed (ἐλυτρώθητε) by the price of the "precious blood . . . of Christ," "as of a lamb

8. Hubbard casts doubt on how central the "price" is to the concept of redemption by noting that Israel is redeemed from Egypt by military power rather than a purchase price. Morris acknowledges that "the idea of the price paid tends to fade when Yahweh is the subject of the verb," but that it is not entirely absent. Instead, we ought to see "a reference to price in the insistence that Yahweh's redemption is at the cost of the exertion of His mighty power" (Morris, *Apostolic Preaching of the Cross*, 26).

9. Note that each of its other uses in the Old Testament carries a connotation of redemption (Pss 111:9; 130:7) and ransom (Isa 50:2). Barnes comments, "God was redeeming his people and thus making a distinction between them and between those who were not his people. This places particularity at the very heart of God's redemption of his people from Egypt" (Barnes, *Atonement Matters*, 69).

10. BDAG, 606; Silva, ed., "λυτρόω," *NIDNTTE*, 3:179–87.

11. BDAG, 14, 343; Silva, ed., "ἀγοράζω," *NIDNTTE*, 1:139–40.

12. Morris, *Apostolic Preaching of the Cross*, 12. Morris also notes, "It is important to realize that it is this idea of payment as the basis of release which is the reason for the existence of the whole word group. Other words were available to denote simple release. Men could (and often did) go on using λύω, or ῥύομαι, etc." (Morris, *Apostolic Preaching of the Cross*, 12). Deissman states, "When anybody heard the Greek word λύτρον, 'ransom,' in the first century, it was natural for him to think of the purchase-money for manumitting slaves" (Deissman, *New Testament Background*, 327).

unblemished and spotless" (1 Pet 1:18–19; cf. Rom 3:24–25; Titus 2:14). Indeed, Paul says, we have redemption through his blood (τὴν ἀπολύτρωσιν διὰ τοῦ αἵματος αὐτου), which Paul equates with the forgiveness of sins (Eph 1:7; cf. Col 1:14). The note of efficacy is struck here, as redemption is to be identified with the forgiveness of sins; the bondage from which sinners are released by the shedding of Christ's blood in their stead is their need to pay for their own sins. Redemption does not merely provide for forgiveness but actually accomplishes it.[13] The redeemed are the forgiven, for Christ has *obtained* eternal redemption (Heb 9:12) by his death (9:15).[14]

The (ἐξ)αγοράζω word group paints the same picture. These terms come from the noun ἀγορά, which means "marketplace" (Matt 20:3; Luke 7:32; Acts 17:17). Thus, to redeem is to purchase out of the marketplace. Because sinners are enslaved to sin (cf. John 8:34; Rom 6:16–18), they need to be thus redeemed. Therefore, we read that "Christ redeemed [ἐξαγοράζω] us from the curse of the law" (Gal 3:13; cf. 4:4–5), which required death for disobedience (Deut 27:26; Gal 3:10; cf. Jas 2:10). Christ has redeemed his people from this curse of spiritual death and destruction "by becoming a curse for us" (Gal 3:13), that is, by bearing the penal sanctions of that curse in the place of his people on the cross. The result is that those who should have been cursed now go free; they receive "the blessing of Abraham" and "the promise of the Spirit through faith" (Gal 3:14). Christ's substitutionary death not only purchases redeemability; it necessarily frees the slave. As Büschel puts it, "In this liberation from the curse of the Law, the essential point is that it confers both an actual and also a legally established freedom ensuring against any renewal of slavery."[15] It is to violate the semantic value of this word to suppose that those who are redeemed might ever be subject to the slavery from which they are redeemed.[16] Indeed, since Christ *redeemed*

---

13. O'Brien, *Ephesians*, 106.

14. Thus, "λύτρωσις may be used for the most effective deliverance"; ἀπολύτρωσις thus speaks of "obtaining release by payment of a ransom" (Morris, *Apostolic Preaching of the Cross*, 41). The aorist participle εὑράμενος in Heb 9:12 ought to be taken as antecedent ("having obtained," NASB; cf. Hughes, *Hebrews*, 328n84) rather than coincident ("thus securing," ESV; cf. O'Brien, *Hebrews*, 322n92). This signifies that the sufficiency and finality of Christ's once-for-all obtainment of redemption on the cross—in contrast to the priests who offered often (cf. Heb 9:6)—is what qualified him to enter the heavenly holy of holies. Redemption is not secured by Christ's heavenly intercession, but by his atoning death through the price of his shed blood. Note verse 15: "a *death* has taken place for the redemption of the transgressions." The death of Christ itself effects redemption; it is not merely preliminary only to be completed by his intercession, and still less by the decision of sinful man.

15. Büschel, "ἀγοράζω," *TDNT*, 1:126.

16. Morris writes, "It is wrong to separate the legal status, gained by the complete discharge of the claims the law had upon us, from the resultant life. The only redemption Paul knew was one in which the redeemed had received the gift of the Holy Spirit, and in which they lived as those who had been adopted into the family of God" (Morris, *Apostolic Preaching of the Cross*, 59). Thus, application cannot be separated from accomplishment, such that there are those who are redeemed who do not receive the gift of the Holy Spirit. If we are to bind ourselves to the biblical definitions, a universal redemption would thus imply a universal salvation. As Owen says, "Universal redemption, and yet many to die in captivity, is a contradiction irreconcilable in itself" (Owen, *Death of Death*, 258).

his people from the curse of the law, they who undergo the curse of the law cannot be said to have been redeemed by him.

Further, those redeemed from the slavery of sin immediately become the possession of God. The redeemed man is not his own but has been "bought [ἠγοράσθητε] with a price" (1 Cor 6:20); though no longer a slave of sin, he is nevertheless a slave of righteousness (Rom 6:18). The liberty into which the slave is freed is paradoxically slavery to God. As Morris notes, "The whole point of this redemption is that sin no longer has dominion; the redeemed are saved to do the will of their Master."[17] To suppose that any whom Christ has redeemed not only continue in their slavery to sin but do not faithfully live as slaves of God is to suggest the sovereign God does not receive that for which he pays. Not only does this contradict the biblical definition of redemption, which, as has been demonstrated, "does not mean simply to put down a price but actually to gain possession of something,"[18] but it is also a state of affairs that could only result from a lack of wisdom or a lack of power on God's part, which are unthinkable.

Therefore, since Scripture defines the redemption Christ accomplished by his death as the efficacious securing of freedom by the payment of a price, which must necessarily issue in freedom from sin, slavery to God and righteousness, the reception of the Holy Spirit, and the inheritance of eternal glory, it cannot be that such redemption was accomplished for all without exception. Many do perish under the curse of the law; it cannot be that Christ has redeemed them from that curse if they themselves must suffer it. Those purchased by the precious blood of Christ can never fail to enjoy the freedom obtained for them by their substitute. Biblical evidence of the particularity of redemption comes in Rev 5:9, where Christ is praised by the heavenly host for having "purchased [ἠγόρασας] for God with Your blood men from [ἐκ] every tribe and tongue and people and nation." Had Christ purchased every person in the history of the world without exception, John would not have said that he purchased *men from* every tribe but simply that he purchased every tribe. The four nouns would have been accusatives of direct object rather than the objects of the preposition ἐκ.[19] Further, these very same purchased ones are those whom Christ has made to be a kingdom of priests who will reign upon the earth (Rev 5:10), demonstrating once again that application necessarily follows accomplishment. Yet again, because not all without exception will reign on the earth, it is legitimate to conclude that not all have thus been purchased by Christ.

Thus Chafer, and Shultz, who cites him with approbation, runs contrary to the biblical doctrine of redemption when he says, "There is, then, a redemption which *pays the price*, but does not of necessity *release* the slave."[20] Such demonstrates the

---

17. Morris, *Apostolic Preaching of the Cross*, 62.

18. Wells, *Price for a People*, 134.

19. Barnes, *Atonement Matters*, 90.

20. Chafer, "For Whom Did Christ Die?," 313; cf. Shultz, "Defense," 148–150. Shultz's citation of Chafer is in his footnote 177.

incompatibility of a universal atonement with an efficacious redemption. If redemption is pressed to be of universal *extent*, and yet not all without exception finally enjoy the release from their captivity, the only recourse is to modify the *nature* of redemption as presented in Scripture. It is, at bottom, to convert redemption into redeemability. Yet such a weakening of the substance of the atonement is too high a price to pay for broadening its extent. John Murray captures it memorably:

> What does redemption mean? It does not mean redeemability, that we are placed in a redeemable position. It means that Christ purchased and procured redemption. This is the triumphant note of the New Testament whenever it plays on the redemptive chord. . . . It is to beggar the concept of redemption as an effective securing of release by price and by power to construe it as anything less than the effectual accomplishment which secures the salvation of those who are its objects.[21]

The notion of a redemption that pays the price but does not release the slave would have been unrecognizable to the biblical authors. For the family of a slave to pay his ransom while he yet remained in slavery would have been a contradiction of justice and a violation of the law of God (cf. Lev 25:47–55). Further, if the purchase of redemption does not release the slave, it must be asked what in fact does secure their release. The answer to that question is uniformly found to be the sinner's faith.[22] Ultimately, proponents of universal atonement—even the MIV—must come to place the decisive work of salvation in man's decision rather than in Christ's work.

Penal Substitution

What each of these motifs illustrates is that Christ's atoning work was most fundamentally a work of penal substitution. That is, his sacrifice frees sinners from guilt because

---

21. Murray, *Redemption Accomplished and Applied*, 63. Spurgeon's comments are also apposite: "A redemption which pays a price, but does not ensure that which is purchased—a redemption which calls Christ a substitute for the sinner, but yet which allows the person to suffer—is altogether unworthy of our apprehension of Almighty God" (Spurgeon, *Metropolitan Tabernacle Pulpit*, 49:39). Indeed, Owen's incredulity is warranted: "Redemption is the freeing of a man from misery by the intervention of a ransom. . . . Now, when a ransom is paid for the liberty of a prisoner, is it not all the justice in the world that he should have and enjoy the liberty so purchased for him by a valuable consideration? . . . Can it possibly be conceived that there should be a redemption of men, and those men not redeemed? that a price should be paid, and the purchase not consummated? . . . A price is paid for all, yet few delivered; the redemption of all consummated, yet few of them redeemed; the judge satisfied, the jailer conquered, and yet the prisoners inthralled!" (Owen, *Death of Death*, 261).

22. For example, "Christ actually did redeem the false teachers, but they are not in Christ through faith . . . and therefore they do not subjectively experience that redemption" (Shultz, "Defense," 149). And again, "Christ's atonement actually accomplished reconciliation, redemption, and propitiation for all people, but all people are not saved because all people do not subjectively appropriate what Christ has done for them. In order to experience the reconciliation and redemption that Christ has accomplished in the atonement, one must be in Christ through faith" (154).

he bore that guilt in their place (Isa 53:4–6; 1 Pet 2:24). His blood effects the propitiation of God's wrath against sinners because he bore that wrath in their place (Gal 3:13). The death of Christ reconciles God to man by virtue of his own alienation and abandonment (Matt 27:46; Heb 13:12). Jesus redeems sinners from the bondage of their sin by submitting himself, for a time, to the bondage of the death that is the wages of sin (Heb 2:14–15; Rev 1:18; cf. Rom 6:23). He frees sinners from their penalty by becoming a substitute for them, paying that penalty in their place and on their behalf.

In addition to the passages referenced in the previous paragraph, one way Scripture teaches the doctrine of penal substitutionary atonement is by the prepositions it employs to speak of the death of Christ and its intended effects, each one of which has connotations of substitution. First, the term περί generally means "for," or "concerning," but can also "depict the person or thing on whose behalf or in whose interest something takes place."[23] When it is used with the term ἁμαρτία, it can have the sense of "to take away, to atone for."[24] Thus, Paul says that Christ was "an offering for sin [περὶ ἁμαρτίας]" (Rom 8:3); Peter says, "Christ also died for sins [περὶ ἁμαρτιῶν ἔπαθεν] once for all" (1 Pet 3:18); and John says, "He Himself is the propitiation for our sins [περὶ τῶν ἁμαρτιῶν]" (1 John 2:2; 4:10). These texts teach that though man's sin requires them to die under the wrath of God, yet Christ has offered himself to perish under God's wrath in their place.

Second, the preposition διά, when used with the accusative, can mean "because of," "on account of," "for the sake of."[25] This describes substitutionary atonement in several texts. Christ came into the world for the sake of sinners (1 Pet 1:18, φανερωθέντος δὲ . . . δι᾿ ὑμᾶς) and died for the sake of sinners (1 Cor 8:11: δι᾿ ὃν Χριστὸς ἀπέθανεν). In 2 Cor 8:9, Paul says, "For you know the grace of our Lord Jesus Christ, that though He was rich, yet for your sake He became poor [δι᾿ ὑμᾶς ἐπτώχευσεν], so that you through His poverty might become rich." The Son, who was eternally rich in his divine being, possessions, and relations, substituted himself for the sake of those who were destitute of God's blessing by exchanging his riches for their poverty. This exchange he accomplished by his death in their place.

Third, the preposition ἀντί is the strongest marker of penal substitution, for its meaning indicates "that one person or thing is, or is to be, replaced by another," and is best translated "instead of, in place of,"[26] such that a subsequent governor rules "in the place of" (ἀντί) his predecessor (Matt 2:22). Jesus said that he came "to give His life as a ransom for [ἀντί] many" (Matt 20:28; Mark 10:45). While sinners were in bondage to sin and condemned to die under the curse of the law, Jesus gave his life as the ransom price in the place of the lives of his people so that they might go free.

---

23. Harris, *Prepositions and Theology*, 180.

24. BDAG, 797.

25. Wallace, *Greek Grammar beyond the Basics*, 369; cf. BDAG, 223.

26. BDAG, 87.

Finally, the most common preposition used to denote penal substitution is ὑπὲρ, which indicates that "an activity or event is in some entity's interest," and it can be rendered "for," "in behalf of," and "for the sake of."[27] Christ gave his body to be broken and his blood to be poured out on behalf of sinners, such that he was a substitutionary sacrifice that turned away wrath from those for whom he has substituted (Mark 14:24; Luke 22:19–20; John 6:51); he is the good shepherd who laid down his life on behalf of his sheep (John 10:11, 15; 1 John 3:16), which means he died so they do not have to; Christ died for our sins (1 Cor 15:3); one died for all (2 Cor 5:14); he gave himself for our sins (Gal 1:4) and for each of the elect, personally (Gal 2:20); he became a curse in our place, so that we would not suffer the curse of the law (Gal 3:13); he gave himself as a ransom in place of his people (1 Tim 2:6), tasting death for the children God gave him (Heb 2:9, 13); the righteous one died in the place of the unrighteous (1 Pet 3:18). There is scarcely a more well-attested doctrine in all of Scripture than that Jesus Christ suffered and died vicariously in the place of sinners in order to atone for their sins. It is not an exaggeration to say that penal substitution is "the essence of the atonement."[28]

To say that Christ died in the place of, in the stead of, or as the substitute for sinners is to say that he did "everything necessary to save us, endured and exhausted the destructive divine judgment for which we were otherwise inescapably destined, and so won us forgiveness, adoption, and glory."[29] This means that "no such suffering—no God-forsakenness, no dereliction—should remain for us. . . . what Christ bore on the cross was the God-forsakenness of penal judgment, which we shall never have to bear because he accepted it in our place."[30] Those for whom he died can never experience the punishment for which he died. This is just what substitution means. It is to be the surety for another (Heb 7:22), such that one's life is given in place of another. It is impossible that Judah's life should be given as a surety for Benjamin's life and yet both of them die without the perpetration of a profound injustice (Gen 44:32–33). Yet this is precisely what the MIV proposes: that Jesus paid for the sins of even those who finally die in their sins through his penal substitutionary atonement.[31] But this

---

27. BDAG, 1030. See Wallace, *Greek Grammar beyond the Basics*, 383–89.

28. Packer, "Introduction to *Death of Death*," 25.

29. Packer, "What Did the Cross Achieve?," 77.

30. Packer, "What Did the Cross Achieve?," 87. Owen concurs, casting the matter in terms of the intent of the atonement: "For no other reason in the world can be assigned why Christ should undergo any thing in another's stead, but that that other might be freed from undergoing that which he underwent for him" (Owen, *Death of Death*, 246).

31. As Ware writes, "Those in hell, who never put their faith in Christ and so were never saved, are under the just judgment of God for their sin, even though *Christ has paid the penalty for their sin*" (Personal correspondence from Bruce Ware, cited in Piper, "My Glory," 648–89. Shultz says, "Jesus Christ's payment for the sins of the elect and the nonelect through his penal substitutionary atonement is necessary in order to account for the multiple intentions that God had in the atonement" (Shultz, "Defense," 98).

is to equivocate on the meaning of substitution.[32] As Wells reasons, "No death can be substitutionary if both the substitute and the men for whom he dies experience death. A man may die in the hope of helping others, but he is not their *substitute* if they die the death he had hoped to save them from."[33] If Jesus endured the wrath of God in the place of those who will eventually suffer it themselves—indeed, those like Pharaoh and Goliath who were already suffering it while Jesus was on the cross—then he was not their substitute but a co-sufferer. A substitute acts in order to relieve another man of his obligation; it is not a substitution if the so-called substitute acts and the other man's obligation remains.[34] Packer's conclusion is thus warranted:

> Any who take this position [i.e., universal atonement] must redefine substitution in imprecise terms, if indeed they do not drop the term altogether, for they are committing themselves to deny that Christ's vicarious sacrifice ensures anyone's salvation. . . . If we are going to affirm penal substitution for all without exception we must either infer universal salvation or else, to evade this inference, deny the saving efficacy of the substitution for anyone; and if we are going to affirm penal substitution as an effective saving act of God we must either infer universal salvation or else, to evade this inference, restrict the scope of the substitution, making it a substitution for some, not all.[35]

32. Trueman captures it well: "If Christ died in the same substitutionary way for the one who dies in Christ and the one who dies outside of Christ, has Christ really substituted in any meaningful, saving way for anyone? This also points to the so-called 'double jeopardy' argument: if Christ died for everyone's sins, does that not demand either universal salvation or equivocation in order to avoid the problem of the sins of the one who died outside of Christ being punished twice—once on the cross and then again in eternity? . . . We might use the same impressive sounding language . . . , but we are using that language equivocally" (Trueman, "Response to Multiple-Intentions View," 204–5).

33. Wells, *Price for a People*, 84.

34. Niemi, *Greater than Aaron*, 50–51. Niemi gives the following example: "If a player on a sports team enters the field of play for a particular position, and the player already on the field in that position leaves the field of play, a substitution has been made. But if both players are on the field for the same position at the same time, that is *not* a substitution. . . . [If Jesus suffered for Pharaoh or Goliath, t]hat's not substitution; that's parallel punishment" (50–51). Trueman provides another: "If a friend pays my speeding ticket and takes my penalty points on his license, he has substituted for me. If, however, my wife is caught speeding and a friend . . . pay[s] her ticket but my wife still faces exactly the same fine, then she has not really substituted for my wife in the way my friend substituted for me" (Trueman, "Response to Multiple-Intentions View," 204–5).

35. Packer, "What Did the Cross Achieve?," 91. Arminian theologian J. Kenneth Grider remains consistent where Ware and Shultz do not. While Ware and Shultz "redefine substitution in imprecise terms," Grider "drop[s] the term altogether." He regards penal substitution as "foreign to Arminianism," which teaches not "that Christ paid the penalty for our sins" but "that Christ suffered for us," because "what Christ did he did for every person; therefore what he did could not have been to pay the penalty, since no one would then ever go into eternal perdition" (Grider, "Arminianism," 80). Clark Pinnock described his journey from Calvinism to Arminianism (to what would eventually be open theism) as a function of insisting less precisely on substitutionary atonement: "Obviously it caused me to reduce the precision in which I understood the substitution to take place" (Pinnock, "From Augustine to Arminius," 23).

If the *nature* of Christ's atonement was a penal substitutionary sacrifice, then the *extent* of Christ's atonement is limited to those who do not experience the punishment for which Christ offered himself as substitute.

Efficacious Accomplishment

At bottom, the preceding analysis of the nature of the atonement yields the conclusion that Scripture teaches Christ's work on the cross was an efficacious accomplishment that will necessarily be applied to all for whom it was accomplished, not a mere provision whose application is rejected by a great number for whom it was provided. If we are to respect the biblical definitions of expiatory sacrifice, propitiation, reconciliation, and redemption, we are constrained to confess that Christ actually took away sins (cf. John 1:29), actually satisfied God's wrath (Rom 3:25), actually accomplished peace with God (Rom 5:9–10), actually secured the freedom of those captive to the slavery of sin (1 Pet 1:18–19), because he actually became our substitute and bore our sins in his body on the cross (1 Pet 2:24) and a became a curse in our place (Gal 3:13). In other words, Christ actually saved his people on the cross. And since there are some who die in their sins, who experience God's wrath, who must endure God's enmity in hell, who are not freed from bondage, and who must bear their own sins and their own curse (cf., e.g., Matt 7:13–14; 25:41, 46), Christ has not expiated, propitiated, reconciled, redeemed, or substituted on their behalf. That is, the atonement is not universal but is limited to the elect alone.

However, those who hold to a universal atonement while at the same time rejecting universal final salvation aim to evade the charge of an inefficacious atonement. Specifically, the MIV aims to avoid this charge by pointing to the distinction between what they call the "objective" and "subjective" aspects of the atonement.[36] Shultz says, "Christ's atonement actually accomplished reconciliation, redemption, and propitiation for all people, but all people are not saved because all people do not subjectively appropriate what Christ has done for them. In order to experience the reconciliation and redemption that Christ has accomplished in the atonement, one must be in Christ

---

36. Traditionally, this distinction is referred to as the "accomplishment" (objective) and "application" (subjective) of redemption, yet it seems proponents of the MIV do not understand the objective-subjective distinction in precisely the way particularists have understood the accomplishment-application distinction, as will become apparent. Further, it should be noted that in the context of atonement studies, the terms "objective" and "subjective" have traditionally been used to describe the difference between theories of the atonement that terminate primarily on God versus primarily on man. Objective theories of the atonement, like penal substitution, say that God is the object of atonement. An expiatory sacrifice is offered to God; it is God who is propitiated and reconciled, and it is to God that a ransom payment is made for the redemption of sinners. On the other hand, subjective theories of the atonement, like the moral influence theory, hold that man is the object of the atonement. Thus, Jesus' example is said to soften men's hearts with the result that they decide to repent of their sins and trust in him.

through faith."[37] Particularists, then, are guilty of "collapsing the application and the provision of the atonement into the same act when the Bible separates them,"[38] undermining the necessity of saving faith for salvation by suggesting that the elect were saved at the cross,[39] and failing to account for texts that speak of even the elect as under God's wrath until they believe (cf. John 3:36; Eph 2:3).[40]

In response, it must be noted, first, that the particularist does not argue for the collapsing of the accomplishment and application of redemption into the same act. Such would be to suggest that the elect are regenerated, justified, and adopted on the cross, before they ever existed or committed the sins from which they need to be saved. Instead, the particularist recognizes a distinction between redemption accomplished and redemption applied—that the cross secured the certain enjoyment of saving benefits that will not be applied until after the delay of some time.[41] The distinction between particularism and the MIV is that particularism views the cross itself as the sole meritorious or procuring cause of the benefits of salvation. As Scripture says, Christ redeemed us by his *blood* (1 Pet 1:18–19), by his *death* (Heb 9:15), by becoming a curse for us on the *cross* (Gal 3:13); in other words, the elect are said to be redeemed when Christ died, not merely when they appropriate the provisions of salvation by faith. Our sins were borne on the cross (1 Pet 2:24), not when we believed. This is to say that the accomplishment of redemption secures the application of redemption, making it infallibly certain that that which was purchased will be bestowed. The cross secures the elect's absolute *right* to expiation, propitiation, reconciliation, and redemption, even though it does not put them into actual *possession* of those benefits until they are applied. The MIV, on the other hand, holds that the cross made an objective provision that lays the necessary groundwork for later application, but the application of which is ultimately procured by the sinner's faith. Since the gospel can be resisted, in the case of the unbelieving the provision of the cross is rendered ineffectual as its benefits are never applied. Though proponents elsewhere deny that they make the atonement conditional,[42] this is precisely what

37. Shultz, "Defense," 154.

38. Shultz, "Defense," 156.

39. Ware, "Outline," 5; Shultz, "Defense," 156–58.

40. Shultz, "Defense," 156–57.

41. Owen explains and helpfully illustrates the efficacy of the cross and the distinction between right and possession. "He did actually, or *ipso facto*, deliver us from the curse, by being made a curse for us [Gal 3:13]; and the handwriting that was against us, even the whole obligation, was taken out of the way and nailed to his cross [Col 2:14]. It is true, all for whom he did this do not instantly actually apprehend and perceive it, which is impossible: but yet that hinders not but that they have all the fruits of his death in actual right, though not in actual possession, which last they cannot have until at least it be made known to them. As, if a man pay a ransom for a prisoner detained in a foreign country, the very day of the payment and acceptation of it the prisoner hath right to his liberty, although he cannot enjoy it until such time as tidings of it are brought unto him, and a warrant produced for his delivery" (Owen, *Death of Death*, 268).

42. For example, Shultz says, "There is therefore nothing 'conditional' or 'hypothetical' about the

they do when they argue that the benefits of Christ's atonement are suspended until the human condition of believing is fulfilled.[43] Thus, Shultz approvingly cites Shedd, who says, "Atonement, in and by itself, separate from faith, saves no soul. Christ might have died precisely as he did, but if no one believed in him he would have died in vain. . . . It is only when the death of Christ has been actually confided [believed] in as atonement, that it is completely 'set forth' as God's propitiation for sin."[44] Yet this is expressly contrary to Rom 3:25, which states that propitiation consists in the shedding of Christ's blood, not in the sinner's faith in it, and that God set forth Christ as this propitiation on the cross, not repeatedly at the conversion of each individual sinner.[45] To say that atonement does not save apart from faith is to subordinate the atonement's efficacy to the sinner's believing. Though Shultz desires to distinguish the MIV from Amyraldianism and to avoid the language of conditionality, one wonders how Shedd's statement above differs substantially from Amyraut's that "This will to render the grace of salvation universal and common to all human beings is so conditional that without the fulfillment of the condition it is entirely inefficacious."[46] Conceiving of the objective provision of the cross in this way inevitably descends into the very conditionality the MIV is eager to avoid.

Second, it is not only conditionality that is inevitable but also inefficacy itself. Despite protestations that "Christ's atonement actually accomplished reconciliation, redemption, and propitiation for all people,"[47] and that the atonement "accomplishes exactly what God wants it to accomplish,"[48] one witnesses a reversion from the language

---

atonement" (Shultz, *Multi-Intentioned View*, 53).

43. Gibson observes, insightfully, "One cannot escape the fact that each scheme ultimately renders the atonement impotent to save: Christ's acquisition of salvation is left *in suspenso* until a *human* condition is fulfilled. Such a position not only smacks of anthropocentricism—'The center of gravity has been shifted from Christ and located in the Christian. Faith is the true reconciliation with God' [Bavinck, *Reformed Dogmatics*, 3:469]—but it is also contrary to the view that Christ's death is *effective* substitutionary atonement" (Gibson, "Trinitarian Work," 358). Commenting on the same passage in Bavinck, Horton avers, "In this view, then, faith not only receives this reconciliation but accomplishes it, and faith becomes a saving work—the basis of, rather than the instrument of, receiving God's forgiving and renewing grace" (Horton, "Is Particular Redemption 'Good News'?," 113).

44. Shedd, *Dogmatic Theology*, 747.

45. See chapter 6 on "Propitiation," 102–7.

46. French: ". . . entierement inefficacieuse" (Amyraut, *Brief Traitté de la Predestination*, 90).

47. Shultz, "Defense," 154.

48. Shultz, *Multi-Intentioned View*, 53. Though inconsistent (see above on "The MIV and Trinitarian Unity"), at times Shultz attempts to maintain this claim of efficacy by claiming that Christ's death was not intended to secure salvation for all without exception, but that his death was intended to secure other non-saving benefits for the reprobate. Thus, if Christ atones for the sins of the reprobate but it is not in order to save them but to purchase common grace and a genuine gospel offer, then it is no derogation of the efficacy of the atonement when the reprobate are not finally saved. However, it must be asked: If one plans to fail, and he succeeds, which has he done? If the MIV says that God intended the cross to be inefficacious unto the salvation of the reprobate, and Christ efficaciously accomplishes that intention, has he succeeded at failing? Ultimately, given that Scripture casts the divine intent of the atonement as exclusively salvific (see chapter 5), the MIV's explanation is moot and the

of efficacy and accomplishment to the language of provision,[49] though redemption *provided* is something quite different from redemption *accomplished*. Scripture does not say, "By his wounds he provided for your healing," but "By His wounds you were healed" (1 Pet 2:24). While accomplishment denotes certainty and definiteness, provision implies tentativeness and potentiality. Thus, Christ's death did not merely provide redemption. It accomplished redemption; it redeemed. In addition to provision, there is also reversion to the language of possibility. Shultz cites Bloesch as saying, "His reconciliation needs to be fulfilled in the experience of redemption made possible by the Holy Spirit."[50] In the introduction of his book, Shultz says, "When we speak of Christ's atonement . . . we are referring to what Christ accomplished to make salvation possible."[51] Ware says that Christ's death "is a payment for sin that makes *possible* the salvation of people."[52] Because of the mutual incompatibility of its claims, the MIV cannot escape portraying Christ as the very "Possibility-Maker" they desire to avoid.[53]

However, before moving on, we must note the internal incoherence of the view that Christ's death makes the salvation of the reprobate possible. Granting the MIV's scheme for the sake of argument, what does it mean for the atonement to make possible the salvation of those to whom God never wills to grant saving faith? Christ is said to provide salvation for all, such that it is possible for all to be saved on the condition that they believe in Christ. Yet the MIV grants both that it is impossible for any to believe apart from the sovereign gift of God (cf. Eph 2:8; Phil 1:29) and that God does not give this gift to all without exception. Indeed, in the case of the vast majority of people throughout history, he has not providentially ordered that they even hear of the gospel in which they are to believe. In what sense does God will for Christ to make salvation possible for those to whom God has purposed not to grant the faith that is the sole means of appropriating Christ's provision?[54] As Hurrion says, "God renders their salvation impossible, which it is said Christ, by his death, had rendered possible."[55] Further,

---

charge of inefficacy cannot be avoided.

49. Shultz, "Defense," 155n185, 156; cf. Demarest, *Cross and Salvation*, 191, as cited in Shultz, "Defense," 156n196. See also Hammett, "Response to Definite Atonement View," 76, 77.

50. Bloesch, *Jesus Christ: Savior and Lord*, 162, as cited in Shultz, "Defense," 154n191.

51. Shultz, *A Multi-Intentioned View*, 2n4; cf. "Defense," 156. Later, Shultz speaks of Christ's atonement making salvation "available" to sinners (195n103), and possible for all people (206–7, 280).

52. Ware, "Outline," 5, emphasis original.

53. Hammett, "Multiple-Intentions View," 171.

54. Or, as Owen puts it, speaking from God's perspective while aiming to demonstrate the absurdity of this claim, "That is, I do will that that shall be done which I do not only know shall never be done, but that it cannot be done, because I will not do that without which it can never be accomplished" (Owen, *Death of Death*, 242).

55. Hurrion, *Particular Redemption*, 57. All species of hypothetical universalism, which, based on their argumentation (if not their admission), would include the MIV, fail as a coherent system because they aim to hold three propositions together, only two of which can be harmonized: (1) God intends to make the salvation of the reprobate possible by Christ's universal provision; (2) God never intends to save anyone apart from their believing; and (3) God never intends to grant the reprobate faith.

the genesis of the problem is not located in God's providence but must be traced all the way back to his decree. In what sense, we must ask, is the salvation of the reprobate possible? If the Father's election is determinative of salvation such that those whom the Father chooses cannot fail to be saved (cf. Rom 8:29–30), then his non-election (or reprobation) is just as determinative of damnation such that those whom he does not choose cannot fail to perish in their sins (Rom 9:22–23; 1 Pet 2:8; Jude 1:4; cf. John 17:12). Since it is not even hypothetically possible for the decree of God to be overturned (Job 42:2; Ps 33:10–11; Isa 46:9–10; Dan 4:35; Eph 1:11), it is not even hypothetically possible for the reprobate to be saved. This leads Blocher to exclaim, "Talk of 'possibility' is not innocent! Possibility is no self-evident notion, and nurtures sophistry. Taken absolutely, according to Aristotelian genealogy, it is pagan; incompatible with biblical monotheism. . . . In what sense is any event 'possible' if God did not decree it? In what sense is the salvation of the non-elect 'possible' if it has been absolutely certain from the foundation of the world that they shall not be saved?"[56]

Ultimately, talk of provisions and possibility leads to striking comments concerning the impotence of the cross. We have already cited Shedd as saying the atonement of itself saves no one unless faith is added to it.[57] Shultz also approvingly cites Hiebert, who, commenting on Titus 2:11–14, says, "The adjective rendered 'that brings salvation' *(soterios)* asserts its saving efficacy. The dative 'to all men' may equally be rendered 'for all men,' thus stressing the universality of the salvation provided. Salvation is available for all, but its saving effect is dependent upon the personal response of faith."[58] Though Hiebert begins with a commitment to the efficacy of Christ's saving mission, after erroneously interpreting "all men" to mean all without exception, he must quickly speak not of salvation accomplished but "provided" and "available." The salvation that began as efficacious now has "its saving effect dependent upon the personal response of faith." Within a span of two sentences, the efficacy of Christ's work is exported to man's faith, demonstrating that a universal atonement is mutually exclusive with an efficacious atonement. Shultz also cites Picirilli, who objects to the notion that "propitiation, say, or reconciliation were actually finished on the cross,"[59] for such would mean they could not be described as children of wrath before having come to faith (Eph 2:3; cf. John 3:36). The substance of this objection will be addressed below, but for now consider: if propitiation and reconciliation were not "actually finished on the cross," but only upon the sinner's conversion, one cannot avoid casting Christ's cross work as ineffectual and incomplete until it is granted its efficacy by the sinner's faith. Indeed, Hammett asserts, "That propitiation, and all Christ did on the cross, though provided to all, remains of no value, ineffectual, useless, until subjectively

56. Blocher, "Jesus Christ the Man," 576.

57. See footnote 44 in this chapter and the related body of text.

58. Hiebert, *Titus*, 440.

59. Picirilli, *Grace, Faith, Free Will*, 94, as cited in Shultz, "Defense," 156n197.

appropriated."[60] Similarly, Ware asks, since saving faith is required for salvation, "How can it be said of the death of Christ *in itself* that by his death *alone* he saved those for whom he died?"[61] These are striking denials of the efficacy of Christ's cross and are at variance with the teaching of Scripture as surveyed above. The glory of Christ's efficacious accomplishment of salvation is undermined, and man's response in faith is exalted. Packer's conclusion is poignant but, it seems, inescapable:

> We want (rightly) to proclaim Christ as Savior, yet we end up saying that Christ, having made salvation possible, has left us to become our own saviors. It comes about in this way. We want to magnify the saving grace of God and the saving power of Christ. So we declare that God's redeeming love extends to everyone, and that Christ has died to save every man, and we proclaim that the glory of divine mercy is to be measured by these facts. And then, in order to avoid universalism, we have to deprecate all that we were previously extolling, and to explain that, after all, nothing that God and Christ have done can save us unless we add something to it; the decisive factor that actually saves us is our own believing. What we say comes to this—that Christ saves us with our help; and what that means, when one thinks it out, is this—that we save ourselves with Christ's help.[62]

But what about the substance of the objection? How can particularists claim that Christ has efficaciously satisfied the wrath of the Father against the sins of the elect in the first century, while at the same time submitting to Scripture's claims that

60. Hammett, "Multiple-Intentions View," 164–65.

61. Ware, "Outline," 5, emphasis original. Note also Shultz's comments exporting the efficacy of the atonement to the Spirit's application of redemption rather than the Son's accomplishment: that "accomplish[es God's] particular purpose in the atonement" (Shultz, *Multi-Intentioned View*, 138), and that this is what "makes the redemption that Christ secured on the cross effective" (Shultz, *Multi-Intentioned View*, 148; cf. 140). Similarly, Hammett speaks of the cross "remov[ing] obstacles to fellowship with God," a fellowship that is effected only by the subjective application of the Spirit (Hammett, "Multiple-Intentions View," 174). Chafer claims, "Christ's death does not save either actually or potentially; rather it makes all men savable" (Chafer, "For Whom Did Christ Die?," 325). Lightner declares that he rejects the view "that the work of Christ on the cross was effective in itself" (Lightner, "For Whom Did Christ Die?," 162).

62. Packer, "Saved by His Precious Blood," 128–29. Hurrion captures it this way: "According to our opponents, Christ's purchase . . . as they say, procured God a right and power to save men on what conditions he pleased; so that when it is said, that God was reconciled, it is only meant that he was reconcilable, and Christ did not procure salvation, but only a salvability; he was but a titular Savior, a Savior without salvation, and a Redeemer without redemption: Christ is only the remote cause, but man the immediate cause; Christ the potential but man the actual cause of his own redemption: Is this honorable to Christ?" (Hurrion, *Particular Redemption*, 16). Bavinck says, "In the guise of honoring the work of Christ, the proponents of universal atonement began to weaken, diminish, and limit it. For if Christ made satisfaction for all, then the acquisition of salvation does not necessarily imply its application. . . . In other words, what alone remains for Christ to accomplish is not the reality but the possibility of salvation, not actual reconciliation but potential reconcilability, 'the salvable state.' . . . The most significant part of the work of salvation, that which really effects salvation, is still left for us to do. . . . What they gain in quantity—and then only seemingly—they lose in quality" (Bavinck, *Reformed Dogmatics*, 3:467–68).

even the elect, before they believe, come into this world "dead in trespasses and sins" (Eph 2:1), being by nature "children of wrath" (Eph 2:3; cf. John 3:18, 36)? Do not particularists, as is accused, "inconsistently make the atonement ineffectual until it is actually applied"?[63] No, they do not.[64] In the first place, this argument fails to take into account the distinction between the divine *sentence* of wrath and the actual enduring of the *execution* of that sentence. The only sense in which unbelievers are under divine wrath before they perish in their sins is that that wrath would certainly break over their heads if they did not trust in Christ alone for salvation before their death. However, for the elect that is an impossibility, because the Father's election and the Son's atonement ensure that the Spirit will regenerate them and grant them saving faith. Yet those who are already condemned in hell for their sins are under divine wrath in an entirely different sense; in the former case wrath was threatened, whereas in this case it has become a reality. Those who fail to make this distinction are guilty of "collaps[ing] the notion of eschatological judgment into present, spiritual experience."[65] Thus, ironically, it is not the particularist who collapses accomplishment into application, but it is the MIV proponent who collapses sentence into execution. As Piper writes, "The wrath that hung over us in our pre-conversion state and which would have broken upon us for real in hell after the eschatological day of judgment, if we had not believed in Christ, broke on Christ two thousand years ago. Thus, there are not two judgments for our sin here, only one."[66]

Second, the key to understanding why this objection presents no challenge to particularism is adequately understanding the relationship between the accomplishment and application of redemption.[67] The cross actually accomplished the satisfaction of God's wrath; once again, propitiation is said to have been made in Christ's blood (Rom 3:25), which was spilled once for all in the first century. As a result, every person for whom Christ died obtained the right to have the wrath of God removed from him, a right that was not procured upon any condition, but absolutely, by the merit of Christ. Thus, the atonement secured—made certain and definite—that the elect would come into possession of the propitiation Christ purchased for them. However, God has decreed that they do not come into possession of that which is their right *immediately* upon its accomplishment. But the delay between the accomplishment and the application does not render the accomplishment ineffectual or its application the less inevitable. Piper provides a helpful illustration of a prisoner whose death sentence had been carried out on a willing substitute a week earlier. Though his penalty had been paid, the

---

63. Strehle, "Systems of the Sixteenth and Seventeenth Centuries," 278. This passage is cited both by Shultz ("Defense," 158n203) and Hammett ("Multiple-Intentions View," 165).

64. In this section, I am indebted to the work of Piper, "My Glory," 649–52.

65. Carson, *John*, 214.

66. Piper, "My Glory," 650. That is, whereas the MIV proposes two judgments for the same sins, particularism does not.

67. See footnote 41 in this chapter and the related discussion in the body of the text.

paperwork for his release requires time to process, and thus he is not released immediately. The man's freedom has been purchased, but it is not applied until the paperwork is fully processed and the guards open the cell to set the man free. Piper comments, "This scenario does not constitute a 'double payment'; it merely demonstrates a delay between the one payment and its application."[68]

In the case of this prisoner, a substitute had satisfied the requirement of justice by dying in his place, and thus the penalty he owed could never break over his head. Its *execution* had already taken place in his substitute. Nevertheless, in the intervening week, the prisoner remained under the *sentence* of that death penalty until his paperwork could be processed and the efficacious propitiation could be applied to his case. A week prior, his release was not merely *provided* for or made *possible*; it was rendered *certain*, even though it was not applied immediately. Owen's illustration is helpful as well: "As, if a man pay a ransom for a prisoner detained in a foreign country, the very day of the payment and acceptance of it the prisoner hath *right* to his liberty, although he cannot *enjoy* it until such time as tidings of it are brought unto him, and a warrant produced for his delivery."[69] The cross has purchased the *right* of our redemption, though we do not enjoy the *possession* of it until it is applied through the regenerating work of the Spirit.

As a biblical illustration of this reality, consider Paul's comments concerning Israel in Rom 11:28–29. He tells the believers in the church of Rome, "From the standpoint of the gospel they [Israel] are enemies for your sake, but from the standpoint of God's choice they are beloved for the sake of the fathers; for the gifts and the calling of God are irrevocable." Because the unbelieving nation currently rejects the gospel, they are considered the enemies of the followers of Christ. Nevertheless, because God has chosen them (κατὰ ... τὴν ἐκλογὴν), they are nevertheless beloved (ἀγαπητοί). God's wrath abides on them, in the sense that it threatens to break upon them if they fail to repent, and yet love abides on them as well. These on whom the wrath of God abides are his *beloved*, even before they have come to faith in Christ. And yet this does not make God's choice of them any less effectual unto their salvation; there is simply a time delay between the election that renders their salvation certain and their possession of that salvation. What a marked difference between the pre-converted elect and those suffering condemnation in hell, who in no sense can be called God's beloved.

Finally, none of this means that particularists present saving faith as unnecessary, as Lightner charges.[70] The death of Christ efficaciously accomplishes the

68. Piper, "My Glory," 650–51. Piper also notes, "The *one* penalty for the elect person's sins was judicially paid for by Christ when he propitiated God's wrath at the cross; but the *application* of that wrath-removing event is not applied immediately but only at the point of saving faith" (Piper, "My Glory," 650–51).

69. Owen, *Death of Death*, 268, emphasis added.

70. "Even though those who accepted the limited view pay lip service to the need for faith, the fact remains that if their view of the design of the atonement is true, faith is meaningless and without purpose" (Lightner, *Death Christ Died*, 124).

salvation of the elect, rendering their possession of that salvation certain, though not immediate. Yet this makes the ministry of the Holy Spirit in regeneration and the responsibility of the elect to believe not a whit less necessary, for those are the means by which the elect will be put into possession of Christ's accomplishment. This is made plain by looking further back in the order of salvation to election.[71] Considering the golden chain of redemption in Rom 8:29–30, it is agreed that God's foreknowledge of the elect renders their salvation certain; not one whom God foreknows will fail to be saved. Why, then, does Paul not stop there? If foreknowledge can be said to *save* the elect—in the sense of rendering the possession of their salvation infallibly certain—why mention anything of predestination? Is it not rendered "meaningless and without purpose"?[72] Apparently not in Paul's mind. Further, does the Father's foreknowledge and predestination, which undeniably make the salvation of the elect certain, render the death of Christ superfluous? No, there is no salvation without the cross, and that reality makes election no less certain or necessary. In the same way, just as the plan of redemption does not render unnecessary the accomplishment of redemption, neither does the accomplishment of redemption render unnecessary the application of redemption. In fact, not only does Christ's death not make faith unnecessary; it makes faith *certain* by purchasing it for the ones the Father has chosen. As Wells says, ". . . foreknowledge, predestination, death of Christ, preaching of the gospel, calling, faith, justification and glorification. Each is necessary; each renders the following links certain. Yet none can be left out."[73]

These objections being removed, then, we must conclude that efficacy is essential and inherent to the biblical doctrine of atonement. Christ has actually—not potentially, provisionally, or hypothetically—accomplished the salvation of his people by dying in their place. Indeed, as Isaiah prophesied, "My servant will succeed!" (Isa 52:13, NET; יַשְׂכִּיל).[74] And as Christ himself announced, "It is finished!" (John 19:30). As Motyer notes, if "the work of Christ only made salvation possible rather than actually secured salvation," then "'finished' only means 'started' and 'succeed' only means 'maybe, at some future date, and contingent on the contribution of others.' 'Finished' is no longer 'finished' and 'success' is no longer a guaranteed result. This is far from both the impression and the actual terms of Isaiah's forecast."[75] Yet those who failed to esteem the Servant for who he was (Isa 53:3–4) were healed and

---

71. Wells, *Price for a People*, 132–33.

72. Lightner, *Death Christ Died*, 124.

73. Wells, *Price for a People*, 133.

74. Motyer argues for this translation: "שׂכל in Qal, 'to behave wisely' (cf. 1 Sam. 18:30), but, contextually, to succeed in battle; the Hiphil blends acting with prudence with acting effectively/successfully (e.g., Josh. 1:7–8). שׂכל in 52:13 is balanced with 'by his knowledge' in 53:11. The Servant knows exactly what to do, does it, and succeeds in what he undertakes" (Motyer, "Stricken for the Transgression," 251n5). Compare *HALOT*, 3:1328, which gives "to have success" as the proper gloss for שׂכל in Isa 52:13.

75. Motyer, "Stricken for the Transgression," 251–52.

made to see (Isa 53:5) based on nothing but the substitutionary atonement of the Servant: "He was pierced through for our transgressions, He was crushed for our iniquities; the chastening for our well-being fell upon Him, and by His scourging *we are healed.*" He was not potentially pierced or provisionally crushed; his chastening did not bring a potential peace, nor his wounds a provisional healing. No, Christ was actually crushed; he actually "bore our sins in His body on the cross." His wounds did not make us healable. They did not put us into a state in which we might be healed if we activated the hypothetically universal scope of Christ's wounds. Rather, by his wounds his people were healed (1 Pet 2:24). His death actually accomplished the spiritual healing of those for whom he died.[76]

And it is in this efficacy that the glory of Christ's atonement consists, for Christ says to the Father, "I *glorified* You on the earth, *having accomplished* the work which You have given Me to do" (John 17:4). As Piper says, "This glory was not the glory of a salvation made *available*, but a salvation made *real* and *effective* in the lives of 'his own.'"[77] The cross did not purchase possibilities or create opportunities, but certainties. It did not make men savable; it saved them. And in this efficacious accomplishment does its glory consist. As Packer says, "His precious blood really does 'save us all.'"[78]

---

76. MacArthur and Mayhue, eds., *Biblical Doctrine*, 549; cf. Trueman, "Definite Atonement View," 42. Spurgeon famously noted that because of the intrinsic worth and efficacy of Christ's sacrifice, those for whom he died "not only may be saved, but are saved, must be saved, and cannot by any possibility run the hazard of being anything but saved" (Spurgeon, "Particular Redemption," 4:135).

77. Piper, "My Glory," 642.

78. Packer, "Saved by His Precious Blood," 123. The full quote is: "He insists that the Bible sees the cross as revealing God's power to save, not his impotence. Christ did not win a hypothetical salvation for hypothetical believers, a mere possibility of salvation for any who might possibly believe, but a real salvation for his own chosen people. His precious blood really does 'save us all;' the intended effects of his self-offering do in fact follow, just because the cross was what it was. Its saving power does not depend on faith being added to it; its saving power is such that faith flows from it. The cross secured the full salvation for all for whom Christ died."

8

The Great High Priest of the New Covenant

ONE OF THE MOST overlooked areas of biblical and theological inquiry in the debate over the extent of the atonement is the high priestly ministry of Christ.[1] The author of Hebrews in several places identifies Christ as "a merciful and faithful high priest in things pertaining to God," intimately linking this high priesthood with his mission "to make propitiation for the sins of the people" (Heb 2:17). He is "the Apostle and High Priest of our confession" (3:1), "a great High Priest who has passed through the heavens," (4:14) who can "sympathize with our weaknesses" (4:15). Christ did not seize this office for himself (5:5), but the Father designated him a high priest according to the order of Melchizedek (5:10; 6:20; cf. 7:15, 17), a priesthood that he holds permanently (7:24), and by virtue of which he always lives to intercede for his people (7:25). The church has "such a high priest, who has taken His seat at the right hand of the throne of the Majesty in the heavens" (8:1; cf. 7:26), a "high priest of the good things to come [who] entered through the greater and more perfect tabernacle" (9:11). Further, he is identified as the mediator of the New Covenant (Heb 8:6; 9:15; 12:24; cf. 1 Tim 2:5; Heb 7:22). Thus, to fail to discuss the extent of the atonement apart from the Bible's teaching concerning the identity of Christ as the mediator and priest of the New Covenant is to take the extent of the atonement out of context, as it were. The work of mediation that Christ accomplished can never be divorced from—indeed, it can only be understood in light of—his identity as mediator.

When one considers that Christ's atoning work is rooted in his identity as the great high priest and mediator of the New Covenant, the nature of the priesthood and the nature of the New Covenant shed much light on the extent of the atonement. In particular, one finds that from the inception of the priesthood, the twofold priestly function of sacrifice and intercession are so inextricably linked that their

---

1. That is not to say that it is a novel argument. Wellum notes ("New Covenant Work of Christ," 518–19nn4–5) that the argument for particular redemption from Christ's priestly ministry is presented in Owen, *Death of Death*; Turretin, *Institutes of Elenctic Theology*, 2:403–86; Bavinck, *Reformed Dogmatics*, 3:455–75; Berkhof, *Systematic Theology*, 361–405; Barnes, *Atonement Matters*; and Horton, *Christian Faith*, 486–520). Wellum also notes, however, that this argumentation is rarely addressed by critics of particular redemption, referencing Lake, "He Died for All," 31–50; Miethe, "Universal Power of the Atonement," 71–96; Demarest, *Cross and Salvation*, 189–93. Trueman laments this in his response to Hammett (Trueman, "Response to Multiple-Intentions View," 205).

objects are coextensive; that is, the priest never fails to intercede on behalf of those for whom he has offered sacrifice, nor does he intercede for those for whom he has not offered. Consistent with this, it will be shown that Scripture teaches the same is true for Christ the great high priest: he offers himself as sacrifice for the very same number for whom he intercedes before the Father, the latter of which Scripture explicitly identifies as particular and not universal. Further, because Christ holds his priesthood strictly in relationship to the New Covenant, and because the New Covenant does not embrace all without exception, another argument emerges in favor of understanding the extent of Christ's mediation to be limited to the elect. Finally, a due consideration of the efficacy of Christ's priestly work will demonstrate that application necessarily follows from impetration; that is, the high priest's salvific accomplishments cannot fail to be applied to those for whom they are accomplished. Since it is evident that they are not applied to all, it will be shown to be reasonable that they have not been accomplished for all.

The Unity of Christ's Priestly Work of Sacrifice and Intercession

By identifying Christ as high priest of New Covenant believers, the New Testament identifies him as the antitype and fulfillment of that to which the Levitical priesthood and sacrificial system looked forward.[2] It is therefore essential to understand the conceptual framework of this system in order to properly understand Christ's atoning work. Now, there is not a one-to-one correspondence between the two; whereas the Levitical priests were priests according to the order of Aaron, Jesus is a priest according to the order of Melchizedek (Heb 7:11). Thus, one ought to expect some discontinuity between the two orders. However, except for where those discontinuities are explicitly noted in the text (e.g., Heb 7:23–27; 10:11–12), it is right to see a basic continuity between the high priesthood of the Old Covenant and Christ's high priesthood in the New Covenant.

The Old Testament Priest: Sacrifice and Intercession

The fundamental duty of the high priest was to represent his people before God by offering gifts and sacrifices for their sins (Heb 5:1; 8:3). He was a mediator of the expiation and propitiation that Yahweh would accomplish for his people (Heb 2:17). But the high priest's duty of offering sacrifices was not limited to simply slaying the animal; the priest's work was not complete until he had sprinkled the blood on the altar in the tabernacle. That is to say, the high priest's duty was the twofold work of sacrifice (the offering of the substitutionary animal) and intercession (the sprinkling

---

2. Portions of this section are adapted from the author's contributions to MacArthur and Mayhue, eds., *Biblical Doctrine*, 552–53.

of its blood on the altar).[3] Thus, throughout the opening seven chapters of Leviticus, which detail the laws for the various sacrifices Israel was to offer via the ministry of the priests, there is the prescription for both sacrifice and intercession, both slaying and sprinkling: "He shall [a] slay the young bull before the LORD, and Aaron's sons the priests shall offer up the blood and [b] sprinkle the blood around on the altar that it is at the doorway of the tent of meeting" (Lev 1:5); "He shall [a] slay it on the side of the altar . . . and Aaron's sons the priests shall [b] sprinkle its blood around the altar" (Lev 1:11); "He shall lay his hand on the head of his offering and [a] slay it at the door way of the tent of meeting, and Aaron's sons the priests shall [b] sprinkle the blood around on the altar" (Lev 3:2; see also 3:8, 13; 4:6–7, 15–18, 25, 30, 34; 5:9; 7:2; 17:5–6). As these references show, the works of sacrifice and intercession were inextricably linked; the offering of the sacrifice was inseparable from the application of the blood of the sacrifice to the altar. As Wellum observes, "the priest applies the sacrificial blood for everyone who brings his offering to him, and there is not a single sacrifice where the blood is not applied to the worshiper. . . . the OT priest also intercedes for all those he represents."[4]

This inextricable union of the priestly duties of sacrifice and intercession was not evident merely in the daily sacrifices, but it was preeminent in the exercises of the Day of Atonement. Aaron was to slay one goat as a sin offering to atone for the sins of Israel (Lev 16:9), but the death of the goat of sacrifice was not the end of the high priest's labors. After slaughtering the goat, he was to "bring its blood inside the veil" into the holy of holies, and "sprinkle it on the mercy seat and in front of the mercy seat" (16:15; cf. 16:18–19). It was not merely the death of the goat but also the intercessory sprinkling of its blood in the immediate presence of God that accomplished atonement for Israel's sins. The very same blood of the sacrificial offering was applied to the altar, indicating no division between the accomplishment of the atoning sacrifice and its application to the people for whom it was offered.[5] Further, along with the goat of sacrifice, the high priest also had to offer a bull as a sin offering for his own sins, which also required slaughtering (16:11) and sprinkling (16:14). In addition, however, Aaron was to ignite incense while in the holy of holies so that a cloud of smoke would cover the mercy seat (16:13). And the fire that would ignite the incense was to come from "the coals of fire from upon the altar before the LORD" (16:12). As Niemi observes, "Aaron took hot coals from the place of sacrifice and used them to start the fire of intercessory incense. The former served as the basis for the latter."[6]

3. Technically, it was not even the priest who slayed the animal, but the worshiper, so as to identify the sinner with the animal that was to die in his place for his sin (see, e.g., Lev 1:5, 11; 3:2, 8; 4:15, 24, 29, 33). As Wellum notes, the only exception is when a sin offering is made on behalf of the priest himself (4:3–4), or when the burnt offering is one of birds (1:14–16) (Wellum, "New Covenant Work of Christ," 526n26).

4. Wellum, "New Covenant Work of Christ," 526.

5. Wellum, "New Covenant Work of Christ," 525.

6. Niemi, *Greater than Aaron*, 65.

These rituals demonstrate that the high priest's work of sacrifice is inextricably linked with his work of intercession. Owen comments, "To offer and to intercede, to sacrifice and to pray, are both acts of the same sacerdotal office, and both required in him who is a priest; so that if he omit either of these, he cannot be a faithful priest for them: if either he does not offer for them, or not intercede for the success of his oblation on their behalf, he is wanting in the discharge of his office by him undertaken."[7] What must be observed from this is that the scope of the priestly work of sacrifice is identical to the scope of the priestly work of intercession. The high priest did not slay the goat of sacrifice as an offering on behalf of a greater number than for whom he sprinkled its blood on the altar. He did not, for example, offer the goat as a provisional atonement for the sins of the Gentile world, only to then intercede with the sprinkling of blood on behalf of Israel alone. The same was true even of the scapegoat; Aaron did not provisionally confess over the head of the scapegoat the sins of everyone throughout the Gentile world, only to then have Israel's sins alone banished into the wilderness. No, the sins imputed to the scapegoat were those very same sins carried out of the holy presence of God, namely, Israel's alone. The scope of the intercession was identical to and grounded in the scope of the sacrifice. They are coextensive, "two sides of the same atoning coin, both accomplished on behalf of Israel alone."[8]

Christ the Great High Priest: Sacrifice and Intercession

In coming to the New Testament and considering the high priestly ministry of Christ, we find this same inextricable link between the twofold work of sacrifice and intercession. As the great high priest of the New Covenant, Christ "through the eternal Spirit offered Himself without blemish to God" (Heb 9:14; cf. 7:27) in the voluntary laying down of his life as a sacrifice for the sins of his people (9:26, 28). But in addition to this offering, the great high priest also rose from the grave and entered into the heavenly tabernacle to intercede on behalf of his people: "For Christ has entered, not into holy places made with hands, which are copies of the true things, but into heaven itself, now to appear in the presence of God on our behalf" (9:24, ESV). Just as the high priest of the Old Covenant would appear in the presence of God in the holy of holies to sprinkle the blood of the sacrifice on

---

7. Owen, *Death of Death*, 183.

8. MacArthur and Mayhue, eds., *Biblical Doctrine*, 552. As Trueman says, "The priest slays the goat as an offering for the people of Israel, and then he enters behind the veil and sprinkles the blood for precisely the same people. It is not that the animal is sacrificed for everyone indiscriminately and then offered for the Israelites in particular. The slaughter and the sprinkling (the sacrifice and the cleansing attached to it) are two sides of the same coin, covering the sins of the same group of people. The same applies to the scapegoat: The same sins placed on his head are carried from the presence of God and into the wilderness. There is no narrowing scope between the two actions. Indeed, one might say that with both goats there is in each case only one overall act of atonement that involves several actions" (Trueman, "Definite Atonement View," 44).

the altar, so also Christ our great high priest entered into the presence of God in the heavenly tabernacle to present his own blood before the Father (9:11–12), pleading, as an advocate for his people, the merits of his sacrifice so that all the blessings he has purchased by his death should in due time be effectually applied to those for whom he purchased them (Rom 8:34; Heb 7:25; 1 John 2:1–2).[9]

This intimate link between Christ's sacrifice and his intercession is evident in numerous passages. First, in Heb 9:12, we read that "through His own blood, [Christ] entered the holy place once for all, having obtained eternal redemption." It is on the basis of having already obtained eternal redemption through the blood shed in his death (9:12, 15) that Jesus may enter into the heavenly sanctuary to intercede for his people.[10] It is on the basis of having "offered Himself without blemish to God" that he can appear in the presence of God to secure the effectual cleansing of believers' consciences from dead works to serve the living God (9:14). In both cases, it is evident that the scope of both actions is coextensive: just as it is with the high priest of Israel, the Messiah's blood shed as a sacrifice is the very blood brought into the heavenly tabernacle for intercession, indicating that both priestly actions are performed for the same people.

Second, in 1 John 2:1–2, the apostle John writes to the churches under his care to warn them against the libertinism of the docetic Gnostics (cf. 3:7–10; 4:1–6) and to encourage them to make war with sin (2:1, 3–6). But in the case that these believers do sin, they ought not to despair, for "if anyone sins, we have an Advocate with the Father, Jesus Christ the righteous" (2:1), praying that their faith should not fail but that they should persevere to the end. On what basis, though, does their advocate engage in his heavenly intercession? The next verse explains, "And He Himself is the propitiation for our sins" (2:2). It is because Christ has turned away the wrath of God from these believers once for all by his substitutionary sacrifice on the cross that his advocacy with the Father on their behalf is efficacious. Sinning believers need not despair of their salvation because the advocate who pleads for them before the Father in heaven is he who has accomplished an efficacious propitiation on their behalf, having extinguished in himself the wrath against those very sins they had been committing. The inextricable link between sacrifice and intercession is evident once again; Christ

---

9. Owen comments, "And what doth he there appear for? Why, to be our advocate, to plead our cause with God, for the application of the good things procured by his oblation unto all them for whom he was an offering" (Owen, *Death of Death*, 176).

10. The aorist participle εὑράμενος in Heb 9:12 ought to be taken as antecedent ("having obtained," NASB; cf. Hughes, *Hebrews*, 328n84) rather than coincident ("thus securing," ESV; cf. O'Brien, *Hebrews*, 322n92). This signifies that the sufficiency and finality of Christ's once-for-all obtainment of redemption on the cross—in contrast to the priests who offered often, cf. 9:6—is what qualified him to enter the heavenly holy of holies. Redemption is not secured by Christ's heavenly intercession, but by his atoning death through the price of his shed blood. Note verse 15: "a *death* has taken place for the redemption of the transgressions." The death of Christ itself effects redemption; it is not merely preliminary only to be completed by his intercession.

intercedes for everyone for whom he is a propitiation, and he is a propitiation for everyone for whom he intercedes.

Finally, the same link between the death and intercession of Christ as the ground of believers' assurance is evident in Rom 8:28–39, where Paul surveys the order of salvation from beginning to end—from the Father's election in eternity past (8:29–30), to the atoning work of Christ (8:32–34), all the way through to the justification (8:33), perseverance, and glorification (8:35–39) of the children of God. The question of assurance is in the foreground, for Paul asks, "If God is for us, who is against us?" (8:31). "Who will bring a charge against God's elect? God is the one who justifies; who is the one who condemns?" (8:33). Upon what basis can these believers be assured that nothing will separate them from the love of Christ (8:35)? The answer is: "Christ Jesus is He who died, yes, rather, who was raised, who is at the right hand of God, who also intercedes for us" (8:34). Note how Paul coordinates the death, resurrection, and intercession of Christ; they are each functions of the unified mediatorial work of Christ, such that all three must be performed for the very same number as the others. Further, the "us" for whom Christ intercedes are the "us all" of verse 32: "He who did not spare His own Son, but *delivered Him over for us all*, how will He not also with Him freely give us all things?" The ones for whom Christ presently intercedes are those for whom the Father delivered over his Son to death. It could never be that he would do the greater work in laying down his life for them, winning all the blessings of redemption by enduring the agonies of divine wrath in his own soul, only to fail to do the lesser work of interceding on their behalf, ensuring the communication of all he purchased.[11] Those for whom he offers himself as sacrifice are those for whom he intercedes.[12]

Limited Intercession

Given that the dual functions of Christ's priestly ministry must be coextensive, a key question comes to the fore: Does Christ intercede before the Father on behalf of all men without exception or on behalf of the elect alone? To suppose the former would lead to several unbiblical conclusions. If Christ appeared before the Father in heaven to intercede for the salvation of the reprobate, he would be asking for something out

11. As Morris says, "He has done the greater thing in giving up his Son; how can he not now do the less?" (Morris, *Romans*, 336). Or Cranfield: "Since God has done the unspeakably great and costly thing, we may be fully confident that He will do what is by comparison far less" (Cranfield, *Romans 1–8*, 436).

12. Owen helpfully summarizes the argument: "So, then, it is evident that both these are acts of the same priestly office in Christ: and if he perform either of them for any, he must of necessity perform the other for them also; for he will not exercise any act or duty of his priestly function in their behalf for whom he is not a priest: and for whom he is a priest he must perform both, seeing he is faithful in the discharge of his function to the utmost in the behalf of the sinners for whom he undertakes. These two, then, oblation and intercession, must in respect of their objects be of equal extent, and can by, no means be separated" (Owen, *Death of Death*, 183–84).

of accord with the Father's will, for the reprobate are those to whom the Father, in his inscrutable wisdom, has chosen not to grant salvation (cf. Rom 9:22). The Son's will would be opposed to the Father's will—a theological impossibility for those who share the identical divine essence and thus the identical divine will.[13] Further, the Father would be constrained to refuse to grant the Son's request—another theological impossibility, for the Father always answers the prayers of the Son (John 11:42), especially given the Father's promise to grant the Son's request to give him the nations as his inheritance (Ps 2:8).

Besides this, however, Jesus himself explicitly denies that he intercedes on behalf of all without exception. In the appropriately named High Priestly Prayer of John 17, offered by the great high priest on the eve of his sacrificial offering, Jesus intercedes before the Father on behalf of those for whom he will soon offer himself as sacrifice (cf. 17:19).[14] He prays that the Father will preserve their salvation even in the midst of hostile forces (17:11, 15), for their unity (17:11, 21–23), for their sanctification (17:17), and for their eventual glorification (17:24). And at the outset of his intercession on their behalf, he identifies for whom he is praying, saying, "I ask on their behalf; *I do not ask on behalf of the world*, but of those whom You have given Me; for they are Yours" (17:9). "The world" is opposed to those who belong to the Father ("Yours"), whom he has given to Jesus ("whom You have given Me"), which can refer to none other than the elect, whose salvation the triune God designed in eternity past in the council of salvation (Eph 1:4–5; 2 Tim 1:9; cf. John 6:37, 39; 10:29; 17:2, 6, 20; Rom 8:33).[15] Here, upon the very precipice of his high priestly work of atonement, engaging in his high priestly work of intercession, Jesus explicitly refuses to intercede on behalf of the reprobate. Therefore, since the priestly work of sacrifice and intercession are so inextricably linked as to be coextensive, and since it is unthinkable that Christ would refuse to intercede for those for whom he has shed (or, as in the present case, for whom he is about to shed) his precious blood, it must be concluded that the extent of the atonement—like the extent of Christ's intercession—is limited to the elect.[16]

13. Trueman observes, "Father and Son cannot have adversarial wills, for that would require them to be different gods; nor can the Father simply overrule the Son against his will, for that would require a situation where the Son is clearly subordinate to the Father—a species of Arianism" (Trueman, "Definite Atonement View," 47).

14. The language of priestly consecration is present in John 17:19 (cf. Exod 28:41; 29:1; Lev 16:2–6). As the high priest of his people, Jesus declares that he sanctifies or consecrates himself in preparation for the ultimate day of atonement.

15. "The world" cannot merely be "unbelievers," because Jesus also prays for those who will eventually believe in him as a result of the disciples' preaching (17:20), who must then be unbelievers before they believe. Even those who have not yet come to faith are "Yours" (i.e., the Father's), whom the Father has given to the Son, whom the Son "has" (John 10:16), on whose behalf the Son intercedes. These are none other than the elect (Rom 8:33), and thus "the world" is none other than the non-elect.

16. It should also be noted that, by John 17, where Jesus limits the extent of his priestly intercession, the reader is not long removed from Jesus' interaction with the Pharisees in John 10, in which we have a series of statements from Jesus that limits the extent of his priestly offering. Jesus categorically declares that he lays down his life for his sheep (10:14–15), those whom the Father had given him

As Trueman notes, "If the Father's intention ["those whom You have given Me"] and the Son's intercession ["I ask on their behalf; I do not ask on behalf of the world"] are focused on the same group of people, and if the blood of Christ constitutes part of that intercession [Heb 9:11–15], then the death of Christ on the cross and his intercession are bound together like two sides of the same coin. This is perhaps one of the most critical elements of the case for particular redemption."[17]

Most non-particularists grant that Christ's intercession is limited to the elect alone. However, they maintain their universalism by positing that the scope of Christ's offering is universal even though the scope of his intercession is particular.[18] Yet this can only be permissible if one divorces Christ's mediatorial work from the entire biblical concept of priesthood—brazenly dividing the priestly work of sacrifice from intercession, which Scripture uniformly unites. It also requires the Son to refuse to intercede on behalf of those for whom he has died. This simply cannot be squared with the passages examined above (Heb 9:11–15; 24–27; 1 John 2:1–2; Rom 8:31–34).

Proponents of the MIV object to this argument by conceding that the scope of priestly offering and priestly intercession are coextensive, but then by offering Jesus' prayer from the cross as evidence of Christ's priestly intercession for the non-elect. Jesus interceded for the elect in John 17, but, the argument goes, he also interceded for the non-elect when he prayed for his crucifiers, "Father, forgive them; for they do not know what they are doing" (Luke 23:34). Shultz argues,

> Concerning Christ's intercession, it is certainly a part of his ministry toward believers (John 17; Rom 8:34; Heb 7:25; 1 John 2:1), but does this demand that Christ never prays for the nonelect? This does not seem to be the testimony of Scripture, which records Christ praying for the forgiveness of those who crucified him (Luke 23:34), Paul praying for his lost Israelite brethren (Rom 9:1–5—why would Paul pray for unbelievers when Christ would not?), and Paul's instruction to pray for all people (1 Tim 2:1–2).[19]

(10:29). Within a span of a few words, Jesus addresses the Pharisees and says, "But you do not believe because *you are not of My sheep*" (10:26). For Jesus to say that he lays his life down for his sheep, and then immediately to identify certain persons to be not of his sheep, is to teach that he did not lay down his life for them, and so not for all without exception.

17. Trueman, "Definite Atonement View," 46.

18. Lightner argues that Christ does not intercede for any but who are believers, and therefore the argument against unlimited atonement from a limited intercession is fallacious. He limits the intercession of Christ, therefore, to his heavenly intercession (Lighnter, *Death Christ Died*, 102–4). However, John 17 is an example of priestly intercession during Christ's *earthly* ministry in which he prays for those who will eventually come to faith through the disciples' preaching (17:20), who are thus not yet believers. Douty makes a similar argument, but retreats from the language of efficacy to the language of provision (Douty, *Only for the Elect?*, 32–38), necessarily casting Christ's atonement as ineffectual, as, we have argued, all non-particularists must eventually do (unless they embrace universal final salvation).

19. Shultz, "Defense," 155n195; cf. Hammett, "Multiple-Intentions View," 165–66.

In the first place, it should be noted that Paul's prayers for unbelievers have no bearing on the question, because the particularist argument is not that Christ never intercedes for unbelievers as such, but rather that he never intercedes for the reprobate. Shultz here confuses the unbelieving with those who finally perish in unbelief. Indeed, particularists grant that Christ prays for unbelievers in John 17:20 when he prays for those sheep who have not yet come into the fold (cf. John 10:16) but who will come to faith through the disciples' message. Secondly, Shultz here assumes his interpretation of 1 Tim 2:1–2, namely, that by "all men" Paul, rather unrealistically, urges prayers for every individual without exception, rather than for all kinds of people without distinction—for example, kings and all who are in authority (2:2). That this is Paul's intent is confirmed by John's instruction forbidding Christians to pray for one committing a sin leading to death (1 John 5:16). A final, intransigent impenitence is indeed a sin that leads to spiritual death (John 8:24), and, given that Jesus knew all men (John 2:24–25) and those who would never believe in him (John 6:64), it would have been a violation of 1 John 5:16 for him to pray for their salvation. John 17:9 is an explicit statement that he does not do so.

But does Luke 23:34 constitute priestly intercession for the reprobate—intercession that must ultimately be ineffectual? Several lines of response lead to a negative answer. In the first place, it must be granted that there is limitation in Jesus' prayer, for the most that can be said is that he prayed for only those present at his crucifixion. It cannot even be that Christ was praying for everyone who was involved in his crucifixion, for that would include Judas Iscariot, who was the son of perdition (Mark 14:21), destined to perish eternally. Jesus would not have prayed for the salvation of one whom he knew the Father never intended to save (cf. 1 John 5:16).[20] Secondly, among those who were present at the crucifixion, Jesus prayed only for those of his crucifiers who were acting ignorantly. This is the basis of his petition: "Forgive them; *for* [γὰρ] they do not know."[21] While some of those present certainly acted in ignorance (Acts 3:17), the text does not say that each one there was ignorant. There is no reason to deny that those who acted in ignorance and who thus were the beneficiaries of this prayer did indeed receive God's forgiveness through repentance and faith at a later time, demonstrating themselves to have been among the elect even while yet unbelieving. Third, there is good reason to believe that his prayer was indeed effectual unto the salvation of those involved in and present at the crucifixion. The centurion saw all that had happened and "began praising God, saying, 'Certainly this man was innocent'" (Luke 23:47), and, "Truly this man was the Son of God!" (Mark 15:39; cf. 15:44–45). When Peter preached the gospel on Pentecost, he named as his hearers those who crucified Jesus (Acts 2:23, 36); Luke tells us that "they were pierced to the heart" (2:37), and that "those who had received his word were baptized; and that day there were added about three thousand souls" (2:41). In his next sermon, Peter

20. Carson, *Love in Hard Places*, 78.

21. BDAG, 189.

preaches the gospel to those whom he says "put to death the Prince of life" (3:15), and Luke records that "many of those who had heard the message believed; and the number of the men came to be about five thousand" (4:4). Eventually, even "a great many of the priests were becoming obedient to the faith" (6:7). There is no reason not to believe that the intercession of the great high priest, Jesus Christ, was effectual unto the salvation of those for whom he prayed, especially since there were many thousands who believed the apostles' message just a short while later.[22] Finally, it may be that Jesus was praying not for their forgiveness unto salvation, but simply that the Father would delay the judgment that their wicked acts immediately deserved. In this case, "Christ's prayer is answered by the Father showing his patience and forgiveness by not bringing full judgment [immediately], thus allowing history to continue and God's ultimate purpose to save his elect to be realized."[23]

Ultimately, there is no reason to suppose that Luke 23:34 is an instance of Christ interceding unto salvation for the reprobate, much less *all* the reprobate, which is the burden of proof that must be met by those holding to a universal intercession. The objection from the MIV fails, and thus the argument for particularism from priestly unity stands.[24]

The Particularity of Christ's New Covenant Mediation

As noted above, Christ is not only a great high priest in fulfillment of the Levitical priesthood, but he is the great high priest of the New Covenant in particular. This is seen especially in the way the author of Hebrews presents the inseparable unity of priesthood and covenant. He argues that the Levitical priesthood could not have

22. Hammett calls such an interpretation "unlikely," saying, "Certainly there were a number of Jews converted in the early church, but to suppose that every single one of those present at the cross, involved in Jesus' crucifixion, were among them, is an assumption that seems inherently implausible" (Hammett, "Multiple-Intentions View," 166n71). However, it is considerably more plausible than the alternative, namely, that Christ (1) intercedes unto salvation on behalf of those for whom his Father never chose and to whom he will never grant saving faith; and (2) fails in his intercession unto salvation, which is entirely contrary to the doctrine of priestly intercession even in the Old Testament, let alone in the great high priest of a better covenant enacted on better promises, even the sovereign Lord of glory himself.

23. Wellum, "New Covenant Work of Christ," 531. Carson grants that it could be that "the Father showed his forbearance and forgiveness by not wiping them out on the spot" (Carson, *Love in Hard Places*, 78). Wellum also refers to Schilder, *Christ Crucified*, 129–47.

24. Letham's comments provide an apt summary: "Christ's role as High Priest is a whole. It is one unified movement of grace towards humanity whereby he takes our place in obeying the Father, in atoning for our sins and bringing us to God. He makes very clear that he prays for us besides dying for us. This is a dominant theme in his high-priestly prayer to the Father in John chapter 17. In that prayer he says to the Father that he does not pray for the world but for those whom the Father had given him. . . . His intercession is limited. He prays for his own and not for the world. It follows that his atoning death is intended for those the Father had given him and not for all in an indiscriminate fashion. If we see the intercession as particular and the cross as universal, we are positing a disruption in the heart of Christ's high-priestly work" (Letham, *Work of Christ*, 236–37).

been perfect and therefore awaited a fulfillment in Christ because there always was a promise for another priest to arise according to the order of Melchizedek rather than Aaron, and that it was on the basis of the Levitical priesthood that the people received the law (Heb 7:11), that is, the laws of the Mosaic Covenant (Exod 19:5; 24:7–8; cf. Deut 29:21). He then comments, "For when the priesthood is changed, of necessity there takes place a change of law also" (Heb 7:12). A change of priesthood requires a change of law, which is to say, a change of covenant (7:18–19). In this case, the change from the Aaronic priesthood to the Melchizedekian priesthood is the change from the Mosaic Covenant to the New Covenant, for "Jesus has become the guarantee [ἔγγυος, "made a surety," KJV] of a better covenant" (7:22), "the mediator [μεσίτης] of a better covenant, enacted on better promises" (8:6), that is, "the mediator [μεσίτης] of a new covenant" (9:15; 12:24).

Thus, that Christ is the great high priest of the New Covenant is absolutely essential to and inseparable from his work of atonement. It is *as* this New Covenant priest that Christ offers and intercedes for his people. His mediatorial work is the mediation of the New Covenant. His atoning death is the death that is required by a covenant (Heb 9:16–17). His blood is the blood of the New Covenant (Matt 26:28; Mark 14:24; Luke 22:20; 1 Cor 11:25; Heb 10:29; 12:24; 13:20), and thus it is the promises of the New Covenant that Christ's blood purchases. Christ is the messenger of the covenant (Mal 3:1b) and is himself even prophesied to be the covenant (Isa 42:6; 49:8). Christ's work of atonement cannot be abstracted from the New Covenant. What he accomplishes in his priestly mediation of sacrifice and intercession, he accomplishes as the priest of the New Covenant. As Waldron and Barcellos put it, "Jesus' whole work was a covenant work; His blood covenant blood, His priesthood covenant priesthood, His office as Mediator a covenant office."[25] Thus, the nature, design, and extent of the atonement of Christ cannot be rightly understood without reference to the New Covenant.

Three questions immediately arise. First, how is this covenant established with those who partake of its benefits? Second, what are the promises, or benefits, of this covenant that Christ is said to purchase? Third, for whom is this covenant designed; is its scope universal or particular?

Union to the Covenant Head

First, the New Covenant is established by virtue of persons' union to Christ, the head of the covenant.[26] Every spiritual blessing that will ever be communicated to mankind is communicated "in Christ" (Eph 1:3), that is, in the believer's union with Christ, who has purchased all the spiritual blessings that he will communicate to

---

25. Waldron with Barcellos, *Reformed Baptist Manifesto*, 59–60.

26. Portions from the following paragraphs are adapted from the author's contributions to MacArthur and Mayhue, eds., *Biblical Doctrine*, 602–7, 615–18.

his people (cf. Rom 8:32).[27] The Father has chosen them in Christ (1:4); they are the Father's adopted children through Christ (1:5); they have redemption by virtue of their union with Christ (1:7); they have obtained an inheritance because of their union with Christ (1:10–11); and they are sealed with the Holy Spirit for the day of redemption by their union to Christ (1:13). It is only as his people are *in him* that he becomes to them wisdom, righteousness, sanctification, and redemption (1 Cor 1:30); it is only *in Christ* that men are made new creations by the new birth (2 Cor 5:17); it is only as one is "found in Him" (Phil 3:9) that he is "justified in Christ" (Gal 2:16), such that there is now "no condemnation for those who are *in* Christ Jesus" (Rom 8:1); the saints are "sanctified in Christ Jesus" (1 Cor 1:2; cf. Rom 7:4; Eph 4:15–16), will persevere in faith in Christ (Rom 8:38–39), will die in Christ (1 Thess 4:16), and will be raised to glorification in Christ (1 Cor 15:20–22).

Scripture often represents union with Christ as the relationship between the head and the body. Christ is the head of his covenant people and they are his body (Rom 12:5; 1 Cor 12:27; Eph 1:22–23; Eph 5:23, 29–30), in such a way that what happens to the head is said to happen to the body, and vice versa. Thus, to unite the body of a believer, who is in union with Christ, to a prostitute is to unite Christ with that prostitute (1 Cor 6:15–17). Intertwining the metaphor of head and body with the metaphor of husband and bride (both illustrating union), Paul notes that because the husband and wife have become one flesh (Eph 5:31), husbands ought to love their wives as their own bodies (Eph 5:28a). Indeed, there is such a union that a husband's love for his wife is love for himself (Eph 5:28b). So also, Christ, the head and husband of his body and bride, the church (cf. Eph 5:23; 5:32), loves the church as his own body, nourishing it and cherishing it (Eph 5:28–29). Once again, by virtue of this union, what happens to the head happens to the body, and what happens to the body happens to the head.

Paul teaches this very truth in Rom 5:12–21, where he compares and contrasts the two covenant heads of humanity: Adam and Christ. When Adam sinned, the death that he deserved was passed on to all people because in that same moment all people sinned (Rom 5:12).[28] In what sense can it be said that all people—that is, every one of Adam's natural posterity, which would include people who are being born even at the present time—sinned when Adam sinned? Paul is teaching that Adam's sin *was* the people's sin; that is, all people were reckoned to have sinned by virtue of their

27. Lincoln comments, "Believers experience the blessings of the heavenly realms not only through Christ's agency but also because they are incorporated into the exalted Christ as their representative, who is himself in the heavenly realms" (Lincoln, *Ephesians*, 22).

28. The three aorist verbs in Rom 5:12—εἰσῆλθεν, διῆλθεν, and ἥμαρτον—appear in parallelism and thus must be interpreted in the same way. While the gnomic aorist can be rendered in the proverbial present, the context disallows such an interpretation here, because it is not Paul's intent to say, "Just as through one man sin *enters* the world." Sin does not enter the world as if progressively or iteratively; it *entered* the world at a specific point in the past—namely, the moment that Adam sinned in the garden. Therefore, context demands that the other aorist verbs in this verse be interpreted in the same way: "Through one man sin entered into the world, and death [entered] through sin, and so death spread to all men, because all sinned."

union with Adam as their head. As 1 Cor 15:22 says, "*In* Adam all die." By virtue of the union between Adam and his posterity, the guilt of his sin is counted to be theirs, and so in union with him they bear the punishment of condemnation and death (Rom 5:15–17). Thus, Paul says, "As through the one man's disobedience, the many were made sinners" (Rom 5:19a). That is, they were constituted, reckoned, counted, or imputed to have committed the sin of Adam.[29] Adam was the representative head of humanity, such that God counted the actual disobedience of Adam against all who were in him, that is, all who were united to him. In the same way, Paul says, "Even so through the obedience of the One the many will be made righteous" (Rom 5:19b). Just as Adam is the representative head of the old humanity and his sin brought condemnation to all who were united to him, so also is Jesus the representative head of the new humanity and his obedience brought justification and righteousness to all who are united to him. As Moo comments, "There exists a life-giving union between Christ and his own that is similar to, but more powerful than, the death-producing union between Adam and his own."[30] Indeed, back to 1 Cor 15:22: "For as *in* Adam all die, so also *in* Christ all will be made alive." That is, all humanity was reckoned to be united with Adam as their representative in such a way that his disobedience counted as their disobedience and brought condemnation on them. In the same way, all those in Christ are united to the last Adam (cf. 1 Cor 15:45) as their representative in such a way that his obedience counts as their obedience and brings righteousness to them. What happens to the head happens to the body.

This means that all that Christ accomplishes as the mediator of the New Covenant—both in his life of earthly ministry and in his death, resurrection, and ascension—he does in union with his body. As seen, it is by virtue of this union that his righteousness is imputed to his people (Rom 5:19); believers become the righteousness of God *in him* (2 Cor 5:21). But this union is also the ground upon which their sin is justly imputed to Christ, for Scripture teaches that his people died with him and in him (Rom 6:6, 8; 2 Cor 5:14; Col 2:20; 3:3), were buried with him (Rom 6:4; Col 2:12), have been raised with him (Col 3:1), and have even been seated in the heavenly places with him "in Christ Jesus" (Eph 2:6). This union, then, is such that his life is their life, his punishment their punishment, his death their death, his resurrection their resurrection, his righteousness their righteousness, and his ascension and glorification

29. The term καθίστημι often unmistakably means "to appoint" (Acts 6:3; Titus 1:5; Heb 5:1; 7:28; 8:3). "Therefore, one could translate Rom. 5:19, 'through the one man's obedience the many were *appointed* sinners,' that is, legally established as sinners. Such an 'appointment' is akin to, if not identical with, imputation" (MacArthur and Mayhue, eds., *Biblical Doctrine*, 617n141; cf. Piper, *Counted Righteous in Christ*, 108–9).

30. Moo, *Romans*, 318. Thus, Paul's use of "many" and "all" have nothing to do with universalizing the scope of Adam's or Christ's federates. Rather, they are used in contrast with the "one" to illustrate the principle of corporate solidarity, or representative headship—i.e., that the actions of the one head affect the many, namely, all who are united to him. Thus Moo: "Paul's point is not so much that the groups affected by Christ and Adam, respectively, are coextensive, but that Christ affects those who are his just as certainly as Adam does those who are his" (Moo, *Romans*, 343).

their ascension and glorification. Everything Christ accomplished with respect to his New Covenant priestly ministry during his earthly sojourn, his people are said to have done in him. It is not as if Christ performed his work of mediation without reference to anyone in particular, and then only after they came to faith they were credited with his actions; no, they are said to have been crucified *with* him (cf. Rom 6:6) and to have died *in* his death (2 Cor 5:14). Though they had not yet been born, God nevertheless counted his people to be in union with their Savior throughout the accomplishment of his redemptive work. The body was always reckoned to be united to the head.[31]

Indeed, this union originates even unto eternity past, before anything had existed, for "He chose us *in Him* before the foundation of the world" (Eph 1:4); "grace . . . was granted us [i.e., to the elect] *in Christ Jesus* from all eternity" (2 Tim 1:9). Though the Father elected his chosen before they existed, he is said to have done so in Christ—to have granted grace in union with Christ. This means that from all eternity there was never a time when God contemplated the elect apart from their vital union to Christ Jesus.[32] Union with Christ is the matrix that encompasses all the doctrines of soteriology, from the Father's election (redemption planned), to Christ's atoning death and resurrection (redemption accomplished), to the believer's conversion (redemption applied), through to the believer's glorification (redemption consummated).

Therefore, since (a) all of Christ's atoning work is inextricable from his role as the high priest of the New Covenant (e.g., Matt 26:28), since (b) all the blessings purchased by Christ to be bestowed by the Father are enjoyed only through union with him (Eph 1:3), and since (c) that covenant is entered into only by virtue of union with Christ, we must ask: With whom is Christ united? Are all people without exception united to Christ, or is his union limited to the elect alone? The answer is the latter. There is no biblical sense in which a non-elect person can be said to be united to Christ, and therefore such a person cannot be said to have been chosen in Christ, to have died with Christ, risen with Christ, or to have been raised with Christ. Therefore, Christ's atonement is limited to those who are united to him, namely, the elect alone.

Proponents of the MIV have averred, as Shultz, that Jesus is indeed "united with all people in his incarnation and his death."[33] Shultz offers no argumentation for this claim apart from the citation of several references that do not comment at all upon a supposed universal union between Christ and all people. He loosely relates this to

---

31. Packer notes, ". . . ontologically and objectively, in a manner transcending bounds of space and time, Christ has taken us with him into his death and through his death into his resurrection" (Packer, "What Did the Cross Achieve?," 86).

32. This is not to teach the doctrine of eternal justification, for this mystical union is not actualized in the sinner's experience until he is converted. Until then he is "separate from Christ" and "without God in the world" (Eph 2:12), having need to be brought near (Eph 2:13). Nevertheless, the language of the above passages must be respected. The elect's mystical union with Christ is real in at least some sense from eternity (Eph 1:4; 2 Tim 1:9) and throughout the ministry of the Lord (e.g., Rom 5:18–19; 6:4–8).

33. Shultz, "Defense," 144.

Christ being the fulfillment of the prophecy in Ps 8:4–6, quoted in Heb 2:6–8. The connection is not made explicit, but it seems Shultz is arguing that Christ is united with all men in his incarnation by virtue of sharing a common humanity with them. Yet this seems to follow a line of argumentation that is common to Barthian theologians, which supposes that Christ cannot be said to have assumed a true human nature if he did not represent all humanity in his mediation.[34] Macleod's response is apposite: "His humanity is that of Everyman. But he is not Everyman. He is the man, Christ Jesus; and the only humanity united to him hypostatically is his own."[35] It simply does not follow that in order to have been truly human, Christ had to represent all men without exception in his mediation.[36] Indeed, in the very same passage to which Shultz refers, the author qualifies the universalistic language of Heb 2:9 and limits Christ's work to "the many sons" (2:10), "those who are sanctified" (2:11), his "brethren" (2:11–12, 17), and "the children whom God has given" him (2:13–14). In denying that he gives help to angels, he does not say, "But he gives help to the posterity of Adam," but rather, "But He gives help to the descendant of Abraham" (2:16). It is not to all humanity considered as sons of Adam, but to the new humanity, as the seed of Abraham, whom Christ gives his saving help. This demonstrates that man's union to Christ is not by virtue of his incarnation, but by virtue of his covenant headship. And since he does not communicate the blessings of the New Covenant to everyone through his flesh, the non-elect cannot be said to have been united to him in his incarnation and death.

Further, considering the foregoing biblical analysis, such a universal union is an impossibility. Even Shultz limits the reprobates' union with Christ to his incarnation and death, and not to his resurrection, ascension, and session. However, Paul says that there is no one united with Christ in his death who is not also united with him in his resurrection: "For if we have become united with Him in the likeness of His death, certainly we shall also be in the likeness of His resurrection, ... Now if we have died with Christ, we believe that we shall also live with Him" (Rom 6:5, 8). There is no such thing as union with Christ in his death without union with Christ in his resurrection. And yet it is agreed that no non-elect person will ever be raised to spiritual life with Christ; no one who has finally rejected the gospel will rise unto a resurrection of life on the new earth after the pattern of Christ's own bodily resurrection. If common humanity is

34. See, e.g., Torrance, *Atonement*, xliv–xlv.

35. Macleod, *Person of Christ*, 202.

36. What is interesting about this contention, however, is that it demonstrates that non-particularists recognize the need for the benefits of Christ's death to be grounded in a union with Christ to his people. Some, like John Davenant and Richard Baxter, posited that that union was grounded in an "evangelical covenant" made by God to all humanity whereby he promises salvation on the condition of repentance and faith (Davenant, *Dissertationes duae*, 17; Baxter, *Universal Redemption of Mankind*, 26). Though the MIV does not posit a sophisticated covenantal structure for Christ's universal mediation, they attempt to fill that gap by the union between Christ and humanity by virtue of his common flesh. In either case, Christ is never said to be the mediator of any covenant but the New Covenant. He occupies no priesthood but the Melchizedekian priesthood. And therefore the work of his mediation is limited to the blessings and the blessed ones of the New Covenant.

the ground of Christ's union to all without exception, and since neither Christ nor the reprobate are any less human after Christ's death than before it, why should that common humanity not also be the ground of Christ's union with all men in his resurrection and ascension? If common humanity is the basis of this union, what could sever that union short of the loss of that common humanity? No, there will never be a reprobate person who is united with Christ in his resurrection, and therefore no reprobate person has ever been united to Christ in his death.[37]

Besides this, as was shown, the believer's union with Christ encompasses all points of the plan of salvation, even the election of the Father in eternity past (cf. Eph 1:4; 2 Tim 1:9). In fact, it is that pretemporal election that *establishes* the union between Christ and his people. From the inception of union with Christ, that union has always been discriminating and particular, limited to those whom the Father has chosen to save. As Gibson observes, "If union with Christ traverses all four moments of redemption, then one cannot introduce particularity into the atonement at the point of application . . . . Christ's atoning death is for a particular group of people precisely because it is an 'in-union-with' death. The scope of redemption accomplished and redemption applied is therefore necessarily coextensive."[38]

The Blessings of the New Covenant

If Christ's blood is the blood of the New Covenant, then what his blood accomplishes in his atoning death is to purchase the promises and blessings of the New Covenant. What, then, are these promises and blessings? At minimum, they include spiritual cleansing (Ezek 36:25); the removal of a heart of stone and the implanting of a heart of flesh (Ezek 11:19; 36:26), which is to say the regeneration that births saving faith in the heart; the permanent indwelling of the Holy Spirit in the heart (Ezek 36:27); the writing of the law on the heart (Jer 31:33) so as to ensure obedience (Ezek 11:20; 36:27); the knowledge of God (Jer 31:34) and restoration to a proper relationship with him (Ezek 11:20; Jer 31:33); and the forgiveness of sins (Jer 31:34). These are the blessings that were obtained by the great high priest and mediator of the New Covenant when he shed his blood—the blood of the covenant (cf. Matt 26:28)—on behalf of those united to him.

Thus, who are those who receive the benefits of these New Covenant promises? It can only be those who actually experience the spiritual cleansing, regeneration, faith, Spirit-indwelling, obedient life, and forgiveness of sins that was purchased

37. David and Jonathan Gibson comment, "This is why the particularity of the atonement cannot be introduced at the point of application, for we were united to Christ in his death and resurrection *prior* to appropriating the benefits of his atonement by faith—which means the scope of redemption accomplished and applied are necessarily coextensive" (Gibson and Gibson, "Sacred Theology," 49). Ferguson adds, "If we are united to Christ, then we are united to him at all points of his activity on our behalf" (Ferguson, "Reformed View," 58).

38. Gibson, "Trinitarian Work," 359–60.

for them. To suppose that Christ died to purchase non-saving benefits for all without exception is "to remove the work of Christ from its new covenant context. . . . Christ's atoning work cannot be extended to all people without also extending the new covenant benefits and privileges to all, which minimally includes regeneration, forgiveness of sins, and the gift of the Spirit."[39] It is to make him something other than the mediator of the New Covenant, to conceive of his blood as something other than the blood of the New Covenant. But Scripture never does this. Christ dies as the priest of the New Covenant, and not of any other covenant.

On the other hand, if one aims to retain the New Covenant context in which Christ's priestly work is accomplished while still claiming a universal offering but restricting the benefits of the New Covenant to the elect, one will have to say that Christ merely provisionally obtained these blessings for all without exception but then fails to apply them to those for whom he obtained them. Yet this will not do. As Owen says, "The sole end why Christ procured any thing by his death was that it might be applied to them for whom it was so procured. . . . Every one for whom Christ died must actually have applied unto him all the good things purchased by his death."[40] Indeed, it could be no other way, for the unity of the priestly functions ensure that Christ does not sacrifice (i.e., accomplish redemption by his death) for anyone for whom he fails to intercede (i.e., apply redemption by his intercession). The unity of sacrifice and intercession ensures that application necessarily follows upon accomplishment. To divide provision from application is to militate against the biblical teaching concerning the very nature of priestly ministry.[41] The high priest of the New Covenant purchases the regeneration, faith, and Spirit-indwelling of those whom he represents on the altar and in the tabernacle of God. Piper observes,

> The blood of Christ did not merely purchase possibilities; it purchased actualities. The faith of God's chosen and called was purchased by "the blood of the covenant" (Matt. 26:28). The promise of the new covenant, that a heart of unbelief would be replaced by a heart of faith (Ezek. 11:19; 36:26), was invincibly obtained by the death of Jesus. The term *definite atonement* refers to this truth—when God sent his Son to die, he had in view the definite acquisition of a group of undeserving sinners, whose faith and repentance he obtained by the blood of his Son. This is a divine purpose in the cross—to

39. Wellum, "New Covenant Work of Christ," 522. In personal correspondence, Wellum adds this comment: "One cannot think of Messiah's work apart from the Messiah having the Spirit (Isa 11:2; 42:1; 61:1; etc.) and then pouring out the Spirit on his people (Ezek 36:25–27; Joel 2:28–29; etc.). The linkage between Messiah and his people is organic, and it is impossible to think of Christ's work without the application work of the Spirit. All of this is part of the New Covenant promise that is fulfilled in the New Testament." Thus, all those for whom Christ satisfied the wrath of God cannot fail to be put into possession of that propitiation by the work of the Spirit. To suppose that one for whom Christ propitiated must suffer the wrath of God is to divorce the work of the Son from the work of the Spirit.

40. Owen, *Death of Death*, 181.

41. As do Demarest, *Cross and Salvation*, 189–93; Douty, *Only for the Elect?*, 58–60; Lightner, *Death Christ Died*, 124–35; and Shultz, "Defense," 155–56.

purchase and create the saving faith of a definite, freely chosen, unworthy, rebellious group of sinners.[42]

To speak of purchasing *and creating* the saving faith of a definite group of sinners is to speak of a united work of impetration (sacrifice) and application (intercession), and to say that the latter necessarily follows from the former. This has been the pattern of priestly ministry from its inception, and the New Testament only gives further support to regard it as true of Christ's priestly ministry. Our great high priest does not merely die for the beneficiaries of the New Covenant; rather, *by* his death he secures the benefits of that covenant for his people, which includes the Spirit's *application* of those very benefits Christ purchased by his death.[43] Therefore, every one for whom Christ has died cannot fail to be saved.

The Scope of the New Covenant

What, then, is the design and extent of the New Covenant? From the preceding discussion, we are constrained to conclude that it is particular and not universal. The New Covenant is not made with all without exception; its provisions are not to make salvation possible for all, but to effectively purchase and apply regeneration, forgiveness of sins, and Spirit-indwelling. As the high priest of the New Covenant, who always efficaciously accomplishes his goals, Christ represents only those to whom he is united, to whom the blessings of the New Covenant are actually eventually communicated. Thus, the New Covenant community cannot be regarded as all people without exception, but only those who eventually partake of those promises. Since the New Covenant itself is not universal, and since Christ cannot die except as the high priest and head of the New Covenant, therefore the extent of his atoning death is not universal but particular. He offers and intercedes on behalf of his people, the elect, alone.

This is consistent with the nature of the New Covenant itself, which in every place is an announcement of God's intention to sovereignly and unilaterally bring the stated blessings upon his people. One counts no less than ten first-person singular verbs in Ezek 36:24–27 that describe Yahweh's sovereign actions to accomplish and put into effect the stipulations of the New Covenant. The same is true of the quotation of Jer 31 in Heb 8:8–12. "I will" remains the constant refrain of the sovereign God. No mention is made of the conditions that man must fulfill in order to participate in this covenant; the promise is that God will fulfill those conditions himself: "I will put My laws into their minds, and I will write them on their hearts, and I will be their God, and they shall be My people" (Heb 8:10). This distinguishes the New Covenant from the Old: in the New Covenant, God *grants* what he requires. Given that the nature of the New Covenant is that its condition—faith—is granted by grace, the members

42. Piper, "My Glory," 642–43.
43. Wellum, "New Covenant Work of Christ," 538.

of the covenant are only those in whom that condition is eventually fulfilled. But, of course, not all men have faith (2 Thess 3:2), and therefore the covenant is made not universally but only with those who will eventually enjoy its blessings.

The Old Covenant Priest and the Mixed Community of Israel

In response to the argument that the high priest of the New Covenant only mediates on behalf of those who belong to the New Covenant, non-particularists raise the objection that on the Day of Atonement the high priest of Israel offered sacrifice and interceded for both believers and non-believers, since not everyone in the nation was a genuine believer and follower of Yahweh. The atonement, then, was offered for "all" of the assembly but was only effective for the remnant of believing ones. In the same way, it is argued, Christ's atonement was offered for all without exception but is effective only for those who appropriate it by faith.[44]

In response, several things must be noted. First, the ministry of the Levitical priesthood was strikingly particular. It should be remembered that the author of Hebrews describes the high priest as those "taken from among men" and "appointed on behalf of men in things pertaining to God" (Heb 5:1). Both of these designations point to the representational nature of the priesthood. That the high priest was taken from among men meant that he stood in solidarity with them; and that he was appointed on behalf of men meant that he was there to represent the interests of his fellow sinners before a holy God. And the sinners the Levites represented were limited to the covenant people of Israel. This was vividly illustrated by the vestments of the high priest, whose breastplate contained twelve precious stones that were to correspond with the names of the twelve tribes of Israel (Exod 28:17–21). When Aaron was to enter the holy place to minister on behalf of the people in the presence of God, he was to "carry the names of the sons of Israel in the breastpiece of judgment over his heart" (Exod 28:29). This was an intensely personal representation of particular people. The high priest took names into the holy of holies, and they were the names of the tribes of the nation of Israel. There is never an indication anywhere in the Old Testament that a priest of Israel sacrificed or offered for the Gentile nations or the world in general. As Wellum notes, "The covenantal blessings of atonement are provided only for those within the covenant community."[45]

Recognizing that even in Israel the priestly mediation was limited to the covenant community is paramount for understanding why the mixed community of Israel poses no challenge to the doctrine of particularistic priestly ministry. Those making this objection frame the comparison between Old and New Covenants as if the believing remnant of Israel corresponded to the church, and as if the unbelievers in Israel corresponded to the unbelieving world in the present age. But this is an apples-to-oranges

---

44. For an example of this argument, see Driscoll and Breshears, *Death by Love*, 179.

45. Wellum, "New Covenant Work of Christ," 525.

comparison. Instead, the proper analogy is that the covenant community of Israel corresponds to the covenant community of the church, while the Gentile nations surrounding Israel correspond to the unbelieving world in the present age. For both covenants, the high priest only offers and intercedes on behalf of the covenant community. On the Day of Atonement, Aaron and his descendants did not slay a goat on behalf of the Egyptians. There was no blood sprinkled on the altar for the Canaanites. The text is plain: the high priest made atonement "because of the impurities of *the sons of Israel* and because of *their* transgressions in regard to all *their* sins" (Lev 16:16); "for himself and for his household and *for all the assembly of Israel*" (16:17); Aaron laid his hands on the head of the scapegoat and confessed over it "all the iniquities of *the sons of Israel*, and all *their* transgressions in regard to all *their* sins" (16:21). The priestly ministry was limited to the covenant community alone.[46]

It is true, however, that the covenant community of Israel was comprised of both believers and unbelievers in Yahweh. The Mosaic Covenant was a national covenant, such that all Israelites—elect and reprobate, believing and unbelieving—enjoyed the benefits of the covenant made with the nation. Carson calls this a "tribal-representative" structure, such that when the nation's leaders obeyed Yahweh the entire nation was blessed according to the provisions of the covenant, and when they disobeyed the entire nation was chastised.[47] One need only think of righteous Daniel praying prayers of confession for his people, though he had not personally participated in their sins (Dan 9:8, 11–12). Even the wicked rulers sometimes enjoyed the blessings of the covenant. Ahab was a wicked king who did not know Yahweh (1 Kgs 16:30–33), yet he nevertheless would have received the covenant sign of circumcision (Gen 17:10) and would therefore have been privileged to eat the Passover (Exod 12:43–45, 48–49), and he lived in the land promised to David as the reigning king of Israel (cf. 2 Sam 7:10). He experienced the blessings of the national covenant even though he did not know the Lord. This would have included the blessings of the Day of Atonement, in which the Lord granted that his wrath against Israel's sin would be temporarily (Heb 9:9–10; 10:1–4), though truly (Heb 9:13), propitiated (cf. Rom 3:25–26), so that his anger would not consume them and cut them off from his presence forever. The Day of Atonement was never a mechanism for individuals' personal salvation, for it had always been impossible for the blood of bulls and goats to take away sins (Heb 10:4). Rather, the Day

46. McCall and Osborne object that "the same sacrifices apply to both Israelites and non-Israelites," and thus non-Jews had access to atonement and so it could not have been limited to the covenant community (McCall with Osborne, "Response to Definite Atonement View," 70). Citing Num 15:25–29, they note that the text says, "One and the same law applies to everyone . . . whether a native-born Israelite or a foreigner residing among you (15:29 NIV)." But even here, they cannot escape the language of "the foreigner residing *among you*," which speaks of a proselyte convert to Judaism who was a part of the assembled congregation of Israel. The argument is not that atonement was made only for ethnic Israelites, but that it was made for the covenant nation of Israel, which included both native-born Israelites and foreign converts. The point depends not on ethnic distinctions but covenantal distinctions.

47. Carson, *Showing the Spirit*, 150–58; cf. Wellum, "New Covenant Work of Christ," 536.

of Atonement accomplished their ceremonial cleansing (Lev 16:30) and graciously fit them to continue to sojourn in the presence of their holy God.[48] In this sense, even the unbelieving and the reprobate—so long as they belonged to the covenant nation—had their sins cleansed on the Day of Atonement.

However, there is marked discontinuity between the Mosaic Covenant community and the New Covenant community. The Mosaic Covenant community was by definition mixed; both true believers and unbelievers made up the covenant nation. That is, each man had to teach his neighbor and each man his brother, saying, "Know the LORD" (Jer 31:34). Evangelism was a necessity within the covenant community of Israel. But a chief distinction between the Old and New Covenants is that the New Covenant community "will *not* teach again, each man his neighbor and each man his brother, saying, 'Know the LORD,'" for *they will all know Me*, from the least of them to the greatest of them,' declares the LORD, 'for I will forgive their iniquity, and their sin I will remember no more" (Jer 31:34). By definition, the New Covenant community is comprised only of believers—only of those who know the Lord, only of those who have the law written on their hearts, only of those who experience the full forgiveness of sin. There is no "remnant" within the New Covenant community. Because of this, the priestly mediation of the high priest of the New Covenant will not include any except those who are his people. Unbelievers were embraced under the Old Covenant priesthood because unbelievers were embraced as a part of the Old Covenant community, so long as they belonged to the nation by circumcision. But because the New Covenant community necessarily excludes those who do not know Yahweh, the priestly mediation of the New Covenant is limited only to Christ's people.

By suggesting that Christ might undertake his priestly ministry for those who do not finally come into possession of the blessings of the New Covenant, proponents of the MIV make the New Covenant no more effective than the Old Covenant. Wellum explains, "If the promise of forgiveness, which is at the heart of the new covenant (Jer 31:34), is given to all humanity but not all are saved, then how is the new covenant more effectual than the old? Parallel to the old, there [would be] covenant members within the new covenant who fail to receive what the covenant was intended to achieve, namely, eternal salvation."[49] But this is precisely what both Jeremiah 31 and Hebrews 8 declare cannot be the case. It directly contradicts the central argument of the book of Hebrews, namely, that Christ is a better covenant mediator than Moses and that the New Covenant is better than the Old, for Christ as the mediator of the New Covenant efficaciously brings all his people to salvation. Wellum continues, "In other words, there is no 'remnant' in the new covenant: all within it know God and experience

---

48. Wellum notes, "God never intended the sacrificial system to effect *ultimate* salvation; they functioned as types/shadows of a greater Priest and sacrifice to come (Heb. 10:1–18). Yet with that said, the Passover and later sacrifices were efficacious in that they preserved the life of the firstborn in Exodus, and later, they purified the people, the priest, and the dwelling of God" (Wellum, "New Covenant Work of Christ," 525).

49. Wellum, "New Covenant Work of Christ," 534.

regeneration and justification. . . . Thus, due to Christ's priestly work we have a full, effective, and complete salvation, unlike the types and shadows of the old."[50]

The Relationship between Impetation and Application

By now it has been made apparent that impetration (i.e., Christ's procuring of blessings by his death) and application (i.e., Christ's applying of blessings by his intercessory ministry and the sending of the Holy Spirit) are coextensive.[51] The latter necessarily and irrevocably follows from the former. This was foreshadowed in the Levitical priestly ministry by the fact that the very same blood of the sacrifice was sprinkled on the altar on behalf of the same worshiper, and it was the result of the intercessory application that the benefits of the sacrifice were enjoyed by the worshiper. The blood of sacrifice did not merely remove obstacles between the worshiper and God, such that on the basis of priestly intercession the sinner might appropriate a provisional atonement so as to subjectively enjoy its benefits. No, by slaying the animal and sprinkling its blood, the priest "effected something in the very dwelling place of God. By this action the priest made the people acceptable to God by applying the sacrificial blood to the altar."[52] Martin is correct when he notes, "For whomsoever a Levitical priest sacerdotally officiated, he was completely successful—completely successful in averting evil, or procuring the privilege, which his official office contemplated."[53] And if Christ is the greater fulfillment of the Levitical priestly office, his priestly ministry must be viewed with no less efficacy. To deny this would be to subjugate Christ's priesthood to Levi's, to say that it is inferior with respect to its efficacy.

But such a disjunction between impetration and application—in which impetration is redefined as a provision that hangs suspended upon man's decision, rather than an achievement once for all accomplished and which must necessarily be applied—is precisely how the MIV maintains a universal impetration with a particular application.[54] This substantiates Martin's inference that "The moment we take up with the theory of a 'general reference' of the atonement—the moment we abandon the elemental principle of individual personal relations—we close against ourselves the

---

50. Wellum, "New Covenant Work of Christ," 537.

51. So Owen: "For by impetration we mean the meritorious purchase of all good things made by Christ for us with and of his Father; and by application, the actual enjoyment of those good things upon our believing; — as, if a man pay a price for the redeeming of captives, the paying of the price supplieth the room of the impetration of which we speak; and the freeing of the captives is as the application of it" (Owen, *Death of Death*, 222).

52. Wellum, "New Covenant Work of Christ," 525.

53. Martin, *Atonement*, 43.

54. For example, Shultz, "Defense," 154–56. See above on "Efficacious Accomplishment," noting especially where proponents of the MIV and their supporters revert to language of provision and possibility which is not necessarily applied.

very gate of entrance into the scriptural doctrine of priesthood, and the glorious realm of truth into which it leads."[55]

This truth is not merely an inference from the doctrine of the priesthood but is confirmed throughout the text of Scripture by those passages that intimately unite the accomplishment and the application of redemption. Space does not permit to reproduce all the passages that testify to this union between accomplishment and application, but a survey of several texts must suffice. In the first place, in the great Servant Song of Isaiah 53, which so clearly outlines the coming Savior's substitutionary atonement, there are at least two references to the inextricable unity between his accomplishment and his application. The first comes in verse 5: "He was pierced through for our transgressions, He was crushed for our iniquities; the chastening for our well-being fell upon Him, and by His scourging we are healed." His being pierced, crushed, chastened, and scourged refer to the accomplishment of redemption by his death, and that accomplishment necessarily and efficaciously issues in the application of healing to the people. There is no mention of appropriation by faith, though certainly that is not to be dismissed. But in Isaiah's mind the substitutionary suffering of Christ itself is what accomplishes the healing of his people. Thus, those for whom he was scourged are necessarily those who come into possession of spiritual healing, even if not immediately. A second instance occurs in verse 11: "By His knowledge, the Righteous One, My Servant, will justify the many, as He will bear their iniquities." The justification of the many, which speaks of the application of redemption, is causally grounded in the Servant's bearing their iniquities, which speaks of his impetration by sacrifice. It is the Savior's bearing their iniquities that issues in their justification. Once again, subjective appropriation is not in Isaiah's view; the bearing of iniquity results in the application of justification, even if not immediately. Those whose sins Christ has borne must come into possession of justification.

This connection is also evident in Rom 4:25, where Paul writes that Christ "was delivered over because of our transgressions, and was raised because of our justification." Christ's being delivered over in death refers to the accomplishment of redemption, whereas the justification of sinners relates to its application. There is no reason to suppose that the "our" in the second half of the verse refers to a different number than the "our" in the first half of the verse, and so it is sound to conclude that Christ has died for the transgressions of the same number for whose justification he has been raised; indeed, his resurrection being but the necessary continuation of his priestly offering (i.e., he could not faithfully discharge his priestly ministry unless he had been raised from the grave and conquered death; Heb 7:23–24), the application of sinners' justification is the inevitable fruit of Christ's impetration.

In Rom 5:9–10 Paul writes, "Much more then, having now been justified by His blood, we shall be saved from the wrath of God through Him. For if while we were enemies we were reconciled to God through the death of His Son, much more, having

55. Martin, *Atonement*, 43.

been reconciled, we shall be saved by His life." Reference to sinners' justification speaks of the application of redemption; and that justification is accomplished "by His blood," a reference to the accomplishment of redemption in the blood of Christ's sacrificial offering. A third moment of redemption, redemption consummated, is indicated by the future tense: "we shall be saved by His life." The combination of Christ's reconciling death and the reception of that reconciliation in application ensures the consummation of redemption in glory.[56]

In the golden chain of redemption as presented in Rom 8:29–34, we find reference to four moments of salvation, though three immediately: God's foreknowledge and predestination (8:29) refer to redemption planned in eternity past by the Father; mention of calling and justification (8:30) speak of redemption applied to the sinner at conversion; glorification (8:30) speaks of redemption consummated. Gibson is right to observe that "the demonstrative pronoun τούτους ('these'), the sustained use of καὶ ('also'), and the repetition of the key verbs (προώρισεν, ἐκάλεσεν, ἐδικαίωσεν) point to an exact correspondence between those who are foreknown, predestined, called, justified, and glorified. The extent of salvation at each stage is the same."[57] Once again, there is no mention of man's duty or the necessity of subjective appropriation. Though again we do not claim that one is justified or glorified apart from faith, the overwhelming emphasis is on what God himself accomplishes in the salvation of sinners, he being the subject of all these verbs. Finally, though redemption accomplished is absent from the chain of verses 29 and 30, it appears before long, in verse 32: "He who did not spare His own Son, but delivered Him over for us all, how will He not also with Him freely give us all things?" The delivering over of the Son speaks of redemption accomplished by Christ's death, and Paul here views the death of Christ in itself—without a reference in this line of thought even to redemption applied—as the ground upon which he will consummate our redemption by giving us "all things," of which glorification is certainly one. The death of Christ is of such efficacy that it may be spoken of as itself producing its intended effect of bringing sinners into possession of "all things." Thus, those for whom Christ was delivered over—namely, the "us" of verse 31, the "these" of verses 29–30, "God's elect" of verse 33—cannot fail to come into possession of all spiritual blessings.[58] Since the reprobate do not come to possess these blessings, Christ died for the elect alone.[59]

---

56. As Gibson puts it, "the synergy of redemption accomplished and redemption applied together *guarantees* redemption consummated: if God has already done the most difficult thing—reconcile and justify us by Christ's death—*how much more* (πολλῷ οὖν μᾶλλον) will he rescue us on the last day of his wrath" (Gibson, "Trinitarian Work," 359).

57. Gibson, "Trinitarian Work," 340.

58. Gibson, "Trinitarian Work," 340–42.

59. Several other passages might be multiplied. Gal 1:4 says of Christ, "who gave Himself [redemption accomplished] to deliver us [redemption applied] according to God's will [redemption planned]." Second Timothy 1:9–10 says of the Father, "who has saved us and called us with a holy calling [redemption applied], not according to our works, but according to His own purpose and

Therefore, for the MIV and other non-particularists to introduce disjunction between the impetration and application of Christ's priestly work[60] is not only to go against the whole tenor of the biblical doctrine of priesthood; it is also to militate against these texts that so intimately wed the accomplishment of redemption to its application, oftentimes unmistakably identifying the latter as the immediate causal result of the former. Those for whom Christ offers are the same number as those for whom he intercedes; the ones for whom he accomplishes redemption are those to whom he applies it. Thus, the MIV's concepts of a redeemed sinner who is not delivered from his slavery, of an object of Christ's propitiatory work who must bear God's wrath for eternity, and of a reconciled sinner who must be banished from God's presence forever in hell are each utter impossibilities.

---

grace which was granted us in Christ Jesus from all eternity [redemption planned], but now has been revealed by the appearing of our Savior Christ Jesus [redemption accomplished], who abolished death and brought life and immortality to light [the hope of redemption consummated] through the gospel." Titus 3:4–7 says, "But when the kindness of God our Savior and His love for mankind appeared [redemption accomplished], He saved us, not on the basis of deeds which we have done in righteousness, but according to His mercy, by the washing of regeneration and renewing by the Holy Spirit [redemption applied], whom He poured out upon us richly through Jesus Christ our Savior [redemption accomplished], so that being justified by His grace [redemption applied] we would be made heirs according to the hope of eternal life [redemption consummated]." Hebrews 10:10 says, "By this will we have been sanctified [redemption applied] through the offering of the body of Jesus once for all [redemption accomplished]."

60. For example, when Shultz says, "All people are objectively reconciled to God, but not all people are subjectively reconciled to God, and therefore not all people are saved" (Shultz, "Reconciliation of All Things," 449), he is arguing that Christ has impetrated for those to whom the fruits of his impetration will not be applied. If Christ has secured "objective reconciliation," he cannot fail to ensure "subjective reconciliation" for that same number (Gibson, "Trinitarian Work," 345).

9

Key Particularistic Texts

HAVING SET THE WORK of Christ's atonement in the context of the foregoing argumentation—the unity between all three persons of the Trinity in their eternal plan of salvation; the singular salvific intention of God in sending the Son to die for sinners; the efficacious nature of the expiation, propitiation, reconciliation, and redemption accomplished by Christ in history; and the unified work of sacrifice and intercession particularly and efficaciously accomplished by Christ as the high priest of the New Covenant—it is now legitimate to appeal to several texts that identify a particular people as the objects of the atoning work of Christ.

Consistent with the particular, definite, and effective nature and design of the atonement presented throughout the whole of Scripture, we come to the New Testament and discover that the prophesied Messiah's mission is particular, definite, and effective. Consider the following seven particularizing designations:

1. His people: Joseph is commanded to name him Jesus, "for He will save *His people* from their sins" (Matt 1:21). The offspring he was promised to see as the immediate result of rendering himself a guilt offering (Isa 53:10) are those to whom his coming and saving work have special, definite reference. They are his people, who, though they may not yet presently believe in him, will, by virtue of their being his, will inevitably come to saving faith (Acts 18:10). Thus, Christ "gave Himself for us to redeem us from every lawless deed, and to purify for Himself *a people for His own possession*, zealous for good deeds" (Titus 2:14). Such designations cannot justly be applied to all without exception but only to those who finally come to a saving knowledge of Christ, i.e., the elect.

2. Many: The Son of Man came to "give His life as a ransom for *many*" (Matt 20:28; Mark 10:45)—not for all—a comment that echoes the promise of Isa 53:12, that the Suffering Servant would bear "the sin of *many*." It is not surprising, therefore, that Jesus identifies the blood he would shed—the blood of the New Covenant (Luke 22:20; 1 Cor 11:25)—as that which would be "poured out for *many* for forgiveness of sins" (Matt 26:28; Mark 14:24). In his ministry as a great high priest who comes to make propitiation for the sins of his people (Heb 2:17), he

thus undertakes to bring "*many* sons to glory" through his sufferings (Heb 2:10), "having been offered once to bear the sins of *many*" (Heb 9:28).

3. Sheep: In John 10, Jesus refers to himself as "the good shepherd" (cf. Matt 26:31; Heb 13:20; 1 Pet 2:25; 5:4; Rev 7:17) who "lays down His life for the *sheep*" (John 10:11; cf. Heb 13:20), emphasizing the personal bond and union that exists between him and those for whom he gives his life. They are his own (John 10:14; cf. 10:3–4), whom he calls by name (10:3), for whom he lays down his life (10:15). The sheep are distinguished from the goats (Matt 25:32–33), the former identified as those who will be saved (25:34) and the latter as those who will perish (25:41).

4. Children of God: In John 11, Caiaphas, the high priest, "prophesied that Jesus was going to die for the nation, and not for the nation only, but in order that He might also gather together into one *the children of God* who scattered abroad" (11:51–52). Those scattered abroad could not refer to those presently believing in Jesus, for they had not yet heard the good news of what Christ had accomplished in Israel. Nevertheless, they are regarded as the children of God, that is, the sheep of another fold (John 10:16; cf. 17:20), those who belong to God by virtue of his eternal choice of them for salvation. Because "both He who sanctifies" (i.e., Christ, whose death sanctifies) "and those who are sanctified" (i.e., the beneficiaries of Christ's sanctifying death) "are all from one Father; [therefore] He is not ashamed to call them *brethren*" (Heb 2:11), "the children whom God has given" to the Son (Heb 2:13). It is not the case that all without exception are the children of God (cf. John 8:42, 44); the brethren of Christ are only those with whom he will praise God in the assembly of the righteous (Heb 2:12).

5. Friends: As the greatest expression of the love of the Father (cf. 1 John 4:10), Jesus demonstrates the greatest love a man can have in that he "lay[s] down his life for his *friends*" (John 15:13), a designation that cannot be applied to those who finally perish as his enemies (cf. 1 Cor 15:25; Phil 3:18).

6. Church: In his farewell address to the Ephesian elders at Miletus, Paul charges his brothers to "shepherd the *church* of God which He"—that is, Christ, God the Son—"purchased with His own blood" (Acts 20:28). Christ has purchased the church by his redemptive death—not every tribe, tongue, people, and nation, but "men *from* every tribe, tongue, people and nation" (Rev 5:9). He is the great bridegroom of the church (Rev 19:7; cf. John 3:29), who "loved the *church* and gave Himself up for *her*" (Eph 5:25). It is the eschatological assembly of the Lord, and not those excluded from that assembly for eternity, for whom Christ has given himself in his atoning death.

7. Elect: As Paul instructs the Romans concerning the blessings of salvation, extending from eternity past ("foreknew" and "predestined," Rom 8:29) to

eternity future ("glorified," 8:30), he identifies those for whom the Father "did not spare His own Son but delivered Him over" (8:32) as "God's elect" (8:33), those to whom he will give all things (8:32), and those on whose behalf Christ has not only died but has been raised and now presently intercedes (8:34).

The Negative Inference Fallacy?

In response to these particularizing designations in Scripture, the non-particularist charges that such argumentation is an instance of the negative inference fallacy. In other words, it does not follow from a comment that Christ has come to save his people that he has not come to save those who are not his people. Put another way, John 10 may say that Christ dies for his sheep, but it does not say he dies *only* for his sheep.[1] Especially given the fact that Scripture elsewhere casts Christ as giving his life for "the world" and dying as a ransom for "all," we do not have warrant to read these texts that emphasize Christ's work for the elect to the exclusion of his supposed work for the non-elect.

Several lines of response may be offered to this objection. In the first place, appealing to the universalizing designations of Christ's death is a significant objection that deserves thorough interaction. Part 3 is devoted to the MIV's handling of those passages that say that Christ died for "all," "the world," and, seemingly, those who finally perish. They cannot merely be dismissed or overlooked. However, the particularist does believe that no text, properly interpreted, teaches that Christ died for all without exception. References to "all" and "the world" need to be interpreted in their context, and, when they are, will be shown to be in harmony with particularism, because, in the overwhelming majority of cases, they mean not all without exception, but all without distinction. When the universalistic texts are shown not to have genuinely universal significance, as part 3 will demonstrate, this accusation of the negative inference fallacy becomes little more than an argument from silence, because although there is no text that says Christ did *not* die for the goats, neither are there texts that say Christ *did* die for the goats.

Second, the particularist does not offer these particularizing designations as proof for his position apart from the biblical and theological framework established in the previous chapters of part 2. This argument is more than lobbing proof texts, aiming to cancel out "alls" with "manys." Rather, it is to set these texts in the context of the purpose and nature of the atonement: namely, that the persons of the Trinity are

---

1. Broughton Knox is representative when he says, "The Bible certainly affirms that Christ laid down his life for his sheep, and that he purchased his church with his own blood; but nowhere is the sentiment expressed negatively, i.e., that he died for his sheep only, or that redemption is to be spoken of the elect only" (Knox, "Aspects of the Atonement," 263). See also Allen, "Atonement: Limited or Universal?," 79; Lightner, *Death Christ Died*, 62; and Miethe, "Universal Power of the Atonement," 73, for this argument.

perfectly united in intending the atonement exclusively for the salvation of a particular people, which Christ effectively accomplishes in union with his people as the great high priest of the New Covenant. Viewed against that backdrop, these passages are far more than proof texts; they are the coherent conclusion of the whole Bible's doctrine of particular and effective atonement.[2] Those who hold to universal atonement do not merely have to demonstrate why "all" means all without exception; they must also explain how such an interpretation coheres with Trinitarian unity in salvation, with Scripture's exclusive emphasis on a single salvific intention for the atonement, with the unity of the high priestly work of sacrifice and intercession, and with the efficacious nature of the Bible's terms for atonement. The extent of the atonement is not a matter of the interpretation of a handful of disparate verses; it is a matter of the whole Bible's doctrine of the purpose and nature of the atonement as well. For this non-particularism has no satisfactory answer.

Third, it is an unreasonable and inconsistent standard for non-particularists to require that the word "only" or some such equivalent appear in a passage for one to legitimately interpret an expression as necessarily discriminating. Applying this standard to other texts would lead to undesirable conclusions. For example, God does not say that he will make a great nation of and multiply *only* Abraham's seed (cf. Gen 12:2; 15:5). But no one supposes that the biblical writers would have to explicitly discriminate in such a way for the reader to understand that Abraham's descendants alone would be the covenant nation of Yahweh.[3] Owen offers the examples of John 14:6 and Col 2:9.[4] Though Christ does not say, "I am the *only* way, the *only* truth, and the *only* life" in John 14:6, we need not doubt that this is his intent. Though Paul does not say, "For in *only* him all the fullness of Deity dwells in bodily form," we ought not to leave open the possibility that there was another in whom the fullness of deity may have dwelt. The nature of these categorical statements, along with their contexts, gives us enough reason to read them as particularizing and discriminating, even without the appearance of terms like "only" or "alone."

Fourth, while it is important for particularists to demonstrate how the universalistic language related to Christ's death harmonizes with particularism, it is a greater problem for the universalist to explain why the writers of Scripture would ever employ particularistic language with regard to the objects of Christ's death if they believed he died for all without exception. Since the elect for whom Christ died were not yet "gather[ed] together into one" but were "scattered abroad" in many places and in different generations (John 11:52; cf. 10:16; 17:20), it is understandable that this particular group would be called "the world," even though they do not include every individual who has ever lived. But it is difficult to explain why, if Christ died for all without exception, the writers of Scripture would ever limit the scope of his death

2. MacArthur and Mayhue, eds., *Biblical Doctrine*, 547.

3. Gibson, "For Whom Did Christ Die?" 292.

4. Owen, *Death of Death*, 245.

with necessarily exclusive designations like "sheep," "church," "friends," and "many."[5] In other words, Paul's comment that "through one act of righteousness there resulted justification of life to *all men*" (Rom 5:18) may be explained by the context of Paul's argument of corporate solidarity between the two heads of humanity: Adam and Christ. The "all" to whom justification of life results are not all without exception; to deny this is to embrace universal final salvation. Rather, considering the context, the "all" of Rom 5:18b refers to all who are united to Christ as their representative head, just as the first half of the verse refers to all who were united to the first Adam as their representative head and thus received his condemnation. This is only confirmed by Paul's reversion to "many" in the following verse. The "many" are the "all" in contrast to the "One" (Rom 5:19b). However, if the love of God manifest in the death of Christ is truly magnified most by its universal breadth, what reason could any biblical author have to refer to the extent of Christ's death in particularizing terms? Why not *always* say "all," or "world"? Why *ever* limit the death of Christ to his "people," his "sheep," the "church," etc.? If Christ purchased for God with his blood *every* tribe, tongue, people, and nation, why should John limit that purchase by saying he merely purchased "men *from* every tribe and tongue and people and nation" (Rev 5:9)? The onus thus lies just as much on the non-particularist to explain particularistic language as it does on the particularist to explain universalistic language.

Ephesians 5:22–33: Divine Monogamy

Finally, the contexts in which these particularizing designations appear demonstrate that they ought to be understood as necessarily exclusive.[6] In Ephesians 5, when Paul makes Christ's sacrificial love for the church the pattern for a husband's love for his wife, we cannot escape the conclusion that he intends that Christ's death for the church is exclusive to her (5:25–27). It cannot be disputed that husbands must love their wives in a way that is special and different from the way they love all others. If (a) Christ's love for the reprobate issued in his laying down his life to atone for their sins just as it had in the case of his own bride, the elect, and if (b) husbands are called to love their wives after that pattern, then (c) the measure of a husband's love to his wife would be indistinguishable from the measure of their love to any other woman. Surely Paul did

---

5. See Hodge, *Atonement*, 425. Cunningham makes the same argument: "There is one great and manifest advantage which the doctrine of a limited atonement possesses over the opposite doctrine, viewed with reference to the comparative facility with which the language of Scripture can be interpreted, so as to accord with it; and this is, that it is much more easy to understand and explain how, in accordance with the ordinary sentiments and practice of men, general or indefinite language may have been employed, when strict and proper universality was not meant, than to explain why limited or definite language should ever have been employed, if there was really no limitation in the object or destination of the atonement" (Cunningham, *Historical Theology*, 2:340).

6. Portions of the following paragraphs are adapted from the author's contributions to MacArthur and Mayhue, eds., *Biblical Doctrine*, 547, 553–54.

not intend to endorse polygamy, yet it is difficult to understand how such a position would be avoided if it is not granted that Christ's dying love for his bride, the church, and her alone, is unique and distinguishing. As Gibson explains, "Paul's description of Christ as the Head and Husband of his body and bride, the church, assumes an organic union, such that when he dies, he dies united to his body and bride in a way that necessarily rules out other people or another organic entity—unless one wishes to entertain the thought of polygamy."[7] That is, the doctrine of union with Christ, which cannot be divorced from one's thinking concerning the nature and extent of the atonement, coupled with the exclusive imagery of the marital union, constrains the reader to interpret Eph 5:25–27 in particularistic, exclusive terms. Both the context and the language itself constrain us to understand that the church, as the bride of Christ, is the only one for whom he gives himself up in his atoning, sanctifying death.

Romans 8:28–39: All Good Things for God's Elect

In this section of Romans 8, Paul comments on the broad sweep of God's salvation, from foreknowledge and predestination (8:29), to calling and justification (8:30), all the way through to glorification (8:30). As demonstrated above,[8] the objects of each verb are the same: all those who are foreknown and predestined are eventually called, justified, and glorified. The Father's election necessarily issues in the regeneration, justification, and eventual glorification of all those whom he has chosen. The chain of 8:29–30 speaks of the plan of redemption (foreknown and predestined), the application of redemption (called and justified), and the consummation of redemption (glorified), but Christ's accomplishment of redemption is noticeably absent.

Yet Paul takes up the accomplishment of redemption beginning in verse 31, when he asks, "What then shall we say to these things? If God is for us, who is against us?" That is to say, if the God whose foreknowledge, predestination, calling, and justification necessarily issue in glorification, and we have been the beneficiaries of his grace, what ought to be our reaction? At this point, Paul ties in the accomplishment of redemption with the rest of the phases of redemption, showing that the atoning death of Christ is as efficacious in securing the consummation of redemption as the other elements. He argues from the greater to the lesser: "He who did not spare His own Son, but delivered Him over for us all, how will He not also with Him freely give us all things?" (8:32). Those for whom the Father delivered over his Son to death cannot fail to receive "all things" from him as well. In context, these "all things" include every benefit necessary to ensure perseverance in faith until final glorification (cf. 8:35–39).

But who is the referent of "us all" for whom the Father has delivered over his Son as an atoning sacrifice? It is only reasonable to believe that they are the same "us" of verse

---

7. Gibson, "For Whom Did Christ Die?" 292–93.

8. See the comments on Rom 8:29–34 under the heading, "The Relationship between Impetration and Application," in chapter 8.

31, which are in turn the "those" foreknown, predestined, called, justified, and glorified of verses 29 and 30. Moving forward, Paul asks another rhetorical question similar to the one he asked in verse 31. This time, though, he names the "us" with the particularizing designation "elect": "Who will bring a charge against God's elect? God is the one who justifies; who is the one who condemns? Christ Jesus is He who died, yes, rather who was raised, who is at the right hand of God, who also intercedes for us" (8:33–34). Therefore, the "those" of verses 29 and 30, the "us" of verse 31, and the "us all" for whom Christ died in verse 32 are the same referent as those called "God's elect" in verse 33—the same "us" for whom Christ presently intercedes "at the right hand of God." Finally, this same "us" appears in verses 35, 37, and 39 as Paul teaches that the same ones will never be separated from the love of God in Christ Jesus (8:35–39).

This has several implications for the extent of the atonement. First, since the reprobate, who finally perish in their sins, do not receive all the saving benefits of God's grace as promised in verse 32, they cannot be those for whom Christ was delivered over in death. Second, since the same number for whom Christ was delivered over are also said to be those for whom Christ intercedes before the Father, and since Christ does not intercede on behalf of the reprobate, they cannot be those for whom Christ was delivered over in death. Third, since the same number for whom Christ was delivered over are those who will never be separated from the love of Christ, those who *are* separated from the love of Christ forever in hell cannot be those for whom Christ was delivered over in death. Finally, since the same number for whom Christ was delivered over are identified as "God's elect," this necessarily excludes all those who are not elect.

The hypothetical universalist's response—i.e., that Christ has died for a greater number than are mentioned in Rom 8:28–39—fails for two reasons. First, it is an argument from silence. To say that there are others for whom Christ died than those mentioned here is foreign to this text, and, as has been demonstrated above and as shall be demonstrated in parts 3 and 4, foreign to the rest of Scripture. Second, it militates against all that has been presented in part 2 of this work: it posits disunity in the Trinity, adds a non-salvific divine intention to the atonement that is nowhere mentioned in Scripture, reduces Christ's accomplishments to inefficacious provisions, and divorces Christ's atoning work from his New Covenant priesthood. Third, when Paul says that Christ was delivered over for "us all," he speaks of *all* for whom Christ was delivered over. If he intended to name only a subset of those for whom Christ died, it is not clear why he would have added the term "all." Finally, such an objection undoes the entirety of Paul's argument in this passage. His whole purpose in Rom 8:28–39 is to give encouragement and assurance to those who are beneficiaries of the atonement of Christ. To do this, he lists the blessings that they enjoy as God's elect and *explicitly grounds them in the death of Christ on their behalf.* If not everyone for whom Christ died is guaranteed to receive those blessings—if someone *could* bring a charge against them or separate them from the love of Christ—why would Paul make Christ's death the very basis of their comfort? It would be no consolation at all. If Christ died for the reprobate as well as the elect, the troubled Roman Christians to whom Paul wrote could respond, "What does Christ's death have to do with my security? He died for everyone without exception, and millions are separated from His love forever in hell!"[9] No, for Paul's argument to hold, the "us all" of Rom 8:32 must refer to everyone for whom Christ died, and this necessarily excludes the reprobate.

John 10:11–30: The Good Shepherd and His Sheep

In John 10, Jesus refers to himself as "the good shepherd" (cf. Matt 26:31; Heb 13:20; 1 Pet 2:25; 5:4; Rev 7:17) who "lays down His life for the *sheep*" (10:11), emphasizing the personal bond and union that exists between him and those for whom he gives his life; they are his own (10:14; cf. 10:3–4), whom he calls by name (10:3), for whom he lays down his life (10:15). In addition, the metaphor of sheep is necessarily discriminating, as Jesus elsewhere employs that word picture to distinguish between those who will finally be saved, the sheep, and those who will finally be lost, the goats (Matt 25:32–33; cf. 25:34, 41). In the next verse, Jesus says, "I have other sheep, which are not of this fold; I must bring them also, and they will hear My voice; and they will become one flock with one shepherd" (10:16). That is to say, the sheep for whom Jesus lays down his life include those other than the disciples who were presently

---

9. MacArthur and Mayhue, eds., *Biblical Doctrine*, 554n72. Hurrion puts it this way: "If we tell a man in distress and anguish of spirit, for his reigning impenitency and unbelief, that Christ died for him, seeing he died for all men, and therefore he may be of good comfort, how easily may he reply, Be it so, that Christ died for all men, and so for me; yet I may perish as well as Cain and Judas: If Christ made my salvation possible by his death, yet I may make my damnation certain by my unbelief. What will it profit me, that Christ died for me, if my own treacherous unbelieving heart shuts me out from salvation? I do not perceive, that he purchased either grace or glory for me; but I am left to my own free will, which I find set against divine things, and bent upon what is evil; I have no absolute promises to plead, no assurance that Christ procured the Holy Spirit to help such as I am, or that Christ loved any man living better than thousands, whom he left to perish in their sins; of what advantage then is it to tell me, that Christ died for me and all men? If Christ had been a propitiation for my unbelief, as well as my other sins, I might have entertained some hope, that I should have been delivered from it; but now, though Christ died for all men, I may perish in my unbelief, as inevitably as if he had died for no man" (Hurrion, "Particular Redemption," 111–12).

Owen's paraphrase is worth noting as well: "If Christ did so buy them, and lay out the price of his precious blood for them, and then at last deny that he ever knew them, might they not well reply, 'Ah, Lord! was not thy soul heavy unto death for our sakes? Didst thou not for us undergo that wrath that made thee sweat drops of blood? Didst thou not bathe thyself in thine own blood, that our blood might be spared? Didst thou not sanctify thyself to be an offering for us as well as for any of thy apostles? Was not thy precious blood, by stripes, by sweat, by nails, by thorns, by spear, poured out for us? Didst thou not remember us when thou hungest upon the cross? And now dost thou say, thou never knewest us? Good Lord, though we be unworthy sinners, yet thine own blood hath not deserved to be despised. Why is it that none can lay any thing to the charge of God's elect? Is it not because thou diest for them? And didst not thou do the same for us? Why, then, are we thus charged, thus rejected? Could not thy blood satisfy thy Father, but we ourselves must be punished? Could not justice content itself with that sacrifice . . . ?'" (Owen, *Death of Death*, 291).

following him as he spoke those words. They are sheep, but they are currently in a different fold; they have not yet come home into the fold of their shepherd, which is to say, they are not currently believing in him. But they are nevertheless Jesus' sheep and will not fail to come to faith in him (10:27–28; cf. 17:20), precisely because they are his sheep, given to him by the Father (cf. 10:29), and for whom he will lay down his life. This means that "Jesus' sheep are a particular set of people that exist before they exercise faith in him."[10] This fact is only underscored by Jesus' comments later in the discourse, where he tells the Pharisees, "But you do not believe because you are not of My sheep" (10:26). It is to be noted that unbelief is not the cause of being excluded from Christ's sheep; Jesus does not say, "You are not My sheep because you do not believe." Rather, not being of Christ's sheep is the explanation of their unbelief. Thus, it is not saving faith that makes one a sheep; saving faith gives evidence that one has already been made a sheep. When one inquires as to how one *is* made a sheep, verse 29 answers, "My Father, who has given them to Me . . ." (John 6:37, 39; 17:2, 6, 9, 24; Heb 2:13). This donation from the Father cannot be distinguished from the Trinitarian council of salvation in which the Father entrusts to the Son's mediation those whom he has chosen to save (Ps 2:8; cf. Ezek 34:23–24). That is to say, the sheep are the elect. Thus, the non-elect are not Christ's sheep, and, consistent with this passage, he does not lay down his life for them.

Those who object to this line of reasoning and claim that Jesus' dying for his sheep does not imply that he died *only* for his sheep ask particularists to provide examples of the language of explicit negation to support their case. Kevin Bauder comments, "The strongest case for Limited Atonement would be made if its proponents could offer specific biblical texts that named particular individuals or groups for whom Christ did *not* die to provide salvation."[11] Trueman rightly responds that this is not a usual way of communicating: ". . . knowing a particular intention does not typically require explicitly denying other intentions. If I leave my house to go to the shops, I do not need to tell my wife that I am not going to the zoo or the restaurant or the theater. That is not how language ordinarily works."[12] However, the kind of language Bauder asks for is present in the narrative of John 10. Jesus' comment to the Pharisees, "But you do not believe because you are not of My sheep" (10:26), is just such a negation. Jesus has categorically declared that he lays down his life for his sheep (10:14–15), and now, within a span of a few verses, he explicitly identifies the Pharisees to be those who are not of his sheep. To say, "I die for the sheep," and "You are not among the sheep," is to say, almost as plainly as can be said, "I do not die for you."[13] As Harmon argues, "It must be stressed that this claim [i.e., that Jesus laying

10. Harmon, "For the Glory of the Father," 277.

11. As cited in Trueman, "Definite Atonement View," 31. One notes Bauder's use of the language of "provision" rather than "accomplishment," consistent with the MIV's view of the inefficacy of the cross.

12. Trueman, "Definite Atonement View," 32.

13. Blocher comments, "The Good Shepherd allegory (John 10) does not only mention that he

his life down for his sheep means not for others] does not exist in a vacuum; it is part of a larger matrix of ideas in this passage that describes the purpose of Christ coming into the world, the means of accomplishing that purpose, and that specifically distinguishes between his sheep and those who are not his sheep."[14] He then quotes Murray, who rightly concludes, ". . . to take the formula 'laying down his life for' out of the relationship in which it occurs and apply it to those who finally perish is to make a distinction that Jesus' own teaching forbids."[15]

Besides John 10:26, another such comment is Jesus' explicit denial that he intercedes on behalf of the world: "I ask on their behalf; I do not ask on behalf of the world, but of those whom You have given me; for they are Yours" (John 17:9). Keeping in mind the unity between the high priestly work of sacrifice and intercession—i.e., the high priest intercedes for the exact same number for whom he offers sacrifice—a denial of priestly intercession is tantamount to a denial of priestly oblation. Thus, it is evident that Jesus' statement about laying his life down for his sheep does necessarily exclude the goats. It is the intent of Jesus' words, supported both by the immediate context of the passage and the greater biblical context of the doctrine of the atonement, that he died only for his sheep.

---

gives his life for his sheep (vv. 11, 15). Almost polemically, it delimits the category of these sheep: they are his own (ἴδια, repeated), whom he calls individually by name (v. 3), and who distinguish themselves from others by responding to *his* voice (v. 5), who are also found in the other 'fold,' the nations (v. 16), and of whom he severely tells the Jewish leaders, 'you are *not* my sheep' (v. 26)—with such an emphasis in the whole discourse, the declaration 'I lay down my life for the sheep' takes on a particular resonance" (Blocher, "Jesus Christ the Man," 563). Thus Harmon rightly concludes, "As the Good Shepherd, Jesus lays down his life for a particular group of people (his sheep) in distinction from others (those who are not his sheep)" (Harmon, "For the Glory of the Father," 277).

14. Harmon, "For the Glory of the Father," 277–28n30.

15. John Murray, "Atonement and the Free Offer," 76.

Part 2 Summary and Conclusion

THE AIM OF PART 2 was to set the exegetical debate between particularism and universalism in the context of the whole Bible's theology of atonement, and thereby to make a positive case for particularism against the claims of the MIV. Too often the discussion jumps immediately to the interpretation of proof texts isolated from this larger biblical framework. Divorced from that framework, in many instances there is little basis for deciding whether "all" means all without exception or all without distinction apart from adding up the commentators who agree with one's own interpretation or simply being tilted in the direction of one's theological presuppositions. What breaks the stalemate is setting these exegetical decisions in the context of the entirety of Scripture's teaching on doctrines intimately related to the extent of the atonement. The fruit of these chapters has been to demonstrate that the Bible teaches that Christ died as a substitute for the elect alone.

We began in eternity past, linking the redemptive work of Christ accomplished in time to the pretemporal Trinitarian council of salvation, in which (a) the Father appointed the Son as mediator on behalf of those he had chosen, giving them to the Son and entrusting him with the accomplishment of their salvation by his work of vicarious, representative, penal substitution; (b) the Son agreed to carry out that work in accordance with the Father's plan; and (c) the Spirit agreed to conceive the Son in the virgin's womb, sustain and empower him throughout his earthly mission through to his death and resurrection, and then apply the salvation the Son would accomplish in accordance with the Father's will. In this eternal plan of salvation, the consubstantial persons of the Trinity are perfectly united both in their saving intention and saving acts, the will of the three being one and their external operations being inseparable. It was demonstrated that the Son did not engage in his atoning mission unilaterally but rather in strict obedience to the eternal Trinitarian plan. It was shown that the Father intended to save only the elect, that the Spirit regenerates only the elect, and that therefore the Son atoned only for the elect. Though the MIV claims to preserve Trinitarian unity by introducing general intentions on behalf of the Father and the Spirit, these were demonstrated to be lacking biblical support and theological coherence.

Having understood that the persons of the Trinity must be perfectly united in their intentions for the atonement, we turned to consider what precisely those intentions were. Contrary to the claims of the MIV, it was demonstrated that Scripture uniformly and repeatedly names a single divine intention—even if expressed in various ways and with multiple facets—for Christ's atonement, namely, salvation. It was found that there is not a single mention of providing salvation or making salvation possible; nor is there any text anywhere in Scripture that identifies the intent of the atonement as purchasing common grace, a genuine gospel offer, or cosmic renewal. The divine intention for Christ's sin-bearing, wrath-propitiating atonement was to save the people of God, and nothing more. While there are indirect non-saving benefits that result from the atonement and that are enjoyed by all, the purchased benefits of the atonement are to be distinguished from its indirect results. In light of this, the groundwork was laid to challenge the legitimacy of the MIV's so-called general intentions of the atonement, which will come in part 4.

Having determined the design or purpose of the atonement to be the salvation of sinners, we then turned to examine what precisely Scripture says it was that Christ actually accomplished in dying. It was discovered that he accomplished exactly what the triune God intended: the expiation of sin, the propitiation of wrath, the reconciliation of God and man, and the redemption of captives to sin, all by means of a penal substitutionary atonement. It was found that Scripture knows nothing of the MIV's redefinitions of these motifs—a substitute and those for whom he substituted punished for the same crimes, a propitiation that leaves men to suffer the wrath of God for eternity, a reconciliation that leaves men separated from God forever, and a redemption that never frees the slaves. Jesus did not come to make men savable, but to actually take away their sins; not to make God placable, but to efficaciously extinguish his wrath against sinners; not to make God reconcilable to man upon a condition he might choose to impose, but to abolish the ground of the enmity between sinners and the holy God; not to make men redeemable, but to deliver them from their bondage. In short, the atonement was discovered to be not a provision, potentiality, or possibility, but an efficacious accomplishment. The MIV's attempts to maintain a commitment to the efficacy of the atonement were shown to be internally inconsistent, as proponents of the MIV were shown to steadily revert from the language of accomplishment to the language of provision and possibility.

Then these atoning accomplishments of Christ were set in the light of his role as the great high priest and mediator of the New Covenant. As the fulfillment of the Levitical high priest, whose twofold ministry of sacrifice and intercession were intimately related, Christ was shown to have offered himself as sacrifice for the same persons for whom he performs his priestly intercession. Given his explicit denial of interceding on behalf of the reprobate, reserving that privilege only to his people whom the Father had given him, it was found to be a reasonable inference that his offering was correspondingly limited to the same number. Further, since Christ performs his priestly mediation as the mediator of the New Covenant alone—his blood being none other than the blood of the covenant—it was demonstrated that he purchased none other than the blessings of the New Covenant, which include regeneration, the forgiveness of sins, and the indwelling of the Spirit, and not common grace, a universal offer, or cosmic renewal. Given that the New Covenant was not made with all without exception, that its benefits are enjoyed only by those who are united to Christ, that these saving realities do not accrue to all without exception, and that the application of these benefits necessarily follows upon their accomplishment, yet another line of evidence was discovered to support a biblical doctrine of particular redemption.

Finally, having elucidated the biblical and theological framework of the purpose and nature of the atonement, several texts of Scripture were considered that cast Christ's atonement in explicitly particularizing terms. Christ has died for his "people," the "many," his "sheep," the "children of God," his "friends," his "bride" the "church," and "God's elect." The common accusation that such particularizing designations do not necessarily rule out his having died for others was found to be wanting, and the terms understood in their contexts were discovered to be necessarily discriminating and exclusive. Given this, the particularity of the atonement was shown to be a biblical doctrine.

However, Scripture also uses universalistic terms to speak of the death of Christ. Any proper defense of particular redemption will therefore need to explain how passages describing Christ's death for "all men" and the "whole world" can be harmonized with the principles of particularism outlined in chapters 4–9. Indeed, the entirety of the positive case for the MIV rests upon these universalistic passages. In chapters 10–12, the MIV's handling of these passages will be examined and it will be demonstrated that none of them supports a universal intention in the atonement.

PART 3

A Particularist Response to the Multiple Intentions View's Interpretation of Universalistic Texts

THE THESIS OF THE present volume is that the multiple intentions view of the extent of the atonement (MIV) misinterprets key passages related to the scope of Christ's atoning death by failing to adequately frame them in the context of the whole of Scripture's teaching concerning the design and nature of the atonement. Too often, the debate concerning *whom* the atonement is for prematurely leaps to arguments over proof texts divorced from the biblical framework of what the atonement *is* and what it was *designed* to accomplish. Isolated from that framework, there appears to be little basis for deciding whether, for example, the term "whole world" in 1 John 2:2 means everyone without exception who has ever lived in the world or a specific group of individuals scattered throughout the whole world, apart from assertions of one's own theological precommitments buttressed by dueling references to disagreeing commentators.

Therefore, in chapters 4–9 I aimed to set the exegetical debate between particular and universal redemption in that biblical context, bringing Scripture's teaching concerning the *purpose* of the atonement and the *nature* of the atonement to bear on sound exegetical interpretation of the *extent* of the atonement. The result was a biblically faithful and theologically sound positive argument for the doctrine of particular redemption. By considering Scripture's teaching (a) that the three persons of the Trinity are perfectly united in the intention and accomplishment of salvation, (b) that the intention of the atonement is presented in exclusively salvific terms, (c) that the atonement is a fundamentally efficacious saving accomplishment rather than a provisional work, (d) that the atonement is a work of Christ's high priestly ministry, which is necessarily particularistic, and (e) that the atonement is cast in explicitly particularistic terms, it was demonstrated that, contrary to the claims of the MIV, the Bible teaches that Christ died as an atoning sacrifice for the elect alone, and not for all without exception.

While the preceding positive case for particular redemption is sufficient to establish it as a biblical doctrine, it is nevertheless true that Scripture also employs universalistic terms like "all" and "world" to denote the scope of Christ's redemptive accomplishments. Therefore, any legitimate defense of particularism must explain how passages describing Christ's death for "all men" and "the whole world" can cohere with the tenets of particular redemption propounded in part 2. Besides this, the MIV seizes upon the so-called plain meaning of these universal designations, interprets them in an absolutely universal sense, and concludes that, rather than interpreting the particularistic texts in light of the universalistic ones (unlimited atonement), and rather than interpreting the universalistic texts in light of the particularistic texts (particular atonement), we should receive both texts at face value. The particularistic texts speak to the particular intentions of the atonement, they say, while the universalistic texts speak to the universal, or general, intentions of the atonement. The whole of the MIV's case that there are general intentions in the atonement rests upon interpreting these universalistic passages to refer to all without exception, to elect and reprobate alike.[1]

However, universalistic language—terms like "all" and "world"—is not self-interpreting. Many passages of Scripture contain universalistic language that cannot rightly be interpreted to refer to every individual without exception (e.g., John 12:19; Rom 5:18). They must be interpreted faithfully in the contexts in which they appear, and in a manner that coheres with the exegetical conclusions of the rest of Scripture's teaching on the atonement. Therefore, the aim of the next three chapters is to examine the key universalistic passages that the MIV claims support universal intentions in the atonement, and to demonstrate that when interpreted faithfully, in their context, according to grammatical-historical exegesis, and considering the whole of Scripture's teaching concerning the design, nature, and extent of the atonement, none of these texts ought to be interpreted in an absolutely universal sense. Therefore, none of these texts should be understood to teach what the MIV claims, namely, that Christ died in some sense for all people without exception. Instead, the proper interpretations of each of these texts are consistent with the doctrine of particular redemption.

The MIV's case for universal intentions in the atonement centers around the interpretation of three categories of universalistic texts: (1) those that speak of Christ's death for "all" or "all men"; (2) those that speak of Christ's death for "the world" or "the whole world"; and (3) those that seem to speak of Christ dying for those who finally perish in their sins. Shultz discusses the following texts in his defense of universal intentions in the atonement: Isa 53:4–6; John 1:29; 3:16–17; 4:42; 6:51; 12:46–47; 2 Cor 5:14–15, 18–21; 1 Tim 2:4–6; 4:10; Titus 2:11; Heb 2:9; 2 Pet 2:1; 1 John 2:2; and 4:14. He groups them into the following four categories: Isa 53:4–6, Johannine literature,

---

1. Shultz writes, "The idea that Christ paid for the sins of the elect and nonelect is necessary in order to account [for] the general intentions that God had in the atonement" (Shultz, "Defense," 100).

Pauline literature, and the General Epistles.[2] The above threefold categorization (i.e., "all," "world," and "perishing" texts) is preferable, however, because the arguments for an absolutely universal interpretation depend on the lexemes themselves, not necessarily a particular author's handling of specific terms. Thus the same argument is made from each "all" text, and so with the other categories.

Further, it ought also to be noted that, for the sake of space restraints, and also to reduce redundancy, I will not provide a thorough refutation of the MIV's handling of all fifteen texts cited above. Instead, I have chosen the seven most significant texts that pose the greatest challenges to particular redemption: four of the "all" texts (Isa 53:4–6; 2 Cor 5:14–15; 1 Tim 2:4–6; and 1 Tim 4:10), which will be addressed in chapter 10; two of the "world" texts (John 3:16–17 and 1 John 2:2), which will be addressed in chapter 11; and one of the "perishing" texts (2 Pet 2:1), which will be addressed in chapter 12. The principles discovered from the exegesis of these texts will be briefly applied to each of the other texts Shultz mentions, though perhaps only in passing or in footnotes. This does not weaken any argument set forth in part 3; nor does it leave any argument of the MIV unaddressed or unanswered.

2. Shultz, "Defense," 100.

10

Christ's Death for "All"

THE FIRST CATEGORY OF texts marshaled in support of a universal extent of the atonement employ the word "all" to refer to the scope of Christ's death. If the Lord has caused the iniquity of us *all* to fall on Christ (Isa 53:6), if one died for *all* (2 Cor 5:14), if Christ gave himself as a ransom for *all* (1 Tim 2:6) and is thus named the Savior of *all men* (1 Tim 4:10), how could one escape the conclusion that Christ has atoned for the sins of all without exception?

However, perhaps nothing has been more injurious to fruitful progress in the debate over the extent of the atonement than the unwarranted assumption that the "plain" or "natural" meaning of the term πᾶς is all without exception.[1] Any attempt, therefore, to interpret "all" in anything other than an absolutely universal sense is derided as reading into or overturning the plain meaning of the text. It is often asserted that "all means all," as if the proper significance of "all" is self-evident and needs no interpretation.[2] Yet this begs the question, for Scripture often uses the term "all" to signify something other than all people without exception. In fact, a far more common meaning of "all" in Scripture is "all without distinction," "all kinds," "all of some sorts," or "some of all sorts."[3]

Indeed, there are several occurrences of the term in Scripture that cannot possibly mean all without exception, as in Rom 5:18, in which Paul says, ". . . even so through one act of righteousness there resulted justification of life to all men [πάντας ἀνθρώπους]." If "all men" must mean all people without exception, this verse would commit one to the doctrine of universal final salvation, which is contradictory to other passages of Scripture (e.g., Matt 7:13; 25:46; see also Rom 11:32). Similarly, in Peter's quotation of Joel 2:28 in Acts 2:17, he cites the Lord's prophecy that "I will pour forth of My Spirit on all mankind"—literally, "upon all flesh [ἐπὶ πᾶσαν σάρκα]." Yet this cannot mean that God will pour out the Holy Spirit upon all people without

---

1. For example, after citing a number of universalistic passages, Polhill exclaims, "I know not what could be more emphatic to point out the universality of redemption" (Polhill, "Divine Will Considered," 166).

2. For example, see George, *Amazing Grace*, 94, as in Hammett, "Multiple-Intentions View," 152.

3. BDAG, 782–84. See especially use 5, which gives the glosses "every kind of, all sorts of."

exception, for the Spirit is given only to those in Christ (e.g., Eph 1:13).[4] In other passages, it is so evident that "all" does not mean all without exception that translators add the words "kinds of" to their translation of πᾶς. Thus, Luke reports that Peter saw πάντα τὰ τετράποδα καὶ ἑρπετὰ τῆς γῆς (Acts 10:12), literally, "all the four-footed animals and creeping things of the earth." Yet many faithful translations, such as the NASB, ESV, NKJV, NET, and NIV, render the verse, "and there were in it all *kinds of* four-footed animals," etc. Though Paul writes that the love of money is ῥίζα . . . πάντων τῶν κακῶν, (1 Tim 6:10), literally, "a root of all the evils," many translations properly render the phrase, "a root of all *sorts of* evil" (NASB) or "all kinds of evil" (CSB, NKJV). Such examples may be multiplied: not all without exception will hate Christ's disciples (Matt 10:22); the Pharisees did not tithe every garden herb without exception (Luke 11:42; cf. Luke 18:12); the stronger brother does not have faith to eat all things without exception, even that which is inedible (Rom 14:2); and the Corinthians did not enjoy all knowledge without exception (1 Cor 1:5). Thus, the mere presence of the term "all" is not sufficient to warrant an absolutely universal interpretation. Like anything else, universal language must be properly interpreted according to its context and consistently with the rest of scriptural teaching.

It is sometimes objected that the designations "all without exception" and "all without distinction" are extrabiblical categories imposed upon the text of Scripture, and thus are illegitimate in unbiased exegesis. However, both designations are derived from Scripture itself. In 1 Cor 15:27, Paul says, "For He has put all things in subjection under His feet. But when He says, 'All things are put in subjection,' it is evident that He is excepted who put all things in subjection to Him." Paul quotes from Ps 8:6, where the Father is said to have subjected "all things" to man. Paul then applies this to the man Jesus, when in the eschaton all things are put into subjection to him. However, Paul does not want to be misunderstood as saying that the Father himself will also be put in subjection to the Son, and so he qualifies the universalistic language and tells his readers that it does not have an absolutely universal referent: the Father is *excepted* from the "all things" that are put in subjection to the Son. In other words, Paul teaches the Corinthians that the "all things" of Ps 8:6 does not mean all things without exception.

Similarly, we may look to the text of Scripture for a foundation for the category of "all without distinction." In Rom 3:22, Paul teaches that "the righteousness of God through faith in Jesus Christ" is "for *all* those who believe." Then he adds, "for there is *no distinction*; for *all* have sinned and fall short of the glory of God" (3:22–23). Paul's intention is surely to bring all sentient sinners to account before the bar of God's justice (3:19–20). However, it is not technically true that every human being without

---

4. See also Gen 6:13: "Then God said to Noah, 'The end of all flesh [כָּל־בָּשָׂר, παντὸς ἀνθρώπου] has come before Me.'" "All flesh" cannot signify every human being alive at that time; still less can it mean every human being throughout history, as universalists allege, because Noah and his family members were not destroyed in the flood.

exception has sinned and falls short of the glory of God, for Christ himself is a human being and never sinned. Paul's point is that there is no distinction between Jew and Gentile when it comes to human sinfulness (cf. 3:29–30). It is not as if Gentiles may be excused because they did not have the Law; nor may Jews be excused because they were the chosen people of God. All without distinction have sinned against God, and thus all without distinction are welcome to the righteousness of God through faith. He makes a similar point in Rom 10:11–12: "For the Scripture says, '*All* those believing in Him will not be disappointed.' For there is *no distinction* between Jew and Greek; for the same Lord is Lord of *all*" (author's translation). By using the term "all" in this last occurrence of 10:12, Paul does not intend to say that Christ is the Lord of all persons without exception, for it is only "those *believing in Him*" [πᾶς ὁ πιστεύων ἐπ' αὐτῷ] that are in view here. Instead, Paul uses the term "all" to remove any distinction between Jews and Gentiles. It is not as if Jews have one Lord and Gentiles have another. The same Lord is Lord of all without distinction.

Therefore, "all without exception" and "all without distinction" are biblical categories that ought to be brought to bear on the exegesis of universalistic language. As MacArthur and Mayhue conclude, "'All' is not a self-defining expression. While it may legitimately be understood to speak of every person who has ever lived (i.e., all without exception), it may also legitimately be understood to speak of all kinds of people throughout the world (i.e., all without distinction)."[5] The proper interpretation of "all" depends on context, together with the sound exegetical conclusions of the rest of Scripture. When the "all" passages marshaled by the MIV in support of universal intentions of the atonement are subjected to sound, contextual exegesis, it will be found that none of them supports an unlimited atonement.[6]

Isaiah 53:4–6

The first text to which Shultz[7] turns to establish that there are universal intentions in the atonement is Isaiah 53, that *locus classicus* where the prophet foretells of the penal substitutionary sacrifice of the Suffering Servant.[8] Given that the Servant suffers not for his own sins but for the sins of others, the question to be answered is: For whose sins

5. MacArthur and Mayhue, eds., *Biblical Doctrine*, 555.

6. MacArthur and Mayhue, eds., *Biblical Doctrine*, 555.

7. Ware does not treat Isaiah 53 in his handout, yet it is to be expected that Shultz, self-consciously developing a constructive defense of the MIV from Ware's outline, would include texts not referenced in Ware's text. Hammett makes only a passing reference to Isa 53:4–6 as an argument for universal atonement but does not expound upon it (Hammett, "Multiple-Intentions View," 154n34). Given that the other texts he cites are developed more thoroughly in Shultz's work, it seems clear that Hammett sees his essay as a self-conscious distillation of Shultz's dissertation and monograph. Thus, it is reasonable to assume that in engaging Shultz, we are satisfactorily engaging the MIV position on this text.

8. Shultz stipulates that Isaiah 53 identifies Christ's suffering as a work of penal substitution, with which I heartily agree. See Shultz, "Defense," 101n10, 102n15; cf. Jeffery, Ovey, and Sach, *Pierced for Our Transgressions*, 52–67.

does the Servant suffer? Shultz focuses specifically on the third of the five stanzas of the fourth Servant Song, namely 53:4–6, as it is, he claims, "the one that speaks to the extent of the atonement."[9] In particular, it is verse 6 that states, "the LORD has caused the iniquity of us all to fall on Him." Seizing upon the term "all," Shultz here finds support for a universal intention in the atonement. He provides three lines of argumentation for this conclusion, which may be summarized as (a) the identity of the first-person plural pronouns throughout the passage, (b) the parallelism of the two halves of verse 6, and (c) the universality of the "nations" in the near and wider context. We will demonstrate, however, that these arguments fail to establish Shultz's proposed conclusion of universality, and will show how a proper interpretation of Isaiah 53 actually supports particularism rather than a universal intention in the atonement.

First, Shultz rightly argues that the first-person plural pronouns throughout the chapter[10] refer neither to the "nations" of 52:13–15 nor to the collective voice of the prophets, but rather to the nation of Israel.[11] Thus, "Isaiah is describing what the Servant does on the behalf of and in the place of the nation of Israel."[12] However, in the very next sentence, Shultz claims that this supports "an unlimited extent of the Servant's sacrifice."[13] But it is unclear how this can be, given that "Israel" is a very particularizing designation that necessarily excludes the "many nations" of 52:15. "Israel" does not refer to all without exception, and thus to claim it as support for universalism is tenuous on its face. Shultz's argument for that claim, however, is that the nation of Israel consisted of both believers and unbelievers, both the elect and the reprobate. Thus, the Servant is predicted to suffer in the place of elect and reprobate alike.[14]

In response, it must be noted that Shultz employs apples-to-oranges comparisons when seeking to draw parallels between (a) the Old and New Covenants as well as between (b) the communities of those respective covenants. The Old Covenant was made with Israel as a nation, and as such, membership in that covenant was no indicator of personal salvation. The New Covenant is made with the elect of God, and, as such, the promise was that each member of the New Covenant community would, by definition, know Yahweh (Jer 31:34). Shultz presents the analogy as if believing Israelites are to the church as unbelieving Israelites are to present-day unbelievers; Christ is said to die for

---

9. Shultz, "Defense," 102. While it is true that verses 4–6 address the extent of the atonement, commentary on the scope of the Servant's work is by no means limited to "the one" stanza. There is also mention of "many nations" (52:15), "my people" (53:8), "His offspring" (53:10), and, simply, "the many" (53:11, 12).

10. For example, "*our* message" (53:1), "*we* did not esteem Him" (53:3), "*our* transgressions" (53:5), and "All of *us* like sheep" (53:6).

11. Shultz, "Defense," 103; cf. Oswalt, *Isaiah 40–66*, 381.

12. Shultz, "Defense," 103.

13. Shultz, "Defense," 103–4.

14. "If the servant bore the sins of the entire nation of Israel, he bore the sins of both the elect remnant and those who rejected God. Those who hold to particular redemption are forced to understand Isaiah as only speaking of the elect remnant in 53:4-6" (Shultz, "Defense," 104).

both groups. However, the scriptural analogy is that the covenant community of Israel is to the covenant community of the church as the Gentile nations are to present-day unbelievers. As demonstrated in chapter 8, for both covenants the high priest offers and intercedes on behalf of the covenant community alone.[15]

Besides this conflation, Shultz's analysis fails to understand that while the first-person plural pronouns do refer to the nation of Israel, they refer not to the nation of the eighth century BC in Isaiah's day, nor even to the nation of the first century AD in Christ's day, but rather to the repentant Israel of the eschaton. The Israel of Isaiah 53 is the Israel on whom has been poured the Spirit of grace and of supplication, so that they will look back upon the one they have pierced and mourn for him as for an only son (Zech 12:10; cf. 13:1). It is the day in which the sons of Israel will have repented and will have sought Yahweh, their God, and the Son of David, their King (Hos 3:5); the day when their deliverer will have come to them from Zion and will have removed ungodliness from Jacob (Ps 53:6; cf. Rom 11:26), when every rebel will be purged from them (Ezek 20:38); the day when all Israel will be saved (Rom 11:25). Broader contextual considerations indicate that those addressed in Isaiah 53 are those addressed in the opening verses of chapter 40, where God calls the prophet to "Speak kindly to Jerusalem" and to tell her that "her warfare has ended, [and] that her iniquity has been removed" (40:1–2). It cannot be said of the reprobate that their warfare has ended and their iniquity has been removed; indeed, there is no peace and no comfort for the wicked (48:22; 57:21; 66:24). The near context makes this unmistakable. The "we" in Isaiah 53 confess that they once saw no majesty in their Messiah (v. 2), but despised him and did not esteem him (v. 3). Yet they also confess their sins (vv. 4–6) amid penetrating instruction concerning his atoning work, of which they regard themselves to be beneficiaries (vv. 4–9). The chapter reads like a conversion testimony, and, seen in this light, as Trueman says, it "assumes the personal conversion of the speaker."[16] As MacArthur concludes,

> [Isaiah] is prophesying the collective response of the Jewish people when they finally see, understand, and *believe* that the one they rejected truly is the promised Messiah. . . . In other words, we need to understand this passage not merely as a description of the crucifixion per se; it is literally the lament of repentant Israel at a future time when the Jewish people will look back on the Messiah whom they had for so long rejected, and they will finally embrace him as their Lord and King. Isaiah 53 gives voice prophetically to the dramatic confession of faith that the believing remnant of Israel will make at that time."[17]

Thus, Shultz is wrong to conclude that the mixed community of the nation of Israel is the object of the Servant's atoning work. Isaiah 53 is the confession of the nation

---

15. See "The Old Covenant Priest and the Mixed Community of Israel," in chapter 8.

16. Trueman, "Definite Atonement View," 48–49.

17. MacArthur, *Gospel According to God*, 38, 39.

of Israel after they have been granted repentance and faith in their Messiah. As such, that the first-person plural pronouns refer to the nation of Israel does not constitute evidence for universality in the atonement. Just the opposite; it demonstrates that Christ atones for the sins of "His offspring," whom he will see as the reward for his sufferings and whom he will justify (53:11).

The second argument Shultz proffers concerns the parallelism of the two halves of verse 6, namely, that the "all" who "have gone astray" and the "us" who have each "turned to his own way" (v. 6a) are the "us all" whose iniquity God caused to fall on Christ (v. 6b).[18] He cites Erickson with approbation, who argues, "The extent of what will be laid on the suffering servant exactly parallels the extent of sin."[19] Since all without exception have sinned against the Lord (not just the elect remnant), and since the iniquity of the same "all" is laid upon Christ, therefore, it is argued, Christ has atoned for the sins of all without exception.

In response, we must observe that neither Shultz nor Erickson could consistently read universalistic language with the methodology they employ here without embracing universal final salvation. For example, to be consistent, they would have to say that the extent of justification "exactly parallels" the extent of human sin (Rom 3:24), that the extent of justification of life "exactly parallels" the extent of the transmission of Adam's guilt and corruption (Rom 5:18), and that the resurrection of the righteous extends to every person who died in Adam (1 Cor 15:22). However, neither of these men would affirm that all without exception are justified or that all without exception will be made alive in Christ.[20] They rightly bring to bear the rest of Scripture's teaching concerning the limited extent of those finally saved (e.g., Matt 7:13; 25:46) on the interpretation of these passages, and thus they understand the universalistic language not to have an absolutely universal sense. The same course should be followed in Isa 53:6. One must consider the rest of Scripture's teaching concerning the particularity of the atonement's design and the efficacy of the atonement's nature (see part 2), and thus interpret the universalistic language of Isaiah 53 not to mean "all without exception" but "all of a certain class"—namely, the eschatological nation of Israel, who has repented and trusted in Messiah (cf. Zech 12:10). While it is true that all without exception have gone astray from the Lord in sin, all without exception are not in view in this passage. Verse 6 is the

18. Shultz, "Defense," 104.

19. Erickson, *Christian Theology*, 847.

20. Shultz himself later argues for such a limitation of the universalistic language of Rom 3:24. After quoting the passage, he writes, "All people who repent of their sin and trust in the truth of the gospel are justified by God" (Shultz, "Defense," 202). One must note, however, that Rom 3:23–24 does not say, "For all have sinned and fall short of the glory of God, and *all who repent and believe in the gospel* are justified as a gift by His grace." The subject of the former phrase is not even repeated: the very same "all" who "have sinned" are those "being justified as a gift by His grace through the redemption which is in Christ Jesus." Yet Shultz instinctively brings the exegetical conclusions of other passages of Scripture (i.e., passages which refute universal final salvation, e.g., Matt 7:13) to bear on his interpretation of universalistic language in Rom 3:24. He is right to do that here, and he ought to interpret the universalistic language in Isa 53:6 in a similar fashion.

confession of the sinfulness of *all those making the confession*, namely, the elect remnant of Israel, repentant at long last, as demonstrated above.[21]

Shultz's third argument for universality in the atonement on the basis of Isaiah 53 is that Isaiah teaches that the Servant will also be a light to the nations (42:6; 49:6; cf. 42:1, 4; 52:13–15); that is, his ministry is "not only for Israel, but for all people."[22] Interestingly, Shultz here interprets "all" not to mean all without exception (which he would need to do in order to make his case for a universal atonement) but all without distinction. He argues that the Servant's work is achieved not on behalf of Israel alone, but also for the nations—that is to say, not for all individuals without exception, but for all peoples without distinction.[23] Though this concession undermines his case for a universal atonement, Shultz concludes his section on Isaiah 53 by simply asserting his position as if it has been proven: "Isaiah 53 proclaims that the elect and the nonelect from all races have their sins paid for by the Servant's substitutionary sacrifice."[24] This conclusion simply does not follow from the evidence presented.

On the other hand, rather than supporting a universal intention in the atonement, Isaiah 53 supports an exclusively particular redemption. It does so by presenting the atonement accomplished by the Servant as being both (a) efficacious—that is, accomplishing its intention, namely, the salvation of those for whom atonement is made, not making salvation possible—and (b) particular—that is, accomplished on behalf of a specific group of persons rather than all people without exception.

The efficacy of the atonement of Isaiah 53 is established in several ways. In the first place, the successfulness of the Servant's ministry is stated at the outset of the song: "Behold, My Servant will succeed" (52:13). Though many translations render שכל here as "act wisely" (ESV, CSB, NIV) or "deal prudently" (KJV, NKJV), and though it has that connotation in the Qal stem (e.g., 1 Sam 18:30), in the Hiphil, as here, it is better rendered "prosper" (NASB) or "succeed" (NET) (e.g., Josh 1:7–8).[25]

---

21. As Wells puts it, "It is true, of course, that all the men and women in the world have gone astray, but Isaiah speaks for the godly remnant. It is for this same group that he speaks when he says, 'The Lord has laid on him the iniquity of us all' (v. 6). He does not mean, 'The Lord has laid on Christ the iniquity of each man who ever lived.' He speaks for his community. 'For the transgression of my people he was stricken' (v. 8)" (Wells, *Price for a People*, 74). See also Trueman, "Definite Atonement View," 49n43.

22. Shultz, "Defense," 105. Despite having identified the referent of the first-person plural pronouns as "the nation of Israel" (103), just two pages later he argues that "the passage is referring to the sins of humanity instead of just the sins of Israel" (105). This inconsistency is the sign of a failed argument.

23. He goes on to say this very thing: ". . . Jesus thought of himself as the Suffering Servant who gave his life for all peoples. Christ is the Servant who dies for Israel's sins, but he also dies for the sins of the Gentiles in order to bring together both Gentiles and Jews into the church, the people of God (Eph 2:11-22)" (Shultz, "Defense," 105–6). This is to argue that Jesus died for all peoples without distinction, not all individuals without exception, conceding that universalistic language ought sometimes to be interpreted distributively rather than absolutely.

24. Shultz, "Defense," 106.

25. Here I follow Motyer's analysis, who notes that in the Hiphil שכל "blends acting with prudence

This especially fits the context of battle in 52:12: a soldier will undertake a great conflict and will be successful. This confident declaration of certain victory at the outset of the song is matched by statements of efficacy toward its conclusion: the Servant will see his offspring, prolong his days, and see the prosperity of the Father's good pleasure (53:10); he "will see it and be satisfied," and "will justify the many" (53:11); he will have a portion with the great and will share in the spoils of victory (53:12). This forms an *inclusio*, providing a striking emphasis upon the theme of the Servant's success in his undertakings.[26] Those whose sins the Servant bears in himself (53:4-6, 11) will not fail to be justified (53:11). The Servant's suffering does not merely procure the *opportunity* for justification depending on the sinner's response—a concept reminiscent in Shultz's comment that Christ's death inaugurated the New Covenant, which is "*potentially* for all people."[27] Instead, this suffering efficaciously accomplishes the justification of all those for whom the Servant suffers. Since not all without exception are finally justified, the Servant does not suffer in the place of all without exception.

Another way in which Isaiah underscores the efficacy of atonement in this passage is to insist that the Servant's suffering itself, and not any response subsequent to that suffering, accomplishes its intended ends. The "we" who make the confession had been blind to the attractiveness of Christ (53:2); their estimation of him was not in accordance with his objective worthiness (53:3), but was that he was cursed of God (53:4b). This is the very blindness to the glory of Christ that characterizes all unbelievers (cf. 2 Cor 4:4). In this state of affairs, the Servant is said to have borne their sin and carried their sorrows (Isa 53:4a)—which is to say, "while we were yet sinners, Christ died for us" (Rom 5:8). Then, with no explanation or intervening human action, this people's blindness is replaced with penetrating insight into the penal substitutionary atonement of Christ (53:5-6), as they see themselves to be beneficiaries of such an atonement ("for *our* transgressions," "for *our* iniquities," etc.; 53:5a). Most significantly, they attribute their own subjective spiritual healing directly to the scourging of the Servant (53:5b). As Peter's gloss puts it, it was by his *wounds* that we are healed (1 Pet 2:24). The wounds *themselves* accomplish healing; they do

---

with acting effectively/successfully" (Motyer, "Stricken for the Transgression," 251n5). Compare this to *HALOT*, 3:1328, which gives "to have success" as the proper gloss for שׂכל in Isa 52:13.

26. "The most obvious feature is the repetition of the opening theme—supreme success, total victory—in the closing verse; a literary device known as *inclusio*" (Blocher, *Songs of the Servant*, 60–61).

27. Shultz, "Defense," 106. Note once again the MIV's injection of the concept of potentiality amidst Scripture's clear statements of efficacy. Motyer's comments are apposite: "In a word, Isaiah's 'Behold! My Servant will succeed!' matches the great cry, 'It is finished' (τετέλεσται) at Calvary (John 19:30) and forces us, at the start of our study of Isaiah 53, to enquire what 'finished' means in John and what 'succeed' means in Isaiah. On any 'open-ended' view of the atonement—that is, that the work of Christ only made salvation possible rather than actually secured salvation—'finished' only means 'started' and 'succeed' only means 'maybe, at some future date, and contingent on the contribution of others.' 'Finished' is no longer 'finished' and 'success' is no longer a guaranteed result. This is far from both the impression and the actual terms of Isaiah's forecast . . ." (Motyer, "Stricken for the Transgression," 251–52).

not merely make sinners *healable* if they would meet the conditions for subjectively appropriating the atonement provided. Motyer summarizes, "The atonement *itself*, and not something outside of the atonement, is the cause for any conversion," and so "it is the atonement that activates conversion, not vice versa (cf. Titus 3:3–5). . . . In a word, his death, that and nothing else, ensures the results of redemption applied."[28] This runs contrary to the MIV's model of the atonement as a provision accomplished for all, the enjoyment of the benefits of which depends upon the sinner's response of faith. Thus, if all those for whom the Servant suffers are saved by his atoning death— healed by his very wounds—then only those who actually experience spiritual healing can be said to be objects of his atonement.

Besides its efficacy, the particularity of the atonement is explicitly affirmed throughout the passage. Just as the author emphasizes the efficacy of the Servant's atonement by means of an *inclusio* (see above), so also does he emphasize the particularity of the atonement by an *inclusio*: the beginning of the song speaks of the "many" who were astonished (52:14) and the "many nations" who will be "sprinkled" (52:15), while the end of the song speaks of the "many" who will be "justified" (53:11), and the "many" whose sin the Servant bore (53:12). If Isaiah's intent was genuinely to extend the atonement to all without exception, it is puzzling that he would use the limiting designation "many." Shultz responds to this in two ways. First, he claims that if "many" does not mean all without exception, verse 11 is at odds with verse 6, which does speak of "all of us" and "us all." However, such an interpretation would only be at odds if one misinterprets verse 6 as Shultz has. As shown above, the "all of us" in verse 6 refers not to every individual who has ever lived, but rather to "my people" (53:8), namely, the eschatological remnant of Israel confessing their faith in Messiah at the end of the days (cf. Zech 12:10). These are elect believers only, the true Israel of God, purged of the unbelievers among them (Ezek 20:38). With this in mind, it is perfectly natural to expect a particularizing designation such as "many" throughout the rest of the passage, which is precisely what is found.[29] Shultz's second response is

---

28. Motyer, "Stricken for the Transgression," 261–62, emphasis original. Trueman makes the same observation: "What is interesting is that this is not rooted in any response of the speaker to the events but rather seems to be the direct result of the work of the Servant. . . [T]he suffering of the Servant in itself brings effective benefits to those for whom the Servant suffered" (Trueman, "Definite Atonement View," 49).

29. Further, to adopt Shultz's reasoning, one could turn the tables and just as easily claim, "If one refuses to read 'all' in verse 6 to mean 'many,' one is pitting verse 6 against verse 11." But it is much easier to explain why a universal designation like "all" does not mean all without exception than it is to explain why a naturally limiting designation like "many" ought to be understood as universal. A. A. Hodge offers such an explanation: "Particular and definite expressions must limit the interpretation of the general ones, rather than the reverse. It is plainly far easier to assign plausible reasons why, if Christ died particularly for his elect, they being as yet scattered among all nations and generations, and undistinguishable by us from the mass of fallen humanity to whom the gospel is indiscriminately offered, he should be said in certain connections to have died for the world or for all, than it can be to assign any plausible reason why, if he died to make the salvation of all possible, he should nevertheless be said in any connection to have died for the purpose of certainly saving his elect" (Hodge,

to assert that Isaiah's use of "many" in 53:11–12 is "not meant to be restrictive in any sense,"[30] but "refers to a great host of people that cannot be numbered, and is *therefore* emphasizing the unlimited extent of Christ's ransom."[31] Particularists have no quarrel with identifying the "many" as a great host that cannot be numbered,[32] but it simply does not follow that an innumerable host refers to all individuals without exception throughout human history. Instead, these "many" are the "seed" that the Servant will see as part of his reward (53:10), a very significant designation that identifies the beneficiaries of the atonement as the Son's spiritual children, which could never refer to those who finally perish in unbelief. These "many" who are the Servant's "seed" are the "many sons" whom Christ will bring to glory (cf. Heb 2:10), "the children whom God has given [Him]" (Heb 2:13), namely, the elect of God.[33]

Besides this, Motyer insightfully observes the literary parallelism between 53:4–6 and 53:10–12, which he argues links the two three-verse paragraphs very strongly.[34] First, the former paragraph climaxes with the term וַיהוָה (53:6), which is precisely how the latter paragraph begins (53:10). Also, the two paragraphs have seven significant words in common:

1. The root חָלָה appears in the opening line ("griefs," v. 4; "grief," v. 10).

2. The Hiphil form of פָּגַע appears in the final line ("to fall," v. 6; "interceded," v. 12).

3. נָשָׂא appears in verse 4 ("He Himself bore") and in verse 12 ("He bore the sin of many").

4. סָבַל appears in verse 4 ("He carried") and in verse 11 ("He will bear").

5. דָּכָא appears in verse 5 ("He was crushed") and in verse 10 ("pleased to crush").

6. עָוֹן appears in verse 5 ("our iniquities") and in verse 10 ("their iniquities").

7. A form of פשׁע appears in verse 5 ("transgressions" and in verse 12 ("transgressors").

Motyer concludes from these data that the straying sheep whose iniquities were laid upon the Servant in verses 4–6 are the very same individuals as "the many" in verses 10–12, who are not only the objects of the *accomplishment* of the Servant's atonement but also objects of its *application* (i.e., they are justified, in relationship

---

Atonement, 425).

30. Shultz, "Defense," 105n27. He offers no argumentation for this claim but includes a citation to Oswalt, *Isaiah 40–66*, 403–8, who does not discuss the extent of the atonement explicitly.

31. Shultz, "Defense," 105n27, emphasis added.

32. For example, see Young, *Isaiah 40–66*, 355, a particularist, who identifies the "many" as "a great multitude that no man can number."

33. See "Particular Election, Particular Redemption" in chapter 4 for how the "giving" of these children to the Son by the Father speaks of sovereign election.

34. Motyer, "Stricken for the Transgression," 265.

to the Servant after his resurrection, etc.). This is significant, because it means that the atonement is not accomplished on behalf of anyone to whom it is not eventually applied; application certainly follows accomplishment, and that by virtue of the *nature* of the accomplishment itself. Isaiah 53 rules out the MIV's claim that the atonement is provided on behalf of those to whom it might never be applied. It also means that "the many" may retain its expansiveness—an innumerable multitude from every nation (Rev 7:9)—while at the same time as retaining its particularity.

In summary, then, Isaiah 53 offers no evidence for a universal intention in the atonement. Its universalistic language cannot be interpreted to be absolutely universal, i.e., to mean all without exception, but rather must be understood to refer to all of a certain class, namely, the elect Israelites comprising the eschatological remnant, who make this confession of repentance and faith in Messiah in the last days. The efficacy of the atonement, along with the particularizing designations throughout the passage ("many," "my people," "His offspring"), lead the interpreter to see that the atonement accomplished by the Servant's sufferings is a thoroughly particular atonement.

2 Corinthians 5:14–15

A second text containing the word "all" marshaled by the MIV in support of a universal intention in the atonement is 2 Cor 5:14–15, where Paul declares that "one died for all, therefore all died; and He died for all, so that they who live might no longer live for themselves, but for Him who died and rose again on their behalf."

Shultz's[35] case for interpreting the "alls" in this text to mean that Jesus died to pay for the sins of all people without exception centers on whether "they who live" in verse 15 refers to the same or different individuals as the "all" for whom Jesus died in verses 14 and 15. Both particularists and MIV supporters agree that "they who live" is a reference to believers, that is, to those who experience spiritual life in Christ as a result of being made alive by the grace of regeneration (cf. Rom 6:4; Eph 2:5).[36] If these οἱ ζῶντες are the same individuals as the πάντων . . . οἱ πάντες . . . πάντων, then Paul would be teaching that the "all" for whom Christ died are only those who eventually rise to spiritual life in him. However, if οἱ ζῶντες refers to a narrower class of individuals than do the πάντων . . . οἱ πάντες . . . πάντων, then Paul would be teaching that Christ died for all without exception, but only a subset of those for whom he died will enjoy the application of the benefits purchased by a universal atonement. Relying much on the

---

35. Once again, Shultz best represents the MIV's case for a universal intention in the atonement based on 2 Cor 5:14–15. Ware mentions this text as part of the argumentation for universal atonement (Ware, "Outline," 2), and then adopts this universalist argumentation in support of the MIV (3). Hammett does not discuss 2 Cor 5:14–15 under his heading of the "Pauline 'all' statements" (Hammett, "Multiple-Intentions View," 151–54), but he does mention it in a footnote as a text that can also be cited in support of the MIV (154n34). Thus, to deal with Shultz's argumentation is to deal with the MIV interpretation for 2 Cor 5:14–15.

36. Shultz, "Defense," 123–24, especially footnote 82. Also see Harris, 2 *Corinthians*, 421.

commentary of Murray Harris, Shultz asserts that οἱ ζῶντες does indeed refer to a category of people distinct from the "all" for whom Christ died. The only argumentation he provides for this claim, however, is the following rhetorical question: "If Paul had meant to indicate that 'all' and 'they who live' were the same group of people, then why did he not simply continue to use the world 'all'?"[37] In other words, the shift from "all" to "they who live" indicates a shift from speaking about one group of people to another. However, this is an exceptionally tenuous foundation on which to base one's case. Not only is it an argument from silence, but there are other plausible answers for why Paul switches from "all" to "they who live." Before a convincing answer emerges, however, the passage as a whole must be examined.

Perhaps the most crucial interpretive key to this text centers on giving full weight to what Paul says is the *effect* of Christ's death on those for whom he died.[38] Specifically, the "all" for whom Christ died are those who have died as a result of his death: ". . . one died for all, *therefore* all died" (ἄρα οἱ πάντες ἀπέθανον, 2 Cor 5:14). That is to say, Christ's death on behalf of "all" *effects* the death of those for whom he died. In what sense can it be said that all those for whom Christ died have died as a result of his death? Scripture answers that those for whom Christ dies are *united* with him, he being the head and they being the body (cf. Rom 12:5; 1 Cor 12:27; Eph 1:22–23; 5:23, 29–30), such that what happens to him as the head can be said to have happened to his body in union with him (e.g., 1 Cor 6:15–17).[39] This includes, perhaps especially, Christ's people dying with him in his death, such that his death to sin counts for them. Colossians 2:20 speaks of believers having "died with Christ [ἀπεθάνετε σὺν Χριστῷ] to the elementary principles of the world." Colossians 3:3 says believers "have died [ἀπεθάνετε] and your life is hidden with Christ [σὺν τῷ Χριστῷ] in God." Most significantly, Rom 6:1–11 details how the believer's union to Christ in his death (ὅσοι ἐβαπτίσθημεν εἰς Χριστὸν Ἰησοῦν, εἰς τὸν θάνατον αὐτοῦ ἐβαπτίσθημεν, Rom 6:3) means that we have died to sin in union to Christ (ἀπεθάνομεν τῇ ἁμαρτίᾳ, v. 2). Because he himself died to sin in his death (Rom 6:10), and because our old self was crucified with him so that our slavery to sin would end (Rom 6:6), therefore our death in and with Christ is a death to the penalty and power of sin (cf. 1 Pet 2:24; 4:1–2).[40]

---

37. Shultz, "Defense," 124. He adds a similar assertion from Harris: "The very addition of the expression οἱ ζῶντες suggests that a new, distinct category is being introduced" (Harris, *2 Corinthians*, 421).

38. Gibson comments, "An undue focus on the word πάντες can neglect the important conjunctive ἄρα. In many ways the meaning of the verse turns on this one word: Christ died for all, *therefore* all died. The point that Paul wishes to make, inter alia, is that Christ's death *effects* the spiritual death of others, such that (καὶ) he died for all so that (ἵνα) those who live (having died in Christ) should no longer live for themselves but for him who died for them and rose again (v. 15)" (Gibson, "For Whom Did Christ Die?," 303).

39. See the discussion under "Union to the Covenant Head," in chapter 8, pages 141–46.

40. Shultz objects to understanding the death of "all" in 2 Cor 5:14 in this way: "The death that the all died was not a death to sin or self, as this would indicate that all of humanity is saved" (Shultz, "Defense," 124n85). However, this is only so if one wrongly interprets the "all" to refer to all without

These are the theological themes that Paul discusses in 2 Cor 5:14–15. The text concerns the believer's union with Christ, his consequent death to sin and self, and his resurrection to a newness of life (cf. Rom 6:4) lived no longer for himself but for Christ (2 Cor 5:15). Thus, Paul states that because the "one died for all," *therefore* the "all" who were united to him died with him—died to sin and died to self. This mystical union with Christ in his death predates even one's own faith union, as the elect are reckoned to have been united to Christ even before the foundation of the world, when they were chosen *in him* (Eph 1:4), when "grace . . . was granted [them] *in Christ Jesus* from all eternity" (2 Tim 1:9). Just as the actions of the one man, Adam, had legal implications for all those who were united to him (even before they had existed), so also did the actions of the second man, Christ, have legal implications for all those who are untied to him (even before many of them had existed) (Rom 5:15–19; 1 Cor 15:22, 45, 47). It is this concept of corporate solidarity, or representative headship, by means of union between the head and the body, that explains Paul's use of universalistic language in 2 Cor 5:14–15.[41] The one-for-all motif does not indicate absolute universality, but corporate solidarity between the one and the many, signaling that the actions of a single "one" affect the "all" whom he represents.

These same themes are at play in Rom 5:18–19, where Paul uses the terms "all" and "many" *interchangeably* in consecutive verses. This does not indicate that Paul believed in a universal justification of all without exception (Rom 5:18), but only a particularistic "making righteous" of others (Rom 5:19). These two verses describe the same work of justification on behalf of the same people, whom Paul calls "all men" in verse 18 and "the many" in verse 19. This shows that in contexts of corporate solidarity and representative headship, universal language is not intended to indicate all people without exception, but rather to contrast the "all" or the "many" with the "one" who represents them. Just as we ought not to conclude from Rom 5:18 that all without exception are justified, neither ought we to conclude from 2 Cor 5:14–15 that all without exception are those for whom Christ died. Christ died for the "all" who were in him, those who died with him at the cross and who are

---

exception. Refer to the body of this section for my refutation of that interpretation. Shultz goes on to rightly reject Barnett's view that the death "all" die as a result of Christ's death for them is a potential death (Barnett, *2 Corinthians*, 289–91). Nothing in the text warrants the injection of the concept of potentiality. Paul does not say, "One died for all, therefore all *potentially* died," but rather, simply, "therefore all *died*." Then, however, Shultz offers his own view, that of both Harris (*2 Corinthians*, 422) and Tasker (*2 Corinthians*, 86), namely, that this is the death that all *deserve* to die because of their sin. Once again, however, the text simply does not say that. Paul does not say, "One died for all; therefore it is evident that all *deserved* to die." In order to retain what they see as the plain meaning of the term "all," the MIV proponents must aggressively alter the plain meaning of the phrase "therefore all died."

41. Gibson comments, "The allusion back to Romans 5:12, 15–19 through the εἰς-πάντες motif does not necessitate interpreting πάντες as referring to everyone, since in the Romans passage πάντες is circumscribed by either Adam or Christ: in relation to the former, the whole of mankind is certainly included—all sinned and died because of their union with Adam—but not so in relation to the latter, unless one opts for universalism" (Gibson, "For Whom Did Christ Die?," 302–3).

eventually raised to walk in newness of life as believers.[42] This cannot and does not describe all people without exception, but only the elect of God, given to the Son, who are eventually regenerated by the Spirit.

This exposes the key weakness of the MIV's argument in 2 Cor 5:14–15. The linchpin of its position in this text is the proposition that the "alls" of verse 14 are a broader category than "they who live" in verse 15. However, this would mean that some who die in Christ fail to rise with him to newness of life. Indeed, Shultz cites Harris to this effect: "While all persons died, in one sense, when the Man who represented them died, not all were raised to new life when he rose."[43] Yet this is absolutely precluded by Paul's comments in Romans 6, where he says that there is no one united with Christ in his death who is not also united with him in his resurrection: "For if we have become united with Him in the likeness of His death, certainly we shall also be in the likeness of His resurrection, ... Now if we have died with Christ, we believe that we shall also live with Him" (Rom 6:5, 8). There is no such thing as union with Christ in his death without union with Christ in his resurrection.[44] No one dies with Christ by virtue of a union with him, who then, by a severing of that union, fails to rise together with him. That is precisely why Paul speaks of resurrection to spiritual life immediately after he mentions their spiritual death to sin (2 Cor 5:14–15; cf. 5:17): the "all" who "died" *are* "they who live."[45] Earlier in his presentation, Harris argues

42. As Gibson captures it, "In Paul's soteriology, Christ's death *for* people cannot be viewed in separation from his union *with* those same people" (Gibson, "Trinitarian Work," 355). Others who interpret the text this way include Bavinck, *Reformed Dogmatics*, 3:465; Berkhof, *Systematic Theology*, 396; Letham, *Work of Christ*, 241; Hurrion, *Particular Redemption*, 84–87; Owen, *Death of Death*, 238–40; and Wells, *Price for a People*, 76–82. Shultz acknowledges most of these references in "Defense," 122n78.

43. Harris, *2 Corinthians*, 423; cf. Shultz, "Defense," 124–5n86.

44. Shultz cites both Letham and Murray, whose argumentation in favor of this point ought to be repeated here. Letham says, "In approaching this passage, we recall that Paul consistently sees Christ's death and resurrection as a unity. Here Christ is said to rise in union with those who live for him and not for themselves. In other words, he rises in union with his believing people. For his death to be other than in union with these would introduce a disruption into what everywhere else Paul maintains as a unity. The context is governed by the theme of Christ's union with his people and can hardly support a different reference" (Letham, *Work of Christ*, 241). Murray says, "But elsewhere [Paul] makes perfectly plain that those who died in Christ rise again with him (Rom 6:8). Although this latter truth is not stated in so many words in [2 Cor 5:14–15], it is surely implied in the words, 'he (Christ) died for all in order that those who live should not henceforth live unto themselves but unto him who died for them and rose again.' If we were to suppose that the expression 'all who live' is restrictive and does not have the same extent as the 'all' for whom Christ died, this would bring us into conflict with the explicit affirmations of Paul in Romans 6:5, 9 to the effect that those who have been planted in the likeness of Christ's death will be also in the likeness of his resurrection and that those who died with him will also live with him. The analogy of Paul's teaching in Romans 6:4–8 must be applied to 2 Corinthians 5:14, 15. Hence those referred to as 'those who live' must have the same extent as those embraced in the preceding clause, 'he died for all.' And since 'those who live' do not embrace the whole human race, neither can the 'all' referred to in the clause 'he died for all' embrace the entire human family" (Murray, *Redemption Accomplished and Applied*, 71–72).

45. As Gibson correctly observes, "Moreover, as verse 15 goes on to explain, Christ died *and was*

that the phrase ὑπὲρ αὐτῶν indicates that Christ represented those on whose behalf he was raised. But he also argues that the phrase ὑπὲρ πάντων indicates representation (in addition to substitution) as well.[46] This would seem to demand that Christ's "representation must surely function in *both* his death and his resurrection,"[47] a thought only strengthened by Paul's identifying Christ in verse 15 as τῷ ὑπὲρ αὐτῶν ἀποθανόντι καὶ ἐγερθέντι—with ὑπὲρ governing both ἀποθανόντι and ἐγερθέντι, indicating their inseparability. Gibson's conclusion is inescapable:

> There seems to be an inconsistency here on Harris's part. At times he seems to suggest an implicit union with Christ in both phases of Christ's death and resurrection, and at other times he wishes to allow for a disjunction between them: union with Christ in his death but not in his resurrection. But, as Paul says in Romans, "For if we have been united with him in a death like his, we shall certainly be united with him in a resurrection like his" (6:5). Note what the apostle argues here: if union with Christ occurred in his death, then union with Christ in his resurrection necessarily follows. There can be no disjunction.[48]

What, then, of Shultz's original question? If the "alls" of 2 Cor 5:14 are identical to "they who live" in 2 Cor 5:15, why does Paul switch from one designation to the other? Why does he not simply say, "One died for all, therefore all died; and he died for all, so that *all* might no longer live for themselves"? Why does Paul shift to identify these "all" who died in Christ as "they who live"? The answer is twofold. First, it is because he wants to emphasize that those who are united with Christ in his death do not *stay* dead, but rise with him to walk in newness of life—precisely as he does in Rom 6:3–8. The "all" for whom Christ died are the "all" who died to sin in union with him. Second, it is because when Paul calls the elect the "all" for whom Christ died, he refers to them in their relation to Christ at the time of the *accomplishment* of redemption, whereas

----

raised for believers (τῷ ὑπὲρ αὐτῶν ἀποθανόντι καὶ ἐγερθέντι). If his death for all resulted in the spiritual death of all, then surely by implication his being raised would result in the resurrection of all, something Paul makes explicit elsewhere (Rom. 6:1–11)" (Gibson, "For Whom Did Christ Die?," 304, emphases original). Consult this portion of Gibson's chapter for a full refutation of Harris on this point.

46. Harris, *2 Corinthians*, 422.

47. Gibson, "For Whom Did Christ Die?," 304.

48. Gibson, "For Whom Did Christ Die?," 304–5. Elsewhere he writes, "When [2 Cor 5:15] is read in correspondence with Romans 6:4–5, it is hard to reconcile how in Paul's soteriology there can be those who died with Christ but who are *not* raised with him to walk in newness of life and to live for him" (Gibson, "Trinitarian Work," 355).

Shultz, however, attempts to evade this conclusion by appealing to the charge of the negative inference fallacy (see chapter 9, "The Negative Inference Fallacy?," on pages 239–43). Just as the MIV argues, for example, in John 10 that Christ's declaration that he dies for his sheep does not rule out that he dies for the goats, so here Shultz argues that Rom 6 speaks of believers only whereas 2 Cor 5:14–15 speaks of both believers and unbelievers (Shultz, "Defense," 125n86). But this is nothing but special pleading. There is no indication that Paul is speaking about the reprobate in 2 Cor 5, which is a celebration of the work of Christ on behalf of his people, the elect, whose substitutionary atonement (vv. 14–15a) issues in his people's sanctification (v. 15), regeneration (vv. 16–17), reconciliation (vv. 18–20), and justification (vv. 19, 21).

calling them "they who live" refers to the elect in their relation to Christ at the time when that redemption has been *applied* to them. Though the elect are never considered apart from their federal union with Christ,[49] yet there is a time before their faith union, that is, before that time when they are put into possession of all the benefits purchased for them by Christ's once-for-all sacrifice. In other words, there are those for whom Christ has died who, prior to their regeneration, cannot be characterized as "they who live," but rather as those who are "dead in [their] trespasses and sins" (Eph 2:1) and who continue living for themselves and not for Christ. By designating the "all" for whom Christ died as "they who live," Paul shifts from the accomplishment of redemption to its application, not from a larger group to a smaller one.

Hence falls the last of the MIV's arguments for a universal intention on the basis of 2 Cor 5:14–15. Rather than teaching that Christ died for all without exception only to raise a portion of them to newness of life, Paul teaches that Christ's death for all who are united to him effects their spiritual death to sin and self, and that his resurrection—by virtue of that same union—guarantees that all the benefits of the redemption accomplished will be fully applied to everyone for whom they were obtained. Thus, the love of Christ, which compels Paul to radically sacrificial ministry (cf. v. 14), is not a general, potential love conditioned upon the sinner's response. It is a personal, actual love for each of the sheep whom the shepherd knows by name—a love that *purchases* the sinner's believing response and bestows it upon him by grace. The particularity of the gospel love of Christ is what makes it personal, and thus what makes it precious.[50]

1 Timothy 2:3–6

A third text used by proponents of the MIV[51] to support a universal intention in the atonement has been called a commonly employed weapon in the arsenal of those opposed to definite atonement.[52] That text is 1 Tim 2:3–6, where Paul says that prayer on behalf of all men "is good and acceptable in the sight of God our Savior, who desires all

49. That is, the elect's union with Christ is said to encompass all aspects of redemption: its plan in the Father's election (Eph 1:4; 2 Tim 1:9), its accomplishment in the Son's atonement (Rom 6:3–4a; Gal 2:20; Col 2:20), and in its application in the Spirit's regeneration (Rom 6:4b; Eph 2:5). Once again, refer to the discussion under "Union to the Covenant Head," in chapter 8.

50. Piper celebrates, "He loved *me*. He gave himself for *me*. The preciousness of this personal love is muted where it is seen as an instance of the same love that Christ has for those who finally perish" (Piper, "My Glory," 641).

51. Ware mentions 1 Tim 2:6 in his list of key texts for both the unlimited atonement view and the multiple intentions view, but offers no commentary on the text (Ware, "Outline," 2, 3). Shultz develops Ware's outline and argues that 1 Tim 2:3–6 refers to atonement for "all people" rather than merely "all kinds of people," i.e., for all without exception (Shultz, "Defense," 131–36). Hammett lists 1 Tim 2:6 (and 4:10) as the two exemplars of "The Pauline 'all' statements" that "indicate clearly a universal or general intention in the atonement" (Hammett, "Multiple-Intentions View," 151; cf. 151–54).

52. Gibson, "For Whom Did Christ Die?," 311. See, for example, Demarest, *Cross and Salvation*, 191; Marshall, "Universal Grace and Atonement," 61–63; Picirilli, *Grace, Faith, Free Will*, 133–37; Towner, *Timothy and Titus*, 183–86.

men to be saved and to come to the knowledge of the truth. For there is one God, and one mediator also between God and men, the man Christ Jesus, who gave Himself as a ransom for all, the testimony given at the proper time." The two instances of universalistic language make this a relevant text for the question of the extent of the atonement. If God "desires *all* men to be saved," and if Christ has given himself as "a ransom for *all*," how can anyone deny that the atonement is for all without exception?

The key to answering that question is to remember that universalistic language is not self-interpreting and that, depending on the context, the term "all" often means all without distinction, all kinds, or some of all sorts, rather than all without exception, absolutely everyone, or all of all sorts. Context is central in determining which interpretation is proper.[53] In this case, Paul's intent is impossible to discern apart from understanding the historical context in which 1 Timothy was written, for he writes, in part, to confront false teachers who were teaching "strange doctrines" (1:3) and turning from sound doctrine to "fruitless discussion" (1:6). Because these false teachers are characterized (1) by a preoccupation with myths (1:4; 4:7; cf. Titus 1:14) and genealogies (1:4 cf. Titus 3:9) (2) as "wanting to be teachers of the Law" (1:7; cf. Titus 3:9), and (3) as relating in some way to Jewishness (e.g., "those of the circumcision," Titus 1:10; "Jewish myths," Titus 1:14), commentators believe that they were "primarily but not exclusively Jewish."[54] Commentators also see a dominant theme of exclusivism in the false teaching Paul confronts in the Pastoral Epistles. The esoteric nature of "speculation" concerning "myths and genealogies" leads some to detect a proto-Gnostic element, and conclude that the churches in Ephesus and Crete were dealing with "a kind of Judaizing Gnosticism."[55] Because a staple of Gnostic and proto-Gnostic thought was an elitism that looked down upon the uninitiated, and because Jewish legalists naturally regarded Israel as the people of God to the exclusion of the Gentiles, both particularist and universalist commentators agree that Paul is concerned in the Pastorals to refute this exclusivist false teaching.[56]

53. Portions of the following are adapted from the author's contributions to MacArthur and Mayhue, eds., *Biblical Doctrine*, 557–58.

54. Knight, *Pastoral Epistles*, 12; cf. 10–12, 26–28. See also Towner, *Timothy and Titus*, 41–50; and Marshall, *Pastoral Epistles*, 44–51.

55. Dibelius and Conzelmann, *Pastoral Epistles*, 3. Kelly notes, "It is in fact unrealistic to look to the well-known Gnostic, or near Gnostic, systems of the second century for light on the teaching that provoked the Pastorals. . . . It is best defined as a Gnosticizing form of Jewish Christianity. . . . There is no need . . . to look outside the first century, or indeed the span of Paul's life, for such an amalgam of Jewish and Gnostic traits in the Levant" (Kelly, *Pastoral Epistles*, 12).

56. From the particularist side, Schreiner writes that "a mirror reading of 1 Timothy suggests that in this epistle the apostle Paul confronts some kind of exclusivism heresy" (Schreiner, "Problematic Texts," 376). From the universalist side, Gordon Fee notes, "The concern [in 1 Tim 2:3–4] is simply with the universal scope of the gospel over against some form of heretical exclusivism and narrowness" (Fee, *1 and 2 Timothy, Titus*, 64). And Towner reasons, ". . . the reason behind Paul's justification of this universal mission is almost certainly the false teaching, with its Torah-centered approach to life that included either an exclusivist bent or a downplaying of the Gentile mission. . . . Paul's focus is on building a people of God who incorporate all people regardless of ethnic, social, or economic

In light of this historical context, the particularist argues that it would be very natural for Paul to employ universalistic language in the Pastorals—such as "all men" and "ransom for all," in 1 Tim 2:4 and 6—in order to undermine this exclusivist false teaching rather than to identify all without exception as the objects of God's saving intention and Christ's atoning work.[57] In other words, by speaking of Christ giving "Himself as a ransom for *all*," Paul does not intend to say that Christ has stood in the place of, and received the punishment due to the sins of, every individual who has ever lived throughout history. Rather, he intends to say that the benefits of Christ's sin-bearing substitutionary atonement are not restricted to an elitist sect but are enjoyed by all kinds of people throughout the whole world.[58]

Such a case is only strengthened by the verse immediately following, in which Paul identifies himself as one "appointed a preacher and an apostle . . . as a teacher of the Gentiles in faith and truth" (2:7). Such a reference to his mission to the Gentiles indicates that Paul is using universalistic language to include all people groups, not to identify every individual without exception. He uses the term "all" in this very way in Acts 22:15, where he reports that Christ has charged him to "be a witness for Him to *all men* [πάντας ἀνθρώπους; the identical phrase in 1 Tim 2:4]." No one would contend that Paul testified to the truth of the gospel to every individual in history without exception. Instead, he defines what he means by "all men" several verses later in Acts 22:21: "And He said to me, 'Go! For I will send you far away to the *Gentiles* [εἰς ἔθνη; cf. ἐθνῶν, 1 Tim 2:7]."[59] Paul's mission to the Gentiles mirrors the Father's saving intentions and Christ's atoning accomplishments: not for all men without exception, but for all men without distinction—Gentiles as well as Jews, the οἱ πολλοί as well as the so-called elite.[60]

---

backgrounds . . ." (Towner, *Timothy and Titus*, 177).

57. However, such reasoning is by no means restricted to particularist commentators. Marshall, who held to an unlimited atonement, wrote, "This universalistic thrust is most probably a corrective response to an exclusive elitist understanding of salvation connected with the false teaching" (Marshall, *Pastoral Epistles*, 420).

58. Reading "all kinds" for πάντας/πάντων is not unprecedented even within the confines of this same epistle, as it is virtually universally agreed that πάντων τῶν κακῶν (1 Tim 6:10) does not refer to, literally, "all the evils." That is to say, the love of money is not the root of every single instance of evil in the world. Rather, the meaning is that "the love of money is a root of *all kinds* of evils" (ESV) or "*all sorts* of evil" (NASB). Depending on the context, it is entirely appropriate to interpret πᾶς as "all kinds."

59. Schreiner, "Problematic Texts," 377.

60. Baugh offers three other arguments in favor of the "all kinds" or "all without distinction" interpretation by demonstrating that the Jew/Gentile distinction is in view. First, God's desire for the salvation of all is grounded by the assertion that there is "one God, and one mediator" (1 Tim 2:5), similar to Rom 3:29–30, where Paul reasons that "since . . . God . . . is one" therefore he is not "the God of Jews only" but is "the God of Gentiles also." There is to be "*no distinction* between Jew and Greek; for the same Lord is Lord of *all*" (Rom 10:12). In Paul's own words, the unity of God shows that he is the Lord of *all without distinction*, i.e., both of Jew and Greek. His point is not to identify "all" as meaning all without exception. Second, Baugh argues that the reference to "the testimony given at the proper time" (1 Tim 2:6) emphasizes the eschatological movement in redemptive history from the

Such a line of reasoning is only further strengthened by observing that the first use of "all" in 1 Timothy 2 occurs in Paul's instruction to pray on behalf of "all men [πάντων ἀνθρώπων]" (2:1), whom he immediately identifies as "kings and all who are in authority" (2:2). That is, Paul wants the church to pray on behalf of all kinds and classes of people—not only for people like them, who are poor and despised in the world, but also for the rulers and authorities, who despise them. The believers would need such an encouragement regarding their political leaders, since "it seemed somewhat absurd to pour out prayers to God for an almost hopeless class of men (not only strangers all to the body of Christ, but intent upon crushing his Kingdom with all their strength)."[61] A similar case emerges in Titus 2:1–11, where the phrase "all men," identifying those to whom salvation has been brought, is necessarily defined by the immediately preceding list of different *classes* of people: older men (2:2), older women (2:3), young women (2:4), young men (2:6), and bondslaves (2:9). Since not all men without exception are actually saved, it is best to interpret πᾶσιν ἀνθρώποις (2:11) as "all *kinds* of men," that is, people in every station of life as enumerated in the previous verses. Correspondingly, the same concept is at play in 1 Tim 2:3–6. Mention of classes of people defines the referents of πάντας ἀνθρώπους (2:4) and πάντων (2:6). Given all of this, Paul's universalistic language in 1 Tim 2:3–6 is best interpreted as the Father intending to save, and the Son atoning for, "all kinds of people"—people from different social classes (rulers versus common people), from different ethnicities (Jews versus Gentiles), and even from different moral backgrounds ("the chief of sinners," 1:15, as opposed to others).[62] Nothing in the historical or literary context gives the interpreter a reason to interpret the universalistic language in an absolutely universal sense.

The MIV's case against such an understanding of 1 Tim 2:3–6 centers on undermining the argumentation for interpreting "all men" and "ransom for all" to refer to all kinds of people or all people without distinction. Unfortunately, a significant portion of their presentation is characterized by question-begging and fallacious appeals

---

single nation of the Jews to all the nations. It is not that salvation has come to every individual, but rather it has come to every people group. Third, in Titus 1:1–3, Paul "explains that his own apostolic commission to the Gentiles is the confirmation of God's eschatological purpose to include Gentiles in salvation through Christ" (Baugh, "Savior of All People," 339–40).

61. Calvin, *Institutes*, 3.24.16. Thus Calvin says elsewhere, "Let us be clear, however, that Paul is not speaking here of each and every individual, but of all sorts and conditions of men. . . . He means that God who in times past chose a certain people for himself now wishes to show mercy to everyone, including those who had been denied, as it were, the hope of salvation. . . . The apostle, then, is not suggesting that God wants to save each and every person, but that the promises which before had been made to one nation only are now spread throughout the world. . . . And just as Paul in this verse has all peoples in mind, so too he has in view all conditions of men, as if to say: 'God wishes to save kings and magistrates as well as the humblest of men'" (Calvin, "Gospel Call," 188, 189).

62. Gibson, "For Whom Did Christ Die?," 313. Similarly Schreiner: "The focus on all kinds of people ensures that whatever gender, class, economic status, social standing, or moral history, *no one* is excluded from God's salvation. The 'all without distinction' position is an expansive, all-inclusive one, and should not be understood otherwise" (Schreiner, "Problematic Texts," 377n10).

to authority in the place of sound exegetical argumentation. Hammett begins his discussion by saying, "Taken *at face value*, the wording of 1 Tim 2:6 . . . seems to indicate *clearly* a universal or general intention in the atonement."[63] These assertions of the clarity of the text beg the question, as it is precisely the proper definitions of the terms "all men" and "all" that are disputed in this discussion. As argued at the outset of this chapter, universalistic language is not self-interpreting; it is not as if the face-value meaning of "all" is all without exception, while interpreting it to mean all without distinction is an unnatural imposition on the text. Both are acceptable definitions of the term, depending on the context.[64] As justification, Hammett makes a fallacious appeal to authority, adding that "a number of interpreters take it that way," (i.e., as indicating a universal or general intention in the atonement) and, later, that commentator I. Howard Marshall "see[s] no reason to restrict the meaning of *all*."[65] One might wish to ask Marshall whether fundamentally altering the nature of the term ἀντίλυτρον from an actual to a potential ransom payment is sufficient reason for such a restriction,[66] but in any case his failure to perceive such a reason is not an argument that one does not exist. Hammett goes on to cite professed particularist Timothy George begging the question in the same manner: ". . . it is better to say that 'all means all,' even if we cannot square the universal reach of Christ's atoning death with its singular focus."[67] Again, the claim that "all means all" begs the question, assuming that the default definition of "all" is all without exception. This assumption remains not only unproven but unargued in Hammett's discussion of the text, which unfortunately ends with these comments. Shultz commits the same fallacy when he represents the universalist interpretation of "all men" as simply "all people," and opposes "all people" to "all kinds of people."[68] "All people" is no more of a specific designation than "all men;" both phrases may just as likely refer to all people without distinction—i.e., Gentiles as well as Jews—as to all people without exception. Similarly, it is precisely the particularist's contention that an author of Scripture may use the phrase "all people" to signify all kinds of people rather than all people without exception. To assume without argument that the universalistic marker means all without exception is to assume what must be proven. It is to offer no sound argument against the interpretation of the text presented above.

Fortunately, Shultz moves on from such question-begging to make his case that "all men" in 1 Tim 2:4 and "all" in 1 Tim 2:6 refer to all people without exception rather than all kinds of people without distinction. First, he interacts with Baugh's three arguments for seeing a Jew-Gentile distinction in the passage (see above), noting that

63. Hammett, "Multiple-Intentions View," 151.

64. Baugh, "Savior of All People," 339n33.

65. Hammett, "Multiple-Intentions View," 151, 152.

66. See the discussion on 1 Tim 2:6 in "The Salvific Intention of the Atonement," in chapter 5.

67. George, *Amazing Grace*, 94, as in Hammett, "Multiple-Intentions View," 152.

68. Shultz, "Defense," 133, 135.

the second and third arguments, though valid, can be understood just as well if "all" is read as all without exception.[69] Shultz's response to the first argument is confusing, and thus ought to be reproduced in its entirety:

> That there is only one God and one Mediator demonstrates that God desires the salvation of Gentiles as well as Jews, but it also stands in opposition to the synagogue's beliefs that God hates the sinner, that God only wants to save the righteous, and that salvation is only for a select few who have the right knowledge (cf. the statement that God wants all to come to the knowledge of the truth in v. 4).[70]

Up until this point, Shultz has done nothing but affirm the point that Baugh has made. This is precisely the kind of exclusivism that Paul is writing to combat: salvation is not merely for the Jews but also for the Gentiles. However, Shultz concludes from this, "Therefore v. 5 does not support the meaning of 'all sorts of people,' but rather indicates that God desires the salvation of all people without exception; sinners as well as the righteous and Gentiles as well as Jews."[71] It is difficult to see how such a conclusion follows from the foregoing premises. Sinners and righteous persons, Jews and Gentiles, are *sorts* of people. Paul is not speaking individualistically; he is speaking precisely of *kinds* of peoples (though not of sinners and righteous persons, but of elect and non-elect sinners). Ultimately, then, Shultz offers no refutation of the particularist exegesis of 1 Tim 2:3–6.[72]

As he turns to make his case for the "all without exception" interpretation, he offers four arguments. First, Shultz rightly argues that the πάντων ἀνθρώπων of verse 1, the πάντας ἀνθρώπους of verse 4, and the ὑπὲρ πάντων of verse 6 ought to be understood in the same sense. But then he argues that the "all men" on behalf of whom we are called to pray refers to all people without exception. He sees this as an inescapable conclusion, for otherwise "the instruction for prayer is reduced to praying for the elect groups of people within all the groups of people in the world, as Christ was the ransom only for those people. This is clearly not the intent of the passage."[73] Now, on the one hand, Shultz is right to say that Paul's intent is not to urge prayer for the elect qua elect; he is not enjoining the church to pray for the chosen *as* the chosen (though given his comment in 2 Tim 1:10 it would not be unprecedented). Again, his point is simply not to exclude any class of people from the church's prayers. But if one were to ask Paul whether these "all men, . . . kings and all who are in authority" (2:1–2) do happen to be the elect, it seems unavoidable that he would

69. Shultz, "Defense," 134nn119–20.

70. Shultz, "Defense," 134n118.

71. Shultz, "Defense," 134n118.

72. He has, however, argued against the "all kinds" interpretation for the πάντων ἀνθρώπων of verse 1, but because he repeats that argument in his case for a universalist interpretation of verses 4 and 6, it is not addressed here but below.

73. Shultz, "Defense," 134n116.

answer in the affirmative. He urges prayer on their behalf not only to the end that the church might live a tranquil and quiet life (2:2), but also that these rulers may be saved, which salvation God desires for them (2:4), and which Christ has suffered to achieve (2:6). The question must then be asked: Are those whom God desires to save elect or non-elect? Would Paul call the church to pray for the salvation of anybody except those whom God has determined to save? Would he call them to ask God to save those in whom he has purposed to display his judgment? What would it mean for God, who accomplishes whatever he pleases (Isa 46:9–10; Pss 115:3; 135:6), to desire the salvation of those whom he has purposed not to save,[74] except that he is benevolent and wishes good upon all his creatures? God's preceptive will, or will of command, is that all should repent and believe (Acts 17:30); his optative will, or will of disposition, is that none of his creatures should perish (Ezek 18:31–32; 33:11); but his decretive will is to save only those whom he has chosen (Job 42:2; Ps 33:10–11; Dan 4:35; Eph 1:11).[75] It is God's decretive will that is in view when Paul speaks of God desiring all men to be saved. Paul's point is that God's decree is that all kinds of men, not merely the elite, will come to a knowledge of the truth, and that therefore, on that basis, we ought to pray for all kinds of men to be saved.

Shultz seems to regard it as ludicrous that Paul would ever suggest that there is an individual for whom we ought not to pray, still less an entire class of persons, namely, the reprobate. However, the apostle John teaches that there is a sin leading to death—likely the sin of apostasy (cf. Heb 6:4–6; 10:26–31)—for which believers ought not to pray (1 John 5:16). Further, Jesus himself, in his High Priestly Prayer, refused to pray for the world, but prayed only on behalf of those whom the Father had given him (John 17:9). Such is an instance in which Jesus prayed "only for the elect." One wonders whether the Lord would escape Shultz's censure if he were to apply it consistently. Given, then, that there are sins for which believers are not to pray, and given that Jesus himself refused to pray for the salvation of the non-elect, but only of the elect,[76] it is not unthinkable for Paul to mean, by urging prayer for the salvation of "all men, for kings and all those in authority," that the church ought to pray that the Lord would save his chosen from within all classes of society, as well as from all ethnicities throughout the world.

Still further, if (a) Shultz is right to propose that we understand the "alls" of verses 1, 4, and 6 in the same way, and if (b) those of verses 4 and 6 refer to all individuals without exception throughout human history (for according to him, that

74. See "Multiple Intentions?" in chapter 5, and "Efficacious Accomplishment," in chapter 7. Owen's question provides a helpful summary: "If he would have had [all without exception] come to the knowledge of the truth, why did he show his word to some and not to others, without which they could not attain thereunto?" (Owen, *Death of Death*, 346).

75. For these three designations of God's will, see MacArthur and Mayhue, eds., *Biblical Doctrine*, 558–59. These distinctions in our speaking of God's will are expertly argued from Scripture in Piper, "Are There Two Wills in God?," 107–31.

76. See "The Unity of Christ's Priestly Work of Sacrifice and Intercession," in chapter 8.

is the extent of God's saving desire and Christ's universal atonement), then (c) one would have to conclude that Paul is urging that believers pray for the salvation of every individual without exception throughout human history. But this is impossible for any finite being to accomplish, as it would not only require virtual omniscience to pray, personally, for every individual who has ever lived, but it would also require a virtually infinite amount of time to enumerate each one by name.[77] In light of this consideration, it is not only unlikely, but absurd, to suppose that Paul means by ὑπὲρ πάντων ἀνθρώπων (2:1) all without exception. Instead, for this reason and the reasons discussed above, it is best to understand him to refer to all without distinction or all kinds of people, and so throughout the passage.

A second argument Shultz offers in favor of his universalistic interpretation is that "God is the only God and Christ is the only Mediator, and therefore God is the God of all and Christ is the Mediator for all."[78] This is to equivocate on the meaning of the words "of" and "for." God is the God of all in the sense that he is their creator, lawgiver, and judge, but he is not "God [their] Savior" (1 Tim 1:1; cf. 1 Tim 2:3). So also, Christ is the mediator for all in the sense that he is the only mediator available to the human race (1 Tim 2:5), but he is not the mediator for any but those who partake in the new covenant (Heb 8:6; 9:15; 12:24).[79] It is also to equivocate on the meaning of "ransom" (ἀντίλυτρον), which Shultz, along with all non-particularist interpreters, must interpret to mean potential ransom, or else be committed to universal final salvation. But there is no hint of potentiality to be found anywhere in this text, nor in any context in which the λυτρ- word group is used in the Scripture.[80] He is not the ransom payment for those who are not set free and must still pay for their own sins. It does not follow that because Christ is the only mediator *available* to all that he *has* mediated on behalf of all.

Third, Shultz rightly reasons that 1 Tim 2:6 is an allusion to Jesus' comment in Matt 20:28 and Mark 10:45 that the Son of Man came "to give His life a ransom for many." Citing Marshall, however, he argues that "many" does not mean "only some

---

77. Gibson, "For Whom Did Christ Die?," 312. As White observes memorably, "Paul is not instructing Timothy to initiate never-ending prayer meetings where the Ephesian phone book would be opened and every single person listed therein would become the object of prayer. The very next phrase explains Paul's meaning: 'for kings and all who are in authority'" (White, *Potter's Freedom*, 140).

78. Shultz, "Defense," 135.

79. See chapter 8 for why Christ's identity as the Mediator of the New Covenant requires his atonement (i.e., his work of mediation) to be particular rather than universal.

80. Gibson, "For Whom Did Christ Die?," 314. Schreiner comments, "The verse and context say nothing about Christ being the *potential* ransom of everyone. The language in verse 6—'who gave himself' (ὁ δοὺς ἑαυτόν)—is a typically Pauline way of referring to the cross, and always refers to Christ's actual self-sacrifice for believers (Rom. 8:32; Gal. 1:4; 2:20; Eph. 5:2; Titus 2:14). It stresses that Christ gave himself as a ransom so that at the cost of his death he actually purchased those who would be his people" (Schreiner, "Problematic Texts," 379). See also the section on "Redemption" in chapter 7.

as opposed to all," but rather "a great many as opposed to a few."[81] However, the intertextual connection does not stop with Matt 20:28 and Mark 10:45, but rather presses all the way back to Isa 53:11–12, upon which those two texts are based. As argued in the above treatment of Isaiah 53, the "many" of that text are "not only those for whom the Servant makes atonement, but they are coextensive with 'the many' who are justified by the Servant (v. 12)."[82] In other words, "the referent of 'many' in Isaiah 53, though it encompasses an undefined but numerous group of people, is still necessarily limited—it refers to those for whom redemption is both accomplished *and* applied—and therefore cannot refer to every single person."[83] This undoes Shultz's argument for reading either the "many" of Mark 10:45 or the "all" of 1 Tim 2:6 as meaning all without exception.

Shultz calls his fourth argument "perhaps the most decisive one," and it is an appeal to the "clearly" universal meaning of 1 Tim 4:10. The two texts ought to use universalistic language in a similar manner, and since "it is extremely difficult to understand 'all men' as 'all sorts of men'" in 4:10, one ought not to read that interpretation in 2:4 and 6. However, as Shultz argues his case for the absolute universality of πάντων ἀνθρώπων in 4:10, he makes significant appeal to consistency with 2:3–6.[84] Though he provides other arguments for both texts, this dependence on fallacious circularity should not go unobserved. His other arguments for 2:3–6 have been answered above; the others for 4:10 will be addressed below.

In fine, then, Shultz's objections to the "all without distinction" interpretation and his positive case for the "all without exception" interpretation are both shown to be unsatisfactory. In 1 Tim 2:3–6, Paul speaks in expansive, universalistic terms in order to undermine the exclusivism of a Gnostic-like sect of Judaistic false teachers, not to teach that Christ has atoned for the sins of every individual without exception. All kinds of people were welcome to God's salvation, from rulers to commoners, from Jews to Gentiles, for "Christ died for *particular men in all those categories of men* whom God wills to save."[85]

1 Timothy 4:10

Along with 1 Tim 2:3–6, Paul's comments just a few chapters later in 1 Tim 4:10 serve as one of the most oft-employed texts marshaled in defense of a universal aspect of the atonement. The text identifies the "living God" (θεῷ ζῶντι) as the "Savior" (σωτήρ) "of all men" (πάντων ἀνθρώπων), but as "especially" (μάλιστα) the Savior of "believers" (πιστῶν). The proper significance of nearly each one of these terms is highly

81. Shultz, "Defense," 136n126; cf. Marshall, "Universal Grace and Atonement," 59.

82. Gibson, "For Whom Did Christ Die?," 314.

83. Schreiner, "Problematic Texts," 379.

84. Shultz, "Defense," 138. See also footnote 134 on that page.

85. Reymond, *New Systematic Theology*, 693.

contested among interpreters, and not only among those who disagree on the extent of the atonement. Any satisfactory interpretation of this passage (1) must fit the context and the flow of Paul's argument; (2) must interpret the term σωτήρ in a manner consistent with its semantic range, which is exclusively soteriological within the Pastoral Epistles (cf. 1 Tim 1:1; 2:3; Titus 1:3; 2:10; 3:4); (3) ought not to assign multiple senses of σωτήρ to its single occurrence in this verse unless clearly warranted;[86] (4) must interpret the phrase πάντων ἀνθρώπων in a manner consistent with its semantic range; (5) ought to preserve the distinction between "all men" and "believers," which seems required by the term μάλιστα; (6) must interpret μάλιστα in a manner consistent with its semantic range; (7) must preserve the efficacious character of the atonement, not reducing it to a possibility, potentiality, or bare provision;[87] and (8) must not read into the text concepts and constructs not present in the text itself. Advocates of both particular redemption and unlimited atonement do not always agree on the proper interpretation of each of these components of the text. For this reason, before discussing the MIV's handling of this text, a survey of the various interpretations of this verse is warranted. There are no fewer than six.

The first view is *genuine universalism*, that is, that God is the Savior of all men in the sense that he actually rescues all without exception from eternal torment and brings them to salvation in heaven. While this view would satisfy a number of the above criteria—e.g., it allows a soteriological interpretation of σωτήρ, does not require one sense of σωτήρ for "all men" and another for "believers," and preserves the atonement's efficacy—nevertheless, it fails to preserve an adequate distinction between "all men" and "believers." If God saves all people without exception, it would be superfluous to add that he is "especially" the Savior of believers. Further, the testimony of the rest of Scripture rules out universal final salvation by its insistence on the reality of eternal punishment for some (e.g., Matt 7:13; 25:46).

A second view might be termed the *potential-actual view*. Held by Arminians, Anglicans, so-called modified Calvinists, and proponents of the MIV,[88] this view holds that God is *potentially* the Savior of all people without exception, insofar as Christ has made a universal payment for the sins of all, but is *actually* the Savior of believers only (hence "especially"), since Christ's universal-potential atonement is only received by those who believe. This view is attractive in that it satisfies a number of the above interpretive issues: σωτήρ is understood in its natural soteriological sense, πάντων ἀνθρώπων may be understood as all people without exception, a distinction is preserved between "all men" and "believers," and so on.

---

86. It is generally agreed that, if at all possible, one ought not to require that a single occurrence of a word be understood in two distinct senses unless the context clearly requires it.

87. See "Efficacious Accomplishment," in chapter 7.

88. Marshall, "For All, for All," 322–46; Knox, "Aspects of the Atonement," 260–66; Demarest, *Cross and Salvation*, 191–93; Ware, "Outline," 2, 3; Shultz, "Defense," 139; Hammett, "Multiple-Intentions View," 152–54.

However, it also falls short in a number of key areas. In the first place, the nearest antecedent of "Savior" is "the living God," a title that refers most conspicuously to the Father rather the Son (1 Tim 3:15; cf. Matt 16:16; 26:63).[89] In addition, the title "God our Savior," which would represent a blending of the two titles in 1 Tim 4:10, occurs several times in the Pastoral Epistles and is often notably distinguished from Christ the Son, thus referring to God the Father.[90] Given this, as well as a notable absence of any mention of the atonement of Christ, it remains to be demonstrated that the atonement is in view here at all.[91] It may be responded that God is not Savior apart from Christ,[92] and that is true if indeed spiritual salvation is in view; however, that is disputed, as some interpret "Savior" to refer to the Father's providential protection in the present life rather than his spiritual salvation unto eternal life. Besides this, however, the potential-actual view artificially reads the theological construct of potentiality into the text where it simply is not. Nothing in 1 Tim 4:10, neither explicitly nor implicitly, gives the reader leave to read out a distinction between a potential provision and an actual application; such a distinction must be read into the text.[93] Further, as a consequence, the potential-actual view necessarily denigrates the efficacy of the atonement as that which merely potentially atones, or provides the possibility for atonement, rather than that which effectively accomplishes salvation. In part 2, it was demonstrated that the whole of Scripture insists that the efficacy of the atonement is inherent to its nature. There is no biblical ground for a potential or possible

89. In addition to this, Steven Baugh makes a compelling case that Paul uses the phrase θεῷ ζῶντι as "a polemical aside aimed at the false veneration of men who were no longer living, yet who were publicly honored as gods and Saviors upon the Ephesian inscriptions" (Baugh, "Savior of All People," 338; cf. 335–38).

90. In 1 Tim 1:1, Paul speaks of "the commandment of God our Savior, and of Christ Jesus," distinguishing the two. The same is true for Titus 1:3. In 1 Tim 2:3, "God our Savior" is to be identified with the "one God" in 2:5, who is distinguished from "the man Christ Jesus," indicating that the Father is in view here. In Titus 3:4, the kindness and love of "God our Savior" is said to appear when he saved believers according to his mercy (3:5), by the regeneration of the Holy Spirit, who was richly poured out upon believers through "Jesus Christ our Savior" (3:6). Once again, a distinction between "God our Savior" and "Jesus Christ our Savior" indicates that by "God our Savior" Paul intends God the Father.

91. Owen asks rhetorically, "Is there any word here spoken of Christ as mediator? Is it not the 'living God' in whom we trust that is the Saviour here mentioned, as the words going before in the same verse are? And is Christ called so in respect of his mediation?" (Owen, *Death of Death*, 190). See also Hurrion, *Particular Redemption*, 94; and Gibson, "For Whom Did Christ Die?," 319.

92. As Hammett argues, "Christ's atonement must be involved, for Paul and the New Testament know of no salvation apart from the cross" (Hammett, "Multiple-Intentions View," 153).

93. Baugh reasons, "The notion of a potential, universal atonement is introduced by the Arminian theologian at this point. God is (potentially) Savior of all people, because Christ's atonement was accomplished for the sake of all individuals. But the notion of a potential application of the atonement is at the very least not clearly implicit in the passage as it stands" (Baugh, "Savior of All People," 332). So also Hurrion: ". . . the text does not say that God *may be*, by virtue of certain remote conditions and possibilities, the Savior of all men, he actually *is so* at present. Now, if it can be proved, that all mankind are actually saved from sin, death, and hell, the dispute is at an end at once. . ." (Hurrion, *Particular Redemption*, 95).

atonement.[94] Further, it is gratuitous to say that God is the Savior of men who are never in fact saved—indeed, in many cases, of men whom God in his providence has never sent word either of the gospel, by which they may be saved, or of the Savior, in whom they must believe to be saved.[95] Reading the construct of potentiality into the text and denigrating the efficacy of the atonement constitute an exegetical burden that the potential-actual view cannot bear, and therefore it must be rejected.

A third view of 1 Tim 4:10 may be termed the *malista view* in light of its unique interpretation of the term μάλιστα in the passage in question. Though the term has the elative sense of "especially"[96] (as it is translated in every New Testament occurrence by the NASB), T. C. Skeat has famously argued that it should be translated in an appositional sense, as "namely" or "that is."[97] Skeat employs examples from the Greek papyri and argues that it is possible for certain New Testament occurrences of μάλιστα to be read appositionally rather than as elative. Applying such a reading to the text in question, Paul would be saying that God is the Savior of all kinds of men, *that is*, those who believe in him. Such an interpretation satisfies a number of the interpretive criteria listed above: it fits the context of Paul's encouragement to Timothy by reminding him that God is faithful to save those who believe in him; it maintains a soteriological sense of σωτὴρ for both πάντων ἀνθρώπων and πιστῶν; it allows a reading of πάντων consistent with its semantic range, namely, "all kinds;"[98] and, most significantly, it preserves the efficacy of the atonement and does not inject foreign theological constructs into the text. It also provides an efficient solution to the question of the extent of the atonement, harmonizing nicely with particularism, since the "all men" of whom God is Savior are identified as those who believe in him, and those alone.[99]

However, this view stands or falls on its unique interpretation of μάλιστα, and it seems evident that Skeat's proposal does not make the best sense of the lexical data in Scripture. A thorough refutation of Skeat is outside the scope of this present work, but Vern Poythress has undertaken such a refutation.[100] He demonstrates that each of Skeat's examples—both in the papyri and in the New Testament—are either ambiguous, and thus should not be accepted in the place of a previously established

94. See chapters 6 and 7.

95. Owen is typically incisive here: ". . . how strange it seems that Christ should be the Saviour of them who are never saved, to whom he never gives grace to believe, for whom he denies to intercede, John 17:9. . . . To me nothing is more certain than that to whom Christ is in any sense a Saviour in the work of redemption, he saves them to the uttermost from all their sins of infidelity and disobedience, with the saving of grace here and glory hereafter" (Owen, *Death of Death*, 191, 192).

96. BDAG, 613.

97. Skeat, "Especially the Parchments," 174.

98. See the above argumentation on 1 Tim 2:3–6, as well as the rendering of "all kinds" for πάντων in 1 Tim 6:10.

99. Particularist George Knight takes this view (Knight, *Pastoral Epistles*, 203–4), as does Arminian I. Howard Marshall (Marshall, "Universal Grace and Atonement," 55).

100. Poythress, "Meaning of μάλιστα," 523–32.

meaning, or flatly mistaken.[101] Though Shultz does not seem to be aware of Poythress's refutation of Skeat, and though his own argumentation against this view is lacking,[102] he is not convinced by this novel reading of μάλιστα either. It is also significant that Paul has elsewhere unmistakably intended to communicate the idea of "that is," or "namely," and has done so by means of the phrase τοῦτ' ἔστιν, which is the common means of expressing that idea (Rom 7:18; 9:8; 10:6, 7, 8; Phlm 1:12). There would be no reason to deviate from this and use μάλιστα, a word with the settled semantic range of "especially," to achieve what τοῦτ' ἔστιν accomplishes.[103]

A fourth view of 1 Tim 4:10 might be termed the *monotheistic exclusivism view*. This view states that, by saying that God is the Savior of all people, Paul intended to say that the living God of the Bible (as opposed to false deities; cf. Josh 3:10; 1 Sam 17:26; Jer 10:10; Dan 6:25–27; Acts 14:15; 1 Thess 1:9), because he is the only God and Savior in the world, is the only Savior available for all of mankind. The world has no other Savior to turn to except to the living God. Then, by adding "especially of believers," Paul intended that this God actually saves only those who believe. Though this sounds somewhat similar to the potential-actual view, proponents of the monotheistic exclusivism view are careful to distinguish the former from the latter. Schreiner takes this view, and qualifies, "This interpretation should not be confused with one that suggests two levels to the atonement: Christ dies for everyone to make them redeemable, and he dies for the elect to actually redeem them. This introduces an unwarranted split-level into the atonement."[104] Hence Schreiner rejects the potential-actual view and, notably, by extension, the MIV. He continues, "The issue in 1 Timothy 4:10 is . . . the twin truths that God (the Father) is the *available* Savior for all kinds of people—God's salvific stance—while at the same time being the *actual* Savior for only those who believe (in Christ)."[105] In other words, the living God is the only Savior *for* all kinds of people, but he is the Savior *of* only believers.

Positively, this view maintains a soteriological sense of σωτήρ, allows a reading of πάντων consistent with its semantic range (i.e., "all kinds"), interprets μάλιστα within *its* semantic range, preserves a distinction between "all men" and "believers," and preserves the efficacy of the atonement by not arguing that Christ has died in a potential or ineffectual sense for the reprobate. However, the monotheistic exclusivism view has two significant marks against it. First, if at all possible, it is desirable to avoid interpreting a single occurrence of a word in two distinct senses. Yet this view does not interpret σωτήρ in the same sense for both πάντων ἀνθρώπων and πιστῶν.

---

101. Schreiner, "Problematic Texts," 380. See Schreiner's summary analysis of Poythress's refutation of Skeat: Schreiner, "Problematic Texts," 380–82.

102. Shultz, "Defense," 137n129.

103. Gibson, "For Whom Did Christ Die?," 317.

104. Schreiner, "Problematic Texts," 386.

105. Schreiner, "Problematic Texts," 386. Barnes also takes this view: "It seems that the understanding that God is the only Saviour of mankind and of all kinds of men—whoever will come, seems [*sic*] to have the least amount of problems" (Barnes, *Atonement Matters*, 213).

God is interpreted to be the Savior of all men in a sense (i.e., he is available to save them) that is distinct from the way he is the Savior of believers (i.e., he actually saves them). Instead, the distinction that μάλιστα makes between πάντων ἀνθρώπων and πιστῶν seems not to be qualitative but a matter of degree. If μάλιστα is to retain its proper force, God has to be the Savior of all men in the same sense as he is the Savior of believers, but only to a greater degree. Such is not the case in the monotheistic exclusivism view. Secondly, perhaps the chief failure of this view is that it injects the foreign construct of *availability* into the text where it is not. One strains to find any concept of the availability of salvation in 1 Tim 4:10 or its surrounding context, whether explicitly or implicitly.[106] While it is true that God is the only Savior available to mankind, and while Paul implicitly makes a similar point in 1 Tim 2:5 (see the above treatment), it is not clear that such is in view in 4:10. Thus, while not impossible, this interpretation leaves something to be desired.

A fifth view of this text may be termed the *providential preservation view*, which argues that eternal, spiritual salvation is not in view in this text at all. Rather, the sense in which Paul identifies God as a Savior in 1 Tim 4:10 is that he is the providential preserver and deliverer of all men from the dangers of physical, temporal life on earth.[107] Given, as argued above, that the referent of σωτήρ is God the Father rather than Christ the Son, and that there is no explicit mention of the atonement in the near context, it would be reasonable to interpret σωτήρ in the only other sense in which the Father is a Savior, namely, that by his providential care he is the rescuer and preserver of life for all his creatures. He is the God "who gives life to all things" (1 Tim 6:13; cf. Acts 17:25), who is "good to all, [whose] mercies are over all His works" (Ps 145:9; cf. v. 17), who "causes His sun to rise on the evil and the good, and sends rain on the righteous and the unrighteous" (Matt 5:45; cf. Luke 6:35), who "gave you rains from heaven and fruitful seasons, satisfying your hearts with food and gladness" (Acts 14:17; cf. Ps 104:27–28), and who "open[s] [his] hand and satisf[ies] the desire of every living thing" (Ps 145:16). Though all men without exception—the elect as well as the reprobate—have sinned against God, he "has not immediately visited his justice on them as he did with the fallen angels (cf. Rom 3:25; 2 Pet 2:4). Even the reprobate enjoy a temporary stay of execution and thus experience the joys of life in a world infused with the common grace of God."[108] Even in the uncertainties of life,

---

106. Hurrion's comments are worth repeating here: ". . . the text does not say that God *may be*, by virtue of certain remote conditions and possibilities, the Savior of all men, he actually *is so* at present." (Hurrion, *Particular Redemption*, 95).

107. So Baugh: "This passage does not, in fact, relate to the atonement directly, or even to eternal salvation, but to God's gracious benefactions to all of humanity, i.e., his common grace. . . . [It relates to] God's care for all of humanity during our time upon earth" (Baugh, "Savior of All People," 331, 333). This seems to be the historic Reformed interpretation of the passage, as it is shared by Calvin (*Epistles to Timothy, Titus, and Philemon*, 111–12), Owen (*Death of Death*, 190–92), Hurrion (*Particular Redemption*, 94), Fairbairn (*1 & 2 Timothy and Titus*, 184–85), Berkhof (*Systematic Theology*, 443–44), and Grudem (*Systematic Theology*, 598n38).

108. MacArthur and Mayhue, eds., *Biblical Doctrine*, 558.

the reprobate are nevertheless rescued out of countless calamities: unknown numbers of car accidents, plane crashes, violent attacks and robberies, or one of ten thousand other disasters whose danger God's enemies never even know to be imminent—yet God rescues even his enemies from such dangers.

In what way, then, is God the Savior "especially" of believers? Paul's argument seems to be that if he is so kind to all men—even to his enemies—as to preserve their lives from danger and bless them with goodness during their time on earth, how will he fail to rescue believers from whatever dangers may befall them as a result of their faithfulness to him in ministry to a hostile world?[109] This fits the context of Paul's argument very well, perhaps better than all the preceding views, as it seems that Paul is encouraging Timothy and the believers in Ephesus to persevere amidst the opposition that will come a result of their laboring and striving (εἰς τοῦτο γὰρ κοπιῶμεν καὶ ἀγωνιζόμεθα) in ministry to a hostile world.[110] By this means, they are encouraged to press on, for they know that if God rescues even unbelievers from temporal danger, he surely will not fail to rescue them from whatever distresses would undermine his purposes for them.[111]

This view has much to commend itself. It seems to fit the context better than any of the previous alternatives, as discussed above. It maintains the same sense of σωτήρ in the case of both πάντων ἀνθρώπων and πιστῶν; it properly distinguishes between πάντων ἀνθρώπων and πιστῶν, but does so while honoring the force of μάλιστα, positing a distinction between them that is genuinely one of degree and not kind (i.e., he rescues unbelievers from temporal dangers because he is kind by nature, but he especially rescues believers because they are the apple of his eye); it allows πάντων ἀνθρώπων to have an absolutely universal sense, which, while rare, is legitimately within the semantic range of the term. Significantly, it preserves the efficacy of the atonement (particularly because the view argues that this verse does

109. As Calvin says, "And if there is no man who does not feel the goodness of God towards him, and who is not a partaker of it, how much more shall it be experienced by the godly, who hope in him? Will he not take peculiar care in them? Will he not more freely pour out his bounty on them? In a word, will he not, in every respect, keep them safe to the end?" (Calvin, *1 Timothy*, 111–12). Fairbairn adds, ". . . in them [believers] the character of God as Saviour reaches its proper culmination. Put in the form of an argument, the idea might be thus expressed: If in that character God does so much for sinful and unbelieving men, how much may He not be justly expected to do for His own chosen people, who are partakers of His grace, and have trusted in His word! In *their* case there is nothing to hinder the outgoings of His loving-kindness, or to restrain the riches of His beneficence, but everything rather to encourage them to expect all from His hand" (Fairbairn, *1 & 2 Timothy and Titus*, 185).

110. These two verbs describing the Christian ministry speak of the ongoing "tremendous efforts and exertions in the proclamation of the gospel" (Rienecker and Rogers, *Linguistic Key*, as cited in Knight, *Pastoral Epistles*, 202).

111. Owen explains, ". . . the words render a reason why, notwithstanding all the injury and reproaches wherewith the people of God are continually assaulted, yet they should cheerfully go forward to run with joy the race that is set before them; even because as God preserveth all . . . , so that he will not suffer any to be injured and unrevenged, Gen 9:5, so is he especially the preserver of them that do believe; for they are as the apple of his eye, Zech. 2:8; Deut. 32:10" (Owen, *Death of Death*, 191).

not comment on the atonement), and it reads no foreign constructs, such as possibility or availability, into the text.

The one mark against the *providential preservation view* is that it requires a non-soteriological reading of σωτήρ. As mentioned above, in every other occurrence of σωτήρ—not only in the Pastoral Epistles, but in the whole of the New Testament—it is clearly used in a soteriological sense, i.e., to indicate spiritual salvation unto eternal life. It is never used in the sense of rescuing or delivering someone from temporal dangers.[112] It is granted that this is a difficulty; however, it is by no means insurmountable. In the first place, though σωτήρ is not used in a non-soteriological sense in the New Testament, it is so used in the Septuagint. Othniel and Ehud, the judges who "delivered" Israel from the hands of their oppressors, were called "saviors" (σωτῆρα, Judg 3:9, 15; cf. Neh 9:27). God himself was described as the one "who delivers [Israel] from all your calamities and your distresses" (ὃς αὐτός ἐστιν ὑμῶν σωτὴρ ἐκ πάντων τῶν κακῶν ὑμῶν καὶ θλίψεων ὑμῶν, 1 Sam 10:19). Further, the cognates of σωτήρ, such as σῴζω and σωτήρια, are used both in the Septuagint and in the New Testament to refer to non-soteriological deliverance and preservation. In Ps 36:6 (LXX 35:7), it is said of God, "You preserve [σώσεις] man and beast." Since God does not save beasts in a soteriological sense, the English properly renders יָשַׁע as "preserve" (NASB, CSB, NKJV, etc.; see also Judg 6:14; 2 Sam 3:18; 2 Kgs 13:5; Obad 1:21). Significantly, Paul himself uses the terms σῴζω and σωτηρία in Acts 27:31 and 34, respectively, to refer to the preservation of physical life aboard the ship on his journey to Rome, and again to the preservation of his physical life from the hands of Nero (Phil 1:19). When one adds to this biblical usage Steven Baugh's case for σωτὴρ as a reference to a benefactor or patron in light of the Greek inscriptions at Ephesus, where Timothy was presently ministering,[113] it seems clear that a non-soteriological use of σωτήρ may be legitimate in this instance and that Schreiner's concerns are overstated.[114]

A sixth and final view on 1 Tim 4:10 may be considered a variation of the previous, namely, the *temporal-eternal view*. This view holds that God is the Savior of all men in the same way as the providential preservation view—namely, that he providentially orders their circumstances so as to preserve their life, rescue them from numerous dangers, etc., out of his kindness to them as his creatures. However, unlike the previous, this view holds that God is the Savior "especially" of believers in that he not only rescues them from temporal dangers like all other people, but he extends that rescue and deliverance all the way into eternity by blessing them with

112. Schreiner objects, ". . . there is a not a single instance in the Pastorals where the salvation word group refers to anything besides spiritual salvation. In other words, the term never means preservation, nor does it focus on material blessings" (Schreiner, "Problematic Texts," 383).

113. Baugh, "Savior of All People," 333–38.

114. That is, ". . . Baugh does not consider how 'salvation' and 'Savior' are used elsewhere in the Pastorals, and he wrongly resorts to how the word is used in inscriptions in Ephesus instead of relying on the nearer and more important context—the Pauline usage in the Pastoral Epistles" (Schreiner, "Problematic Texts," 384).

spiritual salvation from sin. He is thus "the Benefactor and Preserver of all men in this life and of believers in the life to come."[115] As Kent explains, "As applied to unbelievers it includes preservation and deliverance from various evils and the bestowal of many blessings during this life. To believers, however, this salvation does not end with earthly life but goes on for all eternity."[116]

This view has the advantage over the previous of interpreting σωτήρ in a soteriological sense—i.e., of spiritual salvation—to represent God's saving action toward believers. It avoids the difficulty of reading σωτήρ in a way that it is not used anywhere else in the New Testament, let alone the Pastoral Epistles. However, gaining that advantage comes at the cost of sacrificing consistency in reading σωτήρ in the same sense for both πάντων ἀνθρώπων and πιστῶν. Marshall raises this concern when he observes that it "requires that the term be understood very awkwardly in two different senses with the two nouns that are dependent upon it, in a this-worldly nonspiritual sense with the former and in an eschatological spiritual sense with the latter."[117] He argues that the context of 1 Timothy 4 "can only refer to spiritual life; nothing suggests that the writer was thinking of length of physical life as the result of godliness."[118] This is a curious comment, however, because the reference to "worldliness" and "godliness" in 4:7, along with the commentary on profit for "the present life and also for the life to come" in 4:8, seem to be strong contextual foundations for a comment embracing both the temporal and eternal in 4:10. Blocher observes,

> The immediate context, from verse 7b, introduces the duality: bodily exercise does bring some profit—we could speak of a temporal 'salvation'—but the exercise of godliness is fruitful at both levels, earthly and (Paul could have said) *malista* heavenly. Paul does not restrict the benefits of godliness to the higher level, since some affect also life in the body. The duality obtains with God the Father's saving work: it secures the goods of present life *for all* (common grace . . .), and life of the coming age *for believers only*.[119]

Thus, these comments in the immediately preceding context set the stage for reading God's saviorhood in a twofold sense. It is not that this view necessarily requires God to be a qualitatively different Savior for all than he is for believers. Rather, what is in view is his nature as a preserver, protector, and benefactor in general. The character of

---

115. Foerster, "σωτήρ," *TDNT*, 7:1017, as cited in Gibson, "For Whom Did Christ Die?," 318n110.

116. Kent, *Pastoral Epistles*, 154. Kent also quotes Purdy, whose comments are worth reproducing: "God is the Saviour of all men in that on a temporal basis he gives them life and strength, awakens within them high ideals, provides for their pleasure and sustenance, and graciously allows them to live for a time in the light of his countenance. God is specially the Saviour of believers in that he has a special call for them, answers their prayers, and provides for their well-being, not only in this life but also in the life which is to come" (Purdy, "Saviour of All Men," 48).

117. Marshall, "For All, for All," 327.

118. Marshall, "Universal Grace and Atonement," 55.

119. Blocher, "Jesus Christ the Man," 565–56.

beneficence that causes him to deliver friend and enemy alike from temporal dangers is that same character of beneficence that he expresses in eternally saving his chosen ones. As MacArthur comments, "In both cases, He is their Savior and there is a saving that He does on their behalf. In this life, all men experience to some degree the protecting, delivering, sustaining power of God. Believers will experience that to the fullest degree for time and for all eternity."[120]

What, then, is the MIV's response to these various handlings of 1 Tim 4:10? In the first place, Ware seems to align very closely with the potential-actual view outlined above when he says, "So, there is a sense in which Christ is savior of unbelievers (i.e., he died for their sin, though they reject his payment on their behalf), yet a special sense in which he is savior of believers (by faith, they receive Christ's payment for their own sin)."[121] Hammett embraces the potential-actual view outright by using the language of "divine provision and human appropriation."[122]

As has often been the case, Shultz's presentation is the most substantive representative of the MIV on this text. He presents five arguments. First, he agrees that "preserver and provider" fit the semantic domain of σωτήρ, as Baugh has shown, but struggles to accept that interpretation because of the exclusively soteriological use of σωτήρ in the Pastorals.[123] As has been demonstrated above, however, σωτήρ is used non-soteriologically in both the Septuagint and in the extrabiblical Greek of Paul's day, and its cognates are so used throughout the New Testament, including in Pauline usage. Second, he claims that Paul is "repeating the same thought he introduced in 1 Timothy 2:3–6: the gospel is for all people without exception."[124] He follows this with a citation of Mounce, who argues that 4:10 "closely parallels" 1 Tim 2:3–4 "in its description of God as Savior and as making the offer of salvation to all."[125] However, this argument relies upon interpreting 2:3–6 in a manner that has been demonstrated above to be unbiblical. Though the particularist believes "the gospel is for all people without exception" in that we ought to "mak[e] the offer of salvation to all," neither 2:3–6 nor 4:10 speaks a word of the gospel offer to all without exception. Paul's comments in 2:3–6 speak of God's willingness to save all kinds of people and Christ's ransom on behalf of persons of all classes and ethnicities. In 4:10 Paul speaks of the Father's providential kindness to both elect and reprobate alike,

---

120. MacArthur, 1 Timothy, 168.

121. Ware, "Outline," 2. Note that Ware conflates "God," i.e., the Father, with "Christ" as the Savior in view in this passage, and that he imports the atonement, which, as shown above, is not present in the immediate context.

122. Hammett, "Multiple-Intentions View," 153. Also unique to Hammett's contribution is his erroneous claim that John Owen does not discuss 1 Tim 4:10 in his Death of Death; see Owen, Death of Death, 190–92.

123. Shultz, "Defense," 138.

124. Shultz, "Defense," 138.

125. Mounce, Pastoral Epistles, 256.

culminating in the salvation of the elect. Both Shultz and Mounce attempt to make both texts say more than they actually say.

Shultz's third argument is that the potential-actual view fits the soteriological context of the passage, leaning on Marshall's claim that Paul's words "can only refer to spiritual life."[126] Yet this has been challenged above, as there are temporal-eternal cues in the immediately preceding context in verses 7 and 8. Fourth, Shultz argues that reading σωτήρ to refer to common grace would mean that God would have to bestow more (μάλιστα) common grace on believers than unbelievers, which undermines the very notion of common grace. Yet this is not so. The commonality identified by the term "common grace" does not mean that God bestows his kindness on all in equal measure, but rather that he bestows his kindness on friend and enemy alike. It would seem self-evident that a child who grows up in the house of believing parents, of high social standing, and with adequate access to quality educational opportunities can be said to have received more of God's kindness than one who grows up in poverty and never hearing the gospel. As part of the same argument, Shultz, citing Marshall's comment addressed above, goes on to express concern that σωτήρ should be understood in two different ways in the same verse.[127] But once again, the temporal-eternal view does not require God to be a Savior in two totally different senses; rather, the same divine attributes of kindness and goodness express themselves in two different ways depending on the recipient. The distinction is in the beneficiary, not in the benefactor.

Finally, then, Shultz's fifth argument is that God "acts as Savior toward all people, but especially toward believers." That is, "God desires the salvation of all people, and he has provided that salvation for all people in the ransom of Christ, but he acts as Savior toward believers in a much more profound, deeper sense because it is only they who enter a saving relationship with him."[128] Thus, "acting as Savior" toward unbelievers is represented as desiring their salvation. However, such an interpretation strains the language. It is simply not proper to speak of someone as the "savior" of people whom he *desires* to save but whom he does not in fact save. In fact, in God's case, it lies within his power to *act as Savior*—i.e., actually to act to save such persons—and yet he chooses not to so act. Because the MIV redefines the nature of the atonement from an efficacious accomplishment to a potential provision, it must also redefine what it means for God to be a Savior; that is, he is a Savior of men not saved. In point of fact, the language of 1 Tim 4:10 "indicates rather what God actually *is* to men, what they actually receive from Him, than what He reveals Himself as ready and willing to give them."[129] This reveals yet another instance of the MIV's willingness to redefine the nature of the atonement in order to preserve an unnecessary absolutely universal interpretation of "all."

126. Marshall, "Universal Grace and Atonement," 55; Shultz, "Defense," 138.

127. Shultz, "Defense," 139; cf. Marshall, "For All, for All," 327.

128. Shultz, "Defense," 139.

129. Fairbairn, *1 & 2 Timothy and Titus*, 185.

In summary, then, there are at least four interpretations of 1 Tim 4:10 that are consistent with particularism, as described above: the *malista* view, the monotheistic exclusivism view, the providential preservation view, and the temporal-eternal view. While the present author finds it difficult to decide between the final two views and sides tentatively with the temporal-eternal view, it must be noted that all four of these views present fewer exegetical and theological problems, and are all thus more acceptable, than the potential-actual view promoted by the MIV. In a real sense, for the purposes of this project, one does not need to decide which of the four particularist interpretations he finds most compelling; he needs only to see that any of them are more biblically preferable than the MIV's interpretation. When rightly divided, 1 Tim 4:10 provides no support for a universal intention in the atonement.[130]

130. Shultz goes on to discuss two other texts that use the word "all," in support of a universal intention in the atonement: Titus 2:11 and Heb 2:9. Space limitations prevent a full refutation of each. However, comments on Titus 2:11 may be found in the discussion of 1 Tim 2:3–6. Like 1 Timothy 2, Titus speaks of various classes of people (e.g., older men, young women, bondslaves, etc.), and then uses πᾶσιν ἀνθρώποις (Titus 2:11) to mean "all *kinds* of men," that is, people in every station of life as outlined in the previous verses. A similar phenomenon is at play in Heb 2:9, which, though it speaks of Jesus tasting death "for everyone," immediately follows with a statement of the atonement's efficacy: it is that which does not fail to bring "many sons to glory" (Heb 2:10). Besides this, the rest of the paragraph identifies this "everyone" with several particularizing designations: "brethren" (2:11–12), "the children whom God has given Me" (2:13; cf. John 17:2, 6, 9, 20, 24), and "the descendant of Abraham" (2:16), the believer (cf. Gal 3:9), rather than the seed of Adam. Neither text supports a universal intention in the atonement.

11

Christ's Death for the "World"

IN ADDITION TO THOSE texts that speak of Christ's death on behalf of "all," a second set of texts set forth in support of a universal intention in the atonement speak of the atonement on behalf of the "world," or the "whole world." Because the term "world" is such a strikingly universal designation, it is argued, to say that Christ "takes away the sin of the world" (John 1:29), or that the atonement is the result of the love of God for the world (John 3:16), or that Christ is "the propitiation for our sins; and not for ours only, but also for those of the whole world" (1 John 2:2) is to say that that Christ has paid for the sins of all people without exception who have ever lived in the world. These "world" texts, then, become a key argument for proponents of the MIV seeking to demonstrate a universal intention in the atonement.

However, as was shown with the term "all," "world" is a term that is not self-interpreting; its meaning cannot simply be presupposed. Just as "all" can mean all without distinction, and thus does not necessarily refer to all people without exception, so also can the reference to the "world" be taken in numerous different senses—not only in an absolutely universal sense as referring to all people who have ever lived in the world, but also, for example, to refer to a large subset of people within the world at a given time, or to a select group of people scattered throughout the whole world, or to signify the inclusion of Gentiles where some sort of Jewish exclusivism would have been expected. In this chapter, it will be demonstrated that the two strongest "world" texts employed by the MIV, John 3:16 and 1 John 2:2, when properly interpreted according to their respective contexts, do not support a universal intention in the atonement, but rather harmonize with the biblical picture of the design and nature of a particular atonement as presented in part 2.

κόσμος in Johannine Literature

The word "world" translates the Greek term κόσμος, which is an overwhelmingly Johannine term. Used 186 times in the New Testament, 105 occurrences of κόσμος (56 percent) appear in the Gospel of John (78), the Johannine Epistles (24), and Revelation

(3),[1] compared to nine occurrences in Matthew, three in Mark, three in Luke, one in Acts, 47 in the Pauline Epistles, and 19 in the General Epistles.[2] Much of the discussion of texts concerning Christ's atonement for the "world" centers on the proper meaning of the term κόσμος, especially as it appears in Johannine literature.

At least seven categories of meaning for the term κόσμος emerge from a survey of John's writings.[3]

1. In its most basic sense, the word denotes orderliness, and hence the cosmic universe is that which God has brought into order as opposed to chaos.[4] The term "cosmetic" thus signifies adornment, beautifying the human face, for example, by bringing orderliness (cf. κόσμος in 1 Pet 3:3).[5] Therefore, it is recognized that one of the most common meanings for κόσμος is the whole created order, or the universe at large. This is the world that "was made through" Christ (John 1:10), that is, all things that have come into being (John 1:3).

2. A second category is perhaps a subset of the first; namely, κόσμος refers to this world, the inhabitable earth, a designation that is not surprising since for mankind this earth, humanity's habitation, is the most significant aspect of the whole created order.[6] This is how the term is used in its first occurrence in John 1:10, where John tells us that Jesus "was in the world," that is, walking and living and conversing with others upon the earth.[7]

3. Related to this, then, thirdly, κόσμος may also denote every individual who has ever lived upon the earth, or all without exception, such as in Rom 3:19, where Paul says that the function of the law is "that every mouth may be closed and all the world may become accountable to God."[8]

4. A fourth category of meaning for κόσμος identifies a subset of mankind in the world—not all people without exception, but simply a reference to an indistinct large number of people.[9] Hence the Pharisees' exasperated comment concerning Jesus that "the world has gone after Him" (John 12:19), which surely could not have meant all people who had ever lived in the world, nor even all the people

1. Harmon, "For the Glory of the Father," 281. A disputed reference is in Matt 13:35, which is supported by the majority of manuscripts. See Carson, "Matthew," 323–24.

2. Morris, *John*, 111. Morris excludes the reference in Matt 13:35 and so lists 185 total occurrences, with eight in Matthew.

3. Morris's caveat is worth repeating: "The boundaries between the classifications are not hard-and-fast. John moves freely from one to another, or even uses the term in ways that may evoke more than one of its possible meanings" (Morris, *John*, 113).

4. BDAG, 561.

5. Morris, *John*, 111.

6. Morris, *John*, 111–12.

7. E.g., Owen, *Death of Death*, 306.

8. Moo, *Romans*, 205–6.

9. Morris, *John*, 112.

alive in the world at that time (for they themselves had not "gone after" Jesus), but meant rather a large group of the community in Israel (cf. John 7:4; 18:20).

5. A fifth category designates a subset of mankind particularly as they are conceived as hostile to God.[10] Thus κόσμος takes on a particularly negative connotation, having become a world whose orderliness and beauty has been corrupted because of sin. The world, in this sense, hates the disciples of Christ because the world hated Christ (John 15:18–19). In this sense, the world is distinct from Christ's people and thus cannot include them (cf. also John 17:9). Indeed, the world cannot know the children of God because it did not know the Son of God (1 John 3:1).[11]

6. Related to this, a sixth category of meaning for κόσμος includes what is known as the world system, a reference to the powers of darkness in opposition to Christ (1 John 2:15–17; 4:5) under the rule of Satan (1 John 5:19), who is called "the ruler of this world" (John 12:31; 14:30; 16:11).[12]

7. A seventh use of κόσμος designates the Gentile world in contrast to the Jewish people. Because the Jews of Jesus' day regarded the Gentiles as ceremonially unclean in accordance with the stipulations of the Mosaic Covenant, and because they regarded themselves as the special people of God's own possession (cf. Deut 7:6), the coming Messiah's ministry to the Gentiles was a scandal to many (see even Gal 2:11–14). Thus, the New Testament emphasizes that Jesus is not merely the Savior of the Jews, but of the world of the Gentiles as well—something that surprised Nicodemus, the teacher of Israel (3:16–17; cf. 3:9–10), the Samaritans, once considered unclean (John 4:40–42), and the elitist false teachers of Ephesus (1 John 2:1–2). Related to this, κόσμος also seems at times to denote an indistinct number of people spread out through different climes of the world, and particularly believers throughout the world (Rom 1:8; Col 1:6).

The above categories do not by any means represent an exhaustive classification of the varied meanings of κόσμος. In fact, because of the term's importance for the question of the extent of the atonement, many exegetes commenting on this issue

10. Herman Sasse designates the world in this sense as "the sum of the divine creation which has been shattered by the fall, which stands under the judgment of God, and in which Jesus Christ appears as the Redeemer" (Sasse, "κόσμος," *TDNT*, 3:894).

11. See Carson, who argues, notably, "Although some have argued that for John the word *kosmos* ('world') sometimes has positive overtones ('God so loved the world', 3:16), sometimes neutral overtones (as here; cf. also 21:24–25, where the 'world' is simply a big place that can hold a lot of books), and frequently negative overtones ('the world did not recognize him', 1:10), closer inspection shows that although a handful of passages preserve a neutral emphasis the vast majority are decidedly negative. There are no unambiguously positive occurrences. The 'world', or frequently 'this world' (e.g., 8:23; 9:39; 11:9; 18:36), is not the universe, but the created order (especially of human beings and human affairs) in rebellion against its Maker (e.g., 1:10; 7:7; 14:17, 22, 27, 30; 15:18–19; 16:8, 20, 33; 17:6, 9, 14)" (Carson, *John*, 122–23).

12. Barnes, *Atonement Matters*, 198.

provide their own taxonomy of meanings for κόσμος. To briefly survey a representative sample, consider that Morris includes four categories: (1) the universe at large, (2) this world, i.e., the earth, (3) the majority of people, or a large number of people, and (4) people in opposition to Christ;[13] Harmon has three categories: (1) the stage of God's redemptive work through Christ, (2) the scope of God's redemptive work, which he argues to be all without distinction, and (3) a sharp distinction between God's people and the world;[14] Barnes lists five categories: (1) mankind, or the totality of mankind in a general way, (2) mankind as hostile to God, (3) the world system that opposes God and is the realm of Satan's reign, (4) earth, the physical habitation of man, and (5) that which is from the earth, i.e., what is material, with no moral significance;[15] Pink provides seven categories: (1) the universe as a whole, (2) the earth, (3) the world system, (4) the whole human race, (5) humanity minus believers, (6) Gentiles in contrast from Jews, and (7) believers only;[16] and Owen offers five general uses: (1) the world containing all else, (2) the world contained, that is, people in the world, (3) the world corrupted, (4) a worldly estate or condition of men or things, and (5) the world accursed.[17]

The foregoing analysis serves to demonstrate the flexibility of the term κόσμος, especially as it occurs in its Johannine contexts, and that it is therefore illegitimately simplistic "to assert, as some advocates of 'universal atonement' do, that 'world means world' as if it were self-evident that κόσμος refers to all without exception rather than all without distinction."[18] There are many instances in which κόσμος cannot signify all without exception, that is, every person who has ever lived in the world, or even every person alive in the world at the time. In John 1:10, John tells us that "the world did not know Him," which cannot mean that no one throughout the history of the world knew Jesus in a saving manner, or else none would be saved, and just two verses later John speaks of those who received him and believed in his name (1:12). When Jesus says that he speaks the things that he has heard from the Father "to the world" (8:26), he does not mean all without exception, but rather those he meets and speaks with as he ministers openly in Israel. When John says that "the whole world lies in the power of the evil one" (1 John 5:19), he does not intend to include himself and other believers, who by their faith in the Son of God overcome the world (cf. 15:4), and whom the evil one does not touch (5:18). Thus even the strikingly universal designation "whole world" indicates a number less than all without exception. Therefore, naked appeals to the so-called plain meaning of "world" to argue for absolute universality simply

13. Morris, *John*, 111–13.

14. Harmon, "For the Glory of the Father," 282–87.

15. Barnes, *Atonement Matters*, 197–98.

16. Pink, *Sovereignty of God*, 253–54.

17. Owen, *Death of Death*, 303–7.

18. Harmon, "For the Glory of the Father," 287. Harmon lists Miethe as an example: Miethe, "Universal Power of the Atonement," 71–96.

will not satisfy the demand of faithful biblical exegesis. The best meaning for κόσμος must be determined by the context of the passage in question. When the context is thus allowed to speak, it is discovered that Scripture does not anywhere teach that Jesus has atoned for the sins of all without exception. Rather, the context indicates that another of the plausible renderings for κόσμος fits better.

The MIV and κόσμος

Before moving directly to address the texts themselves, a comment is necessary concerning Shultz's own handling of the use of κόσμος in Johannine literature. While he begins by acknowledging that "world" does not always refer to all without exception, he insists that sometimes it does, and therefore a genuinely universal meaning ought not to be dismissed—a notion with which no particularist would disagree.[19] He then argues that John uses κόσμος in three ways, namely, to refer to (1) the totality of creation, (2) the world of humanity, by which he likely means humanity considered generally, and (3) the world of humanity that is "in opposition to God, that is lost and separated from its creator."[20] He offers no defense of this paradigm aside from a citation of (a) Carson stating his unique position on the overwhelmingly negative connotations of κόσμος and (b) a 2006 ETS paper on the subject,[21] and he engages in no discussion of any other taxonomy of the Johannine uses of κόσμος.

Then, Shultz makes the following claim: "There is no place in the Gospel of John where the term *kosmos* is used to refer to a limited group of people, such as believers or the elect, or Gentiles as opposed to Jews."[22] This is a striking claim, considering the many examples offered above. If κόσμος never refers to a limited group of people, ought we to believe that Jesus spoke to all people without exception (John 8:26) or that every individual in Israel followed after Jesus (John 12:19)? Regrettably, such a claim seems to be baseless.[23] However, citing Owen, who sees κόσμος as sometimes identifying the elect (e.g., John 3:16; 4:42; 6:51), Shedd, who interprets κόσμος as sometimes referring

19. Shultz, "Defense," 107.

20. Shultz, "Defense," 107.

21. Carson, *John*, 122–23; Harris, "Out-of-This-World Experience," 7–10.

22. Shultz, "Defense," 107–8.

23. Pink's comments serve as an apt rebuke: "'World means *world*'. True, but we have shown that 'the world' does not [always] mean the whole human family. The fact is that 'the world' is used in a *general* way. When the brethren of Christ said, 'Shew Thyself to *the world*' (John 7:4), did they mean 'shew Thyself to *all mankind*'? When the Pharisees said, 'Behold, *the world* is gone after Him' (John 12:19), did they mean that '*all the human family*' were flocking after Him? When the apostle wrote, 'Your faith is spoken of throughout *the whole world*' (Rom. 1:8), did he mean that the faith of the saints at Rome was the subject of conversation by every man, woman, and child on the earth? When Rev. 13:3 informs us that '*all the world* wondered after the beast', are we to understand that there will be no exceptions? What of the godly Jewish Remnant, who will be slain (Rev. 20:4) rather than submit? These, and other passages which might be quoted, show that the term 'world' often has a *relative* rather than an *absolute* force" (Pink, *Sovereignty of God*, 203, emphases original).

to believers (e.g., John 6:33, 51), and Berkhof, who reads κόσμος as distinguishing the nations from Israel in John 1:29; 6:33; and 6:51, Shultz dismisses all of these claims by an appeal to Marshall, who, he says, "offers a good response to these interpretations." Marshall claims, "It is not possible to limit 'world' to mean 'all without distinction but not all without exception'; the plain sense of the sayings is that salvation is available for all and is offered to all and can be received by those who believe."[24] This, however, is not an exegetical argument; it is merely an assertion. It is by no means self-evident that "the plain sense of the sayings" are as Marshall claims. It is difficult to understand how Shultz can regard this as a good response to particularist claims when neither he nor Marshall offers any engagement of particularist exegesis on this point.[25]

Shultz goes on to briefly discuss the following texts: John 1:29; 4:42, 6:33; 6:51; and 12:47. He asserts that in each the universality of κόσμος makes it unmistakable that Jesus' atoning death is unlimited in extent.[26] For John 1:29, Shultz offers no argumentation aside from a quotation of Bruce, who himself employs the language of "all without distinction" rather than "all without exception." He says, "The 'world' embraces all without distinction of race, religion, or culture."[27] This is exactly right, and perfectly at home with a particularist understanding of John 1:29. Jesus is not merely a parochial Savior; the Messiah has come not only for the Jews but also for the Gentiles. But that he takes away the sins of Gentiles as well as Jews does not mean that he takes away the sins of *all* Gentiles and Jews without exception. Such would be to mistake an indefinite expression for a universal expression, as if the comment that "Christ died for the ungodly" (Rom 5:6) meant that Christ died for *all* the ungodly without exception. Further, to declare Christ to be "the Lamb of God who *takes away the sin of the world*" (John 1:29) is to attribute to him an *efficacious* expiatory atonement. If Christ actually takes away the sin of the "world," and the "world" must be understood to refer to all without exception, we must embrace universal final salvation. The only way to avoid such a conclusion is to denigrate the efficacy of the atonement by tampering with the language of John 1:29. In such a case, "takes away" must be redefined to mean potentially taking away or bringing the possibility of taking away. Not only does such a construct need to be imported into the text (for it is not what the text says), but it stands in contradiction to the unified teaching of Scripture concerning the definite intent and actual efficacy of the Christ's atonement.[28] The same interpretive move is made concerning John 6:33 and 6:51, where Christ's claim

24. Marshall, "For All, for All," 338.

25. This is an example of the stalemate that often occurs in the context of this debate, for apart from the biblical framework of the design and nature of the atonement as presented in part 2, there is little basis from which to argue that "all" means "all without exception" versus "all without distinction" aside from question-begging assertions about the "plain meaning" of disputed terms.

26. Shultz, "Defense," 108–10.

27. Bruce, *Gospel of John*, 53.

28. See chapter 5 on the salvific intention and effect of the atonement. Also see chapter 6 on the nature of the atonement as expiatory sacrifice.

that he is the bread of God from heaven who "*gives* life to the world" is redefined as "he has come to *offer* life to all people who are lost."[29] While particularists agree that Jesus offers eternal life to all without exception, this text does not speak of what he *offers* but of what he *gives*. But if Jesus *gives* eternal life to all without exception, we cannot avoid universal final salvation. Thus, the MIV modifies the nature of the atonement from life that is *given* to life that is merely *offered*.[30]

The same is true for John 4:42. Though Shultz acknowledges that the universal note sounded in this passage is to indicate that Christ is not only the Savior of Jews but also of Gentiles, he seems not to understand that he makes the case for all without distinction rather than all without exception. While Jesus is the Savior of Jews and Gentiles alike, Jesus is in fact not the Savior of all people without exception, for not all people without exception are saved. As Owen comments memorably, "A Saviour of men not saved is strange,"[31] a quip that makes the point with rhetorical power: we strain the meaning of the term "Savior" when we say that Christ is the Savior of those who are not finally saved from sin, death, and judgment. Rather, John 4:42 makes the point that Koester makes, whom Shultz quotes for support, namely, that this comment signifies that "Jesus transcended national boundaries; . . . he was a figure of universal significance."[32] Such a claim is happily affirmed by particularists, as it provides an explanation for why one might interpret κόσμος to refer to people throughout the whole world, Jew and Gentile alike, as opposed to every person without exception.[33]

After this specious argumentation, Shultz concludes with an assertion of his thesis: Jesus died "as an atoning sacrifice that paid for the sins of all people so that all people might be saved."[34] Responding to Grudem's notion that "world" refers to

---

29. Shultz, "Defense," 109.

30. The same is the case with John 6:51, which says, "If anyone eats of this bread, he will live forever; and the bread also which I will give *for the life of the world* is My flesh." Shultz modifies this by saying, "He means that he gives his life (i.e., he dies) so that all people *might* have life" (Shultz, "Defense," 110, emphasis added). But Jesus' words include no such uncertainty. In laying down his life, Jesus aims at the eternal life of the world. Unless he fails of his intention, "the world," whoever they are, must receive the eternal life Jesus died to give them. "The world" in this text must refer to those who actually receive eternal life, i.e., the elect who eventually believe. They are called "the world" to emphasize that the Messiah's salvation is not limited to the Jews but is for those throughout the whole world. This is also true for Shultz's handling of John 12:47, in which Jesus' comment that he has come to "save the world" is reinterpreted as "Jesus makes salvation *available* to all people" (Shultz, "Defense," 110). For further discussion on both John 6:51 and 12:47, see "The Salvific Intent of the Atonement" in chapter 5.

31. Owen, *Death of Death*, 327.

32. Koester, "Savior of the World," 668.

33. Harmon reasons, "In arguing that the extent of the atonement is 'universal,' frequent appeal is made to the Johannine literature. This is quite understandable as there are a number of texts that emphasize the universal scope of God's redemptive work through Christ. However, when understood within the larger context of John's writings, these texts are best understood as emphasizing that the atonement extends beyond Jews to include people from every tribe and tongue" (Harmon, "For the Glory of the Father," 281).

34. Shultz, "Defense," 110.

sinners in general rather than every sinner who ever lived, Shultz asserts, "There is no warrant in these verses for making a distinction between sinners in general and all sinners, other than a preconceived notion of particular redemption."[35] Such comments are representative of the whole of Shultz's attempt to handle the Johannine use of κόσμος. There has been no exegesis, only assertions about the "clear" meaning of texts, supported only with other assertions from commentators who happen to agree with Shultz's conclusions. Sadly, this marks much of the MIV's approach to textual interpretation.[36] But it must be said that making assertions about the plain meaning of Scripture, supported only by commentators who happen to agree, is not exegesis. As such, it exposes the MIV's exegetical case as a tenuous foundation, unable to bear the weight of its proponents' claims.

John 3:16–17

Having outlined the numerous ways in which the apostle John employs the term κόσμος, we may now come to its particular occurrence in John 3:16–17. Jesus says, "For in this way [οὕτως γὰρ] God loved the world [ἠγάπησεν ὁ θεὸς τὸν κόσμον], that [ὥστε] he gave his only begotten Son, that [ἵνα] everyone believing in him [πᾶς ὁ πιστεύων εἰς αὐτὸν] shall not perish, but have eternal life. For God did not send the Son into the world to judge the world, but that the world might be saved [ἵνα σωθῇ ὁ κόσμος] through him."[37]

The principal matter in question is the identity of the "world." Who is this "world" that the Father loved? Those who see a universal intention in the atonement find support for their view by seeing an absolutely universal referent of "world." God's love for the world reveals that "God's saving will" is "for all people without distinction or exception."[38] According to proponents of the MIV, the text "so clearly expresses" an absolute universality—it is "so plain" that all without exception are intended—that minimal argumentation is necessary.[39] However, it is my contention

35. Shultz, "Defense," 110n40.

36. Hammett's argument on John 3:16 reduces to the following: "Numerous commentators on the Gospel of John think 'world' refers to 'humanity' and the verses containing 'world' sound a strong 'universal note'" (Hammett, "Multiple-Intentions View," 150). But the opinions of commentators do not decide the meaning of biblical texts. One must demonstrate from the text itself, rather than from assertions of commentators, that one's view makes the best sense of the text. Then, as if to illustrate his methodology, he misquotes a comment from Bruce to the effect that "world" in John 3:16 means Christ was given "for all, without distinction or exception." What Bruce actually says is, "he was given so that all, without distinction or exception, *who repose their faith on him* . . . might be rescued from destruction and blessed with the life that is life indeed" (Bruce, *Gospel of John*, 89–90, emphasis added). Saying, "Everyone without exception *who believes* will be saved" is consistent with particularism, and is entirely different from saying, "Everyone without exception will be saved."

37. Author's translation.

38. Shultz, "Defense," 111.

39. Shultz, "Defense," 111, 112.

that both the context of the passage as well as the rest of the Scripture's teaching concerning the atonement demand that we reject the MIV's handling of John 3:16.

In the first place, one must consider the nature of the love with which God has so loved the world. In simplest terms, the verb ἀγαπάω signifies to desire and act for the benefit of the beloved. Jesus' comments in Luke 6:35 illustrate this definition, as the command to "love your enemies" is followed with the appositional phrase "and do good." Plainly, then, to love one's enemies is to do good to them, to benefit them. J. I. Packer, commenting on the love of God signified by ἀγαπάω, writes, "It is a purpose of doing good to others," and "[it] takes the initiative in giving help where help is required, and finds its joy in bringing others benefit."[40] Doing good and bringing benefit is of paramount importance. Indeed, Packer says, such love is "measured . . . by what of its own it gives, for the fulfilling of its purpose."[41] In other words, such love does not consist in mere fond affection or an impotent wish to see the beloved benefited. Instead, divine love consists in the determinative act of God's will to purpose to accomplish the benefit of his beloved. As Carson comments, "The Greek construction behind *so loved that he gave his one and only Son* (*houtōs* plus *hōste* plus the indicative instead of the infinitive) emphasizes the intensity of the love, and insists that the envisaged consequence really did ensue."[42] That is, it is an unmistakable mark of this divine love that its "envisaged consequence"—its intended aim or determined purpose—is brought to fruition. Almighty God is not a frustrated lover. His love is always efficacious.

One must ask, then: In John 3:16, what is the benefit God intends to accomplish for his beloved "world" by so loving them in this way? The benefit he purposes (ἵνα) as the effect of his love is that all who believe in the Son (πᾶς ὁ πιστεύων εἰς αὐτὸν) would not die in their sins (μὴ ἀπόληται) but rather be saved unto everlasting life (ἀλλ' ἔχῃ ζωὴν αἰώνιον).[43] The elaborative comment in verse 17 serves only to emphasize this point: the Father sent the Son in order to save the world (ἵνα σωθῇ ὁ κόσμος) through him.[44] Thus, the intended benefit that God purposes to accomplish by his love of the

40. Packer, "Love of God: Universal or Particular?," 278.

41. Packer, "Love of God: Universal or Particular?," 278.

42. Carson, *John*, 204.

43. Carson writes, "His ultimate purpose is the salvation of those in the world who believe in him" (Carson, *John*, 206).

44. The means by which he accomplishes this purpose is the giving of his Son over to death (ἔδωκεν; cf. παρέδωκεν, Rom 8:32) in order to accomplish atonement. Note that the subjunctive introduces no uncertainty into this action. In fact, the subjunctive in a ἵνα clause commonly expresses the purpose of an action that efficaciously achieves its intended result. As Wallace says, "We must not suppose that this use of the subjunctive necessarily implies any doubt about the fulfillment of the verbal action on the part of the speaker. . . . Not only is ἵνα used for result in the NT, but also for purpose-result. That is, it indicates *both the intention and its sure accomplishment*. . . . In other words, the NT writers employ the language to reflect their theology: what God purposes is what happens and, consequently, ἵνα is used to express both the divine purpose and the result" (Wallace, *Greek Grammar beyond the Basics*, 472, 473).

world in John 3:16 is nothing other than salvation itself. Given that divine love must accomplish its purpose, we must conclude that none are objects of this divine love but those who finally receive its intended, purposed benefit of salvation itself, namely, all the believing ones (πᾶς ὁ πιστεύων), that is, the elect alone.[45] The "world," then, in John 3:16 does not refer to all without exception; in fact, it refers to the elect alone.

Why, then, does Jesus use the universalistic term "world" if those he intended to describe are none other than the elect? The answer resides in the context, for in this discourse upon God's salvation of sinners Jesus is speaking with Nicodemus, "a man of the Pharisees" and "a ruler of the Jews" (John 3:1). Given the prevailing Jewish particularism of his day, Nicodemus believed that the saving mercies of God were confined to his own nation.[46] As Morris comments, "The Jew was ready enough to think of God as loving Israel, but no passage appears to be cited in which any Jewish writer maintains that God loved the world."[47] As Jesus proclaims the gospel of salvation to "*the* teacher of Israel" (John 3:10), he declares that God's love extends not only to the nation of Israel, but also to men and women throughout the entire world, without distinction. Gentiles, as well as Jews, who believe in Christ for salvation will not perish but have eternal life.[48] Believers are often the only ones intended by universalistic language, such as when the Spirit is said to be poured forth on "all mankind" (Acts 2:17)—which can only refer to those in whom the Spirit dwells, i.e., elect believers alone—or when they are called "all the families of the earth" (Gen 12:3) or "all nations" (Gal 3:8). Such is also the sense of κόσμος in John 4:42; 6:33; 6:51; and 12:47.

There is a second reason why Jesus uses κόσμος in John 3:16. Not only is he contradicting Nicodemus's Jewish particularism, insisting that the gospel is for all

45. Owen comments, ". . . seeing all love in God is but *velle alicui bonum*, to will good to them that are beloved, *they* certainly are the object of his love to whom he intends that good which is the issue and effect of that love; but now the issue of this love or good intended, being *not perishing*, and *obtaining eternal life* through Christ, happens alone to, and is bestowed on, only elect believers: therefore, they certainly are the object of this love, and they alone" (Owen, *Death of Death*, 324, emphases original). John Murray thus concludes, "There is, after all, nothing in this text [John 3:16] to support what it is frequently supposed to affirm, namely, universal atonement. What it actually says is akin to definite atonement. Something is made infallibly certain and secure—all believers will have eternal life" (Murray, "Atonement and the Free Offer," 80).

46. To substantiate this point, Harmon cites von Schlatter, *Evangelist Johannes*, 48–49. See also Carson, *John*, 205; Köstenberger, *John*, 67–68; MacArthur and Mayhue, eds., *Biblical Doctrine*, 560; Pink, *Sovereignty of God*, 203; and Ryle, *Expository Thoughts on John*, 111.

47. Morris, *John*, 203.

48. Pink adds, "'God so loved the world,' then, signifies, God's love is *international* in its scope. But does this mean that God loves every individual among the Gentiles? Not necessarily, for as we have seen, the term 'world' is general rather than specific, relative rather than absolute" (Pink, *Sovereignty of God*, 203). Harmon provides a helpful summary: "In contrast to the Jewish particularism that characterized many within Israel at the time, Jesus stresses that the scope of God's redemptive purposes extends beyond the Jewish people to incorporate the entire world. This conclusion is reinforced by the larger context. In fact, the next time κόσμος is used after 3:16–19 is in 4:42, where it clearly emphasizes the scope of Jesus' work (see above). So Jesus is emphasizing to this *Jewish* ruler that *whoever* believes, whether Jew or Gentile, has eternal life" (Harmon, "For the Glory of the Father," 284).

peoples without distinction throughout the whole world; he is also commenting on the miserable condition of the objects of his saving love while they remain in their sinful state. As noted above, κόσμος often denotes the corrupt moral character of those living in the world, particularly their hostility to God and the things of God. Hence Carson is correct when he says, "Therefore when John tells us that God loves the world (3:16), far from being an endorsement of the world, it is a testimony to the character of God. God's love is to be admired not because the world is so big but because the world is so *bad*."[49] By calling those whom the Father intends to save by Christ's death "the world," Jesus identifies them as "earthly, lost, miserable, corrupted,"[50] in desperate need of God's loving kindness, which accurately describes even the elect before they repent and trust in Christ.

Now, this is not to say, crassly, that "the world" *means* the "elect." We are not here arguing that "elect" is a proper gloss for of the word κόσμος, as if ἐκλεκτός were its synonym or a cognate of some sort. Rather, it is to say that "elect" is the proper *referent* of the word κόσμος in this context. The *sense* of κόσμος in John 3:16 is "those lost, miserable, corrupt sinners, underserving of God's love and favor, Jews and Gentiles alike, scattered throughout the whole world." That is, Jesus uses the term κόσμος to identify the beneficiaries of his saving work as (a) those lost in sin (i.e., the negative connotation of κόσμος) and (b) Gentiles as well as Jews (i.e., the international connotation of κόσμος). Carson's comment, then, quoted by Shultz, is a mischaracterization of the particularist position: "Clever exegetical devices that make 'the world' a label referring to the elect are not very convincing."[51] Owen explains that he has not set out to prove that "by the *world* is meant the *elect* as such; for though we conceive the persons here designed directly men in and of the world, to be all and only God's elect, yet we do not say that they are here so considered, but rather under another notion, as men scattered over all the world, in themselves subject to misery and sin. . . . [They] materially are [the] elect, though not considered under that formality."[52] That is to say, we ought not merely to substitute the term "elect" when we read the term "world." Jesus' intention was not to comment on whether those of whom he was speaking were elect or reprobate. However, if we were to ask, "Who is this 'world' whom God has so loved? Who are these lost sinners scattered throughout the whole world, Jew and Gentile alike? Are they elect, reprobate, or a

---

49. Carson, *John*, 123, emphasis added. He is also right to observe, "In fact, the 'world' in John's usage comprises no believers at all. Those who come to faith are no longer of this world; they have been chosen out of this world (15:19)" (123). But it must be noted that the "world" is in fact comprised of the *elect*, for the elect, before they come to saving faith, are as much the "world" as any reprobate enemy of the gospel.

50. Owen, *Death of Death*, 328.

51. Carson, *Love of God*, 75; cf. Shultz, "Defense," 111n45. Hammett cites Elwell to the same effect: "There is not one place in the entire NT where 'world' means 'church' or 'the elect'" (Elwell, "Atonement, Extent of," 116). His criticism is answered here.

52. Owen, *Death of Death*, 325–26.

mix of both?," we are shut up to answer that they are the elect alone, for God's purposeful, efficacious love intends their salvation through faith in Christ, and those so loved cannot fail to be saved. And since none but the elect will be saved, the κόσμος of John 3:16 refers to the elect alone.[53]

It must be mentioned, however, that not all particularists agree with this reading of κόσμος in John 3:16. Many particularists are content to interpret "world" as an indefinite expression referring to humanity in general.[54] On the above reading, which regards the "world" to refer to the elect alone, there is a single referent for the object of God's saving actions throughout the verse: "For in this way God loved the world [i.e., the elect who are scattered throughout the world], that He gave His only begotten Son, that everyone believing in Him [i.e., the elect who are brought to faith in Christ] shall not perish, but have eternal life [i.e., the elect escape judgment and are saved]." On the reading that takes "world" to refer to humanity in general, however, there must be at least one another group added to this verse: "For in this way God loved the world [i.e., the totality of fallen humanity, elect and reprobate], that He gave His only begotten Son, that everyone believing in Him [i.e., the elect who are brought to faith in Christ] shall not perish, but have eternal life [i.e., the elect escape judgment and are saved]." In this case, it was God's love for the whole of humanity—elect and reprobate alike—that motivated him to send Christ to die

53. Lightner's objection that "If 'world' means elect only, then it would follow that he 'of the elect' that believeth may be saved and he 'of the elect' that believeth not is condemned (cf. John 3:18)" (Lightner, *The Death Christ Died*, 70) does not in fact follow. In the first place, as has been argued, the particularist's case is not that "world" *means* "elect," so that one might just read "elect" wherever one sees "world." Lightner, then, is arguing with a phantom, as Owen himself noted: ". . . three pretended arguments they bring to disprove that which none went about to prove. . . . So that all those vain flourishes which some men make with these words, by putting the word *elect* in the room of the word *world*, and then coining absurd consequences, are quite beside the business in hand" (Owen, *Death of Death*, 325–26).

Secondly, Lightner's objection assumes that a biblical author never employs κόσμος in different senses in the same context, which is false. It is evident that different senses of the term are used even in its three instances in the single verse of John 1:10: "He was in the world," that is, Jesus was in the inhabitable earth, "and the world was made through Him," that is, the entire created order, the whole universe (cf. John 1:3), "and the world did not know Him," that is, many (but not all) men living upon the earth at that time did not know him, for some did know him, as John says after the following verse (John 1:12–13). So also John 3:17: "For God did not send the Son into the world," that is, into the inhabitable earth, "to judge the world," that is, to judge all people within the world, "but that the world might be saved through Him," which, because God always accomplishes his intentions, refers only to that world of men that will eventually be saved, namely, the elect.

The particularist, then, affirms without hesitation what Lightner says we must reject: "He who believes in Him is not judged; he who does not believe has been judged already" (John 3:18). None of that is at odds with understanding κόσμος to refer to yet-unbelieving elect persons scattered throughout the whole world; nor does it logically lead to proposing the possibility of elect persons being damned. Lightner's objection simply does not follow.

54. So Calvin, "Christ brought life, because the Heavenly Father loves the human race, and wishes that they should not perish" (Calvin, *John*, 123; Carson, *John*, 205); and MacArthur, "He loved the evil, sinful world of fallen humanity. . . . World is a nonspecific term for humanity in a general sense" (MacArthur, *John 1–11*, 115).

as an atonement. But, since they are particularists, they grant that Christ died only for the sins of the believing ones (πᾶς ὁ πιστεύων). Thus, the object of God's love is conceived to be wider than the object of Christ's death.

This position is not the most convincing for several reasons. Particularly, it is difficult to understand how it can be an act of the love of God to *the reprobate* to send Christ into the world to bring eternal life to *all the believing ones*.[55] The reprobate by definition are those who will never believe; indeed, they are those to whom God has chosen never to grant the sovereign gift of saving faith (Eph 2:8; Phil 1:29), for in his inscrutable wisdom he has elected not to save them (Rom 9:21–23; cf. 1 Pet 2:8). How, then, can it be an act of love to those who will never believe to send Christ to accomplish the salvation of only those who will believe? It is to say, "God so loved *all* in such a way that only *some* of them will enjoy the benefits of his love."[56] Given that divine love always secures its design—given that "the measure of love is what it *really gives* to the really needy and undeserving"[57]—how can those who fail to receive salvation be said to be so loved? Further still, it is not only that many who are supposedly thus loved are never granted the faith to believe in Christ. Throughout the history of the world, the Lord of providence has so ordered the circumstances of life such that vast numbers of those whom he is said to love in the sending of Christ never hear one word of Christ. Owen wonders,

> Strange! that the Lord should so love men as to give his only-begotten Son for them, and yet not once by any means signify this love to them, as to innumerable he doth not!—that he should love them, and yet order things so, in his wise dispensation, that this love should be altogether in vain and fruitless!—love them, and yet determine that they shall receive no good by his love, although his love indeed be a willing of the greatest good to them![58]

In other words, what love is it to those who not only never *believe* the gospel, but who, by the providential ordering of God, never even *hear* of the gospel, nor even of the Christ whose coming is supposedly designed to be a signal of God's eminent love for them? This introduces an incongruity that cannot be solved while maintaining that the "world" of John 3:16 extends beyond the elect.

Therefore, the MIV's case for a universal intention in the atonement may not rest at all upon John 3:16–17, for it has been shown that the universality thought to

55. It should be noted that the present author does not intend to deny God's love for the reprobate, for assuredly his love of benevolence and beneficence are over all his works (cf. Ps 145:9; Matt 5:45; Acts 14:17; etc.). What is denied is that the universal love of God is intended here in John 3:16.

56. Paraphrasing Owen, *Death of Death*, 329. Thus, when Shultz summarizes his position on the text by saying, "In John 3:16-17 God is declaring his love towards sinful humanity, and out of this love he sends his Son to die in the place of sinful humanity so that sinful humanity might be saved and have eternal life" (Shultz, "Defense, 111–12), he runs afoul of this problem, for which he has not given an answer.

57. Packer, "Love of God," 286.

58. Owen, *Death of Death*, 328.

be signified by the term κόσμος is not the true sense of this passage. Instead, by the "world," Jesus identifies the objects of God's love to be only those sinners—scattered throughout the entire world, Gentiles as well as Jews—who will eventually be brought to enjoy the fruits of that love, namely, to the salvation God aimed at in sending his Son. Since only the elect will be thus saved by faith in Christ, it is only the elect here indicated by the term "world." Far from presenting a challenge to particular redemption, then, John 3:16–17 serves as further support for it.

1 John 2:2

One of the most hotly debated passages of Scripture as it concerns the extent of the atonement is 1 John 2:1–2, where the apostle John writes to the churches of Asia Minor, "My little children, I am writing these things to you so that you may not sin. And if anyone sins, we have an Advocate with the Father, Jesus Christ the righteous; and He Himself is the propitiation for our sins; and not for ours only, but also for those of the whole world."[59] John writes to the churches in order that his instruction might keep them from sinning (2:1a), for the one who knows Christ keeps his commandments (1:6–7; 2:3–6). While genuine Christians do not make a practice of sinning (3:4, 8–9), it is nevertheless inevitable that believers engage in instances of sin in this life (1:8, 10). In the case of those believers who are troubled by their own sinfulness, John desires to encourage them by pointing to Christ's present priestly ministry in heaven on their behalf: he is their advocate with the Father, the righteous one who pleads for the unrighteous (2:1b), on the basis of his perfectly sufficient propitiation accomplished on their behalf (2:2a). John then encourages these believers by saying that Christ is not the propitiation for their sins only, but also the propitiation for the sins of the whole world (2:2b). That is, a statement concerning the *nature* of the atonement (it is a work of propitiation) is followed by a statement concerning the *extent* of the atonement (it is for the whole world). Both the meaning of the atonement as a propitiation as well as the identity of the "whole world"—especially in contrast to "our" and "ours"—lie at the heart of this verse's contribution to the debate on the extent of the atonement.

In the first place, the reader is right to interpret "our sins" to refer to the sins of believers, for the "our" of verse 2 is also the "we" who have an advocate with the Father in verse 1, whom John also calls "My little children." As a result of this, however, many non-particularist interpreters see the contrast between "ours only" and the "whole world" and assume that the way in which the "whole world" stands in opposition to "ours" is that "our sins" refers to the sins of believers and "those of the whole world" refers to the sins of unbelievers.[60] This consideration is strengthened by the fact that

59. Portions of this section are adapted from the author's contributions to MacArthur and Mayhue, eds., *Biblical Doctrine*, 561–62.

60. Shultz is representative when he says, "In stating that the Son has propitiated the sins of the whole world, John emphasizes that Christ's propitiation for sin is not only for believers (or the elect),

κόσμος often refers to the world in opposition to Christ, as outlined above. Thus, John seems to be saying that Jesus is the propitiation for the sins of believers, but not for believers only, but also for the sins of the entire unbelieving world. That is, Jesus atones for the sins of the elect and reprobate alike, all people without exception.

While intuitive on a superficial level, such a universalistic interpretation immediately presents the interpreter with a challenge. If Christ is the propitiation for the sins of all without exception, it must necessarily follow that all without exception must finally be saved. That is because the meaning of the term ἱλασμός is to efficaciously satisfy God's wrath against sin.[61] For those for whom Christ is a propitiation, God's holy anger against their sin has been extinguished. If the wrath of God breaks over the head of a sinner in eternal judgment, that means God's wrath was *not* satisfied by a propitiation for that sinner. This is manifestly not the case for all without exception. Not all will finally be saved; there will be some who will have the wrath of God against their sins poured on upon them in hell (Matt 7:13; 25:46; 2 Thess 1:9; Rev 21:8). Therefore, Christ has not been the propitiation for the sins of all without exception.

At this point, the interpreter faces two options. First, one might interpret the *nature* (or substance) of the atonement in light of its *extent* (or scope). That is to say, one might insist that the "whole world" means all without exception, and, in a corresponding interpretive move, modify the nature of the atonement by redefining the term "propitiation" to mean a potential propitiation.[62] The death of Christ is "sufficient to deal with the sins of the whole world, but . . . his sacrifice does not become effective until people believe in him."[63] That is, sins are *not* "dealt with" by the death of Christ per se, for Christ's atonement is *ineffective* until the sinner believes.[64]

---

but also for the sins of all people, elect and nonelect" (Shultz, "Defense," 116).

61. Shultz argues explicitly that a universal payment for sin need not entail universalism (Shultz, "Defense," 151–59). However, his argumentation has been refuted in chapters 6 and 7. For a biblical defense specifically of the above definition of propitiation, see chapter 6, pages 102–7. Owen offers a helpful summary: propitiation is "that which was done or typically effected by the mercy-seat—namely, to appease, pacify, and reconcile God in respect of aversation of sin. . . . [It is] to turn away anger by an atonement. . . . that whereby the law is covered, God appeased and reconciled, sin expiated, and the sinner pardoned; whence pardon, and remission of sin is so often placed as the product and fruit of his blood-shedding, whereby he was a 'propitiation,' Matt. xxvi. 28; Eph. i. 7; Col. i. 14; Heb. ix. 22; Rom. iii. 25, v. 9; 1 John i. 7; 1 Pet i. 2; Rev. i. 5" (Owen, *Death of Death*, 334).

62. Donald Lake, whom Shultz cites with approbation, writes that Christ's atonement has a "universal potentiality" (Lake, "He Died for All," 39). Shultz speaks of sins made "forgivable on the basis of the atonement" (Shultz, "Defense," 116–17), but this is not what "propitiation" means. If Christ's death only makes sins forgivable, what then actually forgives sins? The answer seems to be that the sinner's believing is the decisive agent in obtaining the forgiveness made available by Christ's death. According to Scripture, however, forgiveness is not found in the sinner's faith but in the Savior's blood (Eph 1:7).

63. Kruse, *Letters of John*, 75, also cited by Marshall, "For All, for All," 338, on whom Shultz often leans throughout this section.

64. Hence Wells is correct when he observes, "When Christ is said to do these things [e.g., to propitiate] for 'all' or for 'the whole world' we must either reduce the redemption words, making them say much less than they say, or reduce the universal terms such as 'all' and 'the whole world'" (Wells, *Price for a People*, 52).

However, there are at least three significant problems with such an interpretive move. First, it militates against everything Scripture teaches concerning the efficacious nature of propitiation. As was proven in chapters 6 and 7, not a single occurrence of the כָּפַר and ἱλάσκομαι word groups indicates that the atonement ought to be understood as a potential, provisional, or possible atonement. There is no exegetical basis for interpreting propitiation to be anything other than the perfectly efficacious satisfaction of divine wrath.[65]

A second problem with this interpretation is that it puts asunder what God has joined together, namely, Christ's twofold high priestly work of sacrifice and intercession. That John begins 2:2 with καί necessarily links the present verse, speaking of Christ's propitiation, to the previous verse, which speaks of Christ's advocacy, or present intercession.[66] This demonstrates that the former (propitiation) is the ground and foundation of the latter (advocacy), for it is not as if our advocate pleads the innocence of his people before the Father; he above all knows that they are guilty. He seeks the application of their pardon on the basis of his own atoning work for them.[67] Sinning believers need not despair of their salvation because the advocate who pleads for them before the Father in heaven has accomplished an efficacious propitiation on their behalf, having extinguished in himself the wrath against the very sins they had been committing. It is as if the Son says, "Yes, Father, they have sinned, but I have made satisfaction for their sins by bearing your wrath in their place. Pardon them afresh, in view of a perfectly effective propitiation made on their behalf."[68] However, the universalist position separates this inseparable work of priestly ministry. On the one hand, Christ is the propitiation for all without exception, but he is only the heavenly advocate for believers.[69] Not only does this sever what John links in 1 John 2:1–2, but it also stands at odds with the whole of Scripture's teaching that the work of the high priest is a unified work of sacrifice and intercession. Neither the priests of the Old Covenant nor Christ, the great high priest of the New Covenant, to whom the Old Covenant priests pointed, could ever offer sacrifice on behalf of those for whom they refused to intercede; nor could they intercede for those for whom they had not sacrificed. Contrary to

---

65. Once again, see "Propitiation" in chapter 6, as well as "Efficacious Accomplishment" in chapter 7.

66. Pink, *Sovereignty of God*, 257.

67. Boice, *Epistles of John*, 50. Owen explains, "For them the apostle affirmed that Christ is a *propitiation*; that he might show from whence ariseth, and wherein chiefly, if not only, that advocation for them, which he promiseth as the fountain of their consolation, did consist,—even in a presentation of the atonement made by his blood" (Owen, *Death of Death*, 335).

68. Kruse makes the same argument: "And the idea of the atoning sacrifice here is in juxtaposition with the idea of advocacy. Jesus is the one who speaks to the Father in our defence when we sin. This suggests that he is, as it were, pleading for mercy for sinners, and this in turn suggests that his role as the atoning sacrifice is to secure that mercy; that is, he is, in this context, the propitiation for our sins" (Kruse, *Letters of John*, 73–74); cf. Barnes, *Atonement Matters*, 226.

69. As Shultz says, "The use of *paraclete* here to describe Jesus denotes his intercessory ministry for believers" (Shultz, "Defense," 115n57).

proponents of the MIV, Christ advocates for everyone for whom he is a propitiation, and he is a propitiation for everyone for whom he advocates.[70]

A third problem with modifying the nature of the atonement to fit a universal extent is that it wholly overturns the flow of the apostle John's argument, bringing his point to nothing. As mentioned, John writes to the churches in Asia Minor to comfort sinning believers tempted to discouragement over their failures. True believers need not fear that instances of sin imperil their souls, because Jesus the righteous is their advocate with the Father, who pleads for them on the basis of the propitiation he has made on their behalf. It is as if John says, "Take heart, little children, for though your failings are many, yet Christ has made an end to your wrath by his propitiatory death, and presently pleads the merits of that sufficient sacrifice in the throne room of heaven!" However, if Christ is the propitiation for the sins of all without exception—for the reprobate as well as the elect[71]—what could stop these troubled believers from asking John what difference such propitiation makes, since Christ is the propitiation for those who nevertheless bear the punishment of their sins for eternity? How could the propitiation of Christ be the ground of consolation for discouraged sinning believers, assuring them of their pardon and certain hope of heaven, if Christ is that very same propitiation for millions in hell? Owen aptly asks, "Will that be any refreshment unto me which is common unto me with them that perish eternally? Is not this rather a pumice-stone than a breast of consolation?"[72] Such an interpretation undoes the whole of John's argument at this point in the letter.

The alternative to interpreting the substance of the atonement in light of its scope, and thus interpreting "whole world" to mean all without exception, is to interpret the scope of the atonement in light of its substance. That is to say, one must insist that "propitiation" means the same thing it has meant throughout the rest of Scripture—i.e., the efficacious satisfaction of divine wrath. Given that, those for whom Christ is such a propitiation can never fail to have their sins forgiven through faith in Christ (cf. Rom 3:25); that is to say, they are none other than the elect alone. As a result, the "whole world" must be interpreted to mean the elect of God scattered throughout the whole world, without distinction. The contrast between "our sins" and "the sins of the whole world" is not a contrast between believers and unbelievers, or between elect and reprobate; rather, it is a contrast between the believers to whom John is presently writing and (a) the other believers alive at that time as well as (b) the elect who would

70. See "The Unity of Christ's Priestly Work of Sacrifice and Intercession" in chapter 8.

71. As Shultz says: "It is also important to note that Christ is the propitiation for 'our sins' (believers) *in the same way* that he is the propitiation for 'the sins of the whole world' (unbelievers)" (Shultz, "Defense," 116n59).

72. Owen, *Death of Death*, 333. Hurrion asks, along the same lines, "But what comfort can it be to a poor dejected Christian, oppressed with his guilty fears, to tell him, that Christ loved and died for all men alike; for Cain and Judas, as well as for any others . . . ? . . . Is this the doctrine of the gospel? Is this strong consolation? May not the poor distressed soul say, Miserable comforters are ye all?" (Hurrion, *Particular Redemption*, 76).

become believers as time progressed (cf. John 10:16; 17:20). Such an interpretation of "whole world" not only avoids doing violence to the words, grammar, context, and authorial intent of 1 John 1–2; it makes the best sense of each.

First, interpreting "whole world" to refer to all of God's people scattered throughout the whole world makes good lexical sense. As has been demonstrated above, there are multiple senses in which Scripture uses the term κόσμος, and one of those senses is to denote an indistinct number of people spread throughout the world. This is also the case when the term "whole" is added; there are several instances in which it is unmistakable that "whole world" or its equivalent cannot refer to all without exception. In Rom 1:8, Paul says that the faith of the Roman Christians is being proclaimed ἐν ὅλῳ τῷ κόσμῳ, literally, "in the whole world." However, it is plain that not every individual alive on the earth at the time of Paul's writing had heard of the Romans' faith. In fact, some translators render the phrase, "your faith is being proclaimed *throughout* the whole world," in order to properly give the sense (e.g., NASB, KJV, NKJV, NET). In Col 1:6, Paul says that the gospel is constantly bearing fruit and increasing, καθὼς καὶ ἐν παντὶ τῷ κόσμῳ, "just as in all the world also." But of course, at the time of the writing of the Epistle to the Colossians in the AD 60s, the gospel had not even gone into every area of the world, let alone borne fruit in such, and still less had it borne fruit in every individual in the world without exception. Further, those in whom the gospel *had* borne fruit would have had to be restricted to believers, for the gospel does not bear fruit in those who remain dead in their trespasses. Here, then, is an occurrence of "all the world"—surely an equivalent of "whole world"— which refers exclusively to the elect throughout the world.[73] Later in this very letter, John will say that "the whole world [ὁ κόσμος ὅλος] lies in the power of the evil one" (1 John 5:19), which of course must exclude John himself and the believers to whom he writes, for "the evil one does not touch" the one born of God (5:18; cf. 4:4). Given that the expression itself does not constrain the exegete to interpret "whole world" in every instance as all without exception—indeed, given that it often must refer to a limited number within the world—it is not out of accord with sound principles of lexical analysis to interpret it as "all throughout the world" in 1 John 2:2.

Second, such an interpretation makes good contextual sense, given the nature of the false teaching John wrote to combat in the churches of Asia Minor.[74] Much has been written concerning the identity of the false teachers who had gone out

73. Similar examples can be multiplied where the phrases are conceptual parallels, even though not lexically identical. Luke speaks of Augustus's census of πᾶσαν τὴν οἰκουμένην, "all the world" (Luke 2:1, ESV), which cannot refer to all without exception. John speaks of the hour of testing soon to come upon τῆς οἰκουμένης ὅλης, "the whole world" (Rev 3:10). Yet the Philadelphians were promised to be kept from such a tribulation, and thus were excepted from the number indicated by "the whole world." In Rev 12:9, John speaks of the dragon who deceives τὴν οἰκουμένην ὅλην, "the whole world," but which of course could not include those tribulation saints who remained faithful to the end. See Owen, *Death of Death*, 335.

74. "Anyone seeking to make sense of the Letters of John really needs to have a working hypothesis concerning the events which lie behind them" (Kruse, *Letters of John*, 1).

from the believers (proving that they were never really of the people of God, 2:19), though the only area of agreement seems to be that certain conclusions are beyond our reach.[75] What can be discerned from a mirror reading of 1 John is that these false teachers seemed to have claimed to have such fellowship with God that they were sinless (1:6, 8, 10), while at the same time, somewhat paradoxically, disregarding the commands of Christ (2:3–6), walking in patterns of unrighteousness (3:4–9), and acting in an unloving manner toward other professing Christians (3:10–23; 4:7–8, 11–12; 4:20–5:1). It seems they disregarded the claims of Christ because they did not believe he was the promised Messiah (2:22), nor the Son of God (5:1, 5, 10–12, 20). Still further, they did not believe that Jesus came in the flesh (4:2; cf. 2 John 7). And to punctuate it all, they seemed to have claimed for themselves a kind of anointing from the Holy Spirit that gave them access to secret or deeper knowledge than was available to other Christians (2:20, 27; cf. 4:1).

When one adds all those elements together and surveys the era of the late first century, it is likely that these false teachers were the forerunners to what later became known as Gnosticism.[76] Marked by a radical dualism that regarded matter as inherently evil, this would make sense of their denials of Jesus' coming in the flesh, as well as their indifference to deeds done in the body while claiming a higher spiritual life divorced from behavior. It would also make sense of their claim to exclusive knowledge, or γνῶσις, from which "Gnostic" derives, leading them to arrogantly consider themselves the spiritual elite above the rest.[77] This had an effect on the churches for which John was responsible: "The secessionists' insistence that they had a special anointing of the Spirit (which had led them to go beyond the primitive Christian gospel) made those remaining in the author's community wonder whether they lacked that anointing (2:20, 27) and therefore also lacked the spiritual insight which the secessionists claimed to have."[78]

75. For example, after extensive discussion, Schnackenburg concludes, "The Christology of the antichrists in the Johannine epistles also can no longer be described with certainty or precision" (Schnackenburg, *Johannine Epistles*, 23).

76. Guthrie comments, "If we restrict the term Gnosticism to those developed second-century systems of thought which absorbed within their pagan background certain Christian ideas, and by this means threatened the orthodox church, our epistle would seem to belong to a stage somewhat before these developed Christian Gnostic systems, although there were many straws to indicate the direction of the mental winds which were surrounding the church" (Guthrie, *New Testament Introduction*, 865). Schnackenburg is also helpful: "The heresy which occasioned 1 and 2 John cannot be parallel with any other manifestation of heresy known from that era. Yet it has affinities with more than one such movement. . . . The Christology of the antichrists in the Johannine epistles also can no longer be described with certainty or precision. But it is one example of that pseudo-Christian tendency which manifested itself in Gnosticism and was such a threat to the church" (Schnackenburg, *Johannine Epistles*, 23).

77. "It seems most likely that the opponents were Christians who felt that they had moved beyond the elementary stages of orthodox theology to a new position which called orthodox affirmations into question. . . . Relying on their belief that they were inspired by the Spirit and claiming a direct knowledge of God, they thought they no longer needed Jesus or his teaching" (Marshall, *Epistles of John*, 21).

78. Kruse, *Letters of John*, 16. MacArthur adds, "Since they viewed themselves as the spiritual

Consider the implications this has for the discussion at hand. John was writing to believers who were being harassed by false teachers who had recently seceded from their ranks, plying the heresies of an incipient proto-Gnosticism, which included claims of sinless perfectionism and the notion that the key to true spirituality lay in a secret knowledge possessed only by the elite. Therefore, as John encourages these believers, who are tempted to despair because they find themselves not to be sinless as the false teachers claim to be, when he writes concerning the extent of Christ's atoning work, he repudiates all vestiges of exclusivism and speaks of the Savior's accomplishment in the most universalistic of terms. Jesus is not the propitiation for "our" sins only—whether the sins of the proto-Gnostic elites rather than the sins of common Christians like them, whether the sins of the churches in Asia Minor rather than the sins of believers scattered throughout the whole world, or whether the sins of the believers alive in that day rather than the sins of those who would eventually come to faith in Christ. No, Jesus is the propitiation for the sins of God's elect people scattered throughout the entire world, in all times and in all places.[79] Thus, the reason for universalistic language with respect to the atonement is not to indicate that Christ died for all without exception, but rather that he died for all without distinction, all

---

elite, who alone had true spiritual knowledge, Gnostics scorned the unenlightened ones bereft of such knowledge" (MacArthur, *1–3 John*, 9).

79. Harmon reasons, "So in the face of opponents who viewed themselves as a spiritual notch above everyone else, John responds by emphasizing that when Christ died 'it was not for the sake of, say, the Jews only or, now, of some group, gnostic or otherwise, that sets itself up as intrinsically superior. Far from it. It was not for our sins only, but also for the sins of the whole world'" (Harmon, "For the Glory of the Father," 285, quoting Carson, *Difficult Doctrine*, 76).

kinds and classes of people throughout the whole world.[80] Such an interpretation has enjoyed widespread support throughout the history of the church.[81]

Thirdly, the particularist interpretation of "the whole world" not only makes good lexical and contextual sense, but it also makes good grammatical sense. Considering the structure of 1 John 2:2, one observes the following general syntactical formula:

[1]   a comment concerning Christ's atonement   +

[2]   for   +

[3]   a particular group (X)   +

80. This explanation does not commit one to the notion that the recipients of the letter and/or the false teachers were primarily Jewish. Many particularists have argued, even persuasively, that "whole world" intends to include Gentiles as well as Jews under the scope of Christ's atonement (see, e.g., Bavinck, *Reformed Dogmatics*, 3:465; Owen, *Death of Death*, 331–32; Pink, *Sovereignty of God*, 258–59). Attempted refutations of the particularist position, therefore, often argue that such a Jewish audience is unlikely (see, e.g., Douty, *Death of Christ*, 122–5; Marshall, "For All, for All," 338; Shultz, "Defense," 117–18, especially footnote 62). Sometimes a refutation of the Jew/Gentile proposal is mistaken to be a refutation of the particularist interpretation as a whole. It should be noted that the particularist position does not rise and fall with whether or not the audience and/or false teachers were Jewish.

Several other proposals harmonious with particularism have been offered as explanations for the universalistic language. Shultz ("Defense," 117–20) provides a helpful survey of these views, which we may summarize as follows: "whole world" indicates (1) Gentile as well as Jewish believers, as above; (2) that Christ's propitiation is not limited to believers alive at that time, but extends to God's people throughout all generations; (3) that Jesus is the only propitiation *for* the whole world; (4) that Jesus is available to the whole world; (5) that Christ's propitiation is not limited to one nation but is for the elect throughout all nations; and (6) that in the last day Christ will have a saved world to present to the Father, since all his enemies will be destroyed. While all of these are plausible—and while, as Shultz notes, many commentators believe multiple may be in view at the same time (Shultz, "Defense," 120n68; cf., e.g., Murray, *Redemption Accomplished and Applied*, 72–75)—I find views 2 and 5 to be most convincing. Something of a complement of those positions is argued for in the body of the text above. Shultz's response to view 2 is simply to say that it is difficult to understand how one arrives at this meaning (Shultz, "Defense," 118n63). Shultz does not even attempt to respond to view 5 in his discussion (119n66).

Hammett believes that "the variety of [particularists'] suggestions" concerning the precise reason for universalistic language in 1 John 2:2 "betrays the uncertainty of their exegesis" (Hammett, "Multiple-Intentions View," 151). However, it does not follow that, since there are multiple alternative interpretations that make better sense of a text than the universalist proposal, therefore none of those interpretations are sound. It may be clear that "whole world" *cannot* mean all without exception, even if there are multiple plausible explanations for what it does mean.

81. Calvin wrote, "I pass over the dreams of the fanatics, who make this a reason to extend salvation to all the reprobate and even to Satan himself. Such a monstrous idea is not worth refuting. Those who want to avoid this absurdity have said that Christ suffered sufficiently for the whole world but effectively only for the elect. This solution has commonly prevailed in the schools. Although I allow the truth of this, I deny that it fits this passage. For John's purpose was only to make this blessing common to the whole Church. Therefore, under the word 'all' he does not include the reprobate, but refers to all who would believe and those who were scattered through the various regions of the earth" (Calvin, *Catholic Epistles*, 173). The Dutch Annotations comment: Not for ours only, "namely, the Apostles and other believers who now live," but also for the sins "of all men in the whole world out of all Nations, who shall yet believe in him" (Haak, *Dutch Annotations*). See also Smeaton, *Apostles' Doctrine of the Atonement*, 460; Wells, *Price for a People*, 56; MacArthur, *1–3 John*, 49.

[4] "and not for X only, but also . . ."   +

[5] a larger group.

That is, "[1] And He Himself is the propitiation [2] for [3] our sins; [4] and not for ours only, but also [5] for those of the whole world." Interestingly, there is at least one other text in the writings of the apostle John that fits this very same syntactical formula: John 11:49–52. John reports Caiaphas's prophecy about Christ's death, namely, that one man would die for the people and the whole nation not perish (11:50). Then John comments, "Now he did not say this on his own initiative, but being high priest that year, he prophesied that [1] Jesus was going to die [2] for [3] the nation, [4] and not for the nation only, but in order that He might also gather together into one [5] the children of God who are scattered abroad" (11:51–52). Consider the parallel structure:

> John 11:51–52: ". . . Jesus was going to die *for* THE NATION, **and not for** THE NATION **only, but** in order that He might **also** gather together into one the children of God who are scattered abroad."

> 1 John 2:2: "And He Himself is the propitiation *for* OUR SINS; **and not for** OURS **only, but also** for those of the whole world."

The first four elements of the syntactical formula are virtually identical in each verse. The one difference occurs in the fifth element: "the children of God who are scattered abroad" (John 11:52) and "the whole world" (1 John 2:2). Despite the formal variation, however, the syntactical parallel gives good reason to see both elements as substantively synonymous. That is, when John writes 1 John 2:2, there is a precedent for the syntax he uses in a passage written only several years earlier in his Gospel. Therefore, it is reasonable to conclude that when John spoke of "the whole world" in 1 John 2:2, he had in mind the same group of people indicated by "the children of God who are scattered abroad" in John 11:52. Thus, the point is that Jesus would not atone for the sins of only one particular group in one place and alive at one time—whether the Jews (John 11:51) or the believers in Asia Minor (1 John 2:2)—rather, he would atone for the sins of "the children of God" scattered throughout all times and places. He would die not only for the sheep whom his Father had given him (John 10:14–15; cf. 10:29) who were alive at that time, for he says, "I have other sheep, which are not of this fold; I must bring them also, and they will hear My voice; and they will become one flock with one shepherd" (John 10:16). Notice that Jesus does not say he *will* have other sheep, but rather that he *presently has* other sheep who do not belong to the fold to whom he was then ministering. This can refer only to the elect of God who would eventually come to faith through the preaching of the gospel (cf. John 17:20).[82] While this syntactical

---

82. And so Owen: "If it might be granted that in the first branch all believers then living were comprehended, who might presently be made partakers of this truth, yet the increase or accession must be, by analogy, only those who *were to be* in after ages and remoter places than the name of Christ had

parallel is not a conclusive proof of particularism of itself, taken together with the lexical and contextual arguments, it makes good sense of the passage if "whole world" refers to the elect scattered throughout the world.

Fourthly, the particularist interpretation is sound not only lexically, contextually, and grammatically, but also doctrinally. In Rev 5:9, John writes of the atonement of Christ in a manner that is necessarily particularistic: "And they sang a new song, saying, 'Worthy are You to take the book and to break its seals; for You were slain, and purchased for God with Your blood men from every tribe and tongue and people and nation.'" If Christ had redeemed every person who ever lived, there would have been no reason for John to say that he purchased men "from," or "out of" (ἐκ), every tribe and tongue, etc. Especially if the greatness of the atonement were truly to be measured by its breadth, as is so often claimed by advocates of unlimited atonement, there would be no reason for John not to say that Christ *purchased every tribe* and tongue, etc. Put in the language of the present discussion, John says that Jesus purchased all without distinction, not all without exception. It is difficult to accept that if John believed in a universal redemption, he would have taken the opportunity to restrict the object of Christ's redemption to men "out of" every tribe, rather than extend it to every tribe itself.

Finally, an efficacious yet particular atonement fits more naturally with the argument John is making than a universal yet inefficacious atonement. Because Christ's atonement actually satisfies God's wrath against sinners, the troubled believers in the churches of Asia Minor can be perfectly confident that, even though they still struggle with instances of sin, they are not lost as the heretical perfectionists allege. Rather, they have an advocate with the Father who pleads the merits of his perfectly sufficient propitiatory sacrifice. They cannot object (as they could in the case of a universal atonement) that some of the beneficiaries of such a propitiation still perish under the weight of their sins, because he offered his propitiatory sacrifice in their stead alone; he did no such thing for those who bear their own wrath for eternity.

In summary, the particularist interpretation of "the whole world" in 1 John 2:2 fits the lexical choices, context, grammar, doctrine, and authorial intent of the passage in a manner superior to the universalist interpretation. It does not contradict any other passage of Scripture, (as the MIV interpretation does by redefining propitiation), it coheres nicely with other passages John wrote concerning the atonement, and it avoids the undesirable interpretive conclusions of either universal final salvation or an inefficacious propitiation, one of which is unavoidable if "whole world" must refer to all without exception. Therefore, the particularist interpretation is both biblically and theologically preferable, and this text offers no support for a universal intention in the atonement.[83]

---

then reached unto,—even all those who, according to the prayer of our Saviour, John 17:20, should believe on his name to the end of the world" (Owen, *Death of Death*, 338).

83. Shultz also offers 2 Cor 5:18–19 as support for a universal intention in the atonement. Paul

12

Christ's Death for Those Who Will Finally Perish

IN ADDITION TO TEXTS that state that Christ died for "all" and texts that state that Christ died for the "world," a final set of passages is brought forth by opponents of particularism. It is claimed that these verses teach that Christ died for people who finally perish for their sins in hell. Since such persons are eternally condemned, they are evidently not among the elect. And if Scripture says that Christ died for them, then it would seem that at least some for whom Christ died were not elect.[1] His atoning death, therefore, could not be considered inherently efficacious, as has been argued throughout this book, and that would fit with the MIV's concept of the atonement as a provision that must be subjectively appropriated by faith in order to be effective.[2]

There are at least three such texts in the New Testament: Rom 14:15; 1 Cor 8:11; and 2 Pet 2:1.[3] While the former two passages are significant and worthy of

---

writes, "Now all these things are from God, who reconciled us to Himself through Christ and gave us the ministry of reconciliation, namely that God was in Christ reconciling the world to Himself, not counting their trespasses against them, and He has committed to us the word of reconciliation." Space limitations prohibit an extensive engagement, but briefly, this text ought to be interpreted as the other "world" texts. That is, as the immediate context suggests, "world" ought to be interpreted not as "all without exception" but "all without distinction throughout the world." Paul defines divine reconciliation as "not counting their trespasses against them." The only ones whose trespasses are not counted against them are those who receive the blessing of justification (Rom 4:4–8), i.e., the elect alone. This reading is also confirmed by verse 18, as "the world" that is reconciled to God through Christ (5:19) is coextensive with the "us" who are reconciled to God through Christ (5:18), i.e., the elect who eventually believe. Paul uses universalistic language to emphasize the expansiveness of Christ's work of reconciliation—that it extends to those actually reconciled throughout all the world—not to indicate that it extends to every individual who has ever lived, even those who remain alienated from God through all eternity.

1. "[These texts] do not precisely claim Christ's atonement is universal, but they do claim Christ died for some who will finally perish. Thus, they affirm Christ died for more than just the elect and thus imply a general or universal atonement" (Hammett, "Multiple-Intentions View," 155).

2. As Hammett says, "The view that this essay defends is that Christ 'bought' the false teachers in a soteriological sense; that is, they were included in the universal provision Christ made on the cross. But they never personally appropriated that provision, so they were never saved" (Hammett, "Multiple-Intentions View," 155).

3. Some treatments also include Heb 10:29, as Hammett, "Multiple-Intentions View," 155; cf. Owen, *Death of Death*, 364–68 for a response as to why that text does not teach that Christ has died for those who perish eternally.

engagement, 2 Pet 2:1 is often claimed to be the clearest and most definitive text that teaches that Christ died for those who perish.[4] One writer claims that "no assertion of universal redemption can be plainer than" 2 Pet 2:1.[5] For the sake of space constraints, the present discussion will thus be limited to 2 Pet 2:1 alone.[6] The text states: "But false prophets also arose among the people, just as there will also be false teachers among you, who will secretly introduce destructive heresies, even denying the Master who bought them, bringing swift destruction upon themselves." Those who see a universal intention in the atonement seize upon Peter's comment that false teachers—heretics of the vilest sort[7]—were "bought" (ἀγοράζω) by "the Master" (ὁ δεσπότης), which they interpret to mean that Christ the Master has redeemed even non-elect false teachers by his atoning death. However, challenges to that interpretation have come by questioning the proper significance of both δεσπότης and ἀγοράζω. The bearing that 2 Pet 2:1 has on the extent of the atonement centers

---

4. Shultz notes, "Advocates of unlimited atonement consider 2 Peter 2:1 to be one of the strongest statements supporting an unlimited redemption, because the verse seems to be saying that Christ died for those who deny him, and are therefore lost. Therefore Christ's atonement is not only explicitly said to be for who do not believe in him, it is said to be for the worst kind of heretics who deny Christ and his atonement" (Shultz, "Defense," 146–47). Hammett agrees: "While Rom 14:15, 1 Cor 8:11, and Heb 10:29 are occasionally claimed as supporting this idea, a much clearer and more widely used text is 2 Peter 2:1" (Hammett, "Multiple-Intentions View," 155). Ware says that this text "refers clearly to unregenerate people as 'denying the Master who bought (aor. act. prtc. of agoradzo, 'to redeem') them, bringing swift destruction upon themselves'" (Ware, "Outline," 2).

5. Alford, *Alford's Greek Testament*, 4:402.

6. Nevertheless, brief comments on the Rom 14:15 and 1 Cor 8:11 are in order (adapted from the author's contributions to MacArthur and Mayhue, *Biblical Doctrine*, 563). In both texts, Paul is concerned that by exercising his Christian liberty, a believer with a stronger conscience may cause another believer with a weaker conscience to stumble. He warns the stronger brother not to "destroy" (ἀπόλλυμι) "him for whom Christ died," or "the brother for whose sake Christ died." If one for whom Christ died can be "destroyed"—a term often used to describe eternal punishment (e.g., Rom 2:12; 1 Cor 1:18)—then Christ's death must not be inherently efficacious; some for whom he died may also perish in their sins.

However, the authors of Scripture "can refer to those who may finally perish as, for a time, visibly possessing all the descriptions of genuine believers" (Gibson, "For Whom Did Christ Die?," 322). Smeaton calls this "the judgment of charity" (Smeaton, *Apostles' Doctrine of the Atonement*, 447). That is, since these apostates claimed to belong to the people of God, they were regarded as true believers according to their profession. For example, John calls Judas one of Jesus' disciples (John 12:4), and the author of Hebrews warns the "brethren" against falling away, though the church includes a mix of believers and unbelievers (e.g., Heb 3:12–4:7). Thus, while the abuse of Christian liberty has the potential to "hurt" (Rom 14:15) and "wound the conscience" (1 Cor 8:12) of the weaker brother, a true brother for whom Christ died will never finally be lost (Rom 8:35–39; cf. John 10:27–30; Phil 1:6). If such a person does fall away from the faith, they reveal themselves to have never truly been a brother in the first place (1 John 2:19). Paul speaks of such "brothers" according to their profession; they are *so-called* brothers, but were never chosen by the Father, redeemed by the Son, or regenerated by the Spirit.

7. Lightner, *Death Christ Died*, 75.

around whether δεσπότης refers to the Father or the Son, and whether ἀγοράζω refers to soteriological redemption or temporal deliverance.[8]

Master (δεσπότης)

The Greek term δεσπότης occurs ten times in the New Testament, and its basic meaning is "one who has legal control and authority over persons, such as subjects or slaves," as a lord, master, or sovereign.[9] In four occurrences, δεσπότης clearly refers to the master in a master-slave relationship: slaves must regard their masters as worthy of honor (1 Tim 6:1), never disrespecting them, even if they are also Christians (1 Tim 6:2); they must submit to their masters, even when they are unreasonable (Titus 2:9; 1 Pet 2:18). There are three unambiguous references to God the Father as the δεσπότης who exercises sovereign authority over all the cosmos, denoting him as the Lord of creation (Acts 4:24), the Lord of providence (Luke 2:29), and the Lord of judgment (Rev 6:10). A disputed reference is 2 Tim 2:21, which speaks of either the Father or the Son as the Master over the household of the church, with professing believers of the visible church pictured as honorable or dishonorable vessels within the house (2 Tim 2:20). If the genuine believer cleanses himself from "wickedness" (2:19) and "ungodliness" (2:16), he will be revealed to be an honorable vessel useful to his Master (2:21), rather than an apostate like the "men who have gone astray from the truth" (2:18).[10] In Jude 4, δεσπότης seems clearly to refer to Christ. While Jude intended to write of the common salvation shared by all Christians, he nevertheless felt the necessity to exhort these believers to contend for the faith once for all delivered to the saints (v. 3), for, he says, false teachers have surreptitiously infiltrated their ranks and, by their false doctrine and licentious lifestyle, they do "deny our only Master and Lord, Jesus Christ." Given the soteriological context ("common salvation," "faith once for all delivered to the saints"), as well as the Granville-Sharp construction τὸν μόνον δεσπότην καὶ κύριον ἡμῶν Ἰησοῦν Χριστὸν, it is reasonable to conclude that Christ is here referred to as δεσπότης.[11]

The final occurrence of δεσπότης comes in 2 Pet 2:1, where it is disputed as to whether the "Master who bought" the false teachers refers to the Father or the Son. Owen argues that δεσπότης does not commonly refer to Christ, who is far more often called κύριος. Further, since δεσπότης speaks of servants and subjection, and since the work of Christ in redemption is much more consistently expressed in more endearing

---

8. Long, *Definite Atonement*, 84–85.

9. BDAG, 220. Davids comments, "'Sovereign' is a far less usual title, which refers either to a sovereign power, such as the Roman emperor or God, or to the head of a household, who held life-and-death power over his family, including his slaves" (Davids, *Jude and 2 Peter*, 221).

10. Chang reasons, "If a Christian frees himself from any association with apostates, he will become a useful servant for his Master. Thus it is not too much to say that the nuance of slave owner is also present in 2 Timothy 2:21, at least in a metaphorical sense" (Chang, "Second Peter 2:1," 53).

11. Wallace, *Greek Grammar beyond the Basics*, 270–90.

terms, Owen believes that the Father is in view of 2 Pet 2:1.[12] Nettles agrees, arguing that "the use of δεσπότης indicates a measured precision in pointing to God as rightful sovereign over all by virtue of sovereign creative power, his might in controlling the affairs of history, and his sureness to take retribution on those who seek to suppress his truth and oppose or ignore his purposes."[13] If Christ is thus not the Master spoken of in 2 Pet 2:1, it is unlikely that his atonement would be signified by the term ἀγοράζω. The force of the objection to particular redemption on the basis of this text would thus be significantly weakened. However, it is unlikely that δεσπότης refers to the Father and not to Christ, especially because the parallel between the Epistle of Jude and 2 Pet 2 is so strong.[14] Given that Jude 4 refers to Christ as the δεσπότης denied by false teachers, and given the thematic parallels between Jude and 2 Pet 2, it is reasonable to conclude that Christ is the δεσπότης denied by the false teachers in 2 Pet 2:1.[15]

However, Gary Long argues that although δεσπότης in 2 Pet 2:1 refers to Christ the Son, it does not refer to Christ with particular respect to his office and function as *mediator*, but rather to his sovereignty as the Lord of creation, providence, and judgment alongside the Father. He argues that of the twenty occurrences of δεσπότης in the Septuagint alongside the ten occurrences in the New Testament, the term never refers to the Father or to the Son as mediator. Even in Jude 4, Long reasons, where δεσπότης *is* used of Christ, it does not speak of Christ in his capacity as redeemer but as sovereign Lord, owner of each member of the human race. When Christ is referred to as mediator, he argues, Scripture employs either one of his redemptive titles (e.g., the Lamb of God) or speaks of the price laid down for the purchase of redemption (e.g., his blood).[16] As a result, then, though Christ is the δεσπότης who bought the false teachers, his buying them ought not to be understood in a soteriological sense. Rather, it refers to *acquiring* them, in a manner similar to the way the Father acquired the false prophets of Israel when he delivered the entire nation from slavery in Egypt (cf. Deut 32:5–6; 2 Pet 2:1, 13).[17] Like the false prophets who were delivered from

12. Owen, *Death of Death*, 363.

13. Nettles, *By His Grace and for His Glory*, 301.

14. In 2 Pet 2:1, false teachers secretly introduce destructive (παρεισάξουσιν) heresies, whereas in Jude 4, certain persons have crept in unnoticed (παρεισέδυσαν). In 2 Pet 2:1, they deny the Master who bought them (καὶ τὸν ἀγοράσαντα αὐτοὺς δεσπότην ἀρνούμενοι), whereas in Jude 4 they deny our only Master and Lord, Jesus Christ (τὸν μόνον δεσπότην καὶ κύριον ἡμῶν Ἰησοῦν Χριστὸν ἀρνούμενοι). In 2 Pet 2:1 they bring swift destruction (ἀπώλειαν) upon themselves, whereas in Jude 4 they have been marked out for condemnation (κρίμα).

15. Bauckham, *Jude, 2 Peter*, 240; Chang, "Second Peter 2:1," 53–54; Davids, *2 Peter and Jude*, 221; Long, *Definite Atonement*, 85; Schreiner, *Jude, 2 Peter*, 329; Shultz, "Defense," 148.

16. Long, *Definite Atonement*, 85–86.

17. Long argues, "In II Peter 2:1, Peter intentionally alludes to the phrase 'thy father that hath bought thee' in Deuteronomy 32:6. Immediately following [that] phrase . . . are the words 'hath he not *made thee*, and *established* thee?' The three Hebrew words translated 'bought,' 'made,' and 'established' are significant in the sovereign creation view for, in the Hebrew, they mean, in context, 'to acquire,' 'to make,' or 'to constitute and 'to establish' a nation. . . . Although the Greek word translated 'bought' or 'acquire' in Deuteronomy 32:6 is *ktaomai* and not *agorazō*, a word study of these two terms reveals

their outward slavery, so also these false teachers were delivered from their outward corruption, having externally "escaped the defilements of the world" (2 Pet 2:20), that is, by no longer associating with pagan idolatry and worldly immorality. Also like the false prophets, however, their association with the people of God did not mean they were genuine believers, and after a time they denied the Master who acquired them. Thus, Long claims, 2 Pet 2:1 poses no threat to particular redemption, because Christ's spiritual redemption from sin is not in view here.

Long's case is persuasive but ultimately unconvincing, not only because it depends on a reading of ἀγοράζω that is lexically indefensible, as will be demonstrated below, but also because it is difficult to accept that 2 Pet 2:1 provides no reference to Christ as mediator. Since, as argued above, 2 Pet 2:1 is parallel with Jude 4, and since the context of Jude 4 is clearly soteriological given its reference to "common salvation" (Jude 3) and "the grace of our God" (Jude 4), it is legitimate to read the δεσπότης of 2 Pet 2:1 as the δεσπότης of Jude 4, namely, the Master as Savior and not merely the Master as creator.[18] Thus, if particular redemption will survive the scrutiny of 2 Pet 2:1, it will do so by means other than Long's explanation.

Bought (ἀγοράζω)

That leads to the examination of a second key word in this verse. What does Peter mean by saying that Christ the Master has bought these false teachers who deny him? We have already observed one proposal, namely, Long's *sovereign creator view*, which reads ἀγοράζω in the sense of κτάομαι, speaking of Christ as creator rather than redeemer. Another proposal might be termed the *temporal deliverance view*, and it reads ἀγοράζω to refer to physical deliverance from the corruption of the world. After all, Peter goes on to say of these same false teachers, "For if, after they have escaped the defilements of the world by the knowledge of the Lord and Savior Jesus Christ, they are again entangled in them and are overcome, the last state has become worse for them than the first" (2 Pet 2:20). In what sense have false teachers "escaped the defilements of the world"? Well, whether they were converted out of pagan idolatry, out of lecherous immorality, or even out of the self-righteousness legalism of Mosaic ceremonialism, the outward reform of their behavior and their association with the people of God

---

that they are closely related and are used interchangeably in both the Old and New Testaments [cf. 2 Sam 24:21, 24; 1 Chr 21:24; cf. 2 Kgs 22:6; 2 Chr 34:11].... Therefore, the point that Peter seems to be making in referring to Deuteronomy 32:6 in II Peter 2:1 is that just as God had sovereignly acquired Israel out of Egypt (including 'his children' as well as the 'spot' among them which was 'a perverse and crooked generation,' Deut. 32:5) in order to make her a covenant nation spiritually and nationally because he had created her for this purpose, so Christ, the sovereign Lord, acquired the false teachers (spots and blemishes, II Pet. 2:13) in order to make them professing members of the New Covenant outwardly and individually in the flesh, because he had created them for this purpose" (Long, *Definite Atonement*, 94–95). Also see Nettles, *By His Grace and for His Glory*, 301–2.

18. Chang, "Second Peter 2:1," 59.

would indeed constitute something of an escape from the defilements of the world. Owen argues that "their buying was only in respect of this separation from the world, in respect of the enjoyment of the knowledge of the truth; . . . [It is] a deliverance, by God's dispensations towards them, from the blindness of Judaism or Paganism, by the knowledge of the gospel."[19] Thus, by their temporary, outward identification with the people of God, these false teachers can be said to have been delivered out of the external corruptions of the world—not by the spiritual redemption of Christ, but by the providential deliverance of God the Father. Similar to the false prophets of Israel (cf. 2 Pet 2:1a), who were "a perverse and crooked generation" (Deut 32:5) and yet nevertheless were "bought" (קָנֶךָ, ἐκτήσατό) by their Father out of slavery in Egypt and were "created" (עָשֹׁךָ, ἐποίησέν) and "established" (וַיְכֹנְנֶךָ, ἔκτισέ) as a covenant nation alongside the people of God (Deut 32:6), so also were these false teachers internally "stains and blemishes" (2 Pet 2:13) though externally associated with the pure bride of Christ.[20] Like the sovereign creator view, then, the temporal deliverance view interprets ἀγοράζω in a non-soteriological sense.[21]

However, both views face a lexical challenge at precisely this point. The term ἀγοράζω means to buy or purchase.[22] Of the thirty times it occurs in the New Testament, twenty-four times it comes in a non-soteriological context, in reference to buying and selling common commercial purchases, such as buying food (Matt 14:15; Mark 6:36–37; Luke 9:13; John 4:8; 6:5; 13:29), spices (Mark 16:1), oil (Matt 25:9–10), land (Matt 13:44; 27:7; Luke 14:18), precious stones (Matt 13:46; Rev 3:18), cloth (Mark 15:46), or a sword (Luke 22:26). In the other six instances, the object bought or purchased is said to be a person, and in each instance (reserving judgment on 2 Pet 2:1 since it is under dispute) salvation is in view. Paul tells the Corinthians, "For you have been bought with a price" (ἠγοράσθητε γὰρ τιμῆς, 1 Cor 6:20), and,

---

19. Owen, *Death of Death*, 363.

20. Grudem articulates this view well: "In line with this clear reference to false prophets in the Old Testament, Peter also alludes to the fact that the rebellious Jews turned away from God who 'bought' them out of Egypt in the exodus. From the time of the exodus onward, any Jewish person would have considered himself or herself one who was 'bought' by God in the exodus and therefore a person of God's own possession. In this sense, the false teachers arising among the people were denying God their Father, to whom they rightfully belonged. So the text means not that Christ had redeemed these false prophets, but simply that they were rebellious Jewish people (or church attenders in the same position as the rebellious Jews) who were rightly owned by God because they had been brought out of the land of Egypt (or their forefathers had), but they were ungrateful to him. Christ's specific redemptive work on the cross is not in view in this verse" (Grudem, *Systematic Theology*, 600).

21. Shultz claims that such a view requires that the false teachers of 2 Peter be understood as Jews, and notes that that is unlikely. "Peter would not have claimed that the exodus was accomplished for Gentiles as well as Jews" (Shultz, "Defense," 150n178). But this objection does not follow. The false teachers do not have to be Jews in order to be compared to false prophets in Israel. Both groups would have consisted of professing believers in Yahweh who were outwardly delivered from the corruption of the world through an external association with the visible people of God. In this way, Peter appeals to the exodus as an example from which the present church may learn (cf. Rom 15:4; 1 Cor 10:1, 6).

22. BDAG, 14.

"You were bought with a price" (τιμῆς ἠγοράσθητε, 1 Cor 7:23). John praises the Lamb who was slain, who "purchased for God with Your blood [ἠγόρασας τῷ θεῷ ἐν τῷ αἵματί] men from every tribe and tongue and people and nation" (Rev 5:9). And in Rev 14:3–4, John speaks of "the one hundred and forty-four thousand who had been purchased from the earth [οἱ ἠγορασμένοι ἀπὸ τῆς γῆς]," that is, those who "have been purchased from among men [ἠγοράσθησαν ἀπὸ τῶν ἀνθρώπων] as first fruits to God and to the Lamb." This survey shows that when the object of ἀγοράζω is a person, it is always used in a soteriological sense.[23] Since the object of ἀγοράζω in 2 Pet 2:1 is the false teachers, a personal object, it is reasonable to conclude that Peter intends ἀγοράζω in a soteriological sense.

How, then, ought we to understand Peter's intent? What does it mean for Christ the Master to redeem, in a soteriological sense, false teachers who nevertheless perish eternally in their sins? There are at least four proposals.[24] The first we might call the *loss of salvation view*, which views the false teachers as having been genuinely bought by the blood of Christ in atonement and having repented of their sins and trusted in Christ for salvation. They have "escaped the defilements of the world by the knowledge of the Lord and Savior Jesus Christ" (2 Pet 2:20) and have "known the way of righteousness" (2:21). Subsequent to this genuine conversion, however, they become entangled by false doctrine and loose living (2:20), and they finally abandon their salvation, "turn[ing] away from the holy commandment" (2:21) and denying the Master who bought them (2:1).[25] However, while this view has the advantage of reading 2 Pet 2 in a straightforward manner, it fails to adequately account for the rest of Scripture's clear teaching that those who are genuinely saved can never be lost. Christ's sheep cannot be snatched out of the hand of the Father, who is greater than all (John 10:29), nor of the hand of the Son, the good shepherd, to whom the Father has given them (John 10:28). Every sinner who is justified will also be glorified (Rom 8:30), for nothing "will be able to separate us from the love of God, which is in Christ Jesus our Lord" (Rom 8:35–39). No one who was united with Christ in his death (something that must be said of all those forgiven of their sins) will fail to be united with him in the likeness of his resurrection (Rom 6:5, 8).[26] For these reasons, the loss of salvation view is not a biblically viable option.

23. Contra Long, who mistakenly argues, "Of its thirty occurrences in the New Testament, *agorazō* is never used in a soteriological context (unless 2 Pet 2:1 is the exception) without the technical term 'price' (*timēs*—a technical term for the blood of Christ) or its equivalent being stated or made explicit in the context (see 1 Cor 6:20; 7:23; Rev. 5:9; 14:3, 4)" (Long, *Definite Atonement*, 87). Revelation 14:3–4 speaks of the 144,000 who were purchased from the earth, but it makes no mention of a purchase price or of the blood of Christ, whether in those verses or in the near context.

24. I am indebted to Schreiner, "Problematic Texts," 388–92, for the general summaries of the following views.

25. Marshall, *Kept by the Power of God*, 169–70.

26. For an extended defense of the doctrine of the perseverance of the saints, see MacArthur and Mayhue, eds., *Biblical Doctrine*, 644–49; Schreiner and Caneday, *Race Set before Us*; Horton, "Classical Calvinist View," 23–42; and Grudem, "Perseverance of the Saints," 133–82.

A second proposal might be termed the *non-saving redemption view*. Douglas Kennard rightly insists that, given its usage, ἀγοράζω must be interpreted in a soteriological sense. However, he claims that the redemption denoted by ἀγοράζω is not to be equated with salvation. Peter uses the terminology for redemption differently than the apostle Paul, and thus "Petrine redemption is not to be equated with Petrine salvation. . . . In Peter, one can be soteriologically redeemed without having been saved . . . [and so] the redemption of an individual does not guarantee that he shall be ultimately saved."[27] In other words, this view is to be distinguished from the loss of salvation view in that, while on that view those who are redeemed are saved and then lost, according to Kennard, those who are redeemed are not necessarily ever saved. Shultz gives some countenance to this construct of non-saving redemption when he speaks of the term "'bought' referring to soteriological redemption, but not to actual salvation."[28] The main problem with this view, however, is that it depends upon a thoroughly novel understanding of redemption. Throughout Scripture, when the terms גָּאַל and פָּדָה in the Old Testament and λυτρόω, (ἀπο)λύτρωσις, (ἀντί)λύτρον, and (ἐξ)αγοράζω in the New Testament are used soteriologically, they never refer to something short of accomplished salvation.[29] Indeed, the concept of a soteriological redemption distinct from actual salvation approaches incoherence. Kennard's proposal that in Peter's writing one is redeemed when a changed life results is a total redefinition of the biblical concept of redemption.[30] While Peter does emphasize that redemption results in transformation (1 Pet 1:18; 2 Pet 2:1, cf. 2:20–21), Peter's two comments on redemption do not constitute a sufficient body of lexical data that should be distinguished from the rest of Scripture's usage of the terms for redemption.[31] Ultimately, therefore, Kennard's proposal is unconvincing as it lacks sufficient exegetical support.[32]

A third view that takes ἀγοράζω soteriologically is referred to by proponent Andrew Chang as the "spiritual redemption view."[33] However, it may be more accurate to describe this as the *provisional redemption view*. This position holds that Christ has paid the redemption price of his blood in order to purchase all people without

27. Kennard, "Petrine Redemption," 401.

28. Shultz, "Defense," 147.

29. See chapter 7 on the nature of the atonement as redemption.

30. Kennard, "Petrine Redemption," 404.

31. Thus Kennard's claim that "Peter does not use Paul's exhaustive redemption concept, which includes features such as justification, forgiveness, and the ultimate departure from the sinful body" (Kennard, "Petrine Redemption," 399) is unconvincing.

32. Schreiner also notes that Kennard's reading "separates election from redemption" by arguing, like Arminianism, that both elect and non-elect may be redeemed, but, unlike Arminianism, that the elect will certainly be saved (Schreiner, "Problematic Texts," 389). That is, this view fundamentally undermines trinitarian unity in salvation, for the Father's election extends to a different group than the Son's redemption. For more on the necessity of Trinitarian unity in relation to the extent of the atonement, see chapter 4.

33. Chang, "Second Peter 2:1," 60; cf. Long, *Definite Atonement*, 87; Schreiner, "Problematic Texts," 389.

exception, but only those who appropriate that provision by faith experience its benefits.[34] Thus, "the all-merciful and all-just God made provision for all human beings, but . . . some go to hell because of their unwillingness to appropriate the provision."[35] Shultz adopts a version of this view, but, rather than the language of provision and appropriation, he employs the construct of objective and subjective redemption: "Christ actually did redeem the false teachers, but they are not in Christ through faith (they deny him with their words and their actions) and therefore they do not subjectively experience that redemption."[36] He appeals to his own proposal concerning objective and subjective reconciliation and seeks to apply that paradigm to redemption: "Just as Christ objectively reconciled the world but not all people are subjectively reconciled to him, Christ objectively redeemed the world, though all are not subjectively redeemed by him. As Chafer states, . . . 'There is, then, a redemption which pays the price, but does not of necessity release the slave.'"[37]

There are two significant problems with this provision-appropriation, or objective-subjective, paradigm. The first is that it fails to consider all of what Peter says concerning these false teachers. They are not only said to have been bought by the Master (2 Pet 2:1), but they are also said to "have escaped the defilements of the world by the knowledge of the Lord and Savior Jesus Christ" (2:20), and to "have known the way of righteousness" (2:21). It would seem a sound principle that we ought to interpret these statements concerning the false teachers in the same way. That is, in whatever sense the false teachers have been bought, in that sense they have escaped the defilements of the world and have known the way of righteousness. But neither Chang nor Shultz is consistent on this point, for it is admitted that Peter does not mean to teach that the false teachers *provisionally* escaped the defilements of the world but did not actually do so as a result of their failure to appropriate Christ's provisional redemption. Peter does not mean to teach that these false teachers only *objectively* knew the way of righteousness but did not subjectively experience that knowledge. Therefore, it is unsound to conclude that Peter is teaching that Christ only *provisionally* or *objectively* redeemed the false teachers. Schreiner is correct when he observes, "It is evident from

---

34. "By paying His blood as the ransom on the cross, Christ has bought all human beings and owns them. . . . What leads men to hell is their unwillingness to accept God's invaluable provision made for them" (Chang, "Second Peter 2:1," 60, 61).

35. Chang, "Second Peter 2:1," 59. In passing, it is worth noting that by denigrating the efficacy of the atonement, Chang shifts the decisive cause of salvation from God to man, for if it is ultimately man's unwillingness to appropriate the provision that causes him to go to hell, it follows that it is ultimately man's *willingness* to appropriate the provision that causes him to go to heaven. In this way man becomes his own co-savior. As Packer says, ". . . after all, nothing that God and Christ have done can save us unless we add something to it; the decisive factor that actually saves us is our own believing. What we say comes to this—that Christ saves us with our help; and what that means, when one thinks it out, is this—that we save ourselves with Christ's help" (Packer, "Saved by His Precious Blood," 128–29).

36. Shultz, "Defense," 149.

37. Shultz, "Defense," 149–50n177, citing Chafer, "For Whom Did Christ Die?," 313.

Peter's language that the false teachers gave every indication initially that they were truly Christians. Chang's view [and, by extension, Shultz's view], lacks inner coherence and consistency, for he fails to integrate what Peter says about the false teachers being bought by Christ (v. 1) with their knowing Christ as Lord and Savior (v. 20) and knowing the way of righteousness (v. 21)."[38]

A second problem with the provisional redemption view is that, ultimately, Chang's and Shultz's doctrine of redemption is also, like Kennard's, a non-saving redemption. A provisional redemption is not an actual, efficacious redemption. An "objective" redemption that leaves the one redeemed still in his state of slavery is not the redemption Scripture teaches was accomplished by Christ's cross work. The notion of a redemption that pays the price but does not release the slave, as Chafer posits, would have been unrecognizable to the biblical authors, who invariably present the doctrine of redemption as an efficacious accomplishment that secures the release of those for whom the price is paid.[39] Whether by Chang's *provisional* model or the MIV's *objective-subjective* model, redemption gets watered down to mere redeemability.[40] Startling claims are made concerning the cross's inefficacy, such as Chang's comment that "The Cross itself actually does not save anyone."[41] Hammett asserts, "That propitiation, and all Christ did on the cross, though provided to all, remains of no value, ineffectual, useless, until subjectively appropriated."[42] Similarly, Ware asks, since saving faith is required for salvation, "How can it be said of the death of Christ *in itself* that by his death *alone* he saved those for whom he died?"[43] These striking denials of the cross's efficacy, over and against the Scripture's consistent picture of the cross as that by which Christ actually accomplishes salvation rather than merely provides it, demonstrate that such an interpretation is not a viable handling of 2 Pet 2:1.

---

38. Schreiner, "Problematic Texts," 390.

39. See chapter 7 on the nature of the atonement as redemption and as an efficacious accomplishment.

40. Murray captures the heart of the problem: "What does redemption mean? It does not mean redeemability, that we are placed in a redeemable position. It means that Christ purchased and procured redemption. This is the triumphant note of the New Testament whenever it plays on the redemptive chord. . . . It is to beggar the concept of redemption as an effective securing of release by price and by power to construe it as anything less than the effectual accomplishment which secures the salvation of those who are its objects" (Murray, *Redemption Accomplished and Applied*, 63).

41. Chang, "Second Peter 2:1," 59.

42. Hammett, "Multiple-Intentions View," 164–65.

43. Ware, "Outline," 5, emphasis original. Note also Shultz's comments exporting the efficacy of the atonement to the Spirit's application of redemption rather than the Son's accomplishment: that "accomplish[es God's] particular purpose in the atonement" (Shultz, *Multi-Intentioned View*, 138), and that this is what "makes the redemption that Christ secured on the cross effective" (148; cf. 140). Similarly, Hammett speaks of the cross "remov[ing] obstacles to fellowship with God," a fellowship which is effected only by the subjective application of the Spirit (Hammett, "Multiple-Intentions View," 174).

A fourth view, which might be called the *phenomenological view*[44] (also sometimes called the *Christian charity* view),[45] best explains all of Peter's language concerning the false teachers (both in verse 1 and in verses 20–22).[46] This view holds that Peter is speaking of the false teachers according to their outward appearance, for a time, as professing believers. These false teachers were "among you" (2:1), part of the visible church.[47] As Schreiner observes, "It was not as if outsiders who never claimed to be Christians arrived and began to propagate teachings contrary to the gospel. On the contrary, the false teachers were insiders who departed from what they were first taught."[48] This is evident, for, again, these false prophets are described as those who have escaped the defilements of the world only to then once again be entangled in them and overcome by them (2:20). They are described as having known the way of righteousness only to turn away from the holy commandment (2:21) and return like a dog to its vomit and a sow to the mire (2:22). This is describing those who gave every appearance that they had a saving knowledge of Christ, professing to belong to him, who then defected from the fellowship of the faithful, proving that they never really belonged to Christ in the first place (1 John 2:19; cf. Matt 7:21–23). Therefore, Chang's comment that "The text gives no evidence that these false teachers professed to be believers"[49] and Shultz's comment that "the text gives no evidence that these false teachers professed to be believers, and much evidence that they did not"[50] are both proved to be without warrant. Shultz gives no examples of the "much evidence" that he claims exists for why the false teachers were not professing believers, and he does not at that point consider verses 20–22 in his exposition of 2:1. However, when he finally does examine 2:20–21, Shultz contradicts his own claim, saying, "These false teachers are unbelievers who once made false professions of faith without ever experiencing regeneration."[51] This is not to be missed. Shultz explicitly contradicts the whole tenor of his previous argument within the span of thirty pages. Neither Chang nor Shultz provide any other argument against the phenomenological view, and the one they do provide does not stand up to exegetical scrutiny.

44. Barnes, *Atonement Matters*, 220–21.

45. Chang, "Second Peter 2:1," 59; Long, *Definite Atonement*, 89; cf. Shultz, "Defense," 150–51, 151n181.

46. Schreiner, "Problematic Texts," 390.

47. Davids reasons, "Also notice that the false teachers are 'among you.' Unlike the opponents in Jude (Jude 4), these are not people who have 'secretly slipped in among you' but people who already existed 'among you.' Jude never considers those he opposes part of the Christian community. They are interlopers in his eyes, although they may have passed themselves off as Christians. 2 Peter views the false teachers as indeed part of the community, but a part that has left the true faith" (Davids, *Jude and 2 Peter*, 219).

48. Schreiner, "Problematic Texts," 391.

49. Chang, "Second Peter 2:1," 56; cf. 60.

50. Shultz, "Defense," 151n181.

51. Shultz, "Defense," 182.

Therefore, we ought to conclude that Peter speaks of these false teachers *as if* they were believers, charitably speaking of them according to their profession of faith—what others had supposed them to be—even though he knows they were never believers in the first place.[52] Scripture often speaks of those within the visible church with this judgment of charity, ascribing to them all the titles and privileges that only truly belong to those who are genuine believers.[53] Hence Judas is called a disciple (John 12:4) though he is nevertheless the son of perdition. So also the author of Hebrews warns his congregation against apostasy (e.g., Heb 3:12–14)—thus acknowledging that there are unbelievers among them, for no genuine Christian can truly fall away (cf., e.g., John 10:27–28; Rom 8:28–39)—while also calling them "brethren" (Heb 3:12) and even "holy brethren" (Heb 3:1). Thus, these false teachers, who professed to be believers but were never believers to begin with, never *really* and *truly* "escaped the defilements of the world by the knowledge of the Lord and Savior Jesus Christ" (2 Pet 2:20); they merely *appeared* to have done so. They had never *really* and *truly* "known the way of righteousness" (2:21), but only *appeared* to have known it. Peter speaks the same way in 2:1. They had never *really* and *truly* been bought by the one they once claimed as their Master, but only *appeared* to have been so redeemed.[54]

52. So Owen says, "Neither is it more certain that the apostle speaketh of the purchase of the wolves and hypocrites, in respect of the reality of the purchase, and not rather in respect of that estimation which others had of them,—and, by reason of their outward seeming profession, ought to have had,—and of the profession that themselves made to be purchased by him whom they pretended to preach to others" (Owen, *Death of Death*, 364). Smeaton says as well, "These false teachers are described according to their own profession and the judgment of charity. They gave themselves out as redeemed men, and were so accounted in the judgment of the church while they abode in her communion. This is simple and natural. The passage by no means affirms that any but the true church or the sheep of Christ are truly bought by the atoning blood" (Smeaton, *Apostles' Doctrine of the Atonement*, 447).

53. Trueman comments, "Appearance of true faith is not an alien concept in the New Testament. It is present in the parable of the Sower (Mark 4:1–20) and also in the Pastoral Epistles (e.g., 2 Tim 2:16–19). Here in 2 Peter, their ultimate return to their former ways indicates that they were never really changed (2:22). In everyday linguistic use, for example, it is not uncommon for those who believe strongly in perseverance still to speak about friends who were Christians and who now repudiate the faith as having fallen away. The reference is to appearance, not to spiritual reality" (Trueman, "Definite Atonement View," 37).

54. Hammett objects that such a view rejects 2 Pet 2:1 for what it says, for though the text *says* Christ bought the false teachers, proponents of the phenomenological view say Christ did not really buy them. He regards this as "a commitment to a theological position [requiring] one to deny what a verse straightforwardly appears to affirm," and thus suggests that "the theological position needs reexamination" (Hammett, "Multiple-Intentions View," 157).

However, if Hammett were to apply such a standard consistently, he would do away with virtually all interpretation of Scripture and harmonization of apparent contradictions. Deut 6:4 says that God is one. If, in exposition, the comment was made that God is also three, Hammett would likely not counsel the expositor to re-examine his theological commitment to the Trinity. In John 14:28, Jesus says the Father is greater than he is. Yet it would be proper for someone treating that verse to speak of the sense in which it is true that the Father is greater than Jesus, but also of the sense in which it is true that their greatness is coequal. Such would not require a re-examination of one's theological commitment to the deity of Christ and the hypostatic union. The same could be said of the theological commitment to

Therefore, 2 Pet 2:1 does not teach that Christ has atoned for the sins of those who will finally perish. As a result, it provides no support for a universal intention in the atonement, and thus it poses no contradiction to the doctrine of particular redemption.

---

non-universalism when considering Rom 5:18, which speaks of justification of life to all men.

When a superficial reading of a passage of Scripture contradicts the sound exegetical conclusions drawn from other portions of Scripture, care must be taken to see that the text be interpreted in a way that (a) does not do violence to the words, grammar, or context of the passage in question, but also (b) does not do violence to the words, grammar, or context of any other passage of Scripture. The MIV's handling of 2 Pet 2:1 undermines Scripture's teaching concerning the nature of redemption, reducing it to a provision rather than an efficacious accomplishment of salvation. Therefore, the faithful interpreter must seek for a way to understand Peter's words that is consistent with his intent in 2 Peter 2 without undermining the rest of Scripture's teaching. The phenomenological view achieves this.

Part 3 Summary and Conclusion

THE CASE FOR THE MIV is built upon there being both general and particular intentions in the atonement. The general intentions of the atonement are supposedly established by those texts that cast the scope of Christ's death as universal: for "all" (e.g., 1 Tim 2:6) for the "world" (e.g., John 3:16; 1 John 2:2), and for those that finally perish (e.g., 2 Pet 2:1).

However, in part 3, it has been demonstrated that when interpreted in their context, according to grammatical-historical exegesis, and consistently with the exegesis of the rest of Scripture's teaching concerning the nature and design of the atonement, no text genuinely teaches that Christ died to atone for the sins of all without exception. Texts mentioning Christ's death for "all" and for the "world" were shown to refer to all without distinction rather than all without exception—those chosen by God *throughout* the whole world. In each case, the referent is limited by the context to those who eventually partake in the benefits of the salvation purchased by the atonement. Texts that seem to indicate that Christ died for those who finally perish, thus implying that his atonement was not inherently efficacious unto salvation for all those for whom it was offered, were shown to teach no such thing.

Not one of the texts propounded by the MIV lends any credence to an absolutely universal scope to Christ's sacrifice. Without such evidence, the MIV has no grounds for seeing a universal intention in the atonement, and thus it fails as an adequate analysis of the Bible's teaching on the extent of the atonement.

PART 4

A Particularist Response to the So-Called General Intentions of the Atonement

THE DISTINGUISHING CLAIM OF the multiple intentions view of the extent of the atonement (MIV) is that rather than conceiving of the atonement as having *either* particular *or* universal intentions, one ought to say that both are true: there are *multiple* intentions for the atonement. This is said to cohere with the diversity of biblical terminology regarding the extent of the atonement; that is, the reason one reads that the Son of Man gave "His life as a ransom for *many*" (Matt 20:28) as well as that he gave "Himself as a ransom for *all*" (1 Tim 2:6) is because Christ has died for the many (the elect) *and* for all (the elect and the reprobate) in different senses. There are, therefore, according to the MIV, both particular and general intentions for the atonement; Jesus died for the elect to accomplish God's particular intentions, and he died for all without exception to accomplish the general intentions.[1]

The concept of general intentions in the atonement is predicated upon the death of Christ paying for the sins of all people without exception. As Shultz has said, "The idea that Christ paid for the sins of the elect and nonelect is necessary in order to account [for] the general intentions that God had in the atonement."[2] However, after setting forth the MIV's case in their own words in part 1, parts 2 and 3 have demonstrated that, according to Scripture, there is no such universal atonement provided by Christ's death on behalf of all without exception; rather, there is only a particular atonement accomplished by Christ's death on behalf all those—and only those—whom the Father had given him. Part 2 set the debate concerning the *extent* of the atonement in the framework of Scripture's teaching concerning the *purpose* and *nature* of the atonement. By understanding what Scripture says the atonement *is* and what it is *for*, it was proven that *whom* it was for must necessarily be limited to the elect. The MIV fails by conceiving of the purpose and nature of the atonement in a manner fundamentally at odds with the biblical data. Part 3 then examined the MIV's interpretations of the universalistic passages, that is, those texts of Scripture that cast the scope of Christ's

1. Ware, "Outline," 3, 4; Shultz, "Defense," 10–12; Hammett, "Multiple-Intentions View," 149.

2. Shultz, "Defense," 100.

death in universal terms such as "all" or "world." Through contextual, grammatical-historical exegesis of each of those texts, it was shown that none of them genuinely teaches that Christ died to atone for the sins of all without exception. Without such a universal atonement, the claim that there are general intentions in the atonement has no foundation. And without general intentions in the atonement, the claim that there are multiple intentions in the atonement also has no foundation. Thus, the thesis of the present work is vindicated: by failing to adequately frame the issue in the context of Scripture's teaching concerning the purpose and nature of Christ's mediating work (part 2), the MIV bases its conviction that there are general intentions in the atonement on a mishandling of the universalistic texts (part 3).

Though the case for the general intentions fails de facto with the refutation of a universal payment for sins, it is nevertheless necessary to examine the MIV's biblical and theological argumentation for the general intentions. Part 4, then, will demonstrate that the MIV's argumentation for the so-called general intentions of the atonement falls short of biblical scrutiny on its own terms.

A Review of the General Intentions

The general intentions for the atonement proposed by the MIV have been set forth in part 1. Nevertheless, a brief review is in order. Recall the following table from part 1, which presents the multiple intentions of the atonement according to our three primary interlocutors.

	Ware	Shultz	Hammett
1	Limited Scope	Secure Salvation for the Elect	Particular
2	Limitless Scope	(Pay for All Sins)	Universal
3	*Bona fide* Offer	Legitimize Universal Gospel Call	
4	Just Condemnation	Additional Basis for Condemnation	
5		Provide Common Grace	
6		Supremely Reveal God's Character	
7	Cosmic Triumph	Cosmic Triumph	Cosmic

In addition to a (1) particular intention in the atonement for the elect, which Ware, Shultz, and Hammett all affirm,[3] each proponent of the MIV offers several other general intentions. (2) Ware's "limitless scope purpose" has Christ "paying the penalty for the sin of all people [to make] it possible for all who believe to be saved,"[4] which corresponds loosely to Hammett's "universal intention," namely, "to provide forgiveness of sins for all."[5] Shultz emphasizes a universal payment for all sin, and he would

---

3. Ware, "Outline," 4; Shultz, "Defense," 237ff; Hammett, "Multiple-Intentions View," 169ff.

4. Ware, "Outline," 4.

5. Hammett, "Multiple-Intentions View," 149.

agree that this universal payment makes provision for the forgiveness of all people on the condition that they believe,[6] but he does not list the provision of forgiveness as a proper general intention. It seems best to see this represented in Shultz's claim that (3) such a universal payment is necessary for there to be a genuine universal gospel call,[7] which corresponds to Ware's "bona fide offer purpose."[8] Though he does not list it as a proper intention, Hammett sees the universal well-meant offer of the gospel as fitting "much more easily and completely into a view that at least includes a universal intent of the atonement to provide a sacrifice for the sins of all."[9] (4) Shultz develops Ware's "just condemnation purpose" and declares that Christ died for all without exception in order "to provide an additional basis of condemnation for those who reject the gospel."[10] Unique to his own presentation, Shultz also claims that a universal payment for all sins was designed (5) to purchase common grace for all as well as to (6) supremely reveal the character of God.[11] Finally, (7) all three proponents cite a cosmic intention in the atonement, wherein Jesus conquers all sin by his universal atonement, reconciling the cosmos to himself through the blood of his cross.[12]

In proposing to demonstrate that these so-called general intentions of the atonement are not genuinely grounded in a universal payment for the sins of all without exception, it must be noted that the present writer does not deny the existence of these benefits. The particularist has solid ground upon which to present a universal, genuinely offered gospel call to all without exception (e.g., Acts 17:30–31). So also does he have every reason to subscribe to the doctrine commonly called "common grace"—that is, that God is kind to both elect and reprobate alike, sending forth his mercies (short of salvation) upon all without exception (e.g., Matt 5:45). The particularist also has no quarrel with the notion that the sinner's unbelief and rejection of the gospel message increases the ground of his condemnation (e.g., John 12:48; 1 John 5:10) or with the notion that the cross supremely reveals God's character (e.g., Rom 3:24–26; 5:8). What is denied is that these benefits are proper and direct purchases of the atonement. Particularists have always acknowledged that "there are certain blessings short of salvation, which are the fruits of the work of Christ, which may terminate upon any and all men, and which do in fact substantially benefit some who will never attain unto salvation,"[13] a point that Shultz acknowledges.[14] There may be benefits that indirectly accrue to the reprobate as a result of the atonement made solely for the

---

6. Shultz, "Defense," 158–60.

7. Shultz, "Defense," 162–78.

8. Ware, "Outline," 4.

9. Hammett, "Multiple-Intentions View," 169.

10. Shultz, "Defense," 161, 178–83.

11. Shultz, "Defense," 183–95 and 195–203, respectively.

12. Ware, "Outline," 4; Shultz, "Defense," 203–22; Hammett, "Multiple-Intentions View," 184–88.

13. Nicole, "Case for Definite Atonement," 199.

14. Shultz, "Defense," 98.

elect,[15] but the results of the atonement must not be conflated with the atonement itself. The cross did not *purchase* these benefits by means of a universal atonement; rather, God may be kind to even his enemies simply because that is an expression of his own character, and Christ's particular redemption may have universal effects or results without requiring that it be a universal redemption.[16]

Hammett himself acknowledges this distinction between the indirect results of the cross, on the one hand, and a proper purpose or intention of the cross, on the other. He self-consciously differs with Shultz on what should and should not be considered a veritable intention of the atonement. Of the universal gospel call and the additional basis for condemnation, he says that these "seem more like results or outcomes of the universal intention of the atonement rather than separate and additional purposes or intentions of the atonement."[17] This distinction will figure prominently in the discussion of both common grace and cosmic triumph in the following chapters, as it will be argued that both of these are indirect results of the atonement rather than constituent aspects inherent to the atonement.

---

15. MacArthur and Mayhue give an example of this: "If God had not intended to save sinners through Christ's atonement, it is likely that he would have immediately visited justice on sinful man as he did the fallen angels (2 Pet. 2:4). Yet because God intended to save his people through Christ in the fullness of time, even those whom he will not ultimately save will have enjoyed the benefits of common grace, divine forbearance, and a temporary reprieve from divine judgment" (MacArthur and Mayhue, eds., *Biblical Doctrine*, 544).

16. This distinction is important to maintain but is often misunderstood. Snoeberger is representative of such misunderstanding when he casts as hyper-Calvinists those who deny that common grace, etc., are properly *intentions* of the atonement because they are not properly substitutionary. He contrasts such a position with those who see the non-saving benefits resulting from the cross as "bona fide benefits of the atonement" and not merely "spillover benefits of God's particular redemptive impulse" (Snoeberger, "Introduction," 14–15n43).

While Snoeberger is correct to observe a substantive difference between the men he references (Hoeksema and Engelsma on the one hand, and Murray and Mouw on the other), he is wrong to relegate genuine single-intentionality to hyper-Calvinism, for non-hyper-Calvinist particularists also believe that non-substitutionary, non-saving benefits of the cross are indirect benefits resulting from a particular atonement. He is also wrong to characterize John Murray as one who believes that the atonement purchased universal non-saving benefits rather than their simply being indirect results of an exclusively particular redemption. More will be said in the ensuing discussion, especially in the discussion of common grace, but Murray says, for example, "It is true that many benefits accrue from the redemptive work of Christ to the non-elect in this life. . . . But this is not to say that the atonement, in its specific character as atonement, is designed for the reprobate. It is one thing to say that certain benefits accrue to the reprobate from the atonement; it is entirely different to say that the atonement itself is designed for the reprobate. And the fallacy of the latter supposition becomes apparent when we remember that it is of the nature of the atonement to secure benefits which the reprobate never enjoys. In a word, the atonement is bound up with its efficacy in respect of obedience, expiation, propitiation, reconciliation, and redemption. When the Scripture speaks of Christ as dying for men, it is His vicarious death on their behalf that is in view and all the content which belongs to the atonement defines the significance of the formula 'died for.' Thus we may not say that He died for all men any more than that He made atonement for all men" (Murray, *Atonement*, 30).

17. Hammett, "Multiple-Intentions View," 186.

Notwithstanding differences between proponents of the MIV, some more superficial and others more substantive, it seems wise to take Shultz's presentation as representative of the MIV's position on general intentions, as his dissertation and monograph are a conscious development of Ware's brief handout and a significant resource for Hammett's essay.[18] However, for the sake of space limitations, part 4 will interact with only three of Shultz's five general intentions (which are shared by all three men)—those with the strongest biblical and theological argumentation: the genuine universal gospel call, the provision of common grace, and cosmic triumph over all sin.[19] It will be demonstrated that a genuine universal gospel call, common grace, and eschatological cosmic triumph are each consistent with an exclusively particular redemption, especially when viewed as indirect results of the atonement rather than direct purchases of the atonement itself. It will also be shown that the MIV's case for these benefits being proper purposes in and purchases of the atonement is neither biblically nor theologically justifiable. Thus, it will be shown that the so-called multiple intentions of the atonement are no such thing, and in this manner particularism will be vindicated.

18. Relevant material is also presented in Shultz's 2008 article, "God's Purposes for the Nonelect," 145–63.

19. Nevertheless, a brief comment on each of the other two so-called general intentions is warranted. In the case of the "just condemnation purpose" (Ware) or the provision of an "additional basis of condemnation" (Shultz), it is argued that sinners are only justly condemned for rejecting a gospel that was truly and sincerely offered to them. Besides being based on an unsound inference that ability is a prerequisite for responsibility (contra Rom 9:19), it will be shown in the discussion of the genuine universal gospel call that the particularist does believe that the promise of the gospel—"If you believe, you will be saved"—is truly and sincerely offered to sinners indiscriminately, without respect to whether they are elect or reprobate. The truthfulness of that promise is a sufficient basis for the righteous punishment of those who reject the gospel in unbelief. But may we genuinely say that Christ died for people in order to justify their condemnation? Is this how Scripture presents the purpose of the sending and dying of the Son? Quite the opposite, in fact. John 3:17 explicitly contradicts this notion when it says, "For God did *not* send the Son into the world to judge [ἵνα κρίνῃ] the world, but that the world might be saved through Him." Luke 9:56 also notes, "For the Son of Man did not come to destroy men's lives, but to save them." While it is true that judgment *results* from Christ's mission (e.g., John 5:27; 9:39), it is not proper to say that a *purpose* and *intention* of the death of Christ was to increase the condemnation of the reprobate. (For more on how John 3:17 does not contradict John 9:39, see "The Divine Intention for the Son's Atonement" in page 80, footnote 21.

Shultz also argues that Christ made a universal payment for the sins of all people in order to supremely demonstrate the character of God. While it is true that the cross magnifies both the love and justice of God (cf. Rom 3:21–26; 5:8), the Son does not have to pay for everyone's sins in order sufficiently demonstrate the character of God. For Christ to suffer as a substitutionary, propitiatory sacrifice on behalf of one sinner would be an infinite expression of the love and justice of God. It does not follow that he must suffer in the place of all without exception for God to display his character. Further, though the cross displays the character of God to all indiscriminately, not all without exception behold the character of God revealed in the gospel with the eyes of faith. Many sinners remain blind to the gospel of the glory of Christ (2 Cor 4:4); the word of the cross remains "a stumbling block" and "foolishness" to those who are perishing (1 Cor 1:18–23), as Hammett himself observes (Hammett, "Multiple-Intentions View," 191). It cannot be said that the supreme display of the character of God is a *universal* intention of the cross if it is only those who are actually saved who accurately perceive God's character revealed therein.

13

A Genuine Universal Gospel Call, Part 1

ONE OF THE MOST common objections to the doctrine of particular redemption is that it hinders—or at least is inconsistent with—offering the gospel, fully and freely, to all without exception.[1] If Christ did not pay for the sins of all people without exception, how can the preacher of the gospel call all people without exception to believe in Christ for salvation? If Christ did not die for all, it is claimed, then salvation is not available to all, and that must necessarily limit the extent of the offer of salvation. At the very least, it is objected, God cannot *sincerely* and *genuinely* call a man to believe in Christ if he has not given Christ to die in his place in particular. Indeed, what does the preacher of the gospel call a man to believe if not that Christ has purchased his salvation by his substitutionary death on the cross?

However, the overwhelming majority of the proponents of particular redemption have always held that while the extent of Christ's atonement is limited to the elect, Scripture clearly enjoins believers to proclaim to all people the good news of forgiveness of sins through repentance and faith in Christ. Though a minority of particularists have indeed rejected a universal well-meant gospel offer, supporters of particularism have been history's ablest defenders of the indiscriminate preaching of the gospel, giving evidence that there is no practical contradiction between particular redemption and universal evangelism.

Nevertheless, this does raise a number of questions. How can such an offer of salvation through faith in Christ's sacrifice be sincere? Can God be said to genuinely offer salvation to those in whose place he did not send his Son to die? If so, what ought we to make of the doctrine of the sufficiency of the atonement? How can the atonement be sufficient for all if Christ has not died for all, at least in some sense? Further, how can we call people to believe in an atonement that might not have been

---

1. David Allen claims that particularism "provides an insufficient ground for evangelism by undercutting the well-meant gospel offer" (Allen, "The Atonement: Limited or Universal?" 107). Lightner asserts, "Limited atonement runs aground when it comes to sharing the gospel of God's saving grace" (Lightner, *The Death Christ Died*, 153). Molinist Kenneth Keathley and Arminian Roger Olson also make the same claim (Keathley, *Salvation and Sovereignty*, 207; Olson, *Against Calvinism*, 137). See also Chafer, "For Whom Did Christ Die?," 315–16; Douty, *Only for the Elect?*, 45–49; Marshall, "For All, for All," 345–46; Miethe, "Universal Power of the Atonement," 83–85; and Picirilli, *Grace, Faith, Free Will*, 115–18.

accomplished for them? That is, what is the warrant of faith, if not a universal atonement? What is it that we call people to believe when we proclaim the gospel? Do we tell people, indiscriminately, that Christ died specifically and personally for them? How could we do that except on the basis of a universal atonement? These and other questions will be answered in this chapter and the next.

The MIV's Case

In the first place, however, let us consider the case that proponents of the multiple intentions view make in support of the claim that a genuine universal gospel offer necessitates a universal atonement. According to Ware, "Christ died for the purpose of securing the *bon[a] fide* offer of salvation to all people everywhere."[2] He argues, "Since we are commanded to preach the gospel to all people . . . , the unlimited atoning sacrifice of Christ renders this offer of salvation fully and uncompromisingly genuine."[3] This implies that the offer of salvation cannot be "fully and uncompromisingly genuine" unless Christ died for all those to whom the offer is made. Of note, this reasoning is identical to Ware's articulation of what he calls the "unlimited atonement view," or the "classic Arminian position," which he represents as arguing thus: "Since the offer of salvation is clearly to go to all people . . . , there must be a payment made on behalf of those to whom the gospel offer is extended. If no payment has been made for the non-elect, then we cannot say to the non-elect that God offers salvation *to them*."[4] In Ware's thinking, as well as, it seems, what Ware understands to be the Arminian position, the extent of the gospel call cannot exceed the extent of the atonement.

What is largely presented as an implication in Ware's brief handout Shultz develops and makes explicit. He begins by asserting that "Jesus' payment for the sins of all people, elect and nonelect, was necessary for the universal gospel call to take place."[5] In agreement with Ware and the Arminian position, Shultz argues that the gospel cannot "be genuinely and rightly offered to all people" unless "Christ died to provide the basis by which all people could be saved" if they believe.[6] After giving a largely unobjectionable survey of the nature of the universal gospel call,[7] Shultz

2. Ware, "Outline," 4.

3. Ware, "Outline," 4.

4. Ware, "Outline," 2.

5. Shultz, *Multi-Intentioned View*, 92. This material is also presented in Shultz's 2010 article, "Why a Genuine Universal Gospel Call," 111–23.

6. Shultz, *Multi-Intentioned View*, 90. It is important to be precise here. The particularist agrees that Christ's death, by virtue of its intrinsic infinite sufficiency, provides the basis upon which all sinners without exception are called to salvation through repentance and faith. Shultz, however, grounds the universal gospel offer not in the intrinsic sufficiency of Christ's death but in a substitutionary, atoning death for the sins of all without exception. This distinction will be explored below.

7. One quibbles with the use of Ps 22:27 as an instance of a universal gospel call, as this verse is simply a declaration, not a summons, that all the families of the earth will worship Yahweh. Also,

supports these claims by means of four arguments. First, he argues that the content of the gospel as summarized in 1 Cor 15:1–5 shows that the universal gospel call is based on a universal atonement. Paul says the gospel he preached to the Corinthians is that "Christ died for our sins according to the Scriptures" (15:3). Since he would have been preaching this gospel to the Corinthians in order that they would come to faith, it is reasonable to conclude that they were unbelievers when they heard this message. Thus, Paul preached, "Christ died for *our* sins" to unbelievers, and, Shultz argues, "the word 'our' includes both the preacher and those to whom he is preaching. If the atonement was only for the elect, to preach this message to the nonelect would at best be giving them a false hope and at worst would be untrue."[8] On this basis, Shultz concludes that the statement "Christ died for *our* sins" means that Christ died for *all* sins, and therefore he claims that "part of the gospel message is telling unbelievers that 'Jesus died for you.'"[9]

Second, Shultz argues that the motivation for preaching the gospel, as outlined in 2 Cor 5:11–21, shows that the universal gospel call is based on a universal atonement. Since Paul declares that the love of Christ controls him—that is, constrains him to preach the gospel even in the midst of difficulty—on the basis of having concluded that "one died for all" (2 Cor 5:14), therefore, Paul's motivation for universal evangelism was a universal atonement. Shultz cites Barnett for support, who explains, "Paul's sense of ongoing compulsion to evangelize ('controls') arose from his considered judgment ('we are convinced') when he understood that '[Christ had] died for all.'"[10] Further, in addition to speaking of Christ's death for "all," Paul also goes on to ground his earnest appeals in gospel preaching (5:20) in a universal reconciliation: "God was in Christ reconciling the world to Himself, not counting their trespasses against them" (5:19). Thus, Shultz argues, "God wrought a universal reconciliation, therefore he issues a universal gospel call, and therefore Christians are to be ambassadors for him . . . . Christians ought to take the gospel to all people because Christ died for all people."[11]

Third, Shultz argues that the Spirit's work in the gospel call as summarized in John 16:7–11 indicates that the universal gospel call is based on a universal atonement. In the first place, Jesus says that the Holy Spirit will come to "convict *the world* concerning sin and righteousness and judgment" (16:8). Shultz argues that "the world" here refers

---

Shultz's reasoning, borrowed from Oswalt, that monotheism necessarily implies a universal atonement, is unconvincing. Oswalt claims, "If the Lord is the sole God of the whole world and if he is a savior (v. 21), then he must be the savior of the whole world as well" (Oswalt, *Isaiah 40–66*, 223). Oswalt may merely be claiming that the only God of the world is also thereby the only Savior the world has, but the conclusion Shultz draws—namely that on the basis of monotheism the one God actually saves the whole world—simply does not follow from the premises.

8. Shultz, *Multi-Intentioned View*, 93; cf. Shultz, "Defense," 168.

9. Shultz, *Multi-Intentioned View*, 93.

10. Shultz, *Multi-Intentioned View*, 94; cf. Barnett, *2 Corinthians*, 288.

11. Shultz, *Multi-Intentioned View*, 94.

to "all unbelievers."[12] Thus, the Spirit's ministry of conviction of sins is supposed to be universal. Further, Shultz argues that this ministry of the Spirit is "explicitly connected" and "tied to" and "occurs because of" Christ's atonement.[13] After all, it is only because Christ "went away" (cf. 16:7) from his disciples through his death, resurrection, and ascension that the Spirit could be sent to them: "for if I do not go away, the Helper will not come to you" (16:7). Shultz concludes, "Since the Holy Spirit's work of taking the gospel to all unbelievers, elect and nonelect, is based upon Christ's atonement, it seems that Christ's atonement cannot be limited to the elect."[14]

Shultz's fourth and final argument is not really an argument, but merely a reassertion of the premise he must prove, namely, that the genuineness of a universal gospel call simply *must* be grounded in a universal provision of atonement. He states, "If Christ did not pay for the sins of the non-elect, then it is impossible to genuinely offer salvation to the non-elect, since there is no salvation available to offer them. . . . There must be a genuine payment for all people, who can, if they so choose, receive it."[15]

As mentioned above, Hammett believes the universal gospel call is better conceived as a result or outcome of the atonement rather than a proper general purpose or intention of the atonement.[16] Nevertheless, he regards Shultz's argument that 1 Cor 15:3 "assumes a universal provision of the cross" as "an excellent point."[17] Apart from quoting Shultz, his comments are brief, but he concludes, "It seems that gospel preaching, according to Paul, either includes or assumes that Christ died for the sins of those to whom we preach."[18] If the universal gospel call does not necessitate a universal atonement, at the very least, Hammett says, "the preaching of the gospel to all fits much more easily and completely into a view that at least includes a universal intent in the atonement to provide a sacrifice for the sins of all."[19]

Ultimately, the key assumption operative in all three MIV proponents' presentations of this objection—as well as in Arminian, Molinist, four-point Calvinist, and hypothetical universalist versions of the objection—is that the universality of God's gospel call requires a universal provision made by Christ on the cross.[20] However, if this

12. Shultz, *Multi-Intentioned View*, 95.

13. Shultz, *Multi-Intentioned View*, 96.

14. Shultz, *Multi-Intentioned View*, 96. Shultz cites Lightner for support, who says, "The Holy Spirit's work could not reach out beyond the elect if the death of Christ did not have this universal scope since the Spirit's ministry was procured in and through the cross" (Lightner, *The Death Christ Died*, 130–31). Note that in order for this point to stand, "the world" must refer at least in part to the reprobate, which requires Shultz to argue that the conviction spoken of here does not necessarily lead to conversion. Both of these conclusions are disputed both in chapter 4 (see "The Spirit's Conviction Not Universal") and in chapter 14 (see "Universal Conviction?").

15. Shultz, *Multi-Intentioned View*, 98.

16. Hammett, "Multiple-Intentions View," 186.

17. Hammett, "Multiple-Intentions View," 168–69.

18. Hammett, "Multiple-Intentions View," 169.

19. Hammett, "Multiple-Intentions View," 169.

20. As Nicole summarizes, "With one voice these people [i.e., non-particularists] say that since

assumption can be shown to be biblically groundless, the objection to particularism on the basis of a universal offer fails. The remainder of this chapter and the next are dedicated to demonstrating that this is precisely the case. The assumption that a universal offer requires a coextensive provision is not warranted by the biblical text, and in fact there are many scriptural principles that demand such an assumption be rejected.

The Universal Gospel Call: Biblical and Reformed

In the first place, it must be unequivocally affirmed that the universal gospel call is a biblical doctrine.[21] The good news of "repentance for the forgiveness of sins" must be "proclaimed in [Jesus'] name to all the nations" (Luke 24:47; cf. Matt 28:19), that is, to all individuals without distinction or exception (cf. Acts 17:30).

Proper preaching of the gospel message requires the verbal proclamation of at least three components. First, there must be an explanation of the facts of the helplessness of sinful man to save himself in the light of breaking the holy law of God (1 John 1:5–8; Rom 3:23; 6:23), along with the gracious act of God in sending the Son into the world to accomplish redemption by his obedient life, his substitutionary sin-bearing death on the cross, and his resurrection from the dead (Rom 5:6–8; 1 Cor 15:1–5; 2 Cor 5:21; 1 Pet 2:24). Second, in addition to explaining the facts, the gospel message requires an earnest call for sinners to repent of their sins and trust in the work of Christ alone for their righteousness. The gospel preacher calls men to "repent and believe the gospel" (Mark 1:15); he "solemnly testif[ies] to both Jews and Greeks of repentance toward God and faith in our Lord Jesus Christ" (Acts 20:21; cf. 1 Thess 1:9). Third, along with this summons to repentant faith, there must be communicated the promise of the forgiveness of sins and eternal life for all who believe. The gospel preacher thus promises that "whoever believes in Him shall not perish, but have eternal life" (John 3:16), that repentance leads to "the forgiveness of sins" and "the gift of the Holy Spirit" (Acts 2:38), that they who "repent and return" will have their "sins . . . wiped away" and will enjoy "times of refreshing . . . from the presence of the Lord" (Acts 3:19), and that "through [Jesus] everyone who believes is freed from all things, from which you could not be freed through the Law of Moses" (Acts 13:38–39).

Scripture tasks followers of Jesus with proclaiming this gospel—the facts of salvation, the summons to repentance and faith, and the promise of forgiveness—to all people without distinction or exception. Some theologians, ostensibly attempting to protect what they deem to be logical implications of particularism, have suggested that since God intends to save only those he has chosen, therefore the gospel should be preached only to the elect. When confronted with the difficulty of distinguishing the

---

God's gospel call is universal, provision made by Christ must be universal as well" (Nicole, "Covenant, Universal Call," 407).

21. Portions of the following are adapted from the author's contributions to MacArthur and Mayhue, eds., *Biblical Doctrine*, 571–76.

elect from the reprobate, these theologians have responded by seeking for identifying marks of election, such as godly sorrow and contrition for sin.[22] Not only has that position been strongly refuted by particularists of many stripes,[23] and not only does it rest on the very same assumption of the non-particularists,[24] but it is simply contrary to the unified testimony of Scripture. The God who chooses to save only some (Rom 9:14–23) nevertheless reveals himself in Scripture as in some sense fervently desiring the repentance and salvation of the wicked. He has no "pleasure in the death of the wicked," but prefers the wicked to "turn from his ways and live" (Ezek 18:23; cf. 18:32; 33:11).

Thus, God himself issues numerous indiscriminate calls to sinners to repent, believe, find forgiveness, and be saved from sin and judgment. In Isa 45:22, the Lord issues a universal call: "Turn to Me and be saved, all the ends of the earth." The phrase כָּל־אַפְסֵי־אָרֶץ signifies a genuinely universal scope,[25] and the imperative פְּנוּ makes clear that all who hear this call are responsible and duty-bound to obey.[26] With even greater exuberance, Yahweh issues a similar call in Isa 55:1: "Ho! Every one who thirsts, come to the waters; and you who have no money come, buy and eat.

22. This was the substance of the Marrow Controversy in the eighteenth-century Scottish churches. For a helpful digest of the relevant issues, see VanDoodewaard, *Marrow Controversy and Seceder Tradition*.

23. It is of note that those within the Marrow Controversy who saw the universal gospel offer as incompatible with particular redemption were the hyper-Calvinists, whereas the orthodox Calvinists, such as Edward Fisher, Thomas Boston, and Ralph and Ebenezer Erskine, among others, defended the notion that the gospel should be preached to all without exception, even though Christ did not die for all without exception. See Fisher, *Marrow of Modern Divinity*. In the following century, Charles Spurgeon, an unambiguous particularist, was also a distinguished defender of the universal offer of the gospel; on that see Murray, *Spurgeon v. Hyper-Calvinism*. Recently, particularist Donald Macleod took up this cause as well in Macleod, *Compel Them to Come In*.

24. That is, the assumption that the atonement and the gospel offer must be coextensive. Hyper-Calvinists and others who deny the universal gospel offer reason that since (a) the atonement and the offer must be coextensive, and since (b) the atonement is limited to the elect, therefore (c) the gospel offer must be limited to the elect, so far as we can discern them. Conversely, non-particularists insist that since (a) the atonement and the offer must be coextensive, and since (b) the gospel offer must be universal, therefore (c) the atonement must be universal. Ironically, both hyper-Calvinism and universalism rest on the same faulty presupposition—that a universal offer is incompatible with a particular atonement, or, said another way, that the offer and the atonement must be coextensive. It is only particularism that avoids both sides of this unbiblical incompatibilism and demonstrates that a sincere universal offer need not be coextensive with the atonement itself. Clark makes this point when he says, "In this regard, the approach of the Synod of Dort is in contrast to that of both the Remonstrants and the modern critics of the well-meant offer [i.e., hyper-Calvinists]. Rather than making deductions from the revealed fact of God's sovereign eternal decree, the Synod was committed to learning and obeying God's revealed will, even if it seems paradoxical to us" (Clark, "Janus," 174). See footnote 55 on page 264.

25. Young comments, ". . . the reference is to men individually. If the ends of the earth turn unto God, it is only because the individual men who make up the ends of the earth have themselves turned. There is a stress upon individual conversion" (Young, *Isaiah 40–66*, 215–16). Motyer adds, "The fugitives are not a restricted company; any who wish may escape the peril of idolatry and find salvation by 'turning their faces' to the Lord" (Motyer, *Isaiah*, 366).

26. Young, *Isaiah 40–66*, 216.

Come, buy wine and milk without money and without cost." The singular כָּל־צָמֵא individualizes the summons, while the plural imperative לְכוּ generalizes it.[27] This summons is issued to all and every one; despite their poverty, they are invited to freely partake of the refreshing waters of salvation. The summons is repeated in verses 6 and 7, with the promise appended: "Seek the LORD while He may be found; call upon Him while He is near. Let the wicked forsake his way and the unrighteous man his thoughts; and let him return to the LORD, and He will have compassion on him, and to our God, for He will abundantly pardon." In this earnest entreaty, Yahweh's prophet represents him as eagerly desiring to bestow compassion and forgiveness upon any who would turn to him for salvation.

Jesus also, as the image of the invisible God and exact representation of his nature, expresses the compassion of his Father as he invites "all who are weary and heavy-laden" to come to him for rest (Matt 11:28–30). As God, the Lord Jesus knew who the elect and reprobate were, including Judas, the son of perdition who would betray him (John 6:64; cf. 17:12), but this did not keep him from offering the promises of the gospel to all indiscriminately: rest was available to *all* the weary. Accordingly, Jesus' parables demonstrate that the call of salvation goes out to a greater number than who actually respond in faith (Matt 22:2–14; Luke 14:16–24), for though there be many who are called, there are but a few who are chosen (Matt 22:14). That is to say, as MacArthur and Mayhue put it, "many are invited to partake in the feast of the blessings of eternal life, yet because the Father has only chosen some and not all, few are effectually called [unto salvation]. Therefore, many who are invited reject the external call."[28] Thus, Christ himself presents the gospel being proclaimed to elect and reprobate alike. He also makes it clear that men are duty-bound to believe the gospel when he states that it is "the work of God, that you believe" in him (John 6:29). Jesus says this to the crowds whom he had fed the previous day (6:22, 24), which includes those who had grumbled at his teaching (6:41–42), and even those whom Jesus himself declares he knew did not believe (6:64) and who ultimately reject him (6:66). Thus, Jesus commands faith from those he knew would not believe; he issues a universal gospel call to all those he teaches, without distinction or exception.

So also does the Lord commission his servants to preach the gospel to all without exception. The apostle John repeats Jesus' emphasis in John 6 in his first epistle, where he declares, "This is His commandment, that we believe in the name of His Son Jesus Christ" (1 John 3:23). This is the very principle of "duty-faith" that hyper-Calvinism repudiates;[29] God *commands* all indiscriminately to believe on Christ. Or

---

27. Motyer, *Isaiah*, 453.

28. MacArthur and Mayhue, eds., *Biblical Doctrine*, 576. Nicole also captures the thought well: "Since, then, the gospel call was addressed to some who did not respond positively, it is plain that the extent of the call is greater than that of the appropriate acceptance" (Nicole, "Covenant, Universal Call," 406).

29. Once again, see VanDoodewaard, *Marrow Controversy*; and Murray, *Spurgeon v. Hyper-Calvinism*, for more on the history and principles of this debate.

as Paul says at the close of his sermon on Mars Hill, "God is now declaring to men that *all people everywhere* should repent" (Acts 17:30). Though not all people everywhere will repent (cf. Matt 7:13; 2 Thess 3:2), they are nevertheless commanded by God to do so. Followers of Jesus must plead with sinners in a manner that reflects the urgency of the heart of the triune God (cf. Ezek 33:11), and as Paul models in 2 Cor 5:20 when he styles himself an ambassador Christ, begging sinners to be reconciled to God through repentant faith in Jesus. There can be no doubt that the universal, sincere gospel call is a biblical doctrine.[30]

However, how does this universal gospel offer cohere with the particularity of the gospel itself? As presented in chapter 4, the gospel has a Trinitarian-particularist shape: the Father elects some and not all; the Spirit regenerates some and not all; and it is the contention of this present work that the Bible just as clearly teaches that the Son atones for some and not all. How, then, can one preach the gospel to all and not merely some? In response, it must be first observed that Scripture presents no conflict between the particularity of salvation and the universality of gospel proclamation. In fact, Scripture often presents both truths in the very same context without a hint of irony or tension. The universal call to repentance and faith in Isa 55:1–7 (as discussed above) comes on the heels of the fourth Servant Song, in which the Servant is said to justify *the many* by bearing their iniquities. These many are the Servant's offspring, whose salvation is made certain by his substitutionary death in their place (Isa 53:10–12).[31] Thus, while the Servant atones for many, not all, the call to repent goes out to all, and not merely some.

A further example comes in Romans 9, as Paul teaches about the discriminating God who chooses to save sinners according to his own good pleasure, owing to nothing in sinners themselves (9:11, 16). He is the God who exults in his own sovereign freedom and says, "I will have mercy on whom I have mercy, and I will have compassion on whom I have compassion" (9:15; cf. Exod 33:19)—the God who "has mercy on whom He desires, and [who] hardens whom He desires" (9:18). Then, in the very next chapter, after these unqualified declarations of absolute sovereignty in salvation, God says, "All the day long I have stretched out My hands to a disobedient and obstinate

---

30. It should go without saying that the God who issues such earnest calls for repentance—as well as who commissions his ministers to issue those same calls—is *sincere* in his overtures of grace. Some reason that such a universal call cannot be genuine in light of the Father's particular election. But such an accusation is the product of an extrabiblical rationalism being foisted upon the text of Scripture. Both concepts are biblical: the Father has chosen some, and not all, for all who are foreknown and predestined are called, justified, and glorified (Rom 8:29–30), and, at the very same time, the God who does all that he pleases (Pss 115:3, 135:6; Isa 46:10) takes no pleasure in the death of the wicked (Ezek 18:23, 32; 33:11). MacArthur and Mayhue's conclusion is apt: "While it may be difficult to understand how statements of compassion toward the nonelect can be reconciled with the doctrines of sovereign election and particular redemption, it is not an option to conclude that God does not mean what he says!" (MacArthur and Mayhue, eds., *Biblical Doctrine*, 575).

31. For an exegetical defense of particularism in Isaiah 53, see chapter 10.

people" (10:21). The outstretched arms of God signify his earnest, compassionate desire for those to whom they are outstretched to turn and be reconciled to him.[32]

So also, in Matthew 11, just before Jesus issues that tender, searching invitation for all the weary and heavy-laden to come to him and find rest for their souls, he makes what may be his most unambiguous comments in support of the doctrine of absolute divine sovereignty. He praises—he does not just state it, but he praises—the Father, whom he addresses as the sovereign Lord of heaven and earth, for *hiding* his salvation from some and revealing it to others (Matt 11:25). Such discriminating sovereignty, he says, is simply according to the Father's good pleasure (Matt 11:26; cf. Eph 1:5), and thus unconditional (cf. Rom 9:11). Then he declares that no one knows the Father except the Son, as well as "anyone to whom the Son wills to reveal Him" (Matt 11:27). Salvation, which consists in the knowledge of the Father (John 17:3), is the sovereign prerogative of the Son; the Son will reveal the Father to no one but those to whom the Father has given him (cf. John 6:39; 17:2). And then in the very next verse comes that beloved invitation: "Come to Me, all who are weary and heavy-laden, and I will give you rest" (Matt 11:28). As John Murray puts it, "It is on the crest of the wave of divine sovereignty that the unrestricted summons comes to the labouring and heavy laden."[33]

These texts all illustrate that the sovereignty of God in particular election, particular atonement, and particular regeneration is not merely *compatible* with the universal call of the gospel; rather, such particularistic sovereignty is the *foundation* upon which the universal call of the gospel is based. Not only does particularism pose no obstacle to the indiscriminate proclamation of the gospel, but Scripture presents the latter flowing out of the former.[34] (That is because the only atonement that can serve as a thoroughly solid foundation for such a full and free offer is an *efficacious* atonement; and, barring universal final salvation, an efficacious atonement is necessarily a particular atonement.) Thus, the evangelist ought to be no more conflicted about holding fast to the twin truths of sovereign particularism and universal gospel preaching than were the prophet Isaiah (Isa 53:10–12; cf. 55:1–7), the apostle Paul (Rom 9:11–18; cf. 10:21), or the Lord Jesus himself (Matt 11:25–27; cf. 11:28–30).[35]

Not only is the universal gospel call a biblical doctrine consistent with biblical particularism, but the mainstream of Reformed particularists have always recognized this. Contrary to the claims of some hyper-Calvinists, faith in the universal offer of the gospel is not "moderate Calvinism," nor, contrary to the claims of

---

32. Cranfield comments, "The spreading out of the hands, in Ps 143.6 a gesture of supplication, is here a gesture of appealing welcome and friendship" (Cranfield, *Romans*, 2:541).

33. Murray, "Atonement and the Free Offer," 81.

34. Murray writes, "The lesson is that it is not merely conjunction of differentiating and sovereign will with free overture, but that the free overture comes out from the differentiating sovereignty of both Father and Son" (Murray, "Atonement and the Free Offer," 82).

35. Murray, "Atonement and the Free Offer," 82. Murray rightly concludes, "The doctrines of particular election, differentiating love, [and] limited atonement do not erect any fence around the offer of the gospel" (81).

non-particularists, is faith in a limited atonement "extreme Calvinism." As a matter of historical record, belief in particular redemption and a sincere, well-meant, universal offer of the gospel is *historic* Calvinism.

There is no better measure of such a claim than to turn to the Canons of the Synod of Dort, which synod was convened to establish consensus upon the doctrine of the Reformed churches in Europe amidst the threat of burgeoning Arminianism.[36] Under the Second Head of doctrine, concerning the satisfaction of Christ, the Synod asserted the particularity of Christ's atonement while at the same time commending that the gospel be proclaimed "promiscuously" and "seriously":

> . . . that the quickening and saving efficacy of the most precious death of his Son *should extend to all the elect*, for bestowing *upon them alone* the gift of justifying faith, thereby to bring them infallibly to salvation: that is, it was the will of God, that Christ by the blood of the cross, whereby he confirmed the new covenant, should effectually redeem out of every people, tribe, nation, and language, all those, *and those only*, who were from eternity chosen to salvation, and given to him by the Father.[37]

> The promise of the Gospel is that whosoever believeth in Christ crucified shall not perish, but have everlasting life. This promise, together with the command to repent and believe, ought to be declared and published to all nations, *and to all persons promiscuously and without distinction*, to whom God out of His good pleasure sends the Gospel.[38]

> As many as are called by the Gospel are unfeignedly [Lat. *serio*] called; for God hath most earnestly and truly declared in His word what will be acceptable to Him, namely, that all who are called should comply with the invitation. He, moreover, seriously [Lat. *serio*] promises eternal life and rest to as many as shall come to Him and believe in Him.[39]

Like the Scriptures themselves, the Synod found no conflict in affirming that the death of Christ "extend[s] to all the elect" and to "them alone," while at the same time declaring that the promises of the gospel are "seriously" and "unfeignedly" meant on God's part—that is, he sincerely promises salvation to all who repent and believe—and ought to be preached "promiscuously and without distinction."

This was also the conclusion of the Formula Consensus Helvetica, the Swiss confession of 1675, which explicitly rejected any form of universal atonement while at the same time declaring that "the external call itself, which is made by the preaching of

---

36. On the historical setting and doctrinal conclusions of the Synod of Dort, see De Jong, *Crisis in the Reformed Churches*; and Hyde, *Grace Worth Fighting For*.

37. Schaff, *Creeds of Christendom*, 587 (II/8), emphasis added.

38. Schaff, *Creeds of Christendom*, 3:586 (II/5), emphasis added.

39. Schaff, *Creeds of Christendom*, 3:589 (III&IV/8).

the Gospel, is on the part of God also, who calls, earnest and sincere."[40] R. Scott Clark has ably demonstrated that the free offer of the gospel has been well represented in Reformed tradition, citing Calvin, Olevianus, Wollebius, Ames, as well as the Synod of Dort.[41] This has continued into the twentieth and twenty-first centuries, as particularists continue to hold to both a particular redemption and a universal offer.[42] These facts justify Macleod's conclusion, who says, "Belief in the full, free and indiscriminate offer of the gospel has been a core dogma of Reformed orthodoxy from the beginning. It has not merely been conceded. It has been insisted on, as a dogma of such importance that any doctrine inconsistent with it would have to be instantly jettisoned."[43] Bavinck rightly concurs: "However much it might seem that the confession of election and limited atonement might require something else, the Reformed as a rule maintained the universal offer of grace."[44] It is plain, then, both that Scripture teaches that the gospel ought to be offered freely to all without exception and that the majority of particularist theologians have also believed this.

What Makes an Offer Genuine?

While opponents of particularism are quick to grant that this is so[45]—namely, that particularists do believe in a universal gospel call—they struggle to understand how they can justify such a belief in a manner consistent with their particularism.[46] How can God's offer of salvation be genuine if the Father does not choose to save all and if the Son does not die to pay the penalty of sin for all? Such a question leads us to inquire as to what constitutes a genuine offer.

The God of Truth Does Not Feign Sincerity

In the first place, it must be observed that God is a God of truth. He is not a God who reveals himself by his word in order to deceive his people by that revelation. Given that Scripture unmistakably presents God as sincerely offering and earnestly desiring the salvation of the wicked (as shown above), it falls to us to take him at his word and trust in his truthfulness and sincerity. No faithful follower of Christ can countenance the notion that God is insincere in his overtures of grace to whomever those overtures

40. Helvetic Consensus Formula 19, 318.

41. Clark, "Seriously and Promiscuously" 89–104.

42. Nicole, "Covenant, Universal Call," 410; Murray, "Atonement and the Free Offer," 59–85; Berkhof, *Systematic Theology*, 397–98; Packer, *Evangelism and the Sovereignty of God*, 67–69; Packer, "Saved by His Precious Blood."

43. Macleod, "*Amyraldus redivivus*," 220.

44. Bavinck, *Reformed Dogmatics*, 4:35.

45. E.g., Shultz, "Defense," 165–66.

46. E.g., Shultz, "Defense," 174–75.

are sent. And yet that is what must be admitted if this objection is to hold: that God is not only insincere, but that he deceptively feigns sincerity in offering salvation to sinners whom he ultimately has not decreed to save.[47]

But as Dort affirmed, God is "serious" in his offer of salvation to the lost. To say that he "take[s] no pleasure in the death of the wicked, but rather that the wicked turn from his way and live" (Ezek 33:11) is to say that God takes pleasure in—he delights in—the repentance of the wicked. As God's voice is heard in the proclamation of the gospel and the promise of salvation to the believing sinner, one does not merely hear the announcement of God's preceptive will—that is, what he commands to take place by virtue of his own righteousness. God is not merely declaring to sinners that it is right to believe the gospel and wrong to disbelieve it. Instead, he is also communicating his own disposition and desire that those who hear the gospel believe in it. A sinner's repentance pleases God, and another sinner's stubborn refusal to repent (though decreed by him) in a true sense displeases him. Murray comments that such statements as Ezek 33:11 reveal "not at all the 'seeming' attitude of God but a real attitude, a real disposition of lovingkindness inherent in the free offer to all."[48] He does not issue the call of salvation to any sinner in bad faith, as if secretly hoping the sinner will refuse.[49] To accuse him of such, or to assert that such a proposition follows consistently from either his choosing to save only some or Christ's dying for that same particular number, is to blaspheme the God of love and truth as wicked and deceptive. God's universal gospel offer can be sincere ultimately because it is the God of truth who offers it, and his sincerity cannot be called into question.

The Will of God: Decretive, Preceptive, Optative

But how else might this seeming contradiction be explained? On the one hand, God declares that he takes no pleasure in the death of the wicked (Ezek 18:23; 33:11). At the same time, God declares that "He does whatever He pleases" (Ps 115:3), saying, "My purpose will be established, and I will accomplish all my good pleasure" (Isa 46:10). None of his plans are ever frustrated (Ps 33:11; cf. Job 42:2; Dan 4:35). One might expect from these two premises, therefore, that the wicked never perish. If the God who does whatever he pleases takes no pleasure in the death of the wicked, but

---

47. MacArthur and Mayhue, eds., *Biblical Doctrine*, 575.

48. Murray, "Free Offer of the Gospel," 114.

49. Berkhof's comments are apposite: "The external calling is a calling in good faith, a calling that is seriously meant. It is not an invitation coupled with the hope that it will not be accepted. When God calls the sinner to accept Christ by faith, He earnestly desires this; and when He promises those who repent and believe eternal life, His promise is dependable. This follows from the very nature, from the veracity, of God. It is blasphemous to think that God would be guilty of equivocation and deception, that He would say one thing and mean another, that He would earnestly plead with the sinner to repent and believe unto salvation, and at the same time not desire it in any sense of the word" (Berkhof, *Systematic Theology*, 462).

rather takes pleasure in their repentance, it would seem to follow that every wicked person repents unto eternal life. But the wicked do die; sinners perish in their unbelief and go to eternal punishment (e.g., Matt 7:13; 25:46). And indeed, they do so by the eternal decree of the very God who is said to desire their repentance (Rom 9:20–23; Eph 1:11; 1 Pet 2:8). How can this be?

The answer lies in observing a distinction in the way in which Scripture speaks of the divine will. First, God's will of decree, or *decretive* will, signifies what he has infallibly decreed shall come to pass. This is the "good pleasure" (Isa 46:10) or "eternal purpose" (Eph 3:11) whereby he "works all things after the counsel of His will" (Eph 1:11). Second, God's will of command, or *preceptive* will, signifies what he has commanded his creatures to do. This speaks of mankind's duty as laid down in the imperatives of Scripture. Third, God's will of disposition, sometimes called his "*optative* will,"[50] signifies what is pleasing to him, revealing what he is positively disposed to.[51] While one at first might suppose that the content of these aspects of God's will would be identical, upon reflection it is plain that God has sovereignly determined some events to come to pass by his decretive will that he has prohibited by his preceptive will.

For example, the Lord clearly forbids Adam from eating of the tree of the knowledge of good and evil (Gen 2:17). However, Adam does eat from the tree, precipitating man's fall into sin and the need for God's grace in the provision of the seed of the woman (Gen 3:15). Yet we know that it was God's eternal purpose to rescue mankind from sin through the ministry of God the Son incarnate (1 Pet 1:20; cf. Ps 2:7–8; Matt 25:34; John 17:2, 24; Eph 1:4; Rev 13:8). If Christ was foreknown before the foundation of the world, if the elect were chosen in Christ before the foundation of the world, and if the elect were given to Christ by the Father before the foundation of the world, then it was God's plan for sin to corrupt mankind by Adam's fall, through which he would magnify his grace in Christ unto eternity (Eph 2:7). Thus, while it was *against* God's preceptive will for Adam to eat the fruit, it was *according* to God's decretive will that that very act was brought to pass. God may be said *not* to have willed according to his preceptive will what he *had* willed according to his decretive will.[52] Such examples could be multiplied. It was against the preceptive will of God for Joseph's brothers to sell him into slavery out of jealousy (Gen 37:28; cf. 37:11). Yet

---

50. *Optative* describes the grammatical mood of verbs expressing a wish or desire. For example, in 2 Thess 3:16 Paul wishes God's peace upon the believers using the optative mood when he says, "Now may the Lord of peace Himself continually grant [δῴη] you peace in every circumstance." Peter does the same in 1 Pet 1:2: "May grace and peace be multiplied [πληθυνθείη] to you." See Wallace, *Greek Grammar Beyond the Basics*, 480–84.

51. One of the best presentations of this concept comes from John Piper, "Are There Two Wills in God?," 107–31. Piper focuses particularly on the decretive and preceptive wills. One finds a reference to the "optative will" of God in MacArthur and Mayhue, eds., *Biblical Doctrine*, 559.

52. John Murray describes this phenomenon in this way: "God himself expresses an ardent desire for the fulfillment of certain things which he has not decreed in his inscrutable counsel to come to pass. This means that there is a will to the realization of what he has not decretively willed, a pleasure towards that which he has not been pleased to decree" (Murray, "Free Offer of the Gospel," 131).

Joseph declares that it was not his brothers who sent him to Egypt, but God, in order to preserve life (Gen 45:5–8). What God prohibited by his preceptive will he ordained to take place by his decretive will in order to accomplish his good purposes (cf. Gen 50:20). Similarly, it was against the preceptive will of God for Judas to betray Jesus, for the Sanhedrin to find him guilty of sin, for Pilate to give him over to be crucified, and for the soldiers to torture and crucify him. Each of those men sinned by violating the law of God for their part in the murder of Jesus. However, Isa 53:10 says, "Yet it was the will of the Lord to crush him" (ESV). Though against his preceptive will, the Father ordained by his decretive will the crucifixion of the Son in order to accomplish the salvation of his people (cf. Acts 2:23; 4:27–28).

In the same way, God commands by his preceptive will that all men everywhere repent and believe the gospel (Acts 17:30). By his optative will, he represents his own disposition toward all those made in his image—namely, that he desires none of them to perish, and that when they do, his disposition is not one of maniacal delight in their ruin, but of fatherly grief (Ezek 18:23, 32; 33:11; cf. Matt 23:37). Nevertheless, by his decretive will, before the foundation of the world, according to his inscrutable wisdom, he has determined to save only those whom he sovereignly sets his love upon, and to leave the rest to justly perish in their sins (Rom 8:28–30; 9:20–23; Eph 1:4; cf. John 17:9). And the key point is: his decretive will to save only some does not in any way mitigate (a) his preceptive will, by which he commands all to repent, or (b) his optative will, by which he sincerely desires their repentance. In other words, Scripture reveals God as willing and as not willing the same event, albeit in different senses. One will represents what he commands and is positively disposed to; another will represents what he has, in his own wisdom, determined to efficaciously bring to pass. Thus, though God sovereignly determines to cause his people grief (Lam 3:32), yet he does not do so "willingly" (Lam 3:33). Christ weeps over Jerusalem's unbelief (Luke 13:34) while possessing the power to reveal the Father to anyone he chooses (Matt 11:27). It is God who grants repentance unto salvation (2 Tim 2:25), but that same God takes no pleasure in anyone's death (Ezek 33:11). As Murray puts it, "the Lord represents himself . . . as earnestly desiring the fulfilment of something which he had not in the exercise of his sovereign will actually decreed to come to pass."[53] This is not a contradiction; it is a biblical reality concerning the will and ways of the incomprehensible God.

When one applies this to the sincere, universal, well-meant offer of the gospel, it becomes plain that the offer belongs to the realm of God's preceptive and optative will, while the concepts of unconditional election and particular redemption belong to the realm of God's decretive will. God wills the salvation of all people in one sense (hence the universal offer), while he does not will the salvation of all people in another sense (hence particular election and particular redemption); and the existence of one of these senses of God's will does not cancel out the other. The benevolent compassion of God (toward even the reprobate) that issues in the universal call of

53. Murray, "Free Offer of the Gospel," 119.

the gospel is an expression of God's preceptive and optative will, whereas his determination not to save those very same persons is the execution of his sovereign, decretive will.[54] Particular redemption and the universal gospel offer, then, are no more contradictory than God forbidding the crucifixion by his preceptive will and his ordaining the crucifixion by his decretive will.[55]

Pressing further, the fact that Christ has not atoned for the sins of all without exception (which proponents of the MIV deny) no more undermines a universal gospel offer than the fact that the Father has not chosen to save all sinners without exception, or the fact that the Spirit does not grant repentance and faith to all without exception (both of which proponents of the MIV affirm). Non-particularists claim that it is illegitimate to offer salvation to those for whom Christ did not die; in order for such an offer to be genuine, Christ must have provided an atonement for their sins that can be appropriated by faith. But in affirming unconditional election and irresistible grace, proponents of the MIV (along with so-called four-point Calvinists) must concede that the Father offers salvation to those whom he has not chosen, and to whom, in his sovereign wisdom, he chooses not to grant saving faith. If God cannot sincerely offer the gospel to those for whom Christ did not die, how can he sincerely offer the gospel to those whom he has not chosen, or to those whom the Spirit will never grant

---

54. As Piper says, "What this means is that the sincere offer of the gospel and definite atonement are not contradictory. God desires the salvation of the lost, but he does not save all of them. Another way to say it is that there are what appear to be 'levels'" in God's willing. At one level, he sincerely *desires* that everyone be saved. And at another deeper level, his wisdom counsels otherwise, to save only some. . . . "God does not delight in the death of the wicked, as Ezekiel says, and yet, for wise and holy reasons, he withholds the working of his power to 'grant them repentance'" (Piper, "My Glory," 662).

55. Reformed orthodoxy has captured this phenomenon in the distinction between archetypal theology (*theologia archetypa*) and ectypal theology (*theologia ectypa*). Archetypal theology is theology as God knows it, while ectypal theology is theology as it is revealed by God to mankind and as mankind understands it. Clark ably summarizes this notion in Luther, Calvin, Junius, Polanus, and Wollebius (Clark, "Janus," 149–80). This concept of the "secret" and "revealed" will of God, or archetypal and ectypal theology, lay at the foundation of Reformed theology's harmonization of the universal gospel offer (ectypal theology) with a particular election and particular redemption (archetypal theology).

It was the failure to properly distinguish these concepts that led both hyper-Calvinism and Remonstrant Arminianism to hold to an incompatibility between particular redemption and universal gospel preaching. The opponents of the universal offer prioritized the archetypal theology of God's unconditional election and the Son's particular redemption at the expense of the ectypal theology of the universal gospel offer, reasoning that since God had only chosen some and since Christ had only died for some, the gospel should only be offered to those. Like the proponents of the MIV, the Remonstrants prioritized the ectypal theology of the universal offer at the expense of the archetypal theology of God's decree, reasoning that since the gospel must be offered to all, it could not be that Christ had only died for some. Ironically, both hyper-Calvinism and Arminianism make the same error, albeit in opposite directions. That error is the failure to distinguish archetypal theology from ectypal theology, the decretive will from the preceptive will; it is to assume that particularism in the atonement rules out universalism in the offer, and vice versa. In reality, and in a manner analogous to God's sovereignty and man's responsibility, these are not contradictory but are perfectly compatible. See footnote 24 on page 255.

the faith that is the condition by which they may lay hold of the benefits of Christ's provision?[56] Blocher captures the problem well:

> The difficulty Hypothetical Universalism defenders denounce looks more psychological than analytical. One *feels* that God cannot "sincerely" offer Judas or Jezebel a cancellation of their debts as a benefit from the cross, if the price was not paid for them on the cross. But the same difficulty arises when one thinks that God offers Judas or Jezebel (code names for any non-elect individuals) something they are unable to get, since *they are unable to repent.* God has decided *not* to operate repentance in their hearts—this truth, Reformed theologians who hold to Hypothetical Universalism acknowledge. (And God has foreknown *with absolute certainty* that Judas and Jezebel will not repent.)[57]

In other words, if the MIV's objection succeeds against particular redemption, it also succeeds against unconditional election and irresistible grace, and thus proves too much for those who affirm the latter two. But, in fact, the objection does not succeed. Just as the proponents of the MIV have no trouble offering the gospel to those the Father may not have chosen and to whom the Spirit may not grant faith, they should have no trouble offering the gospel to those for whom Christ may not have died. Those are matters of the decretive will of God, whereas the revealed will of God is that faithful followers of Christ must call all without exception to repent and believe.

The Prerequisite for a Genuine Offer

Thus far we have considered that a God of truth cannot offer anything but in a sincere manner, and that this God's sovereign determination not to save all and thus not give Christ to die for all is not in contradiction to his sincere offer of salvation to all. But why is God's offer genuine? What makes an offer genuine? And what about the universal offer of the gospel fits that definition? Along with many non-particularists, the MIV claims that God's offer of salvation to all indiscriminately can only be genuine if there is a coextensive provision—only if Christ has paid the penalty for their sins to make them savable, provisionally procuring their salvation, which

56. As Piper puts it, "If God's foreknowledge cancels the sincerity of his invitations, then there are no sincere invitations at all. In other words, even the Amyraldian and Hypothetical Universalist must deal with the issue that God commands everyone everywhere to repent and believe the gospel (Acts 17:30–31), while also granting repentance and faith to only some (Phil. 1:29; 2 Tim. 2:25)" (Piper, "My Glory," 661). Bavinck also captures this: "If it be objected that God nevertheless offers salvation to those to whom he has decided not to grant faith and salvation, then this is an objection equally applicable to the position of our opponents. For in that case, God also offers salvation to those whom he infallibly knows will not believe" (Bavinck, *Reformed Dogmatics*, 4:37).

57. Blocher, "Jesus Christ the Man," 565–66. Nicole makes the same point: ". . . some opponents urge, an offer cannot be held to be sincere unless there is some expectation that it may be favorably answered. . . . all alike hold that God foreknows all things and would be unable to offer the gospel sincerely to those he knows will refuse" (Nicole, "Covenant, Universal Call," 408–9).

they may lay hold of by believing.[58] But this is not so. An offer is genuine so long as "if the terms of the offer be observed, that which is offered be actually granted."[59] For God to genuinely offer salvation to sinners on the condition of repentant faith, it must be that if any sinner repents of sin and believes in Christ, God will infallibly and without exception save that sinner.

Roger Nicole has famously illustrated the failure of the coextensive provision principle by considering that a department store might send three hundred thousand circulars to the surrounding neighborhoods to advertise a sale on a washing machine, but it would be inappropriate to accuse it of insincerity or unethical practices if it does not have a supply of three hundred thousand washing machines, equal to the number of circulars sent out. Nicole explains, "All that the customer really has the right to expect is that if he/she appears at any of the stores listed within the time stated and with the appropriate amount of cash he/she will be sold the object advertised at the price stipulated."[60] Because the store managers have a reasonable expectation that not everyone who received a circular will be interested in buying a washing machine, they do not need to have a coextensive provision for the offer to be genuine. It is granted that no analogy is perfect, but this one does illustrate that coextensive provision is not a prerequisite for a genuine offer.

Instead, Nicole argues, the essential prerequisite for a sincere or genuine offer of anything is that if the terms of the offer are met, that which is offered must be granted as promised. It is difficult to find any quarrel with such a statement. If person A offers X to person B on condition Y, that offer is genuine if when B performs Y, A gives X to B. Applied to the gospel, God's offer to sinners is that if anyone repents and believes in Christ, he will be saved: ". . . everyone who beholds the Son and believes in Him will have eternal life" (John 6:40).[61] And it is precisely the case that if anyone repents and believes in Christ, God will save him. There never has been, nor will there ever be, a case in which a sinner comes to Christ in repentance and faith and is refused salvation—for *any* reason, least of all that there was insufficiency in Christ's atoning death in his case. Piper captures it well when he writes, "An offer is valid if the one who offers always and without fail gives what is offered to everyone who meets the terms of the offer. This God does without fail. No one ever believed on Jesus and then perished (John 3:16)."[62] Indeed, Christ himself says emphatically, ". . . the one who comes to Me I will certainly not [οὐ μὴ] cast out" (John 6:37b).

---

58. See Shultz, *Multi-Intentioned View*, 98.

59. Nicole, "Covenant, Universal Call," 409–10.

60. Nicole, "Covenant, Universal Call," 408.

61. Caspar Olevian defined the genuine offer in this way: "to offer with intention that the offer should be fulfilled if the recipients meet the condition of trust in Christ" (as cited in Clark, "Janus," 169).

62. Piper, "My Glory," 658–59.

But what if one for whom Christ has not died on the cross should come to Christ in faith? Such a scenario is impossible, for the only ones who come to Christ in faith are the elect—those whom the Father has given him. Jesus says this in the first half of that very same sentence: "All that the Father gives Me will come to Me" (John 6:37a). All those—and only those—that the Father has given to the Son will come to the Son. Only the elect, chosen before the foundation of the world in Christ (cf. Eph 1:4) and given to Christ as his sheep (John 10:14–15; cf. 10:29), are granted saving faith. It is that same number for whom Christ lays down his life in atonement (John 6:39; 10:15; 17:2, 6, 9). The perfect unity of the sovereign saving will of the persons of the Trinity ensures that no sinner comes to Christ in faith and is refused salvation, since the very act of coming is purchased by Christ's atoning death and given by the Father's sovereign appointment. The reprobate will never meet the conditions of the offer; that Christ did not die for them does not diminish the sincerity of the offer.

It is noteworthy is that both archetypal and ectypal theologies are present in John 6:37, without a hint that Jesus believes they are contradictory. "All that the Father gives Me" defines those for whom Christ died as the elect, while "the one who comes to Me" defines that very same number without distinction amidst the mass of sinful mankind to whom the gospel is offered. That the Father gave the Son a *particular* number for whom to lay down his life (John 6:37a) in no way obviates the universal call to all sinners without distinction (John 6:37b). As Packer says, "The two truths stand side by side in these verses, and that is where they belong. They go together. They walk hand in hand. Neither throws doubt on the truth of the other. Neither should fill our minds to the exclusion of the other."[63] It is certainly not a lie to tell sinners that whoever believes will not perish but have eternal life.[64] We may tell them that Christ has accomplished a full atonement; he has purchased forgiveness and righteousness and salvation for *everyone* that his Father has given him; and he promises that whoever comes to him in faith he will never cast away. He has never refused salvation to anyone who has met those conditions. There is no insufficiency in his accomplishment, and the promise is dependable that all who believe will be saved. This offer of salvation is fully and completely genuine—"totally sincere and without any deceit at all."[65] Thus, contrary to Shultz's claim, it is *not* "impossible to genuinely offer salvation to the non-elect, since

---

63. Packer, *Evangelism and the Sovereignty of God*, 101.

64. Owen asks with incisive poignancy, "What do the preachers of the gospel offer to them to whom the word is preached? Is it not life and salvation through Christ, upon the condition of faith and repentance? And doth not the truth of this offer consist in this, that every one that believeth shall be saved? And doth not that truth stand firm and inviolable, so long as there is an all-sufficiency in Christ to save all that come unto him? Hath God intrusted to ministers of the gospel with his intentions, purposes, and counsels [i.e., his decretive will, archetypal theology], or with his commands and promises [i.e., his preceptive will, ectypal theology]? Is it a lie, to tell men that he that believeth shall be saved, though Christ did not die for some of them?" (Owen, *Death of Death*, 393).

65. Piper, "My Glory," 661.

there is no salvation available to offer them."[66] Christ has made a full atonement for sins; he has not merely made men savable or provided a possibility of salvation, but he has accomplished salvation for all the Father has given him. And in the same breath he freely offers that salvation to all who come to him. There is no contradiction between a particular redemption and a genuine universal gospel offer.

The Sufficiency of the Atonement

At least in part, the genuineness of the universal offer of salvation is grounded in the perfect sufficiency of Christ's atoning work. Christ's death is sufficient for all such that if it were the Father's intention to save every individual ever created, Christ would not be required to suffer any more than he already has suffered, for truly he *could* not suffer any more than he has, since his sufferings were infinite. But how can the atonement of Christ be infinitely sufficient—sufficient to save all without exception—if he has not at least in some sense atoned for all without exception? If one denies any universality to the atonement itself, can one also hold to the universal sufficiency of the atonement?

Particular Redemption, Universal Sufficiency

In the first place, it must be observed that as a matter of historical record those who held strongly to a particular redemption did also often hold just as strongly to the infinite sufficiency and worth of the death of Christ. From a historical perspective, Bavinck observes, ". . . all the particularists without exception confess the universality of the sacrifice of Christ as it pertains to its inner value. Even those who object to the formulation that Christ died 'sufficiently' for all and 'efficaciously' for the elect still fully recognize that the substance of Christ's merit is completely sufficient for the atonement of the sins of all people."[67] Cunningham agrees, saying, "First, the advocates of a limited or definite atonement do not deny, but maintain, the infinite intrinsic sufficiency of Christ's satisfaction and merits . . . sufficient to have purchased pardon and reconciliation for the whole race of fallen man."[68] A more recent historical theologian, Donald Macleod, does not hesitate to speak just as exhaustively, saying, "All Reformed theologians have agreed on the infinite *inherent* sufficiency of the sacrifice of Christ: sufficient in itself to redeem the whole world and many worlds besides."[69] The evidence for such a historical assessment is profuse, though perhaps it is sufficient to inquire of John Owen's view of the sufficiency of the death of Christ, as there has hardly been a more staunch defense of particularism than Owen's *The Death*

66. Shultz, "Why a Genuine Universal Gospel Call," 122.

67. Bavinck, *Reformed Dogmatics*, 3:464.

68. Cunningham, *Historical Theology*, 2:331.

69. Macleod, "Definite Atonement and the Divine Decree," 426.

of Death in the Death of Christ. In that very work Owen writes, "The first thing that we shall lay down is concerning the dignity, worth, preciousness, and infinite value of the blood and death of Jesus Christ . . . sufficient in itself for the redeeming of all and every man, if it had pleased the Lord to employ it to that purpose; yea, and of other worlds also."[70] If God had made a thousand worlds and intended to redeem each individual in each of those worlds, the atonement accomplished by the death of the Son of God on the cross would be sufficient to save every one of them.[71] This has been the unified voice of the ablest proponents of particular redemption.

Intrinsic Sufficiency

But again, how can the atonement be sufficient for those for whom Christ did not die? The key to understanding particularism's affirmation of the infinite sufficiency of the atonement is to recognize that it is an *intrinsic* sufficiency of which they are speaking. That is to say, nothing needs to be added to Christ's sacrifice of himself in death to infallibly secure the salvation of all those who trust in him (John 19:30; Heb 7:26–28; 9:11–12, 25–28; 10:10–14). To illustrate this, consider the hypothetical scenario that if God had determined to add to the number of the elect (an acknowledged impossibility), Jesus would not have had to suffer more than he suffered on the cross. The sufferings he underwent on Calvary would not need to be increased in some way for God to justly apply the merits of his sacrifice to the account of another sinner. This is because, in truth, the sufferings Christ experienced on Calvary *could* not have been increased. There was no more suffering for him to endure than what he already endured, for he suffered in the place of sinners, who were infinitely guilty for having offended an infinitely holy God, and thus he bore an infinite outpouring of wrath to satisfy the demands of infinite justice. Further, Christ himself was also infinitely righteous, as the substitute satisfying infinite wrath must have been in order for his sacrifice to be acceptable before God. His righteousness could not have been increased to sweeten the sacrifice or make it more worthy than it already was. His was the blood of God (Acts 20:28), infinitely precious, as of a lamb unblemished and spotless (1 Pet 1:18–19; cf. Heb 9:12–14), offered to the Father by the eternal Spirit of holiness (Heb 9:14), able to justify from all things (Acts 13:38–39; cf. 1 John 1:7), in which blood redemption itself consists (Eph 1:7; Rev 1:5). Thus, the infinite sufficiency of Christ's atonement arises from (a) the dignity and value of the person who made the sacrifice—the infinitely righteous Son of God—as well as from (b) the infinitude of the punishment he endured and the payment that he rendered by his penal substitutionary death.[72]

In the same way, if God had determined to save fewer persons than he did, Christ would not have needed to suffer any less, for a single sin against the infinitely holy

---

70. Owen, *Death of Death*, 295.
71. Owen, *Death of Death*, 297.
72. Owen, *Death of Death*, 296.

God would have demanded an infinite punishment and thus an infinitely righteous substitute. So also, if God had determined to save more persons than he did, Christ would not have needed to suffer any more, for since his sufferings were infinite and his righteousness infinitely acceptable, he *could* not have suffered any more.[73] The eighteenth-century Scottish minister Adam Gib captured this in memorable fashion when he said, "Thus, though our Lord came to redeem only a part of mankind, He did not come to fulfil only a part of the law, or to bear only a part of its curse; . . . Were all mankind betaking themselves to this atonement and righteousness at the bar of the Law and justice, nothing further could be found requisite there for the justification and salvation of them all."[74]

This infinite *intrinsic* sufficiency is what particularists affirm by confessing that Christ's death was sufficient for all. The once-for-all sacrifice offered on Calvary could have satisfied the wrath of God on behalf of the sins of all without exception, and, as is often confessed, of thousands of worlds besides. But what actually makes the atonement a satisfaction for anyone is not its sufficiency, but rather the purpose and design of God in giving the Son over to make that atonement.[75] Owen explains, "It was in itself of infinite value and sufficiency to *have been made a price* to have bought and purchased all and every man in the world. That it did formally become a price for any is solely to be ascribed to the purpose of God, intending their purchase and redemption by it."[76] In other words, the infinite sufficiency of the atonement does not consist in Christ having made satisfaction for the sins of all those for whom his death is sufficient; his death is sufficient for all not on the basis of the Father's actually having *intended* that sacrifice in some sense for all persons. Rather, the sufficiency arises from what the atonement was in itself: the infinitely righteous Savior bearing the infinite wrath of God with perfect efficacy.[77]

73. Cunningham captures this truth well: "They regard His sufferings and death as possessed of value, or worth, sufficient to have purchased pardon and reconciliation for the whole race of fallen man. The value or worth of His sacrifice of Himself depends upon, and is measured by, the dignity of His person, and is therefore infinite. Though many fewer of the human race had been to be pardoned and saved, and atonement of infinite value would have been necessary, in order to procure for them these blessings; and though many more, yea, all men, had to be pardoned and saved, the death of Christ, being an atonement of infinite value, would have been amply sufficient, as the ground of basis of their salvation" (Cunningham, *Historical Theology*, 2:331).

74. Gib, *Present Truth*, 2:154.

75. As Owen says, ". . . its being a price for all or some doth not arise from its own sufficiency, worth, or dignity, but from the intention of God and Christ using it to that purpose" (Owen, *Death of Death*, 296).

76. Owen, *Death of Death*, 296 Andrew Fuller voices the same argument: "If I speak of [the death of Christ] *irrespective of the purpose of the Father and the Son, as to the objects who should be saved by it,* merely referring to what it is in itself sufficient for, and declared in the gospel to be adapted to, I should think that I answered the question in a scriptural way by saying, It was for *sinners as sinners*; but if I have respect to the *purpose* of the Father in giving his Son to die, and to the *design* of Christ in laying down his life, I should answer, It was for the elect only" (Fuller, "Six Letters," 321a, emphasis original).

77. Cunningham says, "We know nothing of the amount or extent of Christ's sufferings in

Against Ordained Sufficiency

This understanding of sufficiency is in stark contrast with the definition offered by many non-particularists. Though it is not always stated (perhaps even because it is not always consciously held), those who see a contradiction between universal sufficiency and particular redemption define sufficiency as what hypothetical universalist John Davenant called "ordained sufficiency" (*sufficientia ordinate*). As Macleod explains, Davenant asserted, "By God's ordination and deliberate intention Christ was offered for the redemption of all mankind and *accepted* for the redemption of all mankind. The sufficiency, he claims, is not confined to the intrinsic nature of the sacrifice but is extended to the divine intention: in the act of offering himself, it was Christ's intention to redeem all men."[78] Davenant derided the doctrine of intrinsic sufficiency as a "bare sufficiency" (*nuda sufficientia*) and insisted that the Scriptures "speak of the death of Christ so as to refer its universal efficacy not to the mere dignity of the sacrifice offered, but to the act and intention of the offering."[79] Moore explains that for Davenant, as well as all hypothetical universalists, the sufficiency of the atonement "involves the will of God that Christ's sufficient death should set the foundation for a two-staged reconciliation and should render all men salvable—in other words, the formal establishment of a potential redemption for all without exception."[80] Macleod observes that according to Davenant the intention of Christ to redeem all men "was conditional in the sense that Christ's redemptive act had to be completed by an additional act, external to the sacrifice itself, namely faith."[81]

The problems with such a view are almost immediately apparent. In the first place, as demonstrated chapter 5, Scripture simply does not speak of the Father's intention in the death of Christ as rendering all men "salvable," nor of the actual efficacy of Christ's sacrifice as establishing a "potential redemption" for anyone.[82] Such a revision of the nature of the atonement rests upon interpreting the universalistic texts in an absolutely universal sense, an exegetical case shown to have failed in part 3.[83] Even the notion of "the formal establishment of a potential" *anything* is suspect, for what would it mean to formally establish that which is not actual? Though seemingly sympathetic with Davenant's conclusions, Moore captures the failure of the hypothetical

---

themselves. Scripture tells us only of *their relation to the law, in compliance with the provision of which they were inflicted and endured.* This implies their infinity, in respect of intrinsic legal worth or value; and this, again, implies their full intrinsic sufficiency for the redemption of all men, if God had intended to redeem and save them" (Cunningham, *Historical Theology*, 2:331, emphasis original).

78. Macleod, "Definite Atonement and the Divine Decree," 426; cf. Davenant, "Dissertation," 2:403.

79. Davenant, "Dissertation," 2:410–11.

80. Moore, "Extent of the Atonement," 139.

81. Macleod, "Definite Atonement and the Divine Decree," 426

82. See chapter 5.

83. See part 3.

universalist system when he observes, "If Owen was emptying the *sufficientia* of any real meaning [which we deny he does], Davenant was emptying the *satisfactio* of any real meaning."[84] He is exactly right; in an attempt to universalize the extent of the atonement, even the best of hypothetical universalists must empty the satisfaction Christ accomplished down to a potential redemption.

Further, if universal sufficiency is based on an intention to save all men, but that intention is conditional such that Christ's redemptive act had to be completed by the additional act of faith, any notion of sufficiency is undermined. X is sufficient for Y if nothing other than X is required to obtain Y. Under the hypothetical universalist proposal, the atonement is *not* sufficient for the salvation of all men apart from the added condition of faith.[85] Besides this, since, under Davenant's scheme, the condition of faith is not part of the "ordained sufficiency" of the atonement, God's appointment of the death of Christ as a means to save all men was not accompanied by the "determinate will in God of producing that end by those means."[86] Macleod captures the essence of Davenant's argument when he observes,

> There was no divine resolve actually to save all men, but only a "general sufficiency" to effect the salvation of all. It is hard to distinguish this "general sufficiency" from the "mere" sufficiency with which Davenant had professed himself dissatisfied. God ordained the means by which all people might be saved, but he did not ordain the grace by which all could avail themselves of these means.[87]

David Allen, a contemporary proponent of such an understanding of sufficiency, which he calls "extrinsic sufficiency," proposes something similar. He writes, "*Extrinsic Sufficiency* speaks to the atonement's actual infinite ability to save all and every human, and this because God, indeed, wills it to be so, such that Christ, *in fact*, made a satisfaction for all humankind."[88] Thus, on this proposal, we are left with God willing the atonement to be sufficient to do that which God never wills to be done. By God's will, Christ has died to satisfy the wrath of God on behalf of sinners such that they may be saved if they believe, but—in the very same act of willing—God does *not* will to grant the faith by which those sinners activate the "ability" of the atonement to save them. It is easy to sympathize with those who regard the duality inherent to

---

84. Moore, "Extent of the Atonement," 141.

85. Some will object that since sinners are not saved at the moment Christ dies, and since faith is necessary for a sinner to be saved, therefore even particularists face the problem of an insufficient atonement. However, this is a failure to understand the difference between impetration and application—redemption accomplished and redemption applied—which is discussed in chapter 7 ("Efficacious Accomplishment") in chapter 8 ("The Relationship between Impetration and Application").

86. Davenant, "Tract," part I, as cited in Macleod, "Definite Atonement and the Divine Decree," 426.

87. Macleod, "Definite Atonement and the Divine Decree," 426.

88. Allen, "Atonement: Limited or Universal?," 64, emphases original.

hypothetical universalism as double-mindedness, resulting in "a confused Christ" with a "split personality," who dies to make men savable on a condition that he sovereignly determines never to grant them.[89] Turretin's critique is apposite, representing the confused Christ in this manner: "I desire that to come to pass which I not only know will not and cannot take place, but also what I am unwilling should take place because I refuse to communicate that without which it can never be brought to pass as it depends upon myself alone."[90] Not only does "ordained" or "extrinsic" sufficiency fail to maintain an atonement that is actually sufficient to accomplish its ends; it also undermines the wisdom of God.[91]

"Sufficient for All, Efficient for the Elect"?

This distinction between intrinsic sufficiency and ordained sufficiency accounts for why both particularists and universalists (whether Arminians or hypothetical universalists) can subscribe to the popular maxim that the death of Christ is sufficient for all but efficient only for the elect,[92] as well as for why proponents of the MIV believe that there is agreement between their position and particularism on the sufficiency of the atonement.[93] The phrase is ambiguous, because it fails to distinguish between not only an *efficiency* based on a limited intention versus a limited appropriation,[94] but also between a *sufficiency* based on the intrinsic worth of the person of Christ and the value of his sufferings (intrinsic) versus the intention and will of God in the death of Christ (ordained, or extrinsic). Particularists affirm the former while Arminians, hypothetical

---

89. Gibson, "Trinitarian Work," 369.

90. Turretin, *Institutes of Elenctic Theology*, 2:467.

91. Allen objects that intrinsic sufficiency is "not *actually* sufficient or able to save any others" but the elect, because "God did not intend for the death of Christ to satisfy for all" (Allen, "Atonement: Limited or Universal?," 63). However, Allen wrongly presupposes, without argument, that no sufficiency is "actual" sufficiency except an "ordained" or "extrinsic" sufficiency rooted in a universal atonement. This simply does not follow, for the reasons stated in the body of this section. Intrinsic sufficiency is indeed a real, actual sufficiency to save anyone and everyone. But since all agree that none will *actually* be saved except the elect, the discussion is by nature hypothetical. For Allen, the *atonement* is hypothetically universal, while for particularists, the atonement's *sufficiency* is hypothetically universal, because God's intention is to save only his elect.

92. This phrase has its origins in the work of the medieval theologian Peter Lombard, who wrote that Christ offers himself "for all, with respect to the sufficiency of the ransom, but for the elect alone with regard to its efficiency, because it effects salvation for the predestined alone" (*pro omnibus, quantam ad pretii sufficientiam; sed pro electis tantum quantum ad efficaciam, quia praedestinatis tantum salutem effecit*) (Lombard, *Sentences*, 3.20.5; 2:128).

93. Ware writes, "All agree that if God wanted to save all people or provide salvation for all people, the value of Christ's payment for sin was sufficient (because of its infinite value for the sin of the world. In brief, his death is sufficient for all" (Ware, "Outline," 1). Shultz states that "both positions generally agree that Christ's death is sufficient for all sin and is efficacious for all who truly believe" (Shultz, "Defense," 6).

94. Archibald, "Comparative Study," 366.

universalists, and proponents of the MIV affirm the latter.[95] Thus, Naselli is right to conclude, "It is not helpful when people define their position with the phrase 'sufficient for all, efficient for the elect.' . . . Arminians, hypothetical universalists, and Calvinists alike have used that elastic phrase to describe their positions; so using it to define one's position results in confusion rather than clarity and precision."[96]

Particularists, then, happily affirm that the atonement was sufficient for all, because there is nothing deficient in the atonement for anyone.[97] No one who comes to Christ in faith finds anything lacking in his person and work with respect to their salvation, and nothing more would have to be accomplished—no more wrath poured out, no more suffering endured—if God intended to save just one more sinner than the company he chose before the foundation of the world. Thus, the atonement *is* sufficient

95. Owen brings much clarity to this question: "Hence may appear what is to be thought of that old distinction of the schoolmen, embraced and used by divers protestant divines, though by others again rejected,—namely, 'That Christ died for all in respect of the sufficiency of the ransom paid, but not in respect of the efficacy of its application;' or, 'The blood of Christ was a sufficient price for the sins of all the world;'—which is most true, as was before declared: for its being a price for all or some doth not arise from its own sufficiency, worth, or dignity, but from the intention of God and Christ using it to that purpose, as was declared; and, therefore, it is denied that the blood of Christ was a sufficient price and ransom for all and every one, not because it was not *sufficient* [for anyone], but because it was not a *ransom* [for everyone]. And so it easily appears what is to be owned in the distinction itself before expressed. If it intend no more but that the blood of our Savior was of sufficient value for the redemption of all and every one, and that Christ intended to lay down a price which should be sufficient for their redemption, it is acknowledged as most true. But the truth is, that expression, 'To die for them,' holds out the intention of our Saviour, in the laying down of the price, to have been their redemption; which we deny, and affirm that then it could not be but that they must be made actual partakers of the eternal redemption purchased for them, unless God failed in his design, through the defect of the ransom paid by Christ, his justice refusing to give a dismission upon the delivery of the ransom" (Owen, *Death of Death*, 296, emphases added).

96. Naselli, "Conclusion," 219. Rather than outright denying the sufficiency of the atonement, as he is often accused of, Beza came to the same conclusion: "Indeed, that 'Christ died for the sins of all men sufficiently, but not efficiently'— even if it is true by the strict sense, nevertheless it is stated quite stiffly and ambiguously, no less than ignorantly" ("Illum enim, 'Christus mortuus est pro omnium hominum peccatis Sufficienter, sed non Efficienter,' et si recto sensu verum est, dure tamen admodum et ambigue non minus quam barbare dicitur") (Beza, *Ad Acta*, 217). Godfrey comments, "Beza granted that if rightly understood the classical formulation of Lombard's *Sentences* was acceptable but he indicated that it was probably better for theological clarity to abandon the distinction. Beza was concerned about the ambiguity of the statement and felt that the particularity of God's saving intention in Christ could be better stated without this distinction. Christ died for all men only in the sense that his death was of infinite value. His death was not for all men individually either with respect to the intention of the Father in sending his Son to die or with respect to the actual effect of the death" (Godfrey, "Reformed Thought on the Extent of the Atonement to 1618," 142).

97. Turretin says, "For it is confessed by all that since its value is infinite, it would have been entirely sufficient for the redemption of each and every one, if God had seen fit to extend it to the whole world. And here belongs the distinction used by the fathers and retained by many divines—that Christ 'died sufficiently for all, but efficiently for the elect only.' For this being understood of the dignity [i.e., intrinsic sufficiency] of Christ's death is perfectly true (although the phrase would be less accurate if referred to the will and purpose of Christ) [i.e., ordained or extrinsic sufficiency]. But the question properly concerns the purpose of the Father in delivering up his own Son and the intention of Christ in dying" (Turretin, *Institutes of Elenctic Theology*, 2:458–59).

for the reprobate—not because Christ has actually paid for their sins to put them in a savable state, or because the Father intended a general non-saving benefit by Christ's death, but because the intrinsic worth of the person of Christ and the merit of his sufferings are sufficient to save any sinner who comes to him.[98]

The Warrant of Faith

If, then, the sufficiency of the atonement consists in its intrinsic value and worth, and not in a universal satisfaction grounded in a general divine intention, it is on the ground of that intrinsic sufficiency that the gospel may be preached to all indiscriminately. Even though the atonement has not been offered *for* all men, the good news of repentance for the forgiveness of sins may be offered *to* all men. In other words, the warrant of faith—the reason any sinner has warrant for repenting of his sins and believing in Christ for salvation—is not the knowledge that Christ has died in the place of that sinner in particular. Rather, such a warrant consists in three other truths.[99]

The first truth is the one insisted upon in the previous point, namely, the infinite sufficiency of Christ's atonement. Sinners are warranted to believe the gospel because Christ is uniquely and precisely suited to their need. The Lord Jesus Christ by his death and resurrection has accomplished salvation (a) for men and women, as opposed to angels or other creatures (Heb 2:16–17), and (b) for sinners, as opposed to righteous persons (Luke 5:32; cf. 1 Tim 1:15). Christ died to save human beings who are sinners; thus, if anyone is a human being and a sinner, he has warrant to trust in Christ to save him, for the infinite sufficiency of his atonement is such that he is "able to save to the

---

98. Cunningham explains, "But after controversy had thrown its full light upon the subject, orthodox divines generally refused to adopt this mode of stating the point, because it seemed to ascribe to Christ a *purpose* or *intention* of dying in the room of all, and of benefiting all by the proper effects of His death, as an atonement or propitiation; not that they doubted or denied the intrinsic sufficiency of His death for the redemption of all men, but because the statement—whether originally so intended or not—was so expressed as to suggest the idea, that Christ, in dying, desired and intended that all men should partake in the proper and peculiar effects of the shedding of His blood. Calvinists do not object to say that the death of Christ—viewed objectively, apart from His purpose or design—was sufficient for all, and efficacious for the elect, because this statement in the first clause merely asserts its infinite intrinsic sufficiency, which they admit; whereas the original scholastic form of the statement . . . [could be interpreted to] indicate that, when He died, *He intended* that all should derive some saving and permanent benefit from His death" (Cunningham, *Historical Theology*, 2:332, emphasis original).

99. John Hurrion offers a helpful summary of these three: "There are three things which lay a sufficient foundation for ministers to call all their hearers to believe, and for any of them to hearken to the call: [1] One thing is, *Christ's ability to save, to the uttermost, all who come to God by him*, Heb. 7:25. Another things is, [2] *God's command*, 1 John 3:23, *that men believe in Christ*; this is *the work of God*, John 6:29, that which he requires, and that which he is pleased with: Besides these, there is [3] the gracious declaration and assurance; 'That whosoever believes shall not perish; and that Christ will in no wise cast out him that comes to him,' chapter 3:16; 6:37. Upon these grounds, the apostles pressed men to 'believe in Christ,' and preached to them forgiveness of sins, Acts 13:38; through faith in his blood" (Hurrion, *Particular Redemption*, 100–101, emphases original).

uttermost those who draw near to God through him" (Heb 7:25, ESV). Nothing is lacking in the person or work of Christ to save those who will believe; therefore, any who believes is welcome to Christ and will find him and his atonement perfectly sufficient to avail for him for forgiveness of sins and righteousness before God.

Secondly, gospel preachers may summon their hearers to faith in Christ—and those hearers have sufficient warrant to answer that summons by believing—on the ground that God himself commands them to do so. In the first place, God commands his servants to preach the gospel to every creature (Mark 16:15), and in so doing he makes indiscriminate gospel preaching a matter of Christian obedience, regardless of whether we can comprehend how such a universal call harmonizes with a particular election and/or a particular redemption. One need not trouble himself with how he might consistently call a sinner to faith in Christ without knowing if the man to whom he is speaking is one of the elect for whom Christ died. Such would be the error of making God's decretive will, rather than his preceptive will, the rule of our duty. As Owen counsels, "A minister is not to make inquiry after, nor to trouble himself about, those secrets of the eternal mind of God, namely,—whom he purposeth to save, and whom he hath sent Christ to die for in particular. It is enough for them to search his revealed will, and thence take their *directions*, from whence they have their *commissions*."[100] In calling men and women to believe the gospel, the preacher does not comment on whether God has chosen or Christ has died for his hearers; he simply makes known to them that God commands them, and so it is their duty, to repent and believe in Christ.[101] This leads us to observe, in the second place, that God not only commands his ministers to preach the gospel to all, but he also commands all without exception to repent and believe the gospel themselves. Paul declares, "having overlooked the times of ignorance, God is now declaring to men that all people everywhere should repent" (Acts 17:30; ESV: "he commands all people everywhere to repent"); and so John with him, "This is His commandment, that we believe in the name of His Son Jesus Christ" (1 John 3:23; cf. John 6:29). It is the duty of all without exception to believe, even though the Father has not purposed to save—nor has Christ died to save—all without exception. Those who object to God's sincerity on the basis that he cannot unfeignedly command contrary to his own decree forget the distinction between his decretive and preceptive will, as well as run afoul of a number of scriptural examples of that very scenario. For example, through Moses God command Pharaoh to let his people go (Exod 5:1), but he has decreed to harden (and then actually does harden) Pharaoh's heart in order to magnify his own power

---

100. Owen, *Death of Death*, 300, emphasis original.

101. Owen explains, "The external offer is such as from which every man may conclude his own duty; none, God's purpose, which yet may be known upon performance of his duty. Their objection, then, is vain, who affirm that God hath given Christ for all to whom he offers Christ in the preaching of the gospel; for his offer in the preaching of the gospel is not declarative to any in particular, neither of what God hath done nor of what he will do in reference to him, but of what he ought to do, if he would be approved of God and obtain the good things promised" (Owen, *Death of Death*, 300).

in him (Rom 9:17; cf. Exod 4:21; 7:3).[102] Thus, it is evident that God's commands (i.e., his preceptive will) are not necessarily indicative of his purpose or intention (i.e., his decretive will). He may sincerely command all without exception to believe in Christ even though he has not elected, nor has Christ died for, all without exception. God is no more insincere in offering the gospel to those for whom Christ did not die than he is insincere in commanding Pharaoh to release Israel from bondage. But all without exception have warrant to believe in Christ on the grounds that God himself has made it their duty by commanding them to do so.

Third, sinners have a warrant to believe in Christ not only because of the sufficiency of the atonement and the command of God, but also because God has set forth the inviolable promise that whoever does repent and believe in Christ will indeed have eternal life (John 3:16). There is an unbreakable connection between faith and salvation. As demonstrated above,[103] no sinner will ever come to Christ in faith and find that there is no atonement for him, for Christ promises that the one who comes to him in faith he will certainly not cast out (John 6:37). Thus, every sinner has warrant to believe that if he comes to Christ in faith, he will not be turned away. He has no need to concern himself with whether the Father has chosen him for salvation from before the foundation of the world, nor whether the Son has died specifically and personally for him two thousand years ago. Here is warrant enough to believe: Christ is able to save all who believe in him; God commands sinners to believe in him; and God promises that all who believe shall be saved.

In eighteenth-century Scotland, the Reformed churches wrestled mightily with the question of the warrant of faith. All were formally committed to both unconditional election and particular redemption, but a disagreement arose as to whether the non-elect had as much of a warrant to believe the gospel as the elect did. If God had not chosen to save some, how could they rightly be called to believe without imputing to them an ability that Scripture declares they do not have?[104] Following from that, the question arose as to whether the gospel should be proclaimed to all people indiscriminately or only to those who had demonstrated signs of their election—namely, signs that God was preparing them to receive salvation by granting them sorrow for sin. And following from *that*, individuals began to concern themselves with discovering evidence of their own election before coming to Christ and resting on him in full faith for the forgiveness

---

102. Owen, *Death of Death*, 299–300. See above "The Will of God: Decretive, Preceptive, Optative," pages 261–65.

103. See "The Prerequisite for a Genuine Offer," pages 265–68.

104. Iain Murray explains, "Hyper-Calvinism argues that sinners cannot be required to do what they are not able to do, namely, to believe in Christ for salvation. The ability to believe belongs only to the elect, and that at the time determined by the Spirit of God. So for a preacher to call all his hearers to immediate repentance and faith is to deny both human depravity and the sovereignty of grace" (Murray, *Spurgeon v. Hyper-Calvinism*, 71).

of sins. They did not believe they had warrant to believe in Christ unless they had evidence that they were one of the elect for whom Christ died.[105]

Though he was not one of the original Marrow Men who refuted this encroaching hyper-Calvinism, Adam Gib, a minister in the Scottish Secession Church birthed from the theology of the Marrow Men, wrote what some have hailed as "one of the best theological pieces on the Call of the Gospel [sic] in relation to the Atonement [sic] that Church history has bequeathed to us."[106] His design was to defend the principles of the Secession Church against the claims of the Church of Scotland, which had fallen to the preparationism and hyper-Calvinism described above. In his treatise, he rightly argues that the warrant for coming to Christ in faith has nothing to do with whether or not sinners are elect, nor with whether Christ has died for them in particular, nor with whether they can discern the grace of God in their hearts preparing them to believe, but only with whether such a one is a "mankind-sinner." Gib writes, ". . . these promises, as laid out to men in the Gospel, do abstract from all regard to any as elect,—to any, more than others; or they have a respect to them only as *sinners*, mankind-sinners."[107] In other words, Gib rightly observes what was presented above, namely, that Christ died for men and women—for "mankind"—and not any other of God's creatures (Heb 2:16–17), and that he died for sinners (1 Tim 1:15) and not the righteous (Luke 5:32). Thus, it is to mankind-sinners *as such* that the gospel is offered. Sometimes it is asked what the particularist offers the reprobate in gospel preaching. However, if we understand the biblical nature of the gospel offer, *nothing* is offered to the reprobate qua reprobate, nor is anything offered to the elect qua elect. One is not offered the gospel on the basis that he is elect, and one is not refused the gospel on the basis that he is reprobate. The offer of the gospel is issued to mankind-sinners *as such*.

Gib's influence is felt throughout the Reformed tradition, as many particularist theologians have been careful to reiterate this very notion. Nicole, perceiving the danger of preparationism, says, "To suggest that there are certain prerequisites to be fulfilled before one can be addressed with the call of the gospel is very mischievous. The only prerequisite Scripture knows is that one should be a member of *fallen humanity* [i.e., mankind-sinners], and this applies to every man, woman, or child who can at all be reached with the good news of the gospel."[108] Bavinck declares, "The gospel is preached to *humans* not as elect or reprobate but *as sinners*, all of whom need redemption."[109] Packer writes, "The invitation is for sinners only, but for sinners universally; it is not for sinners of a certain type only, reformed sinners or sinners

---

105. For more on the Marrow Controversy, see Fisher, *Marrow of Modern Divinity*; and VanDoodewaard, *Marrow Controversy and Seceder Tradition*.

106. Fentiman, "Warrant of Faith," 1. This work by Gib is *The Present Truth: A Display of the Secession Testimony*.

107. Gib, *Present Truth*, 156.

108. Nicole, "Covenant, Universal Call," 405–6, emphasis added.

109. Bavinck, *Reformed Dogmatics*, 4:36, emphasis added.

whose hearts have been prepared by a fixed minimum of sorrow for sin; but for *sinners as such*, just as they are."[110] Most recently, Macleod comments, "We don't have two separate forms of the gospel, one for the elect and one for the reprobate. We have one gospel, with one very specific address: 'To sinners.' And by the same token it is the fact that he is a sinner, not the fact that he is elect, that gives the sinner the right to believe that all its glorious promises are for him."[111]

At this point, Gib makes an argument that proves decisive for the relationship between particular redemption and the warrant of faith. He observes, "God did not make an election of any persons separately from Christ; he did not by one act choose some to everlasting life and by another act give them to Christ for being brought to life, but all was by one act: they were chosen in him (Eph. 1:4)."[112] In other words, that the elect were chosen *in Christ* means that the decree of election is not separate from the decree of the salvation of sinners by Christ's mediation. The Father's decision to save particular sinners *is* the decision to save those particular sinners *by* Christ's work of mediation, and thus the sheep are said to be "given" to Christ by the Father (cf. John 10:14–15; 10:29). That means that the ones chosen by the Father and the ones redeemed by the Son are not separate groups, but are coextensive. The elect *are* the ones for whom Christ died, and those for whom Christ died *are* the elect. Therefore, asking, "Did Jesus die specifically and personally for me?" is equivalent to asking, "Am I elect?" And the point is: the answer to neither of those questions is the warrant of faith. Gib reasons,

> The particular objective destination and intention of our Lord's death cannot [therefore] belong to the ground of the Gospel call, or of faith,—any more than election can do; while these are materially the same thing. As people are not to make any inquiry whether they be among the elect; before they venture to believe in Christ: This is just the same thing, upon the matter, with saying,— that they are not to make any inquiry, whether they be among the persons for whom, or in whose names, Christ shed his blood; before they venture to receive and rest upon Him in the Gospel offer.[113]

Thus, just as the hyper-Calvinists were wrong to conclude that one has no warrant to believe the gospel until he can discern that he is elect, so also are the non-particularists wrong to conclude that one has no warrant to believe the gospel until he can be assured that Christ died specifically and personally for him.[114] In fact, since an assurance of personal interest in the blood of Christ belongs only to the one who believes—that is, since no one in a state of unbelief may suppose he possesses those benefits of Christ's

110. Packer, *Evangelism and the Sovereignty of God*, 98, emphasis added.

111. Macleod, *Compel Them to Come In*, 48.

112. Gib, *Present Truth*, 158.

113. Gib, *Present Truth*, 158–59.

114. This illustrates once again how hyper-Calvinism and Arminianism commit the same incompatibilist error, albeit in the opposite direction. See footnotes 24 and 55 of this chapter.

work that are only received by faith—then to say that a sinner must believe Christ died specifically for him *in order to come* to Christ is to say that he must believe he is saved before he believes. This is to say that one must believe before he believes, and that the warrant for believing is one's belief, which is a logical absurdity.[115]

Therefore, the gospel is to be offered to sinners not on the basis that they are elect, nor on the basis that Christ died specifically for them, but on the basis that (a) they are mankind-sinners as such, that (b) Christ has accomplished a fully sufficient redemption for mankind-sinners, that (c) God commands them as mankind-sinners to believe on Christ for salvation, and that (d) God promises that all mankind-sinners who believe on Christ for salvation will indeed lay hold of forgiveness, righteousness, and eternal life. This is consistent with the examples of gospel preaching in the New Testament. As Packer has famously observed, "The New Testament never calls on any man to repent on the ground that Christ died specifically and particularly for him. The basis on which the New Testament invites sinners to put faith in Christ is simply that they need Him, and that He offers Himself to them, and that those who receive Him are promised all the benefits that His death secured for His people."[116] Here, then, is warrant enough for every sinner to believe. Knowledge of the extent of the atonement has nothing to do with the warrant of faith.

---

115. Gib says, ". . . the declarations of grace about an interest in Christ and his blood [i.e., that he has borne our griefs, carried our sorrows, was wounded for our transgressions, and so on]; . . . : Though these, and such other declarations, are to be set forth in the dispensation of the Gospel,—for being applied by faith upon the foresaid general right; yet they can never be applied to any person in a state of unbelief. They are not to be reckoned true of every one *before* he believe, as the reason why he should believe, for they hold true only of such as are in due time made to believe" (Gib, *Present Truth*, 175).

116. Packer, *Evangelism and the Sovereignty of God*, 69.

14

A Genuine Universal Gospel Call, Part 2

IN THE PREVIOUS CHAPTER, we took up a key objection from the MIV, namely, that a particular redemption is inconsistent with a universal gospel offer. It was shown that a universal gospel call has always been affirmed by the mainstream of those who hold to classic particular redemption, because they ground the genuineness of an offer to be a function not of coextensive provision, but of the granting of what is offered when the terms of the offer are satisfied. In this chapter, we address implications of what has gone before—specifically, what sinners are called to believe in the gospel message, whether or not the evangelist should tell unbelievers that Christ died for them in particular, whether particularism or universalism makes the better gospel offer, and the extent of the Holy Spirit's convicting work in the world.

What Sinners Are Called to Believe in the Gospel

If an individual's warrant for believing the gospel is not the specific knowledge that Christ has died individually and personally for *that* individual's sins, but is rather rooted in the intrinsic sufficiency of the atonement itself, then the content of the gospel to be proclaimed is not, "Christ died for *your* sins, in particular," or "Believe that Christ died for your sins."[1] This is because when calling unbelievers to faith, preachers of the gospel are not calling sinners to believe first of all that Christ died for them in particular or for their sins in particular. Instead, the evangelist calls the unbeliever to believe that he is a sinner liable to the judgment of a holy God; to believe that he is unable to atone for his own sins by any of his own doing; to believe that Christ the God-man is the only and all-sufficient Savior of sinners by his life, death, and resurrection; to trust in Christ and his atoning work for salvation; and then, finally, after all of the previous, to assure himself that all that Christ has done belongs to him by virtue of his faith union to Christ.

1. As Packer says, "Our task in evangelism is to reproduce as faithfully as possible the New Testament emphasis. To go beyond the New Testament, or to distort its viewpoint or shift its stress, is always wrong. . . . The gospel is not 'believe that Christ died for everybody's sins, and therefore yours,' any more than it is 'believe that Christ died only for certain people's sins, and so perhaps not for yours.' The gospel is 'believe on the Lord Jesus Christ, who died for sins, and now offers you himself as your Savior'" (Packer, *Evangelism and the Sovereignty of God*, 70).

A key issue in the debate over this question of the universal gospel call is apprehending this proper ordering of these logically distinct psychological acts of faith. Francis Turretin helpfully explains that while the gospel call certainly commands the sinner to believe in Christ, this call does not demand that such saving faith "exercise . . . all its acts immediately and at the same time."[2] There are certain truths that our minds must apprehend and act faith upon before other truths are to be believed. Several theologians have made this observation, and it is illuminating to consider their various proposals for what sinners are commanded to believe in the universal offer of the gospel.

In two separate sections in his *The Death of Death in the Death of Christ*, John Owen outlines the progression of truths that sinners believe when they exercise saving faith. He explains, "There is an order, natural in itself and established by God's appointment, in the things that are to be believed; so that until some of them are believed the rest are not required."[3] Just as a man climbing a ladder cannot start at the fifth rung, but must climb each rung in order, so also does the believer ascend in faith upon particular truths in a particular order. Owen's first outline consists of five steps. Sinners are to believe (1) "that salvation is not to be had in themselves, . . . nor by the works of the law;" (2) "that there is salvation to be had in the promised seed;" (3) "that Jesus of Nazareth, who was crucified by the Jews, was this Saviour, promised before; and that there is no name under heaven given whereby they may be saved besides his;" (4) the gospel "requires a resting upon this Christ . . . as an all-sufficient Saviour, with whom is plenteous redemption, and who is able to save to the utmost them that come to God by him;" and then, (5) "these things being firmly seated in the soul (and not before), we are every one called in particular to believe the efficacy of the redemption that is in the blood of Jesus towards our own souls in particular."[4]

Later, Owen introduces a slightly different though substantially similar outline. Sinners must believe (1) "that the gospel [is] the word of God, [contains] his will, and that Jesus Christ, therein revealed, is the wisdom and power of God unto salvation"; (2) "that there is an inseparable connection, by God's appointment, between faith and salvation"; (3) "that there be a particular conviction, by the Spirit, of a redeemer to their souls in particular; whereby they become weary, heavy laden, and burdened"; (4) that there must be "a serious full recumbency and rolling of the soul upon Christ in the promise of the gospel, as an all-sufficient Saviour, able to deliver and save to the utmost them that come to God by him."[5] Before getting to the final step, Owen pauses to observe that up to this point no sinner is required by the gospel call to determine whether Christ has died for him in particular, but only to be "fully assured that his

---

2. Turretin, *Institutes of Elenctic Theology*, 2:477.

3. Owen, *Death of Death*, 407.

4. Owen, *Death of Death*, 314–15.

5. Owen, *Death of Death*, 407–8.

death shall be profitable to them that believe in him and obey him."[6] Then, he says, "after all this, and not before, [5] it lies upon a believer to assure his soul, according as he finds the fruit of the death of Christ in him and towards him, of the good-will and eternal love of God to him in sending his Son to die for him in particular."[7] Thus, according to Owen, the gospel call does not consist first of all in calling sinners to believe that Christ has died for them in particular, for such a conviction is a matter of the assurance of their salvation, not the initial laying hold of salvation. Assurance cannot precede faith itself, for, as Packer says, "it is to be inferred from the fact that one *has* believed, not proposed as a reason why one *should* believe."[8] Thus, a universal atonement is not necessary to ground a genuine gospel call.

A contemporary of Owen's, Turretin offers a similar ordering of the acts of faith, observing that "the command to believe in Christ embraces many things *before* we come to the ultimate consolatory act by which we believe that he died for *us*."[9] He goes on:

1. First, we are commanded to believe all that the Scripture reveals to us concerning our misery and inability to secure our own salvation. Hence arises a salutary despair of ourselves and an acknowledgement of the necessity of a remedy.

2. Second, they who thus despair of themselves are commanded to believe that Christ, the Son of God, is the alone all-sufficient Savior given by God to men, in whom they can obtain perfect salvation and remission of sins who sincerely fly to him and are led to repent seriously of their sins.

3. Third, they who are thus contrite and penitent and despairing of themselves are commanded to fly and to come to Christ as the rock of salvation, to embrace his merit as all-sufficient, to include and sweetly rest upon it, from it alone expecting remission of sin, righteousness and salvation.

4. Fourth and finally they, who perceive that they do repent and rest upon Christ truly and solely, are then at length bound to believe that Christ died for them and that on account of his death their sins are remitted.[10]

Similar to Owen, Turretin highlights the necessity to assent to the facts of our own sinfulness and inability to save ourselves, the exclusivity and all-sufficiency of Christ to save all who come to him, and the need to embrace Christ and rest upon his work in dependent faith; and only then to believe that Christ has died particularly for us.

6. Owen, *Death of Death*, 408.
7. Owen, *Death of Death*, 408.
8. Packer, "Saved by His Precious Blood," 130–31, emphasis added.
9. Turretin, *Institutes of Elenctic Theology*, 2:478.
10. Turretin, *Institutes of Elenctic Theology*, 2:478.

	Owen (314–15)	Owen (407–08)	Turretin
1	Salvation not in self or law	Gospel is God's Word; Christ is the power of God unto salvation	Our misery in sin and inability to save ourselves
2	Salvation in the promised seed	Faith in Christ always brings salvation	
3	Christ alone is this Savior	A sensible need of a Savior	Christ alone is the all-sufficient Savior
4	Rest on Christ as all-sufficient	Rest on Christ as all-sufficient	Come to Christ in restful faith
5	Christ's blood avails for me personally	Christ's blood avails for me personally	Christ died for me personally

Owen and Turretin on the Order of the Acts of Faith

Turretin also discusses these acts of faith in terms of their being either the direct acts or the reflex act of faith. The first moment of faith is (1) the *direct act* of believing the facts of the gospel, which consists in both (a) assenting to the truths concerning God, the sinner himself, Christ, and repentance and faith, and (b) fleeing to Christ and trusting him as an all-sufficient Savior. The second moment of faith is (2) the *reflex act*, in which the sinner believes he *has* exercised the direct act of faith—that is, he is persuaded and assured that he truly believes and thus all the promises of the gospel belong to him by virtue of union with Christ.[11] Our faith in the notion that Christ has died specifically and particularly for *us* is a reflex act of faith that is *consequent* upon the direct act of fleeing to Christ and entrusting ourselves to him for salvation.[12] We are simply to repent and believe in Christ, and then, being assured that we have repented and believed, we must believe about ourselves what Scripture says is true of those who repent and believe—namely, that all that Christ has accomplished in his labor to save sinners he accomplished specifically and personally for us.

Therefore, by confusing the reflex act of faith with the direct acts of faith, non-particularists misunderstand the universal gospel call as a call to believe that Christ died specifically and personally for "you," and thus wrongly conclude that such a

11. Turretin, *Institutes of Elenctic Theology*, 2:477.

12. So Turretin: ". . . this command does not immediately and in the first instance demand of us the faith by which we believe that Christ died for us, but the faith by which we fly to Christ, embrace him and rest upon him (which is nothing else than the movement by which the repenting sinner, dejected under a sense of his misery and aroused by the call of the gospel, renouncing every other remedy and trust, flies to Christ as the rock of salvation and with his whole heart earnestly desires and seeks the grace offered in the gospel). . . . If I am conscious that I have exercised this (which is the formal act of faith), then I can and ought to elicit the other act of faith by which I believe that Christ died for me (repenting and flying to him), which is called the consequent act because it follows the direct by which I believe in Christ and take myself to him as the only and all-perfect Savior; and the consolatory act because it pours into the soul of the believer unspeakable joy and consolation. Therefore since no one can have this special and reflex act of faith unless the other preceding acts have been exercised together with the desire of true repentance, it appears that all are not bound to believe that Christ died for them, but only believers and penitents (i.e., all who, through the knowledge of sin and a sense of the divine wrath, are contrite in heart, fly to Christ and seek from him remission of sins and rely on his merit alone for salvation)" (Turretin, *Institutes of Elenctic Theology*, 2:478).

call is invalid unless Christ has died for everyone. However, Scripture never issues the call of the gospel in this way; the apostles and early disciples never call people to faith on the basis that Christ has died specifically and personally for them. Instead, they call sinners to believe that Christ is the promised Messiah and that he alone is the source of salvation through repentance and faith.

Should We Say, "Christ Died for You"?

The question is inevitably asked, then, should preachers of the gospel tell unbelievers, "Christ died for you," as part of their evangelistic proclamation? I believe a consistent particularist ought to answer "no" to that question. Not only, as we have observed, is such phraseology absent from any New Testament example of gospel proclamation, but the meaning of the phrase "died for"—i.e., the *nature* of the atonement—requires that the extent of the atonement be limited to those who actually partake of its saving benefits. To ask, "For whom did Christ die?" is to ask, "For whom did Christ offer himself to the Father as a substitutionary sacrifice for sins? For whose sins has Christ propitiated the wrath of the Father? To whom did Christ reconcile the Father? Whom did Christ redeem from the slavery of sin by the ransom price of his blood?" Parts 2 and 3 have proven that the answer to those questions is that Christ has sacrificed, propitiated, reconciled, and redeemed the elect alone, for they alone are those whose guilt is finally canceled, the ones against whom God's wrath is finally extinguished, those who are finally brought to eternal fellowship with God and who are finally released from the bondage of sin and death. Thus, as Murray says, ". . . when we think of Christ's 'dying for' in the substitutionary terms which are its proper import, we must say that he did not die for those who never become the beneficiaries of that substitution; he did not 'die for' the non-elect."[13] As a result, telling someone that Christ died for them is virtually equivalent to telling that person the Father has chosen them for salvation from before the foundation of the world. While that is a glorious truth that ought to be openly rehearsed to and celebrated by Christians, it is not something that belongs in an evangelistic conversation; still less is it a component of the apostolic proclamation of the gospel. While the unbeliever to whom one is speaking may indeed be one whom the Father has chosen and thus one for whom Christ has died, he also might not be. Because the election status of the unbeliever is unknown to the evangelist, to tell such a one that Christ has died for them may indeed be untrue. Nicole's conclusion is therefore correct: it is "not strictly legitimate [to tell sinners, 'Christ died for you']

---

13. Murray, "Atonement and the Free Offer," 69. So Cunningham as well: "But this position [saying Christ died for you] does not at all correspond with the proper import of what Scripture means when it tells us that Christ died for men. This, *as we prove against the Socinians*, implies that He put Himself in their legal position, that He made satisfaction to God's justice for their sins, or that He purchased redemption for them; and this, we contend, does not hold true of any but those who are actually at length pardoned and saved" (Cunningham, *Historical Theology*, 2:369, emphasis original).

unless there is some assurance that the people involved are among the elect";[14] or, as Murray says, "It cannot be declared to men indiscriminately that, in the proper sense of the term, Christ died for them."[15] As an alternative, Nicole recommends the following, which is wholly consistent with particular redemption: "God in his unfathomable mercy has been pleased to love sinners such as you and me, and he invites you to repent and believe in Jesus Christ. If you do so, you will find that the work of Christ avails for you, and you will be saved."[16]

While all non-particularists would object to this conclusion, even some particularists, who believe that Christ did not atone for the sins of all without exception, nevertheless believe that one should not balk at telling sinners indiscriminately that Christ has died for them as part of their evangelistic proclamation. For example, Wayne Grudem writes, "In that sense the sentence ['Christ died for your sins'] is simply understood to mean, 'Christ died to offer you forgiveness for your sins' or 'Christ died to make available forgiveness for your sins.' The important point here is that sinners realize that salvation is available for everyone and that payment of sins is available for everyone."[17] It is true that salvation is available for everyone on the basis of the sufficiency of Christ's payment—though specifically for everyone who repents and believes in Christ. However, the scriptural meaning of the phrase "Christ died for your sins" is not that Christ died to offer forgiveness or Christ died to make forgiveness available. Scripture never casts the intention or the effect of the atonement in these terms.[18] Christ has not died to make forgiveness *available*; he has died to make forgiveness *actual*. That is, by his death, he has definitively *secured* the forgiveness of sins for all whom the Father gave to him, by giving his life as the sacrificial ransom price for their redemption. In other words, though Christ has indeed died in such a way that forgiveness may be received by any who repents and believes, it was not the purpose of his death to constitute the *availability* of that forgiveness (what hypothetical universalists called the "evangelical covenant").[19] The availability of salvation is not the proper fruit of the death of Christ; the proper fruit is the securing of the salvation of the elect. That Christ's infinitely (intrinsically) sufficient death brings salvation within reach to any who might repent and believe is something of a byproduct or result of the atonement; it is not a proper divine intention of the atonement.

---

14. Nicole, "Covenant, Universal Call," 410.

15. Murray, "Atonement and the Free Offer," 84.

16. Nicole, "Covenant, Universal Call," 410. Blocher echoes this when he writes, "On rigorous definite atonement grounds it is adequate to tell anyone, 'Christ invites you: "Come to me"'; if you do so, you will find that he paid for your sins on the cross, and thus lifted your condemnation for ever.' Not an awful distance [from what the non-particularist proclaims]!" (Blocher, "Jesus Christ the Man," 569).

17. Grudem, *Systematic Theology*, 602.

18. See chapter 5.

19. Davenant, *Dissertationes duae*, 17; Baxter, *Universal Redemption*, 26.

Similarly, particularist Andrew Naselli writes, "A Calvinist can tell a non-Christian, 'Jesus died for you,' because non-Christians generally understand the conjunction 'for' in that sentence to mean that the benefits of Jesus's death are available if they repent and believe."[20] However, believers ought to take cues concerning their evangelistic word choice from the precepts and example of Scripture, not from what they think unbelievers will understand by their extrabiblical words. In the first place, it is uncertain how one could verify that Naselli's supposition—namely, that unbelievers understand "for" to indicate that Jesus has died in such a way that salvation is available to them rather than to indicate that Jesus has actually paid for their sins—is correct. My own evangelistic conversations lead me precisely to the opposite conclusion; in my experience, unbelievers have supposed Jesus' death on the cross for the world gives them license to live how they please. Either way, unbelievers' understanding is not the rule of our evangelistic language; God's word is. And not only does Scripture never record the phrase "Jesus died for you" in evangelistic conversation, but also, as argued above and in previous chapters (especially in part 2), the scriptural meaning of "died for" is not making salvation available, but rather *accomplishing* salvation and *securing* its application.

Shultz's argument that "part of the gospel message is telling unbelievers that 'Jesus died for you'"[21] is based in Paul's summary of his gospel preaching in 1 Cor 15:1–5, particularly in his comment that "Christ died for our sins" (15:3). Since the word "our" includes both the preacher and the hearers of the gospel, and since the gospel is preached to unbelievers (and not merely the elect) in order to bring them to faith, therefore Christ has died for unbelievers as well as believers.[22] In the first place, it must be observed, however, that the proper antithesis is not between the elect and unbelievers, but between the elect and the reprobate. There is such a thing as elect unbelievers, since all those whom God has chosen for salvation do not enter the world believing the gospel but must come to faith as a result of the regenerating work of the Holy Spirit. Nevertheless, it is true, as Shultz notes, that Paul's proclamation of the gospel would have fallen upon the ears of both elect and non-elect sinners.[23]

Second, Shultz writes, "If the atonement were limited only to the elect, than [*sic*] how could Paul and the early church preach to a group of unbelievers that 'Christ died for our sins'?"[24] He seems to assume that as Paul wrote 1 Corinthians 15 he was quoting back to the Corinthians the precise words he used when he evangelized them as unbelievers. This is by no means self-evident, and Shultz does not argue for this. It seems much more probable that rather than providing a verbatim quotation of his evangelistic message, Paul was summarizing for the believing community in

---

20. Naselli, "Conclusion," 226.

21. Shultz, *Multi-Intentioned View*, 93.

22. Shultz, *Multi-Intentioned View*, 93; cf. Shultz, "Defense," 168.

23. Shultz, "Defense," 168.

24. Shultz, "Defense," 168.

Corinth—his "brethren," who "received" the gospel, who were presently standing in the gospel (15:1), whom he regards as "saints" (15:2), and "saved" (15:2)—the foundational message of Christianity upon which their faith was presently grounded.[25] "Our," in 1 Cor 15:3, then, refers to "we who have believed in Jesus, myself as well as you Corinthian believers," and perhaps even those who accompanied him on his missionary journeys.[26] It is not their common humanity that Paul has in mind as he speaks to them in this passage, but the common bond they share by virtue of union to Christ, and thus the common share they have in the benefits of his death. That Paul tells those presently believing in Christ that "Christ died for *our* sins" cannot legitimately be used as support for the notion that Christ died for the sins of elect and reprobate alike. Besides this, commentators have noted that the phrase "for our sins" is likely an allusion to Isaiah 53, in which the Suffering Servant is described as having been "pierced through for our transgressions" and "crushed for our iniquities."[27] If this is connection is legitimate, then all the particularity and efficacy of the atonement inherent in Isaiah 53[28] ought to color what "died for" means in 1 Cor 15:3, further indicating that Paul believes Christ has died for the elect alone.

If one were to stipulate the MIV's proposal that part of the gospel is telling an unbeliever, "Christ died for you," one must ask what the real significance of such a statement is on MIV terms. While one feels the rhetorical and affective value of being able to tell an unbeliever, "Christ died for you," what does it truly mean to say that Christ has died for *you* when Christ has died for *everyone*, even those who spend eternity in hell under the judgment of God for their sins? In this scenario, the fact of Christ's death for such a one makes no definitive difference concerning their actual salvation; on this scheme, Christ has died for plenty of people who nevertheless perish in their sins. Surely the declaration that Christ has died for a particular sinner is meant to instill hope and consolation in that sinner—consolation that God has pitied his miserable state, and hope that he may be free from the penalty and power of his sins. But no sinner can draw any sound, substantive hope or consolation by being told that something is true of him that is also true of those who never find forgiveness. Since the atonement of non-particularism, including the MIV, reduces itself to providing the opportunity of salvation—merely making salvation *available*—the knowledge that Christ has died for me personally cannot bring any solid ground of comfort. Christ may have died for me, yes; "but shall the fruits of his death be certainly applied unto all them for whom he died? If not, I may perish for ever."[29]

25. Fee, *1 Corinthians*, 721–22.

26. Blocher, "Jesus Christ the Man," 568.

27. "The language 'for our sins' is a direct reflection of the LXX of Isa. 53. . . . The plural 'our sins' occurs in vv. 4, 5, and 6; 'for sins' occurs in v. 10 and 'their sins' in vv. 11 and 12. Some have doubted that this reflects the LXX since the LXX does not use the preposition ὑπέρ; but it does use περὶ, and these two have become nearly interchangeable in *koine*" (Fee, *1 Corinthians*, 724, 724n55).

28. See the exegesis of Isa 53:4–6 in chapter 10.

29. Owen, *Death of Death*, 418. As Turretin wisely notes, "It is false that a ground of consolation

As was argued in chapters 6 and 7, such a redefinition of "died for" empties Christ's death of its genuinely substitutionary value.[30] As Trueman memorably illustrates, "What does it mean to say to someone, 'Christ died for you,' if that fact, in and of itself, makes no difference? 'I paid your mortgage, but the bank is still going to foreclose on your loan and repossess your house' seems a rather nonsensical situation, but it has clear parallels with this matter."[31] No genuine consolation or solace can be derived from such an ineffectual payment. If Jesus' payment for sins does not guarantee the sinner's forgiveness, what are non-particularists really intending to communicate by telling him that Jesus died for him? It seems *availability* is the answer to that question, and yet the particularist may preach Christ as available to all who come to him in repentance and faith. If proponents of the MIV desire to tell sinners, "Christ died for you," but they admit that God has genuinely *saving* intentions for the elect alone, the substance of their proclamation is reduced to the following: "Christ died for you (but the real saving intention of God might not apply to you because of God's sovereign election)."[32] Though they would never voice this to the unbeliever, what they mean by their declaration is, "Christ died for you, but he may not have died for you with the intention of actually saving you; he may have died for you with the intention of only making you savable." Though Shultz claims that "the gospel [is] preached to unbelievers to lead them to salvation,"[33] on his scheme the universal intentions of the gospel do not include the intention to actually save the reprobate. If someone says, "Christ died for you," but they cannot *mean* that Christ died for you with the intention of saving you, of what meaningful use is the phrase at all? Trueman rightly observes, "Hypothetical universalism looks like sleight of hand at this point—Calvinism without the pain."[34]

In summary, then, the evangelist ought not to tell unbelievers, "Christ died for you," as part of his gospel proclamation. First, the biblical meaning of the phrase "died for" is inextricable with those saving accomplishments secured by Christ's death, and

---

can be drawn from the absolute universality of the death of Christ because no solid consolation can be drawn from that which is common to the godly and ungodly (nay to the innumerable multitudes who have been and shall be damned equally with those who shall be saved). For since he may be supposed to have died even for Judas and Pharaoh (who have perished notwithstanding), how can the fear of damnation be taken away from me by this?" (Turretin, *Institutes of Elenctic Theology*, 2:480). So also Owen: "If you give me no more to comfort me than what you give, or might have given, to Judas, can you expect I should receive settlement and consolation? Truly, miserable comforters are ye all, physicians of no value, Job's visitors,—skillful only to add affliction unto the afflicted" (Owen, *Death of Death*, 417).

30. See chapter 7, "Penal Substitution."

31. Trueman, "Definite Atonement View," 59. Elsewhere he rightly concludes that "the language of substitution seems to be rather equivocal, even meaningless, when the substitution is both universal and not, in itself, effective" (Trueman, "Definite Atonement View," 59).

32. Trueman, "Definite Atonement View," 210.

33. Shultz, "Defense," 168.

34. Trueman, "Response to Multiple-Intentions View," 210.

these he did not accomplish for all without exception. Second, Scripture never records an instance in which the apostles or early disciples preached the gospel by employing such a phrase, Shultz's handling of 1 Cor 15:3 notwithstanding. Finally, given non-particularism's redefinition of the nature of the atonement in order to accommodate a universal scope, the true value of telling someone that Christ died for them is significantly diminished, nearly to the point of reducing such a declaration to deception or mockery. *In fine*, the MIV's gospel proclamation is *not*, "Christ has died to infallibly secure your salvation," but only, as particularism's, "Believe in the Lord Jesus, and you will be saved" (Acts 16:31).[35]

Particularism Makes the Better Offer

But the fact that the particularist does not tell the unbeliever, "Christ died for you," does not diminish or impoverish the genuine offer of the gospel. In fact, by maintaining the particularity of the atonement, one maintains its all-powerful efficacy, and this only strengthens the confidence of the preacher of the gospel to proclaim it with joy and freedom.[36] This is because the evangelist offers Christ to the sinner in all his sovereign power to *save* (not merely to provide or make possible), with the fullness of his finished work undergirding their hopes for salvation. And, as Murray writes, if it is this Christ that is offered, "the only doctrine of the atonement that will ground and warrant this overture is that of salvation *wrought* and redemption *accomplished*"—not merely salvation made *possible* and redemption *provided*.[37] Murray goes on:

> And the only atonement that measures up to such conditions is a definite atonement. In other words, an atonement construed as providing the possibility of salvation or the opportunity of salvation does not supply the basis required for what constitutes the gospel offer. It is not the *opportunity* of salvation that is offered; it is salvation. And it is salvation because Christ is offered and Christ does not invite us to mere opportunity but to himself.[38]

As was proven in chapters 6 and 7, the atonement offered by proponents of the MIV is one that is ultimately inefficacious, securing only the possibility of salvation. Christ has provided for the salvation of sinners to be enjoyed by them on the condition that they repent and believe.[39] But this shifts the burden of salvation away from

---

35. Bavinck, *Reformed Dogmatics*, 4:36.

36. Packer writes, "In actual fact, just because he recognizes that divine mercy is sovereign and free, he is in a position to make far more of the offer of Christ in his preaching than is the expositor of the new gospel; for this offer is itself a far more wonderful thing on his principles than it can ever be in the eyes of those who regard love to all sinners as a necessity of God's nature, and therefore a matter of course" (Packer, "Saved by His Precious Blood," 133).

37. Murray, "Atonement and the Free Offer," 82, emphasis added.

38. Murray, "Atonement and the Free Offer," 82–83, emphasis original.

39. See Chapter 7, "Efficacious Accomplishment."

the definitive accomplishment of Christ and onto the response of man. As Shultz characterizes the free offer, "There must be a genuine payment for all people, who can, if they so choose, receive it."[40] The onus is shifted back on the sinner, whose choice to believe or disbelieve becomes the decisive determining factor in salvation.[41] Horton captures this reality when he says, ". . . if Christ died for every person and yet many are finally lost, then the good news proclaimed to the world is not, 'Christ has taken away all of your sins,' but 'Christ has made your remission possible if you fulfill certain conditions.'"[42] In such a case, as Bavinck notes, "Whether salvation actually becomes a reality for a person depends on that person herself or himself. Faith is a condition, a work, which alone turns a possible salvation into an actual salvation, and so leaves a person forever in doubt, at least till death."[43]

On the other hand, a particular atonement grounds a full and free offer of *real* rather than *hypothetical* salvation. As Nicole writes, "It does not expect the fulfillment of an unrealizable condition on the part of the sinner as a prerequisite for salvation,"[44] but it directs all attention to Christ, who himself has accomplished every condition required for salvation, purchasing even faith itself and sovereignly guaranteeing that all for whom he died will apprehend every benefit secured for them by his death. As Packer says, "It is the glory of these [gospel] invitations that it is an omnipotent King who gives them," not a "baffled Savior, balked in what he hoped to do by human unbelief."[45] Contrary to a scenario in which all people can, if they so choose, receive

40. Shultz, "Defense," 177.

41. Such a position logically entails synergism and the Arminian doctrine of prevenient grace. While it is true those who hold to the MIV reject these doctrines, they do so inconsistently. Proponents of the MIV would say that the repentant faith that is the condition for appropriating the benefits of Christ's death is granted as a gift of the Spirit's irresistible grace to totally depraved sinners, granted only to those whom the Father unconditionally chose to save. But the language of "if they so choose" is thus revealed to be a bit misleading, for the MIV confesses that the ultimately determinative choice to grant faith belongs to God himself. Whatever is thought to be gained by the universality of Christ's atonement is taken away by the particularity of both election and the conferring of saving faith. Why should the MIV claim that "it is impossible to genuinely offer salvation to the non-elect, since there is no salvation [i.e., atonement] to offer them" (Shultz, "Defense," 177), but not also object that it is impossible to offer salvation to the non-elect, since God wills to never give them the faith that is the sole condition by which they might benefit from the saving provision of Christ? Such objections against particular redemption, if valid, would also succeed against unconditional election and irresistible grace. That the MIV affirms unconditional election and irresistible grace shows that such objections are not true concerns, and thus that they do not apply to the atonement either.

42. Horton, "Is Particular Redemption 'Good News'?," 125.

43. Bavinck, *Reformed Dogmatics*, 4:36. Owen writes, ". . . so far from being the bottom of any solid consolation unto them whose due it is, that it is directly destructive of, and diametrically opposed unto, all those ways whereby the Lord hath declared himself willing that we should receive comfort from the death of his Son, drying up the breast from whence, and poisoning the streams whereby, it should be conveyed unto our souls" (Owen, *Death of Death*, 419).

44. Nicole, "Covenant, Universal Call," 410.

45. Packer, "Saved by His Precious Blood," 132–33. He says elsewhere, ". . . for gospel invitations to sinners never honor God and exalt Christ more, nor are more powerful to awaken and confirm faith, than when full weight is laid on the free omnipotence of the mercy from which they flow" (136).

a universal yet inefficacious payment for sins,[46] the preacher of a definite atonement preaches "the effective action of God to reach out and to save what was lost, not merely God's establishing the right conditions whereby somebody can be saved if they so wish."[47] Because the Father always accomplishes his good pleasure (Isa 46:10), and because he has guaranteed his Servant's success (Isa 52:13; 53:10–11), and because Christ declares that he will lose none whom the Father has given him (John 6:39), and because the Spirit will grant saving faith to all for whom Christ purchased it by his atoning death (Titus 3:4–6; cf. John 16:14), the elect will indeed come to Christ in faith. Under this scheme, the concept of saving faith is not a condition that determinatively grounds salvation; it is merely the empty hand that embraces all the fullness of Christ and his finished work in an act of restful dependence on and eager trust in him alone.[48] Hence Horton says, "The 'once and for all' accomplishment of Christ in his saving work at the cross leaves nothing for sinners to complete by their own actions, whether their decision or effort (Rom. 9:12–16)."[49]

Consequently, he continues, "the evangelistic appeals in the New Testament are unhesitatingly joyful and full of comfort. All who embrace this gift are assured that Christ's work *has already* secured their salvation, the benefits of which they now receive through the gracious work of the Spirit that was included in Christ's purchase of his people."[50] The preacher of the gospel founded upon a definite atonement may rest absolutely assured that his proclamation will be effective according to the purpose of God, whether for conversion or hardening (Isa 55:8–9). The Father *has* many people in these cities (Acts 18:10), and the Son *has* other sheep whom he must bring into the fold also (John 10:16); therefore the preacher must not fear but go on speaking the gospel courageously (Acts 18:9). It is, in fact, a particular redemption that provides the only sure and sound motivation for gospel preaching.

Shultz claims that the motivation for gospel preaching is grounded in a universal atonement. Paul writes that the love of Christ compels him to sacrificial gospel ministry, and that such a compulsion is founded upon the conclusion that "one died for all" (2 Cor 5:14).[51] However, it was demonstrated in chapter 10 that the "all" for whom the one died are the all who died to sin and self in him, as an immediate consequence of his death: "one died for all, *therefore* all died" (2 Cor 5:14).[52] Contrary to Shultz's claim, then, that "Christ's payment for all people is the motivation for preaching the gospel," it is actually a particular redemption that motivates all of Paul's gospel labors. Rather than teaching that Christ died for all without exception only to raise a portion of them

46. Shultz, "Defense," 177.

47. Trueman, "Definite Atonement View," 60–61.

48. Bavinck, *Reformed Dogmatics*, 4:36.

49. Horton, "Is Particular Redemption Good News?," 126.

50. Horton, "Is Particular Redemption Good News?," 126.

51. Shultz, "Defense," 169.

52. See the exegesis of 2 Cor 5:14–15 in chapter 10.

to newness of life, Paul teaches that Christ's death for all who are united to him *effects* their spiritual death to sin and self, and that his resurrection—by virtue of that same union—guarantees that all the benefits of the redemption accomplished will be fully applied to everyone for whom they were obtained. Thus, when he exclaims that it is the love of Christ that compels him to radically sacrificial ministry (2 Cor 5:14), that love, expressed in the gospel of his atonement, is *not* a general love for all without exception, hypothetically suspended upon their response, which love may leave the majority of them to die in their corruption. Instead, it is a personal, actual love for each of the sheep that the shepherd knows by name—a love that definitively secures the sinner's believing response and bestows it upon him by grace. Paul may sing of this love, "*My name* is graven on his hands; *my name* is written on his heart," in a way that is not true of those who finally perish. "The Son of God loved *me* and gave Himself up for *me*" (Gal 2:20), particularly and personally. Such a love, Paul would say, is measureless, whose breadth and length and height and depth" are beyond tracing out, surpassing all knowledge (Eph 3:18–19). The particularity of the gospel love of Christ is what makes it personal, and thus what makes it precious.[53] That love compels gospel preaching, igniting the fire of urgency that causes Paul to plead with sinners to be reconciled to God (2 Cor 5:20).[54] Particularism makes the better gospel offer.

Universal Conviction?

The previous two subsections have dealt with the first two of Shultz's four arguments for universal atonement on the basis of the universal gospel offer (namely, the content of the gospel, based in 1 Cor 15:1–5, and the motivation for the gospel, based in 2 Cor 5:14–20). Shultz's third argument, grounded in John 16:7–11, concerns the supposedly-universal convicting ministry of the Holy Spirit. His argument is

53. John Piper celebrates, "He loved *me*. He gave himself for *me*. The preciousness of this personal love is muted where it is seen as an instance of the same love that Christ has for those who finally perish" (Piper, "My Glory," 641). Later he says, "*Knowing and experiencing the reality of definite atonement affects us with deeper gratitude.* We feel more thankfulness for a gift given to us in particular, rather than feeling like it was given to no specific people and we happened to pick it up" (Piper, "My Glory," 665, italics original).

54. Shultz also claims that the reconciliation of the "world" in 2 Cor 5:18–20 supports the notion of a universal atonement as the motivation for the gospel. However, this text ought to be interpreted, as the other "world" texts, as indicating not all without exception but all without distinction throughout the world (see chapter 11). The immediate context favors this interpretation, for Paul defines divine reconciliation as "not counting their trespasses against them." The only ones whose trespasses are not counted against them are those who receive the blessing of justification (Rom 4:4–8), i.e., the elect alone. This reading is also confirmed by verse 18, as the "world" that is reconciled to God through Christ (2 Cor 5:19) is coextensive with the "us" who are reconciled to God through Christ (5:18), i.e., the elect who eventually believe. Paul uses universalistic language to emphasize the expansiveness of Christ's work of reconciliation—that it extends to those actually reconciled throughout all the world—not to indicate that it extends to every individual who has ever lived, even those who remain alienated from God through all eternity. Thus, it remains the case that a particular redemption, rather than a universal redemption, grounds and motivates the earnest gospel preaching of the servant of Christ.

twofold. First, when Jesus says that the Holy Spirit will come to "convict *the world* concerning sin and righteousness and judgment" (John 16:8), "world" must refer to "all unbelievers,"[55] by which Shultz means both elect and reprobate. Thus, the Spirit has a convicting ministry among both elect and reprobate, whereas, according to particularism, Christ has an atoning ministry among the elect alone. Such a disjunction would present a disjunction in the saving work of the Trinity, whereas a multi-intentioned view of the cross would cohere more naturally. That is, the Son would atone for the sins of all without exception, even though only the elect will finally be forgiven; correspondingly, the Spirit would convict all unbelievers without exception, even though only the elect will finally be brought to faith.

But does "the world" refer to "all unbelievers" as Shultz claims? To support this claim, he appeals to the context of John 15:18—16:6, which speaks of "the world" as hating Christ (15:18, 25), Christ's people (15:19), and the Father (15:23), as well as persecuting Jesus (15:20) and his people (16:2). He also explains that other passages demonstrate these characteristics are true of all unbelievers (Rom 1:18–32; 3:9–20; Eph 2:1–3).[56] However, though all unbelievers fit the description given in John 15:18—16:6, it does not follow that in 16:7–11 John is necessarily speaking about all unbelievers who ever existed or will exist. Such would be to rely upon an absolutely universalistic interpretation of κόσμος, which is by no means warranted by the term alone; κόσμος may refer to all without exception, but in many contexts it also may refer to all without distinction, as demonstrated in chapter 11.

Further, such a move also relies on conflating the categories of unbeliever and reprobate. There is such a category as elect unbelievers, that is, those chosen by the Father who will not fail to receive salvation but who have not yet come to faith in Christ. Each one of the elect were once part of the unbelieving "world" that Jesus describes in 16:7–11. While it is true that all whom the Spirit convicts in the manner stated in John 16:7–11 are unbelievers, for Shultz's argument to hold he must prove that these unbelievers never come to faith in Christ—that is, that the Spirit's conviction concerning sin and righteousness and judgment does not eventually result in conversion.

How, then, ought one to understand the term ἐλέγχω in John 16:8? Carson[57] and Aloisi[58] provide helpful surveys of the various interpretations of the term in its biblical usage, the nuances of which vary according to context. The word ἐλέγχω can mean to expose (John 3:20; Eph 5:11, 13), to reprove (Matt 18:15; Luke 3:19; 2 Tim 4:2; Titus 1:13; 2:15; Heb 12:15; Rev 3:19), to rebuke (1 Tim 5:20), and to refute (Titus 1:9), but also to convict in the sense of bringing someone to a recognition of wrongdoing (as in John 8:46; 16:8; 1 Cor 14:24; Jas 2:9; Jude 1:15).[59] In some cases, it would seem that the

---

55. Shultz, "Defense," 173; cf. Shultz, *Multi-Intentioned View*, 95.

56. Shultz, "Defense," 173.

57. Carson, "Function of the Paraclete," 547–66.

58. Aloisi, "Paraclete's Ministry, of Conviction," 55–69.

59. BDAG, 314–15.

conviction in view is not necessarily effectual unto salvation, as in the book of Jude, where the "hidden reefs in your love feasts," who are "clouds without water" and "doubly dead" (1:12), who are "mockers, following after their own ungodly lusts" (1:18), are convicted "of all their ungodly deeds which they have done in an ungodly way" (1:15). These are men "for whom the black darkness has been reserved forever" (1:13), and thus their conviction is not effectual unto salvation. However, in other instances, such as in the case of the unbeliever entering the worship gathering in 1 Cor 14:24–25, such a one is "convicted by all," called to account for his sin, and the secrets of his heart are disclosed such that he finally "fall[s] on his face and worship[s] God," which is indicative of conversion.[60] Thus, lexical considerations alone cannot determine whether the Spirit's conviction of John 16:7–11 is effectual unto salvation or not.

However, a key consideration suggests that this conviction is indeed effectual unto salvation. Jesus notes that this convicting ministry of the Holy Spirit is for the disciples' advantage: "But I tell you the truth, it is to your advantage that I go away" (16:7). What "advantage" to the disciples would be accomplished by the Holy Spirit's conviction of the world? Given that Jesus is preparing the disciples for their persecution at the hands of unbelievers (15:18–16:2; cf. 16:32–33), it seems best to see this "advantage" as a reference to the encouragement they would enjoy when the very ones persecuting them would become their brothers in Christ by repenting and trusting in him.[61] An example of this comes in Acts 2:36–38, where Peter's Pentecost sermon indicts the Jews for crucifying the one whom "God has made . . . both Lord and Christ" (2:36). The Spirit's work of conviction is seen in their being "pierced to the heart" and crying out, "Brethren, what shall we do?"—that is, to be saved (2:37; cf. 16:30). Another example is the conversion of Saul, who, when he was converted, was the cause of joyful astonishment: "Is this not he who in Jerusalem destroyed those who called on this name, and who had come here for the purpose of bringing them bound before the chief priests?" (9:21). As a result of the Spirit's ministry of conviction, the disciples were not only spared of the particular persecutions that would have come to them at Saul's hand; they were also mightily encouraged to continue in the work of gospel ministry even amidst other opposition, because the Lord was turning their enemies into their brothers.

However, the disciples would have known none of these advantages if the Spirit's convicting ministry in the world did not result in the eventual conversion of those convicted. If the Spirit convinced unbelievers that they were in sin for refusing to believe in Jesus (John 16:9), that he was indeed righteous as evidenced by his resurrection (16:10), and that therefore their judgment of him was satanically unrighteous (16:11), but such conviction was not effectual unto repentance and faith and was only temporary, one struggles to discern why those very unbelievers would not return to their former course of unrighteousness and continue to persecute Jesus' followers. It

---

60. Fee, *1 Corinthians*, 687.

61. Morris, *John*, 619; cf. Bernard, *John* (as in Morris, *John*, 619n19).

is difficult to see what "advantage" that convicting ministry would be to the disciples. Thus, it seems best to understand this conviction as that which would eventually result in the salvation of its objects, and thus best to understand the "world" whom the Spirit would convict as those elect persons not yet brought to faith, the sheep not yet brought into the fold (10:16; 17:20), but who will not fail to be saved by the good shepherd (10:27–29; cf. 6:39). Contrary to Shultz's claims, then, John 16:7–11 does not teach that the Spirit ineffectually convicts the reprobate but effectually brings the unbelieving elect to repentance and faith in Christ.

The second hinge of Shultz's argument from John 16:7–11 consists in the notion that this ministry of the Spirit is "explicitly connected" and "tied to" and "occurs because of" Christ's atonement.[62] Since the Spirit does not come unless Christ goes away to the Father (16:7), and since he does not go away unless he dies, therefore the Spirit's ministry is grounded in the atonement. If the Spirit's work of conviction is genuinely universal, and if that work is grounded in the atonement, then the atonement must also be genuinely universal in some sense. As Lightner claims, "The Holy Spirit's work could not reach out beyond the elect if the death of Christ did not have this universal scope since the Spirit's ministry was procured in and through the cross."[63]

In the first place, this line of argumentation depends on the previous, namely, that the Spirit's convicting ministry in John 16:7–11 is absolutely universal, working in the elect and reprobate alike—which we have just refuted. Leaving that aside, while Shultz and Lightner are right to see a connection between Christ's death, resurrection, and ascension and the Spirit's coming, they aim to make that connection bear more weight than is warranted by the text. It is simply not the case that everything the Father and Spirit accomplish in the world, short of salvation, must be purchased by the Son's atonement. As will be discussed in the next chapter, on the atonement's relationship to common grace, Jesus does not have to suffer divine wrath in order for the Father justly to be kind to his enemies; such is simply an expression of the Father's own nature (cf. Luke 6:35), not a purchase of the atonement. While indirect benefits do accrue to the reprobate as an indirect result of Christ's particular atonement, the results of the atonement must not be confused with the atonement itself.

Shultz aims to defend the notion that whatever the Spirit does in the world is a direct, purchased benefit of the atonement by observing that the coming of the Spirit is a consequence of Christ's ascension, which is a consequence of his resurrection, which is a consequence of his death. On this basis, it is argued, his death must be universal.[64] Yet it might be observed with the same measure of consistency that Christ's death is "explicitly connected" and "tied to" and "occurs because of" his obedient life, which is itself a consequence of his incarnation, which itself is a consequence of

---

62. Shultz, "Defense," 174; cf. Shultz, *Multi-Intentioned View*, 96.

63. Lightner, *Death Christ Died*, 130–31.

64. Shultz, "Defense," 100, 172–74, 218–19.

the eternal Trinitarian plan of salvation.[65] But it would not be legitimate on this basis to conclude that the ministry of the Spirit was purchased by Christ's incarnation, or by his obedient life of righteousness, or even by his resurrection and ascension, which is a more immediate prerequisite of the Spirit's coming than the atonement is. The Spirit's ministry is as much a result of those other aspects of Christ's work as it is a result of the atonement, and yet, to take the incarnation as an example, Scripture explicitly declares the incarnation to have been designed with exclusively *salvific* intentions (John 3:17; 12:46; 1 Tim 1:15; Heb 10:5–10; 1 John 3:5; 4:9).[66] The Son partook of flesh and blood because the "children" (Heb 2:14) whom the Father had given him (Heb 2:13; cf. John 17:9) were of flesh and blood; he gives help to the seed of Abraham, the believer (cf. Gal 3:9), not to the entire posterity of Adam (Heb 2:16); and "*Therefore*, He had to be made like His *brethren* in all things" in order "to make propitiation for the sins of the people" (Heb 2:17).

Besides all of this, even if it was granted that the Spirit's ministry of conviction extended to sinners who finally perish in their sins, this would still not meet the burden of proof required to demonstrate that the Spirit's convicting ministry of the "world" in John 16:7–11 is an absolutely *universal* conviction. If there is to be a universal intention of Christ's atonement proven by a supposedly universal convicting ministry of the Holy Spirit, the MIV must prove that the Spirit exercises this ministry in all persons throughout history without exception. But it is granted by all sides that, in God's providential control of history, the Holy Spirit has not brought the gospel (which Shultz declares to be the means of this conviction[67]) to the vast majority of persons who have lived, much less to all without exception. If the Spirit's conviction comes by means of the preaching of the gospel, and if the gospel has not been preached to all without exception, the Spirit's ministry of conviction cannot be universal.[68] Therefore, a universal intention in the atonement is not supported by the Spirit's convicting ministry.

65. See chapter 4.

66. See chapter 5.

67. "The Holy Spirit only convicts people through special revelation, or the gospel" (Shultz, "Defense," 181).

68. Strange takes this argument to another level, arguing that if we must accept that atonement is not genuinely offered where there is no provision, it equally follows that atonement is not genuinely offered where there is not *access* to that provision. He asks, "In what is this category of people [i.e., the unevangelized] even salvable if they do not have the opportunity to respond to what was [supposedly] done for them?" (Strange, "Slain for the World?," 593). This very line of reasoning has led several to deny that hearing the gospel is necessary for salvation. Pinnock is representative when he says, "If Christ died for all the opportunity must be given for all to register a decision about what was done for them. They cannot lack the opportunity merely because someone failed to bring the gospel of Christ to them" (Pinnock, *Wideness in God's Mercy*, 157). Lake suggests that God treats the unevangelized according to whether they *would have* believed the gospel if it *had* come to them (Lake, "He Died for All," 43). Without such a denial of the necessity of gospel preaching for salvation (Rom 10:14–17), the atonement must necessarily be limited—if not to the elect, then to those who actually hear the gospel offer. As Strange puts it, ". . . for those who never hear the gospel, not only is universal or 'unlimited'

Conclusion

This leads to a brief review of Shultz's final argument, which is really no argument at all, but merely a reassertion of the premise he has failed to prove, namely, that the genuineness of a universal gospel call simply *must* be grounded in a universal provision of atonement. He states, "If Christ did not pay for the sins of the non-elect, then it is impossible to genuinely offer salvation to the non-elect, since there is no salvation available to offer them. . . . There must be a genuine payment for all people, who can, if they so choose, receive it."[69] Shultz merely asserts that this is true. While he does respond to several particularist explanations to this objection, he does not support this particular claim with any argumentation. He cites others' assertions but offers no arguments.[70]

Therefore, we must judge that the MIV's arguments for a universal intention in the atonement on the basis of a universal gospel call are ultimately unconvincing. Though the Father has chosen some rather than all, and though the Son has atoned for the elect alone, and though the Spirit regenerates that same number, nevertheless particularism maintains (and has historically maintained) that the gospel of repentance for the forgiveness of sins through Christ must be preached to all people indiscriminately and without exception. The genuineness of such an offer has nothing to do with the concept of a coextensive provisional atonement, but rather it is rooted in the character of the God of truth and compassion, whose preceptive and optative wills are to be interpreted as genuine expressions of his desire, even though he decrees otherwise. His offer is genuine because it is he who makes it, and because God will certainly and without fail grant the salvation he offers to any sinner who meets the terms of the offer, namely, if they repent and believe in Christ.

Such an offer may be made on the basis of the intrinsic, infinite sufficiency of the atonement Christ accomplished. Because the Christ who accomplished the atonement was infinitely righteous, and because his infinite suffering paid an infinite price, the atonement is indeed *sufficient* for all without exception even though the

---

atonement susceptible to the claim of *not* presenting a sincere or 'well-meant' offer of the gospel, but actually for this category of humanity, it makes no offer at all . . . " (Strange, "Slain for the World?," 587). Indeed, on the MIV's scheme, we must believe that God gave Christ to die to make all men savable *if* they believe the gospel, and not only does God *not* give the grace without which that condition can never be met (regeneration unto faith), but he also does not so order his providence to send a great majority of them the very message that they must believe. As Owen puts it, "God doth not proffer life to *all* upon the condition of faith, passing by a great part of mankind without any such proffer made to them at all" (Owen, *Death of Death*, 312, emphasis original).

69. Shultz, *Multi-Intentioned View*, 98.

70. Chafer says, "How, it may be urged, can a universal gospel be preached if there is no universal provision? To say on the one hand that Christ died only for the elect and on the other hand that His death is the ground on which salvation is offered to all men is perilously near contradiction" (Chafer, "For Whom Did Christ Die?," 315). Similarly, Lightner asks, "If Christ died only for the elect, then why take that message to the non-elect? An even more sobering question would be, 'Why does God invite all men if Christ did not provide for all?'" (Lightner, *Death Christ Died*, 114).

atonement itself is not *for* all without exception. Every human being who is a sinner is warranted to believe the gospel message of forgiveness of sins through Christ, not because each one is aware that Christ died for them personally, but because Christ's atonement is sufficient to save all who come to him, God commands all to come, and God promises that all who do come will be saved. Thus, in preaching the gospel to all, the servants of God do not tell sinners, "Christ died for you," for Scripture never records gospel preaching to include this phrase as the content of the gospel, but simply teaches that God has been pleased to save sinners through the death and resurrection of Christ, and he welcomes to himself all who come through repentant faith alone. In exercising faith in the gospel, sinners only arrive at the persuasion that Christ has died for them personally after they have exercised the previous acts of faith. They first believe that they are in need of salvation and are totally unable to save themselves, and that Christ alone is the all-sufficient Savior perfectly suited to their need. As a result, they embrace him in dependent, restful trust. Only then, discerning that they have believed in Christ, do they believe what Scripture says about those who have believed—namely, that Christ has died for their sins and that all the blessings of salvation are theirs by virtue of their union with him. This perfect, particular redemption, in which Christ has met every need and fulfilled every condition on the sinner's behalf, and which leaves nothing else for the sinner to accomplish, is the only atonement that can genuinely ground a full and free offer of pardon through faith in Christ. Far from impoverishing the universal gospel offer, particular redemption makes the far *better* offer, for it guarantees the effectiveness of the gospel and magnifies the omnipotence of the king who offers himself to sinners.

15

The Provision of Common Grace

WHILE GOD'S SPECIAL, OR saving, grace is limited in scope to those who actually receive salvation (e.g., John 1:16; Acts 20:24; Rom 3:24; Eph 2:8; Heb 2:9), the doctrine commonly called "common grace" refers to the truth that God is kind and does good to all of his creatures without exception, even those who will not finally be saved. Because God is not only gracious to sinners by rescuing them from their sin, but is also "kind to ungrateful and evil men" (Luke 6:35), there are virtually innumerable blessings that God mercifully bestows even upon those who hate him and never come to him through faith in Jesus Christ. As Ps 145:9 says, "The LORD is good to all, and His mercies are over all His works." Thus, "common grace" refers to "every favour of whatever kind or degree, falling short of salvation, which this undeserving and sin-cursed world enjoys at the hand of God."[1] These blessings typically fall into three broad categories.[2]

First, God's common grace is manifest in his work in the world to restrain sin and evil such that, while the earth is cursed and mankind is helplessly depraved, nature is not as corrupt and men are not as evil as they could possibly be. God works in the hearts of even those who do not belong to him in order to restrain sin, as was the case with Abimelech, to whom God said, "I also kept you from sinning against Me" (Gen 20:6). He also restrains his wrath against sin; his comment that his Spirit would not always "strive with man" (Gen 6:3) implies that his Spirit had been striving with man for a time. While the wickedness of man deserves immediate judgment, the people of Noah's day enjoyed many days of goodness and blessing before the flood finally broke out upon them (Gen 6:5–7). Paul mentions that God "overlooked the times of ignorance" (Acts 17:30), indicating that God held back the thorough exercise of his judgment upon idolatrous rebels as a kindness looking forward to the arrival of Christ (Acts 17:31). Even the judgments God does pour out do not reach their full measure, so that though the ground is cursed because of man's sin and only yields fruit with difficulty (Gen 3:17), nevertheless the ground still does yield the vegetation that sustains both man and beast (Ps 104:14).

---

1. Murray, "Common Grace," 96.
2. The following presentation is adapted from Murray, "Common Grace," 93–119.

Second, common grace is manifest in the good gifts God gives to his undeserving creatures. The creation itself, though cursed because of man's sin, nevertheless receives the bountiful care of its creator, who makes the dawn and the sunset shout for joy, who visits the earth and enriches it (Ps 65:8–9), such that "the earth is satisfied with the fruit of His works" (104:13) and "the earth is full of the lovingkindness of the LORD" (33:5). Even the animals, though not within the purview of God's saving grace, receive the benefits of their own existence through the care of the God of heaven, for "The eyes of all look to You, and You give them their food in due time. You open Your hand and satisfy the desire of every living thing" (145:15–16), giving food "to all flesh" (136:25). Unregenerate men, enemies of righteousness and haters of God, are nevertheless beneficiaries of the sun, which gives light and warmth, and of rain, which waters their crops and provides refreshment, "for He causes His sun to rise on the evil and the good, and sends rain on the righteous and the unrighteous" (Matt 5:45). Though he permitted the wicked nations to walk in the darkness of their sin (Acts 14:16), for the great part of history confining his revelation to a single nation, nevertheless "He did not leave Himself without witness, in that He did good and gave you rains from heaven and fruitful seasons, satisfying your hearts with food and gladness" (Acts 14:17). This "witness" of common grace testifies to his mercy (Luke 6:36) and love (Matt 5:44–45) even to those whom he does not adopt as sons through Christ. Among the most exalted blessings the reprobate receive are the benefits of external association with the people of God, which nevertheless fall short of salvation. Those who finally fall away are described as being at one time "enlightened" by divine wisdom (Heb 6:4) and as having tasted "the good word of God and the powers of the age to come" (6:5). Though such blessings do not ultimately result in their salvation, it is the kindness of God that they should be so near to the apex of his goodness. Besides these things, relative moral good is attributed to those among whom it is said that none does good (cf. Rom 3:10),[3] for even the tax collectors and Gentiles—both indicative of unredeemed sinners[4]—love and do good to their own (Matt 5:46), and through the common grace of the conscience even "the Gentiles who do not have the Law do instinctively the things of the Law" (Rom 2:14–15).[5] "Every good thing and every perfect gift is from above, coming down from the Father of lights" (Jas 1:17),

---

3. The Second London Baptist Confession (16.7) puts it as follows: "Works done by unregenerate men, although for the matter of them they may be things which God commands, and of good use both to themselves and others; yet because they proceed not from a heart purified by faith, nor are done in a right manner according to the word, nor to a right end, the glory of God, they are therefore sinful, and cannot please God, nor make a man meet to receive grace from God, and yet their neglect of them is more sinful and displeasing to God."

4. France, *Matthew*, 227n165, 693–94.

5. Murray also gives the examples of Jehu and Jehoash, who are not to be regarded as genuine believers (see 2 Kgs 10:29 and 2 Chr 24:17–27, respectively), but who nevertheless did "well in executing what is right in My eyes" (2 Kgs 10:30) and "right in the sight of the LORD" (2 Kgs 12:2) (Murray, "Common Grace," 107).

and each of those good things and perfect gifts that fall upon the reprobate represents the exercise of God's common grace.[6]

Thirdly, common grace is manifest by God's patiently restraining his certain judgment upon the reprobate. In God's inscrutable wisdom, he has determined that all those he has not chosen for salvation should be "prepared for destruction" (Rom 9:22) and "appointed" to doom (1 Pet 2:8). As the logical consequence of his election, the decree of reprobation was certain from before the foundation of the world (Rom 9:23; cf. Eph 1:4). In the case of the sinning angels, God immediately visited justice upon them, casting them into hell and committing them to pits of darkness until the final judgment (2 Pet 2:4). However, it is the kindness and longsuffering of God that forestalls the condemnation of the reprobate, with the result that they enjoy the blessings of this life as enumerated above. As Paul warns the self-righteous Jews in Rome against the certain judgment coming for those who practice lawlessness (Rom 2:1–3, 5), he ascribes the forestalling of such judgment to the "riches of His kindness and tolerance and patience," which is designed to lead sinners to repentance (2:4). Similarly, Peter, answering the objection that Christ had been slow to return to earth as promised, calls attention to the coming day of judgment (2 Pet 3:7) and states that his hesitation stems from his patience, desiring that all whom he has chosen for salvation be brought into the fold (3:9) before he destroys the earth with fire (3:7, 10, 12).[7] There are still those whom the Father has chosen, for whom Christ has died, who have not yet been regenerated by the Spirit and thus have not repented and trusted in Christ. Before bringing his judgment upon the reprobate, God must call all his own to himself, and so he is patient toward them. This patience results in a temporary reprieve from justice—a stay of execution—even for those whom he does not intend to save.

---

6. MacArthur and Mayhue capture this eloquently, "Every breath taken, every morsel eaten, every earthly beauty, and every wholesome moment is only possible by God's gracious provision (cf. Job 12:10; Acts 17:28). He is the sole source of all goodness (Ps. 106:1; Mark 10:18; 1 Tim. 4:4; James 1:17). Consequently, all that is good and worthwhile comes from his benevolent hand. Though this world has been devastated by the curse of sin (Rom. 8:20–22), the common grace of God allows sinners to taste of his abundant lovingkindness (see Ps. 34:8)" (MacArthur and Mayhue, eds., *Biblical Doctrine*, 488).

7. This comment reflects the position that in 2 Pet 3:9 the "all" whom the Lord wishes to come to repentance has the same referent as the "you" toward whom God is patient, and that this refers to the elect alone. The "you" of verse 9 are also the "beloved" of verse 8 ("But do not let this one fact escape *your* notice, *beloved*") and verse 1 ("This is now, *beloved*, the second letter I am writing to *you*"), indicating that he regards his recipients to be those within the church, whom he regards as true believers according to the judgment of charity. These recipients, according to 2 Pet 1:1, are "those who have received a faith of the same kind as ours, by the righteousness of our God and Savior, Jesus Christ." The "you" refers to the people of God. Therefore, Peter is teaching that Christ delays his return because he is patient toward those sheep who are his own (cf. John 10:14), whom he *has* (cf. John 10:16) because the Father has given them to him (John 10:29; cf. 6:37, 39; 17:2, 6, 9, 20, 24), for whom he has laid down his life (John 10:15), but who have not yet heard his voice and come into the fold (John 10:16). Thus, the sense of the verse is: "The Lord . . . is patient toward you, beloved brethren, not wishing for any of you [i.e., the sheep given to him by the Father] to perish, but for all of you to come to repentance." See MacArthur and Mayhue, *Biblical Doctrine*, 558–60.

Common Grace and the Atonement

What is the relationship between these good gifts of God's kindness and the atonement of Christ? Proponents of the MIV are divided on the issue. Ware makes no comment on common grace in his handout, indicating that he likely does not regard God's kind benefits to the reprobate to have been purchased by a supposedly universal atonement of Christ. Shultz, however, contends for that very position, stating that "non-salvific grace goes out to the nonelect on the basis of the atonement,"[8] namely, Christ's "intention to pay for all sin."[9] Because Christ has paid for all the sins of all sinners, God may on that basis be kind even to the reprobate. Hammett, on the other hand, while averring that "it makes logical sense that the provision of undeserved benefits to all could be grounded in the universal intention of the cross," hesitates to affirm the point "in the absence of more explicit biblical support."[10]

While some particularists of the hyper-Calvinist stripe have denied common grace altogether, the mainstream of particularism has always affirmed that God is kind to the elect and the reprobate alike, mercifully bestowing good gifts upon even his enemies, as outlined above. Those particularists who affirm common grace (the overwhelming majority) have also acknowledged that the blessings God gives to the reprobate are in some sense consequences of the atonement of Christ.[11] But they reject the notion that these blessings are proper and direct purchases of an atonement that paid for the sins of all people.[12] Cunningham captures it well when he says,

> [I]t is not denied by the advocates of particular redemption . . . that mankind in general, even those who ultimately perish, do derive some advantages or benefits from Christ's death; and no position they hold requires them to deny this. They believe that important benefits have accrued to the whole human race from the death of Christ, and that in these benefits those who are finally impenitent and unbelieving partake. What they deny is, that Christ intended to procure, or did procure, for all men those blessings which are proper and

---

8. Shultz, "Defense," 186.

9. Shultz, "Defense," 187. He says, ". . . each of these elements of common grace is only possible because of Christ's payment for all sin on the cross" (187).

10. Hammett, "Multiple-Intentions View," 191.

11. Turretin writes, "We do not inquire [i.e., dispute] whether the death of Christ gives occasion to the imparting of many blessings even to reprobates" (Turretin, *Institutes of Elenctic Theology*, 2:459). Murray says, "The unbelieving and reprobate in this world enjoy numerous benefits that flow from the fact that Christ died and rose again" (Murray, *Redemption Accomplished and Applied*, 61).

12. Berkhof makes the point, writing, "Reformed theologians generally hesitate to say that Christ by His atoning blood *merited* these blessings for the impenitent and reprobate. At the same time they do believe that important and natural benefits *accrue* to the whole human race from the death of Christ, and that in these benefits the unbelieving, the impenitent, and the reprobate also share" (Berkhof, *Systematic Theology*, 438, emphasis added).

peculiar fruits of His death, in its specific character as an atonement [e.g., redemption, reconciliation, etc.] . . . for all men.[13]

As a result, traditional particularism makes a very clear conceptual distinction between (a) the direct and proper *purchases* or *purposes* of the atonement, on the one hand, and (b) the indirect and consequential *results* of what the atonement did purchase, on the other. The benefits of common grace are said to "flow from,"[14] "flow . . . collaterally and incidentally from,"[15] "accrue from,"[16] or be "related to"[17] the death of Christ; they are said to be "fruits,"[18] "results,"[19] "indirect results,"[20] "consequences,"[21] or "benefits"[22] of the atonement; and the atonement is said to "give occasion for"[23] or "indirectly produce"[24] common grace blessings. But this does not mean that the atonement *purchases* the blessings of common grace as the proper and direct fruit of its nature as an *atonement*, or that the atonement was *intended* for all without exception on this basis. Christ does not need to pay for the sins of all people without exception in order for God to be kind to all people without exception. After enumerating many of the common grace blessings that "are related in one way or another to the atonement and may be said to flow from it," Murray says, "But this is not to say that the atonement, in its specific character as atonement, is designed for the reprobate. It is one thing to say that certain benefits accrue to the reprobate from the atonement; it is entirely different to say that the atonement itself is designed for the reprobate."[25] As was argued above concerning whether one ought to tell unbelievers, "Christ died for you," we must consider what precisely the atonement is *as* an atonement, both in its design and in its nature—that is, it is an expiation of sin and guilt, a propitiation of the wrath of God, a reconciliation of God to man, and a redemption of man from the slavery of sin.[26] And since the atonement is always efficacious in its design, none can be said to be partakers of the atonement who do not finally

13. Cunningham, *Historical Theology*, 2:332–33.

14. Murray, *Redemption Accomplished and Applied*, 61–62; Turretin, *Institutes of Elenctic Theology*, 2:459.

15. Cunningham, *Historical Theology*, 2:333.

16. Berkhof, *Systematic Theology*, 438; Kuiper, *For Whom Did Christ Die?*, 78; Murray, "Atonement and the Free Offer," 69.

17. Murray, "Atonement and the Free Offer," 64.

18. Murray, "Atonement and the Free Offer," 65, 68; Nicole, "Case for Definite Atonement," 199.

19. Kuiper, *For Whom Did Christ Die?*, 78.

20. Berkhof, *Systematic Theology*, 438–39; Kuiper, *For Whom Did Christ Die?*, 84.

21. Cunningham, *Historical Theology*, 2:333; Hodge, *Systematic Theology*, 2:558.

22. Berkhof, *Systematic Theology*, 438; Cunningham, *Historical Theology*, 2:332–33; Murray, "Atonement and the Free Offer," 66, 69.

23. Turretin, *Institutes of Elenctic Theology*, 2:459.

24. Bavinck, *Reformed Dogmatics*, 3:467.

25. Murray, *Atonement*, 30.

26. See chapters 5–7.

find their sin expiated, God's wrath satisfied, their alienation from God overcome and their relationship with him restored, and their release from the bondage of sin effected. This is what the atonement is "in its proper connotation,"[27] and thus none can be said to be partakers of Christ's substitutionary atonement, in its direct and proper sense, who are not finally beneficiaries of his substitution. And since there is no text of Scripture that indicates that common grace is the *intent* or the *effect* of the atonement, there is no compelling reason to consider common grace to be a proper, purchased *purpose* of the atonement, even though common grace benefits may said to be indirect *results* flowing from the atonement.

This distinction between proper purpose and indirect result is observable in the way Scripture speaks about the design of the death of Christ. In John 3:17, Jesus says, "For God did not send the Son into the world to judge the world [οὐ γὰρ ἀπέστειλεν ὁ θεὸς τὸν υἱὸν εἰς τὸν κόσμον ἵνα κρίνῃ τὸν κόσμον], but that the world might be saved through Him."[28] Based on this verse, it may be safely concluded that the Father did not design the Son's saving mission, nor did the Son come into the world on his saving mission (which finds its climax in the atonement), for the purpose of judgment and the destruction of sinners' lives (cf. Luke 9:56). However, Jesus' comment in John 9:39 would seem almost contradictory to his words in 3:17. Jesus says there, "For judgment I came into this world [εἰς κρίμα ἐγὼ εἰς τὸν κόσμον τοῦτον ἦλθον], so that those who do not see may see, and that those who see may become blind." In 3:17, he says he that was not sent for judgment (οὐ . . . ἵνα κρίνῃ), while in 9:39, he says that he did come into the world for judgment (εἰς κρίμα). Unless one is ready to admit a contradiction in Scripture, he would have to admit that there is a sense in which Christ did come for judgment and a sense in which he did not come for judgment. The direct and proper *purpose* (ἵνα) of the coming of Christ into the world was salvific; it was "that the world might be saved through Him" (3:17).[29] However, when Christ is rejected in unbelief, judgment is the necessary *result* (εἰς) (cf. 3:18). As the true light that comes into the world, Christ enlightens every man (1:9); that is, the light of truth "shines on all, and forces a distinction"[30] between those who love darkness, hate the light, and flee lest their deeds be exposed (3:19–20), and those who love the light, practice the truth, and come into the light that their deeds may be manifest as having been wrought in God (3:21). Thus, as Laney concludes, "the purpose of Christ's coming was redemptive. Yet, when His saving work is rejected, judgment results. Even though judgment results from unbelief, condemnatory judgment was not the purpose of the incarnation."[31] A

27. Murray, "Atonement and the Free Offer," 69.

28. A related comment from Jesus in Luke 9:56 confirms the same thought: "For the Son of Man did not come to destroy men's lives [οὐκ ἦλθεν ψυχὰς ἀνθρώπων ἀπολέσαι], but to save them."

29. As He repeats in John 12:47, "For I did not come to judge the world [οὐ γὰρ ἦλθον ἵνα κρίνω τὸν κόσμον], but to save the world [ἀλλ᾽ ἵνα σώσω τὸν κόσμον]."

30. Carson, *John*, 124.

31. Laney, *John*, 82.

distinction emerges, then, between purpose and result. Judgment and condemnation *result* from the incarnation and the cross, but it would be misguided to conclude that such condemnation is a proper purpose or intention for the atonement. Interestingly, Hammett, though himself a proponent of the MIV, grants this distinction between proper purpose and indirect result on precisely these same textual grounds. He says that such judgment "seems more like [a] resul[t] or outcom[e] of the . . . atonement rather than [a] separate and additional purpos[e] or intentio[n] of the atonement. . . . Judgment and condemnation come upon those who reject Christ, but God's purpose in sending Christ was not for him to be rejected."[32]

Such a distinction between purpose, or design, and result has caused some disagreement among particularists as to whether one ought to say that the atonement was in any sense designed for the reprobate. Kuiper argues this point most strongly, observing that, since God is absolutely sovereign and works all things according to his decree, whatever non-saving benefits of common grace indirectly result from the cross nevertheless were indeed *designed* to result from the cross. Kuiper writes, "It is the sheerest folly to say that, while God designed to save the elect through the death of His Son, all other results of the atonement are accidental and lie without the pale of the divine purpose. God purposed everything that comes to pass, all the fruits of the atonement included."[33] While it is certainly true that everything happens by God's design, results of the atonement included, it would be wrong to conclude from Kuiper's use of "design" that common grace was a universal intention of the atonement. In that sense, we ought to say that *every* contingent result of anyone's salvation (in the history of the world) was another distinct divine intention of the atonement. There would not be six or seven multiple intentions of the atonement, but billions of intentions. Further, to use "design" in that sense would also run afoul of the comparison of John 3:17 and 9:39. If one were to use Kuiper's language in support of multiple intentions in the atonement, one would have to say that since God has purposed everything that comes to pass, the judgment of sinners who reject Christ cannot not fall outside the pale of that purpose. But it is difficult to see how one could then account for the explicit negations of John 3:17 and 12:47, namely, that judgment was *not* a purpose for which Christ came into the world. While we must insist that nothing lies outside the purview of God's decree, we must say that God has decreed the salvation of the elect as the proper and direct purpose of the atonement, while he has also decreed that common grace benefits to be indirect results of the atonement.

An illustration from daily life may serve to elucidate this point. Scripture indicates that marriage is an illustration of Christ's relationship to the church; he is the bridegroom and she is his bride (cf. Eph 5:22–33; Rev 19:7–9). In the case of an earthly wedding, the proper and direct purpose of the wedding is for the bride and groom to be joined together in the covenant of marriage. Nevertheless, there are seemingly

32. Hammett, "Multiple-Intentions View," 190.
33. Kuiper, *For Whom Did Christ Die?*, 78.

innumerable other details that come to pass as indirect results or benefits of the ceremony. One example is that the bridesmaids usually purchase dresses for the ceremony, which oftentimes they keep for themselves after the wedding has ended. This is certainly a benefit that results from the marriage of the bride and groom; without the wedding, each bridesmaid would not have gotten a new dress. And such a benefit is certainly *designed*; the bride often expends significant effort with her bridesmaids in picking out dresses that each woman likes, that match the color scheme of the wedding, and that match the style of each other's dresses. But it would not be accurate to say that a *purpose* of the wedding is that the bridesmaids receive new dresses. Nor even would it be proper to say that the marriage was the *primary* purpose of the wedding ceremony while the bridesmaids receiving their dresses was a *secondary* purpose. No, the direct and proper purpose of the wedding is that the bride and groom be married to one another, even if there are spillover benefits—even *designed* spillover benefits—that are enjoyed as indirect results of the wedding.

Such is the case with the atonement and the benefits of common grace. While various blessings for all mankind naturally and necessarily *result* from the death of Christ, those common grace blessings are not a *purpose* or *intention* of the atonement. Therefore, it is wrong to conclude, as Kuiper, that the design of the atonement is properly universal,[34] or, as Hodge, that Christ "died for all . . . that He might secure for men the innumerable blessings attending their state on earth,"[35] or, as Murray says in one place, that "even the non-elect are embraced in the design of the atonement."[36] It is worth noting that Murray contradicts himself within several pages on this point, later (rightly) arguing, "The atonement was designed for those, and those only, who are ultimately the beneficiaries of what it is in its proper connotation. . . . he did not 'die for' the non-elect. . . . it is something entirely different to say that they are the partakers or were intended to be the partakers of the vicarious substitution which 'died for' properly connotes."[37] Elsewhere Murray contends that saying the atonement was designed for the reprobate is a "fallacy," striking the proper balance and saying, "the atonement embraced in its design the bestowment of these benefits upon the reprobate. But this is not to say that the atonement, in its specific character as atonement, is designed for the reprobate."[38] Instead, we ought to understand that while the reprobate "enjoy many benefits that accrue *from* the atonement, they do not partake of the *atonement*" itself.[39] Here Murray captures the reality that the results of the atonement ought not to be considered as the atonement itself. The proper design or purpose of the atonement—what Christ purchased in his death—is the certain

34. Kuiper, *For Whom Did Christ Die?*, 78.

35. Hodge, *Systematic Theology*, 2:558.

36. Murray, "Atonement and the Free Offer," 64.

37. Murray, "Atonement and the Free Offer," 69.

38. Murray, *Atonement*, 30.

39. Murray, "Atonement and the Free Offer," 69, emphasis original.

salvation of the elect. Such a particular purchase then *results* in numerous blessings for even the reprobate, but the results of the atonement are not to be regarded as the atonement. The reprobate are not atoned for, but the definite, efficacious, salvific atonement for the elect does produce benefits for others.[40]

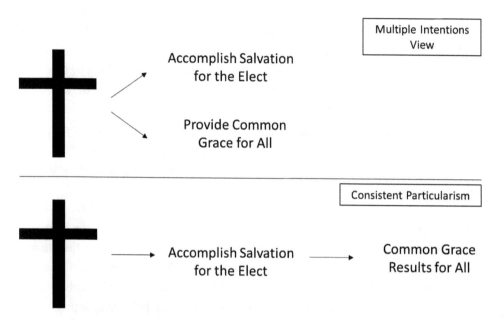

Relationship between Atonement and Common Grace: MIV vs. Particularism

In what specific ways, then, do the benefits of common grace accrue to all men as a *result* of the atonement for the elect, rather than as a purposed or intended *purchase* of the atonement for all without exception? In the first place, as mentioned above, the reprobate are granted a temporary reprieve from judgment as a result of God's plan to save the elect from sin and death (Rom 2:1–5; 2 Pet 3:9). If God had not intended to save anyone, it would seem there would have been no reason to forestall the condemnation due to mankind at all; he would have cast them immediately into hell as he did with the fallen angels (2 Pet 2:4; cf. Heb 2:16).[41] Yet because the Father planned to save the elect through the atonement of Christ, which he would accomplish not immediately upon mankind's commission of sin but in the fullness of time (cf. Gal 4:4), "it became necessary for God to exercise forbearance, to check the course of evil, to promote the development of the natural powers of man, to keep alive within the hearts of men a desire for civil righteousness, for external morality and good order

---

40. Piper, "My Glory," 657.

41. As Bavinck says, ". . . God would no longer have allowed the world and humankind to exist had he not had another and higher purpose for it. . . . For though it is true that Christ did not, strictly speaking, acquire the natural life by his suffering and death, yet the human race was spared on account of the fact that Christ would come to save it" (Bavinck, *Reformed Dogmatics*, 3:470, 471).

in society, and to shower untold blessings upon mankind in general."[42] Just as God blessed Potiphar's house for the sake of Joseph (Gen 39:5), God's intention to save his elect through Christ's atonement results in blessing for the reprobate. This stay of execution allows for a context in which even those who will never be saved know something other than their deserved judgment, for in this divine forbearance they experience the other blessings of common grace in this life.

Secondly, during their lives on earth, the reprobate enjoy the blessings that result from the fruit of the Spirit being worked in those who belong to Christ. It is based upon the efficacy of the atonement of Christ that sinners are raised from spiritual death to walk in newness of life in obedience to him (cf. Rom 6:4), for all the holy acts believers walk in were planned by the Father and purchased by the Son on the cross (Eph 2:10; Titus 2:14). Thus, as believers grow in maturity and increase in bearing the fruit of the Spirit, they are instructed to "do good to all people, and especially to those who are of the household of the faith" (Gal 6:10). Believers act as salt and light upon the earth (Matt 5:13–16), and the influence of their godliness in society thus makes the world a more pleasant place even for the reprobate to live. In places and times where God's providence has ordered the flourishing of his church in society, the idolatrous practices of false religion have been greatly reduced under the influence of the gospel, and the naturally perverse desires and appetites of men have been restrained so that sinners do not give full vent to their lusts.

Thirdly, the universal offer the gospel results only from the accomplishment of Christ in his atoning death for sinners, and the proclamation of the gospel is itself a kindness to all those to whom it is addressed. Though the reprobate will never be saved as a result of the gospel being preached to them (and that by God's design), it is nevertheless a sincere offer of mercy from the God who genuinely takes no pleasure in the death of the wicked. The gospel is good news to whomever it is preached (cf. Rom 10:15), and so, as Murray says, the uninhibited overture of grace is indeed grace to those to whom it comes.[43] It is a grace that millions throughout history have never experienced, passing their days in the darkness of their futile minds (Eph 4:17–18; cf. Rom 1:21–22), unenlightened by the truths of God's special revelation. But for the enemies of God even to hear that he stands willing to do them good; that he is so kindly disposed to mankind that he would send his Son in the weakness of human flesh to stand in the place of sinners, to bear their punishment under the heavy hand of his own wrath; that a God so glorious deigns to be their Savior, to rescue them from their bondage and pardon them from their iniquity, if only they would have him—if only they would repent and trust in Christ—for such a message

---

42. Berkhof, *Systematic Theology*, 438. See also MacArthur and Mayhue, *Biblical Doctrine*, 544. Hodge's comment is also noteworthy: "It is very plain that any plan designed to secure the salvation of an elect portion of a race propagated by generation and living in association, as is the case with mankind, cannot secure its end without greatly affecting, for better or for worse, the character and destiny of all the rest of the race not elected" (Hodge, *Atonement*, 358).

43. Murray, "Atonement and the Free Offer," 63.

even to grace the ears of the impenitent is an infinite condescension of the kind God who takes no pleasure in the destruction of his creatures.

But if these blessings of common grace are only indirect benefits that are results of the atonement, where are they properly grounded? What is the efficient cause of common grace benefits to the reprobate, if not a universal atonement? Scripture consistently indicates that the gifts of common grace are rooted in the character of God. In describing the common grace of God throughout the earth, David roots such goodness in the covenant faithfulness of God: "The earth is full of the *lovingkindness* of the LORD" (Ps 33:5); the God "who gives food to all flesh" does so on the ground that "His *lovingkindness* is everlasting" (136:25). The psalmist later praises God in this way: "You are good and do good" (119:68); in other words, God's *doing* good to all his creatures is grounded in his *being* good as a matter of his own character. David again says, "The LORD is *good* to all, and His *mercies* are over all His works" (145:9). Goodness and mercy are the fount from which even non-saving blessings spring forth unto the sons of men. When Jesus enjoins his followers to love their enemies and pray for their persecutors, the ground of that command is "that you may be sons of your Father who is in heaven," who causes the sun and rain to rise on the evil and the good (Matt 5:44–45).[44] Thus, if Christians do good to their enemies, they will in this way be imitators of their Father, who sends the common grace blessings of sun and rain upon his enemies. In this way, Jesus roots common grace in the Father's *love*. In the parallel text, Luke 6:31–36, Jesus exhorts the disciples to love their enemies, and to do good to them, with the result that they will be acting as sons of God, who himself is *kind* to ungrateful and evil men. This kindness is rooted in the fact that "your Father is *merciful*." In Acts 14:17, Paul recounts to the men of Lystra that God blessed generations of pagans by sending rain, granting fruitful seasons, and satisfying their hearts with food and gladness. This common grace, he says, meant that God "did not leave Himself without a *witness*," indicating that these blessings were testimony of God's kindness and goodness to them.[45] At every turn, Scripture roots the blessings of common grace not in a universal atonement, but in the character of the God who is by nature kind to his enemies. Even Hammett, a proponent of the MIV, differs from Shultz on this point and acknowledges that "the texts usually cited in support of common grace . . . seem to associate common grace more with the character of God (his love and kindness) than with the atonement of Christ."[46]

---

44. Murray writes, "It cannot then be disputed that such benefits as are exemplified in sunshine and rain, bestowed upon the ungodly, flow from God's kindness and mercy. It is because he is kind and merciful that he dispenses these benefits to his enemies. He is beneficent because he is benevolent" (Murray, "Atonement and the Free Offer," 1:66).

45. Murray says, "God did them good . . . [and] behind this doing good and bestowal of blessing, as well as behind the gladness of heart which followed, there was the divine goodness and lovingkindness" (Murray, "Free Offer of the Gospel," 117).

46. Hammett, "Multiple-Intentions View," 190–91.

Some object that it would be unjust for God to show such undeserved kindness to sinners, and that that injustice must be satisfied by the atonement of Christ. Christ must die, therefore, to pay for the goodness God shows the reprobate who deserve nothing but wrath. However, Scripture never gives any indication of this. There is no text or set of texts that indicates that any non-saving benefits are purchased by Christ's cross work. More poignantly, it must be said that it is not an act of injustice for God to act according to his own character. It is not unrighteous for God to be kind to the undeserving; it is good for him to be so. Christ does not need to atone for the Father's kindness. Each human being sinfully spurns the common grace of God in his unbelief, to be sure. In the case of the elect, that sinful disregard of God's goodness will indeed be paid for by Christ's sacrifice as he intercedes for them as their surety on the cross. But in the case of the reprobate, it is not as if their sinful disregard of God's goodness will go unpunished simply because Christ has not atoned for them; rather, they themselves will pay for those sins in hell. No sin will go unpunished, and therefore no injustice will be done. Christ bears that punishment for the elect, but the reprobate will bear it themselves in their destruction.

In summary, then, it is eagerly admitted that common grace flows from and is an indirect result of the atonement. But because the results of the atonement are not to be confused with the atonement—that is, because the distinction between the direct and proper *purpose*, or *intention*, of the atonement must not be conflated with the *results* of the atonement—we ought to regard common grace not as rooted in a universal provision on the cross, but rather in the character of God, who is merciful to his enemies. God does not have to pay, through Christ, for who he is. Thus, that common grace results from the death of Christ is no sound argument for a universal atonement.

Engaging the MIV on Common Grace and the Atonement

In the context of the above scriptural teaching, Shultz's presentation must be evaluated. In the first place, it is worth noting that in much of his presentation, Shultz's claims about the atonement's relationship to common grace are fairly modest. According to Shultz, "common grace . . . is based upon and flows out of Christ's atonement";[47] it is "due . . . to . . . the atonement";[48] "non-salvific grace goes out to the nonelect on the basis of the atonement";[49] and "God's patience in judgment, which is only possible because of the atonement, allows for all people to experience and receive God's good gifts of common grace."[50] Each of these statements fits well within the parameters set by the above presentation and is consistent with particularism. Particularists agree that there is a sense in which common grace is based upon and flows out of the atonement, for,

47. Shultz, "Defense," 185.
48. Shultz, "Defense," 189.
49. Shultz, "Defense," 186; cf. 189, 191
50. Shultz, "Defense," 194–95.

again, if God never intended to save anyone by Christ's sacrifice, it is likely that he would have sent each sinner to immediate destruction as he did with the fallen angels. The atonement for the elect is applied over the course of time, and that results in a forbearance of judgment for all, and thus sets the stage for the enjoyment of the other blessings of common grace. Shultz is aware of this agreement, stating, "Many advocates of particular redemption agree that common grace is a result of the atonement, but do not believe that common grace requires an atonement that pays for the sins of the non-elect. They describe common grace as an indirect benefit to the nonelect that comes about because of Christ's particular atonement for the elect."[51] Thus, Shultz accurately understands the opposing argument.

However, he replies that such a proposal does not do justice to three biblical realities. First, he explains what he means by common grace going to the reprobate "on the basis of the atonement" by quoting Lightner, who claims that the blessings of common grace are "some of Calvary's achievements."[52] But Lightner here confuses what the cross achieves as a proper and direct purchase versus what indirectly results from that achievement. Strictly speaking, though common grace results from the achievement of expiation, propitiation, reconciliation, and redemption for the elect, common grace itself is not a proper achievement of the cross.[53] Neither Shultz nor Lightner argues in light of the distinction between proper achievement and indirect result; each only asserts that if common grace results from the atonement in any way, it must be by a universal payment for sin. Shultz's second reason for rejecting particularism's indirect result argument is because it supposedly does not do justice "to the Holy Spirit's role in common grace."[54] Here, Shultz refers to the same argument from John 16:7–11 that he employed in arguing for a universal atonement on the basis of a universal gospel offer, namely, that whatever the Spirit does in the world is a consequence of Christ's death, resurrection, and ascension. This argument has been refuted above, and thus is without weight in the present discussion as well.[55]

Finally, Shultz claims that the particularist explanation does not explain the various kinds of common grace. He asks, "In what way, for example, would a non-elect person's natural abilities in art or mathematics flow out of an atonement that was only for the elect?"[56] In response, it must be observed once again that unless God

51. Shultz, "Defense," 186.

52. Lightner, *Death Christ Died*, 110.

53. See the immediately preceding discussion on "Common Grace and the Atonement."

54. Shultz, "Defense," 186.

55. See chapter 14 on "Universal Conviction?" After restating the argument, Shultz concludes, "Common grace cannot be reduced to an indirect benefit that results from an atonement only for the elect" because "this would suggest that the Spirit has no role in common grace, because there would be no grounds for his universal work in the atonement" (Shultz, "Defense," 186–87n75). However, this is based upon the faulty and unargued assumption that the Spirit can work in no one's circumstances except those for whom an atonement has been provided. Such an assumption is biblically unwarranted.

56. Shultz, "Defense," 187n77.

planned to save his people through the atonement of Christ, sinners would have been immediately consigned to their eternal punishment. Thus, whatever time a non-elect person devoted to exercising God-given natural abilities was owed, indirectly, to the atonement; without it, he would have been in hell rather than in his present life. Further, beyond the provision of natural life as opposed to immediate judgment, Scripture does not root the natural talents and abilities of mankind in a universal provisional atonement, but, as argued above, in the character of God, who is kind to his enemies. Shultz cites several texts to support the notion that God's giving of natural gifts is owing to a universal atonement,[57] but none of them mentions the atonement, and only one of them relates to the coming of Christ, namely, John 1:9. He claims Christ's enlightenment of every man consists in giving understanding such that "all people are able to know true things about God and the universe,"[58] ostensibly based upon a universal atonement, though he does not specify this. But this is an un-satisfactory interpretation of the passage, for neither the text nor the context of John 1:9 indicates that such enlightenment is rooted in the atonement. Instead, Christ's "enlightens every man" by "forc[ing] a distinction"[59] between the lovers of darkness (3:19–20) and those who practice the truth (3:21). Rather than the atonement, God's common grace benefits to his enemies are a result of his character, as explicitly stated in all the texts Shultz cites (with the exception of John 1:9, which is not related to common grace): God is good to his enemies because he is immutable (Jas 1:17), loving (Matt 5:44–45), beneficent (Acts 14:17), merciful (Ps 145:9) and righteous (Ps 145:17), and compassionate and gracious (Exod 34:6). God does not need to exact a payment for sins in order to be kind to sinners.[60]

Shultz then attempts to leverage an argument from John Murray, who explains that all common grace benefits are dispensed under the universal mediatorial domin-ion of Christ, which dominion Christ exercises "on the basis and as the reward of his finished work of redemption." Murray continues, "Consequently, since all benefits and blessings are within the realm of Christ's dominion and since this dominion rests upon his finished work of atonement, the benefits innumerable which are enjoyed by all men indiscriminately are related to the death of Christ and may be said to accrue from it in one way or another."[61] In response, it must be noted that such argumentation is entirely consistent with particularism (naturally, since Murray is a particularist), so long as one does not attempt to make Murray say what he denies—namely, that the atonement purchases common grace by paying for the sins of the reprobate. Again, the particular-ist does not dispute that common grace may be said to "rest upon" the atonement, be

57. Namely, Exod 34:6; Ps 145:15–16; Matt 5:45; Acts 14:17; Jas 1:16–17; and John 1:9 (Shultz, "Defense," 187–88).

58. Shultz, "Defense," 188.

59. Carson, *John*, 124.

60. Once again, see the immediately preceding discussion on "Common Grace and the Atonement."

61. Murray, *Redemption Accomplished and Applied*, 61–62.

"related to the death of Christ," or "accrue from it in one way or another." But Murray himself argues that the "one way or another" cannot be a universal atonement.[62] Shultz's claim does not follow from Murray's argumentation.

Then, foreshadowing the argument that God's patience in judgment supports a universal atonement, Shultz claims, "The reason that God forestalls his judgment is because his wrath against humanity has been satisfied in the atonement. Therefore every blessing that a person receives . . . is due first and foremost to God's grace displayed in the atonement."[63] This is similar to particularism's claim that common grace indirectly results from the atonement because the reprobate's temporary reprieve from judgment would not exist without an atonement for the elect. However, Shultz goes beyond this and claims that it is God's satisfaction of wrath against humanity (i.e., against all humans without exception) that is the basis of this temporary suspension of judgment. However, not only has a universal propitiation been disproven in parts 2 and 3 of this present work, but the internal incoherence of Shultz's position is present on the face of his argument. If God's wrath has been satisfied against all of humanity via a universal atonement, his judgment (which comes in his wrath against the impenitent) cannot merely be forestalled; it must be eradicated. If judgment is still coming, by definition, wrath has not been satisfied.[64] Thus, Shultz has not proven that God's giving natural gifts to the reprobate requires a universal atonement.

Shultz goes on to argue that God's restraining of sin and evil is further proof that common grace requires a universal atonement. He once again appeals to his argumentation from the work of the Holy Spirit, saying, "It is because this restraining of sin and evil is a work of the Holy Spirit that it results from the atonement, as *all* that the Holy Spirit does to restrain sin is based upon the Son's atoning death."[65] He continues to make the same argument: since the work of common grace is executed by the Spirit, and since the Spirit's work in the world is based on the atonement of Christ, therefore if the Spirit works common grace among the reprobate, it must be that Christ died for the reprobate as well as the elect. We have demonstrated several times how this argumentation does not follow. Not everything the Spirit does in the world is a direct purchase of the atonement. The Father and the Spirit may act on the basis of their own divine character without the Son having to pay a penalty or suffer punishment. God does not need to pay for who he is. This is the only argument Shultz makes in this section about God's restraint of sin.

---

62. E.g., Murray, "Atonement and the Free Offer," 69.

63. Shultz, "Defense," 189.

64. See "Propitiation" in chapter 6 and "Efficacious Accomplishment" in chapter 7.

65. Shultz, "Defense," 191, emphasis added. In his monograph, Shultz removes the phrase "is based upon" and adds "flows from" (Shultz, *Multi-Intentioned View*, 105). The import is unaffected. Without further argumentation, Shultz quickly resorts to a reassertion of his claim: "In the same way that God's natural gifts for the nonelect are a result of the atonement that includes the nonelect, the Holy Spirit's restraining work among the nonelect is only possible because of the atonement for the nonelect" (105).

Shultz then turns to argue his case from a third category of common grace: God's patience in judgment. He briefly treats Rom 3:23–25, which speaks of God's forbearance in passing over sins committed before the coming of Christ, and claims, "It is because of the atonement that God can justly forbear from punishing sin for as long as he desires, because sin has been punished in Christ. Therefore all people are allowed to live this life, even though they are sinners who deserve nothing but damnation, because of Christ's atonement."[66] Shultz argues that God forbears to punish sin on the basis of the atonement, which he believes to be universal. Thus, we may read "sin has been punished in Christ" as "*all* sin has been punished in Christ" or "the sins of all without exception have been punished in Christ." Two responses are necessary, however. First, if all sin—or the sins of all without exception—has been punished in Christ, upon what righteous basis is anyone punished for sins in hell? If such a universal provision is a just basis to forestall judgment, why must this judgment merely be delayed and not remitted entirely? If a universal atonement has so satisfied the demands of righteousness such that God may *delay* judgment, what is insufficient in that satisfaction of righteousness that makes judgment necessary at all? Ultimately, the non-particularist must deny the efficacy of propitiation in order to account for universality.[67] Second, the divine forbearance outlined in Rom 3:23–25 is not the temporary reprieve of judgment that results from common grace. Instead, it is his willingness to declare righteous and receive into heaven those believers under the Old Covenant era who died before the coming of Christ and his sacrifice for sins. As Moo says, "Paul's meaning is rather that God 'postponed' the full penalty due sins in the Old Covenant, allowing sinners to stand before him without their having provided an adequate 'satisfaction' of the demands of his holy justice (cf. Heb. 10:4)."[68] Such an interpretation is validated by the following verse, which speaks of God's righteousness demonstrated in his being "just and the justifier of the one who has faith in Jesus" (Rom 3:26). That is, it is the elect who are in view in this passage. The question Paul is answering is, as Schreiner captures it, "How can God mercifully save people without compromising his justice?"[69] Paul answers that God could, for example, save Moses despite the ultimate inefficacy of the types and shadows (Heb 10:4), because he looked forward to the time when the substance to which those ceremonies pointed would culminate in the efficacious propitiation accomplished by the Messiah. He is not speaking about the forbearance of punishment of the reprobate, for, as a result of their impenitence and unbelief, they perished in their sins and went to their deserved punishment (e.g., Ps 31:17). God's righteousness is not called into question because he punishes the reprobate; whatever temporary reprieve they experience ahead of their judgment they must pay for in hell (as opposed to Christ paying for it on Calvary).

66. Shultz, "Defense," 191–92.

67. Again, refer to the case made in chapters 6 and 7.

68. Moo, *Romans*, 240. See also Morris, *Romans*, 182–84.

69. Schreiner, *Romans*, 198.

No, Paul is vindicating God's righteousness in his allowing the salvation of those who did not bring an adequate satisfaction for sins before the once-for-all sacrifice of Christ was made.[70] He responds by saying that the efficacy of Christ's propitiation is so perfect that it reaches back to the previous age as the proleptic basis upon which God received believing sinners to himself. Therefore, Shultz's argument is foreign to the point of the passage and thus cannot support his claims.

Finally, Shultz appeals to 2 Pet 3:9, stating that "God lovingly delays his judgment because there are people still yet to be saved. . . . God's patience in judgment is bound up with his desire that all people be saved and that all people hear about his salvation in the universal gospel call."[71] However, this interpretation of this verse is not without significant problems. In the first place, the "people still yet to be saved" are the elect alone. When taken into account, this fact shows that no more can be said about 2 Pet 3:9 and common grace than that God's common grace to the reprobate (consisting in a temporary reprieve from punishment) is due only to God's patience toward the elect whom he will bring to faith.[72] As Kuiper says, "God shows mercy to the wicked because of the righteous."[73] The definite atonement accomplished for the elect, as well as the patient forbearance in the bringing of the elect to faith, indirectly results in blessings for the reprobate. This is a far cry from a universal atonement purchasing common grace for the reprobate. Further, when Shultz claims that God's patience in judgment is "bound up with" his desire that all people would hear the gospel and be saved, he fails to reckon with the reality that, by God's own sovereign appointment, all people do *not* hear the gospel; nor will all people be saved. Precisely because God has not so ordered providence to bring the gospel to all people without exception, and because he has not chosen to save all people without exception, we must reject Shultz's conclusion that God's patience in judgment "demonstrates that God has intentions in the atonement for all people, and therefore that the atonement was for all people."[74] Shultz bases his argumentation upon Peter Davids's interpretation of 2 Pet 3:9, which reads as follows:

> However one decides the effect of repentance on the final judgment, it is clear that, according to 2 Peter, if God had his way no one would come under condemnation in that judgment. . . . What he wants is 'everyone'/'all' to come to repentance. It looks as if 2 Peter is saying that God does not wish even the 'scoffers' to perish . . . but rather wants even them to repent. God's will may not be done, but it will not be for lack of trying on his part.[75]

70. Moo, *Romans*, 242.

71. Shultz, "Defense," 193–94.

72. See the above argumentation in "The Provision of Common Grace," particularly in footnote 7 of this chapter.

73. Kuiper, *For Whom Did Christ Die?*, 82.

74. Shultz, "Defense," 194.

75. Davids, *2 Peter and Jude*, 281, cited in Shultz, "Defense," 194n101. It is notable, and encouraging,

It must be observed that though Shultz claims to subscribe to the other four doctrines of grace, the MIV cannot but rest upon argumentation that is fundamentally inimical to those doctrines. To say, "if God had his way," and that "God's will may not be done" despite his "trying" is to imply that his will is thwarted (contrary to Job 42:2) or that his plans are frustrated (contrary to Ps 33:10–11), a notion entirely at odds with the Scripture's testimony to his absolute sovereignty (Pss 115:3; 135:6; Isa 46:10; Dan 4:35; Eph 1:11). It represents a view of salvation—indeed, an entire a worldview—that is in fundamental conflict with the biblical doctrines of God's sovereign grace in salvation. This is noteworthy, because though Shultz claims that the MIV "is not an attempt . . . to incorporate Arminian elements into a Calvinistic soteriology,"[76] it cannot avoid doing just that. The mutual exclusivity of those two systems of theology makes it impossible to compromise on one doctrine and not the others. Shultz's leaning on Davids's exegesis demonstrates that in this case.

Conclusion

Though the most thorough proponent of the MIV claims that universal common grace is grounded in a universal payment for all sins, his arguments for such a claim have been shown to fall short of the biblical standard of scrutiny. God's giving of natural gifts, his restraint of sin and evil, and his patiently forestalling judgment are not the proper and direct purchase of an atonement provided for the reprobate, but rather are the indirect results of an atonement accomplished for the elect, brought to fruition as an expression of the character of a kind God who is merciful to all of his creatures. Though God gives good gifts, short of salvation, to elect and reprobate alike, these good gifts are no argument for a universal atonement, and thus do not support the MIV's claims for general intentions in the atonement.

---

that this quote was left out of Shultz's monograph (Shultz, *Multi-Intentioned View*, 106).

76. Shultz, "Defense," 97.

16

The Cosmic Triumph over All Sin

THE LAST OF THE general intentions of the atonement proposed by the MIV is that Christ has died to pay for the sins of all without exception in order that he might reconcile the cosmos to himself, triumphing over all sin.[1] The central text in the MIV's argumentation for this point is Col 1:19–20, which says, "it was the Father's good pleasure . . . through Him to reconcile all things [τὰ πάντα] to Himself, having made peace through the blood of His cross; . . . whether things on earth or things in heaven [εἴτε τὰ ἐπὶ τῆς γῆς εἴτε τὰ ἐν τοῖς οὐρανοῖς]." According to this verse, the blood shed on Christ's cross accomplished the peace of all creation, which was in a state of hostility against God as a result of the fall (cf. Gen 3:17; Rom 8:20). The object of this work of reconciliation is said to be "all things," a phrase Paul has just employed four other times in Col 1:16–17 to denote the totality of creation—the things "in the heavens and on earth, visible and invisible, whether thrones or dominions or rulers or authorities."[2] Just as, then, the referent of the "all things" that have been created through and for Christ is "as broad as it can possibly be," so also the referent of the "all things" that have been reconciled by Christ's cross is "as broad as it can be, . . . on the widest possible scale; all things everywhere are reconciled to God by the atonement."[3] This includes the material creation, the animal world, humanity, and spiritual beings.[4] This presentation is followed by Shultz's claim that such a universal reconciliation "is only possible if Christ's atonement was for all sin, and not just the sin of the elect."[5] Shultz provides four arguments in favor of this interpretation, the first two of which are also set forth by Ware and Hammett, and the final two of which are unique to Shultz. This chapter will examine each of these arguments and will demonstrate that none of them proves that Christ's cosmic triumph over all sin necessitates a universal atonement.

---

1. Ware, "Outline," 4; Shultz, "Defense," 203–22; Hammett, "Multiple-Intentions View," 184–88.

2. Hammett, "Multiple-Intentions View," 185; cf. Moo, *Colossians and Philemon*, 134–35.

3. Shultz, "Defense," 204–5.

4. Hammett, "Multiple-Intentions View," 185; cf. Melick, *Colossians*, 225.

5. Shultz, "Defense," 205.

Universal Triumph Does Not Require Universal Atonement

The first argument the MIV puts forth is that Christ's conquest over all sin would be incomplete if he did not atone for all sin on the cross. Shultz reasons, "It is difficult to understand, however, how Christ could reconcile all things to himself and triumph over all sin if he did not pay for all sin at the cross. If Christ only paid for the sins of the elect in the atonement, then it would seem that there would be sin that would be outside of his atoning work, and thus there would be sin outside of His [*sic*] cosmic triumph."[6] Shultz is self-consciously following Ware's thought here, who writes, "Were Christ to die for the sin of the elect only . . . this would leave sin that stands outside of his atoning work and hence outside of his victorious triumph over sin."[7] In other words, Christ's conquest over sin would not be total and complete without atoning for all sin.

To be sure, Christ conquers sin's dominion over the elect by making atonement for them. He is, as Ferguson has said, *Christus Victor et Propitiator*.[8] He cancels out the certificate of debt consisting in decrees against those whom he eventually makes alive together with him (Col 2:13–14) by nailing their debt certificate to the cross (Col 2:14). In the case of the elect, then, Christ has disarmed the spiritual authorities that would be hostile against them, rendering them powerless against his people (Col 2:15). As the great high priest of the New Covenant community, Christ makes propitiation for the sins (Heb 2:17) of the children whom God has given him (Heb 2:13), thereby releasing them from the slavery and fear of death (Heb 2:15) and triumphing over the devil who had had the power of death (Heb 2:14). As the apostle John says, "The Son of God appeared for this purpose, to destroy the works of the devil" (1 John 3:8), which he accomplishes by taking away sins through his penal substitutionary atonement (3:5), and freeing his people to practice righteousness through abiding in him (3:6–7).

However, Shultz and Ware seem to proceed on the assumption that the only way in which sin can be conquered and triumphed over is by atoning for sin. Yet this is by no means the case. In the first place, the assumption that Christ must conquer all sin by atonement is explicitly contradicted by at least one key biblical passage: Heb 2:16. In a context that speaks of Christ's incarnation (2:14), suffering (2:10), and death (2:9)—which is both a propitiation of divine wrath (2:17) and a conquest over sin (2:14–15), and the scope of which is particularized by calling the objects of his atoning work his "brethren" (2:11–12) and "the children whom God has given" him (2:13)—the author makes an explicit negation, emphatically declaring that the

6. Shultz, "Defense," 205–6.

7. Ware, "Outline," 4.

8. Ferguson, "*Christus Victor et Propitiator*," 171–89. Shultz acknowledges, "Each Scripture that highlights the *Christus Victor* aspect of the atonement indicates that Christ's payment for sin is the foundation of his victory over Satan" (Shultz, "Defense," 208). On this point, see also Jeffery, Ovey, and Sach, *Pierced for Our Transgressions*, 139–42.

scope of the high priestly work of Messiah does not extend to the angels: "For assuredly [δήπου] He does not give help to angels [οὐ . . . ἀγγέλων ἐπιλαμβάνεται], but He gives help to the descendant of Abraham." Whatever the reconciliation of "all things" means in Colossians 1, then, it cannot mean that Christ has paid for the sins of the fallen angels, for the author of Hebrews explicitly denies that Christ's atonement extended to them. Christ does indeed triumph over the cosmic enemies of God—"the rulers and authorities" (Col 2:15) of the spiritual realm. However, Heb 2:16 teaches that he does not do this by paying for their sins.[9] Thus, the extent of Christ's atonement does not have to be—and indeed is not—coextensive with the extent of his cosmic triumph. Thus, the premise upon which Shultz's first argument is based is shown to be unbiblical.

Hammett seems to lay the groundwork for this point in his identification of death itself as an enemy of Christ's to be defeated. He writes, "Finally, 1 Cor 15:26 identifies the last enemy to be defeated as death. Only by undergoing death could Christ show his victory over it by his resurrection and promise his followers victory over it too (see 1 Cor 15:54–55)."[10] His claim is true. However, presumably, Hammett would not say that death itself is an object of Christ's atonement. Christ did not atone for death; as an abstract, impersonal reality, death did not have sins for which to atone. Christ did not reconcile death to God by a cosmic work of reconciliation. Rather, Christ triumphs over death by freeing the children God had given him from the slavery and fear of death (Heb 2:13–15), and then by casting death itself into the lake of fire at the end of the millennial reign (Rev 20:14). Thus, evidently, Christ may conquer that for which he does not atone. His universal conquest is *based upon* his particular atonement, but it is not the immediate *purchase* of his atonement.[11] If Christ's atonement extends neither to the fallen angels nor to death itself, and yet his triumph is rightly said to extend to both, then the scope of Christ's triumph is, in principle, broader than the scope of the atonement. Consequently, the sins of all people do not have to be paid for in order for Christ to triumph over them. Universal triumph does not require universal atonement.

Since Christ's triumph over his enemies does not require him to atone for their sins, by what means does Christ triumph over the enemies for whose sins he did not atone? While Christ triumphs over the sin of the elect through the atonement, overthrowing the rule of Satan in their lives, he triumphs over the sin of the reprobate through judgment—that is, through the punishment of his enemies, exacting from them the full penalty of their sins, even unto "the last cent" (Matt 5:25–26). As Savior, Christ pays for the sins of the elect on the cross; as Judge, Christ exacts payment for the sins of his enemies under the terrible wrath of God, who themselves will pay for their

9. Blocher, "Jesus Christ the Man," 574.

10. Hammett, "Multiple-Intentions View," 187.

11. For more on this point, see below: "Christ's Reign Is a Consequence of His Obedience, Not His Atonement."

sins in eternal conscious torment. Divine justice is satisfied in the punishment of all sin; but not all sin is punished in precisely the same manner. As Blocher aptly observes, "the everlasting punishment of impenitent sinners *is* the satisfaction of justice."[12] So, while it is true, as Shultz states, that "the reconciliation of all things includes the complete conquering of all of the enemies of the cross,"[13] such a conquest is achieved *both* by turning those enemies into friends via the saving work of atonement *and* by punishing eternally the enemies who refuse to receive that saving work.[14]

Reconciliation Is Incompatible with Eternal Alienation

The second argument advanced by the MIV that aims to prove that Christ's cosmic triumph necessitates a universal atonement is that the reconciliation of Col 1:19–20 is both (a) universal, extending to all creation without exception, and (b) of a different nature or character than the traditional understanding of doctrine of reconciliation. As mentioned above, proponents of the MIV argue that reconciliation is absolutely universal on the basis of the phrases, "all things, . . . whether things on earth or things in heaven," while also pointing to the fact that the means of this universal reconciliation is said to be Christ's work on the cross: "having made peace through the blood of His cross."[15] Then they observe that because the Scriptures rule out the doctrine of universal final salvation, this universal reconciliation of Colossians 1 must not mean the same thing for both elect and non-elect sinners. All without exception are

---

12. Blocher, "Jesus Christ the Man," 574, emphasis original. Russell Moore, whom Shultz quotes with approbation (Shultz, "Defense," 212n156), observes the same point, saying, "Jesus does indeed triumph over all things, making peace through the blood of his cross (Col 1:20), but this peace does not mean the redemption of every individual. Instead, Jesus triumphs over his enemies—as they are consigned to damnation beneath the feet of his sovereign Lordship" (Moore, "Personal and Cosmic Eschatology," 899–900). Aside from acknowledging that the reconciliation of Colossians 1 is of broader scope than the redemption of sinners—something Shultz would not agree with, given his claim of universal redemption—Moore recognizes that for which Shultz seems not to have a category, namely, that Christ triumphs over sin by judgment as well as by atonement.

13. Shultz, "Defense," 207.

14. This, then, is the answer to Shultz's inquiries, "If only the sin of the elect is paid for, how does Christ gain victory over all sin?" and, "How is Christ's victory over Satan and the demonic powers in the atonement through canceling out sins (Col 2:13–15) and taking away sins (1 John 3:4–10) possible if only a portion of sins were cancelled out and taken away?" (Shultz, "Defense," 211). That is, because there are two modes of conquest. The atonement conquers the sins of the elect, and, on the basis of (i.e., as a consequence of) that conquest, Christ will one day conquer the sins of the reprobate by casting them (i.e., the reprobate) into the lake of fire. Though one might object that it is wrong to locate the conquest of sin in the future, given that Col 1:20 speaks of this cosmic reconciliation in the past tense, it is a fact that Shultz himself acknowledges, saying, "Christ's reconciliation of all things is cosmic in scope, and though it is grounded in the atonement it will ultimately take place at the end of time, when Christ delivers up His kingdom to his [sic] Father" (Shultz, "Defense," 207). In the monograph, "Christ's reconciliation of all things" is replaced by "Jesus' victory" (Shultz, *Multi-Intentioned View*, 112).

15. Ware, "Outline," 4.

reconciled through the atonement, but not all are reconciled in the same way. The elect are reconciled "salvifically," while the non-elect are reconciled "in a non-salvific way."[16] Shultz explains this non-salvific reconciliation by distinguishing between subjective, objective, and eschatological aspects of reconciliation:

> While the elect are *subjectively* reconciled to God during this life at the moment of their salvation, the nonelect never experience this aspect of reconciliation. They are *objectively* reconciled in the present only in the sense that God has postponed the full display of His judgment toward them (just as He has done for believers as well) so that they might be saved (Rom 3:25; 2 Pet 3:9). Those who never experience a saving relationship with God, however, will still have a future experience of reconciliation with him. They will participate in an *eschatological* reconciliation.[17]

Thus, according to Shultz, Col 1:20 speaks of the objective reconciliation in which, through Christ's cross, God has postponed judgment and provided the opportunity of salvation. Subjective reconciliation is what one naturally thinks of when considering the reconciliation accomplished by Christ, though even this is not without significant revision. For the MIV, Christ accomplishes objective reconciliation for all on the cross (though this does not put away the enmity between God and sinners), but he does not accomplish salvific reconciliation. Salvific reconciliation is accomplished by the sinner's faith; as Shultz explains, "The elect are salvifically reconciled to God when they accept his objective reconciliation through faith."[18] Ware and Shultz argue that Col 1:21–23 makes this plain, since it highlights the necessity of persevering faith for reconciliation ("if indeed you continue in the faith firmly established and steadfast").[19] "Only then," says Ladd, cited by Shultz, "does reconciliation become effective for the sinner."[20]

However, as demonstrated thoroughly in chapter 6, such a doctrine of reconciliation is a significant redefinition from the biblical presentation. The biblical doctrine of reconciliation speaks to Christ's removal of the ground of the enmity that exists between God and men because of sin (cf. Rom 5:10–11; 2 Cor 5:18–19; Col 1:20–22). According to one lexical source, reconciliation is "the exchange of hostility for a friendly relationship."[21] According to another, reconciliation "expresses the transformation of the relationship (of enmity) between God and human beings that has been brought about by the new Adam, Jesus Christ (Rom 5:12–19)."[22] Even Moo,

16. Shultz, "Defense," 212.

17. Shultz, *Multi-Intentioned View*, 116, emphasis added; cf. Hammett, "Multiple-Intentions View," 186.

18. Shultz, "Defense," 213.

19. Shultz, "Defense," 214–15; cf. Ware, "Outline," 4.

20. Ladd, *Theology of the New Testament*, 496, as cited in Shultz, "Defense," 213.

21. BDAG, 521.

22. Silva (ed.), "ἀλλάσσω," *NIDNTTE*, 1:246. As Barrett says, "To reconcile is to end a relation of

on whom proponents of the MIV rely for their exegesis of Colossians 1, says that reconciliation "refers to the restoration of fellowship between God and sinners."[23] Melick, on whom they also rely heavily, openly acknowledges that for his interpretation of such universal reconciliation to stand, "the common understanding of reconciliation must be broadened."[24] Contrary to Shultz's presentation, reconciliation is not made effective by the sinner's faith but is decisively accomplished by God in the cross work of Christ. In all the occurrences of the verb "to reconcile," God is the subject, whether explicitly (2 Cor 5:18, 19; Col 2:20, 22) or implicitly (Rom 5:10). Sinners do not effect or activate this reconciliation by their believing; they passively *receive* as a gift the reconciliation accomplished by Christ (Rom 5:11). It is through Christ's death on the cross that sinners are reconciled to God (Col 1:22), and not through their faith at the time of their conversion. While it is true that man's hostility to God is not overcome until conversion, Scripture refers to that as having "now *received* the reconciliation" (Rom 5:11).[25] But before they received it—that is, even before their conversion; indeed, while they were yet *enemies* of God—Scripture speaks of a reconciliation *accomplished* by Christ's death.[26]

Shultz's attempted revision of the doctrine of reconciliation into his subjective-objective paradigm, then, does not cohere with the biblical data, for it fails to maintain the unity between the impetration and application that Scripture teaches must characterize Christ's work as the high priest of the New Covenant.[27] When Shultz says, "All people are objectively reconciled to God, but not all people are subjectively reconciled to God, and therefore not all people are saved,"[28] he is arguing that Christ has impetrated for those to whom the fruits of his impetration will not be applied. But as demonstrated in chapter 8, as the great high priest of the New Covenant, Christ cannot fail to apply "subjective reconciliation" to all those for whom he has accomplished "objective reconciliation."[29] Rather than a broadened concept of reconciliation that is ineffective until accomplished by the sinner's faith, Scripture teaches that reconciliation is effectively accomplished by Christ's death, and then is certainly (though not immediately) applied to every one for whom it was accomplished.

---

enmity, and to substitute for it one of peace and goodwill" (Barrett, *2 Corinthians*, 175).

23. Moo, *Colossians*, 134.

24. Melick, *Colossians*, 226.

25. In other words, "now" refers to the subjective application of the benefits of salvation, experienced at conversion, to which Christ's act of reconciliation (again, while we were enemies) is antecedent. Paul also uses the term "now" to refer to the believer's having been justified (Rom 5:9), another aspect of the application of redemption. Thus, Christ's work of reconciliation is *finished* and *accomplished* on the cross, but it is *received* by and *applied* to the believing sinner at conversion. See also "The Relationship between Impetration and Application" in chapter 8.

26. Also see "Efficacious Accomplishment" in chapter 7.

27. Again, see "The Relationship between Impetration and Application" in chapter 8.

28. Shultz, "Reconciliation of All Things," 449.

29. See Gibson, "Trinitarian Work," 345.

Aside from this, however, proponents of the MIV take such a redefinition of reconciliation to startling conclusions. In particular, they argue that Col 1:20 teaches that even the reprobate suffering in the eternal lake of fire are in a sense reconciled to and at peace with God. Ware writes, "So, the reconciliation of Col 1:20 is one in which the rebellion is over, yet God's conquered foes do not share in his glory. In this sense, all those in hell stand reconciled to God, i.e., they are no longer rebels and their sinful disregard for God has been crushed and is ended."[30] In personal correspondence with John Piper, Ware says, "Those in hell, who never put their faith in Christ and so were never saved, are under the just judgment of God for their sin, even though *Christ has paid the penalty for their sin*."[31] According to Ware, then, the MIV entails an understanding of the reconciliation accomplished by Christ's cross wherein one may be reconciled to God and yet not delivered from eternal punishment in hell. Indeed, he says, "This reconciliation must be one which includes a sense in which those outside of Christ, consigned to eternal punishment in hell, are at peace with God."[32] Shultz concurs, averring that the reconciliation spoken of in Col 1:20 does not involve the forgiveness of sins or the reward of eternal life, and so, while they are reconciled, those in hell will be alienated from God for eternity. Thus, reconciliation means that the reprobate "have been decisively subdued to the will of God and can do nothing but serve his purposes. . . . The nonelect in hell will be reconciled in that they are no longer able to rebel against God because they will acknowledge Jesus for who He is."[33] While they are suffering in the lake of fire with Satan, Shultz says, "there will be peace even between God and the nonelect as a result of the atonement."[34]

In response, it must be said that the MIV's redefinition of reconciliation has rendered the biblical concept unrecognizable. Piper is correct when he says that such a redefinition "stretches language to the breaking point," involving the proponents of the MIV "in a worse tangle of linguistic improbability than the ones they are trying to avoid."[35] Proponents of the MIV should be commended for attempting to do justice to the universality of the language in Col 1:20; "all things . . . whether things on earth or things in heaven" cannot be dismissed with a hand-wave. But, as Piper rightly observes, the MIV's proposed solution is worse than the problem. For the sake of interpreting the *scope* of reconciliation in accordance with the plain sense of the phrase "all things," the MIV distorts the *substance* of reconciliation such that it leads to affirming absurdities, such as saying that those eternally alienated from God are reconciled to him, and that those in eternal conscious torment under God's wrath are

---

30. Ware, "Outline," 4.

31. Personal correspondence from Bruce Ware, cited in Piper, "My Glory," 648–49, emphasis original.

32. Personal correspondence from Bruce Ware, cited in Piper, "My Glory," 653.

33. Shultz, "Defense," 214–15.

34. Shultz, "Defense," 216; cf. Ware, "Outline," 4; Hammett, "Multiple-Intentions View," 186.

35. Piper, "My Glory," 653.

at peace with him. While it seems natural to insist that "all" means all, the conclusions such an interpretation leads to—reconciled alienation and peaceful torment—demonstrate that that interpretation is not tenable.

Consider four lines of thought that demonstrate the non-viability of the MIV's exegesis of Col 1:20.[36] First, the concept of being at peace with God is utterly incompatible with suffering under his wrath. The establishment of the sinner's peace with God is concomitant with being justified by faith (Rom 5:1), which cannot be said of those suffering in hell for their sins in impenitence and unbelief. Christ establishes peace through his cross by "abolishing in His flesh the enmity, which is the Law of commandments contained in ordinances" (Eph 2:14–15). This is akin to his "having canceled out the certificate of debt consisting of decrees against us, which was hostile to us; and He has taken it out of the way, having nailed it to the cross" (Col 2:14). It is a contradiction to say that the damned experience this peace while suffering under the very hostility and enmity of the law of decrees Christ was said to abolish by his death. In Revelation, the worshipers of the beast, paradigmatic for those finally lost in sin (cf. Rev 20:10–15), are pictured as being cast into judgment, where they will "drink of the wine of the wrath of God," "be tormented with fire and brimstone," the smoke of whose torment "goes up forever and ever," who "have no rest day and night" (Rev 14:10–11). The eternal absence of rest cannot be reconciled with the concept of peace. Indeed, God says, "There is no peace for the wicked" (Isa 48:22; cf. 57:21). Piper is right to conclude that "to say that blood-bought peace describes the relationship between God and those in hell surely must eventually make a heaven of hell or rob heaven of peace."[37]

Second, it is not true to say that those suffering for their sins in hell are no longer rebels, or that their sinful disregard for God is ended. Shultz claims that the reprobate in hell are not able to rebel because they will finally acknowledge Jesus for who he is: Lord of all creation.[38] While it is true that they will make this begrudging confession as conquered enemies of the rightful king of the world (cf. Phil 2:10–11), it is not true that such a confession is incompatible with continued rebellion. When Christ taught at the synagogue in Capernaum, a demon who possessed a man there cried out, "What business do we have with each other, Jesus of Nazareth? Have you come to destroy us? I know who You are—the Holy One of God!" (Mark 1:24; cf. Luke 4:34). The demon

---

36. The following evaluation of the MIV's doctrine of reconciliation follows Piper's work in "My Glory," 652–56.

37. Piper, "My Glory," 654.

38. Shultz also makes this claim that Satan and his demons are reconciled in the same way (Shultz, "Defense," 216). However, Satan and the demons cannot be the objects of Christ's atoning work of reconciliation, because, as demonstrated above, Heb 2:16 explicitly contradicts this notion, which says that the atonement does not extend to angels, which Satan and the demons are. Further, since the atonement does not extend to angels, but Christ nevertheless rules over Satan and the demons, eventually casting them into the lake of fire (Rev 20:10), creation may be restored and the principalities conquered without there being a payment for their sins.

acknowledged Jesus for who he was—the holy one of God—and yet the text gives no indication that the demon ceased his rebellion against or disregard for Christ. Nor does any other text give reason to suppose that "in hell the recognition of Jesus as Savior and Lord will diminish enmity."[39] "[E]very tongue will confess that Jesus Christ is Lord, to the glory of God the Father" (Phil 2:11). But to those who are "under the earth"—the damned, the demons, and the devil—such a confession will not be the adoring praise of a worshiper at long last, nor the subdued acknowledgment that one was wrong about a matter of no consequence, but rather the despairing admission of a conquered enemy, bowing in resentful defeat to the sovereign king whose power he can no longer deny.[40] There is only reason to expect that such a despairing admission will lead to *greater* rebellion and disregard for their ultimate enemy, who pours out his wrath upon them without mercy. Instead, the only sense in which the rebellion of Christ's enemies is diminished in hell is that it is contained such that they can no longer harm God's people or revel in their sin without consequences. That is, they have been removed from the habitation of God's people and from the presence of his blessing (cf. Matt 8:12; Rev 22:15). Piper is right to conclude, "This is not reconciliation. It is ultimate banishment and alienation. This is not the peace Jesus purchased with his blood. This is the removal of those who would not make peace with God."[41]

This leads to a key observation about the distinction between Col 1:20 and Phil 2:10–11. Ware and Shultz seem to regard both texts as describing the same reality: Christ's final conquest of all things, including his enemies. Ostensibly, if reconciliation can be defined as Christ subduing his enemies under his lordship, Philippians 2 also describes what Colossians 1 calls "reconciliation." However, the concept of reconciliation is notably absent from Phil 2. Further, Philippians 2 contains a phrase that Colossians 1 does not—namely, καταχθονίων, "under the earth." In Philippians, Paul mentions three categories of beings whose knees will bow and whose tongues will confess: "those who are in heaven [ἐπουρανίων] and on earth [ἐπιγείων] and under the earth [καταχθονίων]." In Colossians, there are only two: both the "things in heaven" (τὰ ἐν τοῖς οὐρανοῖς) and the "things on earth" (τὰ ἐπὶ τῆς γῆς) are mentioned as the objects of Christ's reconciliation, but there is no reference to the things *under* the earth. This

---

39. Piper, "My Glory," 654.

40. O'Brien comments on every knee bowing to and every tongue confessing the lordship of Christ: "On the last day every knee will bow and every tongue will 'openly declare' that Jesus alone has the right to rule. For those who, in the here and now, have already bowed the knee to Jesus and confessed him as Lord . . . the acclamation at his parousia would spring from the heart. Others, however, . . . are not depicted as gladly surrendering to God's grace, but as submitting against their wills to a power they cannot resist" (O'Brien, *Philippians*, 250). Kent rightly agrees, "Paul does not imply by this a universal salvation, but means that every personal being will ultimately confess Christ's Lordship, either with joyful faith or with resentment and despair" (Kent, *Hebrews*, 125). It is notable that Philippians 2 does not describe the state of such conquered enemies as reconciled to or at peace with God. The difference between Phil 2:10–11 and Col 1:20 is the presence of the phrase "and under the earth" in the former and its absence from the latter.

41. Piper, "My Glory," 655.

is because in Colossians Paul is envisioning the time *after* the enemies of Christ have been sent to their judgment, "cast out into the outer darkness" (Matt 8:12), "outside" of the new Jerusalem (Rev 22:14–15), with "the dogs and the sorcerers and the immoral persons and the murderers and the idolaters, and everyone who loves and practices lying" (22:15). This realm of existence "outside" the new heavens and the new earth is the "outer darkness" that is "under the earth." It is "real," as Piper observes, "but not part of the new reality. In the new reality all things are reconciled to Christ by his blood."[42] Thus, the "all things" of Colossians 1 is explicitly limited to the "things on earth" and the "things in heaven"—describing only those who stand in a right relationship to God through Christ—because those who are "under the earth" have already been removed in judgment. The enemies of Christ are not the objects of the reconciliation of Colossians 1 because they are not part of the "all things" that remain in the new reality after God has cast the wicked into outer darkness.[43]

One might object that such an interpretation does not do justice to the phrase "all things" in Col 1:20. Aside from allowing the appositive phrase—"whether things in heaven or things on earth," with the notable absence of "things under the earth" (cf. Phil 2:10)—to define "all things," it should be noted that there is biblical precedent for describing this new-creation reality in universal terminology that nevertheless excludes the damned. At the close of Isaiah's prophecy, Yahweh speaks of "the new heavens and the new earth" that will endure in his presence (Isa 66:22). Of that new creation God says, "And it shall be from new moon to new moon and from sabbath to sabbath, all mankind [כָל־בָּשָׂר, literally "all flesh"] will come to bow down before Me" (Isa 66:23). Whereas in Colossians 1 "all things" are reconciled to God through Christ," so in Isaiah 66 "all flesh" will worship God in the new heavens and new earth. However, God continues describing the activity of all mankind who worship him in that place: "Then they will go forth and look on the corpses of the men [הָאֲנָשִׁים] who have transgressed against Me. For their worm will not die and their fire will not be quenched; and they will be an abhorrence to all mankind [כָל־בָּשָׂר]" (Isa 66:24). The worshipers of God in the new creation are described in universal terms ("all mankind"), and yet there is a reference to the damned ("men"), who are distinguished and excluded from "all mankind." This demonstrates that it is possible for Scripture to refer to the eschatological people of God in universal terms while excluding the damned. Just as "all mankind" does not refer to the "men" whose corpses will be an abhorrence to all mankind in Isa 66:23–24, so also "all things" does not refer to "those who are under the earth" in Col 1:20.[44]

42. Piper, "My Glory," 656.

43. Warfield calls this an "eschatological universalism" rather than an each-and-every universalism (Warfield, *Plan of Salvation*, 102). The whole world will indeed be reconciled to God through the atonement of Christ, but the enemies of the gospel will have been cast out of that new world. See also Bavinck, *Reformed Dogmatics*, 3:474–75; and Kuiper, *For Whom Did Christ Die?*, 95–100.

44. Piper summarizes well: Paul "means that the blood of Christ has secured the victory of God over the universe in such a way that the day is coming when 'all things' that are in the *new* heavens

Shultz objects to this interpretation of Col 1:20 for two reasons. He writes, "While it is certainly true that the elect are reconciled, it is difficult to understand the basis for the reconciliation of creation in this argument. This argument is also unable to explain what it means to say that the nonelect are reconciled, as Col 1:20 does."[45] Taking the second claim first, it is simply untrue that Col 1:20 says the non-elect are reconciled. Shultz infers that "all things" implies that the reprobate are included, but such is to beg the question, for that is the very matter in dispute. But since the reprobate are outside the scope of "all things" because they are now "under the earth" (Phil 2:10) and in "outer darkness" (Matt 8:12), and since there is linguistic precedent for the use of such universal language (Isa 66:22–24), Shultz's presumption is unwarranted.

As to how the reconciliation of the elect alone can ground the reconciliation of creation, it is once again necessary to bring to mind the distinction between the atonement itself, on the one hand, and the results of the atonement, on the other. An atonement that has cosmic results is not the same thing as an atonement accomplished for the cosmos. In Col 1:20, Paul is not teaching that the creation is the *object* of Christ's reconciling work of atonement. Rather, he is teaching that Christ's reconciling work of atonement—i.e., the salvation of the elect—has *consequences* for all of creation. Jonathan Gibson captures this well when he writes that "Paul is no more arguing that Christ propitiated God's wrath for every human being than he is arguing that Christ propitiated God's wrath for rocks and birds and stars, or even fallen angels. Rather, Paul is simply stating that one of the eschatological *consequences* of Christ's death is a universal peace among all things on earth and in heaven."[46]

This point becomes clearer when one considers the relationship between mankind and the creation, both with respect to sin and the curse and with respect to redemption and the eradication of that curse. Though creation assuredly groans under the curse of sin (cf. Rom 8:22), the creation has no sin of its own for which atonement is required. Creation was cursed because of man's sin: "Cursed is the ground *because of you*," declared God to Adam (Gen 3:17). It was because of the sin of *man* that "the creation was subjected to futility" (Rom 8:20), such that it would bear thorns and

---

and the *new* earth will be entirely reconciled to God with no rebel remnants. Before that day comes, all those who refuse to be reconciled by his blood will be cast into 'outer darkness' (Matt. 8:12), so that they are not reckoned to be a part of the new heavens and the new earth. The rebels in hell will simply not be part of the 'all things' which fill the new heavens and the new earth. They are 'outside' of the new reality, in the 'darkness'" (Piper, "My Glory," 655, emphasis original).

45. Shultz, "Defense," 205n138.

46. Gibson, "For Whom Did Christ Die?," 310, emphasis added. Bavinck calls the renewal of heaven and earth "the fruit of the cross of Christ," distinguishing it from Origen's universalist heresy, which said that "Christ suffered somewhat for [irrational creatures] and merited something for them" (Bavinck, *Reformed Dogmatics*, 3:471). Kuiper notes that "there is no Scriptural warrant" for Origen's doctrine that "Christ suffered meritoriously for inanimate creatures," but rather, "as the fall of man, the head of creation, affected creation adversely, throwing it into disorder, so Christ, who has atoned for the sins of man, will ultimately destroy also this *consequence* of man's sin" (Kuiper, *For Whom Did Christ Die?*, 97, emphasis added).

thistles and yield produce for food only by great exertion on man's part (Gen 3:18–19). Again, the creation was not morally culpable for this; it was "not willingly" subjected to futility (Rom 8:20) but was cursed by God himself as a result of human sin. Nor was the creation cursed with no plan for its redemption, for the one who subjected it did so "in hope that the creation itself also will be set free from its slavery to corruption" (8:21). But the redemption and renewal of the creation comes about not because it is the direct object of Christ's universal atonement; rather, just as its curse followed man's curse, so also its redemption will follow man's redemption. The creation "waits eagerly" not for an atonement for its sins but "for the revealing of the sons of God" (8:19). The creation will be set free from its slavery to corruption "into the freedom of *the glory of the children of God*" (8:21). As Moo puts it, "It is only with and because of the glory of God's children that creation experiences its own full and final deliverance."[47] Just as the creation was cursed in order to be a suitable habitation for God's curse upon Adam's posterity, so also will the creation be redeemed in order to be a suitable habitation for God's blessing upon the new humanity recreated in Christ, the last Adam. This new humanity is not inclusive of all human beings, still less the animals or the inanimate creation, but rather consists of the elect alone. Accordingly, Rom 8:19–23, read in concert with Gen 3:17–19, "shows that what lies behind the *cosmic* renewal is not a universal provision made by Christ's atonement but a consummated redemption of a *particular* group of people—'the sons of God.'"[48]

Thus, the MIV's case for a universal atonement on the basis of cosmic reconciliation collapses under the weight of the lexical data themselves. Reconciliation is incompatible with eternal alienation. Peace may not be predicated of those suffering in torment for eternity. While such an interpretation seems to safeguard a plain, normal sense of the phrase "all things," it redefines the nature of reconciliation and of peace with God in such a way that, by the principle of the analogy of the faith, it cannot be sustained. Instead, the "all things" of Col 1:20 refers to the elect who are reconciled by the cross of Christ *after* the casting out of the wicked from the new creation (Matt 8:12). This is a faithful handling of the universalistic language (cf. Isa 66:23–24) and does not require a redefinition of the nature of reconciliation. A cosmic reconciliation need not be grounded in a universal atonement; rather, Scripture explicitly teaches that it is a particular redemption that has a universal impact with consequences for the entire cosmos.

---

47. Moo, *Romans*, 517. Significantly, F. F. Bruce, whom Shultz quotes in support of his own position, recognizes this relationship between man and creation, such that the reconciliation of the cosmos in Col 1:20 ought to be understood as the consequence rather than the direct and proper purchase of the atonement. Bruce writes, ". . . it is far more likely that, for Paul, cosmic reconciliation was a corollary of personal reconciliation" (Bruce, *Colossians, Philemon, and Ephesians*, 76–77, as cited in Shultz, "Defense," 214n159).

48. Gibson, "For Whom Did Christ Die?," 310.

Christ Does Not Die to Damn

A third reason the MIV gives for why Christ's cosmic triumph over all sin must be based upon a universal atonement is that both the elect and the reprobate will experience an eschatological resurrection. Citing John 5:26–29, Shultz observes that both the elect ("those who did the good deeds") and the reprobate ("those who committed the evil deeds") will be resurrected, the elect unto "a resurrection of life" and the reprobate unto "a resurrection of judgment" (5:29).[49] He argues that Christ exercises this sovereign summons to all the dead (5:25, 28) by virtue of his being granted such authority from the Father (5:22), which, Shultz reasons, the Father grants to him on the basis of his own resurrection, which "which is a result of his atonement."[50] Since his atonement is inextricably linked to his resurrection, and since his resurrection results in the resurrection of elect and reprobate alike, it must be that he atoned for elect and reprobate alike.

Two brief responses to this first line of argumentation are in order. First, the text from which Shultz argues this point (i.e., John 5) makes no reference to the death or atonement of Christ. While it is undeniable that Christ could not execute lordship over the living and the dead unless he himself rose from the grave (cf. Rom 14:9; Phil 2:8–11; Rev 1:18), this is not the ground given for such lordship in the present passage. Jesus says, "For just as the Father has life in Himself, even so He gave to the Son also to have life in Himself; and He gave Him authority to execute judgment, because He is the Son of Man" (John 5:26–27). Verse 26 highlights the deity of the Son, as Jesus says the Father communicates aseity (a metonym for the divine essence, especially in light of divine simplicity) to the Son in eternal generation. It is, first of all, because Christ is God that he may execute judgment over the dead and the living.[51] Verse 27 highlights the identity of the Son as the divine Messiah, the "Son of Man" of Dan 7:13–14, who would rescue his people. The whole tenor of the context of the passage concerns Jesus' identity as "equal with God" (John 5:18), who exercises all the prerogatives of God. The

---

49. Shultz, "Defense," 217. It is worth noting that neither Ware nor Hammett cite the resurrection of elect and reprobate as an argument for cosmic triumph by universal atonement. With respect to proponents of the MIV, this is unique to Shultz. However, it is not original with him, as Shultz seems to rely on the work of Lightner (Lightner, *Death Christ Died*, 144–45) for this argument.

50. Shultz, "Defense," 218–19. Shultz cites 1 Cor 15:13 to support this last claim: "But if there is no resurrection of the dead, not even Christ has been raised." However, it should be noted that Paul does not make this statement to argue that Christ's resurrection makes possible the resurrection of others—though he does make that point in 1 Cor 15:20–23—but rather to argue that those in Corinth who were doubting the doctrine of the resurrection of the dead (in general) could not do so consistently with their Christian faith, since Christianity is founded upon the belief in the resurrection of the dead, namely, Christ's resurrection from the dead. Other texts Shultz could appeal to in order to support this claim would be Phil 2:8–11, since it is Christ's obedience unto death that is the "very reason" for which "God highly exalted Him" in such a way that every knee will bow and every tongue will confess his lordship. Heb 2:14 and Rev 1:18 also are texts that state Christ has gained authority over death by his own death and resurrection.

51. See Carson, *John*, 256–57.

Messiah's work of mediating between God and men by virtue of his atonement is not unrelated to his lordship over the dead and living—far from it. However, it is worth noting that what is emphasized in this context as the ground of such lordship is his identity as the eternal Son of God and the promised Messiah.

Second, Shultz here is attempting to make the same "result" argument that he employs to argue that the universal gospel call and common grace are indicators of a universal atonement. Since the Spirit's work in the world (through the universal gospel call and through common grace) is a consequence of Christ's "going away" from the disciples (John 16:7), and since that ascension is a result of the resurrection, and since the resurrection is a result of the atonement, therefore Christ's atonement purchases the universal work of the Spirit and is itself universal.[52] But, as observed in the analysis above, saying that such lordship results from the atonement is not the same thing as saying that it is the direct purchase and merited effect of the atonement. We might argue with the same measure of consistency that Christ's death is a result of his obedient life, and that his obedient life is a result of his incarnation, and that his incarnation is result of the eternal Trinitarian plan of salvation. But it would not be legitimate on this basis to conclude that the ministry of the Spirit was *purchased* by his life, his incarnation, or the plan of salvation—and certainly not that the eternal plan of salvation extended to all without exception. The same is true with the lordship conferred upon Christ as a consequence of his obedience unto death and his victorious resurrection. Though these are indeed *consequences* of the atonement, there is a great deal of difference between a direct and proper purchase of the atonement and the consequences or results of that purchase.[53] Shultz must not only prove that Christ's prerogative to judge results as a consequence of his resurrection, which results from his atonement (in which case, *everything* that results from the atonement would be evidence for a universal atonement; but the results of the atonement are not the atonement). Instead, he must prove that Scripture indicates that Christ's prerogative to judge is the direct and proper purchase of the atonement— i.e., that the atonement is the meritorious cause of his lordship, such that we could say that Christ died to purchase the authority by which he would rule as Lord of all creation.[54] This is a burden of proof he never meets.

Moving forward, Shultz turns to 1 Cor 15:21–22 for support, which says, "For since by a man came death, by a man also came the resurrection of the dead. For

52. Shultz, "Defense," 100, 172–74, 218–19.

53. See the argumentation in chapter 14 under "Universal Conviction?" and in chapter 15 under "Common Grace and the Atonement."

54. Owen observes that such authority is not grounded in Christ's work of satisfaction, as if his lordship was the fruit of his propitiation and ransom. He writes, ". . . we deny that it is anywhere in the Scripture once intimated that the ransom paid by Christ in his death for us was the cause of his exaltation to be Lord of all: it was his obedience to his Father in his death, and not his satisfaction for us, that is proposed as the antecedent of this exaltation; as is apparent, Phil. ii. 7–11" (Owen, *Death of Death*, 377–78).

as in Adam all die, so also in Christ all will be made alive." Shultz seems to acknowledge that the "all" who "will be made alive" refers to believers only,[55] but he proceeds to argue, with the help of other sources, that the resurrection of both elect and reprobate is supported by this text. He cites Lighter, who argues that Christ's universal atonement "must be the basis for the future resurrection of all men,"[56] as well as Custance, who argues that the atonement is unlimited "since all men equally will be raised from the dead, freed forever from their present physical defect, and will therefore face judgment in bodies no longer subject to death."[57] Despite Shultz's proviso, the argument seems to be that 1 Cor 15:22 teaches that "all"—i.e., both the elect and reprobate—"will be made alive"—i.e., will be raised from the dead, whether unto life or judgment (cf. John 5:29).

Three responses will demonstrate that such an argument does not prove the MIV's claim. First, there is no proper sense in which resurrection unto eternal death ought to be called being "made alive." In the context of John 5, eternal life is explicitly contrasted with judgment (John 5:24), and while the righteous are resurrected unto life, the wicked are resurrected unto judgment (5:29). Thus, while the Son raises all without exception, those to whom he gives life (5:21) are the elect alone. It is by virtue of Christ's atoning death that he is said to be the Savior of those for whom he died (2 Tim 1:10; Titus 2:13–14; 1 John 4:10, 14). But it is wholly improper to speak of Christ as the Savior of those men whom he damns for eternity. Custance therefore misses the mark when he describes the resurrected reprobate as "freed forever from their present physical defect, . . . in bodies no longer subject to death."[58] Such is to conceive of death as going out of existence rather than the separation of the body and soul from God's presence to bless. The resurrection of the unrighteous unto everlasting judgment can in no sense be described as being "made alive" or being "no longer subject to death." Rather, the reprobate are given bodies that are designed to experience *consummate* death for all eternity. It is no mercy to be resurrected unto damnation. In fact, it would be a mercy if God did not raise the wicked to life—if he left them in their natural body or as a disembodied spirit, for beings in such a state could not withstand the infinite fires of judgment and would be annihilated. To go out of existence is a less severe punishment than to be given a body that may sustain consummate physical punishment for eternity. Though the unrighteous are conscious, their eternal experience cannot be described as "life" in any sense. They are resurrected only to experience everlasting death. If Lightner is correct that Christ, as the last Adam, defeats the power of death through his resurrection, thereby giving

---

55. "Although the context of these verses is concerned with the resurrection of believers . . ." (Shultz, "Defense," 219).

56. Lightner, *Death Christ Died*, 144. Barrick seems to hold a similar position (Barrick, "Extent of the Perfect Sacrifice," 8).

57. Custance, *Sovereignty of Grace*, 171.

58. Custance, *Sovereignty of Grace*, 171.

him the authority to resurrect both the elect and reprobate,[59] it would follow that, in the case of the reprobate, Christ defeated the power of death in order that he might subject men to eternal death. But Christ does not die to damn; he dies to save. It is unthinkable that someone could tell another, "Christ died for you," and mean by it, "Christ died in order to secure his own authority to condemn you to hell." Such a proposition is incoherent, and it is not the testimony of Scripture.

Second, Scripture never gives any indication that Christ must pay for the sins of the reprobate so that he might ultimately raise them unto a resurrection of eternal judgment. The Father requires no payment in order to carry out his justice upon the wicked; there are no barriers to his executing justice upon the wicked that must be overcome by the ministry of Christ. Christ does not have to die for someone in order to earn the right to condemn them. The Father exercises that authority by virtue of his being their creator and judge, not by virtue of Christ having paid for their sins. In fact, it is precisely because there has been no payment for their sins that God's justice demands that the reprobate be resurrected unto eternal damnation. Put simply, Christ does not merit by his atonement the resurrection bodies of the reprobate, in which they will be punished for eternity. Rather, the reprobate themselves, as impenitent and unbelieving sinners, merit their damnation by their sin.

Third, 1 Cor 15:22 says, "For as in Adam all die, so also *in Christ* all will be made alive." This text teaches that, in union with Adam, all people are imputed with his guilt and are reckoned to be sinners (cf. Rom 5:18a, 5:19a). But in union with Christ, those united to Christ will all be counted righteous (cf. Rom 5:18b, 5:19b).[60] The key question is: Are unbelievers united to Christ? No. There is no text in Scripture that refers to an unbeliever as being "in Christ" in any sense. Therefore, if it is only "in Christ" that "all will be made alive," and unbelievers are never in Christ, they cannot be part of the "all" who "will be made alive." There is no union with Christ in which the reprobate partake of a resurrection. As Ciampa and Rosner observe, "the unqualified 'all' of v. 22 who will be made alive is clarified by v. 23 with the phrase 'those who belong to him.'"[61] The raising of the dead unto damnation is not a result of the atonement; it is the judgment of God upon sin. As mentioned earlier, Christ conquers sin not merely by atonement but also by judgment.

Christ's Reign Is a Consequence of Obedience, Not Atonement

Shultz then gives a fourth and final reason, similar and related to the previous, for why Christ's cosmic triumph necessitates a universal atonement. Since Jesus will rule over all creation (not merely the elect), and since his kingly rule is only given to him as "a result of" (or "is based upon") his atonement and resurrection (e.g., Rev 5:11–14), therefore

59. Lightner, *Death Christ Died*, 144–45.

60. Hodge, *1 & 2 Corinthians*, 324–26.

61. Ciampa and Rosner, *1 Corinthians*, 764.

his atonement must be in some sense for all creation. In other words, an atonement that grounds a universal reign must itself be universal.[62]

The problems with such a proposal have been addressed above. In the first place, Shultz once again conflates a result of the atonement with a direct and proper purchase of the atonement. Showing that Christ's kingly authority is "a result of" or "based upon" the atonement is too loose of a connection to argue for genuine universality in the atonement.[63] Secondly, in the most proper sense, Christ's kingly authority is not even the immediate result of the atonement per se, but the result of of the death of Christ as an act of humble submission and obedience to the Father. It is not as if Christ has to render payment in order to purchase or merit the right to reign over all creation as its Lord (as he had to purchase or merit the forgiveness and righteousness of the elect). As God the Son, the Second Person of the Trinity has always possessed and exercised that right. Even in his state of humiliation, he nevertheless held the entire cosmos together (Col 1:17) by the sustaining word of his power (Heb 1:3). Rather, the Son's exaltation over all things, which was a consequence of his death (cf. Phil 2:9), was the Son's restoration to a station of manifest authority that was not surrendered but only veiled during his humiliation.[64] This exaltation and universal dominion, further, is not grounded upon a satisfaction for the sins of all without exception, but grounded upon the Son's obedience to the Father even unto death: "Being found in appearance as a man, He humbled Himself by becoming obedient to the point of death, even death on a cross. For this reason also, God highly exalted Him, and bestowed on Him the name which is above every name" (Phil 2:8–9). Though it may seem to be a distinction without a difference—for Christ's obedient death on the cross is the means by which he rendered satisfaction for sins—yet the emphasis is clear. Paul does not use any of the key terms for atonement in this text; no mention is made of expiation, propitiation, reconciliation, or redemption. Instead, the "very reason" cited for the Son's exaltation is his obedience to the Father.[65]

---

62. Shultz, "Defense," 220–22.

63. See the argumentation in chapter 14 under "Universal Conviction?" and in chapter 15 under "Common Grace and the Atonement."

64. On Christ's exercise of his divine prerogatives in the state of his humiliation, and on the doctrine of the *extra Calvinisticum*, see Riccardi, "Veiled in Flesh the Godhead See," 103–27.

65. Once again, Owen captures the thought helpfully: ". . . we deny that it is anywhere in the Scripture once intimated that the ransom paid by Christ in his death for us was the cause of his exaltation to be Lord of all: it was his obedience to his Father in his death, and not his satisfaction for us, that is proposed as the antecedent of this exaltation; as is apparent, Phil. ii. 7–11" (Owen, *Death of Death*, 377–78). Elsewhere he says, "[Christ's] own exaltation, indeed, and power over all flesh, and his appointment to be Judge of the quick and the dead, was a *consequent* of his deep humiliation and suffering; but that it was the *effect* and *product* of it, procured *meritoriously* by it, that it was the *end* aimed at by him in his making satisfaction for sin, that we deny. Christ hath a power and dominion over all, but the foundation of this dominion is not in his death for all. . . . [His dominion] is not the immediate effect of his death for them, but rather all things are given into his hand out of the immediate love of the Father to his Son, John iii. 35; Matt. xi. 27. That is the foundation of all this sovereignty and dominion over all creatures, with this power of judging that is put into his hand" (204, emphasis added).

One indication that such a distinction—i.e., between (a) the death of Christ as an act of obedience to God and (b) the death of Christ as an act of atonement for sinners—is correct is that Scripture explicitly denies that Christ has atoned for all those beings over which he reigns as Lord. Christ reigns in sovereignty over the angels and demons, and yet Heb 2:16 explicitly denies that Christ has atoned for the angels: "For assuredly He does not give help to angels, but He gives help to the descendant of Abraham" (cf. 2:17, which identifies this "help" as "propitiation"). Since Christ did not atone for the angels and demons, but he does exercise dominion over them, therefore that dominion is not grounded in or purchased by his atonement, but is the proper and immediate effect of the love of the Father (cf. John 3:35) conferred upon him as a reward for his obedience (Phil 2:8–9).

Part 4 Summary and Conclusion

Central to the thesis of the multiple intentions view of the extent of the atonement is that the Father, Son, and Spirit had both particular and universal (or general) intentions for the atonement, and therefore Christ died to pay for the sins of the elect alone, in one sense, and for the sins of all without exception, in several other senses. In part 4, we have examined the MIV's case for the three most convincing general intentions in the atonement: the universal gospel call, the provision of common grace, and the cosmic triumph for all sin. In each case, the truth of these doctrines was affirmed—that is, the particularist does not deny but believes that the gospel ought to be genuinely and earnestly offered to all people without exception; that God is indeed kind to all of his creatures, friend and enemy alike, showering good things upon them out of his abundant mercy; and that Christ will triumph over all creation by conquering all sin.

However, also in each case, these doctrines were shown not to be grounded in a universal payment for the sins of all people. First, the gospel is to be proclaimed to all men not on the basis of a universal provision on behalf of all men, but on the basis of (a) the infinite intrinsic sufficiency of the atonement Christ accomplished, (b) the command of God to all sinners to repent and believe, and (c) the certainty of the promise that all who believe will be saved. Second, common grace flows to elect and reprobate alike not because Christ has purchased such good gifts by paying for the sins of all people, but simply because God's nature is to be kind and merciful to, to give good gifts to, and to love all of his creatures, even his enemies. Scripture consistently names the character of God, and never a universal atonement, as the source and ground of common grace. Finally, Christ's cosmic triumph over all sin is grounded not in an atonement for all sins at the cross, but in the combination of both (a) the atonement for the elect's sins on the cross and (b) the conquest of the reprobate's sin in eschatological judgment. The reconciliation of the cosmos occurs when all the enemies of God have been cast outside the new creation, thus leaving all things reconciled to God, whether the things on earth or the things in heaven (Col 1:20). The redemption of creation is not grounded in a universal atonement, but rather is a result of the particular redemption of the elect. Just as creation was cursed as a consequence of man's sin, so also will creation be redeemed as a consequence of man's redemption. Christ exercises his kingly authority in his eschatological dominion over all things not because he paid for the sins of all things, but because the Father has conferred such dominion upon the Son as a reward for his obedience to him in his earthly mission.

Thus, each line of argumentation for general intentions in the atonement has failed to satisfy the demands of biblical exegesis and theological coherence. This is consistent with the findings of part 2, which demonstrated that Scripture's teaching concerning the design, nature, and scope of the atonement shuts one up to the doctrine of particular redemption, and of part 3, which demonstrated that the universalistic texts often marshaled in support of a universal atonement not only do not support a universal atonement but rather support an exclusively particular atonement. Consequently, the MIV's claims that there are general intentions for the atonement should be rejected. There are not multiple general intentions alongside a particular intention to save the elect; there is only the single, all-encompassing intention for which Christ Jesus came into the world: to save sinners (1 Tim 1:15).

Conclusion

THE PURPOSE OF THIS book was to critically evaluate the biblical and theological claims made by proponents of the multiple intentions view of the extent of the atonement. As the debate concerning the extent of the atonement has continued within the evangelical and Reformed communities, the multiple intentions view presented itself as a novel position answering the controversial question, "For whom did Christ die?" Traditional responses to that question have framed the answer as an either-or proposition. Particularists, or proponents of a particular or definite atonement, have answered that Christ died only for the elect, with the purpose of definitively securing their salvation. Non-particularists, or proponents of a universal or general atonement, have answered that Christ died for each and every person, making it possible for all people without exception to be saved from sin through faith in Christ.

The multiple intentions view claims that, rather than an either-or proposition, the answer to the question "For whom did Christ die?" ought to be a both-and proposition. According to the MIV, both particular redemption and universal atonement are right in what they affirm but wrong in what they deny. The MIV affirms that God had multiple intentions for the Son's atonement—that the Father intended that Christ should die both (a) to make possible the salvation for all without exception and (b) to infallibly secure the salvation of the elect. Christ died for all without exception, *and* he died for the elect alone, in different senses. This position, its proponents argue, does the most justice to all the Bible's teaching—both concerning efficacious nature of the atonement unto salvation and concerning the numerous texts saying Jesus died for all men, the whole world, or even those who finally perish. The particular intention of the cross was to secure the salvation of the elect, but there are multiple other general intentions, short of salvation, that the cross provided for even the non-elect, including making the universal gospel offer possible, providing common grace to all, and the conquest of all sin.

The thesis of this project was that, by failing to adequately frame the issue in the context of Scripture's teaching concerning the nature and purpose of Christ's mediating work, the multiple intentions view bases its conviction that there are general intentions in the atonement on a mishandling of the universalistic texts. This study set out to prove that the Bible's teaching concerning the design and nature of the atonement is foundational to gleaning its teaching on the extent of the atonement, and that rightly exegeting the key passages of Scripture concerning the atonement's design, nature, and extent leads to an affirmation of particular redemption. This study also set out to prove that proponents of the MIV have misinterpreted the universalistic texts, and that their claim on the basis of these texts that Jesus died to pay the penalty for the sins of all people without exception is exegetically unfounded. As a result, this study argued that there is no exegetical or theological basis for the general intentions of the atonement, and therefore the central thesis of the multiple intentions view fails.

Summary

Part 1 was intended to thoroughly lay out the tenets, claims, and arguments of the multiple intentions view in its own words, ensuring that the author of this present critical evaluation properly understood and fairly represented the position he set out to critique. It surveyed the relevant work of three key proponents of the multiple intentions view: Bruce Ware, Gary Shultz, and John Hammett. Ware's classroom handout introducing the multiple intentions view served as a sort of foundational document for the position, which was then thoroughly developed into a dissertation-length constructive work of theology by Shultz, one of Ware's PhD students. Hammett's essay in *Perspectives on the Extent of the Atonement: 3 Views* relied heavily on Shultz's dissertation and subsequent monograph. Between the three, a clear systematic center emerged: God sent Christ, and Christ came to earth, with the intention that Christ would die *both* to make salvation available to all without exception *and* to infallibly secure the salvation of the elect alone. Thus, Jesus paid for the sins of the elect and the reprobate, but in different senses and to accomplish different purposes, or to carry out the multiple intentions named above.

In order to give full voice to those texts that cast the extent of Christ's death in the broadest of terms (e.g., "all," "world," etc.), the MIV has significantly revised the traditional understanding of the nature of the atonement. The achievements of the atonement (i.e., expiation, propitiation, reconciliation, and redemption) are redefined such that they are not the particular accomplishments that will certainly be applied to all those for whom they were purchased, but rather are provisions that may be rejected through unbelief. Thus, there are those whose sins Christ expiated who must bear those same sins in hell for eternity, those for whom Christ propitiates the Father's wrath who suffer under his wrath forever, those reconciled to God who will be alienated from God in the lake of fire, and those redeemed who remain in bondage to sin and death. These benefits of the atonement only become particular and effective through the Holy Spirit's ministry of conversion. In other words, the atonement does not efficaciously atone until it is accepted by faith.

Part 2 began the critical analysis of the MIV. One aspect of the thesis of the present work was that the MIV conducts its exegesis of the extent of Christ's atonement while not taking significantly enough into account the implications of Scripture's teaching concerning the nature and purpose of Christ's atonement. A chief contention of this study, then, was that the scope of the atonement is inextricably linked to the scheme (purpose, design) and substance (nature) of the atonement. Thus, part 2 set the exegetical debate between particular versus universal atonement in the context of the whole Bible's theology of atonement, and made a positive exegetical-theological case for particularism against the claims of the MIV, demonstrating that the Bible teaches that Christ died to atone for the sins of the elect alone, and not all people without exception.

This was done in five broad steps. First, chapter 4 demonstrated that the unity of the Trinity demands a particular redemption. Christ engaged in his atoning mission in strict obedience to the eternal trinitarian plan of salvation, in which the Father appointed the Son as the mediator of the elect and entrusted him with the accomplishment of their salvation. Since the Father intended to save only those whom he has chosen, and since the Spirit regenerates no more than those whom the Father has chosen, it is fitting and necessary that the Son would atone only for the elect. It cannot be that the Son atones for a different number than the Father has chosen or the Spirit regenerates. Such was demonstrated to be the teaching of Scripture. While the MIV is sensitive to the charge of Trinitarian disunity, its claim that both the Father and Spirit also had general intentions in the plan of salvation was shown to be lacking in biblical support.

Chapter 5 then surveyed the explicit statements of Scripture concerning God's intentions in sending the Son into the world and in the Son's coming to accomplish atonement. It was demonstrated that Scripture uniformly and repeatedly names a single divine intention—even if variously expressed—for Christ's atonement, namely, to save sinners. There is not a single instance in which Scripture speaks of a divine intention to "provide salvation," "make salvation possible," "make the gospel offer possible," "provide common grace," or to "renew the creation." Though there are universal consequences or ramifications of the atonement, the single stated divine intention for Christ's atonement was to save those the Father has chosen, and nothing more.

Chapters 6 and 7 proved that the accomplishments of the atonement were precisely in accord with the intentions for the atonement. The substance of the atonement itself was a penal substitutionary sacrifice that expiated man's sin, propitiated God's wrath, reconciled God to man, and redeemed sinners out of bondage. Contrary to the MIV's revisions of these biblical terms for atonement, it was discovered that the atonement was not in any sense a provision, potentiality, or possibility, but an efficacious accomplishment, such that all for whom propitiation was made, for example, could never experience the divine wrath that Christ satisfied on their behalf. Though the MIV denies this, its proponents have nevertheless professed a commitment to the efficacy of the atonement. However, such claims were demonstrated to be internally inconsistent, as they steadily revert from the language of accomplishment to the language of provision and possibility.

Chapter 8 set the accomplishments of the cross in the context of Christ's priesthood. It was proven that, as the great high priest of the New Covenant and the fulfillment of the Levitical priesthood, Christ offered himself as a sacrifice for the same persons for whom he now intercedes in heaven. These two priestly ministries are coextensive. Consequently, Scripture's explicit denials of Christ's intercession on behalf of the non-elect prove that, as Christ intercedes only for his people, so also he offered sacrifice only for his people. Further, since Christ offered this sacrifice as the mediator of the New Covenant (the one whose blood *is* the blood of the covenant), chapter 8 went on to show that Christ purchased none other than the blessings of the New Covenant, which include regeneration, the forgiveness of sins, and the indwelling of the Spirit—and not the universal gospel offer, common grace, or cosmic triumph. Thus, the partakers of these benefits can be none other than those for whom Christ died, and such a number is limited to the elect. Further still, it was demonstrated that Scripture teaches that the application of the blessings purchased by the atonement necessarily follow upon their accomplishment. That is, Christ did not purchase anything for anyone by his atonement that the Spirit does not eventually apply, which means all for whom Christ died must necessarily receive salvation—another line of evidence demonstrating that the atonement is particular and not universal.

Finally, chapter 9 brought the preceding exegetically derived theological framework of the Bible's doctrine of the design and nature of the atonement to bear on the question of the extent of the atonement. Several texts of Scripture were examined that describe the scope of Christ's sacrifice in explicitly particularistic terms: Christ died for the "many," his "people," the "sheep" he calls his own and whom he knows by name, the "children" that God had given him, his "friends," his "bride," and God's "elect." When soundly interpreted in their respective contexts, these terms were shown to be necessarily discriminating and exclusive terms, putting to rest the objection of the negative inference fallacy. The popular argument that emphasis upon the sheep, for example (cf. John 10:11–15), does not exclude the goats was found to be unconvincing. By the end of part 2, the particularity of the atonement was shown to be a biblical doctrine, derived from the sound, contextual exegesis of Scripture, coherent with the exegetical conclusions of the rest of Scripture.

Part 3 examined seven of the thirteen texts proposed by Shultz that the MIV claims establishes universality in the atonement: texts that state that Jesus died for "all" or "all men," texts that state that Jesus died for the "world" or the "whole world," and texts that seem to indicate that Jesus died for those who will finally perish in hell. In chapters 10–12, it was shown that when interpreted in their context, according to grammatical-historical exegesis, and consistently with the exegesis of the rest of Scripture's teaching concerning the nature and design of the atonement, no text genuinely teaches that Christ died to atone for the sins of all without exception. Rather, universalistic language in each case is appropriately restricted by factors in the context of each passage. In many instances, the author employs universalistic language to refer to all without distinction rather than all without exception—that is, to those chosen by God *throughout* the whole world. Texts that seem to indicate that Christ died for those who finally perish, thus implying that his atonement was not inherently efficacious unto salvation for all those for whom it was offered, were shown to teach no such thing.

Ultimately, not one of the texts offered by proponents of the MIV in any way indicates that Christ died to pay for the sins of all people without exception. Instead, each text was demonstrated to be naturally, soundly, and contextually interpreted in a manner consistent with Scripture's doctrine of the atonement as presented in part 2. That is, since part 2 decisively proved that particular redemption best accounts for all of Scripture's teaching on the design, nature, and extent of the atonement, the exegesis of the universalistic texts presented in part 3 was shown not to be strained or inappropriate, but contextually, grammatically, and historically sound. Bereft of any text definitively teaching a universal extent of the atonement, the MIV was left without grounds for its general intentions of the atonement. That is to say, since the general intentions of the atonement are based upon interpreting universalistic texts in an absolutely universal sense, and since those texts were proven not to bear the exegetical weight of that absolutely universal sense, there was found to be no basis for the general intentions, and thus no basis for the multiple intentions view itself.

Though that was so, it was nevertheless necessary to examine the MIV's claims for each of their proposed general intentions. In part 4, we considered the MIV's case for the three most convincing general intentions, namely, the universal gospel call, the provision of common grace, and the cosmic triumph for all sin. It was demonstrated that, though Scripture affirms the truth of these doctrines, the MIV showed none to be grounded in a universal payment for the sins of all people. Instead, chapters 13 and 14 proved that the gospel may be genuinely proclaimed and offered to all without exception, on the basis of the atonement's infinite sufficiency, God's universal command to repent and believe, and the inviolable truth that all who believe will be saved. Chapter 15 showed that common grace is grounded not in a universal provisional atonement, but in the character of God, whose nature is to be kind to his enemies. As to cosmic triumph, chapter 16 demonstrated that while it is true that Christ triumphs over the sin of the elect by his atonement, it is also true that he triumphs over the sin of the reprobate by his judgment. The creation will be redeemed not as the purchase of a universal atonement, but rather as the result of the particular redemption of the elect. Thus, reconciliation will be universal when all the enemies of the gospel have been cast out from the presence of the Lord into outer darkness, leaving nothing in heaven or on earth but the chosen people whose sins Christ conquered on the cross. Thus, consistent with the findings of part 2 and part 3, part 4 found there to be no biblical evidence for general intentions in the atonement. There are not multiple general intentions alongside a particular intention to save the elect; there is only the single, all-encompassing intention for which Christ Jesus came into the world: to save sinners (1 Tim 1:15). Therefore, the exegetical and theological argumentation proffered by Ware, Shultz, and Hammett has failed to bear the weight of their claims, and their central thesis for multiple intentions in the atonement must be rejected.

Areas for Further Study

There are several profitable avenues for further study on the debate over the extent of the atonement. Given the truth that there is nothing new under the sun, combined with the fact that contemporary evangelicals continue to be woefully ignorant of the history of theology, it would be helpful to see more doctoral-level research on the history of the debate over the extent of the atonement. In particular, it would be valuable to see the several views of history placed along a theological spectrum, to isolate the key tenets of each view, and to draw correspondences from the arguments of history to the arguments being advanced by various theologians today. Though the present work, for the sake of focusing on exegetical and theological analysis, did not devote space to a historical study, several discriminate views have begun to become apparent. Moving from the far left of the spectrum to the right, there are advocates of universal final salvation (e.g., Origen); then, the view of the Remonstrants, with the variations of Arminius himself and, later, of Wesley; the four-point Calvinism of Walvoord, Lightner, Erickson, and Demarest; the unique view of Richard Baxter, whose neonomianism was inextricably linked with his doctrine of universal atonement; the French hypothetical universalism of the School of Saumur (e.g., James Cameron, Moises Amyraut); the British hypothetical universalism of James Ussher, John Davenant, and John Preston; the classic particularism of William Perkins, John Owen, Francis Turretin, and some of the later Reformed confessions (especially the developments from the Synod of Dort to the Westminster Assembly and to the Second London Baptist Confession of Faith); and, finally, the varying brands of hyper-Calvinism that would deny either the infinite sufficiency of the atonement or the legitimacy of the universal offer of the gospel, as well as those advocating strains of preparationism. Highlighting the key exegetical and theological moves that distinguish these camps from one another and then identifying these moves in the work of historical and contemporary theology would be fruitful, especially as there currently seems to be an increase of confessionally Reformed thinkers who are open to tying the universal ramifications of the atonement more directly to the atonement itself.

Another area for further study would be to bring the principles vindicated in this volume to bear on what Hammett calls the "Reformed Multiple Intentions" views.[1] Men like William G. T. Shedd, Robert Dabney, and Charles Hodge spoke of the extent of the atonement in ways that many would consider to be inconsistent with their convictions

---

1. Hammett, "Multiple-Intentions View," 188.

concerning Reformed theology. An examination of their writings similar to the present work's analysis of Ware, Shultz, and Hammett would prove valuable to contemporary Reformed theological studies. Related to this, it could be profitable to engage the question as to whether or not the multiple intentions view could be considered to be a Reformed doctrine, given (a) its proponents' affirmation of the other four doctrines of grace, the five *solas* of the Reformation, and the absolute sovereignty of God in all things, and (b) the presence of similar argumentation in some classically Reformed theologians such as Shedd, Dabney, and Hodge, while at the same time noting its departure from the traditional Reformed doctrine of the atonement.

Finally, there is a need for more work to be done on the doctrine of the sufficiency of the atonement, particularly in exploring how the classic Reformed doctrine of the infinite intrinsic sufficiency of the atonement differs from Davenant's doctrine of "ordained sufficiency," or what David Allen calls "extrinsic sufficiency." Proponents of differing views may talk past one another because, while they all affirm the infinite sufficiency of the atonement, each one means something different by "sufficiency" than the other. A robust exegetical examination of the texts that give rise to the categories of intrinsic versus ordained sufficiency would likely move the conversation forward and bring clarity where there has been confusion. Related to this, it would also be helpful for classic particularists who believe in infinite sufficiency to interact further with Nettles, who is suspicious of it.[2]

Final Assessment: Cling to a Perfect Redemption

The atoning work of the Lord Jesus Christ on the cross stands as the very epicenter of Christianity. It is no exaggeration to say that the cross-work of Christ is the very heart of the gospel. Scripture calls the gospel message by which we are saved "the word of the cross" (1 Cor 1:18); unbelievers are "enemies of the cross of Christ" (Phil 3:18–19); Paul summarizes the gospel by saying of the work of Christ on the cross, "Christ died for our sins according to the Scriptures" (1 Cor 15:3); indeed, the cross is the very content of the gospel itself, for Paul says, "We preach Christ crucified" (1 Cor 1:23). John Newton gave wise counsel when he said, "I advise you by all means to keep close to the atonement. The doctrine of the cross is the sun in the system of truth."[3]

While many contemporary evangelicals would agree that the cross of Christ, and the atonement accomplished there, ought to be the perennial object of meditation, many also would object that the *atonement* and the *extent* of the atonement are two different things. *That* Christ died for sins is the heart of the gospel, yes; but *for whom* he died is regarded as an arcane discussion of theology. This conception, however, is profoundly mistaken. If it is agreed that the *nature* of the atonement runs to the very heart of the gospel, then one does not stray far from the heart of the Christian faith

2. Nettles, *By His Grace and for His Glory*, 297–321.

3. Newton, *Sixty-Six Letters*, 62.

when he asks, "*For whom* has Christ accomplished these things?" In fact, if the Son of God has broken the power of sin and death, satisfied the wrath of the Father, and purchased the redemption by which sinners may be freed from divine judgment, there may not be a more significant follow-up question than, "For whom has he done these things?" Sinclair Ferguson aptly captures the practicality of the question of the extent of the atonement when he writes, "How one thinks about the nature, effects, and extent of the atonement has an inevitable impact, directly or indirectly, on preaching, teaching, and pastoral counseling. If part of the minister's task is to help his congregation to sing in joyful wonder in response to the gospel, 'Amazing love, how can it be, That thou my God should'st die for me?' then the meaning of his dying 'for me' cannot be ignored."[4] This means that the extent of the atonement cannot be divorced from the nature of the atonement. What one believes about the former will invariably affect and direct what one believes about the latter. The answer to the question "For whom did Christ die?" has necessary implications on how one answers the question "What did Christ accomplish by his dying?"

While the purpose of this book was to demonstrate the biblical and theological failure of the multiple intentions view of the atonement and to vindicate the doctrine of particular redemption, the underlying burden of this work has not been to exclude people from the breadth of God's love demonstrated through Christ's cross. Instead, the central burden of this work has been to safeguard the substance of the atonement from being weakened by an attempt to universalize its extent. Despite its protestations to the contrary, the MIV has followed other species of non-particularism in redefining the nature of Christ's accomplishments on the cross as a result of extending those accomplishments to all without exception.[5] And that redefinition has reduced those accomplishments to provisions and possibilities, effectively confessing that the cross does not *save* people but only makes them *savable*; their salvation is contingent upon their reception by faith of the offer of salvation. By universalizing the extent of the atonement in significant ways, the MIV has indeed limited its efficacy. Since, on its scheme, atonement has been made on behalf of all without exception, but not all without exception go to heaven, something other than the atonement must become the decisive, determining factor in an individual's salvation—namely, the sinner's response to the atonement. However Christ and the cross are conceived to save sinners, on the MIV's scheme they are only the remote causes of that salvation; the immediate savior is the sinner's response of faith. This proves theologian Stephen Wellum correct when he says, "Ultimately what is at stake in the debate over the extent of the atonement is a Savior who saves, a cross that effectively accomplishes and secures all the gracious promises of the new covenant, and a redemption that does not fail."[6] When one presses

---

4. Ferguson, "Blessèd Assurance, Jesus Is Mine?," 608–9.

5. See especially chapters 6 and 7.

6. Wellum, "New Covenant Work of Christ," 539.

for consistency, the implications of the extent of the atonement strike at the very heart of the nature of the atonement—that is, at the heart of the gospel itself.

This is not to suggest that the proponents of the multiple intentions view of the extent of the atonement deny the gospel. As Ferguson wisely observes, "it is not always the case that individuals are comprehensive and consistent in following through their implications, and it is important not to impute a belief in those implications where they are in fact denied by an individual."[7] Nevertheless, he continues, "It remains proper . . . to point out the logical implications of presuppositions."[8] This is the course the present study has aimed to keep in arriving at these conclusions. This is not to say that the MIV is a heretical doctrine, but that the implications of the MIV, if worked out comprehensively and consistently, lead one to strike at truths that are central to the gospel. Consider the below recapitulation of some of the statements proponents of the MIV have made about the cross and its achievements, along with the statements of those upon whose argumentation they have relied.

In the first place, though proponents of the MIV have stated that they want to rightly portray Christ as Savior rather than just the "Possibility-Maker" of salvation,[9] the mutual exclusivity of an efficacious atonement and an unlimited atonement render this inescapable. Thus, the atonement does not save, or accomplish salvation; it makes salvation possible. In the introduction of his book, Shultz says, "When we speak of Christ's atonement . . . we are referring to what Christ accomplished to make salvation *possible*."[10] Shultz later cites Bloesch with approval, who says, "[Christ's] reconciliation needs to be fulfilled in the experience of redemption made *possible* by the Holy Spirit."[11] Ware goes so far as to say, "We cannot speak correctly of Christ's death as actually and certainly *saving* the elect. No, even here, the payment made by his death on behalf of the elect renders their salvation *possible*."[12]

Second, the inefficacy of the atonement under the MIV scheme is seen in its re-definition of propitiation. The penalty that Christ paid—that is, enduring the wrath of God—in the place of his people, satisfying the demands of justice and propitiating the righteous anger of God, is reconceived as that which did not decisively and determinatively do either of those things. Thus, Ware can claim that there are "those in hell, who never put their faith in Christ and so were never saved, [who] are under the just judgment of God for their sin, even though *Christ has paid the penalty for their sin*."[13]

7. Ferguson, *Whole Christ*, 155n1.

8. Ferguson, *Whole Christ*, 155n1.

9. Hammett, "Multiple-Intentions View," 171.

10. Shultz, *Multi-Intentioned View*, 2n4, emphasis added; cf. 156. Later he speaks of Christ's atonement making salvation "available" to sinners (Shultz, "Defense," 195n103) and "possible" for all people (Shultz, "Defense," 206–7, 280).

11. Bloesch, *Jesus Christ*, 162, emphasis added.

12. Ware, "Outline," 5, emphases original.

13. Personal correspondence from Bruce Ware, as cited in Piper, "My Glory," 648–49, emphasis original.

Rather than an efficacious satisfaction of wrath, the MIV redefines the atonement as the payment of a penalty that may very well still have to be paid—the satisfaction of justice that may very well be aroused and executed upon precisely those for whom the cross was supposed to satisfy justice. This is to make the cross inefficacious.

Third, the reconciliation between God and man that Scripture says was decisively accomplished by the death of Christ has, according to the MIV, been redefined so significantly that those banished from God's presence forever in the lake of fire can be said to be reconciled to God. Ware states, "In this sense, all those in hell stand reconciled to God, i.e., they are no longer rebels and their sinful disregard has been crushed and ended."[14] This also means that there is a sense in which we must declare that those suffering in eternal torment are at peace with God, as Ware says: "This reconciliation must be one which includes a sense in which those outside of Christ, consigned to eternal punishment in hell, are at peace with God."[15] Shultz claims that, while they are suffering in the lake of fire with Satan, "there will be peace even between God and the nonelect as a result of the atonement."[16] According to Hammett, such reconciliation "involves judgment and punishment."[17] To support this claim of a reconciliation compatible with alienation, Shultz appeals to Marshall, who writes, "God and Christ appeal to [unbelievers] to accept the fact that reconciliation has been accomplished *and to complete the action* by taking down the barrier on their side—the barrier of pride and disobedience and hatred of God."[18] Though Marshall speaks of reconciliation accomplished, he does not view such an accomplishment so decisively as to be incompatible with the idea that the action of such a reconciliation must be completed by the unbeliever. That is, in order to universalize the extent of the atonement, Shultz and Marshall must redefine that atonement (in this case, considered as reconciliation) as inefficacious—not an objective work finished on the cross, but an action that has been begun by God yet must be completed by man.

Fourth, the MIV must also redefine the doctrine of redemption. Scripture indicates that the ransom payment of the blood of Christ (1 Tim 2:6; 1 Pet 1:18–19) is the price that effectually secures sinners' release from the bondage of sin (John 8:34; Rom 6:6, 16–18) and the curse of the law (Gal 3:13; 4:4–5).[19] Yet Shultz employs the argumentation of Chafer, who speaks of "a redemption which pays the price, but does not of necessity release the slave."[20] That is, Christ may pay the price of redemption

---

14. Ware, "Outline," 4. Shultz writes, "The nonelect in hell will be reconciled in that they are no longer able to rebel against God because they will acknowledge Jesus for who He is" (Shultz, "Defense," 214–15).

15. Personal correspondence from Bruce Ware, as cited in Piper, "My Glory," 653.

16. Shultz, "Defense," 216; cf. Ware, "Outline," 4.

17. Hammett, "Multiple-Intentions View," 186.

18. Marshall, "Meaning of Reconciliation," 123, emphasis added.

19. See chapter 7 on "Redemption."

20. Chafer, "For Whom Did Christ Die?," 148–50.

for a slave who is never released from the bonds of sin and death. Those whom he redeemed from the curse of the Law by becoming a curse for them (Gal 3:13) may nevertheless still suffer under the curse of the Law. This is not the Scripture's doctrine of redemption, but an alternative that robs it of its efficacy.

Finally, the proponents of the MIV make numerous statements—and also rely on numerous statements of others whose argumentation they employ to support the MIV—that explicitly denigrate the efficacy of the atonement, casting the cross in terms that lead the reader to no other conclusion than that it was ineffective in accomplishing its aims. Shultz approvingly cites Hiebert's comments on Titus 2:11–14, who says, "The adjective rendered 'that brings salvation' *(soterios)* asserts its saving efficacy. The dative 'to all men' may equally be rendered 'for all men,' thus stressing the universality of the salvation provided. Salvation is available for all, but its saving effect is dependent upon the personal response of faith."[21] Hiebert begins with an affirmation of the "saving efficacy" of Christ's mission, but because he wrongly interprets "all men" to refer to all people without exception, he quickly revises his confession of the efficacy of the atonement by speaking not of salvation accomplished but salvation merely *provided* and *available.* Two sentences later, the formerly efficacious salvation now has "its saving effect dependent upon the personal response of faith." In this way, the efficacy of the atonement is exported to man's faith, once again demonstrating that universalizing the extent of the atonement inexorably leads to limiting the efficacy of the atonement. Further, Shultz also cites Picirilli, who rejects the idea that "propitiation, say, or reconciliation were *actually finished* on the cross."[22] But if propitiation and reconciliation were not actually finished on the cross, but only upon the sinner's conversion, the atonement is not completed until granted its efficacy by the sinner's faith. Robert Lightner, one to whom Shultz often turns in defense of his argumentation for the MIV, outright rejects the notion "that the work of Christ on the cross was effective in itself."[23] Chafer, another thinker to whom Shultz often appeals for support, makes the striking statement that "Christ's death *does not save* either actually or potentially; rather it makes all men savable."[24] Shultz appeals to Shedd, who says, "Atonement, in and by itself, separate from faith, saves no soul. Christ might have died precisely as he did, but if no one believed in him he would have died in vain. . . . It is only when the death of Christ has been actually confided [believed] in as atonement, that it is completely 'set forth' as God's propitiation for sin."[25] Similarly, Hammett himself asserts, "That propitiation, and all Christ did on the cross, though provided to all, remains of

21. Hiebert, *Titus,* 440.

22. Picirilli, *Grace, Faith, Free Will,* 94, emphasis added.

23. Lightner, "For Whom Did Christ Die?," 162.

24. Chafer, "For Whom Did Christ Die?," 325, emphasis added.

25. Shedd, *Dogmatic Theology,* 747. For a refutation of Shedd's claim here, see chapter 6 on "Propitiation."

no value, ineffectual, useless, until subjectively appropriated."[26] And finally, Ware asks with seeming exasperated incredulity, "How can it be said of the death of Christ *in itself* that by his death *alone* he saved those for whom he died?"[27]

Each of these statements—whether made by proponents of the MIV themselves or appealed to by them in support of the MIV—illustrates the claim made above: as with all species of non-particularism, by seeking to universalize the extent of the atonement, the MIV redefines the nature of the atonement, and thereby limits the efficacy of the atonement. Among the many reasons for rejecting the MIV presented in this book, this redefinition and weakening of the substance of the atonement is paramount. The particularist who believes that the doctrine of the extent of the atonement is genuinely a matter of consequence is not driven by a desire to exclude certain sinners from the benefits of redemption or the wide scope of God's love for his creatures. The particularist is not ultimately concerned with declaring that there are certain people for whom Christ did not die. Rather, his chief concern is to safeguard the achievements of Christ's cross from being robbed of their power and efficacy, even if by a well-intentioned but ill-fated desire to universalize their extent. In order to be able to say that Christ died for all without exception, the *substance* of the atonement must be reimagined as that which makes men savable rather than that which actually and decisively saves them.[28] Such a conception of the atonement empties the cross of its power and removes the ground of the good news of the gospel message.

Thus, particularism seeks to protect the limited extent of the atonement not as an end in itself, but as a necessary concomitant of an atonement that powerfully and effectively secures the salvation of all for whom it was accomplished. The glory of the atonement consists in its efficacy.[29] The cross did not purchase possibilities or create opportunities, but certainties. It did not make men savable; it saved them. Therefore, above all, what particularists are most concerned to preserve is the fully consistent affirmation of an atonement that actually atones—an atonement of which we can sing, "Dear dying Lamb, Thy precious blood shall never lose its pow'r," and "O perfect redemption, the purchase of blood!" Evangelical Christians must insist upon and cling to a doctrine of the extent of the atonement that yields a *perfect* redemption, whose blood will *never* lose its power. For that reason, the multiple intentions view must be rejected and the single saving intention of the cross must be tenaciously maintained. "It is a trustworthy statement, deserving full acceptance, that Christ Jesus came into the world *to save sinners*" (1 Tim 1:15).

26. Hammett, "Multiple-Intentions View," 164–65.

27. Ware, "Outline," 5, emphasis original.

28. Thus, as Owen says, "What they give on the one hand they take away with the other by suspending the enjoyment of [the benefits of the cross] on a condition by us to be fulfilled, not by [Christ] procured" (Owen, *Death of Death*, 226).

29. Jesus says to the Father, "I *glorified* You on the earth, *having accomplished* the work which You have given Me to do" (John 17:4). As Piper says, "This glory was not the glory of a salvation made *available*, but a salvation made *real* and *effective* in the lives of 'his own'" (Piper, "My Glory," 642).

Bibliography

Alford, Henry. *Alford's Greek Testament*. 4 vols. Grand Rapids: Baker, 1980.

Alexander, Joseph Addison. *Commentaries on the Prophecies of Isaiah*. Grand Rapids: Zondervan, 1980.

Alexander, T. Desmond. *Exodus*. Apollos Old Testament Commentary. Downers Grove, IL: InterVarsity, 2017.

Allen, David L. "The Atonement: Limited or Universal?" In *Whosoever Will: A Biblical-Theological Critique of Five-Point Calvinism*, edited by David L. Allen and Steve W. Lemke, 61–107. Nashville: B&H Academic, 2010.

———. *The Extent of the Atonement: A Historical and Critical Review*. Nashville: B&H Academic, 2016.

Aloisi, John. "The Paraclete's Ministry of Conviction: Another Look at John 16:8–11." *Journal of the Evangelical Theological Society* 47/1 (March 2004) 55–69.

Amyraut, Moïse. *Brief Traitté de la Predestination et de ses principals dependances*. Saumur, France: Jean Lesnier & Isaac Debordes, 1634. 2nd ed., 1658.

Archibald, Paul Noel. "A Comparative Study of John Calvin and Theodore Beza on the Doctrine of the Extent of the Atonement." PhD diss., Westminster Theological Seminary, 1998.

Armstrong, Brian G. *Calvinism and the Amyraut Heresy: Protestant Scholasticism and Humanism in Seventeenth-Century France*. Madison: University of Wisconsin Press, 1969.

———. "The Calvinism of Moise Amyraut: The Warfare of Protestant Scholasticism and French Humanism." ThD diss., Princeton University, 1967.

Arnold, Bill T., and John H. Choi. *A Guide to Biblical Hebrew Syntax*. Cambridge, UK: Cambridge University Press, 2003.

Augustine. *St. Augustine on the Psalms*. Edited by Scholastica Hebgin and Felicitas Corrigan. New York: Paulist, 1960.

Averbeck, Richard E. "כָּפַר." In *New International Dictionary of Old Testament Theology and Exegesis*, edited by Willem VanGemeren, 3:681–82. Grand Rapids: Zondervan, 1997.

Barker, Glenn W. "1, 2, and 3 John." In *The Expositor's Bible Commentary*, edited by Frank E. Gaebelein, 12:293–377. Grand Rapids: Zondervan, 1981.

Barnes, Tom. *Atonement Matters: A Call to Declare the Biblical View of the Atonement*. Darlington, UK: Evangelical Press, 2008.

Barnett, Paul. *The Second Epistle to the Corinthians*. New International Commentary on the New Testament. Grand Rapids: Eerdmans, 1997.

Barrett, C. K. *The Second Epistle to the Corinthians*. Black's New Testament Commentary. London: A & C Black, 1973.

Barrick, William D. "The Extent of the Perfect Sacrifice of Christ." Unpublished article.

Bauckham, Richard. *Jude, 2 Peter*. Word Biblical Commentary 50. Waco, TX: Word, 1983.

Baugh, Steven M. "'Savior of All People': 1 Tim 4:10 in Context." *Westminster Theological Journal* 54 (1992) 331–40.

Bavinck, Herman. *Reformed Dogmatics*. Vol. 2: *God and Creation*. Edited by John Bolt, translated by John Vriend. Grand Rapids: Baker Academic, 2006.

———. *Reformed Dogmatics*. Vol. 3: *Sin and Salvation*. Edited by John Bolt, translated by John Vriend. Grand Rapids: Baker Academic, 2006.

———. *Reformed Dogmatics*. Vol. 4: *Holy Spirit, Church and New Creation*. Edited by John Bolt, translated by John Vriend. Grand Rapids: Baker Academic, 2006.

Baxter, Richard. *Universal Redemption of Mankind by the Lord Jesus Christ: Stated and Cleared by the Late Learned Mr Richard Baxter. Whereunto Is Added a Short Account of Special Redemption, by the Same Author*. 1st ed. London: John Salusbury, 1694.

Beale, G. K. *The Book of Revelation: A Commentary on the Greek Text*. New International Greek Testament Commentary. Grand Rapids: Eerdmans, 1999.

Beasley-Murray, George R. *John*. Word Biblical Commentary 36. Waco, TX: Word, 1987.

Berkhof, Louis. *Systematic Theology*. Grand Rapids: Eerdmans, 1941.

Bernard, J. H. *A Critical and Exegetical Commentary on the Gospel According to St. John*. 2 vols. International Critical Commentary. Edinburgh: T. & T. Clark, 1929.

Blacketer, Raymond A. "Blaming Beza: The Development of Definite Atonement in the Reformed Tradition." In *From Heaven He Came and Sought Her: Definite Atonement in Historical, Biblical, Theological, and Pastoral Perspective*, edited by David Gibson and Jonathan Gibson, 121–41. Wheaton, IL: Crossway, 2013.

———. "Definite Atonement in Historical Perspective." In *The Glory of the Atonement: Biblical, Historical, and Practical Perspectives. Essays in Honor of Roger Nicole*, edited by Charles E. Hill and Frank A. James III, 304–23. Downers Grove, IL: InterVarsity, 2004.

———. "The Three Points in Most Parts Reformed: A Reexamination of the So-Called Well-Meant Offer of Salvation." *Calvin Theological Journal* 35 (2000) 37–65.

Blocher, Henri A. G. "Jesus Christ *the* Man: Toward a Systematic Theology of Definite Atonement." In *From Heaven He Came and Sought Her: Definite Atonement in Historical, Biblical, Theological, and Pastoral Perspective*, edited by David Gibson and Jonathan Gibson, 541–82. Wheaton, IL: Crossway, 2013.

———. *Songs of the Servant: Isaiah's Good News*. Vancouver, BC: Regent College Publishing, 2005.

Bloesch, Donald G. *Jesus Christ: Savior and Lord*. Downers Grove, IL: InterVarsity, 1997.

Blum, Edwin A. "2 Peter." In *The Expositor's Bible Commentary*, edited by Frank E. Gaebelein, 12:257–92. Grand Rapids: Zondervan, 1981.

Bock, Darrell L. *Luke*. Vol. 2: *9:51—24:53*. Baker Exegetical Commentary on the New Testament. Grand Rapids: Baker Academic, 1996.

Boersma, Hans. *A Hot Peppercorn: Richard Baxter's Doctrine of Justification in Its Seventeenth-Century Context of Controversy*. Vancouver, BC: Regent College Publishing, 2004.

———. *Violence, Hospitality, and the Cross: Reappropriating the Atonement Tradition*. Grand Rapids: Baker Academic, 2004.

Boettner, Lorraine. *The Reformed Doctrine of Predestination*. Grand Rapids: Eerdmans, 1932.

Boice, James Montomery. *The Epistles of John: An Expositional Commentary*. Grand Rapids: Baker, 2004.

———. *Foundations of the Christian Faith*. Rev. ed. Downers Grove, IL: InterVarsity, 1986.

Boice, James Montgomery, and Philip Graham Ryken. *The Doctrines of Grace: Rediscovering the Evangelical Gospel.* Wheaton, IL: Crossway, 2002.

Boyce, James Petigru. *Abstract of Theology.* Philadelphia: American Baptist Publishing Society, 1887.

Brakel, Wilhelmus à. *The Christian's Reasonable Service.* 4 vols. Edited by Joel R. Beeke, translated by Bartel Elshout. 1992. Reprint, Grand Rapids: Reformation Heritage, 2011.

Bray, John Stanley. "Theodore Beza's Doctrine of Predestination." PhD diss., Stanford University, 1971.

Brink, Gert van den. "Impetration and Application in John Owen's Theology." In *The Ashgate Research Companion to John Owen's Theology,* edited by Kelly M. Kapic and Mark Jones, 85–96. Surrey, UK: Ashgate, 2012.

Brown, Francis, S. R. Driver, and Charles A. Briggs, eds. *Hebrew and English Lexicon.* Oxford: Clarendon, 1907. Reprint, Peabody, MA: Hendrickson, 1996.

Brown, John. *Hebrews.* Geneva Series of Commentaries. 1862. Reprint, Carlisle, PA: Banner of Truth, 2009.

Brown, Michael. "Not by Faith Alone: The Neonomianism of Richard Baxter." *Puritan Reformed Journal* 3/1 (2011) 133–52.

Bruce, F. F. *The Epistle to the Hebrews.* New International Commentary on the New Testament. Rev. ed. Grand Rapids: Eerdmans, 1990.

———. *The Epistles of John: Introduction, Exposition, and Notes.* Grand Rapids: Eerdmans, 1970.

———. *The Epistles to the Colossians, to Philemon, and to the Ephesians.* New International Commentary on the New Testament. Grand Rapids: Eerdmans, 1989.

———. *The Gospel of John: Introduction, Exposition, and Notes.* Grand Rapids: Eerdmans, 1983.

Büschel, Friedrich. "ἀγοράζω." In *Theological Dictionary of the New Testament,* edited by Gerhard Kittel, 1:125–27. Grand Rapids: Eerdmans, 1964.

———. "λύτρον." In *Theological Dictionary of the New Testament,* edited by Gerhard Kittel, 4:340–49. Grand Rapids: Eerdmans, 1964.

Calvin, John. *Commentaries on the Catholic Epistles.* Translated by John Owen. In vol. 22 of *Calvin's Commentaries.* Grand Rapids: Baker, 2009.

———. *Commentaries on the Epistle of Paul the Apostle to the Hebrews.* Translated by John Owen. In vol. 22 of *Calvin's Commentaries.* Grand Rapids: Baker, 2009.

———. *Commentaries on the Epistle of Paul the Apostle to the Romans.* Translated by John Owen. In vol. 19 of *Calvin's Commentaries.* Grand Rapids: Baker, 2009.

———. *Commentaries on the Epistles of Paul the Apostle to the Philippians, Colossians, and Thessalonians.* Translated by William Pringle. In vol. 21 of *Calvin's Commentaries.* Grand Rapids: Baker, 2009.

———. *Commentaries on the Epistles to Timothy, Titus, and Philemon.* Translated by William Pringle. In vol. 21 of *Calvin's Commentaries.* Grand Rapids: Baker, 2009.

———. *Commentaries on the Four Last Books of Moses Arranged in the Form of a Harmony.* Translated by John King. In vol. 2 of *Calvin's Commentaries.* Grand Rapids: Baker, 2009.

———. *Commentaries on the Second Epistle of Paul the Apostle to the Corinthians.* Translated by John Owen. In vol. 20 of *Calvin's Commentaries.* Grand Rapids: Baker, 2009.

———. *Commentary on the Gospel of John.* Translated by William Pringle. In vol. 17 of *Calvin's Commentaries.* Grand Rapids: Baker, 2009.

————. *Commentary on a Harmony of the Evangelists, Matthew, Mark, and Luke.* Translated by William Pringle. In vol. 16 of *Calvin's Commentaries.* Grand Rapids: Baker, 1996.

————. *Concerning the Eternal Predestination of God.* Translated with an introduction by J. K. S. Reid. London: James Clark, 1961.

————. "The Gospel Call." In *Sermons on 1 Timothy,* translated by Robert White, 187–201. Carlisle, PA: Banner of Truth, 2018.

————. *Institutes of the Christian Religion.* Edited by John T. McNeill, translated by Ford Lewis Battles. 2 vols. 1559. Reprint, Philadelphia: Westminster Press, 1960.

————. "Isaiah 33–66." Translated by John King. In vol. 8 of *Calvin's Commentaries.* Grand Rapids: Baker, 2009.

Carson, D. A. *The Difficult Doctrine of the Love of God.* Wheaton, IL: Crossway, 2000.

————. "The Function of the Paraclete in John 16:7–11." *Journal of Biblical Literature* 98 (1979) 547–66.

————. *The Gospel According to John.* Pillar New Testament Commentary. Grand Rapids: Eerdmans, 1991.

————. *Love in Hard Places.* Wheaton, IL: Crossway, 2002.

————. "Matthew." In *The Expositor's Bible Commentary,* edited by Frank E. Gaebelein, 8:1–599. Grand Rapids: Zondervan, 1984.

————. *Showing the Spirit.* Grand Rapids: Baker, 1987.

Chafer, Lewis Sperry. "For Whom Did Christ Die?" *Bibliotheca Sacra* 137.548 (October–December 1980) 310–26. Reprint of 1948 article.

————. *Systematic Theology.* 8 vols. Dallas: Dallas Seminary Press, 1948.

Chang, Andrew D. "Second Peter 2:1 and the Extent of the Atonement." In *Vital New Testament Issues: Examining New Testament Passages and Problems,* edited by Roy B. Zuck, 206–15. Grand Rapids: Kregel, 1996. Originally published as "Second Peter 2:1 and the Extent of the Atonement." *Bibliotheca Sacra* 142 (1985) 52–63.

Chisholm, Robert B., Jr. *From Exegesis to Exposition: A Practical Guide to Using Biblical Hebrew.* Grand Rapids: Baker, 1999.

Ciampa, Roy E., and Brian S. Rosner. *The First Letter to the Corinthians.* Pillar New Testament Commentary. Grand Rapids: Eerdmans, 2010.

Clark, R. Scott. "Janus, the Well-Meant Offer of the Gospel, and Westminster Theology." In *The Pattern of Sound Doctrine: A Festschrift for Robert B. Strimple,* edited by David VanDrunen, 149–79. Phillipsburg, NJ: P&R, 2004.

————. "Seriously and Promiscuously: The Synod of Dort on the Free Offer of the Gospel." In *The Synod of Dort: Historical Theological, and Experiential Perspectives,* edited by Joel R. Beeke and Martin I. Klauber, 89–104. Göttingen: Vandenhoeck & Ruprecht, 2020.

Clifford, Alan C. *Atonement and Justification: English Evangelical Theology, 1640–1790: An Evaluation.* London: Oxford University Press, 1990.

————. *Calvinus: Authentic Calvinism: A Clarification.* Norwich, UK: Charenton Reformed, 1996.

Clines, David J. A., and John Elwolde, eds. *The Dictionary of Classical Hebrew.* 5 vols. Sheffield, UK: Sheffield Academic, 1995.

Cranfield, C. E. B. *A Critical and Exegetical Commentary on the Epistle to the Romans.* Vol. 1. International Critical Commentary on the Holy Scriptures of the Old and New Testaments. Edinburgh: T. & T. Clark, 1975.

————. *A Critical and Exegetical Commentary on the Epistle to the Romans.* Vol. 2. International Critical Commentary on the Holy Scriptures of the Old and New Testaments. Edinburgh: T. & T. Clark, 1979.

Crisp, Oliver J. "Is Universalism a Problem for Particularists?" *Scottish Journal of Theology* 63/1 (2010) 1–23.

———. "Non-Penal Substitution." *International Journal of Systematic Theology* 9/4 (2007) 415–33.

———. "Penal Non-Substitution." *Journal of Theological Studies* 59/1 (April 2008) 140–68.

Culver, Robert Duncan. *Systematic Theology: Biblical and Historical*. Ross-Shire, UK: Mentor, Christian Focus, 2008.

Cunningham, William. *Historical Theology: A Review of the Principal Doctrinal Discussions in the Christian Church since the Apostolic Age*. Vol. 2. 1862. Reprint, Edinburgh: Banner of Truth, 1960.

Custance, Arthur C. *The Sovereignty of Grace*. Grand Rapids: Baker, 1979.

Dabney, R. L. *Syllabus and Notes of the Course of Systematic and Polemic Theology*. 2nd ed. St. Louis: Presbyterian Publishing Company of St. Louis, 1878.

Daniel, Curt. *The History and Theology of Calvinism*. N.p.: Good Books, 2003.

———. "HyperCalvinism and John Gill." PhD diss., University of Edinburgh, 1983.

Danker, Frederick W., Walter Bauer, William F. Ardnt, and F. Wilbur Gingrich. *A Greek-English Lexicon of the New Testament and Other Early Christian Literature*. 3rd ed. Chicago: University of Chicago Press, 2000.

Davenant, John. "A Dissertation on the Death of Christ, as to Its Extent and Special Benefits: Containing a Short History of Pelagianism, and Shewing the Agreement of the Doctrines of the Church of England on General Redemption, Election, and Predestination, with the Primitive Fathers of the Christian Church, and Above All, with the Holy Scriptures." In *An Exposition of St. Paul to the Colossians*, translated by Josiah Allport, 2:309–569. London: Hamilton, Adams, 1832.

———. *Dissertationes duae: Prima de Morte Christi, quatenus ad omnes extendatur, quatenus ad solos Electos restringatur: Altera de Praedestinatione & Reprobatione*. Edited by Thomas Bedford. 1st ed. Cambridge: Roger Daniel, 1650.

Davids, Peter H. *The First Epistle of Peter*. New International Commentary on the New Testament. Grand Rapids: Eerdmans, 1990.

———. *The Letters of Jude and 2 Peter*. Pillar New Testament Commentary. Grand Rapids: Eerdmans, 2006.

Davies, R. E. "Christ in Our Place—The Contribution of the Prepositions." *Tyndale Bulletin* 21 (1970) 71–91.

De Jong, Peter Y., ed. *Crisis in the Reformed Churches: Essays in Commemoration of the Great Synod of Dort, 1618–1619*. Grandville: Reformed Fellowship, 2008.

Demarest, Bruce A. *The Cross and Salvation: The Doctrine of Salvation*. Foundations of Evangelical Theology. Wheaton, IL: Crossway, 1997.

Denny, James. *The Death of Christ*. London: Hodder and Stoughton, 1911.

Diaballah, Amar. "Controversy on Universal Grace: A Historical Survey of Moïse Amyraut's *Brief Traitté de la Predestination*." In *From Heaven He Came and Sought Her: Definite Atonement in Historical, Biblical, Theological, and Pastoral Perspective*, edited by David Gibson and Jonathan Gibson, 165–99. Wheaton, IL: Crossway, 2013.

Douty, Norman F. *Did Christ Die Only for the Elect?: A Treatise on the Extent of Christ's Atonement*. 1978. Reprint, Eugene, OR: Wipf & Stock, 1998.

Driscoll, Mark, and Gerry Breshears. *Death by Love: Letters from the Cross*. Wheaton, IL: Crossway, 2008.

Dunn, James D. G. *The Epistles to the Colossians and to Philemon*. New International Greek Testament Commentary. Grand Rapids: Eerdmans, 1996.

Earle, Ralph. "1 Timothy." In *The Expositor's Bible Commentary*, edited by Frank E. Gaebelein, 11:339–90. Grand Rapids: Zondervan, 1981.

Edwards, James R. *The Gospel According to Mark*. Pillar New Testament Commentary. Grand Rapids: Eerdmans, 2002.

Ellingworth, Paul. *The Epistle to the Hebrews: A Commentary on the Greek Text*. New International Greek Testament Commentary. Grand Rapids: Eerdmans, 1993.

Elwell, Walter A. "Atonement, Extent of." In *Evangelical Dictionary of Theology*, edited by Walter A. Elwell, 100–101. 2nd ed. Grand Rapids: Baker Academic, 2001.

Erickson, Millard J. *Christian Theology*. Grand Rapids: Baker Academic, 2013.

Fairbairn, Patrick. *1 & 2 Timothy and Titus*. Geneva Series of Commentaries. Carlisle, PA: Banner of Truth, 2002.

Fee, Gordon D. *The First Epistle to the Corinthians*. New International Commentary on the New Testament. Grand Rapids: Eerdmans, 1987.

Fentiman, Travis. "Concerning the Gospel Call and the Warrant of Faith." From *The Present Truth: A Display of the Secession Testimony*. Edinburgh: Fleming and Neill, 1774. https://archive.org/details/AdamGibConcerningTheGospelCallAndTheWarrantOfFaith.

Ferguson, Sinclair B. "'Blessèd Assurance, Jesus Is Mine'?: Definite Atonement and the Cure of Souls." In *From Heaven He Came and Sought Her: Definite Atonement in Historical, Biblical, Theological, and Pastoral Perspective*, edited by David Gibson and Jonathan Gibson, 607–31. Wheaton, IL: Crossway, 2013.

———. "Christus Victor et Propitiator: The Death of Christ, Substitute and Conqueror." In *For the Fame of God's Name: Essays in Honor of John Piper*, edited by Sam Storms and Justin Taylor, 171–89. Wheaton, IL: Crossway, 2010.

———. "The Reformed View." In *Christian Spirituality: Five Views of Sanctification*, edited by Donald L. Alexander, 47–76. Downers Grove, IL: IVP Academic, 1989.

———. *The Whole Christ: Legalism, Antinomianism, and Gospel Assurance—Why the Marrow Controversy Still Matters*. Wheaton, IL: Crossway, 2016.

Fisher, Edward. *The Marrow of Modern Divinity*. 2009. Reprint, Ross-shire, UK: Christian Focus, 2015.

Foerster, Werner. "σωτήρ." In *Theological Dictionary of the New Testament*, edited by Gerhard Friedrich, 7:1003–21. Grand Rapids: Eerdmans, 1971.

Foord, Martin. "God Wills All People to Be Saved—or Does He?: Calvin's Reading of 1 Timothy 2:4." In *Engaging with Calvin: Aspects of the Reformer's Legacy for Today*, edited by Mark D. Thompson, 179–203. Nottingham, UK: Apollos, 2009.

———. "John Owen's Gospel Offer: Well-Meant or Not?" In *The Ashgate Research Companion to John Owen's Theology*, edited by Kelly M. Kapic and Mark Jones, 283–96. Surrey, UK: Ashgate, 2012.

France, R. T. *The Gospel of Matthew*. New International Commentary on the New Testament. Grand Rapids: Eerdmans, 2007.

Fuller, Andrew. "Six Letters to Dr. Ryland Respecting the Controversy with the Rev. A. Booth." In *The Works of Andrew Fuller*, 317–25. Carlisle, PA: Banner of Truth, 2007.

Garland, David E. *2 Corinthians*. New American Commentary 29. Nashville: Broadman and Holman, 1999.

Gatiss, Lee. "A Deceptive Clarity?: Particular Redemption in the Westminster Standards." *Reformed Theological Review* 69/3 (2010) 180–96.

———. *For Us and for Our Salvation: "Limited Atonement" in the Bible, Doctrine, History, and Ministry*. London: Latimer Trust, 2012.

———. "Shades of Opinion within a Generic Calvinism: The Particular Redemption Debate at the Westminster Assembly." *Reformed Theological Review* 69/2 (2010) 101–18.

———. "The Synod of Dort and Definite Atonement." In *From Heaven He Came and Sought Her: Definite Atonement in Historical, Biblical, Theological, and Pastoral Perspective*, edited by David Gibson and Jonathan Gibson, 143–63. Wheaton, IL: Crossway, 2013.

Gentry, Peter J., and Stephen J. Wellum. *Kingdom through Covenant: A Biblical-Theological Understanding of the Covenants*. Wheaton, IL: Crossway, 2012.

George, Timothy. *Amazing Grace: God's Pursuit, Our Response*. 2nd ed. Wheaton, IL: Crossway, 2011.

Gib, Adam. *The Present Truth: A Display of the Secession Testimony*. 2 vols. Edinburgh: Fleming and Neill, 1774.

Gibson, David, and Jonathan Gibson. "Sacred Theology and the Reading of the Divine Word: Mapping the Doctrine of Definite Atonement." In *From Heaven He Came and Sought Her: Definite Atonement in Historical, Biblical, Theological, and Pastoral Perspective*, edited by David Gibson and Jonathan Gibson, 33–53. Wheaton, IL: Crossway, 2013.

Gibson, Jonathan. "For Whom Did Christ Die?: Particularism and Universalism in the Pauline Epistles." In *From Heaven He Came and Sought Her: Definite Atonement in Historical, Biblical, Theological, and Pastoral Perspective*, edited by David Gibson and Jonathan Gibson, 289–330. Wheaton, IL: Crossway, 2013.

———. "The Glorious, Indivisible, Trinitarian Work of God in Christ: Definite Atonement in Paul's Theology of Salvation." In *From Heaven He Came and Sought Her: Definite Atonement in Historical, Biblical, Theological, and Pastoral Perspective*, edited by David Gibson and Jonathan Gibson, 331–73. Wheaton, IL: Crossway, 2013.

Godfrey, W. Robert. "Reformed Thought on the Extent of the Atonement to 1618." *Westminster Theological Journal* 37 (1975–1976) 133–71.

Godfrey, W. Robert. "Tensions within International Calvinism: The Debate on the Atonement at the Synod of Dort, 1618–1619." PhD diss., Stanford University, 1974.

Green, Lowell C. "Universal Salvation (1 Timothy 2:4) according to the Lutheran Reformers." *Lutheran Quarterly* 9 (1995) 281–300.

Grider, J. Kenneth. "Arminianism." In *Evangelical Dictionary of Theology*, edited by Walter Elwell, 82–83. Grand Rapids: Baker, 1984.

Grogan, Geoffrey W. "Isaiah." In *The Expositor's Bible Commentary*, edited by Frank E. Gaebelein, 6:1–354. Grand Rapids: Zondervan, 1986.

Groves, J. Alan. "Atonement in Isaiah 53." In *The Glory of the Atonement: Biblical, Historical, and Practical Perspectives. Essays in Honor of Roger Nicole*, edited by Charles E. Hill and Frank A. James III, 61–89. Downers Grove, IL: InterVarsity, 2004.

Grudem, Wayne. "Perseverance of the Saints: A Case Study from the Warning Passages in Hebrews." In *Still Sovereign: Contemporary Perspectives on Election, Foreknowledge, and Grace*, edited by Thomas R. Schreiner and Bruce A. Ware, 133–82. Grand Rapids: Baker, 2000.

———. *Systematic Theology: An Introduction to Biblical Doctrine*. Grand Rapids: Zondervan, 1994.

Guthrie, Donald. *The Letter to the Hebrews: An Introduction and Commentary*. Tyndale New Testament Commentary. Grand Rapids: Eerdmans, 1983.

———. *New Testament Introduction*. 4th ed. Downers Grove, IL: InterVarsity, 1990.

————. *The Pastoral Epistles*. Grand Rapids: Eerdmans, 1957.

Haak, Theodore. *The Dutch Annotations upon the Whole Bible . . . Ordered and Appointed by the Synod of Dort*. London, 1657.

Hall, Basil. "Calvin against the Calvinists." In *John Calvin*, edited by G. E. Duffield, 19–37. Nashville: Abingdon, 1966.

Hammett, John S. *40 Questions about Baptism and the Lord's Supper*. Grand Rapids: Kregel, 2015.

————. *Biblical Foundations for Baptist Churches: A Contemporary Ecclesiology*. Grand Rapids: Kregel, 2005.

————. "Multiple-Intensions View of the Atonement." In *Perspectives on the Extent of the Atonement: 3 Views*, edited by Andrew David Naselli and Mark A. Snoeberger, 143–94. Nashville: B&H Academic, 2015.

Harmon, Matthew S. "For the Glory of the Father and the Salvation of His People: Definite Atonement in the Snyoptics and Johannine Literature." In *From Heaven He Came and Sought Her: Definite Atonement in Historical, Biblical, Theological, and Pastoral Perspective*, edited by David Gibson and Jonathan Gibson, 267–88. Wheaton, IL: Crossway, 2013.

Harris, Murray J. *Prepositions and Theology in the Greek New Testament*. Grand Rapids: Zondervan, 2012.

————. *The Second Epistle to the Corinthians: A Commentary on the Greek Text*. New International Greek Testament Commentary. Grand Rapids: Eerdmans, 2005.

Harris, R. Laird. "כָּפַר." In *Theological Wordbook of the Old Testament*, edited by Gleason L. Archer Jr. and Bruce K. Waltke, 1:453. Chicago: Moody, 1980.

————. "Leviticus." In *The Expositor's Bible Commentary*, edited by Frank E. Gaebelein, 2:499–654. Grand Rapids: Zondervan, 1990.

Harris, W. Hall, III. "An Out-of-This-World Experience: A Look at 'κόσμος' in the Johannine Literature." Paper presented at the annual meeting of the Evangelical Theological Society, Washington, DC, November 18, 2006.

Harrison, Everett F. "Romans." In *The Expositor's Bible Commentary*, edited by Frank E. Gaebelein, 10:1–172. Grand Rapids: Zondervan, 1976.

Haykin, Michael A. G. "'We Trust in the Saving Blood': Definite Atonement in the Ancient Church." In *From Heaven He Came and Sought Her: Definite Atonement in Historical, Biblical, Theological, and Pastoral Perspective*, edited by David Gibson and Jonathan Gibson, 57–74. Wheaton, IL: Crossway, 2013.

Helm, Paul. *Calvin and the Calvinists*. Edinburgh: Banner of Truth, 1982.

————. "Calvin, Indefinite Language, and Definite Atonement." In *From Heaven He Came and Sought Her: Definite Atonement in Historical, Biblical, Theological, and Pastoral Perspective*, edited by David Gibson and Jonathan Gibson, 97–119. Wheaton, IL: Crossway, 2013.

————. "The Logic of Limited Atonement." *Scottish Bulletin of Evangelical Theology* 3/2 (1985) 47–54.

Hendel, R. "The Exodus in Biblical Memory." *Journal of Biblical Literature* 120 (2001) 601–22.

Hendriksen, William. *Exposition of Galatians, Ephesians, Philippians, Colossians, and Philemon*. New Testament Commentary Grand Rapids: Baker Academic, 1964.

————. *Exposition of the Gospel According to John: Two Volumes Complete in One*. New Testament Commentary. Grand Rapids: Baker Academic, 1953.

————. *Exposition of the Gospel According to Matthew*. New Testament Commentary. Grand Rapids: Baker Academic, 1982.

Henebury, Paul Martin. "Christ's Atonement: Its Purpose and Extent, Part 1." *The Conservative Theological Journal* 9 (March 2005) 87–108.

————. "The Extent of the Atonement, Part 2." *The Conservative Theological Journal* 9 (August 2005) 241–57.

Hiebert, D. Edmond. "Titus." In *The Expositor's Bible Commentary*, edited by Frank E. Gaebelein, 11:419–49. Grand Rapids: Zondervan, 1981.

Hodge, A. A. *The Atonement*. 1867. Reprint, London: Evangelical Press, 1974.

————. *Outlines of Theology*. 1860. Reprint, Carlisle, PA: Banner of Truth, 1991.

Hodge, Charles. *1 and 2 Corinthians*. Geneva Series of Commentaries. Carlisle, PA: Banner of Truth, 1974.

————. *Romans*. Crossway Classic Commentaries. Wheaton, IL: Crossway, 1993.

————. *Systematic Theology*. 3 vols. Grand Rapids: Eerdmans, 1968.

Hoehner, Harold W. *Ephesians: An Exegetical Commentary*. Grand Rapids: Baker Academic, 2002.

Hogg, David S. "'Sufficient for All, Efficient for Some': Definite Atonement in the Medieval Church." In *From Heaven He Came and Sought Her: Definite Atonement in Historical, Biblical, Theological, and Pastoral Perspective*, edited by David Gibson and Jonathan Gibson, 75–95. Wheaton, IL: Crossway, 2013.

Horton, Michael S. *The Christian Faith*. Grand Rapids: Zondervan, 2011.

————. "A Classical Calvinist View." In *Four Views on Eternal Security*, edited by J. Matthew Pinson, 21–42. Grand Rapids: Zondervan, 2002.

————. "Is Particular Redemption 'Good News'?" In *The Synod of Dort: Historical, Theological, and Experiential Perspectives*, edited by Joel Beeke and Martin I. Klauber, 105–31. Göttingen: Vandenhoeck & Ruprecht, 2020.

Hubbard, Jr., R. "גאל." In *New International Dictionary of Old Testament Theology and Exegesis*, edited by Willem A. VanGemeren, 1:789–94. Grand Rapids: Zondervan, 1997.

————. "פדה." In *New International Dictionary of Old Testament Theology and Exegesis*, edited by Willem A. VanGemeren, 3:578–82. Grand Rapids: Zondervan, 1997.

Hughes, Philip Edgcumbe. *The Book of the Revelation: A Commentary*. Grand Rapids: Eerdmans, 1990.

————. *A Commentary on the Epistle to the Hebrews*. Grand Rapids: Eerdmans, 1977.

————. *Paul's Second Epistle to the Corinthians*. New International Commentary on the New Testament. Grand Rapids: Eerdmans, 1962.

Hurrion, John. *Particular Redemption: The End and Design of the Death of Christ*. Carlisle, PA: Banner of Truth, 2017.

Hyde, Daniel R. *Grace Worth Fighting For: Recapturing the Vision of God's Grace in the Canons of Dort*. Lincoln, NE: Davenant, 2019.

Jeffery, Steve, Michael Ovey, and Andrew Sach. *Pierced for Our Transgressions: Rediscovering the Glory of Penal Substitution*. Wheaton, IL: Crossway, 2007.

Johnson, Alan F. "Revelation." In *The Expositor's Bible Commentary*, edited by Frank E. Gaebelein, 12:397–603. Grand Rapids: Zondervan, 1982.

Joüon, Paul. *A Grammar of Biblical Hebrew*. Translated and revised by T. Muraoka. Subsidia Biblica 14/I–II. Rome: Pontifical Biblical Institute, 2000.

Kaiser Jr., Walter C. "Exodus." In *The Expositor's Bible Commentary*, edited by Frank E. Gaebelein, 2:285–497. Grand Rapids: Zondervan, 1990.

Keathley, Kenneth. *Salvation and Sovereignty: A Molinist Approach*. Nashville: B&H Academic, 2010.

Keil, C. F., and F. Delitzsch. *Isaiah*. Translated by James Martin. Biblical Commentary on the Old Testament. Reprint, Peabody, MA: Hendrickson, 2011.

Kelly, J. N. D. *The Pastoral Epistles*. Black's New Testament Commentary. Peabody, MA: Hendrickson, 1993.

Kendall, R. T. *Calvin and English Calvinism to 1649*. Studies in Christian History and Thought. New York: Oxford University Press, 1979.

Kennard, Douglas W. "Petrine Redemption: Its Meaning and Extent." *Journal of the Evangelical Theological Society* 30 (1987) 399–405.

Kent, Homer A., Jr. *The Epistle to the Hebrews: A Commentary*. Winona Lake, IN: BMH, 2002.

————. *The Pastoral Epistles: Studies in 1 and 2 Timothy and Titus*. Rev. ed. Winona Lake, IN: BMH, 1986.

Knight, George W., III. *The Pastoral Epistles: A Commentary on the Greek Text*. New International Greek Testament Commentary. Grand Rapids: Eerdmans, 1992.

Knox, D. Broughton. "Some Aspects of the Atonement." In *D. Broughton Knox: Selected Works*, edited by Tony Payne, 1:260–66. Kingsford, NSW: Matthias Media, 2000.

Koehler, Ludwig, and Walter Baumgartner, eds. *The Hebrew and Aramaic Lexicon of the Old Testament*. Revised by Walter Baumgartner and Johann Jakob Stamm. Translated and edited by M. E. J. Richardson. 2 vols. New York: Brill, 1994–2000.

————. *The Hebrew and Aramaic Lexicon of the Old Testament*. Revised by Walter Baumgartner and Johann Jakob Stamm. Translated and edited by M. E. J. Richardson. Electronic ed., BibleWorks 8. Leiden, Netherlands: Koninklijke Brill NV, 1994–2000.

Koester, Craig R. "'The Savior of the World' (John 4:42)." *Journal of Biblical Literature* 109 (1990) 665–80.

Köstenberger, Andreas J. *John*. Baker Exegetical Commentary on the New Testament. Grand Rapids: Baker, 2004.

Kruse, Colin G. *The Letters of John*. Pillar New Testament Commentary. Grand Rapids: Eerdmans, 2000.

Kuiper, R. B. *For Whom Did Christ Die?: A Study of the Divine Design of the Atonement*. Grand Rapids: Eerdmans, 1959.

Ladd, George Eldon. *A Commentary on The Revelation of John*. Grand Rapids: Eerdmans, 1972.

————. *A Theology of the New Testament*. Edited by Donald A. Hagner. Rev. ed. Grand Rapids: Eerdmans, 1993.

Lake, Donald M. "He Died for All: The Universal Dimensions of the Atonement." In *Grace Unlimited*, edited by Clark H. Pinnock, 31–50. Minneapolis: Bethany House, 1975.

Lane, William L. *The Gospel of Mark*. New International Commentary on the New Testament. Grand Rapids: Eerdmans, 1974.

————. *Hebrews 1–8*. Word Biblical Commentary 47A. Dallas: Word, 1991.

————. *Hebrews 9–13*. Word Biblical Commentary 47B. Dallas: Word, 1991.

Laney, J. Carl. *John*. Moody Gospel Commentary. Chicago: Moody, 1992.

Leith, John H. "Helvetic Consensus Formula." In *Creeds of the Churches: A Reader in Christian Doctrine from the Bible to the Present*, edited by John H. Leith, 308–23. 3rd ed. Louisville: John Knox, 1982.

Letham, Robert. "Theodore Beza: A Reassessment." *Scottish Journal of Theology* 40 (1986) 25–40.

———. "The Triune God, Incarnation, and Definite Atonement." In *From Heaven He Came and Sought Her: Definite Atonement in Historical, Biblical, Theological, and Pastoral Perspective*, edited by David Gibson and Jonathan Gibson, 437–60. Wheaton, IL: Crossway, 2013.

———. *The Work of Christ.* Contours of Christian Theology. Downers Grove, IL: InterVarsity, 1993.

Lightner, Robert P. *The Death Christ Died: A Biblical Case for Unlimited Atonement.* Second edition. Grand Rapids: Kregel, 1998.

———. "For Whom Did Christ Die?" In *Walvoord: A Tribute*, edited by Donald K. Campbell. Chicago: Moody, 1982.

Lincoln, Andrew. *Ephesians.* Word Biblical Commentary 42. Nashville: Thomas Nelson, 1990.

Lombard, Peter. *Sententiae in IV Libris Distinctae.* Grottaferrata, Rome: Collegii S. Bonaventurae ad Claras Aquas, 1981.

Long, Gary D. *Definite Atonement.* 4th ed. N.p., 2014.

MacArthur, John. *1–3 John.* MacArthur New Testament Commentary. Chicago: Moody, 2007.

———. *1 Timothy.* MacArthur New Testament Commentary. Chicago: Moody, 1995.

———. *2 Corinthians.* MacArthur New Testament Commentary. Chicago: Moody, 2003.

———. *Colossians.* MacArthur New Testament Commentary. Chicago: Moody, 1992.

———. *The Gospel According to God: Rediscovering the Most Remarkable Chapter in the Old Testament.* Wheaton, IL: Crossway, 2018.

———. *John 1–11.* MacArthur New Testament Commentary. Chicago: Moody, 2006.

———. "The Love of God for Humanity." *The Master's Seminary Journal* 7 (1996) 7–30.

———. *Revelation 1–11.* MacArthur New Testament Commentary. Chicago: Moody, 1999.

———. *Revelation 12–22.* MacArthur New Testament Commentary. Chicago: Moody, 2000.

MacArthur, John, and Richard Mayhue, eds. *Biblical Doctrine: A Systematic Summary of Bible Truth.* Wheaton, IL: Crossway, 2017.

MacLean, Donald John. *James Durham (1622–1658) and the Gospel Offer in Its Seventeenth-Century Context.* Reformed Historical Theology. Göttingen, Germany: Vandenhoeck & Ruprecht, 2015.

Macleod, Donald. "*Amyraldus redivivus*: A Review Article." *Evangelical Quarterly* 81/3 (2009) 210–29.

———. *Compel Them to Come In: Calvinism and the Free Offer of the Gospel.* Ross-shire, UK: Christian Focus, 2020.

———. "Definite Atonement and the Divine Decree." In *From Heaven He Came and Sought Her: Definite Atonement in Historical, Biblical, Theological, and Pastoral Perspective*, edited by David Gibson and Jonathan Gibson, 401–35. Wheaton, IL: Crossway, 2013.

———. *The Person of Christ.* Contours of Christian Theology. Downers Grove, IL: IVP Academic, 1998.

Marshall, I. Howard. *A Critical and Exegetical Commentary on the Pastoral Epistles.* International Critical Commentary. Edinburgh: T. & T. Clark, 1999.

———. *The Epistles of John.* New International Commentary on the New Testament. Grand Rapids: Eerdmans, 1978.

———. "'For All, for All My Saviour Died.'" In *Semper Reformandum: Studies in Honor of Clark H. Pinnock,* edited by Stanley P. Porter and Anthony R. Cross, 322–46. Carlisle, UK: Paternoster, 2003.

———. *Kept by the Power of God: A Study of Perseverance and Falling Away.* Minneapolis: Bethany, 1969.

———. "The Meaning of Reconciliation." In *Unity and Diversity in New Testament Theology: Essays in Honor of George E. Ladd,* edited by Robert A. Guelich, 117–32. Grand Rapids: Eerdmans, 1978.

———. "Universal Grace and Atonement in the Pastoral Epistles." In *The Grace of God and the Will of Man,* edited by Clark H. Pinnock, 51–69. Minneapolis: Bethany House, 1989.

Martin, Hugh. *The Atonement: In Its Relations to the Covenant, the Priesthood, the Intercession of Our Lord.* Edinburgh: James Gemmell, 1882.

Martin, Ralph P. *2 Corinthians.* Word Biblical Commentary 40. Waco, TX: Word, 1986.

Mayhue, Richard L. "For What Did Christ Atone in Isaiah 53:4–5?" *The Master's Seminary Journal* 6/2 (Fall 1995) 121–42.

McCall, Thomas H., and Grant R. Osborne. "Response to Definite Atonement View." In *Perspectives on the Extent of the Atonement: 3 Views,* edited by Andrew David Naselli and Mark A. Snoeberger, 62–73. Nashville: B&H Academic, 2015.

McGeown, Martyn J. "A Critical Examination of the Amyraldian View of the Atonement." N.d. http://www.cprf.co.uk/articles/amyraldianexamination.htm#.WtfWwy7wapo.

Melick, Richard R., Jr. *Philippians, Colossians, Philemon.* New American Commentary 32. Nashville: Broadman and Holman, 1991.

Metzger, Bruce M. *A Textual Commentary on the Greek New Testament.* 2nd ed. Stuttgart: German Bible Society, 1994.

Miethe, Terry L. "The Universal Power of the Atonement." In *The Grace of God, the Will of Man: A Case for Arminianism,* edited by Clark H. Pinnock, 71–96. Grand Rapids: Zondervan, 1989.

Milgrom, Jacob. *Leviticus 1–16: A New Translation with Introduction and Commentary.* Anchor Bible Commentary 3. New York: Doubleday, 1991.

Milton, Anthony. *The British Delegation at the Synod of Dort.* Woodbridge, UK: Boydell, 2005.

Moo, Douglas J. *The Epistle to the Romans.* New International Commentary on the New Testament. Grand Rapids: Eerdmans, 1996.

———. *Galatians.* Baker Exegetical Commentary on the New Testament. Grand Rapids: Baker Academic, 2013.

———. *The Letters to the Colossians and to Philemon.* Pillar New Testament Commentary. Grand Rapids: Eerdmans, 2008.

Moore, Jonathan D. *English Hypothetical Universalism: John Preston and the Softening of Reformed Theology.* Grand Rapids: Eerdmans, 2007.

———. "The Extent of the Atonement: English Hypothetical Universalism versus Particular Redemption." In *Drawn into Controversie: Reformed Theological Diversity and Debates within Seventeenth-Century British Puritanism,* edited by Michael A. G. Haykin and Mark Jones, 124–61. Göttingen, Germany: Vandenhoeck & Ruprecht, 2011.

Moore, Russell D. "Personal and Cosmic Eschatology." In *Theology for the Church,* edited by Daniel L. Akin, 671–722. Nashville: Broadman and Holman, 2007.

Morris, Leon. *The Apostolic Preaching of the Cross.* 3rd ed. Grand Rapids: Eerdmans, 1965.

———. *The Epistle to the Romans*. Pillar New Testament Commentary. Grand Rapids: Eerdmans, 1988.

———. *The Gospel According to John*. New International Commentary on the New Testament. Grand Rapids: Eerdmans, 1995.

———. *The Gospel According to Matthew*. Pillar New Testament Commentary. Grand Rapids: Eerdmans, 1992.

Motyer, J. Alec. "'Stricken for the Transgression of My People': The Atoning Work of Isaiah's Suffering Servant." In *From Heaven He Came and Sought Her: Definite Atonement in Historical, Biblical, Theological, and Pastoral Perspective*, edited by David Gibson and Jonathan Gibson, 247–66. Wheaton, IL: Crossway, 2013.

Mounce, Robert H. *The Book of Revelation*. New International Commentary on the New Testament. Grand Rapids: Eerdmans, 1997.

Mounce, William D. *Pastoral Epistles*. Word Biblical Commentary 46. Waco, TX: Word, 2000.

Muller, Richard A. "Calvin and the 'Calvinists': Assessing Continuities and Discontinuities Between the Reformation and Orthodoxy, Part 1." *Calvin Theological Journal* 30/2 (1995) 345–75.

———. "Calvin and the 'Calvinists': Assessing Continuities and Discontinuities between the Reformation and Orthodoxy, Part 2." *Calvin Theological Journal* 31/1 (1996) 125–60.

———. "Calvin on Christ's Satisfaction and Its Efficacy: The Issue of 'Limited Atonement.'" In *Calvin and the Reformed Tradition: On the Work of Christ and the Order of Salvation*, 70–106. Grand Rapids: Baker Academic, 2012.

———. *Christ and the Decree: Christology and Predestination from Calvin to Perkins*. Grand Rapids: Baker Academic, 2008.

———. "Davenant and Du Moulin: Variant Approaches to Hypothetical Universalism." In *Calvin and the Reformed Tradition: On the Work of Christ and the Order of Salvation*, 126–60. Grand Rapids: Baker Academic, 2012.

———. *Dictionary of Latin and Greek Theological Terms*. Grand Rapids: Baker Academic, 1985.

———. "A Tale of Two Wills?: Calvin, Amyraut, and Du Moulin on Ezekiel 18:23." In *Calvin and the Reformed Tradition: On the Work of Christ and the Order of Salvation*, 107–125. Grand Rapids: Baker Academic, 2012.

———. "Was Calvin a Calvinist?" In *Calvin and the Reformed Tradition: On the Work of Christ and the Order of Salvation*, 51–69. Grand Rapids: Baker Academic, 2012.

Murray, Iain H. *The Forgotten Spurgeon*. Edinburgh: Banner of Truth, 1973.

———. *Spurgeon v. Hyper-Calvinism: The Battle for Gospel Preaching*. Carlisle, PA: Banner of Truth, 1995.

Murray, John. *The Atonement*. Grand Rapids: Baker, 1962.

———. "The Atonement." In *Collected Writings of John Murray*, 2:142–50. Carlisle, PA: Banner of Truth, 1977.

———. "The Atonement and the Free Offer of the Gospel." In *Collected Writings of John Murray*, 1:59–85. Carlisle, PA: Banner of Truth, 1976.

———. "Calvin on the Extent of the Atonement." *Banner of Truth* 234 (1983) 20–22.

———. "Common Grace." In *Collected Writings of John Murray*, 2:93–119. Carlisle, PA: Banner of Truth, 2009.

———. *The Epistle to the Romans: The English Text with Introduction, Exposition and Notes in Two Volumes*. Grand Rapids: Eerdmans, 1997.

———. "The Free Offer of the Gospel." In *Collected Writings of John Murray*, 4:113–32. Carlisle, PA: Banner of Truth, 1982.

———. *Redemption Accomplished and Applied*. Grand Rapids: Eerdmans, 1955.

Naselli, Andrew David. "Conclusion." In *Perspectives on the Extent of the Atonement: 3 Views*, edited by Andrew David Naselli and Mark A. Snoeberger, 213–27. Nashville: B&H Academic, 2015.

———. "John Owen's Argument for a Definite Atonement in *The Death of Death in the Death of Christ*: A Brief Summary and Evaluation." *Southern Baptist Journal of Theology* 14/4 (2010) 60–82.

Nettles, Thomas J. *By His Grace and for His Glory: A Historical, Theological, and Practical Study of the Doctrines of Grace in Baptist Life*. 2nd ed. Lake Charles, LA: Cor Meum Tibi, 2002.

Newton, John. *Sixty-Six Letters from the Rev. John Newton to a Clergyman and His Family*. Edited by John Coffin. London: Simpkin, Marshall, 1844.

Nicole, Roger R. "C. H. Dodd and the Doctrine of Propitiation." *Westminster Theological Journal* 17 (1955) 117–57.

———. "The Case for Definite Atonement." *Bulletin of the Evangelical Theological Society* 10 (1967) 199–207.

———. "Covenant, Universal Call, and Definite Atonement." *Journal of the Evangelical Theological Society* 38 (1995) 403–11.

———. "John Calvin's View of the Extent of the Atonement." *Westminster Theological Journal* 47 (1985) 197–225.

———. "Moyse Amyraut (1596–1664) and the Controversy on Universal Grace, First Phase (1634–1637)." PhD diss., Harvard University, 1966.

———. *Our Sovereign Savior: The Essence of the Reformed Faith*. Ross-shire, UK: Christian Focus, 2002.

———. "Particular Redemption." In *Our Savior God: Studies on Man, Christ, and the Atonement*, edited by James M. Boice, 165–78. Grand Rapids: Baker, 1980.

Niemi, Josh. *Greater than Aaron: The Supremacy of Christ's Limited Atonement*. N.p., 2019.

O'Brien, Peter T. *Colossians, Philemon*. Word Biblical Commentary 44. Waco, TX: Word, 1982.

———. *The Epistle to the Philippians: A Commentary on the Greek Text*. New International Greek Testament Commentary. Grand Rapids: Eerdmans, 1991.

———. *The Letter to the Ephesians*. Pillar New Testament Commentary. Grand Rapids: Eerdmans, 1999.

———. *The Letter to the Hebrews*. Pillar New Testament Commentary. Grand Rapids: Eerdmans, 2010.

Olley, John W. "'The Many': How Is Isaiah 53:12a to Be Understood?" *Biblica* 68 (1987) 330–56.

Olson, Roger E. *Against Calvinism*. Grand Rapids: Zondervan, 2011.

Osborne, Grant R. "General Atonement View." In *Perspectives on the Extent of the Atonement: 3 Views*, edited by Andrew David Naselli and Mark A. Snoeberger, 81–127. Nashville: B&H Academic, 2015.

———. *Revelation*. Baker Exegetical Commentary on the New Testament. Grand Rapids: Baker Academic, 2002.

Oswalt, John N. *The Book of Isaiah: Chapters 40–66*. New International Commentary on the Old Testament. Grand Rapids: Eerdmans, 1998.

———. "Isaiah 52:13—53:12: Servant of All." *Calvin Theological Journal* 40 (2005) 85–94.

Owen, John. [*Death of Death*] *Salus Electorum, Sanguis Jesu, or, The Death of Death in the Death of Christ*. In *The Works of John Owen*, edited by W. H. Goold, 10:139–428. Edinburgh: Johnstone & Hunter, 1850–1855. Reprint, Edinburgh: Banner of Truth, 1967.

———. *Of the Death of Christ, the Price He Paid, and the Purchase He Made*. In *The Works of John Owen*, edited by W. H. Goold, 10:430–79. Edinburgh: Johnstone & Hunter, 1850–1855. Reprint, Edinburgh: Banner of Truth, 1967.

———. *The Mystery of the Gospel Vindicated and Socinianism Examined*. In *The Works of John Owen*, edited by W. H. Goold, 12:3–617. Edinburgh: Johnstone & Hunter, 1850–1855. Reprint, Edinburgh: Banner of Truth, 1967.

Packer, J. I. "The Atonement in the Life of a Christian." In *The Glory of the Atonement*, edited by Charles E. Hill and Frank A. James, 409–25. Downers Grove, IL: InterVarsity, 2004.

———. *Evangelism and the Sovereignty of God*. Downers Grove, IL: InterVarsity, 1961.

———. "Introductory Essay." In *The Death of Death in the Death of Christ*, by John Owen, 1–25. London: Banner of Truth, 1959. Also published as: "Saved by His Precious Blood: An Introduction to John Owen's *The Death of Death in the Death of Christ*." In *In My Place Condemned He Stood: Celebrating the Glory of the Atonement*, edited by J. I. Packer and Mark Dever, 53–100. Wheaton, IL: Crossway, 2007.

———. "The Love of God: Universal and Particular." In *Still Sovereign: Contemporary Perspectives on Election, Foreknowledge, and Grace*, edited by Thomas R. Schreiner and Bruce A. Ware, 277–91. Grand Rapids: Baker, 2000.

———. "What Did the Cross Achieve?: The Logic of Penal Substitution." In *Celebrating the Saving Work of God: Collected Shorter Writings of J. I. Packer*, 1:85–123. Carlisle, UK: Paternoster, 2000. Also published in *In My Place Condemned He Stood: Celebrating the Glory of the Atonement*, edited by J. I. Packer and Mark Dever, 111–44. Wheaton, IL: Crossway, 2007.

Pao, David W. *Colossians and Philemon*. Zondervan Exegetical Commentary on the New Testament. Grand Rapids: Zondervan, 2012.

Perkins, William. *The Workes of that Famous and Worthy Minister of Christ in the Universitie of Cambridge, Mr. William Perkins*. 2 vols. Cambridge: Cambridge University Press, 1915.

Peterson, David G. "Atonement in the Old Testament." In *Where Wrath and Mercy Meet: Proclaiming the Atonement Today*, edited by David G. Peterson, 1–25. Carlisle, UK: Paternoster, 2001.

Picirilli, Robert E. *Grace, Faith, Free Will; Contrasting Views of Salvation: Calvinism and Arminianism*. Nashville: Randall House, 2002.

Pierce, Madison N. "Hebrews 1 and the Son Begotten 'Today.'" In *Retrieving Eternal Generation*, edited by Fred Sanders and Scott R. Swain, 117–31. Grand Rapids: Zondervan, 2017.

Pink, Arthur W. *The Sovereignty of God*. Grand Rapids: Baker, 1984.

Pinnock, Clark H. "From Augustine to Arminius: A Pilgrimage in Theology." In *The Grace of God, the Will of Man: A Case for Arminianism*, edited by Clark H. Pinnock, 15–30. Grand Rapids: Zondervan, 1989.

———. *A Wideness in God's Mercy: The Finality of Jesus in a World of Religions*. Grand Rapids: Zondervan, 1992.

Piper, John. "Are There Two Wills in God?" In *Still Sovereign: Contemporary Perspectives on Election, Foreknowledge, and Grace*, edited by Thomas R. Schreiner and Bruce A. Ware, 107–31. Grand Rapids: Baker, 2000.

———. *Counted Righteous in Christ: Should We Abandon the Imputation of Christ's Righteousness?* Wheaton, IL: Crossway, 2002.

———. *Fifty Reasons Why Jesus Came to Die.* Wheaton, IL: Crossway, 2006.

———. *Let the Nations Be Glad: The Supremacy of God in Missions.* 3rd ed. Grand Rapids: Baker, 2010.

———. "'My Glory I Will Not Give to Another': Preaching the Fullness of Definite Atonement to the Glory of God." In *From Heaven He Came and Sought Her: Definite Atonement in Historical, Biblical, Theological, and Pastoral Perspective*, edited by David Gibson and Jonathan Gibson, 633–67. Wheaton, IL: Crossway, 2013.

Plumer, William S. *Psalms: A Critical and Expository Commentary with Doctrinal and Practical Remarks.* Geneva Series of Commentaries. Carlisle, PA: Banner of Truth, 1867.

Plummer, Alfred. *A Critical and Exegetical Commentary on the Second Epistle of St. Paul to the Corinthians.* International Critical Commentary. Edinburgh: T. & T. Clark, 1970.

Polhill, Edward. *The Divine Will Considered in Its Eternal Decrees and Holy Execution of Them.* London: Thomas Ward, 1844.

Poythress, Vern S. "The Meaning of μάλιστα in 2 Timothy 4:13 and Related Verses." *Journal of Theological Studies* 53 (2002) 523–32.

Purdy, Warren E. "The Meaning of the Phrase 'Saviour of All Men' in First Timothy 4:10." Unpublished monograph. Grace Theological Seminary, 1954.

Putnam, Frederic Clarke. *Hebrew Bible Insert: A Student's Guide.* 2nd ed. Quakertown, PA: Stylus, 2002.

Rainbow, Jonathan H. *The Will of God and the Cross: An Historical and Theological Study of John Calvin's Doctrine of Limited Redemption.* Allison Park, PA: Pickwick, 1990.

Rehnman, Sebastian. "A Particular Defence of Particularism." *Journal of Reformed Theology* 6 (2012) 24–34.

Reymond, Robert L. *A New Systematic Theology of the Christian Faith.* 2nd ed. Nashville: Thomas Nelson, 1998.

Riccardi, Michael. "Veiled in Flesh the Godhead See: A Study of the Kenosis of Christ." *The Master's Seminary Journal* 30/1 (Spring 2019) 103–27.

Rienecker Fritz, and Cleon L. Rogers. *A Linguistic Key to the Greek New Testament.* Grand Rapids: Eerdmans, 1980.

Rooker, Mark. F. *Leviticus.* New American Commentary 3A. Nashville: Broadman and Holman, 2000.

Ross, Allen P. *Holiness to the Lord: A Guide to the Exposition of the Book of Leviticus.* Grand Rapids: Baker Academic, 2002.

Rouwendal, P. L. "Calvin's Forgotten Classical Position on the Extent of the Atonement: About Sufficiency, Efficiency, and Anachronism." *Westminster Theological Journal* 70/2 (Fall 2008) 317–35.

Ryle, J. C. *Expository Thoughts on John.* Vol. 1. Carlisle, PA: Banner of Truth, 2012.

Ryrie, Charles C. *Basic Theology.* Colorado Springs, CO: Victor, 1986.

Sailer, William S. "The Nature and Extent of the Atonement: A Wesleyan View." *Bulletin of the Evangelical Theological Society* 10 (1967) 189–98.

Sasse, Herman. "κόσμος." In *Theological Dictionary of the New Testament*, edited by Gerhard Kittel, 3:867–98. Grand Rapids: Eerdmans, 1965.

Scaer, David. "The Nature and Extent of the Atonement in Lutheran Theology." *Bulletin of the Evangelical Theological Society* 10 (1967) 179–87.

Schaff, Philip, ed. *The Creeds of Christendom*. Vol. 3: *The Evangelical Protestant Creeds*. 6th ed. 1931. Reprint, Grand Rapids: Baker, 1990.

———. *Nicene and Post-Nicene Fathers*. 1st ser. 14 vols. 1886. Reprint, Peabody, MA: Hendrickson, 1994.

Schaff, Philip, and Henry Wace, eds. *Nicene and Post-Nicene Fathers*. 2nd ser. 14 vols. 1890–1900. Reprint, Peabody, MA: Hendrickson, 1994.

Schilder, Klaas. *Christ Crucified*. Grand Rapids: Eerdmans, 1940.

Schlatter, Adolf von. *Der Evangelist Johannes*. 2nd ed. Stuttgart: Calwer, 1948.

Schnackenburg, Rudolf. *The Johannine Epistles*. Tunbridge Wells, Kent: Burns & Oates, 1992.

Schreiner, Thomas R. *1, 2 Peter, Jude*. New American Commentary 37. Nashville: Broadman and Holman, 2003.

———. "Does Romans 9 Teach Individual Election unto Salvation?" In *Still Sovereign: Contemporary Perspectives on Election, Foreknowledge, and Grace*, edited by Thomas R. Schreiner and Bruce A. Ware, 89–106. Grand Rapids: Baker, 2000.

———. "Does Scripture Teach Prevenient Grace in the Wesleyan Sense?" In *Still Sovereign: Contemporary Perspectives on Election, Foreknowledge, and Grace*, edited by Thomas R. Schreiner and Bruce A. Ware, 229–46. Grand Rapids: Baker, 2000.

———. *Galatians*. Zondervan Exegetical Commentary on the New Testament. Grand Rapids: Zondervan, 2010.

———. "Penal Substitution View." In *The Nature of the Atonement: Four Views*, edited by James Beilby and Paul R. Eddy, 67–98. Downers Grove, IL: InterVarsity, 2006.

———. "'Problematic Texts' for Definite Atonement in the Pastoral and General Epistles." In *From Heaven He Came and Sought Her: Definite Atonement in Historical, Biblical, Theological, and Pastoral Perspective*, edited by David Gibson and Jonathan Gibson, 375–97. Wheaton, IL: Crossway, 2013.

———. *Romans*. Baker Exegetical Commentary on the New Testament. Grand Rapids: Baker Academic, 1998.

Schreiner, Thomas R., and Ardel B. Caneday. *The Race Set before Us: A Biblical Theology of Perseverance and Assurance*. Downers Grove, IL: InterVarsity, 2001.

Schrock, David S. "A Biblical-Theological Investigation of Christ's Priesthood and Covenant Mediation with Respect to the Extent of the Atonement." PhD diss., The Southern Baptist Theological Seminary, 2013.

———. "Jesus Saves, No Asterisk Needed: Why Preaching the Gospel as Good News Requires Definite Atonement." In *Whomever He Wills: A Surprising Display of Sovereign Mercy*, edited by Matthew M. Barrett and Thomas J. Nettles, 77–119. Cape Coral, FL: Founders, 2012.

Shedd, William G. T. *Dogmatic Theology*. Edited by Alan W. Gomes. 3rd ed. Phillipsburg, NJ: P&R, 2003.

Shultz, Gary L., Jr. "A Biblical and Theological Defense of a Multi-Intentioned View of the Extent of the Atonement." PhD diss., The Southern Baptist Theological Seminary, 2008.

———. "God's Purposes in the Atonement for the Nonelect." *Bibliotheca Sacra* 165 (April–June 2008) 145–63.

———. *A Multi-Intentioned View of the Atonement*. Eugene, OR: Wipf & Stock, 2013.

———. "The Reconciliation of All Things in Christ." *Bibliotheca Sacra* 167 (October–December 2010) 442–59.

———. "Why a Genuine Universal Gospel Call Requires an Atonement That Paid for the Sins of All People." *Evangelical Quarterly* 82/2 (2010) 111–23.

Skeat, T. C. "'Especially the Parchments': A Note on 2 Timothy iv.13." *Journal of Theological Studies* 30 (1979) 173–77.

Silva, Moises, ed. "ἀγοράζω." In *New International Dictionary of New Testament Theology and Exegesis*, 1:139–40. Grand Rapids: Zondervan, 2014.

———. "ἀλλάσσω." In *New International Dictionary of New Testament Theology and Exegesis*, 1:242–49. Grand Rapids: Zondervan, 2014.

———. "ἱλάσκομαι." In *New International Dictionary of New Testament Theology and Exegesis*, 2:531–41. Grand Rapids: Zondervan, 2014.

———. "λυτρόω." In *New International Dictionary of New Testament Theology and Exegesis*, 3:179–87. Grand Rapids: Zondervan, 2014.

Smeaton, George M. *The Apostles' Doctrine of the Atonement*. 1870. Reprint, Carlisle, PA: Banner of Truth, 2009.

Snoeberger, Mark A. "Introduction." In *Perspectives on the Extent of the Atonement: 3 Views*, edited by Andrew David Naselli and Mark A. Snoeberger, 1–17. Nashville: B&H Academic, 2015.

Spurgeon, Charles. *The Metropolitan Tabernacle Pulpit*. Vol. 49. Pasadena, TX: Pilgrim, 1977.

———. "Particular Redemption." In *The New Park Street Pulpit*, 4:129–36. London: Alabaster and Passmore, 1856.

Stott, John R. W. *The Letters of John: An Introduction and Commentary*. Tyndale New Testament Commentaries. Grand Rapids: Eerdmans, 1988.

Strange, Daniel. "Slain for the World?: The 'Uncomfortability' of the 'Unevangelized' for a Universal Atonement." In *From Heaven He Came and Sought Her: Definite Atonement in Historical, Biblical, Theological, and Pastoral Perspective*, edited by David Gibson and Jonathan Gibson, 585–605. Wheaton, IL: Crossway, 2013.

Strehle, Stephen A. "The Extent of the Atonement at the Synod of Dort." *Westminster Journal of Theology* 51 (1989) 1–23.

———. "The Extent of the Atonement within the Theological Systems of the Sixteenth and Seventeenth Centuries." ThD diss., Dallas Theological Seminary, 1980.

Strong, Augustus H. *Systematic Theology*. Valley Forge, PA: Judson, 1969.

Suhany, Alan Michael. "John Calvin and the Extent of the Atonement Revisited." Paper presented at the 45th annual meeting of the Evangelical Theological Society, November 20, 1993.

Swanson, Andrew. "The Love of God for the Non-Elect." *Reformation Today* 51 (May–June 1976) 2–13.

Tasker, R. V. G. *The Second Epistle to the Corinthians*. Tyndale New Testament Commentary. Grand Rapids: Eerdmans, 1958.

Tay, Edwin. "Christ's Priestly Oblation and Intercession: Their Development and Significance in John Owen." In *The Ashgate Research Companion to John Owen's Theology*, edited by Kelly M. Kapic and Mark Jones, 159–70. Surrey, UK: Ashgate, 2012.

Thielman, Frank. *Ephesians*. Baker Exegetical Commentary on the New Testament. Grand Rapids: Baker Academic, 2010.

Thiessen, Henry Clarence. *Lectures in Systematic Theology*. Revised by Vernon D. Doerksen. Grand Rapids: Eerdmans, 1997.

Thomas, G. Michael. *The Extent of the Atonement: A Dilemma for Reformed Theology from Calvin to Consensus (1536–1675).* Studies in Christian History and Thought. Blechtley, UK: Paternoster, 1997.

Thomas, Robert L. *Revelation 1–7: An Exegetical Commentary.* Wycliffe Exegetical Commentary. Chicago: Moody, 1992.

———. *Revelation 8–22: An Exegetical Commentary.* Wycliffe Exegetical Commentary. Chicago: Moody, 1995.

Torrance, T. F. *The Atonement: The Person and Work of Christ.* Downers Grove, IL: IVP Academic, 2009.

Towner, Philip H. *The Letters to Timothy and Titus.* New International Commentary on the New Testament. Grand Rapids: Eerdmans, 2006.

Troxel, A. Craig. "Amyraut 'at' the Assembly: The *Westminster Confession of Faith* and the Extent of the Atonement." *Presbyterion* 22 (1996) 43–55.

Trueman, Carl R. "Atonement and the Covenant of Redemption: John Owen on the Nature of Christ's Satisfaction." In *From Heaven He Came and Sought Her: Definite Atonement in Historical, Biblical, Theological, and Pastoral Perspective,* edited by David Gibson and Jonathan Gibson, 201–23. Wheaton, IL: Crossway, 2013.

———. *The Claims of Truth: John Owen's Trinitarian Theology.* Carlisle, UK: Paternoster, 1998.

———. "Definite Atonement View." In *Perspectives on the Extent of the Atonement: 3 Views,* edited by Andrew David Naselli and Mark A. Snoeberger, 19–61. Nashville: B&H Academic, 2015.

———. "The Necessity of the Atonement." In *Drawn into Controversie: Reformed Theological Diversity and Debates within Seventeenth-Century British Puritanism,* edited by Michael A. G. Haykin and Mark Jones, 204–22. Göttingen, Germany: Vandenhoeck & Ruprecht, 2011.

Turretin, Francis. *Institutes of Elenctic Theology.* Edited by James T. Dennison Jr. Phillipsburg, NJ: P&R, 1993.

Ussher, James. *The Judgement of the Late Arch-Bishop of Armagh, and Primate of Ireland.* London: John Crook, 1658.

Van Til, Cornelius. *Common Grace and the Gospel.* Edited by K. Scott Oliphint. 1972. Reprint, Phillipsburg, NJ: P&R, 2015.

VanDoodewaard, William. *The Marrow Controversy and Seceder Tradition.* Reformed Historical-Theological Studies. Grand Rapids: Reformation Heritage, 2011.

Vanhoozer, Kevin. "The Atonement in Postmodernity: Guilt, Goats and Gifts." In *The Glory of the Atonement: Essays in Honor of Roger Nicole,* edited by Charles E. Hill and Frank A. James III, 367–404. Downers Grove, IL: InterVarsity Press, 2004.

Vaughan, Curtis. "Colossians." In *The Expositor's Bible Commentary,* edited by Frank E. Gaebelein. 11:161–226. Grand Rapids: Zondervan, 1981.

Vos, Geerhardus. "The Scriptural Doctrine of the Love of God." In *Redemptive History and Biblical Interpretation: The Shorter Writings of Geerhardus Vos,* edited by Richard B. Gaffin, 425–57. Phillipsburg, NJ: P&R, 1980.

Waldron, Samuel E., and Richard C. Barcellos. *A Reformed Baptist Manifesto.* Palmdale, CA: Reformed Baptist Academic, 2004.

Wallace, Daniel B. *Greek Grammar beyond the Basics: An Exegetical Syntax of the New Testament.* Grand Rapids: Zondervan, 1996.

Waltke, Bruce K., and Michael Patrick O'Connor. *An Introduction to Biblical Hebrew Syntax.* Winona Lake, IN: Eisenbrauns, 1990.

Walvoord, John. *Jesus Christ Our Lord.* Chicago: Moody, 1980.

————. "Reconciliation." *Bibliotheca Sacra* 120 (1963) 3–12.

————. *The Revelation of Jesus Christ: A Commentary.* 1966. Reprint, Chicago: Moody, 1981.

Ware, Bruce A. "*Cur Deus Trinus*?: The Relation of the Trinity to Christ's Identity as Savior and to the Efficacy of His Atoning Death." *Southern Baptist Journal of Theology* 10 (2006) 48–56.

————. "Extent of the Atonement: Outline of the Issue, Positions, Key Texts, and Key Theological Arguments." Course handout, The Southern Baptist Theological Seminary, n.d.

————. "The Extent of the Atonement: Select Support for and Benefits of a 'Multiple Intentions' Understanding." Outline presented at the 62nd annual meeting of the Evangelical Theological Society, November 18, 2010.

————. *Father, Son, and Holy Spirit: Relationships, Roles, and Relevance.* Wheaton, IL: Crossway, 2005.

————. *God's Greater Glory: The Exalted God of Scripture and the Christian Faith.* Wheaton, IL: Crossway, 2004.

————. *God's Lesser Glory: The Diminished God of Open Theism.* Wheaton, IL: Crossway, 2000.

————. *The Man Christ Jesus: Theological Reflections on the Humanity of Christ.* Wheaton, IL: Crossway, 2012.

————. "A Modified Calvinist Doctrine of God." In *Perspectives on the Doctrine of God: Four Views*, edited by Bruce A. Ware, 76–120. Nashville: B&H Academic, 2008.

Warfield, Benjamin Breckenridge. *The Plan of Salvation.* Rev. ed. Grand Rapids, Eerdmans, 1984.

Wells, Tom. *A Price for a People: The Meaning of Christ's Death.* Carlisle, PA: Banner of Truth, 1992.

Wellum, Stephen J. *God the Son Incarnate: The Doctrine of Christ.* Evangelical Foundations of Theology. Wheaton, IL: Crossway, 2017.

————. "The New Covenant Work of Christ: Priesthood, Atonement, and Intercession." In *From Heaven He Came and Sought Her: Definite Atonement in Historical, Biblical, Theological, and Pastoral Perspective*, edited by David Gibson and Jonathan Gibson, 517–39. Wheaton, IL: Crossway, 2013.

White, James R. *The Potter's Freedom: A Defense of the Reformation and a Rebuttal of Norman Geisler's Chosen but Free.* Amityville, NY: Calvary, 2000.

Wilder, Terry L. "The Extent of Christ's Atonement." *Midwestern Journal of Theology* 5/2 (Spring 2007) 48–53.

Wiley, H. Orton. *Christian Theology.* 2 vols. Kansas City, MO: Beacon Hill, 1941.

Williams, Garry J. "The Definite Intent of Penal Substitutionary Atonement." In *From Heaven He Came and Sought Her: Definite Atonement in Historical, Biblical, Theological, and Pastoral Perspective*, edited by David Gibson and Jonathan Gibson, 461–82. Wheaton, IL: Crossway, 2013.

————. "Punishment God Cannot Twice Inflict: The Double Payment Argument *Redivivus*." In *From Heaven He Came and Sought Her: Definite Atonement in Historical, Biblical, Theological, and Pastoral Perspective*, edited by David Gibson and Jonathan Gibson, 483–515. Wheaton, IL: Crossway, 2013.

Williams, Jarvis J. *For Whom Did Christ Die?: The Extent of the Atonement in Paul's Theology.* Milton Keynes, UK: Paternoster, 2012.

Williamson, Paul R. "'Because He Loved Your Forefathers': Election, Atonement, and Intercession in the Pentateuch." In *From Heaven He Came and Sought Her: Definite Atonement in Historical, Biblical, Theological, and Pastoral Perspective*, edited by David Gibson and Jonathan Gibson, 227–45. Wheaton, IL: Crossway, 2013.

Wright, R. K. McGregor. *No Place for Sovereignty: What's Wrong with Freewill Theism.* Downers Grove, IL: InterVarsity, 1996.

Yarbrough, Robert W. *1–3 John.* Baker Exegetical Commentary on the New Testament. Grand Rapids: Baker Academic, 2008.

Young, Edward J. *The Book of Isaiah.* Vol. 3: *Chapters 40–66.* Grand Rapids: Eerdmans, 1972.

Scripture Index

Genesis

1:1	60
1:2	60
2:17	262
3:8	108
3:15	262
3:17–19	329
3:17	300, 318, 328
3:18–19	329
3:22–24	108
6:3	300
6:5–7	300
6:13	174n4
6:14	97n8
9:5	202n111
12:2	159
12:3	217
15:5	159
17:10	100n16, 150
18:14	89
20:6	300
32:20	102
32:30	98
37:11	262
37:28	262
39:5	309
44:32–33	119
45:5–8	263
50:20	263

Exodus

3:7–8	113
3:8	84
4:21	277
5:1	276
6:6	113
7:3	277
8:22–23	114
9:18	257

12:3–7	101
12:4	101
12:12	101
12:13	101
12:29–30	101
12:43–45	100n16, 101, 150
12:48–49	100n16, 101, 150
13:12–15	113
14:30	114
18:4	84
18:8–10	84
19:5	141
20:3–5	103
21:8	113
21:11	113
21:28–30	113
21:30	114
24:3	103
24:7–8	141
24:7	103
28:17–21	149
28:29	149
28:38	82
28:41	81, 137n14
29:1	81, 137n14
29:33	98
29:36–37	98
30:10	98
30:11–16	97n8
30:12	113–14
30:15–16	98
32:1–8	103
32:10	103
32:11–14	103
32:27–28	103
32:30	98, 103
32:32	98, 103
33:19	257
34:6–7	x
34:6	313, 313n57
40:34–38	98

Revelation (*continued*)